C000130387

Chambers FICTION FILE

Compiled and edited by

Roger Prebble

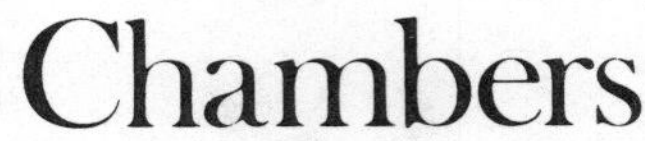

EDINBURGH NEW YORK TORONTO

Published 1992 by W & R Chambers Ltd
43–45 Annandale Street, Edinburgh, EH7 4AZ

British Library Cataloguing in Publication Data
A catalogue record for this book is available from the British Library.

ISBN 0-550-19033-3

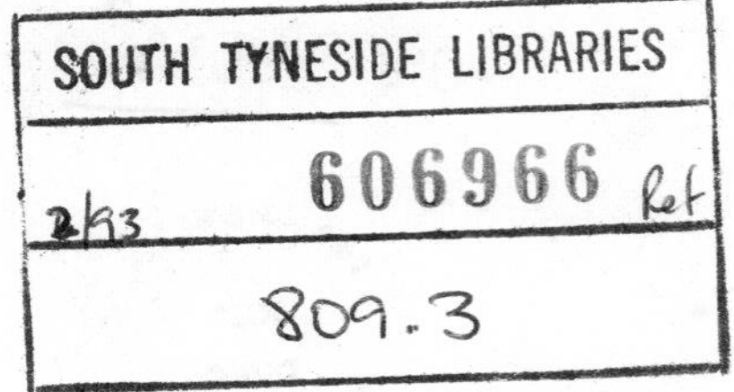

Editorial manager Min Lee

Typeset by Alphaset Graphics, Edinburgh
Printed in England by Clays Ltd, St Ives, plc

CONTENTS

INTRODUCTION	iv
HOW TO USE THIS BOOK	v
AUTHORS	1
TITLES	133
CHARACTERS	446

INTRODUCTION

Whilst there are many admirable reference books available on the vast subject of literature, very few cater for novels in particular and those tomes that do are not designed for the reader who wishes to zone in quickly to a required titbit of information.

Fiction File is concerned solely with novels and collections of short stories; it provides instant access to the relevant facts and figures. You will not find lengthy analyses of 'great' writers within, but an easy-to-use series of alphabetical and chronological check-lists.

Any crossword solver/compiler or quiz buff, or any one of that not insubstantial group of people who just love browsing, will appreciate the instant availability of the reference in this collection.

The book has been divided into three fully cross-referenced sections — authors, titles and characters — allowing access from any item of information already known by the reader. The extremely broad sweep of authors takes in writers from all points of the globe, past and present, while the date range of *Fiction File* runs from the generally accepted origins of the novel in the early 16th century to the very latest 1990s titles both literary and popular.

There is also much additional information — novels' settings; names of literary towns, houses and boats; characters' relationships and occupations — in total an indispensable source for checking all things fictional.

HOW TO USE THIS BOOK

Fiction File is so thoroughly cross-referenced that whether you know the author, the novel title or just a single character, all other information can be pinpointed straight away.

The first section consists of authors arranged alphabetically by surname, and in each case includes a chronological listing of novels. The second section comprises novels alphabetically by title plus, in many cases, a setting and list of characters, together with their relationships/occupations. The third section contains the characters themselves, with a title and author reference.

All else should be self-explanatory, but a brief read-through of the following information may be helpful.

Notes

(a) Authors' real names are also listed and will refer the reader to the better-known pseudonyms.

(b) Where possible, novel titles are in the original language. However, in most cases the equivalent English title is also listed.

(c) Where numbers and forms of names or titles occur at the start of a title (eg 2001, Dr or Mrs), they appear in alphabetical order as if they were spelt out in full.

Authors

A

ABRAHAMS, Peter
(1919–) South African

Song of the City (1945)
Mine Boy (1946)
Path of Thunder (1948)
Wild Conquest (1951)
Tell Freedom: Men of Africa (1954)
A Wreath for Odomo (1956)
Jamaica (1957)
A Night of Their Own (1965)
This Island Now (1966)
The View from Coyoba (1985)

ACHEBE, Chinua
(1930–) Nigerian

Things Fall Apart (1958>
No Longer At Ease (1960)
The Sacrificial Egg (1962)
Arrow of God (1964)
A Man of the People (1966)
Chike and the River (1966)
Girls at War (1972)
How the Leopard Got His Claws (1972)
The Flute (1977)
Don't Let Him Die (1978)

ACKER, Kathy
(1948–) American

The Childlike Life of the Black Tarantula: Some Lives of Murderesses (1975)
Kathy Goes to Haiti (1978)
The Adult Life of Toulouse Lautrec by Henri Toulouse Lautrec (1978)
Great Expectations (1982)
Blood and Guts in High School (1984)
Hello, I'm Erica Long (1984)
Algeria (1985)
Don Quixote: Which Was a Dream (1986)
Empire of the Senseless (1988)
In Memoriam to Identity (1990)

ACKERLEY, J(oseph) R(andolph)
(1896–1967) English

My Dog Tulip (1956)
We Think the World of You (1960)

ACKROYD, Peter
(1949–) English

The Last Testament of Oscar Wilde (1983)
Hawksmoor (1985)
Chatterton (1987)
First Light (1989)

ACTON, Sir Harold
(1904–) English

Peonies and Ponies (1941)
Old Lamps for New (1965)
Tit for Tat (1972) coll

ADAM, Paul (Auguste Marie)
(1862–1920) French

Chair molle (1885)
Être, ou les Feux du sabbat (1888)
Robes rouges (1891)
Le Vice filial (1891)
En décor (1891)
Le Mystère des foules (1895)
La Force du mal (1896)
La Force (1899)
L'Enfant d'Austerlitz (1902)
La Ruse (1903)
Au soleil de juillet (1903)
La Ville inconnue (1911)

ADAMS, Douglas
(1952–) English

The Hitch-Hiker's Guide to the Galaxy (1978)
The Restaurant at the End of the Universe (1980)
Life, the Universe and Everything (1982)
So Long and Thanks for the Fish (1985)
Dirk Gently's Holistic Detective Agency (1987)
Long Dark Tea-Time of the Soul (1988)

ADAMS, Henry Brooks
(1838–1918) American

Democracy (1880)
Esther (1884)

ADAMS, Richard
(1920–) English

Watership Down (1972)
Shardik (1974)
The Plague Dogs (1977)
The Girl in a Swing (1980)

AGEE, James
(1909–55) American

The Morning Watch (1954)
A Death in the Family (1957)

AGNON, S(amuel) Y(osef)
(1888–1970) Israeli

And the Crooked Shall Be Made Straight (1916)
The Bridal Canopy (1922)
Only Afterwards (1947)
In the Heart of the Seas (1948)
A Guest for the Night (1968)

AGOULT, Comtesse d' (Marie de Flavigny)
see **STERN, Daniel**

AIKEN, Conrad (Potter)
(1889–1973) American
Father of Joan Aiken

Blue Voyage (1927)
Great Circle (1933)
King Coffin (1935)
A Heart for the Gods of Mexico (1939)

AIKEN Joan (Delano)
(1924–) American
Daughter of Conrad Aiken

(children's)
The Kingdom and the Cave (1960)
The Wolves of Willoughby Chase (1962)
Black Hearts in Battersea (1964)
Night Birds on Nantucket (1966)
The Whispering Mountain (1968)
The Cuckoo Tree (1971
The Shadow Guests (1980)
The Stolen Lake (1981)

AINSWORTH, William Harrison
(1805–82) English

Rookwood[1] (1834)
Jack Sheppard[1] (1839)
The Tower of London (1840)
Old St Paul's (1841)
Guy Fawkes (1841)
The Lancashire Witches[2] (1848)
Mervyn Clitheroe[2] (1857)

[1] Newgate novels [2] Lancashire novels

AKSAKOV, Sergei Timofeevich
(1791–1859) Russian

The Blizzard (1854)
A Family Chronicle (1856)
The Childhood Years of Bagrov Grandson (1858)

ALAIN-FOURNIER
(1886–1914) French
real name: Henri-Alban Fournier

Le Grand Meaulnes (1913)

ALARCÓN, Pedro Antonio de
(1833–91) Spanish

El sombrero de tres picos (1874)

ALCOTT, Louisa M(ay)
(1832–88) American

(children's)
Moods [1] (1864)
Little Women (1868)
Good Wives (1869)
An Old-Fashioned Girl (1870)
Little men (1871)
Work [1] (1873)
Eight Cousins (1875)
Rose in Bloom (1876)
A Modern Mephistopheles [1] (1877)
Under the Lilacs (1877)
Jack and Jill (1880)
Jo's Boys (1886)

[1] not children's

ALDINGTON, Richard
(1892–1962) English

Death of a Hero (1929)
The Colonel's Daughters (1931)
All Men Are Enemies (1933)
Very Heaven (1937)
Rejected Guest (1939)

ALDISS, Brian W(ilson)
(1925–) English

(science fiction)
The Brightfount Diaries [1] (1955)
Non-Stop (1958)
The Primal Urge (1961)
Hothouse (1962)
Greybeard (1964)
The Saliva Tree (1966)
Report on Probability A (1968)
The Hand-Reared Boy [1] (1970
A Soldier Erect (1971)
The Moment of Eclipse (1971)
Frankenstein Unbound (1973)
Enemies of the System (1978)
Helliconia Spring [2] (1983)
Helliconia Summer [2] (1983)
Helliconia Winter [2] (1985)
Ruins [1] (1986)
Forgotten Life (1988)

[1] not science fiction [2] Helliconia trilogy

ALDRICH, Thomas Bailey
(1836–1907) American

The Story of a Bad Boy (1870)
The Stillwater Tragedy (1880)

ALDRIDGE, James
(1918–) American

Signed With Their Honour (1942)
The Diplomat (1949)
I Wish He Would Not Die (1957)
Goodbye Un-America (1979)

ALEMÁN, Mateo
(1547–1614) Spanish

Guzmán de Alfarache (1604)

ALEXANDER, Lloyd (Chudley)
(1924–) American

(children's)
Time Cat (1963)
The Book of Three [1] (1964)
The Black Cauldron [1] (1965)
The Castle of Llyr [1] (1966)
Tartan Wanderer [1] (1968)
The High King [1] (1968)
The Marvellous Misadventures of Sebastian (1970)
The First Two Lives of Lukas-Kasha (1978)

[1] Prydain cycle

ALEXIS, Willibald
(1798–1871) German
real name: Georg Wilhelm Häring

(historical)
Walladmor (1824)
Schloss Avignon (1827)
Cabanis (1832)

ALEXIS, Willibald (cont.)
Haus Düsterweg [1] (1835)
Zwölf Nächtê [1] (1838)
Die Hosen des Herrn von Bredow (1846–8) 2 vol
Der Wärwolf (1848)
Isegrimm (1854)

[1] not historical

ALGER, Horatio
(1834–99) American

Ragged Dick (1868)
Luck and Pluck (1869)
Tattered Tom (1871)
Phil the Fiddler (1872)
Struggling Upward (1890)

ALGREN, Nelson
(1909–81) American

Somebody in Boots (1935)
Never Come Morning (1942)
The Man with the Golden Arm (1949)
A Walk on the Wild Side (1956)

ALLBEURY, Ted
(1917–) English

(spy/thriller)
A Choice of Enemies (1971)
The Man with the President's Mind (1977)
The Lantern Network (1978)
The Alpha List (1979)
Consequence of Fear (1980)
All Our Tomorrows (1982)
The Girl from Addis (1984)
Children of Tender Years (1985)
The Crossing (1987)
Seeds of Treason (1988)
Deep Purple (1989)
A Time without Shadows (1990)

ALLEN, Grant
(1848–99) Anglo-Canadian

Philista (1884)
The Devil's Die (1888)
The Woman Who Did (1895)

ALLEN, James Lane
(1849–1925) American

A Kentucky Cardinal (1894)
Aftermath (1896)
The Choir Invisible (1897)

ALLEN, (William) Hervey
(1889–1949) American

Anthony Adverse (1933)
Action at Aquila (1938)
It Was Like This (1940)
The Forest and the Fort (1945)

ALLINGHAM, Margery
(1904–66) English

(crime)
Blackerchief Dick [1] (1921)
Crime at Black Dudley (1928)
Police at the Funeral (1931)
Death of a Ghost (1934)
Flowers for the Judge (1936)
The Case of the Late Pig (1937)
Coroner's Pidgin (1945)
More Work for the Undertaker (1948)
The Tiger in the Smoke (1952)
The Beckoning Lady (1955)
Hide My Eyes (1958)
The China Governess (1963)
The Mind Readers (1965)

[1] not crime

ALSOP, Mary O'Hara
see **O'HARA, Mary**

ALTHER, Lisa
(1944–) American

Kinflicks (1976)
Original Sins (1981)
Other Women (1985)'
Bedrock (1990)

AMADO, Jorge
(1912–) Brazilian

The Violent Land (1945)

Gabriella, Clove and Cinnamon (1958)
Tieta (1978)
The Swallow and the Tom Cat (1982)

AMBLER, Eric
(1909–) English

(spy)
The Dark Frontier (1936)
Epitaph for a Spy (1938)
The Mask of Dimitrios (1939)
The Night-Comers (1956)
Passage of Arms (1959)
Dirty Story (1967)
The Intercom Conspiracy (1970)
The Levanter (1972)

AMICIS, Edmondo de
see **DE AMICIS, Edmondo**

AMIS, Sir Kingsley (William)
(1922–) English
Father of Martin Amis

Lucky Jim (1954)
That Uncertain Feeling (1955)
I Like It Here (1958)
Take a Girl Like You (1960)
One Fat Englishman (1963)
The Anti-Death League (1966)
I Want It Now (1968)
Colonel Sun (1968)
as Robert Markham
The Green Man (1969)
Girl 20 (1971)
The Riverside Villas Murder (1973)
Ending Up (1974)
The Alteration (1976)
Jake's Thing (1978)
Russian Hide and Seek (1980)
Stanley and the Women (1984)
The Old Devils (1986)
Difficulties with Girls (1988)
The Folks That Live on the Hill (1990)

AMIS, Martin (Louis)
(1949–) English
Son of Kingsley Amis

The Rachel Papers (1973)
Dead Babies (1975)
Success (1978)
Other People (1981)
Money (1984)
Einstein's Monsters (1987)
London Fields (1989)
Time's Arrow (1991)

ANAND, Mulk Raj
(1905–) Indian

Untouchable (1935)
The Coolie (1936)
Two Leaves and a Bud (1937)
The Village [1] (1939)
Across the Black Waters [1] (1940)
The Sword and the Sickle [1] (1942)
Private Life of an Indian Prince (1953)
Morning Face (1968)

[1] Sikh Peasant trilogy

ANDERSEN, Hans Christian
(1805–75) Danish

The Improvasitore (1835)
OT (1836)
Only a Fiddler (1837)
The Little Match Girl (1848)

ANDERSON, Sherwood
(1874–1941) American

Windy McPherson's Son (1916)
Marching Men (1917)
Winesburg, Ohio (1919)
Poor White (1920)
Many Marriages (1922)
Dark Laughter (1925)
Tar, a Midwest Childhood (1926)
Beyond Desire (1932)
Puzzled America (1935)
Kit Brandon (1936)
Home Town (1940)

ANDRES, Stefan
(1906–70) German

Bruder Lucifer (1932)
Eberhard im Kontrapunkt (1933)
Die unsichtbare Mauer (1934)
Der Mann von Asteri (1939)
Die Reise nach Portiuncula (1954)
Der Versuchung des Synesios (1971) posth

ANDRIC, Ivo
(1892–1975) Yugoslavian

The Bridge on the Drina (1945)
Bosnian Story (1945)
The Woman from Sarajevo (1946)

ANDRZEJEWSKI, Jerzy
(1909–) Polish

Ashes and Diamonds (1948)
The Inquisitors (1957)
He Cometh Leaping on the Mountain (1963)

ANSTEY, F
(1856–1934) English
real name: Thomas Anstey Guthrie

Vice Versa (1882)
The Tinted Venus (1885)
Tourmalin's Time Cheques (1891)
Baboo Jabberjee, BA (1897)
The Brass Bottle (1900)
Only Toys! (1903)
In Brief Authority (1915)

ANTHONY, Evelyn
(1928–) English

(historical)
The Tamarind Seed (1971)
Assassin (1973)
The French Bride (1976)
The Grave of Truth (1980)
The Defector (1980)
as Davinia Graham
Avenue of the Dead (1981)
as Davinia Graham
Albatross (1982)
as Davinia Graham
The Company of Saints (1983)
as Davinia Graham
The Occupying Power (1983)
The Curse of the King (1986)
The Heiress (1987)
The Scarlet Thread (1989)

ANTHONY, Piers
(1934–) American
real name: Piers A Jacob

(science fiction)
Chthon (1967)
A Spell for Chameleon (1977)

ANZENGRÜBER, Ludwig
(1839–89) Austrian

Der Schandfleck (1877)
Der Sternsteinhof (1885)

APPIAH, Peggy
(1921–) Anglo-Ghanaian

The Children of Ananse (1968)

ARAGON, Louis
(1897–1982) French

Le Paysan de Paris (1926)
Les Cloches de Bâle (1933)
Les Beaux Quartiers (1936)
Les Voyageurs de l'impériale (1942)
Aurélien (1945)
Les Communistes (1949–51) 6 vol
La Semaine sainte (1958)
Blanche, ou l'Oubli (1967)

ARCHER, Jeffrey
(1940–) English

Not a Penny More, Not a Penny Less (1976)
Shall We Tell the President? (1977)
Kane and Abel (1979)
The Prodigal Daughter (1982)
First Among Equals (1984)
A Matter of Honour (1985)
As the Crow Flies (1991)

ARDEN, John
(1930–) English
Silence Among the Weapons (1982)

ARÈNE, Paul
(1843–96) French
Jean des figues (1868)
La Gueuse parfumée, récits provençaux (1876)
Au bon soleil (1881)
Le Midi rouge (1895)

ARLEN, Michael
(1895–1956) Anglo-Armenian
real name: Dikran Kuyumjian
Piracy (1922)
The Green Hat (1924)
Hell! Said the Duchess (1934)

AROUET, François Marie
see **VOLTAIRE**

ARTHUR, Ruth M(abel)
(1905–79) English
(romance)
Dragon Summer (1962)
Portrait of Margarita (1968)
After Candlemas (1974)

ASCH, Sholem
(1880–1957) polish-American
The Mother (1930)
Three Cities (1933)
The War Goes On (1936)
Uncle Moses (1938)
Judge Not (1938)
The Nazarene (1939)
The Apostle (1943)
East River (1946)
The Prophet (1955)

ASHFORD, Daisy
(1881–1972) English
The Young Visiters (1919)

ASHTON-WARNER, Sylvia
(1908–78) New Zealand
Spinster (1958)
Three (1970)

ASIMOV, Isaac
(1920–92) American
(science fiction)
Nightfall (1941)
I, Robot (1956)
Foundation [1] (1951)
Foundation and Empire [1] (1952)
Second Foundation [1] (1953)
The Caves of Steel (1954)
The Naked Sun (1957)
Fantastic Voyage (1966)
The Robots of Dawn (1983)
Robots and Empire (1985)
Fantastic Voyage II (1987)
Prelude to Foundation (1988)

[1] Foundation trilogy

ASTURIAS, Miguel
(1899–1974) Guatemalan
The President (1946)
Men of Maize (1949)
The Cyclone (1950)
The Mulatta and Mr Fly (1960)

ATHERTON, Gertrude (Franklin)
(1857–1948) American
The Conqueror (1922)
The Black Oxen (1923)
The Californians (1935)

ATWOOD, Margaret (Eleanor)
(1939–) Canadian
The Edible Woman (1969)
Surfacing (1972)
Lady Oracle (1976)
Life Before Man (1979)
Bodily Harm (1982)
The Handmaid's Tale (1985)
Cat's Eye (1989)

AUCHINLOSS, Louis (Stanton)
(1917–) American

The Indifferent Children (1947)
The Great World and Timothy Colt (1956)
Portrait in Brownstone (1962)
The Rector of Justin (1965)
A World of Profit (1968)
The Book Class (1984)
Exit Lady Masham (1984)
Diary of a Yuppie (1986)

AUDIBERTI, Jacques
(1899–1965) French

Abraxas (1938)
Cent Jours (1947)

AUEL, Jean M(arie)
(1936–) American

The Clan of the Cave Bear [1] (1980)
The Valley of Horses [1] (1983)
The Mammoth Hunters [1] (1985)
The Plains of Passage (1990)

[1] Earth's Children trilogy

AUERBACH, Berthold
(1812–82) German
real name: Moses Baruch Auerbacher

Spinoza (1837) 2 vol
Dichter und Kaufmann (1840) 2 vol
Schwarzwälder Dorfgeschichten (1843–53) 4 vol
Die Frau Professorin (1846)
Neues Leben (1852) 3 vol
Barfüssele (1856)
Joseph im Schnee (1860)
Edelweiss (1861)
Auf der Höhe (1865) 3 vol
Das Landhaus am Rhein (1869) 5 vol
Waldfried (1874) 3 vol
Der Forstmeister (1879) 2 vol

AUERBACHER, Moses Baruch
see **AUERBACH, Berthold**

AUSTEN, Jane
(1775–1817) English

Sense and Sensibility (1811)
Pride and Prejudice (1813)
Mansfield Park (1814)
Emma (1816)
Northanger Abbey (1818) posth
Persuasion (1818) posth
Lady Susan (1871) posth
Love and Friendship (1922) posth
Sanditon (1925) posth unf
The Watsons (1927) posth unf

AUSTER, Paul
(1947–) American

Squeeze Play (1982)
In the Country of Last Things (1987)
Moon Palace (1989)
The Music of Chance (1990)
The New York Trilogy (1990) 3 vol

AUSTIN, Stella
(?–1893) English

Stumps (1873)

AVALLONE, Michael
(1924–) American

(crime)
The Tall Dolores (1956)
The February Doll Murders (1966)
Shoot It Again, Sam (1972)

AVERY, Gillian (Elise)
(1926–) English

(children's)
The Warden's Niece (1957)
Trespassers at Charlecote (1958)
James without Thomas (1959)
The Elephant War (1960)
To Tame a Sister (1961)
The Greatest Gresham (1962)
The Peacock House (1963)
The Italian Spring (1964)
Call of the Valley (1968)
A Likely Lad (1971)

Huck and Her Time Machine (1977)
The Lost Railway [1] (1980)
Onlookers [1] (1983)

[1] not children's

AYMÉ, Marcel
(1902–67) French

La Jument verte (1933)
Les Contes du chat perché (1939)
Le Passe-Muraille (1943)
En arrière (1950)

B

BABEL, Isaak
(1894–1941) Russian

Red Cavalry (1926)

BACCHELLI, Riccardo
(1891–1985) Italian

Il diavolo al Pontelungo (1927)
Il mulino del Po (1938–1940) 2 vol
Bellezza e Unamità (1972)

BAGE, Robert
(1720–1801) English

Mount Henneth (1781)
Barham Downs (1784)
The Fair Syrian (1787)
James Wallace (1788)
Man As He Is (1792)
Hermsprong (1796)

BAGLEY, Desmond
(1923–83) English

(thriller)
The Golden Keel (1963)
High Citadel (1965)
Wyatt's Hurricane (1966)
Landslide (1967)
The Vivero Letter (1968)
The Spoilers (1969)
Running Blind (1970)
The Freedom Trap (1971)
The Tightrope Men (1973)
The Snow Tiger (1975)
The Enemy (1978)
Flyaway (1979)
Bahama Crisis (1980)
Windfall (1982)
The Legacy (1982)
Night of Error (1984) posth

BAGNOLD, Enid (Algerine)
(1889–1981) English

Serena Blandish (1925)
National Velvet (1935)
The Loved and the Envied (1951)

BAINBRIDGE, Beryl
(1934–) English

A Weekend with Claude (1967)
Another Part of the Wood (1968)
Harriet Said (1972)
The Dressmaker (1973)
The Bottle Factory Outing (1974)
Sweet William (1975)
A Quiet Life (1976)
Injury Time (1977)
Young Adolf (1978)
Winter Garden (1980)
Watson's Apology (1984)
Mum and Mr Armitage (1985)
Forever England (1986)
Filthy Lucre (1986)
An Awfully Big Adventure (1989)

BALCHIN, Nigel
(1908–70) English

The Small Back Room (1943)
Mine Own Executioner (1945)
In the Absence of Mrs Petersen (1966)

BALDWIN, James (Arthur)
(1924–87) American

Go Tell It on the Mountain (1953)
Giovanni's Room (1956)
Another Country (1962)
Tell Me How Long the Train's Been Gone (1968)
If Beale Street Could Talk (1974)
Just Above My Head (1979)

BALL, John
(1911–) American

In the Heat of the Night (1965)
Five Pieces of Jade (1972)
Mark One – the Dummy (1974)

BALLANTYNE, R(obert) M(ichael)
(1825–94) Scottish

(adventure)
The Young Fur-Traders (1856)
Ungava (1857)
The Coral Island (1858)
Martin Rattler (1858)
The World of Ice (1860)
The Dog Crusoe (1861)
The Gorilla Hunters (1861)
The Wild Man of the West (1863)
The Lifeboat (1864)
The Lighthouse (1865)
Fighting the Flames (1867)
Deep Down (1868)
The Iron Horse (1871)
Black Ivory (1873)
Pirate City (1874)
Under the Waves (1876)
Post Haste (1880)

BALLARD, J(ames) G(raham)
(1930–) English

(science fiction)
The Drowned World (1962)
The Drought (1965)
The Crystal World (1966)
Crash (1972)
Concrete Island (1972)
High Rise (1975)
Empire of the Sun [1] (1984)

[1] not science fiction

BALZAC, Honoré de
(1799–1850) French

Les Chouans (1829)
Contes drolatiques (1832–7) 3 vol
La Comédie humaine (1842–8) 17 vol

BANKS, Iain
(1954–) Scottish

The Wasp Factory (1984)
The Bridge (1986)
Canal Dreams (1989)

BANKS, Lynne Reid
(1929–) English

The L-Shaped Room (1960)
The Backward Shadow (1970)
The Adventures of King Midas (1974)
Two is Lonely (1974)
Dark Quartet (1976)
Path to the Silent Country (1977)

BANVILLE, John
(1945–) Irish

Nightspawn (1971)
Birchwood (1973)
Doctor Copernicus (1976)
Kepler (1981)
The Newton Letter: An Interlude (1982)
Mefisto (1986)
The Book of Evidence (1989)

BARBEY D'AUREVILLY, Jules-Amédée
(1808–89) French

L'Amour impossible (1841)
La Bague d'Annibal (1843)
Une Vieille Maîtresse (1851)
L'Ensorcelée (1854)
Le Chevalier des Touches (1864)
Un Prêtre marié (1865)
Les Diaboliques (1874) coll
Une Histoire sans nom (1882)
Ce qui ne meurt pas (1884)
Une Page d'histoire (1886)

BARDIN, John Franklin
(1916–) American

(thriller)
The Deadly Percheron (1946)
The Last of Phili Banter (1947)
Devil Take the Blue-Tail Fly (1948)

BARING-GOULD, Sabine
(1834–1924) English

Through Fire and Flame (1868)
Mehalah (1880)
The Gaverocks (1888)
The Broom-Squire (1896)

BARNES, Djuna (Chappell)
(1892–1982) American

Ryder (1928)
Nightwood (1936)

BARNES, Julian (Patrick)
(1946–) English

Metroland (1980)
as D Kavanagh
Before She Met Me (1982)
as D Kavanagh
Fiddle City (1983)
as D Kavanagh
Flaubert's Parrot (1984)
Putting the Boot In (1985)
as D Kavanagh
Staring at the Sun (1986)
A History of the World in 10 1/2 Chapters (1989)
Talking It Over (1991)

BAROJA, Pia
(1872–1956) Spanish

The City of the Discreet (1905)
Paradox King (1906)
The Tree of Knowledge (1911)

BARRÈS, Maurice
(1862–1923) French

Sous l'oeil des barbares [1] (1888)
Un Homme libre [1] (1889)
Le Jardin de Bérénice [1] (1891)
Les Déracinés [2] (1897)
L'Appel au soldat [2] (1900)
Leurs figures [2] (1902)
Au service de l'Allemagne [3] (1905)
Colette Baudoche [3] (1909)
La Colline inspirée (1913)
Le Génie du Rhin (1921)
Un Jardin sur l'Oronte (1922)

[1] Culte de moi novels
[2] Le Roman de l'energie nationale novels
[3] Les Bastions de l'Est novels

BARRIE, J(ames) M(atthew)
(1860–1937) Scottish

Auld Licht Idylls [1] (1888)
A Window in Thrums [1] (1889)
The Little Minister [1] (1891)
Sentimental Tommy (1896)
Tommy and Grizel (1900)
Peter and Wendy (1911)

[1] Thrums novels

BARSTOW, Stan(ley)
(1928–) English

A Kind of Loving (1961)
Ask Me Tomorrow (1962)
Joby (1964)
The Watchers on the Shore (1966)
A Raging Calm (1968)
Right True End (1976)
Brother's Tale (1980)
Just You Wait and see (1986)

BARTH, John (Simmons)
(1930–) American

The Floating Opera (1956)
The End of the Road (1958)
The Sot-Weed Factor (1960)
Giles Goat-Boy (1966)
Chimera (1974)
Letters (1979)
Sabbatical (1982)
Tidewater Tales (1988)

BARTHELME, Donald
(1931–89) American

Come Back, Dr Caligari (1964)
Snow White (1967)
Sadness (1972)
The Dead Father (1975)
Paradise (1986)

BASSANI, Giorgio
(1916–) Italian
The Gold Rimmed Spectacles (1958)
The Garden of the Finzi-Continis (1962)
The Heron (1968)

BASSO, Hamilton
(1904–64) American
Courthouse Square (1936)
Sun in Capricorn (1942)
The View from Pompey's Head (1954)

BASTARD, Lucien
see **ESTANG, Luc**

BATES, H(erbert) E(rnest)
(1905–74) English
The Two Sisters (1926)
The Fallow Land (1932)
Fair Stood the Wind for France (1944)
The Jacaranda Tree (1949)
Love for Lydia (1952)
The Darling Buds of May (1958)

BAUM L(yman) Frank
(1856–1919) American
(children's)
The Wonderful Wizard of Oz (1900)
The Marvelous Land of Oz (1905)
Queen Zixi of Ix (1905)
Ozma of Oz (1907)
Dorothy and the Wizard of Oz (1908)
The Road to Oz (1909)
The Emerald City of Oz (1910)
The Patchwork Girl of Oz (1913)
Tik-Tok of Oz (1914)
The Scarecrow of Oz (1915)

BAUM, Vicki
(1888–1960) Austro-American
Grand Hotel (1930)
Falling Star (1934)
Headless Angel (1948)
The Mustard Seed (1953)
Ballerina (1958)

BAWDEN, Nina
(1925–) English
Odd Flamingo (1954)
Change Here for Babylon (1956)
Devil by the Sea (1957)
Just Like a Lady (1960)
The Secret Passage[1] (1963)
Tortoise by Candlelight (1963)
On the Run[1] (1964)
The White Horse Gang[1] (1966)
The Witch's Daughter[1] (1966)
A Handful of Thieves[1] (1967)
The Runaway Summer[1] (1969)
The Birds on the Trees (1970)
Squib[1] (1971)
Anna Apparent (1972)
Carrie's War[1] (1973)
The Peppermint Pig[1] (1975)
Rebel on a Rock[1] (1978)
Familiar Passions (1979)
The Robbers[1] (1979)
Kept in the Dark[1] (1982)
The Ice House (1983)
The Finding[1] (1985)
Circles of Deceit (1987)
Keeping Henry[1] (1988)
The Outside Child[1] *(1989)*

[1] children's

BAYLY, Ada Ellen
see **LYALL, Edna**

BEACH, Edward
(1918–) American
Run Silent, Run Deep (1955)
Dust on the Sea (1972)

BEAUCHAMP, Kathleen Mansfield
see **MANSFIELD, Katherine**

BEAUVOIR, Simone de
(1908–86) French
L'Invitée (1943)
Le Sang des autres (1944)
Tous les hommes sont mortels (1946)

Les Mandarins (1954)
Les Belles Images (1966)

BECKETT, Samuel (Barclay)
(1906–89) Irish
Murphy (1938)
Molloy (1951)
Watt (1953)
Malone Dies (1956)
The Unnamable (1958)
How It Is (1961)

BECKFORD, William
(1760–1844) English
Vathek (1787)

BEDFORD, Sybille
(1911–) English
The Sudden View (1953)
The Legacy (1956)
A Favourite of the Gods (1962)
A Compass Error (1968)

BEERBOHM, Sir (Henry) Max(imilian)
(1872–1956) English
Zuleika Dobson (1911)

BEHN, Aphra
(1640–89) English
Oroonoko (1688)

BEKESSY, Hans
see **HABE, Hans**

BELL, Acton, Currer & Ellis
see **BRONTË, Anne, Charlotte & Emily**

BELLAMY, Edward
(1850–98) American
Looking Backward: 2000–1887 (1888)

BELLOC, Hilaire (Joseph Hilary Pierre)
(1870–1953) Anglo-French
Emmanuel Burden, Merchant (1904)
Mr Clutterbuck's Election (1908)
The Girondin (1911)
The Green Overcoat (1912)
Belinda (1928)

BELLOW, Saul
(1915–) American
Dangling Man (1944)
The Victim (1947)
The Adventures of Augie March (1953)
Seize the Day (1956)
Henderson the Rain King (1959)
Herzog (1964)
Mr Sammler's Planet (1969)
Humboldt's Gift (1975)
The Dean's December (1982)
More Die of Heartbreak (1987)
The Bellarosa Connection (1989)

BELY, Andrei
(1880–1934) Russian
real name: Boris Nikolaevich Bugayev
The Silver Dove (1909)
Petersburg (1913)
Kotik Letaev (1915–1916) 2 vol

BEMELMANS, Ludwig
(1898–1963) Austro-American
Madeline (1938)
(plus many Madeline novels)
Quito Express (1938)
Hotel Splendide (1941)
The High World (1954)
The Street Where the Heart Lies (1963)

BENCHLEY, Peter (Bradford)
(1940–) American
Jaws (1974)
The Deep (1976)
The Island (1979)
The Girl of the Sea of Cortez (1982)
Q Clearance (1986)

BENEDICTUS, David
(1938–) English

The Fourth of June (1962)
World of Windows (1971)
Twentieth-Century Man (1978)

BENET, Stephen Vincent
(1898–1943) American

Jean Huguenot (1923)
The Devil and Daniel Webster (1937)

BENNETT, (Enoch) Arnold
(1867–1931) English

A Man from the North (1898)
Grand Babylon Hotel (1902)
Anna of the Five Towns (1902)
The Gates of Wrath (1903)
The Old Wives' Tale (1908)
Clayhanger[1] (1910)
Hilda Lessways[1] (1911)
The Card (1911)
These Twain[1] (1915)
The Roll Call (1918)
Mr Prohack (1922)
Riceyman Steps (1923)
Imperial Palace (1930)

[1] Clayhanger trilogy

BENSON, E(dward) F(rederic)
(1867–1940) English
Brother of RH Benson

Dodo (1893)
(plus many Dodo novels)
Queen Lucia (1920)
(plus many Lucia novels)
The Face (1929)

BENSON, R(obert) H(ugh)
(1871–1914) English
Brother of EF Benson

The Lord of the World (1907)
Come Rack! Come Rope! (1912)
The Average Man (1913)

BENSON, Stella
(1892–1933) English

The Little World (1925)
Tobit Transplanted (1931)

BENTLEY, E(dmund) C(lerihew)
(1875–1956) English

(crime)
Trent's Last Case (1913)

BENTLEY, Phyllis
(1894–1977) English

Carr (1929)
Inheritance (1932)
A Modern Tragedy (1934)

BERGER, John (Peter)
(1926–) English

A Painter of Our Time (1958)
The Foot of Clive (1962)
Corker's Freedom (1964)
G (1972)

BERGER, Thomas (Louis)
(1924–) American

Crazy in Berlin (1958)
Reinhart in Love (1962)
Little Big Man (1964)
Killing Time (1967)
Regiment of Women (1973)
Sneaky People (1975)
Who Is Teddy Villanova? (1979)
Arthur Rex: A Legendary Novel (1979)
Neighbors (1980)
Reinhart's Women (1981)
The Feud (1983)
Nowhere (1985)
Being Invisible (1987)
The Houseguest (1988)
Changing the Past (1989)
Orrie's Story (1990)

BERGMAN, Hjalmar
(1883–1931) Swedish
Clownen Jac (1930)

BERKELEY, Anthony
see **ILES, Francis**

BERNANOS, Georges
(1888–1948) French
Sous le soleil de Satan (1926)
La Joie (1929)
Un Crime (1935)
Le Journal d'un curé de campagne (1936)
Nouvelle Histoire de Mouchette (1937)
Monsieur Ouine (1946)

BESANT, Sir Walter
(1836–1901) English
Ready-Money Mortiboy (1872)
with James Rice
The Golden Butterfly (1876)
with James Rice
By Celia's Arbour (1878)
with James Rice
The Steamy Side (1881)
with James Rice
The Chaplain of the Fleet (1881)
with James Rice
All Sorts and Conditions of Men (1882)
Children of Gibeon (1886)

BESTER, Alfred
(1913–) American
(science fiction)
The Demolished Man (1953)
The Stars My Destination (1956)
The Computer Connection (1974)

BEYLE, Henri
see **STENDHAL**

BIANCO, Margery Williams
(1881–1944) American
(children's)
The Velveteen Rabbit (1922)
The Little Wooden Doll (1925)
Poor Cecco (1925)

BIGGERS, Earl Derr
(1884–1933) American
Seven Keys to Baldpate (1913)
The Agony Column (1916)
The House without a Key (1925)
(plus many Charlie Chan novels)

BINCHY, Maeve
(1940–) Irish
Light a Penny Candle (1982)
Echoes (1985)
Firefly Summer (1987)
Circle of Friends (1990)

BIRD, Robert Montgomery
(1806–54) American
Sheppard Lee (1836)
Nick of the Woods (1837)
The Adventures of Robin Day (1839)

BITZIUS, Albert
see **GOTTHELF, Jeremias**

BLACK, William
(1841–1898) Scottish
A Daughter of Heth (1871)
The Strange Adventures of a Phaeton (1872)
A Princess of Thule (1873)
Madcap Violet (1876)
Macleod of Dare (1879)

BLACKMORE, R(ichard) D(oddridge)
(1825–1900) English
Clara Vaughan (1864)

BLACKMORE, RD (cont.)
Cradock Nowell (1866)
Lorna Doone (1869)
The Maid of Sker (1872)
Alice Lorraine (1875)
Springhaven (1877)
Tommy Upmore (1884)

BLACKWOOD, Algernon (Henry)
(1869–1951) English
(occult)
The Empty House (1906)
John Silence (1908)
The Human Chord (1910)
The Wave (1916)
Tongues of Fire (1924)
The Dance of Death (1927)
Shocks (1935)

BLAIR, Eric (Arthur)
see **ORWELL, George**

BLAKE, Nicholas
(1904–72) Anglo-Irish
real name: Cecil Day-Lewis
(crime)
A Question of Proof (1935)
Thou Shell of Death (1936)
There's Trouble Brewing (1937)
The Beast Must Die (1938)
The Smiler with the Knife (1939)
Malice in Wonderland (1940)
The Case of the Abominable Snowman (1941)
Minute for Murder (1947)
The Dreadful Hollow (1953)
The Whisper in the Gloom (1954)
End of Chapter (1957)
The Widow's Cruise (1959)
The Worm of Death (1961)
The Sad Variety (1964)
The Morning After Death (1966)

BLANCHOT, Maurice
(1907–) French
Thomas l'Obscur (1941)
Aminadab (1942)
L'Arrêt de mort (1948)
Celui qui ne m'accompagnait pas (1953)
Le Dernier Homme (1957)
L'Attente, l'Oubli (1961)

BLASCO IBAÑEZ, Vicente
(1867–1928) Spanish
The Cabin (1898)
Blood and Sand (1908)
The Four Horsemen of the Apocalypse (1916)

BLATTY, William Peter
(1928–) American
Which Way to Mecca, Jack? (1961)
The Exorcist (1971)
I'll Tell Them I Remember You (1974)
Legion (1983)

BLISH, James
(1921–75) American
(science fiction)
Earthman Come Home (1955)
A Case of Conscience (1958)
Black Easter of Faust Aleph Null (1968)

BLIXEN, Karen (Christentze)
(1885–1962) Danish
née Dinesen
Out of Africa (1938)
Winter's Tales (1942) coll
Last Tales (1957) coll

BLOCH, Robert (Albert)
(1917–) American
(thriller)
The Scarf (1947)
The Kidnapper (1954)
Shooting Star (1958)
Psycho (1959)
Firebug (1961)
Terror (1962)
The Star Stalker (1968)
The Todd Dossier (1969)

Night-World (1962)
American Gothic (1974)
There is a Serpent in Eden (1979)
Psycho II (1982)
Night of the Ripper (1984)
Unholy Trinity (1986)

BLUME, Judy
(1938–) American

(children's)
Iggie's House (1970)
Are You There God? It's Me, Margaret (1970)
Then Again, Maybe I Won't (1971)
It's Not the End of the World (1972)
Tales of a Fourth Grade Nothing (1972)
Deenie (1973)
Blubber (1974)
Forever (1975)
Wifey [1] (1978)
Superfudge (1980)

[1] not children's

BLYTH, Harry
see **MEREDITH, Hal**

BLYTON, Enid (Mary)
(1897–1968) English

(children's)
The Adventures of the Wishing Chair (1937)
(plus many Wishing Chair books)
Mr Galliano's Circus (1938)
(plus many Galliano books)
The Secret Island (1938)
Naughty Amelia Jane (1939)
(plus many Amelia Jane books)
Five on a Treasure Island (1942)
(plus many Famous Five books)
St Clare's (1943)
(plus many St Clare's books)
The Secret Seven (1945)
(plus many Secret Seven books)
Malory Towers (1946)
(plus many Malory Towers books)
Little Noddy Goes to Toyland (1949)
(plus many Noddy books)

BOLDREWOOD, Rolf
(1826–1915) Australian
real name: Thomas Alexander Browne

Robbery Under Arms (1888)
War to the Knife (1889)

BÖLL, Heinrich
(1917–) German

Der Zug war pünktlich (1949)
Und sagte kein einziges Wort (1953)
Haus ohne Hüter (1954)
Das Brot der frühen Jahre (1955)
Billard um halb zehn (1959)
Die Ansichten eines Clowns (1963)
Gruppenbild mit Dame (1971)
Die verlorene Ehre der Katharina Blüm (1974)
Fürsorgliche Belagerung (1979)

BORGES, Jorge Luis
(1899–1986) Argentinian

Fictions (1944) coll
Labyrinths (1953) coll

BORROW, George
(1803–81) English

The Zincali (1841)
The Bible in Spain (1843)
Lavengro (1851)
The Romany Rye (1857)
Wild Wales (1862)

BOULLE, Pierre
(1912–) French

William Conrad (1950)
The Bridge over the River Kwai (1952)
The Planet of the Apes (1961)

BOURGET, Paul
(1852–1935) French

L'Irréparable (1884)
Cruelle énigme (1885)
André Cornélis (1887)
Le Disciple (1889)

BOURGET, Paul (cont.)
Cosmopolis (1893)
L'étape (1902)
Un Divorce (1904)
L'émigré (1907)
Le Démon de midi (1914)
Le Justicier (1919)
L'échéance (1921)

BOWEN, Elizabeth (Dorothea)
(1899–1973) Anglo-Irish
The Hotel (1927)
The Last September (1929)
Friends and Relations (1931)
To the North (1932)
The House in Paris (1935)
The Death of the Heart (1938)
The Heat of the Day (1949)
A World of Love (1955)
The Little Girls (1964)
A Day in the Dark (1965)
Eva Trout (1969)

BOWLES, Paul
(1910–) American
The Sheltering Sky (1949)
The Delicate Prey (1950)
Let It Come Down (1952)
The Spider's House (1955)
Up Above the World (1966)

BOYD, James
(1888–1944) American
(historical)
Drums (1925)
Marching On (1927)
Bitter Creek (1939)

BOYD, William (Andrew Murray)
(1952–) British
A Good man in Africa (1981)
An Ice-Cream War (1982)
Stars and Bars (1984)
The New Confessions (1987)
Brazzaville Beach (1990)

BRADBURY, Malcolm (Stanley)
(1932–) English
Eating People Is Wrong (1959)
Stepping Westward (1965)
The History Man (1975)
Rates of Exchange (1983)
Why Come to Slaka? (1986)
Cuts (1987)

BRADBURY, Ray(mond Douglas)
(1920–) American
(science fiction)
The Martian Chronicles (1950)
The Illustrated Man (1951)
Fahrenheit 451 (1953)
Dandelion Wine (1957)
Something Wicked This Way Comes (1962)
The Autumn People (1965)
Tomorrow Night (1966)
Long After Midnight (1976)
To Sing Strange Songs (1979)
Death is a Lonely Business (1985)
A Graveyard for Lunatics (1990)

BRADDON, Mary Elizabeth
(1837–1915) English
The Trail of the Serpent (1861)
Lady Audley's Secret (1862)
Aurora Floyd (1863)
The Doctor's Wife (1864)
Henry Dunbar (1864)
Ishmael (1884)

BRADFORD, Barbara Taylor
(1933–) English
A Woman of Substance (1980)
Voice of the Heart (1983)
Hold the Dream (1985)
Act of Will (1986)
To Be the Best (1988)
The Women in His Life (1990)
Remember (1991)

BRAGG, Melvyn
(1939–) English

For Want of a Nail (1965)
The Second Inheritance (1966)
Without a City Wall (1968)
The Hired Man [1] (1968)
A Place in England [1] (1970)
The Nerve (1971)
The Hunt (1971)
Josh Lawton (1972)
The Silken Net (1974)
Autumn Manoeuvres (1978)
Kingdom Come [1] (1980)
Love and Glory (1983)
The Maid of Buttermere (1987)
A Time to Dance (1989)

[1] Cumbrian trilogy

BRAINE, John (Gerard)
(1922–86) English

Room at the Top (1957)
The Vodi (1959)
Life at the Top (1962)
The Jealous God (1964)
Stay With Me Till Morning (1968)
The Queen of a Distant Country (1972)
Finger of Fire (1977)
One and Last Love (1981)

BRINK, André
(1935–) South African

Looking on Darkness (1974)
An Instant in the Wind (1976)
Rumours of Rain (1978)
A Dry White Season (1979)
A Chain of Voices (1982)
The Wall of the Plague (1984)
The Ambassador (1985)
States of Emergency (1988)

BROCH, Hermann
(1886–1951) Austrian

Die Schlafwandler (1930–2) 3 vol
Die unbekante Grösse (1933)
Bergroman (1935)
Der Tod des Vergil (1945)

BRODKEY, Harold (Roy)
(1930–) American

The Runaway Soul (1991)

BROMFIELD, Louis
(1896–1956) American

The Green Bay Tree [1] (1924)
Possession [1] (1925)
Early Autumn [1] (1926)
A Good Woman [1] (1927)
The Strange Case of Miss Annie Spragge (1928)
The Rains Came (1937)
Wild is the River (1941)
Until the Daybreak (1942)
Bitter Lotus (1945)
Colorado (1947)
Mr Smith (1951)

[1] Escape tetraology

BRONTË, Anne
(1820–49) English
early pseudonym: Acton Bell
Sister of Charlotte & Emily

Agnes Grey (1847)
The Tenant of Wildfell Hall (1848)

BRONTË, Charlotte
(1816–55) English
early pseudonym: Currer Bell
Sister of Anne & Emily

Jane Eyre (1847)
Shirley (1849)
Villette (1853)
Emma (1855) unf
The Professor (1857) posth

BRONTË, Emily (Jane)
(1818–48) English
early pseudonym: Ellis Bell
Sister of Anne & Charlotte

Wuthering Heights (1847)

BROOKE, (Bernard) Jocelyn
(1908–66) English

The Scapegoat (1948)
The Military Orchid (1948)
A Mine of Serpents (1949)
The Goose Cathedral (1950)
The Image of a Drawn Sword (1950)
Four Portraits (1954)

BROOKE, Henry
(1703–83) Irish

The Fool of Quality (1770)
Juliet Grenville (1774)

BROOKNER, Anita
(1928–) English

A Start in Life (1981)
Providence (1982)
Look at Me (1983)
Hotel du Lac (1984)
Family and Friends (1985)
A Misalliance (1986)
A Friend from England (1987)
Latecomers (1988)
A Closed Eye (1991)

BROPHY, Brigid (Antonia)
(1929–) Anglo-Irish

Hackenfeller's Ape (1953)
The King of a Rainy Country (1956)
Flesh (1962)
The Finishing Touch (1963)
The Snow Ball (1964)
In Transit (1969)
The Adventures of God in His Search for the Black Girl (1973)
Pussy Owl (1976)
Place without Chairs (1978)

BROSTER, D(orothy) K(athleen)
(1877–1950) English

(historical romance)
Sir Isumbras at the Ford (1918)
The Yellow Poppy (1912)
The Wounded Name (1922)
Mr Rowl (1924)
The Flight of the Heron [1] (1925)
The Gleam in the North [1] (1927)
The Dark Mile [1] (1929)
Ships in the Bay! (1931)
Almond, White Almond (1933)
Child Royal (1937)
The Sea without a Haven (1941)
The Captain's Lady (1947)

[1] Jacobite trilogy

BROWN, Charles Brockden
(1771–1810) American

Wieland (1798)
Arthur Mervyn (1799)
Ormond (1799)
Edgar Huntly (1799)
Clara Howard (1801)
Jane Talbot (1801)

BROWN, George Douglas
see **DOUGLAS, George**

BROWN, George Mackay
(1921–) Scottish

Greenvoe (1972)
Magnus (1973)

BROWNE, T(homas) A(lexander)
see **BOLDREWOOD, Rolf**

BRUNHOFF, Jean de
(1899–1937) French

The Story of Babar (1931)
(plus many Babar books)

BRYHER
(1894–1983) English
real name: (Annie) Winifred Ellerman

The Fourteenth of October (1952)

BUCHAN, John
(1875–1940) Scottish
Baron Tweedsmuir

Sir Quixote of the Moors (1895)
Prester John (1910)
The Power House (1910)
The Thirty-Nine Steps (1915)
Greenmantle (1916)
Mr Standfast (1918)
Huntingtower (1922)
The Three Hostages (1924)
John Macnab (1925)
The Dancing Floor (1926)
Castle Gay (1926)
Witch Wood (1927)
Gap in the Curtain (1927)
The Courts of the Morning (1929)
House of the Four Winds (1934)
The Island of Sheep (1936)
Sick Heart River (1941) posth

BUCK, Pearl
(1892–1973) American
née Sydenstricker

(Chinese)
East Wind, West Wind (1930)
The Good Earth[1] (1931)
Sons[1] (1932)
A House Divided[1] (1935)
The Exile (1936)
The Patriot (1939)
Other Gods (1940)
Dragon Seed (1942)
Imperial Women (1956)
The Three Daughters of Madame Liang (1969)

[1] House of Earth trilogy

BUCKERIDGE, Anthony
(1912–) English

(children's)
Jennings Goes to School (1950)
(plus many Jennings books)

BUGAYEV, Boris Nikolaevich
see **BELY, Andrei**

BUKOWSKI, Charles
(1920–) American

Post Office (1971)
Factotum (1975)
Women (1978)
Ham on Rye (1982)
Hollywood (1989)

BULGAKOV, Mikhail (Afanasevich)
(1891–1940) Russian

The White Guard (1925)
Black Snow (1937)

BULWER-LYTTON, Edward
(1803–73) English
Baron Lytton

Falkland (1827)
Pelham (1828)
The Disowned and Devereux (1829)
Paul Clifford (1830)
Eugene Aram (1832)
Godolphin (1833)
The Last Days of Pompeii (1834)
Rienzi (1835)
Ernest Maltravers (1837)
Zanoni (1842)
The Last of the Barons (1843)
Harold (1848)
My Novel (1853)
What Will He Do With It? (1858)
A Strange Story (1862)
The Coming Race (1871)
Kenelm Chillingly (1873)
The Parisians (1873) unf

BUNIN, Ivan (Alexeievich)
(1870–1953) Russian

The Village (1910)
Sukhodol (1911)

BUNIN, Ivan (cont.)

The Gentleman from San Francisco (1914)
The Life of Arsenev (1927)
The Well of Days (1933)

BUNYAN, John
(1628–88) English

(allegorical)
The Pilgrim's Progress (1678–84) 2 vol
The Life and Death of Mr Badman (1680)
The Holy War (1682)

BURGESS, Anthony
(1917–) English
real name: John Anthony Burgess Wilson

Time for A Tiger [1] (1956)
The Enemy in the Blanket [1] (1958)
Beds in the East [1] (1959)
The Doctor is Sick (1960)
One Hand Clapping (1961)
as Joseph Kell
A Clockwork Orange (1962)
The Wanting Seed (1962)
Honey for the Bears (1963)
Inside Mr Enderby [2] (1963)
as Joseph Kell
Nothing Like the Sun (1964)
The Eve of St Venus (1964)
Tremor of Intent (1965)
Enderby Outside [2] (1968)
MF (1971)
The Clockwork Testament [2] (1974)
1985 (1978)
Earthly Powers (1980)
The End of the World News (1982)
Enderby's Dark Lady [2] (1984)
The Kingdom of the Wicked (1985)
The Piano Players (1986)
Any Old Iron (1988)
The Devil's Mode (1990)

[1] Malayan trilogy [2] Enderby novels

BURNETT, Francis (Eliza) Hodgson
(1849–1924) Anglo-American

That Lass O'Lowrie's (1877)
A Far Barbarian (1881)
Little Lord Fauntleroy (1886)
Sara Crewe (1888)
Two Little Pilgrims' Progress (1895)
The Little Princess (1905)
The Secret Garden (1910)
The Lost Prince (1915)
Robin (1922)

BURNEY, Fanny
(1752–1840) English
Madame D'Arblay

Evelina (1778)
Cecilia (1782)
Camilla (1796)
The Wanderer (1814)

BURROUGHS, Edgar Rice
(1875–1950) American

Tarzan of the Apes (1914)
(plus many Tarzan novels)

BURROUGHS, William (Seward)
(1914–) American

Junkie (1953)
The Naked Lunch (1959)
The Experimentor (1960)
The Soft Machine (1961)
The Ticket That Exploded (1962)
Dead Fingers Talk (1963)
Nova Express (1964)
The Wild Boys (1971)
Exterminator! (1973)
The Last Words of Dutch Schulz (1975)
Cities of the Red Night (1981)

BUTLER, Samuel
(1835–1902) English

Erewhon (1872)
The Fair Haven (1873)
Erewhon Revisited (1901)
The Way of All Flesh (1903) posth

BUTOR, Michel (Marie François)
(1926–) French

Passage de Milan (1954)
L'Emploi du temps (1956)
La Modification (1957)
Degrés (1960)
La Génie du Piev (1960)
San Marco (1963)
Intervalle (1973)

BYARS, Betsy (Cromer)
(1928–) American

(children's)
The Summer of the Swans (1970)
The Eighteenth Emergency (1973)
Goodbye, Chicken Little (1979)
The Night Swimmers (1980)
The Animal, the Vegetable and John D Jones (1982)

BYATT, A(ntonia) S(usan)
(1936–) English
Sister of Margaret Drabble

Shadow of a Sun (1964)
The Game (1967)
The Virgin in the Garden (1978)
Still Life (1985)
Possession (1990)

C

CABELL, James Branch
(1879–1958) American

(fantasy)
The Eagle's Shadow (1904)
The Soul of Melicent (1913)
Figures of Earth (1915)
The Silver Stallion (1917)
Jurgen (1919)
The High Place (1923)
The Music from Behind the Moon (1926)

CABLE, George Washington
(1844–1925) American

The Grandissimes (1880)
Madame Delphine (1881)
Dr Sevier (1885)
Bonaventure (1888)
John March, Southerner (1894)
Bylow Hill (1902)

CAIN, James M(allahan)
(1892–1977) American

(crime)
The Postman Always Rings Twice (1934)
Serenade (1937)
Mildred Pierce (1941)
Love's Lovely Counterfeit (1942)
Career in C Major (1943)
Double Indemnity (1943)
Rainbow's End (1975)
Cloud Nine (1984) posth
The Enchanted Isle (1985) posth

CAINE, Sir (Thomas Henry) Hall
(1853–1931) English

The Shadow of a Crime (1885)
The Deemster (1887)
The Bondman (1890)
The Scapegoat (1891)
The Manxman (1894)
The Christian (1897)
The Eternal City (1901)
The Prodigal Son (1904)
The White Prophet (1909)
The Woman Thou Gavest Me (1913)

CALDWELL, Erskine (Preston)
(1903–87) American

The Bastard (1929)
Poor Fool (1930)
American Earth (1931)
Tobacco Road (1932)
God's Little Acre (1933)
Journeyman (1935)
Some American People (1935)
All-Out on the Road to Smolensk (1942)

CALDWELL, Erskine (cont.)
Sure Hand of God (1947)
A Lamp for Nightfall (1952)
Love and Money (1954)
Jenny by Nature (1961)
Close to Home (1962)
The Last Night of Summer (1963)
Summertime Island (1969)
The Weather Shelter (1970)
Annette (1974)

CALLAGHAN, Morley (Edward)
(1903–) Canadian
Strange Fugitive (1928)
Native Argosy (1929)
It's Never Over (1930)
Broken Journey (1932)
Such Is My Beloved (1934)
They Shall Inherit the Earth (1935)
More Joy in Heaven (1936)
Jake Baldwin's Vow (1948)
The Loved and the Lost (1951)
The Man with the Coat (1955)
The Many Coloured Coat (1960)
That Summer in Paris (1963)
A Fine and Private Place (1975)
A Time for Judas (1983)

CALVINO, Italo
(1923–85) Italian
Il sentiero dei nidi di ragno (1947)
Il visconte dimezzato (1952)
Il barone rampante (1957)
Il cavaliere inesistente (1959)
Le citté invisibili (1972)
Palomar (1983)

CAMUS, Albert
(1913–60) French
L'Étranger (1942)
La Peste (1947)
La Chute (1956)

CANETTI, Elias
(1905–) Bulgarian
Die Blendung (1935)

CANTWELL, Robert (Emmett)
(1908–) American
Laugh and Lie Down (1931)
The Land of Plenty (1934)

CAPEK, Josef
(1887–1945) Czech
Brother of Karel Capek
Stin Kapradiny (1930)

CAPEK, Karel
(1890–1938) Czech
Brother of Josef Capek
The Manufacture of the Absolute (1923)
Hordubal (1933)
The Meteor (1933)
An Ordinary Life (1934)
War with the Newts (1936)

CAPOTE, Truman
(1924–84) American
Other Voices, Other Rooms (1948)
The Grass Harp (1951)
Breakfast at Tiffany's (1958)
In Cold Blood (1966)
Thanksgiving Visitor (1968)

CAREY, Peter (Philip)
(1943–) Australian
Bliss (1981)
Illywhacker (1985)
Oscar and Lucinda (1989)
The Tax Inspector (1991)

CARPENTIER, Alejo
(1904–80) Cuban
El reino de este mundo (1949)
Los pasos perdidos (1953)
El siglo de las luces (1962)

CARR, Philippa
see **PLAIDY, Jean**

CARROLL, Lewis
(1832–98) English
real name: Charles Lutwidge Dodgson

(children's)
Alice's Adventures in Wonderland (1865)
Through the Looking-Glass (1871)
Sylvie and Bruno (1889)

CARTER, Angela
(1940–92) English

Shadow Dance (1966)
Heroes and Villains (1969)
The Infernal Desire Machines of Dr Hoffman (1972)
Nights at the Circus (1984)

CARTLAND, Dame (Mary) Barbara
(1901–) English

Jigsaw (1923)
(plus many romance novels)

CARY, (Arthur) Joyce (Lunel)
(1888–1957) Irish

Aissa Saved (1932)
An American Visitor (1933)
The African Witch (1936)
Castle Corner (1938)
Mister Johnson (1939)
Charley Is My Darling (1940)
The House of Children (1941)
Herself Surprised (1941)
To Be a Pilgrim (1942)
The Horse's Mouth (1944)
The Moonlight (1946)
A Fearful Joy (1949)
Prisoner of Grace (1952)
Except the Lord (1953)
Not Honour More (1955)
The Captive and the Free (1959) posth unf

CATHER, Willa (Sibert)
(1873–1947) American

The Troll Gardens (1905)
Alexander's Bridge (1912)
O Pioneers! (1913)
The Song of the Lark (1915)
My Antonia (1918)
One of Ours (1922)
A Lost Lady (1923)
The Professor's House (1925)
My Mortal Enemy (1926)
Death Comes for the Archbishop (1927)
Shadows of the Rock (1931)
Lucy Gayheart (1935)
Sapphire and the Slavce Girl (1940)

CELA, Camilo José
(1916–) Spanish

San Camilo (1936)
The Family of Pascual Duarte (1942)
Viaje a la Alcarria (1948)
La Colmena (1951)

CÉLINE, Louis-Ferdinand
(1894–1961) French
real name: Louis-Ferdinand Destouches

Voyage au bout de la nuit (1932)
Mort àcrédit (1936)
Bagatelles pour un massacre (1938)
Les Beaux Draps (1941)
D'un château l'autre (1957)
Entretiens avec le professeur Y (1959)
Nord (1960)
Rigodon (1969) posth

CERVANTES (SAAVEDRA), Miguel de
(1547–1616) Spanish

La Galatea (1585)
Don Quixote (1605–15) 2 vol
Persiles y Sigismunda (1617) posth

CHALLANS, Mary
see **RENAULT, Mary**

CHAMISSO, Adelbert von
(1781–1838) Franco-German

Peter Schlemihl (1813)

CHANDLER, Raymond (Thornton)
(1888–1959) American

The Big Sleep (1939)
Farewell, My Lovely (1940)
The High Window (1942)
The Lady in the Lake (1943)
The Little Sister (1949)
The Long Goodbye (1953)
Playback (1958)

CHARTERIS, Leslie
(1907–) Anglo-American
real name: Leslie Charles Bowyer Yin

Meet the Tiger (1928)
(plus many Saint novels)

CHASE, James Hadley
(1906–) English
real name: René Raymond

No Orchids for Miss Blandish (1939)
Mallory (1950)
Why Pick on Me? (1951)
Just Another Sucker (1961)
One Bright Summer's Morning (1963)
This Is For Real (1965)
The Whiff of Money (1969)
An Ace Up My Sleeve (1971)
The Joker in the Pack (1975)
I Hold Four Aces (1977)

CHATEAUBRIAND, (François-René) Vicomte de
(1768–1848) French

Atala (1801)
René (1802)
Les Aventures du dernier Abencérage (1826)

CHEEVER, John
(1912–82) American

The Wapshot Chronicle (1957)
The Wapshot Scandal (1964)
Bullet Park (1969)
The World of Apples (1973)
Falconer (1977)
Oh What a Paradise It Seems (1982)

CHESTERTON, G(ilbert) K(eith)
(1874–1936) English

The Napoleon of Notting Hill (1904)
The Club of Queer Trades (1905)
The Man Who Was Thursday (1908)
The Innocence of Father Brown (1911)
(plus many Father Brown novels)
The Flying Inn (1914)

CHEVALLIER, Gabriel
(1895–1969) French

La Peur (1930)
Clochmerle (1934)
Clochmerle Babylon (1954)

CHILDERS, (Robert) Erskine
(1870–1922) Anglo-Irish

The Riddle of the Sands (1903)

CHOPIN, Kate
(1851–1904) American
née O'Flaherty

At Fault (1890)
The Awakening (1899)

CHRISTIE, Dame Agatha (Mary Clarissa)
(1890–1976) English
Lady Mallowan; née Miller

(crime)
The Mysterious Affair at Styles (1920)
The Murder on the Links (1923)
Poirot Investigates (1924) coll
The Murder of Roger Ackroyd (1926)
The Big Four (1927)

The Mystery of the Blue Train (1928)
The Seven Dials Mystery (1929)
Partners in Crime (1929) coll
Giants' Bread (1930)
as Mary Westmacott
The Murder at the Vicarage (1930)
Peril at End House (1932)
Lord Edgware Dies (1933)
Murder on the Orient Express (1934)
Unfinished Portrait (1934)
as Mary Westmacott
Why Didn't They Ask Evans? (1934)
The ABC Murders (1935)
Cards on the Table (1936)
Murder in Mesopotamia (1936)
Death on the Nile (1937)
Appointment with Death (1938)
Murder Is Easy (1939)
Ten Little Niggers (1939)
Sad Cypress (1940)
Evil Under the Sun (1941)
N or M? (1941)
The Body in the Library (1942)
The Moving Finger (1943)
Absent in the Spring (1944)
as Mary Westmacott
Sparkling Cyanide (1945)
The Hollow (1946)
The Labours of Hercules (1947)
The Rose and the Yew Tree (1948)
as Mary Westmacott
Taken at the Flood (1948)
A Murder Is Announced (1950)
Mrs McGinty's Dead (1952)
They Do It With Mirrors (1952)
After the Funeral (1953)
Hickory Dickory Death (1953)
4.50 from Paddington (1957)
Ordeal by Innocence (1958)
Cat Among the Pigoens (1959)
The Adventure of the Christmas Pudding (1960)
The Pale Horse (1961)
The Mirror Crack'd from Side to Side (1962)
The Clocks (1963)
A Caribbean Mystery (1964)
At Bertram's Hotel (1965)
Third Girl (1966)
Endless Night (1967)
By the Pricking of My Thumbs (1968)
Hallowe'en Party (1969)
Passenger to Frankfurt (1970)
Nemesis (1971)
Elephants Can Remember (1972)
Postern of Fate (1973)
Curtain (1975)
Sleeping Murder (1976)

CHURCH, Richard (Thomas)
(1893–1972) English

The Porch (1937)
The Cave (1950)
Prince Albert (1963)

CHURCHILL, Winston
(1871–1947) American

The Celebrity (1898)
Richard Carvel (1899)
The Crisis (1901)
The Crossing (1904)
Coniston (1906)
Mr Crewe's Career (1908)
A Modern Chronicle (1910)
The Inside of the Cup (1913)
A Far Country (1915)
The Dwelling Place of Light (1917)

CHURCHILL, Sir Winston (Leonard Spencer)
(1875–1965) English

Savrola (1900)

CLANCY, Tom
(1947–) American

The Hunt for Red October (1984)
Red Storm Rising (1986)
Patriot Games (1987)
The Cardinal of the Kremlin (1988)
Clear and Present Danger (1989)
The Sum of All Fears (1991)

CLARKE, Arthur C(harles)
(1917–) English

(science fiction)
Childhood's End (1953)
The City and the Stars (1976)
The Nine Billion Names of God (1967)
2001: a Space Odyssey (1968)
Rendezvous with Rama (1973)
The Fountains of Paradise (1979)

CLARKE, Marcus (Andrew Hislop)
(1846–81) American

Long Odds (1868)
For the Term of His Natural Life (1872)
Felix and Felicitas (1881) unf

CLAVELL, James (du Maresq)
(1922–) Australian

King Rat (1962)
Tai Pan (1966)
Shogun (1975)
Noble House (1981)

CLEARY, Jon
(1917–) Australian

(crime/thriller)
You Can't See Around Corners (1947)
Forests of the Night (1963)
The High Commissioner (1966)
Helga's Web (1971)
Ransom (1972)
A Flight of Chariots (1973)
Peter's Pence (1974)
The Safe House (1975)
Vortex (1977)
A Very Private War (1980)
The Golden Sabre (1981)

CLELAND, John
(1709–89) English

Fanny Hill (1748–1749)
Memoirs of a Coxcomb (1751)
The Surprises of Love (1764)

CLEMENS, Samuel Langhorne
see **TWAIN, Mark**

COCTEAU, Jean
(1889–1963) French

Le Potomak (1913)
Thomas l'Imposteur (1923)
Le Grand Écart (1923)
Les Enfants terribles (1929)

COETZEE, J(ohn) M(ichael)
(1940–) South African

Dusklands (1974)
In the Heart of the Country (1977)
Waiting for the Barbarians (1980)
Life and Times of Michael K (1983)
Foe (1986)

COLETTE
(1873–1954) French
full name: Sidonie-Gabrielle Colette

Claudine à l'école (1900)
(plus many Claudine books)
with 'Willy' Henri Gauthier-Villars, husband
L'Inénue libertine (1909)
La Vagabonde (1910)
L'Entrave (1913)
Chéri (1920)
La Maison de Claudine (1922)
Le Bléen herbe (1923)
La Fin de Chéri (1926)
La Naissance du jour (1928)
Sido (1929)
La Chatte (1933)
Mes Apprentissages (1936)
Le Képi (1943)
Gigi (1943)

COLLIER, John
(1901–80) English

His Monkey Wife (1930)
Defy the Foul Fiend (1934)

COLLINS, Jackie
(1939–) English
Sister of Joan Collins

The World Is Full of Married Men (1968)
The Stud (1970)
Sunday Simmons and Charlie Brick (1972)
Lovehead (1974)
The World Is Full of Divorced Women (1975)
Lovers and Gamblers (1977)
The Bitch (1979)
Chances (1981)
Hollywood Wives (1983)
Lucky (1985)
Hollywood Husbands (1986)
Lady Boss (1990)

COLLINS, Joan (Henrietta)
(1933–) English
Sister of Jackie Collins

Prime Time (1988)
Love and Desire and Hate (1990)

COLLINS, (William) Wilkie
(1824–89) English

Antonina (1850)
Basil (1852)
After Dark (1856)
The Dead Secret (1857)
The Woman in White (1860)
No Name (1862)
Armadale (1866)
The Moonstone (1868)
Man and Wife (1870)
The Law and the Lady (1875)
The Haunted Hotel (1879)
I Say No (1881)
The Guilty River (1886)
Blind Love (1890) posth

COMPTON-BURNETT, Dame Ivy
(1892–1969) English

Dolores (1911)
Pastors and Masters (1925)
Brothers and Sisters (1929)
Men and Wives (1931)
More Women Than Men (1933)
A House and Its Head (1935)
Daughters and Sons (1937)
A Family and a Fortune (1939)
Parents and Children (1941)
Elders and Betters (1944)
Manservant and Maidservant (1947)
Two Worlds and Their Ways (1949)
Darkness and Day (1951)
The Present and the Past (1953)
Mother and Son (1955)
A Father and His Fate (1957)
A Heritage and Its History (1959)
The Mighty and Their Fall (1961)
A God and His Gifts (1963)
The Last and the First (1971) posth

CONAN DOYLE, Sir Arthur
see **DOYLE, Sir Arthur Conan**

CONDON, Richard
(1915–) American

(thriller)
The Oldest Confession (1958)
The Manchurian Candidate (1959)
Some Angry Angel (1960)
A Talent for Loving (1961)
An Infinity of Mirrors (1964)
Any God Will Do (1966)
Ecstasy Business (1967)
Mile High (1969)
Vertical Smile (1971)
Winter Kills (1974)
Money Is Love (1975)
Whisper of the Axe (1976)
Abandoned Woman (1977)
Bandicoot (1978)
Death of a Politician (1979)
The Entwining (1981)
Prizzi's Honor (1982)
A Trembling upon Rome (1983)
Prizzi's Family (1986)

CONNELL, E(van) S(helby)
(1924–) American

Mrs Bridge (1958)

CONNELL, ES (cont.)
The Patriot (1960)
The Diary of a Rapist (1966)
Mr Bridge (1969)
The Connoisseur (1974)
Double Honeymoon (1976)

CONNOLLY, Cyril (Vernon)
(1903–74) English
The Rock Pool (1936)

CONRAD, Joseph
(1857–1924) Anglo-Polish
real name: Teodor Josef Konrad Nalecz Korzeniowski
(nautical)
Almayer's Folly (1895)
An Outcast of the Islands (1896)
The Nigger of the Narcissus (1897)
Lord Jim (1900)
The Inheritors (1901)with Ford Madox Ford
Heart of Darkness (1902)
Romance (1903)
with Ford Madox Ford
Typhoon (1903)
Nostromo (1904)
The Mirror of the Sea (1906)
The Secret Agent (1907)
Under Western Eyes (1911)
Chance (1914)
Victory (1915)
The Shadow Line (1917)
The Arrow of Gold (1919)
The Rescue (1920)
The Rover (1923)

CONSTANT, Benjamin
(1767–1830) French
real name: Henri-Benjamin Constant de Rebecque
Adolphe (1816)

COOK, Robin
(?–) American
(thriller)
Coma (1977)
Sphinx (1979)
Brain (1981)
Godplayer (1983)
Mindbend (1985)
Outbreak (1987)
Mortal Fear (1988)
Mutation (1989)
Harmful Intent (1990)
Vital Signs (1991)

COOKSON, Catherine (Ann)
(1906–) English
Kate Hannigan (1947)
Love and Mary Ann (1961)
Katie Mulholland (1967)
Feathers in the Fire (1971)
The Mallen Girl (1973)
The Mallen Streak (1973)
The Mallen Lot (1974)
Tilly Trotter (1980)
Tilly Trotter Wed (1981)
Tilly Trotter Widowed (1982)
The Gillyvors (1990)

COOLIDGE, Susan
(1835–1905) American
real name: Sarah Chauncy Woolsey
(children's)
What Katy Did (1872)
What Katy Did at School (1873)
Eyebright (1879)
A Guernsey Lily (1880)
What Katy Did Next (1886)
Clover (1888)
In the High Valley (1890)

COOPER, James Fenimore
(1789–1851) American
Precaution (1820)
The Spy (1821)
The Pilot (1823)
The Pioneers [1] (1823)

Lionel Lincoln (1825)
The Last of the Mohicans[1] (1826)
The Prairie[1] (1827)
The Red Rover (1827)
The Wept of Wish-Ton-Wish (1829)
The Water Witch (1830)
The Bravo (1831)
The Heidenmauer (1832)
The Headsman (1833)
Homeward Bound (1838)
Home as Found (1838)
The Pathfinder[1] (1840)
The Deerslayer[1] (1841)
Afloat and Ashore (1844)
Miles Wallingford (1844)
Littlepage Manuscripts (1845)
The Chainbearers (1845)
The Redskins (1846)

[1] Leatherstocking Tales

COOPER, Jilly
(1937–) English

Emily (1975)
Bella (1976)
Harriet (1977)
Octavia (1977)
Prudence (1978)
Imogen (1978)
Lisa & Co (1981)
Riders (1984)
Rivals (1988)
Polo (1991)

COOPER, William
(1910–) English
real name: Harry Summerfield Hoff

Scenes from Provincial Life (1950)
Disquiet and Peace (1956)
Scenes from Married Life (1961)
You Want the Right Frame of Reference (1970)
Scenes from Metropolitan Life (1982)
Scenes from Later Life (1983)

COOVER, Robert (Lowell)
(1932–) American

The Origin of the Brunists (1966)
The Universal Baseball Association, Inc., J. Henry Waugh Prop. (1968)
The Public Burning (1977)
Spanking the Maid (1982)
Gerald's Party (1986)

CORELLI, Marie
(1855–1924) English
real name: Mary Mackay

A Romance of Two Worlds (1886)
Thelma (1887)
Ardath (1889)
Barabbas (1893)
The Sorrows of Satan (1895)
The Mighty Atom (1896)
Zisha (1897)
The Master Christian (1900)
Temporal Power (1902)
God's Good Man (1904)
The Devil's Motor (1910)
Eyes of the Sea (1917)
The Young Diana (1918)
The Secret Power (1921)

CORNWELL, David (John Moore)
see **LE CARRÉ, John**

CORTAZAR, Julio
(1914–84) Franco-Argentinian

Los premios (1960)
62: modelo para armar (1962)
Rayuila (1963)

COX, William Trevor
see **TREVOR, William**

COZZENS, James Gould
(1903–78) American

Confusion (1924)
SS San Pedro (1931)
Men and Brethren (1936)

COZZENS, James Gould (cont.)
Ask Me Tomorrow (1940)
The Just and the Unjust (1942)
Guard of Honour (1948)
By Love Possessed (1957)
Children and Others (1965)
Morning, Noon and Night (1968)

CRAIK, Dinah Maria
(1826–87) English
née Mulock

The Ogilvies (1846)
Olive (1850)
John Halifax, Gentleman (1856)
The Adventures of a Brownie (1872)
The Little Lame prince (1875)

CRANE, Stephen
(1871–1900) American

Maggie: a Girl of the Streets (1893)
The Red Badge of Courage (1895)
The Third Violet (1897)
The Open Boat (1898)
Active Service (1899)
The Monster (1899)

CRAWFORD, F(rancis) Marion
(1854–1909) American

Mr Isaacs (1882)
Adam Johnstone's Son (1895)
Via Crucis (1898)
The Prima Donna (1908)
The White Sister (1909)

CREASEY, John
(1908–73) English

(crime/spy)
Meet the Baron (1937)
(plus many Baron novels)
Introducing the Toff (1938)
(plus many Toff novels)
Gideon's Day (1955)
(plus many Gideon novels)

CRESSWELL, Helen
(1934–) English

(children's)
Jumbo Spencer (1963)
Where the Wind Blows (1966)
The Piemakers (1967)
The Signposters (1967)
The Night-Watchmen (1969)
The Outlanders (1970)
The Beachcombers (1972)
Lizzie Dripping (1973)
The Winter of the Birds (1975)
Ordinary Jack [1] (1977)
Absolute Zero [1] (1978)
Bagthorpes Unlimited [1] (1978)
Bagthorpes v the World [1] (1979)
Dear Shrink (1982)

[1] The Bagthorpe Saga

CRICHTON, Michael
(1942–) American

The Andromeda Strain (1969)
The Terminal Man (1972)

CROLY, George
(1780–1860) Irish

Salathiel (1829)
Marston (1846)

CROMPTON, Richmal
(1890–1969) English
real name: Richmal Crompton Lamburn

The Outlaws (1922)
(plus many William novels)

CRONIN, A(rchibald) J(oseph)
(1896–1981) Scottish

Hatter's Castle (1931)
The Stars Look Down (1935)
The Citadel (1937)
The Keys of the Kingdom (1941)
The Green Years (1944)
Shannon's Way (1948)
Beyond This Place (1953)
Crusader's Tomb (1956)

A Song of Sixpence (1964)
A Pocket Full of Rye (1969)

CROWLEY, Aleister
(1875–1947) English
real name: Edward Alexander Crowley

The Diary of a Drug Fiend (1932)

CUMMINGS, E(dward) E(stlin)
(1894–1962) American

The Enormous Room (1922)

CUNNINGHAM, EV
see **FAST, Howard**

CUSSLER, Clive (Eric)
(1931–) American

(thriller)
The Mediterranean Caper (1973)
Raise the Titanic (1976)
Vixen 03 (1977)
Night Probe (1981)
Pacific Vortex (1983)
Cyclops
Treasure (1988)
Dragon (1990)

D

DAGERMAN, Stig
(1923–54) Swedish

The Games of Night (1947)
A Burnt Child (1948)

DAHL, Roald
(1916–91) Welsh-Norwegian

(children's)
Over to You [1] (1946) coll
Sometime Never [1] (1948)
Someone Like You [1] (1954)
Kiss, Kiss [1] (1960)
James and the Giant Peach (1961)
Charlie and the Chocolate Factory (1964)
The Magic Finger (1956)
Fantastic Mr Fox (1970)
Charlie and the Great Glass Elevator (1972)
Switch Bitch [1] (1974)
Danny the Champion of the World (1975)
The Enormous Crocodile (1978)
My Uncle Oswald [1] (1979)
The Twits (1980)
George's Marvellous Medicine (1981)
The BFG (1982)
Boy [1] (1984)
Matilda (1988)

[1] not children's

DANNAY, Frederick
see **QUEEN, Ellery**

D'ANNUNZIO, Gabriele
(1863–1938) Italian

Il piacere (1889)
L'innocente (1892)
Il trionfo della morte (1894)
Il fuoco (1900)

DAUDET, Alphonse
(1840–97) French

Le Petit Chose (1868)
Fromont jeune et Risler aîné (1874)
Jack (1876)
Le Nabab (1877)
Les Rois en exil (1879)
Numa Roumestan (1881)
L'Évangéliste (1883)
Sapho (1884)
L'Immortel (1888)

DAVIDSON, Lionel
(1922–) English

The Night of Wenceslas (1960)
The Rose of Tibet (1962)
A Long Way to Shiloh (1966)

DAVIDSON, Lionel (cont.)
Making Good Again (1968)
Smith's Gazelle (1971)
The Sun Chemist (1976)
The Chelsea Murders (1978)
Under Plum Lake (1980)

DAVIES, (William) Robertson
(1913–) Canadian

The Salterton Trilogy (1986) 3 vol
The Deptford Trilogy (1983) 3 vol
The Rebel Angels [1] (1981)
What's Bred in the Bone [1] (1985)
The Lyre of Orpheus [1] (1988)
Murther and Walking Spirits (1991)

[1] Cornish Trilogy

DAVIS, Richard Harding
(1864–1916) American

Van Bibber (1892)
Soldiers of Fortune (1897)
The King's Jackal (1898)
Captain Macklin (1902)
The Bar Sinister (1903)
Vera the Medium (1908)
The White Mice (1909)

DAY-LEWIS, C(ecil)
see **BLAKE, Nicholas**

DAZAI, Osamu
(1909–48) Japanese

The Setting Sun (1947)
No Longer Human (1948)

DE AMICIS, Edmondo
(1846–1908) Italian

La vita militare (1868)
Il cuore (1878)

DE BRUNHOFF, Jean
see **BRUNHOFF, Jean de**

DEEPING, (George) Warwick
(1877–1950) English

Love Among the Ruins (1904)
Sorrell and Son (1925)
Old Pybus (1928)
Roper's Row (1929)
Exiles (1950)

DEFOE, Daniel
(1660–1731) English

Robinson Crusoe (1719)
The Farther Adventures of Robinson Crusoe (1719)
The Life and Adventures of Mr Duncan Campbell (1720)
Captain Singleton (1720)
Colonel Jack (1722)
Moll Flanders (1722)
A Journal of the Plague Year (1722)
Roxana (1724)
Memoirs of a Cavalier (1724)

DE FOREST, John William
(1826–1906) America

Miss Ravenel's Conversion (1866)
The Wetherel Affair (1873)
Honest John Vane (1875)
The Bloody Chasm (1881)
A Lover's Revolt (1889)

DEIGHTON, Len (Cyril)
(1929–) English

(spy)
The Ipcress File (1962)
Funeral in Berlin (1965)
Billion-Dollar Brain (1966)
Only When I Larf (1968)
Spy Story (1974)
SS-GB (1978)
Berlin Game [1] (1984)
Mexico Set [1] (1985)
London Match [1] (1986)
Mamista (1991)

[1] Game, Set and Match trilogy

DE LA MARE, Walter
(1873–1956) English
Henry Brocken (1904)
The Return (1910)
The Three Mulla-Mulgars (1910)
Memoirs of a Midget (1921)
The Almond Tree (1923)

DE LA RAMÉE, Maria Louise
see **OUIDA**

DE LA ROCHE, Mazo
(1885–1961) Canadian
Jalna (1927)
(plus many Jalna novels)

DELEDDA, Grazia
(1871–1936) Italian
Elias Portolu (1900)
Cenere (1903)
Nostalgia (1905)
Canne al vento (1913)
Cosima (1937)

DeLILLO, Don
(1936–) American
Americana (1971)
End Zone (1972)
Great Jones Street (1973)
Ratner's Star (1976)
Players (1977)
Running Dog (1978)
The Names (1982)
White Noise (1985)
Libra (1988)
Mao II (1991)

DENNIS, Nigel (Forbes)
(1912–) English
Boys and Girls Come Out to Play (1949)
Cards of Identity (1955)
A House in Order (1966)

DESAI, Anita
(1937–) Indian
née Mazumdar
Cry, the Peacock (1963)
Bye-Bye, Blackbird (1971)
Where Shall We Go This Summer? (1975)
Fire on the Mountain (1975)
Clear Light of Day (1980)
In Custody (1980)
The Village by the Sea (1982)
Baumgartner's Bombay (1988)

DESTOUCHES, Louis-Ferdinand
see **CÉLINE, Louis-Ferdinand**

DEUTSCH, Babette
(1895–) Russo-American
real name: Avrahm Yarmolinsky
Banners (1919)
Honey out of the Rock (1925)
In Such a Night (1927)
Rogue's Legacy (1942)

DE VRIES, Peter
(1910–) American
But Who Wakes the Burglar? (1940)
The Tunnel of Love (1954)
The Tents of Wickedness (1959)
Through the Fields of Clover (1961)
The Glory of the Hummingbird (1975)
Consenting Adults (1980)
The Prick of Noon (1985)
Peckham's Marbles (1986)

DEXTER, Colin
(1930–) English
(crime)
Last Bus to Woodstock (1975)
Last Seen Wearing (1976)
The Silent World of Nicholas Quinn (1977)
Service of All the Dead (1979)
The Dead of Jericho (1981)
The Riddle of the Third Mile (1983)

DEXTER, Colin (cont.)
The Secret of Annexe 3 (1986)
The Wench Is Dead (1989)

DIAZ, Abby Morton
(1821–1904) American

Henry's Letters to His Grandmother (1870)
The Cats' Arabian Nights (1881)

DICKENS, Charles (John Huffham)
(1812–70) English
Great-grandfather of Monica Dickens

Pickwick Papers (1837)
Oliver Twist (1838)
Nicholas Nickleby (1839)
The Old Curiosity Shop (1841)
Barnaby Rudge (1841)
A Christmas Carol [1] (1843)
Martin Chuzzlewit (1844)
The Chimes [1] (1844)
The Cricket on the Hearth [1] (1845)
The Battle of Life [1] (1846)
Dombey and Son (1848)
The Haunted Man [1] (1848)
David Copperfield (1850)
Bleak House (1853)
Hard Times (1854)
Little Dorrit (1857)
A Tale of Two Cities (1859)
The Uncommercial Traveller (1860) coll
Great Expectations (1861)
Our Mutual Friend (1865)
The Mystery of Edwin Drood (1870) unf

[1] Christmas books

DICKENS, Monica (Enid)
(1915–) English
Great-granddaughter of Charles Dickens

Joy and Josephine (1948)
Kate and Emma (1964)
The Room Upstairs (1966)
Last Year When I Was Young (1974)
The Haunting of Bellamy Four (1988)
Closed at Dusk (1990)

DICKINSON, Peter
(1927–) English

Skin Deep (1968)
The Weathermonger [1] (1968)
The Devil's Children [1] (1970)
Sleep and His Brother (1971)
The Dancing Bear [1] (1972)
The Poison Oracle (1974)
The Lively Dead (1975)
The Blue Hawk [1] (1976)
Walking Dead (1977)
Tulku [1] (1979)
The Seventh Raven [1] (1981)

[1] children's

DIDEROT, Denis
(1713–84) French

La Religieuse (1796) posth
Jacques le fataliste (1796) posth
Le Neveu de Rameau (1823) posth

DIDION, Joan
(1934–) American

Run River (1963)
Play It As It Lays (1970)
A Book of Common Prayer (1977)
Democracy (1984)

DISRAELI, Benjamin
(1804–81) English
Earl of Beaconsfield

Vivian Grey [1] (1826)
Popanilla (1827)
The Young Duke (1831)
Contarini Fleming [1] (1832)
Alroy [1] (1833)
Henrietta Temple (1837)
Venetia (1837)
Coningsby [2] (1844)
Sybil [2] (1845)
Tancred [2] (1847)
Lothair (1870)
Endymion (1880)
Falconet (1927) posth unf

[1] trilogy [2] trilogy

DITZEN, Rudolf
see **FALLADA, Hans**

DÖBLIN, Alfred
(1878–1957) German

Berge, Meere und Giganten (1924)
Berlin Alexanderplatz (1929)
Karl und Rosa (1950)

DOCTOROW, E(dgar) L(awrence)
(1931–) American

Welcome to Hard Times (1960)
Big as Life (1966)
The Book of Daniel (1971)
Ragtime (1975)
Loon Lake (1980)
World's Fair (1985)
Billy Bathgate (1989)

DODGSON, Charles Lutwidge
see **CARROLL, Lewis**

DONLEAVY, J(ames) P(atrick)
(1926–) Irish-American

The Ginger Man (1955)
A Fairy Tale of New York (1960)
A Singular Man (1963)
The Beastly Beatitudes of Balthazar B (1968)
The Onion Eaters (1971)
The Destinies of Darcy Dancer, Gentleman (1977)
Schultz (1980)
Leila (1983)
Are You Listening, Rabbi Low? (1987)

DONNADIEN, Marguerite
see **DURAS, Marguerite**

DONNELLY, Ignatius
(1831–1901) American

Caesar's Column (1891)

DOOLITTLE, Hilda
(1886–1961) American

Palimpsest (1926)
Hedylus (1928)
The Hedgehog (1936)
Bid Me to Live (1960)

DOS PASSOS, John (Roderigo)
(1896–1970) American

One Man's Initiation (1917)
Three Soldiers (1921)
Manhattan Transfer (1925)
The 42nd Parallel [1] (1930)
1919 [1] (1932)
The Big Money [1] (1936)
The Adventures of a Young Man [2] (1939)
Number One [2] (1943)
The Grand Design [2] (1949)
Most Likely to Succeed (1954)

[1] USA trilogy [2] District of Columbia trilogy

DOSTO(Y)EVSKY, Fyodor (Mikhailovich)
(1821–81) Russian

Poor Folk (1846)
The Double (1846)
White Nights (1848)
The House of the Dead (1861)
Notes from Underground (1864) coll
Crime and Punishment (1866)
The Idiot (1868)
The Devils (1872)
A Raw Youth (1875)
The Brothers Karamazov (1880)

DOUGLAS, George
(1869–1902) Scottish
real name: George Douglas Brown

The House with the Green Shutters (1901)

DOUGLAS, (George) Norman
(1868–1952) Austro-Scottish

South Wind (1917)
They Went (1920)
In the Beginning (1928)

DOUGLAS, Lloyd C(assel)
(1877–1951) American

Magnificent Obsession (1929)
Green Light (1935)
White Banners (1936)
Dr Hudson's Secret Journal (1939)
Invitation to Live (1940)
The Robe (1942)
The Big Fisherman (1949)

DOYLE, Sir Arthur Conan
(1859–1930) Scottish

(crime/adventure)
A Study in Scarlet (1887)
Micah Clarke (1889)
The Sign of Four (1890)
The Refugees (1891)
The White Company (1891)
The Great Shadow (1892)
The Adventures of Sherlock Holmes (1892) coll
The Final Problem (1893)
The Memoirs of Sherlock Holmes (1894) coll
The Exploits of Brigadier Gerard (1896)
Rodney Stone (1896)
Uncle Bernac (1897)
The Hound of the Baskervilles (1902)
The Return of Sherlock Holmes (1905) coll
Sir Nigel (1906)
The Lost World (1912)
The Poison Belt (1913)
The Land of Mist (1926)
The Case Book of Sherlock Holmes (1927) coll
The Maracot Deep (1929)

DRABBLE, Margaret
(1939–) English
Sister of AS Byatt

A Summer Birdcage (1963)
The Garrick Year (1964)
The Millstone (1965)
Jerusalem the Golden (1967)
The Waterfall (1969)
The Needle's Eye (1972)
The Realms of Gold (1975)
The Ice Age (1977)
The Middle Ground (1980)
The Radiant Way (1987)
A Natural Curiosity (1989)

DREISER, Theodore (Herman Albert)
(1871–1945) American

Sister Carrie (1900)
Jennie Gerhardt (1911)
The Financier [1] (1912)
The Titan [1] (1914)
The Genius (1915)
An American Tragedy (1925)
The Stoic [1] (1947) posth

[1] trilogy

DRUMMOND, June
(1923–) South African

The Boon Companions (1974)
The Patriots (1979)

DuBOIS, William E(dward) B(urghardt)
(1868–1963) American

The Dark Princess (1928)

DUDEVANT, Baronne
see **SAND, George**

DUFFY, Maureen
(1933–) English

That's How It Was (1962)
The Single Eye (1964)
The Microcosm (1966)
The Paradox Players (1967)
Wounds (1969)
Capital (1975)
Londoners (1983)
I Want to Go to Moscow (1986)
Change (1987)

DUHAMEL, Georges
(1884–1966) French

Salavin (1920–1932) coll
Chronique des Pasquier (1933–1945) coll

DUMAS, Alexandre (père)
(1802–70) French
Father of Alexandre Dumas

Isabelle de Bavière (1836)
Pauline (1838)
Acté (1839)
Othon l'Archer (1840)
Le Chevalier d'Harmenthal (1843)
Ascanio (1843)
Cécile (1844)
Les Trois Mousquetaires (1844)
La Fille du Régent (1845)
La Reine Margot (1845)
Le Comte de Monte-Cristo (1845)
Vingt Ans après (1845)
La Guerre des Femmes (1846)
La Dame de Monsoreau (1848)
Le Collier de la Reine (1849)
Le Vicomte de Bragelonne (1850)
La Tulipe noire (1850)
Le Trou de l'enfer (1850)
Ange Pitou (1853)
Ingénue (1854)
La Comtesse de Charny (1855)
Les Companions de Jéhu (1857)
Les Louvres de Machecoul (1859)
Les blancs et les bleus (1868)

DUMAS, Alexandre (fils)
(1824–1895) French
Son of Alexandre Dumas

La Dame aux camélias (1848)
L'Affaire Clemenceau (1864)

DU MAURIER, Dame Daphne
(1907–1989) English
Granddaughter of George Du Maurier

The Loving Spirit (1931)
The Progress of Julius (1933)
Jamaica Inn (1936)
Rebecca (1938)
Frenchman's Creek (1942)
Hungry Hill (1943)
The King's General (1946)
The Parasites (1949)
My Cousin Rachel (1951)
The Birds (1952)
Mary Anne (1954)
The Scapegoat (1957)
The Breaking Point (1959)
The Glass-Blowers (1963)
The Flight of the Falcon (1965)
The Breakthrough (1966)
The House on the Strand (1969)
Don't Look Now (1970)
The Rendezvous (1980)

DU MAURIER, George (Louis Palmella Busson)
(1834–96) Anglo-French
Grandfather of Daphne Du Maurier

Peter Ibbetson (1891)
Trilby (1894)
The Martian (1897) posth

DUNN, Nell
(1936–) English

Up the Junction (1966)
Poor Cow (1967)
The Incurable (1971)
Tears His Head Off His Shoulders (1974)
The Only Child (1978)
Steaming (1981)

DUNSANY, Edward (John Moreton Drax Plunkett)
(1878–1957) Irish
Baron Dunsany

(fantasy)
The Gods of Pegana (1905)
Time and the Gods (1906)
The Sword of Welleran (1908)
The Book of Wonder (1912)
The Travel Tales of Mr Jorkens (1931)
The Curse of the Wise Women (1933)

DUPIN, Amandine Aurore
see **SAND, George**

DURAS, Marguerite
(1914–) French
real name: Marguerite Donnadien

Les Impudents (1942)
La Douleur (1945)
Le Square (1955)
Moderato cantabile (1958)
L'Après-midi de M Andesmas (1962)
Le Vice-Consul (1966)
L'Amante anglaise (1967)
Détruite dit-elle (1967)
L'Amour (1971)
L'Amant (1984)

DURRELL, Lawrence (George)
(1912–91) English

Pied Piper of Lovers (1935)
Panic Spring (1937)
as Charles Norden
The Black Book: an Agon (1938)
Justine [1] (1957)
Balthazar [1] (1958)
Mountolive [1] (1958)
Clea [1] (1960)
Tunc (1968)
Nunquam (1970)
Monsieur [2] (1974)
Livia [2] (1978)
Constance [2] (1982)
Sebastian [2] (1983)
Quinx [2] (1985)

[1] Alexandria Quartet [2] Avignon Quincunx

E

ECO, Umberto
(1932–) Italian

Il nome della rosa (1980)
Foucault's Pendulum (1988)

EDEN, Emily
(1797–1869) English

The Semi-Detached House (1859)
The Semi-Detached Couple (1860)

EDGEWORTH, Maria
(1767–1849) Anglo-Irish

Castle Rackrent (1800)
Belinda (1801)
Leonora (1806)
The Absentee (1812)
Patronage (1814)
Harrington (1817)
Ormond (1817)
Helen (1834)

EDMONDS, Walter D(umaux)
(1903–) American

Rome Haul (1929)
The Big Barn (1930)
Eerie Water (1933)
Mostly Canallers (1934)
Drums Along the Mohawk (1936)
Chad Hanna (1940)
The Matchlock Gun (1941)
The Boyds of Black River (1953)

EDSON, J(ohn) T(homas)
(1928–) English

(western)
Trail Boss (1961)
Waco's Debt (1964)
The Law of the Gun (1966)
Cuchilo (1969)
The Hide and Tallow Man (1974)
Bunduki [1] (1975)
Renegade (1978)
White Indian (1981)

[1] not western

EGGLESTON, Edward
(1837–1902) American

Mr Blake's Walking-Stick (1870)
The Hoosier Schoolmaster (1871)
The End of the World (1872)

The Mystery of Metropolisville (1873)
The Circuit Rider (1874)
Roxy (1878)
The Hoosier Schoolboy (1883)
The Graysons (1888)
The Faith Doctor (1891)

EICHENDORFF, Joseph Freiherr von
(1788–1857) German
Ahnung und Gegenwart (1815)
Das Marmorbild (1819)
Aus dem Leben eines Taugenichts (1826)
Dichter und ihre Gesellen (1834)

ELIOT, George
(1819–80) English
real name: Mary Ann Evans
Scenes of Clerical Life (1858) coll
Adam Bede (1859)
The Mill on the Floss (1860)
Silas Marner (1861)
Romola (1862)
Felix Holt (1866)
Middlemarch (1872)
Daniel Deronda (1876)

ELKIN, Stanley (Lawrence)
(1930–) American
Boswell (1964)
A Bad Man (1967)
The Dick Gibson Show (1971)
The Franchiser (1976)
George Mills (1982)
The Magic Kingdom (1985)

ELLERMAN, (Annie) Winifred
see **BRYHER**

ELLIS, Alice Thomas
(1932–) British
real name: Anna Margaret Haycroft née Lindholm
The Sin Eater (1977)
The Birds of the Air (1980)
The 27th Kingdom (19802)
The Other Side of the Fire (1983)
Unexplained Laughter (1985)
The Clothes in the Wardrobe [1] (1987)
The Skeleton in the Cupboard [1] (1988)
The Fly in the Ointment [1] (1989)
The Inn at the Edge of the World (1990)

[1] trilogy

ELLIS, H(umphry) F(rancis)
(1907–) English
AJ Wentworth BA (1980)
Swan Song of AJ Wentworth (1982)
A Bee in the Kitchen (1983)

ELLISON, Ralph W(aldo)
(1914–) American
Invisible Man (1952)

ENRIGHT, D(ennis) J(oseph)
(1920–) English
Academic Year (1955)
Heaven Knows Where (1957)
Figures of Speech (1965)
The Joke Shop [1] (1976)
Wild Ghost Chase [1] (1978)
Beyond Land's End [1] (1979)

[1] children's

ESTANG, Luc
(1911–) French
real name: Lucien Bastard
L'Interrogataire (1957)
L'Horloger de Cherche-Midi (1959)
Le Bonheur et le salut (1961)
Que ces mots répondent (1964)

EVANS, Caradoc
(1878–1945) Welsh
real name: David Evans
My People (1915) coll
Capel Sion (1916) coll
My Neighbours (1919) coll

EVANS, David
see **EVANS, Caradoc**

EVANS, Mary Ann
see **ELIOT, George**

EWING, Juliana Horatia
(1841–85) English
née Gatty

(children's)
Mrs Overtheway's Remembrances (1869)
A Flat Iron for a Farthing (1872)
Lob-Lie-by-the-Fire (1873)
Six to Sixteen (1875)
Jan of the Windmill (1876)
A Great Emergency (1877)
Jackanapes (1879)
Daddy Darwin's Dovecote (1884)

F

FAIRFIELD, Cecily Isabel
see **WEST, Rebecca**

FALLADA, Hans
(1893–1947) German
real name: Rudolf Ditzen

Bauern, Bonzen und Bomben (1931)
Kleiner Mann was nun? (1932)
Wer einmal aus dem Blechnapf frisst (1934)

FARIGOULE, Louis
see **ROMAINS, Jules**

FARRAR, Frederick William
(1831–1903) English

Eric, or Little by Little (1858)
Julian Home: a Tale of College Life (1859)
St Winifred's, or the World of School (1862)
Three Homes: a Tale for Fathers (1865)

FARRELL, James T(homas)
(1904–79) American

Young Lonigan [1] (1932)
Gas-House McGinty (1933)
The Young Manhood of Studs Lonigan [1] (1934)
Judgment Day [1] (1935)
A World I Never Made [2] *(1936)*
Tommy Gallagher's Crusade (1937)
No Star Is Lost [2] (1938)
Father and Son [2] (1940)
Ellen Rogers (1941)
My Days of Anger [2] (1943)
This Man and This Woman (1951)
The Face of Time [2] (1953)
Tradition and Dream (1964)
New Year's Eve, 1929 (1967)

[1] Studs Lonigan trilogy [2] Danny O'Neill quintet

FAST, Howard (Melvin)
(1914–) American

(historical)
The Children (1935)
The Last Frontier (1941)
Freedom Road (1944)
Spartacus (1951)
Torquemada (1966)
The Immigrants (1972)
The Case of the Poisoned Éclairs (1979) as EV Cunningham

FAULKNER, William (Harrison)
(1897–1962) American

Soldier's Pay (1926)
Mosquitos (1927)
Sartoris (1929)
The Sound and the Fury (1929)
As I Lay Dying (1930)
Sanctuary (1931)
Light in August (1932)
Pylon (1935)
Absalom, Absalom! (1936)
The Unvanquished (1938)
The Wild Palms (1939)
The Hamlet (1940)
Intruder in the Dust (1948)

Requiem for a Nun (1951)
A Fable (1954)
The Town (1957)
The Mansion (1959)
The Reivers (1962)

FEIGE, Albert Otto Max
see **TRAVEN, B**

FEINSTEIN, Elaine
(1930–) English

The Circle (1970)
The Glass Alembic (1973)
The Children of the Rose (1975)
The Shadow Master (1979)
The Survivors (1982)

FERBER, Edna
(1887–1968) American

Dawn O'Hara (1911)
Emma McChesney & Co (1915)
Fanny Herself (1917)
The Girls (1921)
Gigolo (1922)
So Big (1924)
Show Boat (1926)
Cimarron (1929)
American Beauty (1931)
Come and Get It (1935)
Saratoga Trunk (1941)
Giant (1950)
Ice Palace (1958)

FERRIER, Susan (Edmonstone)
(1782–1854) Scottish

Marriage (1818)
The Inheritance (1824)
Destiny (1831)

FEUCHTWANGER, Lion
(1884–1958) German

Die Hässliche Herzogin (1923)
Jud Süss (1925)
Der Erfolg [1] (1930)
Die Geschwister Oppenheim [1] (1933)
Exil [1] (1940)
Simone [1] (1944)

[1] tetralogy

FIELDING, Henry
(1707–54) English
Brother of Sarah Fielding

Shamela Andrews (1741)
The Adventures of Joseph Andrews (1742)
The Life of Jonathan Wild the Great (1743)
The History of Tom Jones (1749)
Amelia (1751)

FIELDING, Sarah
(1710–68) English
Sister of Henry Fielding

The Adventures of David Simple [1] (1744)
Familiar Letters Between the Principal Characters in David Simple [1] (1744)
The Governess (1749)
Volume the Last [1] (1753)
The History of the Countess of Dellwyn (1759)
The History of Ophelia (1760)

[1] David Simple novels

FIGES, Eva
(1932–) Anglo-German

Winter Journey (1967)
B (1972)
Days (1974)
Nelly's Version (1977)
Waking (1981)
Light (1983)
The Seven Ages (1983)
Ghosts (1988)
The Tree of Knowledge (1990)

FIRBANK, (Arthur Annesley) Ronald
(1886–1926) American

Vainglory (1915)

FIRBANK, Ronald (cont.)
Inclinations (1916)
Caprice (1917)
Valmouth (1921)
Santal (1921)
The Flower Beneath the Foot (1923)
Prancing Nigger (1924)
Concerning the Eccentricities of Cardinal Pirelli (1926) posth
The Artificial Princess (1934) posth

FISHER, Dorothea Frances
(1879–1958) American
née Canfield

Gunhild (1907)
The Squirrel-Cage (1912)
Hillsboro People (1915)
The Bent Twig (1915)
The Day of Glory (1919)
The Brimming Cup (1921)
Raw Material (1923)
Her Son's Wife (1926)
The Deepening Storm (1930)
Bonfire (1933)
Seasoned Timber (1939)

FITZGERALD, F(rancis) Scott (Key)
(1896–1940) American

This Side of Paradise (1920)
The Beautiful and Damned (1922)
The Great Gatsby (1925)
Tender Is the Night (1934)
The Last Tycoon (1941) posth unf

FLAUBERT, Gustave
(1821–80) French

Madame Bovary (1857)
Salammbo (1862)
L'Education sentimentale (1869)
La Tentation de Saint Antoine (1874)
Un Coeur simple (1877)
La Légende de Saint Julien l'Hospitalier (1877)
Hérodias (1877)
Bouvard et Pécuchet (1881) posth unf

FLECKER, James (Herman) Elroy
(1884–1915) English

The King of Alsander (1914)

FLEMING, Ian (Lancaster)
(1908–64) English

(spy)
Casino Royale (1953)
Live and Let Die (1954)
Moonraker (1955)
Diamonds Are Forever (1956)
From Russia, with Love (1957)
Dr No (1958)
Goldfinger (1959)
For Your Eyes Only (1960)
Thunderball (1961)
The Spy Who Loved Me (1962)
On Her Majesty's Secret Service (1963)
Chitty-Chitty-Bang-Bang [1] (1964)
You Only Live Twice (1964)
The Man with the Golden Gun (1965) posth
Octopussy (1966) posth
The Living Daylights (1966) posth

[1] not spy

FOGAZZARO, Antonio
(1842–1911) Italian

Daniele Cortis (1885)
Piccolo mondo antico (1895)
Il santo (1905)
Leila (1910)

FOLLETT, Ken
(1949–) English

(thriller)
The Bear Raid (1976)
Storm Island (1978)
Eye of the Needle (1978)
The Key to Rebecca (1980)
The Man from St Petersburg (1982)
On Wings of Eagles (1984)
Lie Down with Lions (1985)
The Pillars of the Earth (1989)
Night Over Water (1991)

FONTANE, Theodor
(1819–98) German

Grete Minde (1879)
L'Adutera (1882)
Graf Petöfy (1884)
Cécile (1887)
Irrungen Wirrungen (1888)
Frau Jenny Treibel (1892)
Effi Briest (1895)
Mathilde Möhring (1906) posth unf

FORD, Ford Madox
(1873–1939) English
real name: Ford Hermann Hueffer

The Shifting of the Fire (1892)
The Inheritors (1901)
with Joseph Conrad
Romance (1903)
with Joseph Conrad
The Fifth Queen and How She Came to Court[1] (1906)
Privy Seal: His Last Venture[1] (1907)
The Fifth Queen Crowned[1] (1908)
The Good Soldier (1915)
Some Do Not[2] (1924)
No More Parades[2] (1925)
A Man Could Stand Up[2] (1926)
The Last Post[2] (1928)
When the Wicked Man (1932)

[1] Fifth Queen trilogy [2] Parade's End tetralogy

FORESTER, C(ecil) S(cott)
(1899–1966) English

(nautical/adventure)
Payment Deferred (1926)
Brown on Resolution (1929)
Plain Murder (1930)
The African Queen (1935)
The General (1936)
The Happy Return (1937)
Ship of the Line (1938)
Captain Hornblower RN (1939)
The Ship (1943)
Lord Hornblower (1946)
Mr Midshipman Hornblower (1950)
Randall and the River of Time (1951)
Hornblower and the Atropos (1953)
The Nightmare (1954)
Hornblower in the West Indies (1958)
Hornblower and the Hotspur (1962)

FORSTER, E(dward) M(organ)
(1879–1970) English

Where Angels Fear to Tread (1905)
The Longest Journey (1907)
A Room with a View (1908)
Howards End (1910)
A Passage to India (1924)
Maurice (1971) posth

FORSYTH, Frederick
(1938–) English

(thriller)
The Day of the Jackal (1971)
The Odessa File (1972)
The Dogs of War (1974)
The Shepherd (1975)
The Devil's Alternative (1979)
The Fourth Protocol (1984)
The Negotiator (1989)
The Deceivers (1991)

FOUQUÉ, Friedrich (Heinrich Karl)
(1777–1843) German
Baron de la Motte

Undine (1811)
Der Zauberring (1813)

FOURNIER, Henri-Alban
see **ALAIN-FOURNIER**

FOWLES, John (Robert)
(1926–) English

The Collector (1963)
The Magus (1966)
The French Lieutenant's Woman (1969)
The Ebony Tower (1974) coll
Daniel Martin (1977)
Mantissa (1982)
A Maggot (1985)

FRAME, Janet (Paterson)
(1924–) New Zealand

Owls Do Cry (1957)
Faces in the Water (1962)
Scented Gardens for the Blind (1963)
A State of Siege (1966)
Intensive Care (1970)
Daughter Buffalo (1972)
Living in the Maniototo (1979)

FRANCE, Anatole
(1844–1924) French
real name: Jacques-Anatole-François Thibault

Le Crime de Sylvestre Bonnard (1881)
Thaïs (1890)
La Rôtisserie de la Reine Pédauque (1893)
Le Lys rouge (1894)
L'Histoire contemporaine (1896–1901) 4 vol
L'Ile des pingouins (1908)
Les Dieux ont soif (1912)

FRANCIS, Dick
(1920–) English

(horse-racing)
Dead Cert (1962)
Nerve (1964)
Odds Against (1965)
For Kicks (1967)
Forfeit (1969)
Bone Crack (1971)
Rat Race (1973)
Slay-Ride (1974)
High Stakes (1976)
Risk (1978)
Trial Run (1979)
Whip Hand (1980)
Reflex (1981)
Twice Shy (1981)
Banker (1983)
Proof (1984)
Bolt (1986)
Hot Money (1987)
Straight (1989)
Comeback (1991)

FRANK, Waldo (David)
(1889–1967) American

The Unwelcome Man (1917)
The Art of the Vieux Colombier (1918)
Our America (1919)
Rahab (1922)
City Block (1922)
Salvos (1924)
Chalk Face (1924)
The Rediscovery of America (1929)
Dawn in Russia (1932)
In the American Jungle (1937)
Summer Never Ends (1941)
Not Heaven (1953)

FRASER, Lady Antonia
(1932–) English
née Pakenham

Quiet as a Nun (1977)
(plus many Jemima Shore novels)

FRASER, George Macdonald
(1925–81) Scottish

Flashman (1969)
(plus many Flashman novels)

FRAYN, Michael
(1933–) English

The Tin Man (1965)
The Russian Interpreter (1966)
Towards the End of the Morning (1967)
A Very Private Life (1968)
Sweet Dreams (1973)

FREELING, Nicholas
(1927–) English

(crime)
Love in Amsterdam (1962)
(plus many Van der Valk novels)

FREEMAN, Mary E(leanor)
(1852–1930) American
née Wilkins

A Humble Romance (1887)

A New England Nun (1891)
Jane Field (1893)
Giles Corey (1893)
Pembroke (1894)
Jerome, a Poor Man (1897)
Silence (1898)
The Love of Parson Lord (1900)
The Portion of Labor (1901)
The Debtor (1905)
Butterfly House (1912)

FRENCH, Marilyn
(1929–) American

The Women's Room (1977)
The Bleeding Heart (1980)
Her Mother's Daughter (1987)

FREYTAG, Gustav
(1816–95) German

Soll und Haben (1855) 3 vol
Die verlorene Handschrift (1864)
Die Ahnen (1873–81) 6 vol

FRISCH, Max (Rudolf)
(1911–) Swiss

Stiller (1954)
Homo Faber (1957)
Mein Name sei Gantenbein (1964)

FROMENTIN, Eugène
(1820–76) French

Dominique (1863)

FROUDE, J(ames) A(nthony)
(1818–94) English

The Nemesis of Faith (1849)

FUENTES, Carlos
(1928–) Mexican

Aura (1962)
Cambio de piel (1967)
Terra nostra (1975)

FUGARD, Athol (Harold)
(1932–) South African

Tsotsi (1980)

FULLER, Henry (Blake)
(1857–1929) American

The Cliff Dwellers (1893)
With the Procession (1895)
The Last Refuge (1900)
Bertram Cope's Year (1919)

FULLER, John (Leopold)
(1937–) English
Son of Roy Fuller

Flying to Nowhere (1983)

FULLER, Roy (Broadbent)
(1912–91) English
Father of John Fuller

The Second Curtain (1953)
Image of a Society (1956)
The Ruined Boys (1959)
The Father's Comedy (1961)
My Child, My Sister (1965)
The Carnal Island (1970)

FURPHY, Joseph
(1843–1912) Australian

Such is Life (1903)
Rigby's Romance (1946) posth
Brolga (1948) posth

G

GABORIAU, Émile
(1832–73) French

(crime)
L'Affaire Lerouge (1866)
Le Crime d'Orcival (1867)
Le Dossier 113 (1867)
Monsieur Lecoq (1869)
Les Esclaves de Paris (1869)
La Corde au cou (1873)

GADDA, Carlo Emilio
(1893–1973) Italian

Il castello di Udine (1934)
Adalgisa (1944)
Quer pasticciaccio brutto de via Merulana (1957) unf
Cognizione del dolore (1963) unf

GADDIS, William
(1922–) American

The Recognitions (1955)
JR (1976)
Carpenter's Gothic (1985)

GALLICO, Paul (William)
(1897–1976) American

The Snow Goose (1947)
The Lonely (1947)
Jennie (1950)
The Small Miracle (1952)
Ludmila (1955)
Flowers for Mrs Harris (1958)
Too Many Ghosts (1961)
Scruffy (1962)
The Hand of Mary Constable (1964)
The Poseidon Adventure (1969)

GALSWORTHY, John
(1867–1933) English

Jocelyn (1898)
Man of Devon (1901) coll
The Island Pharisees (1904)
The Forsyte Saga (1906–21) 3 vol
Fraternity (1909)
The Dark Flower (1913)
A Modern Comedy (1924–28) 3 vol
End of the Chapter (1931–33) 3 vol

GALT, John
(1779–1839) Scottish

The Ayrshire Legatees (1821)
Annals of the Parish (1821)
The Provost (1822)
The Entail (1823)
The Member (1832)

GARCIA MARQUEZ, Gabriel
(1928–) Colombian

La hojarasca (1955)
El coronel no tiene quien le escriba (1961)
La mala hora (1966)
Cien años de soledad (1967)
El otoño del patriarca (1975)
Crónica de una muerte anunciada (1981)

GARDNER, Erle Stanley
(1889–1970) American

(crime/courtroom)
The Case of the Velvet Claws (1933)
(plus many Perry Mason novels)

GARLAND, (Hannibal) Hamlin
(1860–1940) American

Main-Travelled Roads (1891) coll
Jason Edwards: an Average Man (1892)
Rose of Dutcher's Coolly (1895)
The Captain of the Gray-Horse Troop (1902)
Cavanagh, Forest Ranger (1910)

GARNER, Alan
(1934–) English

(children's)
The Weirdstone of Brisingamen (1960)
The Moon of Gomrath (1963)
Elidor (1965)
The Owl Service (1967)
Red Shift (1973)
The Stone Book (1976)

GARNETT, David
(1892–1981) English

Lady into Fox (1922)
A Man in the Zoo (1924)
The Sailor's Return (1925)
Beany-Eye (1935)
Plough over the Bones (1973)

GARNETT, Eve
(1908–) English
(children's)
The Family from One End Street (1937)
Further Adventures of the Family from One End Street (1956)
Holiday at Dew Drop Inn (1962)

GASH, Jonathan
(1933–) English
real name: John Grant
(antiques)
The Judas Pair (1977)
Gold from Gemini (1978)
The Grail Tree (1979)
Spend Game (1980)
The Vatican Rip (1981)
Firefly Gadroon (1982)
The Sleepers of Erin (1983)
The Gondola Scam (1984)
The Tartan Ringers (1986)
Moonspender (1987)
The Very Last Gambado (1989)

GASKELL, Elizabeth (Cleghorn)
(1810–65) English
Mary Barton (1848)
Ruth (1853)
Cranford (1853)
North and South (1855)
Sylvia's Lovers (1863)
Cousin Phillis (1864)
Wives and Daughters (1866) posth unf

GAUTHIER-VILLARS, Henri
see **COLETTE**

GAUTIER, Théophile
(1811–72) French
Mademoiselle de Maupin (1835)
La Morte amoreuse (1836)
Fortunio (1837)

GENET, Jean
(1910–1986) French
Notre-Dame des Fleurs (1944)
Miracle de la rose (1946)
Querelle de Brest (1947)

GERHARDIE, William (Alexander)
(1895–1977) Anglo-Russian
née Gerhardi
Futility (1922)
The Polyglots (1925)
Pending Heaven (1930)
Resurrection (1934)
Of Mortal Love (1936)

GIBBON, Lewis Grassic
(1901–35) Scottish
real name: James Leslie Mitchell
Stained Radiance (1930)
Sunset Song[1] (1932)
Cloud Howe[1] (1933)
Grey Granite[1] (1934)

[1] A Scots Quair trilogy

GIBBONS, Stella (Dorothea)
(1902–89) English
Cold Comfort Farm (1932)
Miss Linsey and Pa (1936)
Nightingale Wood (1946)
Conference at Cold Comfort Farm (1949)
The Shadow of the Sorcerer (1955)
The Snow Woman (1969)
The Woods in Winter (1970)

GIDE, André
(1869–1951) French
L'Immoraliste (1902)
La Porte étroite (1909)
Les Caves du Vatican (1914)
La Symphonie pastorale (1919)
Les Faux-Monnayeurs (1926)
Robert (1930)

GILLIAT, Penelope
(1924–) English
One by One (1965)
What's It Like Out? (1968)
Sunday Bloody Sunday (1972)
Cutting Edge (1978)
Mortal Matters (1983)
Lingo (1990)

GILLOTT, Jacky
(1939–) English
Salvage (1968)
War Baby (1971)
Crying Out Loud (1976)
The Head Case (1979)
Intimate Relations (1980)

GIRAUDOUX, Jean
(1882–1944) French
Simon le pathétique (1918)
Suzanne et le Pacifique (1921)
Siegfried et le Limousin (1922)
Juliette au pays des hommes (1924)
Bella (1926)

GISSING, George (Robert)
(1857–1903) English
Workers in the Dawn (1880)
The Unclassed (1884)
Isabel Clarendon (1886)
Demos (1886)
Thyrza (1887)
A Life's Morning (1888)
The Emancipated (1890)
New Grub Street (1891)
Born in Exile (1892)
The Odd Women (1893)
Sleeping Fires (1895)
The Whirlpool (1897)
The Crown of Life (1899)
Our Friend the Charlatan (1901)
The Private Papers of Henry Ryecroft (1903)
Veranilda (1904) posth
Will Warburton (1905) posth

GLASGOW, Ellen (Anderson Gholson)
(1873–1945) American
The Descendant (1897)
The Voice of the People (1900)
The Battleground (1902)
The Deliverance (1904)
Virginia(1913)
Life and Gabriella (1916)
Barren Ground (1925)
The Romantic Comedians (1926)
They Stooped to Folly (1929)
The Sheltered Life (1932)
Vein of Iron (1935)
In This Our Life (1941)

GLASPELL, Susan
(1882–1948) American
The Glory of the Conquered (1909)
The Visioning (1911)
Fidelity (1915)
Brook Evans (1928)
The Fugitive's Return (1929)
Ambrose Holt and Family (1931)
Norma Ashe (1942)

GLYN, Elinor
(1864–1943) English
née Sutherland
The Visits of Elizabeth (1900)
Three Weeks (1907)
Man and Maid (1922)
Did She? (1934)
The Third Eye (1940)

GODDEN, Rumer
(1907–) English
Chinese Puzzle (1935)
Lady and Unicorn (1937)
Black Narcissus (1939)
Fugue in Time (1945)
The River (1946)
A Breath of Air (1950)
An Episode of Sparrows (1955)
The Greengage Summer (1958)
China Court (1961)

The Battle ofthe Villa Fiorita (1963)
In the House of Brede (1970)
Candle for St Jude (1980)
The Dark Horse (1981)
Thursday's Children (1984)
Coromandel Sea Change (1991)

GODWIN, William
(1756–1836) English
Husband of Mary Wollstonecraft
Father of Mary Shelley

Caleb Williams (1794)
St Leon (1799)
Fleetwood (1805)
Mandeville (1817)
Cloudesley (1830)
Deloraine (1833)

GOETHE, Johann (Wolfgang von)
(1744–1832) German

Die Leiden des jungen Werthers (1774)
Wilhelm Meisters Lehrjahre (1796)
Die Wahlverwandtschaften (1809)

GOGOL, Nikolai Vasilevich
(1809–52) Russian

Dead Souls (1842)

GOLD, Herbert
(1924–) American

Birth of a Hero (1951)
The Man Who Was Not With It (1956)
Salt (1963)
The Fathers (1967)

GOLDING, William (Gerald)
(1911–) English

Lord of the Flies (1954)
The Inheritors (1955)
Pincher Martin (1956)
Free Fall (1959)
The Spire (1964)
The Pyramid (1967)
Darkness Visible (1979)
Rites of Passage [1] (1980)
The Paper Men (1984)
Close Quarters [1] (1987)
Fire Down Below [1] (1989)

[1] trilogy

GOLDMAN, William
(1931–) American

Boys and Girls Together (1964)
Marathon Man (1974)
Control (1982)
The Colour of Light (1984)
Brothers (1986)

GOLDSMITH, Oliver
(1728–74) Irish

The Vicar of Wakefield (1766)

GONCHAROV, Ivan (Aleksandrovich)
(1812–91) Russian

An Ordinary Story (1847)
Oblómov (1859)
The Ravine (1869)

GONCOURT, Edmond de
(1822–96) and
GONCOURT, Jules de
(1830–70) French brothers

En 1851 (1851)
Souer Philomène (1961)
Germinie Lacerteux (1864)
Madame Gervaisais (1869)

GORDIMER, Nadine
(1923–) South African

The Lying Days (1953)
A World of Strangers (1958)
Occasion for Loving (1963)
The Late Bourgeois World (1966)
A Guest of Honour (1970)
The Conservationist (1974)
Burger's Daughter (1979)
July's People (1981)
A Sport of Nature (1987)

GORDON, Richard
(1921–) English
Doctor in the House (1952)
(plus many Doctor novels)

GORE, Catherine (Grace Frances)
(1799–1861) English
née Moody
Theresa Marchmont (1824)
Mothers and Daughters (1831)
Mrs Armytage (1836)
Cecil (1841)
The Banker's Wife (1843)

GORKY (or GORKI), Maxim
(1868–1936) Russian
real name: Alexsei Maksimovich Peshkov
Makar Chudra (1892)
Chelkash (1895)
Twenty-Six Men and a Girl (1899)
Foma Gordeyev (1899)
Konovalov (1903)
The Mother (1907)
Childhood (1913)
Among People (1915)
The Life of a Useless Man (1917)
My Universities (1923)
The Artomonov Business (1925)
The Life of Klim Samgin (1925–36) unf

GOTTHELF, Jeremias
(1797–1854) Swiss
real name: Albert Bitzius
Der Bauernspiegel (1837)
Geld und Geist (1844)
Der Geltstag (1845)
Käthi (1847)

GOULD, Nat(haniel)
(1857–1919) English
(horse-racing)
The Double Event (1891)
(plus many Turf novels)

GRAHAM, Davinia
see **ANTHONY, Evelyn**

GRAHAM, Winston
(1911–) English
Ross Poldark (1945)
(plus many Poldark novels)

GRAHAME, Kenneth
(1859–1932) Scottish
(children's)
The Golden Age (1895) coll
Dream Days (1898) coll
The Wind in the Willows (1908)
Bertie's Escapade (1946) posth

GRAND, Sarah
(1854–1943) Anglo-Irish
real name: Frances Elizabeth Bellenden McFall
The Heavenly Twins (1893)
The Beth Book (1898)

GRANT, John
see **GASH, Jonathan**

GRASS, Günter (Wilhelm)
(1927–) German
Die Blechtrommel (1959)
Katz und Maus (1961)
Hundejahre (1963)
Örtlich betäubt (1969)
Das Treffen in Telgte (1979)
Kopfgeburten (1980)
Die Ratte (1987)

GRAVES, Robert (von Ranke)
(1895–1985) English
Goodbye to All That (1929)
I, Claudius (1934)
Claudius the God (1934)
Antigua, Penny, Puce (1936)
Count Belisarius (1938)

Sergeant Lamb of the Ninth (1940)
Proceed, Sergeant Lamb (1941)
Wife to Mr Milton (1943)
The Golden Fleece (1944)
King Jesus (1946)
The White Goddess (1947)
Two Wise Children (1966)

GRAY, Alasdair (James)
(1934–) Scottish

Lanark: A Life in Four Books (1981)
1982, Janine (1984)
The Fall of Kelvin Walker: A Fable of the Sixties (1985)
McGrotty and Ludmilla: or, The Harbinger Report (1990)

GREEN, Henry
(1905–73) English

Blindness (1926)
Living (1929)
Party Going (1939)
Caught (1943)
Loving (1945)
Back (1946)
Nothing (1950)
Doting (1952)

GREEN, Julien
(1900–) Franco-American

Mont-Cinère (1925)
Adrienne Mesurat (1927)
Léviathan (1929)
Minuit (1936)
Si j'étais vous ... (1947)
Moïra (1950)
Chaque homme dans sa nuit (1960)
L'Autre (1971)

GREENE, (Henry) Graham
(1904–91) English

The Man Within (1929)
The Name of Action (1930)
Rumour at Nightfall (1931)
Stamboul Train (1932)
It's a Battlefield (1934)
England Made Me (1934)
A Gun for Sale (1936)
Brighton Rock (1938)
The Confidential Agent (1939)
The Power and the Glory (1940)
The Ministry of Fear (1943)
The Heart of the Matter (1948)
The Third Man (1950)
The End of the Affair (1951)
The Quiet American (1955)
Loser Takes All (1955)
Our Man in Havana (1958)
A Burnt-Out Case (1961)
The Comedians (1966)
Travels with My Aunt (1969)
The Honorary Consul (1973)
The Human Factor (1978)
Doctor Fischer of Geneva (1980)
Monsignor Quixote (1982)
The Tenth Man (1985)
The Captain and the Enemy (1988)

GREENWOOD, Walter
(1903–74) English

Love on the Dole (1933)
The Secret Kingdom (1938)
Saturday Night at the Crown (1959)

GREY, (Pearl) Zane
(1872–1939) American

(western)
Betty Zane (1903)
Riders of the Purple Sage (1912)
(plus many western novels)

GRIFFIN, Gerald
(1803–40) Irish

The Collegians (1829)

GRILLPARZER, Franz
(1792–1872) Austrian

Das Kloster bei Sendomir (1828)
Der arme Spielmann (1848)

GRIMMELSHAUSEN, Johann (Jakob Christoffel von)
(1622–76) German
Simplicissimus (1669)

GROSSMITH, George
(1847–1912) and
GROSSMITH, Weedon
(1852–1919) English Brothers
The Diary of a Nobody (1892)

GUNN, Nell (Miller)
(1891–1973) Scottish
Grey Coast (1926)
The Lost Glen (1928)
Morning Tide (1931)
Sun Circle (1933)
Butcher's Broom (1934)
Highland River (1937)
Wild Geese Overhead (1939)
The Silver Darlings (1941)
The Well at the World's End (1951)
Bloodhunt (1952)
The Other Landscape (1954)

GUNTHER, John
(1901–70) American
Death Be Not Proud (1949)
The Lost City (1964)

GUTHRIE, Thomas Anstey
see **ANSTEY, F**

GYP
(1850–1932) French
real name: Comtesse de Mirabeau
Petit Bob (1882)
Mademoiselle Loulou (1888)
Mariage de Chiffon (1894)

H

HABE, Hans
(1911–77) Austro-American
real name: Hans Bekessy
Zu spät? (1940)
Ob Tausend fallen (1943)
Off Limits (1955)
Ilona (1960)
Die Mission (1965)
The Poisoned Stream (1969)

HAGGARD, Sir H(enry) Rider
(1856–1925) English
(adventure)
Dawn (1884)
The Witch's Head (1885)
King Solomon's Mines (1885)
She (1887)
Allan Quatermain (1887)
The World's Desire (1890)
Eric Brighteyes (1891)
Nada the Lily (1892)
Montezuma's Daughter (1893)
The Pearl Maiden (1903)
Ayesha (1905)
Queen Sheba's Ring (1910)
The Wanderer's Necklace (1914)

HAILEY, Arthur
(1920–) Anglo-Canadian
(thriller)
The Final Diagnosis (1959)
In High Places (1962)
Hotel (1965)
Airport (1968)
Wheels (1971)
The Money-Changers (1975)
Overload (1979)
Strong Medicine (1984)
The Evening News (1990)

HALL, Adam
(1920–) English
real name: Elleston Trevor

The Quiller Memorandum (1965)
The Warsaw Document (1971)

HALL, James (Norman)
see **NORDHOFF, Charles**

HAMILTON, (Anthony Walter) Patrick
(1904–62) English

Craven House (1926)
The Midnight Bell [1] (1929)
The Siege of Pleasure [1] (1932)
The Plains of Cement [1] (1934)
Hangover Square (1941)
The Slaves of Solitude (1947)

[1] Twenty Thousand Streets under the Sky trilogy

HAMILTON, Charles (Harold St John)
see **RICHARDS, Frank**

HAMILTON, Donald (Bengtsson)
(1916–) American

(crime)
Date with Darkness (1947)
Murder Twice Told (1950)
Night Walker (1954)
Line of Fire (1955)
Death of a Citizen (1960)
(plus many Matt Helm novels)

HAMMETT, (Samuel) Dashiell
(1894–1961) American

(crime/thriller)
Red Harvest (1929)
The Dain Curse (1929)
The Maltese Falcon (1930)
The Glass Key (1931)
The Thin Man (1932)

HAMMOND-INNES, Ralph
see **INNES, Hammond**

HAMSUN, Knut
(1859–1952) Norwegian
real name: Knut Pedersen

Sult (1890)
Mysterier (1892)
Pan (1894)
Markens grøde (1917)

HANDKE, Peter
(1942–) Austrian

Die Hornissen (1966)
Die Angst des Tormanns beim Elfmete (1970)

HANLEY, James
(1901–86) Irish

Drift (1930)
Boy (1931)
Captain Bottell (1933)
The Furys [1] (1935)
The Secret Journey [1] (1936)
Our Time Is Gone [1] (1940)
The Ocean (1941)
What Farrar Saw (1946)
Emily (1948)
A Walk in the Wilderness (1950)
The Closed Harbour (1952)
Levine (1956)
Say Nothing (1962)
Another World (1972)
A Woman in the Sky (1973)
A Kingdom (1978)

[1] Dublin novels

HANSFORD-JOHNSON, Pamela
(1912–) English
Wife of CP Snow

This Bed Thy Centre (1935)
Too Dear for My Possessing (1940)
The Unspeakable Skipton (1959)

HARDY, Thomas
(1840–1928) English

Desperate Remedies (1871)
Under the Greenwood Tree (1872)
A Pair of Blue Eyes (1873)
Far from the Madding Crowd (1874)
The Hand of Ethelberta (1876)
The Return of the Native (1878)
The Trumpet-Major (1880)
A Laodicean (1881)
Two on a Tower (1882)
The Mayor of Casterbridge (1886)
The Woodlanders (1887)
Wessex Tales (1888) coll
A Group of Noble Dames (1891) coll
Tess of the D'Urbervilles (1891)
Life's Little Ironies (1894)
Jude the Obscure (1895)
The Well-Beloved (1897)

HÄRING, Georg Wilhelm
see **ALEXIS, Willibald**

HARLAND, Henry
(1861–1905) American

Mea Culpa (1891)
Grey Roses (1895)
The Cardinal's Snuff-Box (1900)
My Friend Prospero (1904)

HARRIS, Joel Chandler
(1848–1908) American

(children's)
Uncle Remus (1880) coll
Nights with Uncle Remus (1883) coll
Mingo (1884)
Free Joe (1887)
Uncle Remus and His Friends (1892) coll
Mr Rabbit at Home (1895) coll
Sister Jane (1896)
Gabriel Tolliver (1902)
The Tar-Baby (1904) coll
Uncle Remus and Brer Rabbit (1906) coll
Uncle Remus and the Little Boy (1910) coll posth

HARRIS, John Wyndham Parkes Lucas Beynon
see **WYNDHAM, John**

HARRIS, (Theodore) Wilson
(1921–) Anglo-Guyanese

Palace of the Peacock [1] (1960)
The Far Journey of Oudin [1] (1961)
The Whole Armour [1] (1962)
The Secret Ladder [1] (1963)
The Waiting Room (1967)
Ascent to Omai (1970)
The Age of the Rainmakers (1971)
Black Marsden (1972)
Genesis of the Clowns (1975)
The Tree of the Sun (1978)

[1]Guyanan Quartet

HARRIS, Thomas
(1940–) American

Black Sunday (1975)
Red Dragon (1981)
The Silence of the Lambs (1988)

HARTE, (Francis) Bret
(1836–1902) American

The Luck of Roaring Camp (1868)
The Outcasts of Poker Flat (1869)
The Heathen Chinee (1870)
Mrs Skagg's Husbands (1873)
Tales of the Argonauts (1875)

HARTLEY, L(eslie) P(oles)
(1895–1972) English

Night Fears (1924) coll
Simonetta Perkins (1925)
The Killing Bottle (1932) coll
The Shrimp and the Anemone [1] (1944)
The Sixth Heaven [1] (1946)
Eustace and Hilda [1] (1947)
The Boat (1949)

My Fellow Devils (1951)
The Go-Between (1953)
A Perfect Woman (1955)
The Hireling (1957)
Facial Justice (1960)
The Brickfield (1964)
The Beyrayal (1966)
Poor Clare (1968)
The Love-Adept (1969)

[1] trilogy

HAUPTMANN, Gerhart
(1862–1946) German

Bahnärter Thiel (1888)
Fasching (1888)
Der Ketzer von Soana (1918)
Der Phantom (1923)
Wanda (1928)

HAWKINS, Sir Anthony Hope
see **HOPE, Anthony**

HAWTHORNE, Nathaniel
(1804–64) American

Fanshawe (1828)
Twice-Told Tales (1837) coll
Mosses from the Old Manse (1846) coll
The Scarlet Letter (1850)
The House of the Seven Gables (1851)
The Blithedale Romance (1852)
The Marble Faun (1860)

HAY, John (Milton)
(1838–1905) American

The Bread-Winners (1884)

HAZZARD, Shirley
(1931–) Australian

Cliffs of Fall (1963)
People in Glass Houses (1967)
The Bay of Noon (1970)
The Transit of Venus (1980)

HEARN, Lafcadio
(1850–1904) Greco-Irish

Chita (1889)
Youma (1890)

HECHT, Ben
(1892–1964) American

Eric Dorn (1921)
Gargoyles (1922)
A Jew in Love (1930)
A Flag Is Born (1946)

HEIBERG, Hermann
(1840–1910) German

Ausgetobt (1883)
Apotheker Heinrich (1885)
Esthers Ehe (1886)

HEINLEIN, Robert A(nson)
(1907–) American

(science fiction)
Beyond This Horizon (1948)
The Puppet Masters (1951)
Double Star (1956)
Methuselah's Children (1958)
Stranger in a Strange Land (1961)
The Red Planet (1966)
The Menace from the Earth (1968)
The Man Who Sold the Moon (1970)
I Will Fear No Evil (1971)
Time Enough for Love (1973)
The Number of the Beast (1980)
Friday (1982)

HELLER, Joseph
(1923–) American

Catch-22 (1961)
Something Happened (1974)
Good as Gold (1979)
God Knows (1984)
Picture This (1988)

HEMINGWAY, Ernest (Miller)
(1899–1961) American

Torrents of Spring (1926)
The Sun Also Rises (1926)
Men without Women (1927) coll
A Farewell to Arms (1929)
Death in the Afternoon (1932)
The Green Hills of Africa (1935)
To Have and Have Not (1937)
For Whom the Bell Tolls (1940)
Across the River and into the Trees (1950)
The Old Man and the Sea (1952)
Islands in the Stream (1970) posth

HENRY, O
(1862–1910) American
real name: William Sydney Porter

Cabbages and Kings (1904) coll

HENTY, G(eorge) A(lfred)
(1832–1902) English

(children's/historical)
Out in the Pampas (1871)
The Young Franc-Tireurs (1872)
The Young Buglers (1880)
Under Drake's Flag (1883)
With Clive in India (1884)
In Freedom's Cause (1885)
The Bravest of the Brave (1887)
The Lion of St Mark's (1889)
Redskin and Cowboy (1892)
A Roving Commission (1900)
With Roberts to Pretoria (1902)

HERBERT, Sir A(lan) P(atrick)
(1890–1971) English

The Secret Battle (1919)
The Water Gipsies (1930)
Holy Deadlock (1934)

HERBERT, Frank
(1920–86) American

(science fiction)
The Dragon in the Sea (1956)
Dune [1] (1965)
Dune Messiah [1] (1969)
Children of Dune [1] (1976)
God Emperor of Dune [2] (1980)
Heretics of Dune [2] (1982)
Chapter House Dune [2] (1985)

[1] Dune trilogy [2] 2nd Dune trilogy

HERBERT, James
(1943–) English

(horror)
The Rats (1974)
The Survivor (1976)
Fluke (1977)
The Fog (1978)
Lair (1979)
The Dark (1980)
The Jonah (1981)
Shrine (1983)
Domain (1984)
Moon (1985)
The Magic Cottage (1986)
Sepulchre (1987)
Haunted (1988)
Creed (1990)

HERGESHEIMER, Joseph
(1880–1954) American

The Lay Anthony (1914)
Mountain Blood (1915)
The Three Black Pennys (1917)
Gold and Iron (1918)
Java Head (1919)
Linda Condon (1919)
Cytherea (1922)
Balisand (1924)
Tampico (1926)
Swords and Roses (1929)
The Limestone Tree (1931)
Tropical Winter (1933)
The Foolscap Rose (1934)

HERRICK, Robert
(1868–1938) American

The Man Who Wins (1897) coll
The Gospel of Freedom (1898)

The Web of Life (1900)
The Real World (1901)
The Common Lot (1904)
The Master of the Inn (1908)
Together (1908)
The Healer (1911)
One Woman's Life (1913)
Clark's Field (1914)
The World Decision (1916)
Homely Lilla (1923)
Waste (1924)
The End of Desire (1931)
Sometime (1933)

HERZOG, Émile
see **MAUROIS, André**

HESSE, Hermann
(1877–1962) German-Swiss

Peter Camenzind (1904)
Unterm Rad (1906)
Gertrud (1910)
Rosshalde (1914)
Knulp (1915)
Demian (1919)
Siddhartha (1922)
Der Steppenwolf (1927)
Narziss und Goldmund (1930)
Morgenlandfahrt (1932)
Der Glasperlenspiel (1943)

HEWLETT, Maurice (Henry)
(1861–1923) English

(historical)
The Forest Lovers (1898)
Richard Yea-and-Nay (1900)
The Queen's Quair (1904)

HEYER, Georgette
(1902–74) English

(historical/romance/crime)
The Black Moth (1921)
These Old Shades (1926)
The Masqueraders (1928)
Beauvallet (1929)
Devil's Cub (1934)
Regency Buck (1935)
Death in the Stocks (1935)
Behold, Here's Poison (1936)
The Talisman Ring (1936)
Faro's Daughter (1941)
The Reluctant Widow (1946)
Arabella (1949)
The Grand Sophy (1950)
The Quiet Gentleman (1951)
The Toll-Gate (1954)
Bath Tangle (1955)
The Unknown Ajax (1959)

HIBBERT, Eleanor
see **PLAIDY, Jean**

HICHENS, Robert Smythe
(1864–1950) English

The Green Carnation (1894)
The Garden of Allah (1904)
The Call of the Blood (1906)
The Paradine Case (1933)
That Which Is Hidden (1939)

HIGGINS, George V(incent)
(1939–) American

The Friends of Eddie Coyle (1972)
The Digger's Game (1973)
Cogan's Trade (1974)
A City on a Hill (1975)
The Judgment of Deke Hunter (1976)
Dreamland (1977)
A Year or So with Edgar (1979)
Kennedy for the Defense (1980)
The Rat on Fire (1981)
The Patriot Game (1982)
A Choice of Enemies (1984)
Penance for Jerry Kennedy (1985)
Imposters (1986)
Outlaws (1987)
Wonderful Years, Wonderful Years (1988)
Trust (1989)
Victories (1990)

HIGGINS, Jack
(1929–) English
real name: Harry Patterson

(thriller)
Toll for the Brave (1971)
The Savage Day (1972)
The Eagle Has Landed (1975)
The Cretan Lover (1980)
Solo (1980)
Luciano's Luck (1981)
Touch the Devil (1982)
Exocet (1983)
Night of the Fox (1986)
A Season in Hell (1989)

HIGHSMITH, Patricia
(1921–) American

(crime)
Strangers on a Train (1950)
The Talented Mr Ripley (1955)
Ripley Under Ground (1971)
Ripley's Game (1974)
Found in the Street (1986)
Ripley Under Water (1991)

HILL, Susan (Elizabeth)
(1942–) British

The Enclosure (1961)
Do Me a Favour (1963)
Gentleman and Ladies (1968)
A Change for the Better (1969)
I'm King of the Castle (1970)
Strange Meeting (1971)
The Bird of Night (1972)
In the Springtime of the Year (1974)
The Woman in Black: A Ghost Story (1983)
Air and Angels (1991)

HILTON, James
(1900–54) English

Catherine Herself (1920)
Knight without Armour (1933)
The Lost Horizon (1933)
Goodbye Mr Chips (1934)
We Are Not Alone (1937)
Random Harvest (1941)

HINES, (Melvin) Barry
(1939–) English

The Blinder (1966)
A Kestrel for a Knave (1968)
The Gamekeeper (1975)

HOBAN, Russell (Conwell)
(1925–) American

Bedtime for Frances (1960)
The Mouse and His Child (1967)
The Lion of Boaz-Jachin and Jachin-Boaz (1972)
Turtle Diary (1976)
Riddley Walker (1980)

HOFF, Harry Summerfield
see **COOPER, William**

HOFFMAN, Charles Fenno
(1806–84) American

Vanderlyn (1837) unf
Greyslaer (1840)

HOFFMANN, Ernst Theodor Amadeus
(1776–1822) German

Ritter Gluck (1809)
Don Juan (1813)
Der goldene Topf (1814)
Die Elixiere des Teufels (1816)

HOFFMANN, Heinrich
(1809–74) German

(children's)
Struwwelpeter (1847)

HOGG, James
(1770–1835) Scottish

The Private Memoirs and Confessions of a Justified Sinner (1824)

HÖLDERLIN, Friedrich
(1770–1843) German
Hyperion (1799)

HOLMES, Oliver Wendell
(1809–94) American
Elsie Venner (1861)
The Guardian Angel (1867)
A Mortal Antipathy (1884)

HOLT, Victoria
see **PLAIDY, Jean**

HOOD, Thomas
(1799–1845) English
Tylney Hall (1834)

HOOPER, J(ohnson) J(ones)
(1815–62) American
Some Adventures of Captain Simon Suggs (1846)
The Widow Rugby's Husband (1851)

HOPE, Anthony
(1863–1933) English
real name: Sir Anthony Hope Hawkins
A Man of Mark (1890)
The Prisoner of Zenda [1] (1894)
The Dolly Dialogues (1894)
The Chronicles of Count Antonio (1895)
Phroso (1897)
Rupert of Hentzau [1] (1898)
Simon Dale (1898)
The Intrusions of Peggy (1902)
Sophy of Kravonia (1906)
Mrs Maxon Protests (1911)
Little Tiger (1925)

[1] Ruritania novels

HOPE, Laura Lee
(?–?) American
(children's)
Bobbsey Twins (1904)
(plus many Bobbsey Twins books)

HORGAN, Paul
(1903–) American
The Fault of Angels (1933)
No Quarter Given (1935)
Far from Cibola (1938)
The Habit of Empire (1941)
A Distant Trumpet (1960)
Things As They Are (1965)
The Peach Stone (1967) coll
Everything to Live For (1968)
Whitewater (1970)
The Thin Mountain Air (1977)
Mexico Bay (1982)
Under the Sangre de Cristo (1985)

HORNUNG, E(rnest) W(illiam)
(1866–1921) English
The Amateur Cracksman (1899)
(plus many Raffles novels)

HOUSEHOLD, Geoffrey (Edward West)
(1900–88) English
Rogue Male (1939)
Watcher in the Shadows (1960)
Dance of the Dwarfs (1968)
Rough Justice (1982)

HOUSMAN, Laurence
(1865–1959) English
Trimblerigg (1924)

HOWATCH, Susan
(1940–) English
Penmarric (1964)
Shrouded Walls (1972)
Cashelmara (1974)
Call in the Night (1976)
The Rich Are Different (1977)
Sins of the Fathers (1980)
The Wheel of Fortune (1984)
Glittering Images (1986)'
Glamorous Powers (1988)
Ultimate Prizes (1990)
Scandalous Risks (1991)

HOWE, E(dgar) W(atson)
(1853–1937) American
The Story of a Country Town (1883)

HOWELLS, William Dean
(1837–1920) American
Their Wedding Journey (1872)
The Lady of the Aroostook (1879)
The Undiscovered Country (1880)
A Fearful Responsibility (1881)
A Modern Instance (1882)
The Rise of Silas Lapham (1885)
Indian Summer (1886)
The Minister's Charge (1887)
A Hazard of New Fortunes (1890)
The Quality of Mercy (1892)
An Imperative Duty (1893)
A Traveller from Altruria (1894)
The Son of Royal Langbirth (1904)
New Leaf Mills (1913)
Leatherwood God (1916)

HOYLE, Sir Fred(erick)
(1915–) English
(science fiction)
The Black Cloud (1957)
Ossian's Ride (1959)
A for Andromeda (1962)
October the First Is Too Late (1966)
Comet Halley (1985)

HUDSON, W(illiam) H(enry)
(1841–1922) Anglo-American
A Crystal Age (1887)
Fan (1892)
Green Mansions (1904)
A Shepherd's Life (1910)

HUEFFER, Ford Hermann
see **FORD, Madox Ford**

HUGHES, Richard (Arthur Warren)
(1900–76) Anglo-Welsh
A High Wind in Jamaica (1929)
In Hazard (1938)
The Fox in the Attic (1961)
The Wooden Shepherdess (1973)

HUGHES, Thomas
(1822–96) English
(children's)
Tom Brown's Schooldays (1857)
The Scouring of the White Horse (1859)
Tom Brown at Oxford (1861)

HUGO, Victor (Marie)
(1802–85) French
Bug-Jargal (1826)
Notre-Dame de Paris (1831)
Claude Geuex (1834)
Les Misérables (1862)
Les Travailleurs de la mer (1866)
L'Homme qui rit (1869)
Quatre-vingt-treize (1873)

HULME, Keri
(1947–) New Zealand
The Bone People (1984)
Lost Possessions (1985)

HUNT, Irene
(1907–) American
(children's)
Across Five Aprils (1964)
Up a Road Slowly (1966)
No Promises in the Wind (1970)

HUNT, (Isobel) Violet
(1866–1942) English
The Maiden's Progress (1894)
White Rose of Weary Leaf (1908)

HUNTER, Evan
see **McBAIN, Ed**

HUTCHINSON, R(ay) C(oryton)
(1907–75) English

The Unforgotten Prisoner (1933)
Shining Scabbard (1936)
Testament (1938)
Elephant & Castle (1949)
The Stepmother (1955)
A Child Possessed (1964)
Rising (1976) posth

HUXLEY, Aldous (Leonard)
(1894–1963) English

Crome Yellow (1921)
Mortal Coils (1922) coll
Antic Hay (1923)
Those Barren Leaves (1925)
Point Counter Point (1928)
Brave New World (1932)
Eyeless in Gaza (1936)
After Many a Summer (1939)
Time Must Have a Stop (1944)
Ape and Essence (1948)
The Genius and the Goddess (1955)
Brave New World Revisited (1958)
Island (1962)

HUYSMANS, Joris-Karl
(1848–1907) Franco-Dutch

Croquis parisiens (1880)
En ménage (1881)
Avau l'eau (1882)
Arebours (1884)
Là-bas [1] (1891)
En route [1] (1895)
La Cathédrale [1] (1898)
L'Oblat [1] (1903)

[1] Durtal tetralogy

I

IBAÑEZ, Vicente Blasco
see **BLASCO IBAÑEZ, Vicente**

ILES, Francis
(1893–1970) English

(crime)
The Poisoned Chocolates Case (1929)
as Anthony Berkeley
Malice Aforethought (1931)
Before the Fact (1932)

IMLAY, Gilbert
(1754–1828) American

The Emigrants (1793)

INCHBALD, Elizabeth
(1753–1821) English
née Simpson

A Simple Story (1791)
Nature and Art (1796)

INNES, Hammond
(1913–) English
real name: Ralph Hammond-Innes

(thriller)
Wreckers Must Breathe (1940)
Attack Alarm (1941)
Dead and Alive (1946)
Killer Mine (1947)
The White South (1949)
The Angry Mountain (1950)
Campbell's Kingdom (1952)
The Strange Land (1954)
The Mary Deare (1956)
The Doomed Oasis (1960)
Atlantic Fury (1962)
The Strode Venturer (1965)
The Conquistadors (1969)
Levkas Man (1971)
North Star (1974)
The Big Footprints (1977)
Solomon's Seal (1980)
The Black Tide (1982)
High Stand (1985)
Medusa (1988)
Isvik (1991)

INNES, Michael
see **STEWART, JIM**

IRON, Ralph
see **SCHREINER, Olive**

IRVING, John
(1942–) American

Setting Free the Bears (1968)
The Water-Method Man (1972)
The 158-Pound Marriage (1974)
The World According to Garp (1976)
The Hotel New Hampshire (1981)
The Cider House Rules (1985)
A Prayer for Owen Meany (1989)

IRVING, Washington
(1783–1859) American

The Sketch Book (1820) coll
Bracebridge Hall (1822) coll

ISHERWOOD, Christopher (William Bradshaw)
(1904–86) English

All the Conspirators (1928)
The Memorial (1932)
Mr Norris Changes Trains (1935)
Goodbye to Berlin (1939)
Prater Violet (1945)
The World in the Evening (1954)
Down There on a Visit (1962)
A Single Man (1964)
Meeting by the River (1967)

ISHIGURO, Kazuo
(1954–) Japanese

A Pale View of Hills (1982)
An Artist of the Floating World (1986)
The Remains of the Day (1989)

J

JACOB, Piers A
see **ANTHONY, Piers**

JACOBS, W(illiam) W(ymark)
(1863–1943) English

Many Cargoes (1896) coll
At Sunwich Point (1902)
The Monkey's Paw (1902)
Dialstone Lane (1904)
Deep Waters (1919) coll

JAMES, Henry
(1843–1916) American

Watch and Ward (1871)
Roderick Hudson (1876)
The American (1877)
The Europeans (1878)
Daisy Miller (1879)
An International Episode (1879)
Confidence (1880)
Washington Square (1881)
The Portrait of a Lady (1881)
The Siege of London (1883) coll
The Bostonians (1886)
The Princess Casamassima (1886)
The Reverberator (1888)
The Aspern Papers (1888)
The Tragic Muse (1890)
The Other House (1896)
The Spoils of Poynton (1897)
What Maisie Knew (1898)
In the Cage (1898)
The Turn of the Screw (1898)
The Awkward Age (1899)
The Sacred Fount (1901)
The Wings of the Dove (1902)
The Ambassadors (1903)
The Golden Bowl (1904)
The Ivory Tower (1917) posth unf
The Sense of the Past (1917) posth unf

JAMES, M(ontague) R(hodes)
(1862–1936) English
Ghost Stories of an Antiquary (1904) coll

JAMES, P(hyllis) D(orothy)
(1920–) English
(crime)
Cover Her Face (1962)
A Mind to Murder (1963)
Unnatural Causes (1967)
Shroud for a Nightingale (1971)
An Unsuitable Job for a Woman (1972)
The Black Tower (1975)
Death of an Expert Witness (1977)
Innocent Blood (1980)
The Skull beneath the Skin (1982)
A Taste for Death (1986)
Devices and Desires (1989)

JARRELL, Randall
(1914–65) American
Pictures from an Institution (1954)

JEAN PAUL
(1763–1825) German
real name: Johann Paul Friedrich Richter
Hesperus (1795)
Quintus Fixlein (1796)
Titan (1800–1803) 6 vol
Die Flegeljahre (1804–1805) 4 vol unf

JEFFERIES, Richard
(1848–87) English
Wood Magic (1881)
Bevis, the Story of a Boy (1882)

JENSEN, Johannes Vilhelm
(1873–1950) Danish
Den Lange Rejse (1908–1922) 3 vol

JEROME, Jerome K(lapka)
(1859–1927) English
Three Men in a Boat (1889)
Three Men on the Bummel (1900)
Paul Klever (1902)

JEWETT, Sarah Orne
(1849–1909) American
Deephaven (1877) coll
A Country Doctor (1884)
A Marsh Island (1885)
The Country of the Pointed Firs (1896)

JHABVALA, Ruth Prawer
(1927–) Anglo-Polish
To Whom She Will Marry (1955)
Esmond in India (1957)
The Householder (1960)
Get Ready for Battle (1962)
Heat and Dust (1975)
In Search of Love and Beauty (1983)

JOHNS, Captain W(illiam) E(arle)
(1893–1968) English
(children's/war)
The Camels Are Coming (1932)
(plus many Biggles books)
Gimlet Goes Again (1944)
(plus many Gimlet books)

JOHNSON, B(ryan) S(tanley William)
(1933–73) English
Travelling People (1963)
Albert Angelo (1964)
Trawl (1966)
Theunfortunates (1969)
House Mother Normal (1971)
Christy Malry's Own Double-Entry (1973)
See the Old Lady Decently (1975) posth

JOHNSON, Doctor Samuel
(1709–84) English

Rasselas (1759)

JOKAI, Mír
(1825–1904) Hungarian

The Day of Wrath (1850)
The Turks in Hungary (1852)
The Magyar Nabob (1853)
Karpathy (1854)
The New Landlord (1862)
Black Diamonds (1870)
The Modern Midas (1875)
God Is One (1877)
The White Woman of Leutschau (1884)
The Gipsy Baron (1885)
Dr Dumanany's Wife (1891)

JONES, (Everett) LeRoi
(1934–) American

The System of Dante's Hell (1965)

JONES, James
(1921–77) American

From Here to Eternity (1951)
Go to the Widow-Maker (1967)
The Merry Month of May (1971)

JONG, Erica
(1942–) American

Fear of Flying (1974)
How to Save Your Own Life (1978)

JORISCH, Norah
see **LOFTS, Norah**

K

KAFKA, Franz
(1883–1924) Austrian

Die Verwandlung (1915)
Der Prozess (1925) posth
Das Schloss (1926) posth unf
Amerika (1927) posth unf

KANTOR, MacKinlay
(1904–77) American

Diversey (1928)
Long Remember (1934)
Arouse and Beware (1936)
The Noise of Their Wings (1938)
Gentle Annie (1942)
Happy Land (1943)
Andersonville (1955)
Valley Forge (1975)

KARAMZIN, Nikolai Mikhailovich
(1766–1826) Russian

Poor Liza (1792)
Natalia, the Boyar's Daughter (1792)

KÄSTNER, Erich
(1899–1974) German

(children's)
Emil und die Detektive (1929)
Annaluise und Anton (1929)
Pünktchen und Anton (1931)
Fabian [1] (1931)
Das fliegende Klassenzimmer (1933)
Drei Männer im Schnee (1934)
Die Konferenz der Tiere [1] (1949)

[1] not children's

KAVANAGH, D
see **BARNES, Julian**

KAVANAGH, Julia
(1824–1877) Irish

Madeleine (1848)
Nathalie (1850)
Adèle (1858)

KAVANAGH, Patrick
(1905–67) Irish

Tarry Flynn (1948)

KAWABATA, Yasunari
(1899–1972) Japanese

The Dancer of Izu Province (1925)
Red Group of Asakusa (1930)
Snow Country (1935–47)
A Thousand Cranes (1948)
The Sound of the Mountain (1949–54)
Kyoto (1962)
House of the Sleeping Beauty (1969)

KAYE, M(ary) M(argaret)
(1911–) English

Six Bars at Seven (1940)
Death Walks in Kashmir (1953)
Death Walks in Berlin (1955)
Death Walks in Cyprus (1956)
Shadow of the Moon (1957)
Night on the Island (1960)
Trade Wind (1963)
The Far Pavilions (1978)
The Ordinary Princess [1] (1980)
Thistledown [1] (1981)

[1] children's

KAZANTZAKIS, Nikos
(1883–1957) Greek

Toda Raba (1929)
Zorba the Greek (1946)
Christ Recrucified (1954)

KEATING, H(enry R(aymond) F(itzwalter)
(1926–) English

(crime)
Death and the Visiting Fireman (1959)
The Perfect Murder (1964)
(plus many Inspector Ghote novels)

KELL, Joseph
see **BURGESS, Anthony**

KELLER, Gottfried
(1819–90) Swiss

Der grüne Heinrich (1854)
Züricher Novellen (1878) coll
Martin Salander (1886)

KELMAN, James (Alexander)
(1946–) Scottish

The Busconductor Hines (1984)
Chancer (1985)
Greyhound for Breakfast (1987) coll
A Disaffection (1989)
The Burn (1991) coll

KENEALLY, Thomas (Michael)
(1935–) Australian

The Place at Whitton (1964)
The Fear (1965)
Bring Larks and Heroes (1967)
Three Cheers for a Paraclete (1968)
The Survivor (1969)
A Dutiful Daughter (1971)
The Chant of Jimmy Blacksmith (1972)
Passenger (1979)
Schindler's Ark (1982)
A Family Madness (1985)
The Playmaker (1987)

KENNEDY, Margaret (Moore)
(1896–1967) English

The Ladies of Lyndon (1923)
The Constant Nymph (1924)
Red Sky at Morning (1927)
Return I Dare Not (1931)
A Long Time Ago (1932)
Together and Apart (1936)
The Midas Touch (1938)
The Feast (1950)
Troy Chimneys (1953)
The Oracle (1955)
The Heroes of Clone (1957)
The Forgotten Smile (1961)
Not in the Calendar (1964)

KENT, Alexander
(1925–) English
real name: Douglas Reeman

(nautical)
To Glory We Steer (1968)

KENT, Alexander (cont.)
Enemy in Sight! (1970)
Sloop of War (1972)
Richard Bolitho Midshipman (1975)
Passage to Mutiny (1976)
The Inshore Squadron (1979)
Stand into Danger (1981)
Success to the Brave (1983)
Colours Aloft! (1986)
Honour This Day (1987)
The Only Victor (1990)
The Killing Ground (1991)
as Douglas Reeman

KEROUAC, Jack
(1922–69) American
The Town in the City (1950)
On the Road (1957)
The Subterraneans (1958)
The Dharma Bums (1958)
Tristessa (1960)
Big Sur (1962)
Desolation Angels (1965)

KESEY, Ken (Elton)
(1935–) American
One Flew over the Cuckoo's Nest (1962)
Sometimes a Great Notion (1964)
Demon Box (1986) coll

KESSEL, Joseph
(1898–1979) Russo-French
L'Équipage (1923)
Nuits des princes (1928)
Le Coup de grâce (1931)

KEYES, Frances Parkinson
(1885–1970) American
The Old Gray Homestead (1919)
The Career of David Noble (1921)
Queen Anne's Lace (1930)
The Safe Bridge (1934)
Honor Bright (1936)
All That Glitters (1941)
If Ever I Cease to Love (1943)
Came a Cavalier (1948)
Dinner at Antoine's (1949)
Joy Street (1951)
The Royal Box (1954)
Blue Camellia (1957)
The Chess Players (1961)
Three Ways of Love (1964)
The Explorer (1965)

KIMITAKE, Hiraoka
see **MISHIMA, Yukio**

KING, Francis (Henry)
(1923–) English
To the Dark Tower (1946)
The Dividing Stream (1951)
The Widow (1957)
The Custom House (1961)
The Brighton Belle (1968)
Flights (1973)
Hard Feelings (1976)
The Action (1979)

KING, Stephen (Edwin)
(1947–) American
(horror)
Carrie (1973)
Salem's Lot (1975)
Night Shift (1976)
The Shining (1976)
The Stand (1978)
The Dead Zone (1979)
Firestarter (1980)
Danse Macabre (1981)
Cujo (1981)
The Gunslinger (1982)
Christine (1983)
Skeleton Crew (1985)
It (1986)
Misery (1987)
The Tommyknockers (1988)
The Dark Half (1989)
Four Past Midnight (1990)
Needful Things (1991)

KINGSLEY, Charles
(1819–75) English
Brother of Henry Kingsley

Yeast (1850)
Alton Locke (1850)
Hypatia (1853)
Westward Ho! (1855)
Two Years Ago (1857)
The Water-Babies (1863)
Hereward the Wake (1866)

KINGSLEY, Henry
(1830–76) English
Brother of Charles Kingsley

Geoffrey Hamlyn (1859)
Ravenshoe (1862)
Austin Elliott (1863)
The Hillyers and the Burtons (1865)

KIPLING, Rudyard
(1865–1936) English

Plain Tales from the Hills (1888) coll
The Light That Failed (1890)
The Jungle Books [1] (1894–5) 2 vol
Captains Courageous (1897)
Stalky & Co [1] (1899)
Kim (1901)
Just So Stories [1] (1902) coll
Puck of Pook's Hill [1] (1906)
Rewards and Fairies [1] (1910)
Debits and Credits (1926) coll

[1] children's

KITCHIN, C(lifford) H(enry) B(enn)
(1895–1967) English

Streamers Waving (1925)
Mr Balcony (1927)
Death of My Aunt [1] (1929)
Crime at Christmas [1] (1934)
The Birthday Party (1938)
The Auction Sale (1949)
Jumping Joan (1954)
The Secret River (1956)
Ten Pollitt Place (1957)

[1] crime

KNOWLES, John
(1926–) American

A Separate Peace (1959)
Spreading Fires (1974)

KOESTLER, Arthur
(1905–83) Anglo-Hungarian

The Gladiators (1939)
Darkness at Noon (1940)
Scum of the Earth (1941)
Arrival and Departure (1943)
Thieves in the Night (1946)
The Age of Longing (1951)

KOONTZ, Dean R
(1945–) American

(horror)
Star Quest (1968)
(plus many science fiction novels)
The Crimson Witch (1971)
Hanging On (1974)
Prison of Ice (1976)
Night Chills (1977)
Whispers (1980)
The Mask (1981)
Phantoms (1983)
Darkness Comes (1984)
Strangers (1986)
Twilight Eyes (1987)
Watchers (1987)
Lightning (1988)
Midnight (1989)
The Bad Place (1990)

KORZENIOWSKI, Teodor Josef Konrad Nalecz
see **CONRAD, Joseph**

KOSINSKI, Jerzy (Nikodem)
(1933–) Polish-American

The Painted Bird (1965)
Steps (1968)
Being There (1971)
Blind Date (1977)
Passion Play (1979)

KRANTZ, Judith
(?–) American

Scruples (1968)
Princess Daisy (1980)
Mistral's Daughter (1982)
I'll Take Manhattan (1986)
Till We Meet Again (1988)
Dazzled (1990)

KUNDERA, Milan
(1929–) Czech

The Joke (1967)
Life Is Elsewhere (1973)
The Farewell Party (1976)
The Unbearable Lightness of Being (1984)

KUYUMJIAN, Dikran
see **ARLEN, Michael**

L

LA FARGE, Oliver (Hazard Perry)
(1901–63) American

Laughing Boy (1929)
Sparks Fly Upward (1931)
All the Young Men (1935)
The Copper Pot (1942)

LA FAYETTE, Marie-Madeleine
(1634–93) French

La Princesse de Montpensier (1662)
Zaùde (1670)
La Princesse de Clèves (1678)

LAGERKVIST, Pär (Fabian)
(1891–1974) Swedish

Bödeln (1933)
Dvärgen (1944)
Barabbas (1950)

LAGERLÖF, Selma (Ottiliana Lovisa)
(1858–1940) Swedish

Gösta Berlings saga (1891)
Jerusalem (1902)
Nils Holgerssons underbara resa genom Sverige [1] (1907)

[1] children's

LAMBURN, Richmal Crompton
see **CROMPTON, Richmal**

LAMMING, George (Eric)
(1927–) Barbadian

In the Castle of My Skin (1953)
The Emigrants (1954)
Of Age and Innocence (1958)
Season of Adventure (1960)
Water with Berries (1971)
Natives of My Person (1972)

L'AMOUR, Louis
(1908–88) American

Hondo (1953)
Sackett (1961)
How the West Was Won (1962)
(plus many western novels)

LAMPEDUSA, Giuseppe (Tomasi di)
(1896–1957) Italian

Il Gattopardo (1958) posth

LANDON, Letitia Elizabeth
(1802–38) English

Romance and Reality (1831)
Ethel Churchill (1837)

LANG, Andrew
(1844–1912) Scottish

The Mark of Cain (1886)
The Disentanglers (1902)

LARDNER, Ring(old Wilmer)
(1885–1933) American

The Big Town (1921)

LARKIN, Philip (Arthur)
(1922–85) English

Jill (1946)
A Girl in Winter (1947)

LAURENCE, Margaret
(1926–87) Canadian

This Side of Jordan (1960)
The Stone Angel [1] (1964)
A Jest of God [1] (1966)
The Fire-Dwellers [1] (1969)
A Bird in the House [1] (1970)
The Diviners [1] (1974)

[1] Manawaka quintet

LAWRENCE, D(avid) H(erbert)
(1885–1930) English

The White Peacock (1911)
The Trespasser (1912)
Sons and Lovers (1913)
The Rainbow (1915)
Women in Love (1920)
Aaron's Rod (1922)
Kangaroo (1923)
The Plumed Serpent (1926)
Lady Chatterley's Lover (1928)

LAWRENCE, George Alfred
(1827–76) English

Guy Livingstone (1857)
Sword and Gown (1859)
Border and Bastille (1863)

LAXNESS, Halldór
(1902–) Icelandic

Salka Valka (1931–2)
Heimsljós (1937–40) 4 vol
Islandsklukkan (1943–9)
Atómstöðin (1948)
Gerpla (1952)
Brekkukotsannáll (1957)
Paradisarheimt (1960)
Kristnihald undir Jökli (1968)

LEASOR, (Thomas) James
(1923–) English

(crime/thriller)
Not Such a Bad Day (1946)
The Strong Delusion (1951)
NTR: Nothing to Report (1955)
Passport to Oblivion (1964)
Passport to Peril (1966)
Passport in Suspense (1967)
Passport for a Pilgrim (1968)
Never Had a Spanner on Her (1970)
Love-All (1971)
Follow the Drum (1972)
Hosts of Extras (1973)
Mandarin Gold (1973)
The Chinese Widow (1975)
Jade Gate (1976)
The Unknown Warrior (1980)
Open Secret (1982)

LE CARRÉ, John
(1931–) English
real name: David John Moore Cornwell

(spy)
Call for the Dead (1961)
A Murder of Quality (1962)
The Spy Who Came In from the Cold (1963)
The Looking Glass War (1965)
A Small Town in Germany (1968)
The Naive and Sentimental Lover [1] (1971)
Tinker, Tailor, Soldier, Spy (1974)
The Honourable Schoolboy (1977)
Smiley's People (1980)
The Little Drummer Girl (1983)
A Perfect Spy (1986)
The Russia House (1989)
The Secret Pilgrim (1991)

[1] not spy

LEE, Harper
(1926–) American
To Kill a Mockingbird (1960)

LEE, Harriet
(1757–1851) English
Errors of Innocence (1786)
Clare Lennox (1797)

LEE, Laurie
(1914–) English
Cider with Rosie (1959)

LEE, Manfred
see **QUEEN, Ellery**

LE FANU, (Joseph) Sheridan
(1814–73) Irish
(horror)
The Cock and Anchor [1] (1845)
Torlogh O'Brien [1] (1847)
The House by the Churchyard (1863)
Uncle Silas (1864)
Guy Deverell (1865)
The Tenants of Malory (1867)
A Lost Name (1868)
The Wyvern Mystery (1869)
Checkmate (1871)
The Rose and the Key (1871)
In a Glass Darkly (1872) coll
Willing to Die (1873)

[1] not horror

LeGUIN, Ursula
(1929–) American
née Kroeber
(science fiction)
Rocannon's World (1966)
Planet of Exile (1966)
City of Illusions (1967)
A Wizard of Earthsea [1] (1968)
The Tombs of Atuan [1] (1971)
The Farthest Shore [1] (1972)
The Dispossessed (1974)
Always Coming Home (1986)

[1] Earthsea trilogy

LEHMANN, Rosamund (Nina)
(1903–90) English
Dusty Answer (1927)
A Note in Music (1930)
Invitation to the Waltz (1932)
The Weather in the Streets (1936)
The Ballad and the Source (1944)
The Echoing Grove (1953)
A Sea-Grape Tree (1970)

LENNOX, Charlotte (Ramsay)
(1720–1804) Anglo-American
The Life of Harriot Stuart (1750)
The Female Quixote (1752)
Henrietta (1758)
Sophia (1762)
Euphemia (1790)

LENZ, Siegfried
(1926–) Prusso-German
Der Mann im Strom (1957)
Brot und Spiele (1959)
Stadtgespräch (1963)
Deutschstunde (1968)
Das Vorbild (1973)

LEONARD, Elmore
(1925–) American
The Bounty Hunters (1953)
The Law at Randado (1955)
Escape from Five Shadows (1959)
Hombre (1961)
Valdez Is Coming (1969)
The Big Bounce (1969)
The Moonshine war (1969)
Forty Lashes Less One (1972)
Mr Majestyk (1974)
Fifty-Two Pickup (1974)
Swag (1976)
The Hunted (1977)
Unknown Man No. 89 (1977)
The Switch (1978)
Gunsights (1979)
City Primeval (1980)
Gold Coast (1980)
Split Images (1982)

Cat Chaser (1982)
Stick (1983)
LaBrava (1983)
Glitz (1985)
Bandits (1987)
Touch (1987)
Freaky Deaky (1988)
Killshot (1989)
Get Shorty (1990)
Maximum Bob (1991)

LEONOV, Leonid (Maksimovich)
(1899–) Russian

The Badgers (1924)
The Thief (1927)
The River Sot (1929)
Skutarevsky (1932)
The Road to the Ocean (1935)
The Russian Forest (1953)

LERMONTOV, Mikhail (Yurevich)
(1814–41) Russian

A Hero of Our Time (1840)

LEROUX, Gaston
(1868–1927) French

(crime)
Le Mystère de la chambre jaune (1907)
Le Parfum de la dame en noir (1909)
Le Fantôme de l'Opéra (1911)

LESAGE, Alain-René
(1668–1747) French

Le Diable boiteux (1707)
Gil Blas (1715–1735) 4 vol

LESSING, Doris (May)
(1919–) Anglo-Rhodesian
née Tayler

The Grass Is Singing (1950)
Martha Quest [1] (1952)
A Proper Marriage [1] (1954)
A Ripple from the Storm [1] (1958)
The Golden Notebook (1962)
Landlocked [1] (1965)
The Four-Gated City [1] (1969)
Briefing for a Descent into Hell (1971)
Memoirs of a Survivor (1975)
Re: Colonised Planet 5, Shikasta [2] (1979)
The Marriages between Zones Three, Four and Five [2] (1980)
The Sirian Experiments [2] (1981)
The Making of the Representative for Planet 8 [2] (1982)
Documents Relating to the Sentimental Agents in the Volyen
Empire [2] (1983)
The Good Terrorist (1985)
The Fifth Child (1988)

[1] Children of Violence novels
[2] Canopus in Argus Archives novels

LEVER, Charles (James)
(1806–72) Irish

Harry Lorrequer (1839)
Charles O'Malley (1841)
Jack Hinton the Guardsman (1843)
The Knight of Gwynne (1847)
Roland Cashel (1850)
The Dodd Family Abroad (1854)
Sir Jasper Carew (1855)
The Fortunes of Glencore (1857)
Luttrel of Arran (1865)
Lord Kilgobbin (1872)

LEVIN, Meyer
(1905–81) American

Reporter (1929)
Yehuda (1931)
The Old Bunch (1937)
Citizens (1940)
Compulsion (1956)
The Fanatic (1964)
The Settlers (1972)
The Harvest (1978)

LEWIS, C(live) S(taples)
(1898–1963) English

(children's)
Out of the Silent Planet [1] (1938)

LEWIS, CS (cont.)
Perelandra [1] (1943)
That Hideous Strength [1] (1945)
The Lion, the Witch and the Wardrobe [2] (1950)
Prince Caspian: The Return to Narnia [2] (1951)
The Voyage of the Dawn Treader [2] (1952)
The Silver Chair [2] (1953)
The Horse and His Boy [2] (1954)
The Magician's Nephew [2] (1955)
The Last Battle [2] (1956)

[1] science fiction novels [2] Narnia books

LEWIS (Harry) Sinclair
(1885–1951) American

Our Mr Wrenn (1914)
The Job (1917)
Main Street (1920)
Babbitt (1922)
Arrowsmith (1924)
Mantrap (1926)
Elmer Gantry (1927)
The Man Who Knew Coolidge (1928)
Dodsworth (1929)
Ann Vickers (1933)
It Can't Happen Here (1935)
Prodigal Parents (1938)
Gideon Planish (1943)
Cass Timberlane (1945)
Kingsblood Royal (1947)

LEWIS, M(atthew) G(regory)
(1775–1818) English

The Monk (1796)

LEWIS, (Percy) Wyndham
(1882–1957) English

Tarr (1918)
The Childermass [1] (1928)
The Apes of God (1930)
The Revenge for Love (1937)
Monstre Gai [1] (1955)
Malign Fiesta [1] (1955)
Self Condemned (1957)

[1] The Human Age trilogy

LINKLATER, Eric
(1899–1974) Scottish

White Man's Saga (1928)
Poet's Pub (1929)
Juan in America (1931)
The Men of Ness (1932)
Laxdale Hall (1933)
Magnus Merriman (1934)
Juan in China (1937)
The Wind in the Moon [1] (1944)
Private Angelo (1946)
The Pirates in the Deep Green Sea [1] (1949)
The House of Gair (1953)
The Ultimate Viking (1955)
Roll of Honour (1961)
The Voyage of the Challenger (1972)

[1] children's

LIVELY, Penelope (Margaret)
(1933–) English
née Greer

(children's)
Astercote (1970)
The Wild Hunt of Hagworthy (1971)
The Driftway (1972)
The House in Norham Gardens (1974)
A Stitch in Time (1976)
Fanny's Sister (1977)
The Voyage of QV66 (1978)
The Road to Lichfield [1] (1979)
The Revenge of Samuel Stokes (1981)
Judgement Day [1] (1981)
Moon Tiger [1] (1986)
A House Inside Out (1987)
Passing On (1989)

[1] not children's

LLEWELLYN, Richard
(1907–83) Welsh
real name: Richard Doyle Vivian Llewellyn Lloyd

How Green Was My Valley (1939)
None But the Lonely Heart (1943)
The Flame of Hercules(1957)
Up into the Singing Mountain (1963)
Green, Green My Valley Now (1975)

A Night of Bright Stars (1979)
I Stand on a Quiet Shore (1982)

LLOSA, Mario Vargas
see **VARGAS LLOSA, (Jorge) Mario (Pedro)**

LLOYD, Richard Doyle Vivian Llewellyn
see **LLEWELLYN, Richard**

LOCKHART, John Gibson
(1794–1854) Scottish

Some Passages in the Life of Adam Blair (1822)
Reginald Dalton (1823)
Matthew Wald (1824)

LODGE, David (John)
(1935–) English

The Picturegoers (1960)
Ginger You're Barmy (1962)
The British Museum Is Falling Down (1965)
How Far Can You Go? (1980)
Small World (1984)
Nice Work (1988)
Paradise News (1991)

LOFTING, Hugh (John)
(1886–1947) English

(children's)
The Story of Dr Dolittle (1920)
(plus many Dr Dolittle books)

LOFTS, Norah
(1904–) English
real name: Norah Jorisch;
née Robinson

(historical/romance)
I Met a Gypsy (1935)
White Hell of Pity (1937)
Out of This Nettle (1939)
The Brittle Glass (1942)
Jassy (1944)
Silver Nutmeg (1947)
Esther (1950)
The Luteplayer (1951)
Afternoon of an Autocrat (1956)
Scent of Cloves (1958)
The Town House [1] (1959)
The House at Old Vine [1] (1961)
The House at Sunset [1] (1963)
The Concubine (1964)
Bless This House (1968)
Blossom Like the Rose (1970)
Charlotte (1972)
Knight's Acre (1975)
Gad's Hall (1977)
Haunted House (1978)
Day of the Butterfly (1979)
The Claw (1981)

[1] House trilogy

LONDON, Jack (Griffith)
(1876–1916) American

The Son of the Wolf (1900) coll
The Cruise of the Dazzler (1902)
The Call of the Wild (1903)
The Sea-Wolf (1904)
Before Adam (1906)
White Fang (1906)
The Iron Heel (1907)
Martin Eden (1909)
Burning Daylight (1910)
Smoke Bellew (1912)
The Valley of the Moon (1913)
John Barleycorn (1913)

LOOS, Anita
(1893–1981) American

Gentlemen Prefer Blondes (1925)
But Gentlemen Marry Brunettes (1928)
No Mother to Guide Her (1961)

LOTI, Pierre
(1850–1923) French
real name: Julien Viaud

Aziyadé(1879)
Mon frère Yves (1883)
Pêcheur d'Islande (1886)
Matelot (1893)

LOTI, Pierre (cont.)
Ramuntcho (1897)
L'Inde (1903)
Un Pèlerin d'Angkor (1912)

LOVECRAFT, H(oward) P(hillips)
(1890–1937) American
(science fiction/horror)
The Case of Charles Dexter Ward (1928)
At the Mountain of Madness (1931)
The Shadow over Innsmouth (1936) coll
Something About Cats (1949) posth
Dreams and Fancies (1962) coll posth

LOVER, Samuel
(1797–1868) Irish
Rory O'Moore (1836)
Handy Andy (1842)

LOWRY, (Clarence) Malcolm
(1909–57) English
Ultramarine (1933)
Under the Volcano (1947)
Lunar Caustic (1963) posth
Dark As the Grave Wherein My Friend Is Laid (1968) coll posth

LUCAS, Victoria
see **PLATH, Sylvia**

LUDLUM, Robert
(1927–) American
(thriller)
The Scarlatti Inheritance (1971)
The Osterman Weekend (1973)
The Rhinemann Exchange (1975)
The Gemini Contenders (1976)
The Holcroft Covenant (1977)
The Matarese Circle (1978)
The Bourne Identity (1980)
The Parsifal Mosaic (1982)
The Aquitaine Progression (1984)
The Bourne Supremacy (1986)
The Icarus Agenda (1988)
The Bourne Ultimatum (1990)

LURIE, Alison
(1926–) American
Love and Friendship (1962)
Imaginary Friends (1967)
The War between the Tates (1974)
Only Children (1979)
The Truth About Lorin Jones (1988)

LYALL, Edna
(1857–1903) Anglo-Irish
real name: Ada Ellen Bayly
Donovan (1882)
We Two (1884)
In the Golden Days (1885)
Doreen (1895)

LYALL, Gavin (Tudor)
(1932–) English
(thriller)
The Most Dangerous Game (1963)
Midnight Plus One (1965)
Venus With Pistol (1969)
Blame the Dead (1973)
Judas Country (1975)
The Secret Servant (1980)
The Conduct of Major Maxim (1983)

LYLY, John
(1554–1606) English
Euphues (1579–80) 2 vol

LYTTON, Baron
see **BULWER-LYTTON, Edward**

M

MACAULAY, Dame (Emilie) Rose
(1881–1958) English
Abbots Verney (1906)
Views and Vagabonds (1912)
The Lee Shore (1920)

Potterism (1920)
Dangerous Ages (1921)
Told by an Idiot (1923)
Orphan Island (1924)
Crewe Train (1926)
Keeping Up Appearances (1928)
They Were Defeated (1932)
I Would Be Private (1937)
And No Man's Wit (1940)
The World My Wilderness (1950)
The Towers of Trebizond (1956)

MACDONALD, George
(1824–1905) Scottish

Phantastes (1858)
David Elginbrod (1863)
Alec Forbes of Howglen (1865)
Robert Falconer (1868)
At the Back of the North Wind [1] (1871)
The Princess and the Goblin [1] (1872)
Gutta Percha Willie [1] (1873)
The Lost Princess [1] (1875)
The Princess and Curdie [1] (1883)
A Rough Shaking [1] (1891)
Lilith (1895)

[1] children's

MACDONALD, John D(ann)
(1916–86) American

(crime)
The Brass Cupcake (1950)
Nightmare in Pink (1964)
The Last One Left (1967)
Pale Gray for Guilt (1968)
The Scarlet Ruse (1973)

MACDONALD, Ross
(1915–83) Canadian-American
real name: Kenneth Millar

(thriller)
The Dark Tunnel (1944)
The Moving Target (1949)
The Drowning Pool (1950)
The Barbarous Coast (1956)
The Doomsters (1958)
The Galton Case (1959)
The Wycherly Woman (1961)
The Goodbye Look (1969)
The Underground Man (1971)
Sleeping Beauty (1973)
The Blue Hammer (1976)

MACINNES, Colin
(1914–76) English

City of Spades [1] (1957)
Absolute Beginners [1] (1959)
My Love and Justice [1] (1960)
All Day Saturday (1966)
Westward to Laughter (1970)

[1] Visions of London trilogy

MACKAY, Mary
see **CORELLI, Marie**

MACKENZIE, Sir (Edward Morgan) Compton
(1883–1972) English

The Passionate Elopement (1911)
Carnival (1912)
Sinister Street (1913–14) 2 vol
Guy and Pauline (1915)
Sylvia Scarlett (1918)
Coral (1925)
Vestal Fire (1927)
Extremes Meet (1928)
Extraordinary Women (1928)
Figure of Eight (1936)
The Four Winds of Love (1937–45) 4 vol
Whisky Galore (1947)
Echoes (1953)
Thin Ice (1956)
Rockets Galore (1957)
Catmint (1961)

MACKENZIE, Henry
(1745–1831) Scottish

The Man of Feeling (1771)
The Man of the World (1773)
Julia de Roubigné(1777)

MACKINTOSH, Elizabeth
see **TEY, Josephine**

MACLAVERTY, Bernard
(1942–) Irish

Lamb (1980)
Cal (1983)

MACLEAN, Alistair
(1922–87) Scottish

(adventure/thriller)
HMS Ulysses (1955)
The Guns of Navarone (1957)
South by Java Head (1958)
The Last Frontier (1959)
Night without End (1960)
Fear Is the Key (1961)
The Dark Crusader (1961)
The Satan Bug (1962)
as Ian Stuart
Ice Station Zebra (1963)
When Eight Bells Toll (1966)
Where Eagles Dare (1967)
Force 10 from Navarone (1968)
Puppet on a Chain (1969)
Caravan to Vaccares (1970)
Bear Island (1971)
The Way to Dusty Death (1973)
Breakheart Pass (1974)
Circus (1975)
The Golden Gate (1976)
Sea Witch (1977)
Goodbye California (1978)
Athabasca (1980)
River of Death (1981)
Partisans (1982)
Floodgate (1983)
San Andreas (1984)
Santorini (1986)

MACHEN, Arthur (Llewellyn)
(1863–1947) Welsh

(supernatural)
The Great God Pan (1894)
The Hill of Dreams (1907)
Tales of Horror and the Supernatural (1948) coll posth

MAILER, Norman (Kingsley)
(1923–) American

The Naked and the Dead (1948)
Barbary Shore (1951)
The Deer Park (1955)
An American Dream (1965)
Why Are We in Vietnam? (1967)
The Armies of the Night (1968)
Mimi and the Siege of Chicago (1969)
The Prisoner of Sex (1971)
Ancient Evenings (1983)
Tough Guys Don't Dance (1984)

MALAMUD, Bernard
(1914–86) American

The Natural (1952)
The Assistant (1957)
A New Life (1961)
The Fixer (1967)
The Tenants (1971)
Dubin's Lives (1979)
God's Grace (1982)

MALRAUX, André
(1901–76) French

Les Conquérants (1928)
La Voie royale (1930)
Le Condition humaine (1933)
L'Espoir (1937)
Altenburg (1947)

MANKOWITZ, (Cyril) Wolf
(1924–) English

Make Me an Offer (1952)
A Kid for Two Farthings (1953)
My Old Man's a Dustman (1956)
Cockatrice (1963)
The Biggest Pig in Barbados (1965)
Raspberry Reich (1979)

MANN, Heinrich
(1871–1950) German
Brother of Thomas Mann

In einer Familie (1894)
Im Schlaraffenland (1900)

Professor Unrat (1905)
Die kleine Stadt (1909)
Die Armen [1] (1917)
Der Untertan [1] (1918)
Der Kopf [1] (1925)
Ein ernstes Leben (1930)

[1] Kaiserreich trilogy

MANN, Jessica
(1937–) English

(crime)
Mrs Knox's Profession (1972)
The Eighth Deadly Sin (1976)
The Sting of Death (1978)
Deadlier Than the Male (1981)
No Man's Island (1983)
Grave Goods (1984)
A Kind of Healthy Game (1986)

MANN, Thomas
(1875–1955) German
Brother of Heinrich Mann

Der kleine Herr Friedemann (1898) coll
Buddenbrooks (1901)
Tonio Kröger (1903)
Tristan (1903)
Königliche Hoheit (1909)
Der Tod in Venedig (1912)
Das Wunderkind (1914)
Der Zauberberg (1924)
Mario und der Zauberer (1930)
Die Geschichten Jaakobs [1] (1933)
Der junge Joseph [1] (1934)
Joseph in Ägypten [1] (1936)
Lotte in Weimar (1939)
Joseph der Ernährer [1] (1942)
Doktor Faustus (1947)
Der Erwählte (1951)
Felix Krull (1954)

[1] Joseph und seine Brüder trilogy

MANNING, Olivia
(1908–80) English

The Wind Changes (1937)
Artist Among the Missing (1949)
School for Love (1951)
A Different Face (1953)
The Doves of Venus (1955)
The Great Fortune [1] (1960)
The Spoilt City [1] (1962)
Friends and Heroes [1] (1965)
The Play Room (1969)
The Rain Forest (1974)
The Danger Tree [2] (1977)
The Battle Lost and Won [2] (1978)
The Sum of Things [2] (1980)

[1] Balkan trilogy [2] Levant trilogy

MANSFIELD, Katherine
(1888–1923) New Zealand
real name: Kathleen Mansfield Beauchamp

In a German Pension (1911) coll
Prelude (1918)
Bliss (1920)
The Garden Party (1922)
The Dove's Nest (1923) coll posth
Something Childish (1924) coll posth

MANZONI, Alessandro
(1785–1873) Italian

I promessi sposi (1825–7) 2 vol

MARKANDAYA, Kamala
(1923–) Anglo-Indian

Nectar in a Sieve (1954)
A Silence of Desire (1960)
Possession (1963)
A Handful of Rice (1966)
The Coffer Dams (1969)
The Nowhere Man (1972)
Two Virgins (1973)
The Golden Honeycomb (1979)
Pleasure City (1982)

MARKHAM, Robert
see **AMIS, Kingsley**

MARQUAND, John (Phillips)
(1893–1960) American

The Late George Apley (1937)

MARQUAND, George (cont.)
Wickford Point (1939)
HM Pulham, Esq (1941)
Point of No Return (1949)
Sincerely Willis Wayde (1955)

MARQUEZ, Gabriel García
see **GARCIA MARQUEZ, Gabriel**

MARRYAT, Captain Frederick
(1792–1848) English
(nautical)
Frank Mildmay (1829)
Peter Simple (1834)
Jacob Faithful (1834)
Mr Midshipman Easy (1836)
Japhet in Search of a Father (1836)
Snarleyyow (1837)
The Phantom Ship (1839)
Poor Jack (1840)
Masterman Ready [1] (1841)
The Settlers in Canada [1] (1844)
Children of the New Forest [1] (1847)

[1] children's

MARSH, Dame (Edith) Ngaio
(1899–1982) New Zealand
(crime)
A Man Lay Dead (1934)
Enter a Murderer (1935)
Vintage Murder (1937)
Overture to Death (1939)
Surfeit of Lampreys (1941)
Died in the Wool (1945)
Final Curtain (1947)
Swing, Brother, Swing (1949)
Opening Night (1951)
Scales of Justice (1954)
Off with His Head (1957)
False Scent (1960)
Dead Water (1964)
Clutch of Constables (1968)
When in Rome (1970)
Black As He's Painted (1974)
Last Ditch (1977)
Grave Mistake (1978)
Photo-Finish (1980)
Light Thickens (1982)

MARTIN DU GARD, Roger
(1881–1958) French
Devenir (1909)
Jean Barois (1913)
Les Thibault (1922–40) 8 vol

MARTINEAU, Harriet
(1802–76) English
Deerbrook (1839)
The Playfellow [1] (1841) coll

[1] children's

MARTINSON, Harry Edmund
(1904–78) Swedish
Vägen ut (1936)
Vägen till Klockrike (1948)

MASEFIELD, John (Edward)
(1878–1967) English
Captain Margaret (1908)
Multitude and Solitude (1909)
Lost Endeavour (1910)
Jim Davies (1911)
The Street of Today (1911)
The Taking of Helen (1923)
Sard Harker (1924)
Odtaa (1926)
The Midnight Folk [1] (1927)
The Bird of Dawning (1933)
The Box of Delights [1] (1935)
Dead Ned [1] (1938)
Live and Kicking Ned [1] (1939)

[1] children's

MASON, A(lfred) E(dward) W(oodley)
(1865–1948) English
A Romance of Westdale (1895)
Clementina (1901)
The Four Feathers (1902)
At the Villa Rose (1910)
(plus many Inspector Hanaud novels)
Fires over England (1936)

MASSIE, Allan
(1938–) British

Change and Decay in All Around I See (1978)
The Last Peacock (1980)
The Death of Men (1981)
One Night in Winter (1984)
Augustus: The Memoirs of the Emperor (1986)
A Question of Loyalties (1989)
Tiberius (1990)

MASTERS, Edgar Lee
(1868–1950) American

Mitch Miller (1920)
Skeeters Kirby (1923)
Mirage (1924)

MASTERS, John
(1914–83) English

(adventure)
Nightrunners of Bengal (1951)
Bhowani Junction (1954)
To the Coral Strand (1962)
Trial at Monomoy (1964)
The Breaking Strain (1967)
The Rock (1970)
Thunder at Sunset (1975)
Casanova (1976)
Now, God Be Thanked (1979)
Heart of War (1980)
By the Green of the Spring (1981)
The Ravi Lancers (1985) posth

MATTHIESSEN, Peter
(1927–) American

Race Rock (1954)
Partisans (1955)
Raditzer (1961)
A Play in the Fields of the Lord (1965)
Far Tortuga (1975)
Killing Master Watson

MATURIN, Charles (Robert)
(1782–1824) Irish

The Fatal Revenge (1807)
The Wild Irish Boy (1808)
The Milesian Chief (1811)
Women, or pour et contre (1818)
Melmoth the Wanderer (1820)
The Albigenses (1824)

MAUGHAM, Robin
(1916–) English
Nephew of W Somerset Maugham

The Servant (1948)
Behind the Mirror (1955)
The Man with Two Shadows (1958)
The Slaves of Timbuktu (1961)
November Reef (1962)
The Green Shade (1968)
The Barrier (1973)
The Dividing Line (1979)

MAUGHAM, W(illiam) Somerset
(1874–1965) English
Uncle of Robin Maugham

Liza of Lambeth (1897)
Mrs Craddock (1902)
Of Human Bondage (1915)
The Moon and Sixpence (1919)
The Painted Veil (1925)
Cakes and Ale (1930)
Rain (1932)
Theatre (1937)
The Razor's Edge (1944)

MAUPASSANT, Guy de
(1850–93) French

Boule-de-Suif (1880)
Mademoiselle Fifi (1882) coll
Une Vie (1883)
Yvette (1885)
Bel-Ami (1885)
Monsieur Parent (1886) coll
Mont-Oriol (1887)
Pierre et Jean (1888)
Fort comme la mort (1889)
Notre coeur (1890)

MAURIAC, François
(1885–1970) French

L'Enfant chargéde chaînes (1913)
Le baiser au lépreux (1922)
Thérèse Desqueyroux (1927)
La Fin de la nuit (1935)
Les Anges noirs (1936)
Le Sagouin (1950)

MAUROIS, André
(1885–1967) French
real name: Émile Herzog

Bernard Quesnay (1926)
Climats (1928)
Le Cercle de Famille (1932)

McBAIN, Ed
(1926–) American
real name: Evan Hunter

(crime)
The Blackboard Jungle [1] (1954)
as Evan Hunter
Cop Hater (1956)
(plus many 87th Precinct novels)

[1] not crime

McCARTHY, Mary (Therese)
(1912–89) American

The Company She Keeps (1942)
The Oasis (1949)
The Groves of Academe (1952)
A Charmed Life (1955)
The Group (1963)
Birds of America (1971)
Cannibals and Missionaries (1980)

McCULLERS, Carson (Smith)
(1917–67) American

The Heart Is a Lonely Hunter (1940)
Refections in a Golden Eye (1941)
The Member of the Wedding (1946)
The Ballad of the Sad Café(1951) coll
Clock without Hands (1961)

McMURTY, Larry (Jeff)
(1936–) American

Horseman, Pass By (1961)
Leaving Cheyenne (1963)
The Last Picture Show (1966)
Moving On (1970)
All My Friends Are Going to be Strangers (1972)
Terms of Endearment (1975)
Somebody's Darling (1978)
Cadillac Jack (1982)
The Desert Rose (1983)
Lonesome Dove (1985)
Texasville (1987)
Anything for Billy (1988)
Some Can Whistle (1989)
Buffalo Girls (1990)

McEWAN, Ian (Russell)
(1948–) English

First Love, Last Rites (1975) coll
The Cement Garden (1978)
Calabrian Summer (1980)
Sleeping Tiger (1982)
Star of Randevi (1984)
Temple Bells (1985)
The Black Pearl (1988)

McFALL, Frances Elizabeth Bellenden
see **GRAND, Sarah**

McKAY, Claude
(1890–1948) Jamaican

Home to Harlem (1928)
Banjo (1929)
Banana Bottom (1933)

McNEILE, Herman Cyril
see **SAPPER**

MELVILLE, Herman
(1819–91) American

Typee (1846)
Omoo (1847)

Mardi (1849)
Redburn (1849)
White-Jacket (1850)
Moby-Dick (1851)
Pierre (1852)
Israel Potter (1855)
The Piazza Tales (1856) coll
*The Confidence Man*1*: His Masquerade* (1857) unf
Billy Budd, Foretopman (1924) posth

MERCER, Cecil William
see **YATES, Dornford**

MEREDITH, George
(1828–1909) English

The Shaving of Shagpat (1856) coll
The Ordeal of Richard Feverel (1859)
Evan Harrington (1861)
Sandra Belloni (1864)
Rhoda Fleming (1865)
Vittoria (1867)
The Adventures of Harry Redmond (1871)
Beauchamp's Career (1876)
The Egoist (1879)
The Tragic Comedians (1880)
Diana of the Crossways (1885)
One of Our Conquerors (1891)
Lord Ormont and His Aminta (1894)
The Amazing Marriage (1895)

MEREDITH, Hal
(1852–98) American
real name: Harry Blyth

The Missing Millionaire (1893)
(plus many Sexton Blake books)

MÉRIMÉE, Prosper
(1803–70) French

Chronique du règne de Charles IX (1829)
Mosaïque (1833) coll
Colomba (1841) coll
Nouvelles (1852) coll
Dernières Nouvelles [1] (1873) coll

[1] horror

METALIOUS, Grace
(1924–64) American

Peyton Place (1956)
Tight White Collar (1960)
No Adam in Eden (1963)

MEYER, Conrad Ferdinand
(1825–98) Swiss

(historical)
Jürg Jenatsch (1876)
Der Heilige (1880)
Die Richterin (1885)
Angela Borgia (1891)

MICHENER, James A(lbert)
(1907–) American

Tales of the South Pacific (1947)
The Bridges at Toko-Ri (1953)
Sayonara (1954)
Hawaii (1959)
Caravans (1963)
The Source (1965)
Iberia (1968)
The Drifters (1971)
The Fires of Spring (1972)
Centennial (1974)
The Covenant (1980)
Space (1982)
Poland (1983)
Texas (1985)
Journey (1988)
Caribbean (1989)

MILLAR, Kenneth
see **MACDONALD, Ross**

MILLER, Arthur
(1915–) American

Focus (1945)

MILLER, Henry (Valentine)
(1891–1980) American

Tropic of Cancer (1934)
Black Spring (1936)

MILLER, Henry (cont.)
Tropic of Capricorn (1939)
The Colossus of Maroussi (1941)
The Air-Conditioned Nightmare (1945)
Remember to Remember (1947)
Sexus [1] (1949)
Plexus [1] (1953)
Nexus [1] (1960)

[1] Rosy Crucifixion trilogy

MILLER, Walter
(1922–) American

(science fiction)
The Darfsteller (1955)
A Canticle for Leibowitz (1960)

MILLIGAN, Spike (Terence Alan)
(1918–) English

Puckoon (1963)
The Looney (1987)

MILLIN, Sarah Gertrude
(1889–1968) South African

The Dark River (1919)
Adam's Rest (1922)
God's Stepchildren (1924)
Mary Glenn (1925)
The Sons of Mrs Aab (1931)

MILNE, A(lan) A(lexander)
(1882–1956) English

(children's)
Winnie-the-Pooh (1926) coll
The House at Pooh Corner (1928) coll

MILOSZ, Czeslaw
(1911–) Polish

Trzy Zimy (1936)
Ocalenie (1945)
Zniewolony umysl (1953)
Dolina Issy (1955)
Ziemia ulro (1977)
Kroniki (1987)

MIRABEAU, Comtesse de
see **GYP**

MISHIMA, Yukio
(1925–70) Japanese

real name: Hiraoka Kimitake
Confessions of a Mask (1949)
Thirst for Love (1950)
The Sound of Waves (1954)
The Temple of the Golden Pavilion (1956)
After the Banquet (1960)
The Sailor Who Fell from Grace with the Sea (1963)
Sea of Fertility (1965–70) 4 vol

MITCHELL, James Leslie
see **GIBBON, Lewis Grassic**

MITCHELL, Julian
(1935–) English

Imaginary Toys (1961)
As Far As You Can Go (1963)
The White Father (1964)
The Undiscovered Country (1966)

MITCHELL, Margaret
(1900–49) American

Gone with the Wind (1939)

MITCHISON, Naomi (Margaret)
(1897–) Scottish
née Haldane

The Conquered (1923)
When the Bough Breaks (1924) coll
Cloud Cuckoo Land (1925)
Black Sparta (1928) coll
Corn King and Spring Queen (1931)
The Delicate Fire (1933) coll
The Blood of the Martyrs (1939)
The Big House (1950)
Swan's Road (1954)
Memoirs of a Spacewoman (1962)

MITFORD, Mary Russell
(1787–1855) English
Atherton (1854)

MITFORD, Nancy (Freeman)
(1904–73) English
Highland Fling (1931)
Christmas Pudding (1932)
Wigs on the Green (1935)
Pigeon Pie (1940)
The Pursuit of Love (1945)
Love in a Cold Climate (1949)
The Blessing (1951)
Don't Tell Alfred (1960)

MITTELHOLZER, Edgar (Austin)
(1909–65) Guyanan
Corentyne Thunder (1941)
A Morning at the Office (1950)
Shadows Move Among Them (1951)
Children of Kaywana [1] (1952)
The Life and Death of Sylvia (1951)
The Harrowing of Hubertus (1954)
My Bones and My Flute [1] (1955)
Of Trees and the Sea (1956)
A Tale of Three Places (1957)
Kaywana Blood [1] (1958)
A Tinkling in the Twilight (1959)
Latticed Echoes (1960)
Thunder Returning (1961)

[1] Kaywana trilogy

MO, Timothy
(1953–) Anglo-Chinese
The Monkey King (1978)
Sour Sweet (1982)
An Insular Possession (1986)

MOIR, David Macbeth
(1798–1851) Scottish
Mansie Wauch, Tailor in Dalkeith (1828)

MOLESWORTH, Mary Louisa
(1839–1921) English
née Stewart
(children's)
The Cuckoo Clock (1877)
The Tapestry Room (1879)
The Adventures of Herr Baby (1881)
The Children of the Castle (1890)
The Carved Lions (1895)
Peterkin (1902)
The Little Guest (1907)
The Story of a Year (1910)

MONSARRAT, Nicholas (John Turney)
(1910–79) English
(nautical)
Three Corvettes (1945)
The Cruel Sea (1951)
The Story of Esther Costello [1] (1953)
The Tribe That Lost Its Head [1] (1956)
The Ship That Died of Shame (1959)
The Nylon Pirates (1960)
The Kapillan of Malta (1973)
The Master Mariner (1979–80) 2 vol; 1 vol posth

[1] not nautical

MONTAGUE, C(harles) E(dward)
(1867–1928) English
A Hind Let Loose (1910) coll
Rough Justice (1926)

MONTGOMERY, L(ucy) M(aud)
(1874–1942) Canadian
(children's)
Anne of Green Gables (1908)
Anne of Avonlea (1909)
Anne's House of Dreams (1917)
Anne of the Island (1919)
Rilla of Ingleside (1921)
Emily of New Moon (1923)
Anne of Windy Poplars (1936)
Anne of Ingleside (1939)

MONTHERLANT, Henry de
(1896–1972) French

Le Songe (1922)
Les Bestiaires (1926)
Les Célibataires (1934)
Les Chaos et la nuit (1965)
Les Garçons (1969)

MOORCOCK, Michael
(1939–) English

(science fiction)
The Final Programme (1968)
A Cure for Cancer (1971)
The English Assassin (1972)
The Land Leviathan (1974)
The Condition of Muzak (1977)
Gloriana (1978)
The Entropy Tango (1981)
The Steel Tsar (1982)
The Laughter of Carthage (1984)

MOORE, Brian
(1921–) Irish

Judith Hearne (1955)
The Feast of Lupercal (1957)
The Luck of Ginger Coffey (1960)
The Emperor of Ice Cream (1965)
I Am Mary Dunne (1968)
Catholics (1972)
The Doctor's Wife (1976)
The Mangan Inheritance (1979)
The Temptation of Eileen Hughes (1981)
Cold Heaven (1983)
Black Robe (1985)
The Colour of Blood (1987)
Lies of Silence (1990)

MOORE, George (Augustus)
(1852–1933) Anglo-Irish

A Modern Lover (1883)
A Mummer's Wife (1885)
A Drama in Muslin (1886)
A Mere Accident (1887)
Spring Days (1888)
Mike Fletcher (1889)
Esther Waters (1894)
Evelyn Innes (1898)
Sister Theresa (1901)
The Brook Kerith (1916)
Héloise and Abelard (1921)
Aphrodite in Aulis (1930)

MOORE, Doctor John
(1729–1802) Scottish

Zeluco (1786)
Edward (1796)
Mordaunt (1800)

MORAVIA, Alberto
(1907–) Italian
real name: Alberto Pincherle

Gli indifferenti (1929)
Agostino (1944)
La Romana (1947)
L'amore conjugal (1949)
Il conformista (1951)
La noia (1952)
Raconti Romani (1954)
La ciociara (1957)
L'attenzione (1965)
La vita interiore (1978)

MORE, Sir Thomas
(1478–1535) English

Utopia (1516)

MORGAN, Charles (Langbridge)
(1894–1958) English

Portrait in a Mirror (1929)
The Fountain (1932)
Sparkenbroke (1936)
The Voyage (1940)
The Judge's Story (1947)
The River Line (1949)

MORIER, James Justinian
(1780–1849) English

The Adventures of Hajji Baba of Ispahan (1824)
The Adventures of Hajji Baba in England (1828)
Ayesha (1834)

MORITZ, Karl Philipp
(1756–93) German
Anton Reiser (1785–90) 5 vol

MORLEY, Christopher (Darlington)
(1890–1957) American
Parnassus on Wheels (1917)
Shandygaff (1918)
Kathleen (1920)
Where the Blue Begins (1922)
Thunder on the Left (1925)
Off the Deep End (1928)
Swiss Family Manhattan (1932)
Streamlines (1937)
Kitty Foyle (1939)
Thorofare (1942)
The Ironing Board (1949)

MORRIS, William
(1834–96) English
The Dream of John Ball (1888)
News from Nowhere (1891)
The Well at the World's End (1896)

MORRISON, Arthur
(1863–1945) English
Tales of Mean Streets (1894) coll
A Child of the Jago (1896)
Cunning Murrell (1900)
The Hole in the Wall (1902)

MORRISON, Toni (Chloe Anthony)
(1931–) American
née Wofford
The Bluest Eye (1970)
Sula (1974)
Song of Solomon (1977)
Tar Baby (1981)
Beloved (1987)

MORTIMER, John (Clifford)
(1923–) English
Ex-husband of Penelope Mortimer
Charade (1947)
Rumming Park (1948)
Answer Yes or No (1950)
The Narrowing Stream (1952)
Like Men Betrayed (1954)
Rumpole of the Bailey (1978) coll
(plus many Rumpole books)
Paradise Postponed (1985)
Summer's Lease (1988)
Titmuss Regained (1989)

MORTIMER, Penelope (Ruth)
(1918–) English
Ex-wife of John Mortimer;
née Fletcher
Johanna (1947)
A Villa in Summer (1954)
Daddy's Gone A-Hunting (1958)
The Pumpkin Eater (1962)
The House (1971)
Long Distance (1974)
The Handyman (1983)

MOSLEY, Nicholas
(1923–) English
Baron Ravensdale
Accident (1964)
Impossible Object (1968)
Natalie Natalia (1971)

MOTTRAM, R(alph) H(ale)
(1883–1971) English
The Spanish Farm [1] (1924)
Sixty-Four, Ninety-Four [1] (1925)
The Crime of Vanderlynden's
The Banquet (1934) coll

[1] Spanish Farm trilogy

MOWAT, Farley (McGill)
(1921–) Canadian
(children's)
The Dog Who Wouldn't Be (1957)

MOWAT, Farley **(cont.)**
Owls in the Family (1961)
Lost in the Barrens (1965)
Curse of the Viking Grave (1974)

MUIR, Edwin
(1887–1957) Scottish
The Marionette (1927)
The Three Brothers (1931)
Poor Tom (1932)

MULOCK, Dinah Maria
see **CRAIK, Dinah Maria**

MUNRO, Alice (Anne)
(1931–) Canadian
née Laidlaw
Lives of Girls and Women (1971)

MUNRO, H(ector) H(ugo)
see **SAKI**

MUNRO, Neil
(1864–1930) Scottish
John Splendid (1898)
Doom Castle (1901)
The Vital Spark (1906)
The New Road (1914)
Jaunty Jock (1918)
Para Handy (1931) coll posth

MUNTHE, Axel (Martin Fredrik)
(1857–1949) Swedish
The Story of San Michele (1929)

MURDOCH, Dame Iris (Jean)
(1919–) Anglo-Irish
Under the Net (1954)
The Flight from the Enchanter (1956)
The Sandcastle (1957)
The Bell (1958)
A Severed Head (1961)
An Unofficial Rose (1962)
The Unicorn (1963)
The Italian Girl (1964)
The Red and the Green (1965)
The Time of the Angels (1966)
The Nice and the Good (1968)
Bruno's Dream (1969)
A Fairly Honourable Defeat (1970)
An Accidental Man (1971)
The Black Prince (1972)
The Sacred and Profane Love Machine (1974)
A Word Child (1975)
Henry and Cato (1977)
The Sea, The Sea (1978)
Nuns and Soldiers (1980)
The Philosopher's Pupil (1983)
The Good Apprentice (1985)
The Book and the Brotherhood (1987)
The Message to the Planet (1989)

MUSIL, Robert (Elder von)
(1880–1942) Austrian
Der Mann ohne Eigenschaften (1930–43) 3 vol; 1 vol posth unf

MYERS, L(eopold) H(amilton)
(1881–1944) English
The Orissers (1922)
The 'Clio' (1925)
The Near and the Far [1] (1929)
Prince Jali [1] (1931)
The Root and the Flower [1] (1935)
Strange Glory (1936)
The Pool of Vishnu [1] (1940)

[1] The Near and the Far tetralogy

N

NABOKOV, Vladimir (Vladimirovich)
(1899–1977) Russian
Mary (1926)
King, Queen, Knave (1928)
The Eye (1930)

The Defence (1930)
Glory (1932)
Laughter in the Dark (1932)
Despair (1936)
Invitation to a Beheading (1938)
The Gift (1938)
The Real Life of Sebastian Knight (1941)
Bend Sinister (1947)
Lolita (1955)
Pnin (1957)
Pale Fire (1962)
Ada (1969)
Transparent Things (1972)
Look at the Harlequins! (1974)
The Enchanter (1976) posth

NAIPAUL, Sir V(idiadhar) S(urajprassad)
(1932–) Trinidadian
The Mystic Masseur (1957)
The Suffrage of Elvira (1958)
Miguel Street (1959) coll
A House for Mr Biswas (1961)
Mr Stone and the Knights Companion (1963)
The Mimic Men (1967)
In a Free State (1971)
Guerrillas (1975)
A Bend in the River (1979)
Among the Believers (1981)
The Enigma of Arrival (1987)
A Turn in the South (1989)

NARAYAN, R(asipuram) K(rishnaswami)
(1906–) Indian
Swami and Friends (1935)
The Bachelor of Arts (1937)
The Dark Room (1938)
The English Teacher (1945)
Mr Sampath (1949)
The Financial Expert (1952)
The Guide (1958)
The Man-Eater of Malgudi (1961)
The Vendor of Sweets (1967)
The Painter of Signs (1977)
The Tiger for Malgudi (1983)

NEAL, John
(1793–1876) American
Randolph (1823)
Rachel Dyer (1828)
The Down-Easters (1833)

NEMEROV, Howard
(1920–) American
The Melodramatists (1949)
Federigo (1954)
Journal of the Fictive Life (1965)

NESBIT, E(dith)
(1858–1924) English
(children's)
The Prophet's Mantle [1] (1885)
The Story of the Treasure-Seekers [2] (1899)
The Wouldbegoods [2] (1901)
Five Children and It (1902)
The New Treasure-Seekers [2] (1903) coll
The Phoenix and the Carpet (1904)
The Railway Children (1906)
The Enchanted Castle (1907)
The House of Arden (1908)
Harding's Luck (1909)
Salome and the Head [1] (1909)
The Magic City (1910)
The Wonderful Garden (1911)
Wet Magic (1913)
Five of Us and Madeline (1925) coll posth

[1] not children's [2] Bastable Family books

NEWBOLT, Sir Henry (John)
(1862–1938) English
Taken from the Enemy (1892)
The Old Country (1906)
The New June (1909)

NEWBY, P(ercy) H(oward)
(1918–) English
Journey to the Interior (1946)
Agents and Witnesses (1947)
Mariner Dances (1948)

NEWBY, PH (cont.)
The Picnic at Sakhara (1955)
Something to Answer for (1968)
A Lot to Ask (1975)
Feelings Have Changed (1981)
Leaning in the Wind (1986)

NEWMAN, Andrea
(1938–) English
A Share of the World (1964)
A Bouquet of Barbed Wire (1969)
An Evil Streak (1977)
Mackenzie (1980)
A Sense of Guilt (1988)
Triangles (1990)

NEXØ, Martin (Andersen)
(1869–1954) Danish
Pelle (1906–10) 4 vol
Ditte (1917–21) 4 vol

NGUGI, James T
see **THIONG'O, Ngugi Wa**

NICOLSON, Sir Harold (George)
(1886–1968) English
Sweet Waters (1921)
Public Faces (1932)

NIN, Anaîs
(1903–77) American
Winter of Artifice (1939)
Ladders to Fire (1946)
The Four-Chambered Heart (1950)
A Spy in the House of Love (1954)
Cities of the Interior (1959)
Collages (1964)
Little Birds (1979) posth

NIVEN, Larry (Van Cott)
(1938–) American
(science fiction)
Ringworld (1970)
Protector (1973)
The Long Arm of Gil Hamilton (1976)
The Magic Goes Away (1978)
The Patchwork Girl (1980)
The Integral Trees (1983)
Limits (1985) coll
The Smoke Ring (1987)

NOBBS, David
(1935–) English
A Piece of the Sky Is Missing (1965)
The Death of Reginald Perrin (1975)
The Return of Reginald Perrin (1977)
The Better World of Reginald Perrin (1978)
Second from Last in the Sack Race (1983)
A Bit of a Do (1986)
Pratt of the Argus (1988)
Fair Do's (1990)

NOONAN, Robert
see **TRESSELL, Robert**

NORDEN, Charles
see **DURRELL, Lawrence**

NORDHOFF, Charles (Bernard)
(1887–1947) American
The Fledgling (1919)
The Pearl Lagoon (1924)
The Derelict (1928)
Mutiny on the Bounty (1932)
with James Hall
Men Against the Sea (1934)
with James Hall

NORRIS, (Benjamin) Frank(lin)
(1870–1902) American
Moran of the Lady Letty (1898)
McTeague (1899)
The Octopus [1] (1901)
The Pit [1] (1903) posth
Vandover and the Brute (1914) posth

[1] Epic of the Wheat trilogy unf

NORTON, Mary
(1903–) English
(children's)
The Borrowers (1952)
The Borrowers Afield (1955)
The Borrowers Afloat (1959)
The Borrowers Aloft (1961)
The Borrowers Avenged (1982)

NORWAY, Nevil Shute
see **SHUTE, Nevil**

NYE, Robert
(1939–) English
March Has Horse's Ears [1] (1966)
Doubtfire (1967)
Wishing Gold [1] (1970)
Poor Pumpkin [1] (1971)
Falstaff (1976)
Merlin (1978)
Faust (1980)
The Voyage of the Destiny (1982)
The Memoirs of Lord Bron (1989)
[1] children's

O

OATES, Joyce Carol
(1938–) American
Shuddering Fall (1964)
A Garden of Earthly Delights (1967)
Them (1969)
Wonderland (1971)
Do With Me What You Will (1973)
The Poisoned Kiss (1975)
Son of the Morning (1979)
A Bloodsmoor Romance (1982)
Solstice (1985)

O'BRIEN, Edna
(1932–) Irish
The Country Girls (1960)
The Lonely Girl (1962)
Girls in Their Married Bliss (1964)
August Is a Wicked Month (1965)
Casualties of Peace (1966)
A Pagan Place (1970)
Night (1972)
Johnny I Hardly Knew You (1977)

O'BRIEN, Flann
(1911–66) Irish
real name: Brian O'Nolan (O'Nuallain)
At Swim-Two-Birds (1939)
An Béal Bocht (1941)
The Dalkey Archives (1965)
The Third Policeman (1967) posth

O'CONNOR, Edwin
(1918–68) American
The Oracle (1951)
The Last Hurrah (1956)
The Edge of Sadness (1961)
I Was Dancing (1964)
All in the Family (1966)

O'CONNOR, Frank
(1903–66) Irish
real name: Michael Francis O'Donovan
Bones of Contention (1936) coll
Dutch Interior (1940)
Crab Apple Jelly (1944) coll
Traveller's Samples (1950) coll
Domestic Relations (1957) coll

O'CONNOR, (Mary) Flannery
(1925–64) American
Wise Blood (1952)
A Good Man Is Hard to Find (1955) coll
The Violent Bear It Away (1960)

O'DONOVAN, Michael Francis
see **O'CONNOR, Frank**

O'FAOLAIN, Sean
(1900–) Irish
A Nest of Simple Folk (1933)
Bird Alone (1936)
Come Back to Erin (1940)

O'FLAHERTY, Liam
(1897–1984) Irish
The Neighbour's Wife (1923)
Spring Sowing (1924) coll
The Informer (1925)
The Tent (1926) coll
Famine (1937)
Two Lovely Beasts (1948) coll
Insurrection (1950)

O'HARA, John (Henry)
(1905–70) American
Appointment in Samarra (1934)
Butterfield 8 (1935)
Pal Joey (1940)
A Rage to Live (1949)
Ten North Frederick (1955)
Ourselves to Know (1960)

O'HARA, Mary
(1885–1980) American
real name: Mary O'Hara Alsop
(children's)
My Friend Flicka (1941)
Thunderhead (1943)
Green Grass of Wyoming (1946)

OKRI, Ben
(1959–) Nigerian
Flowers and Shadows (1980)
The Landscapes Within (1981)
The Famished Road (1991)

OLIPHANT, Laurence
(1829–88) English
Piccadilly (1870)
Altiora Peto (1883)

OLIPHANT, Margaret
(1828–97) Scottish
née Wilson
Caleb Field (1851)
The Athelings (1857)
Salem Chapel [1] (1863)
The Perpetual Curate [1] (1864)
Miss Marjoribanks [1] (1866)
Phoebe Junior [1] (1876)
A Beleaguered City (1880)
A Little Pilgrim (1882)
Hester (1883)
Effie Ogilvie (1886)
The Second Son (1888)
Kirsteen (1890)
Sir Robert's Fortune (1895)

[1] Chronicles of Carlingford novels

ONIONS, (George) Oliver
(1873–1961) English
Widdershins (1911) coll
Whom God Hath Sundered (1912–1913) 2 vol

O'NOLAN, Brian
see **O'BRIEN, Flann**

ONSTOTT, Kyle
(1897–1978) American
Mandingo (1957)
Drum (1962)
Master of Falconhurst (1964)

O'NUALLAIN, Brian
see **O'BRIEN, Flann**

ORCZY, Baroness (Emmuska Magdalena)
(1865–1947) Anglo-Hungarian
(historical)
The Emperor's Candlesticks (1899)
The Scarlet Pimpernel (1905)
(plus many Pimpernel novels)

ORWELL, George
(1903–50) English
real name: Eric (Arthur) Blair
Burmese Days (1934)
A Clergyman's Daughter (1935)

Keep the Aspidistra Flying (1936)
Coming Up for Air (1939)
Animal Farm (1945)
Nineteen Eighty-Four (1949)

OSBOURNE, Lloyd
see **STEVENSON, Robert Louis**

OUIDA
(1839–1908) English
real name: Maria Louise de la Ramée

Held in Bondage (1863)
Strathmore (1865)
Under Two Flags (1867)
Folle-Farine (1871)
A Dog of Flanders [1] (1872)
Two Little Wooden Shoes (1874)
Moths (1880)
A Village Commune (1881)
Bimbi [1] (1882) coll
In Maremma (1882)

[1] children's

OZICK, Cynthia
(1928–) American

Trust (1966)
The Pagan Rabbit (1971)
Bloodshed (1976)
Levitation (1982)
The Cannibal Galaxy (1983)
The Messiah of Stockholm (1987)

P

PAGE, Thomas Nelson
(1853–1922) American

In Ole Virginia (1887) coll
On Newfound River (1891)
Red Rock (1898)

PALTOCK, Robert
(1697–1767) English

The Adventures of Peter Wilkins (1751)

PARGETER, Edith
see **PETERS, Ellis**

PARKIN, Molly
(1932–) English

Love All (1974)
Uptight (1975)
Switchback (1978)
Up and Coming (1980)
Love Bites (1982)
Breast Stroke (1983)
Cock-a-Hoop (1985)

PASOLINI, Pier Paolo
(1922–75) Italian

Ragazzi di vita (1955)
Una vita violenta (1958)

PASTERNAK, Boris (Leonidovich)
(1890–1960) Russian

Doctor Zhivago (1957)

PATCHEN, Kenneth
(1911–71) American

Memoirs of a Shy Pornographer (1945)
Sleepers Awake (1946)
See You in the Morning (1948)

PATER, Walter (Horatio)
(1839–94) English

The Child in the House (1878)
Marius the Epicurean (1885)

PATON, Alan (Stewart)
(1903–88) South African

Cry, the Beloved Country (1948)
Too Late the Phalarope (1953)
Debbie Go Home (1961) coll
Ah, but Your Land Is Beautiful (1981)

PATTERSON, Harry
see **HIGGINS, Jack**

PAVESE, Cesare
(1908–50) Italian
Il compagno (1947)
La bella estate (1949)
La luna e i falò (1950)

PEACOCK, Thomas Love
(1785–1866) English
Headlong Hall (1816)
Melincourt (1817)
Nightmare Abbey (1818)
Maid Marian (1822)
The Misfortunes of Elphin (1829)
Crotchet Castle (1831)
Gryll Grange (1861)

PEAKE, Mervyn (Laurence)
(1911–68) English
Titus Groan [1] (1946)
Gormenghast [1] (1950)
Titus Alone [1] (1959)

[1] Gormenghast trilogy

PEDERSEN, Knut
see **HAMSUN, Knut**

PERCY, Walker
(1916–90) American
The Moviegoer (1961)
The Last Gentleman (1966)
Love in the Ruins (1971)
Lancelot (1977)
The Second Coming (1980)
The Thanatos Syndrome (1987)

PÉREZ GALDOS, Benito
(1843–1920) Spanish
Doña perfecta (1876)
Fortunata y Jacinta (1887)
Miau (1888)
Angel guerra (1891)

PESHKOV, Aleksei Maksimovich
see **GORKY, Maxim**

PETERS, Ellis
(1913–) English
real name: Edith Pargeter
(crime)
Iron-Bound (1936)
as Edith Pargeter
She Goes to War (1942)
as Edith Pargeter
Reluctant Odyssey (1946)
as Edith Pargeter
Fallen into the Pit (1951)
as Edith Pargeter
Death Mask (1959)
The Scarlet seed (1963)
as Edith Pargeter
The Grass Widow's Tale (1968)
Death to the Landlords! (1972)
The Horn of Roland (1974)
Afterglow and Nightfall (1977)
as Edith Pargeter
A Morbid Taste for Bones (1977)
(plus many Cadfael whodunnit novels)

PETERSEN, Nils
(1897–1943) Danish
Sandalmagernes gade (1931)

PEYREFITTE, Roger
(1907–) French
Les Amitiés particulières (1944)
Les Ambassades (1951)
Les Clés de Saint Pierre (1955)

PEYTON, KM
(1929–) English
real name: Kathleen Wendy Peyton
(children's)
Windfall (1962)
The Maplin Bird (1964)
Thunder in the Sky (1966)
Flambards [1] (1967)
The Edge of the Cloud [1] (1969)

Flambards in Summer [1] (1969)
Pennington's Seventeenth Summer [2] (1970)
The Beethoven Medal [2] (1971)
Pennington's Heir [2] (1973)
Prove Yourself a Hero (1977)
Dear Fred (1981)
Flambards Divided [1] (1982)

[1] Flambards books [2] Pennington trilogy

PEYTON, Kathleen Wendy
see **PEYTON KM**

PHILLIPS, David Graham
(1867–1911) American

The Plum Tree (1905)
Susan Lennox (1917)

PHILLPOTTS, Eden
(1862–1960) English

Lying Prophets (1896)
Children of the Mist (1898)
The Human Boy (1899)

PINCHERLE, Alberto
see **MORAVIA, Alberto**

PIRANDELLO, Luigi
(1867–1936) Italian

L'esclusa (1901)
Il fu Mattia Pascal (1904)
I vecchi e i giovani (1909)

PLAIDY, Jean
(1906–) English
real name: Eleanor Hibbert

(historical/romance)
Beyond the Blue Mountains (1948)
Madame Serpent [1] (1951)
Italian Woman [1] (1952)
Queen Jezebel [1] (1953)
Flaunting Extravagant Queen (1957)
Bride of Pendorric (1963)
as Victoria Holt
Menfreya (1966)
as Victoria Holt
The Shadow of the Lynx (1971)
as Victoria Holt
The Miracle of St Bruno's (1972)
as Philippa Carr
Lord of the Far Island (1975)
as Victoria Holt
The Devil on Horseback (1977)
as Victoria Holt
The Spring of the Tiger (1979)
Lady in the Tower (1986)

[1] Catherine de Medici novels

PLATH, Sylvia
(1932–63) American

The Bell Jar (1963)
as Victoria Lucas, until 1966

PLOMER, William (Charles Franklin)
(1903–73) Anglo-South African

Turbott Wolfe (1926)
Sado (1931)
The Case Is Altered (1932)
The Invaders (1934)
Museum Pieces (1952)

POE, Edgar Allan
(1809–49) American

(crime/horror)
The Fall of the House of Usher (1840)
The Murders in the Rue Morgue (1841)
The Gold Bug (1843)
The Tell-Tale Heart (1843)
The Pit and the Pendulum (1845)
The Premature Burial (1845)
The Cask of Amontillado (1846)

PONTOPPIDAN, Henrik
(1857–1944) Danish

Det forjaettede land (1891–5) 2 vol
Lykke-Per (1898–1904) 3 vol

PORTER, Anne Maria
(1780–1832) English
Sister of Jane Porter

The Hungarian Brothers (1807)
Don Sebastian (1809)

PORTER, Jane
(1776–1850) English
Sister of Anne Maria Porter

(historical)
Thaddaeus of Warsaw (1803)
The Scottish Chiefs (1810)
The Pastor's Fireside (1815)

PORTER, Kathleen Anne
(1890–1980) American

Flowering Judas (1930) coll
Hacienda (1934)
Noon Wine (1937)
Ship of Fools (1962)

PORTER, William Sydney
see **HENRY, O**

POTTER, (Helen) Beatrix
(1866–1943) English

(children's)
The Tale of Peter Rabbit (1901)
(plus many animal books)

POWELL, Anthony (Dymoke)
(1905–) English

Afternoon Men (1931)
Venusberg (1932)
From a View to a Death (1933)
Agents and Patients (1936)
What's Become of Waring (1939)
A Dance to the Music of Time (1951–75) 12 vol
O, How the Wheel Becomes It! (1983)
The Fisher King (1986)

POWYS, John Cowper
(1872–1963) English
Brother of Theodore & Llewellyn Powys

Wood and Stone (1915)
Rodmoor (1916)
Ducdame (1925)
Wolf Solent (1929)
A Glastonbury Romance (1932)
Weymouth Sands (1934)
Maiden Castle (1936)
Morwyn (1937)
Owen Glendower (1940)
Mortal Strife (1941)
Porius (1951)
The Inmates (1952)
Atlantis (1954)
The Brazen Head (1956)
All or Nothing (1960)

POWYS, Llewellyn
(1884–1939) English
Brother of John Cowper & TF Powys

Apples Be Ripe (1930)
Love and Death (1939)

POWYS, T(heodore) F(rancis)
(1875–1953) English
Brother of John Cowper & Llewellyn Powys

Black Bryony (1923)
Innocent Birds (1926)
Mr Weston's Good Wine (1927)
Unclay (1931)

PRÉVOST, Abbé (Antoine-François)
(1697–1763) French

Manon Lescaut (1731)
Mémoires d'un honnête homme (1745)

PRICHARD, Katharine Susannah
(1884–1972) Australian

The Pioneers (1915)
Windlestraws, Working Bullocks (1926)
Coonardoo (1929)

Haxby's Circus (1930)
Intimate Strangers (1937)
The Roaring Nineties [1] (1946)
Golden Miles [1] (1948)
Winged Seeds [1] (1950)

[1] Goldfields trilogy

PRIESTLEY, J(ohn) B(oynton)
(1894–1984) English

Benighted (1927)
Farthing Hall (1929)
with Hugh Walpole
The Good Companions (1929)
Angel Pavement (1930)
Faraway (1932)
Let the People Sing (1939)
Black-Out in Gretley (1942)
Bright Day (1946)
Jenny Villiers (1947)
Festival at Farbridge (1951)
The Magicians (1954)
Lost Empires (1965)
The Image Men (1968)

PRITCHETT, Sir V(ictor) S(awdon)
(1900–) English

Claire Drummer (1929)
Nothing Like Leather (1935)
Dead Man Leading (1937)
Mr Beluncle (1951)
When My Girl Comes Home (1961) coll
The Camberwell Beauty (1974) coll

PROUST, Marcel
(1871–1922) French

À la recherche du temps perdu
(1913–27) 7 vol

PUSHKIN, Alexander (Sergeevich)
(1799–1837) Russian

The Prisoner of the Caucasus (1821)
The Fountain of Bakhchisarai (1826)
Eugene Onegin (1831)
The Queen of Spades (1834)

PUZO, Mario
(1920–) American

The Dark Arena (1955)
The Fortune Pilgrim (1965)
The Godfather (1969)
Fools Die (1978)
The Sicilian (1984)

PYM, Barbara (Mary Crampton)
(1913–80) English

Some Tame Gazelle (1950)
Excellent Women (1952)
Less Than Angels (1955)
A Glass of Blessings (1958)
No Fond Return of Love (1961)
Quartet in Autumn (1977)
The Sweet Dove Died (1979)
An Academic Question (1986) posth
Civil to Strangers (1987) posth

PYNCHON, Thomas
(1937–) American

V (1963)
The Crying of Lot 49 (1966)
Gravity's Rainbow (1973)
Slower Learner (1984) coll

Q

QUEEN, Ellery
Pseudonym of two Americans:
Frederick Dannay (1905–82)
& Manfred Lee (1905–71)

(crime)
The Roman Hat Mystery (1929)
(plus many Ellery Queen novels)

QUENEAU, Raymond
(1903–76) French

Le Chiendent (1933)
Les Enfants du limon (1938)
Saint Glinglin (1948)
Zazie dans le Métro (1959)

QUILLER-COUCH, Sir Arthur (Thomas)
(1863–1944) English
Dead Man's Rock (1887)
Troy Town (1888)
The Splendid Spur (1889)
Noughts and Crosses (1891)
I Saw Three Ships (1892)
The Delectable Duchy (1893)
The Ship of Stars (1899)
The Westcotes (1902)
Hetty Wesley (1903)
Fort Amity (1904)
Poison Island (1907)
Lady Good-for-Nothing (1910)
Foe-Farrell (1918)

QUOIREZ, Françoise
see **SAGAN, Françoise**

R

RAABE, Wilhelm
(1831–1910) German
Ein Frühling (1857)
Drei Federn (1865)
Horacker (1865)
Wunnigel (1879)
Alte Nester (1880)
Hastenbeck (1898)

RABELAIS, François
(1494–1553) French
Gargantua and Pantagruel (1532–52) 5 vol

RADCLIFFE, Ann
(1764–1823) English
née Ward
(Gothic)
The Castles of Athlin and Dunbayne (1789)
A Sicilian Romance (1790)
The Romance of the Forest (1791)
The Mysteries of Udolpho (1794)
The Italian (1797)

RAND, Ayn
(1905–) American
The Fountainhead (1943)
Atlas Shrugged (1957)
We the Living (1959)

RANSOME, Arthur (Mitchell)
(1884–1967) English
(children's)
Swallows and Amazons (1930)
Swallowdale (1931)
Peter Duck (1932)
Winter Holiday (1933)
Coot Club (1934)
Pigeon Post (1936)
We Didn't Mean to Go to Sea (1937)
Secret Water (1939)
The Big Six (1940)
Missee Lee (1941)
The Picts and the Martyrs (1943)
Great Northern? (1947)

RAO, Raja
(1909–) Indian
Kanthapura (1938)
The Serpent and the Rope (1960)
The Cat and Shakespeare (1965)

RAPHAEL, Frederic (Michael)
(1931–) American
The Limits of Love (1960)
The Trouble with England (1962)
Lindmann (1963)
Like Men Betrayed (1970)
April, June and November (1972)
The Glittering Prizes (1976)
Sleeps Six (1979)
Heaven and Earth (1985)

RASPE, R(udolph) E(rich)
(1737–94) German
The Adventures of Baron Münchausen (1785) coll

RAWLINGS, Marjorie Kinnan
(1896–1953) American

South Moon Under (1933)
Golden Apples (1935)
The Yearling (1938)
Cross Creek (1942)
The Sojourners (1953)

RAYMOND, René
see **CHASE, James Hadley**

READ, Miss
(1913–) English
real name: Dora Jessie Saint

Village School (1955)
Thrush Green (1959)
The Fairacre Festival (1969)
The Christmas Mouse (1973)
No Holly for Miss Quin (1976)

READ, Piers Paul
(1941–) English

The Junkers (1966)
Monk Dawson (1969)
The Upstart (1973)
The Professor's Daughter (1975)
A Married Man (1979)
The Free Frenchman (1986)

READE, Charles
(1814–84) English

Peg Woffington (1853)
Christie Johnstone (1853)
It Is Never Too Late to Mend (1856)
The Course of True Love (1857)
The Autobiography of a Thief (1858)
Love Me Little, Love Me Long (1859)
The Cloister and the Hearth (1861)
Hard Cash (1863)
Griffith Gaunt (1866)
Foul Play (1869)
Put Yourself in His Place (1870)
A Terrible Temptation (1871)
A Hero and a Martyr (1874)

REBECQUE, Henri-Benjamin Constant de
see **CONSTANT, Benjamin**

REDGROVE, Peter (William)
(1932–) English

In the Country of the Skin (1973)
The Beekeepers (1980)

REED, Talbot Baines
(1852–93) English

(children's)
The Fifth Form at St Dominic's (1887)
Cock House at Fellsgarth (1891)

REEMAN, Douglas
see **KENT, Alexander**

REEVE, Clara
(1729–1807) English

The Champion of Virtue (1777)
The Two Mentors (1783)
The Exiles (1788)
The School for Widows (1791)
Memoirs of Sir Roger de Clarendon (1793)
Destination (1799)

REID, Forrest
(1875–1947) Irish

The Kingdom of Twilight (1904)
The Garden God (1905)
Following Darkness (1912)
Uncle Stephen [1] (1931)
The Retreat [1] (1933)
Young Tom [1] (1934)

[1] Tom Barber trilogy

REID, (Thomas) Mayne
(1818–83) Irish

The Rifle Rangers (1850)
The Scalp Hunters (1851)
The Boy Hunters (1852)

REID, Mayne (cont.)
The Child Wife (1853)
The Quadroon (1856)
War Trail (1857)
Boy Tar (1859)
The Headless Horseman (1866)

REIZENSTEIN, Elmer
see **RICE, Elmer**

REMARK, Erich Paul
see **REMARQUE, Erich Maria**

REMARQUE, Erich Maria
(1898–1970) German
real name: Erich Paul Remark
Im Westen nichts Neues (1929)
Der Weg zurück (1931)
Drei Kameraden (1938)

REMIZOV, Alexei (Mikhailovich)
(1877–1957) Russian
The Pond (1906)
The Clock (1908)
The Fifth Pestilence (1911)
On a Field Azure (1927) coll

RENAULT, Mary
(1905–83) English
real name: Mary Challans
(historical)
The Charioteer (1953)
The Last of the Wine 1956)
The King Must Die (1958)
The Bull from the Sea (1962)
The Persian Boy (1972)

RENDELL, Ruth (Barbara)
(1930–) English
(crime)
From Doon with Death (1964)
To Fear a Painted Devil (1965)
Vanity Dies Hard (1965)
A New Lease of Death (1967)
Wolf to the Slaughter (1967)
The Secret House of Death (1968)
The Best Man to Die (1969)
A Guilty Thing Surprised (1970)
No More Dying Then (1971)
One Across, Two Down (1972)
Murder Being Done Once (1972)
Some Lie and Some Die (1973)
The Face of Trespass (1974)
Shake Hands For Ever (1975)
A Demon in My View (1976)
A Judgement in Stone (1977)
A Sleeping Life (1978)
Make Death Love Me (1979)
The Lake of Darkness (1980)
Put On By Cunning (1981)
Master of the Moor (1982)
The Speaker of Mandarin (1983)
The Killing Doll (1984)
The Tree of Hands (1984)
An Unkindness of Ravens (1985)
Talking to Strange Men (1987)
The Veiled One (1988)

REYMONT, W(ladyslaw) S(tanislaw)
(1867–1925) Polish
The Comédienne (1896)
The Promised Land (1899)
The Peasants (1902–09) 4 vol
The Year 1794 (1913–18) 3 vol

RHYS, Jean
(1894–1979) Welsh-Dominican
real name: Gwendolen Williams
Quartet (1928)
After Leaving Mr Mackenzie (1931)
Voyage in the Dark (1934)
Good Morning Midnight (1939)
Wide Sargasso Sea (1966)
Tigers Are Better Looking (1968) coll
Sleep It Off, Lady (1976) coll

RICE, Elmer
(1892–1967) American
real name: Elmer Reizenstein
A Voyage to Purilia (1930)
Imperial City (1937)

RICE, James
see **BESANT, Walter**

RICHARDS, Frank
(1876–1961) English
real name: Charles Harold St John Hamilton
(children's)
Billy Bunter of Greyfriars School (1947)
(plus many Billy Bunter books)

RICHARDSON, Dorothy M(iller)
(1873–1957) English
Pilgrimage (1915–38, 1967) 12 vol; 1 vol posth

RICHARDSON, Ethel Florence
see **RICHARDSON, Henry Handel**

RICHARDSON, Henry Handel
(1870–1946) English
real name: Ethel Florence Richardson
Maurice Guest (1908)
The Getting of Wisdom (1910)
Australia Felix [1] (1917)
The Way Home [1] (1925)
Ultima Thule [1] (1929)
The Young Cosima (1939)

[1] The Fortunes of Richard Mahony trilogy

RICHARDSON, Samuel
(1689–1761) English
Pamela (1740–1) 2 vol
Clarissa (1747–8) 8 vol
The History of Sir Charles Grandison (1753–4) 7 vol

RICHLER, Mordecai
(1931–) Canadian
The Acrobats (1954)
Son of a Smaller Hero (1955)
A Choice of Enemies (1957)
The Apprenticeship of Duddy Kravitz (1959)
The Incomparable Auk (1963)
Cocksure (1968)
St Urbain's Horsemen (1971)
Joshua Then and Now (1980)

RICHTER, Conrad (Michael)
(1890–1968) American
The Sea of Grass (1937)
The Trees (1940)
The Fields (1946)
The Town (1950)
The Light in the Forest (1953)
The Lady (1957)

RICHTER, Johann Paul Friedrich
see **JEAN PAUL**

RIDING, Laura
(1901–) American
(historical)
A Trojan Ending (1937)
Lives of Wives (1939)

RITCHIE, Lady Anna Isabella
(1837–1919) English
Daughter of WM Thackeray
Old Kensington (1873)
Mrs Dymond (1885)

RIVIÈRE, Jacques
(1886–1925) French
Aimée (1922)
Florence (1935) posth unf

ROBBE-GRILLET, Alain
(1922–) French
Les Gommes (1953)
Le Voyeur (1955)
La Jalousie (1957)
Dans le labyrinthe (1959)
L'Année dernière à Marienbad (1961)

ROBBINS, Harold
(1912–) American

Never Love a Stranger (1948)
The Dream Merchants (1949)
A Stone for Danny Fisher (1952)
79 Park Avenue (1955)
The Carpetbaggers (1961)
The Adventurers (1966)
The Betsy (1971)
The Pirate (1974)
The Lonely Lady (1976)
Dreams Die First (1977)
Memories of Another Day (1979)
Goodbye Janette (1981)
Spellbinder (1982)
Descent from Xanadu (1984)
The Storyteller (1986)
The Piranhas (1991)

ROBBINS, Tom
(1936–) American
real name: Thomas Eugene Robbins

Another Roadside Attraction (1971)
Even Cowgirls Get the Blues (1976)
Still Life with Woodpecker (1980)
Jitterbug Perfume (1984)
Skinny Legs and All (1990)

ROHMER, Sax
(1886–1959) English
real name: Arthur Sarsfield Ward

(thriller)
Dr Fu Manchu (1913)
(plus many Fu Manchu novels)

ROLFE, Frederick William
(1860–1913) English

Stories Toto Told Me (1898) coll
Hadrian the Seventh (1904)
Don Tarquinio (1905)
The Desire and Pursuit of the Whole (1934) posth

ROLLAND, Romain
(1866–1944) French

Jean-Christophe (1905–12) 10 vol
Clérambault (1920)

ROMAINS, Jules
(1885–1972) French
real name: Louis Farigoule

Mort de quelqu'un (1911)
Le Dieu des corps (1928)
Les Hommes de bonne volonté (1932–47) 27 vol

ROS, Amanda
(1860–1939) Irish
née McKittrick

Irene Iddesleigh (1897)
Delia Delaney (1898)

ROSS, Martin
see **SOMERVILLE, Edith Oenone**

ROTH, Henry
(1907–) American

Call It Sleep (1934)

ROTH, Joseph
(1894–1939) Austrian

Job (1930)
Radetzskymarsch (1932)
Tarabas (1935)

ROTH, Philip (Milton)
(1933–) American

Goodbye Columbus (1959) coll
Letting Go (1962)
When She Was Good (1967)
Portnoy's Complaint (1969)
The Breast (1972)
My Life As a Man [1] (1974)
The Ghost Writer [1] (1979)
Zuckerman Unbound [1] (1981)
The Anatomy Lesson [1] (1983)
The Prague Orgy [1] (1985)
The Counterlife (1986)

[1] Zuckerman novels

ROUSSEAU, Jean-Jacques
(1712–78) French

Julie, ou la Nouvelle Héloïse (1761)
Émile (1762)

RUSHDIE, (Ahmed) Salman
(1947–) Anglo-Indian

Grimus (1975)
Midnight's Children (1981)
Shame (1983)
The Satanic Verses (1988)
Haroun and the Sea of Stories (1990)

RUTHERFORD, Mark
(1831–1913) English
real name: William Hale White

The Autobiography of Mark Rutherford (1881)
Mark Rutherford's Deliverance (1885)
The Revolution in Tanner's Lane (1887)

S

SACKVILLE-WEST, Vita
(1892–1962) English

Heritage (1919)
The Challenge (1923)
The Edwardians (1930)
All Passion Spent (1931)
No Signposts in the Sea (1961)

SADE, Marquis de (Donatien Alphonse François)
(1740–1814) French

Les 120 Journées de Sodome (1784)
Justine (1791)
La Philosophie dans le boudoir (1792)
Juliette (1798)
Les Crimes de l'amour (1800)

SAGAN, Françoise
(1935–) French
real name: Françoise Quoirez

Bonjour Tristesse (1954)
Un Certain Sourire (1956)
Aimez-vous Brahms? (1959)
La Chamade (1966)
Un Profil perdu (1974)
Le Lit défait (1977)
Un Orage immobile (1983)

SAINT, Dora Jessie
see **READ, Miss**

SAINTE-BEUVE, Charles-Augustin
(1804–69) French

Volupté (1834)

SAINT-EXUPÉRY, Antoine de
(1900–44) French

Courrier-Sud (1928)
Vol de nuit (1931)
Terre des hommes (1939)
Pilote de guerre (1942)
Le Petit Prince [1] (1943)

[1] children's

SAKI
(1870–1916) English
real name: H(ector) H(ugh) Munro

Reginald (1904) coll
Reginald in Russia (1910) coll
The Chronicles of Clovis (1911) coll
The Unbearable Bassington (1912)
When William Came (1913)
Beasts and Super-Beasts (1914) coll
The Toys of Peace (1919) coll posth
The Square Egg (1924) coll posth

SALINGER, J(erome) D(avid)
(1919–) American

The Catcher in the Rye (1951)
Nine Stories (1953) coll
Franny and Zooey (1961)
Raise High the Roof Beam, Carpenters (1963)
Seymour: an Introduction (1963)

SALTEN, Felix
(1869–1947) Austrian
real name: Siegmund Salzmann

Olga Frohmut (1910)
Bambi (1923)
Bambis Kinder (1940)

SALTYKOV, Mikhail (Evgrafovich)
(1826–89) Russian

Contradictions (1847)
The Golovlyov Family (1876)

SALZMANN, Siegmund
see **SALTEN, Felix**

SAND, George
(1804–76) French
real name: Baronne Dudevant, (Amandine Aurore Dupin)

Indiana (1832)
Valentine (1832)
Lélia (1833)
Jacques (1834)
Mauprat (1837)
Spiridion (1838)
Consuelo (1843)
La Comtesse de Rudolstadt (1845)
La Mare au diable (1846)
La Petite Fadette (1848)
Les Maîtres Sonneurs (1852)
L'Homme de neige (1856)
Le Marquis de Quntinie (1863)

SANSOM, William
(1912–76) English

Fireman Flower (1944) coll
The Body (1949)
A Young Wife's Tale (1974)

SANTAYANA, George
(1863–1952) Spanish-American

The Last Puritan (1935)

SAPPER
(1888–1937) English
real name: Herman Cyril McNeile

(adventure)
Bulldog Drummond (1920)
(plus many Bulldog Drummond novels)

SARGESON, Frank
(1903–82) New Zealand

Conversations with My Uncle (1936)
A Man and His Wife (1940) coll
I Saw in My Dream (1949)
I for One (1956)
The Hangover (1967)
Joy of the Worm (1969)
Man of England Now (1972)
Sunset Village (1973)

SAROYAN, William
(1908–81) American

The Daring Young Man on the Flying Trapeze (1934) coll
The Trouble with Tigers (1938) coll
The Human Comedy (1943)
One Day in the Afternoon of the World (1964)

SARRAUTE, Nathalie
(1902–) Franco-Russian
née Tcherniak

Tropismes (1939)
Portrait d'un inconnu (1947)
Martereau (1953)
Le Planétarium (1959)
Les Fruits d'or (1963)
Entre la vie et la mort (1968)
Vous les entendez? (1972)

SARTRE, Jean-Paul
(1905–80) French

La Nausée (1938)
Les Chemins de la Liberté(1947–50) 3 vol

SASSOON, Siegfried (Louvain)
(1886–1967) English

Memoirs of a Fox-Hunting Man (1928)
Memoirs of an Infantry Officer (1930)
Sherston's Progress (1936)

SAYERS, Dorothy L(eigh)
(1893–1957) English

(crime)
Whose Body? (1923)
Clouds of Witness (1927)
Unnatural Death (1928)
The Unpleasantness at the Bellona Club (1928)
Lord Peter Views the Body (1929)
The Documents in the Case [1] (1930)
Strong Poison (1930)
The Five Red Herrings (1931)
Have His Carcase (1932)
Murder Must Advertise (1933)
Hangman's Holiday (1933)
The Nine Tailors (1934)
Gaudy Night (1934)
Busman's Honeymoon (1937)
In the Teeth of the Evidence (1940)
Striding Folly (1973) posth

[1] not a Lord Peter Wimsey novel

SCHILLER, Johann (Christoph Friedrich) von
(1759–1805) German

Der Geisterseher (1789) unf

SCHMITZ, Ettore
see **SVEVO, Italo**

SCHNABEL, Johann Gottfried
(1692–1752) German

Die Insel Felsenburg (1731–43) 4 vol

SCHNITZLER, Arthur
(1862–1931) Austrian

Der Weg ins Freie (1908)
Thérèse (1928)

SCHREINER, Olive (Emilie Albertina)
(1855–1920) South African

The Story of an African Farm (1883) as Ralph Iron
Trooper Peter Halket of Mashonaland (1897)
From Man to Man (1926) posth
Undine (1929) posth

SCOTT, Paul (Mark)
(1920–78) English

Johnnie Sahib (1952)
The Alien Sky (1958)
The Chinese Love Pavilion (1960)
The Jewel in the Crown [1] (1966)
The Day of the Scorpion [1] (1968)
The Towers of Silence [1] (1971)
A Division of the Spoils [1] (1975)
Staying On (1977)

[1] Raj Quartet

SCOTT, Sir Walter
(1771–1832) Scottish

Waverley (1814)
Guy Mannering (1815)
The Antiquary (1816)
The Black Dwarf [1] (1816)
Old Mortality [1] (1816)
Rob Roy (1817)
The Heart of Midlothian [1] (1818)
The Bride of Lammermoor [1] (1819)
A Legend of Montrose [1] (1819)
Ivanhoe (1819)
The Monastery (1820)
The Abbot (1820)
Kenilworth (1821)
The Pirate (1821)
The Fortunes of Nigel (1822)
Peveril of the peak (1822)
Quentin Durward (1823)
St Ronan's Well (1823)
Redgauntlet (1824)
The Betrothed [2] (1825)
The Talisman [2] (1825)
Woodstock (1826)
The Highland Widow [3] (1827)

SCOTT, Sir Walter (cont.)
The Two Drovers [3] (1827)
The Surgeon's Daughter [3] (1827)
The Fair Maid of Perth [3] (1828)
Anne of Geierstein (1829)
Count Robert of Paris [1] (1831)
Castle Dangerous [1] (1831)

[1] Tales of My Landlord
[2] Tales of the Crusaders
[3] Chronicles of the Canongate

SEGAL, Erich
(1937–) American

Love Story (1970)
Oliver's Story (1977)
The Class (1985)
Doctors (1988)

SEIDEL, Ina
(1885–1974) German

Das Labyrinth (1922)
Das Wunschfind (1930)
Michaela (1959)

SELBY, Hubert
(1928–) American

Last Exit to Brooklyn (1964)
The Room (1971)
The Demon (1977)
Requiem for a Dream (1979)

SENANCOUR, Étienne (Pivert de)
(1770–1846) French

Obermann (1804)

SERVICE, Robert William
(1876–1958) Canadian

The Trail of '98 (1910)
The Pretender (1915)
The Roughneck (1923)
The House of Fear (1927)

SETON, Anya
(1916–) English

(historical)
My Theodosia (1941)
Dragonwyck (1944)
The Turquoise (1946)
The Hearth and the Eagle (1948)
Fox Fire (1951)
Katherine (1954)
The Winthrop Woman (1958)
Devil Water (1962)
Avalon (1966)
Green Darkness (1972)

SEWELL, Anna
(1820–78) English

Black Beauty (1877)

SEYMOUR, Gerald
(1941–) English

(thriller)
Harry's Game(1975)
The Glory Boys (1976)
Kingfisher (1977)
Red Fox (1979)
The Contract (1980)
Archangel (1982)
In Honour Bound (1984)
Field of Blood (1985)
A Song in the Morning (1986)
At Close Quarters (1987)
Condition Black (1991)

SHARPE, Tom (Ridley)
(1928–) English

Riotous Assembly (1971)
Indecent Exposure (1973)
Porterhouse Blue (1974)
Blott on the Landscape (1975)
Wilt (1976)
The Great Pursuit (1977)
The Wilt Alternative (1979)
Vintage Stuff (1982)
Wilt on High (1984)

SHAW, George Bernard
(1856–1950) Irish

Cashel Byron's Profession (1886)
An Unsocial Socialist (1887)
Love Among the Artists (1900)

SHAW, Irwin
(1913–) American

The Young Lions (1948)
The Troubled Air (1950)
Lucy Crown (1956)
Two Weeks in Another Time (1960)
Voices of a Summer Day (1965)
Rich Man, Poor Man (1970)
Evening in Byzantium (1973)
Nightwork (1975)
Beggarman Thief (1977)
The Top of the Hill (1979)
Bread upon the Waters (1981)

SHELDON, Sidney
(1917–) American

The Naked Face (1970)
The Other Side of Midnight (1974)
A Stranger in the Mirror (1976)
Bloodline (1977)
The Master of the Game (1982)
If Tomorrow Comes (1985)
The Sands of Time (1988)

SHELLEY, Mary
(1797–1851) English
Daughter of William Godwin & Mary Wollstonecraft

Frankenstein (1818)
Valperga (1823)
The Last Man (1826)
Lodore (1835)
Falkner (1837)

SHERRIFF, R(obert) C(edric)
(1896–1975) English

The Fortnight in September (1931)
Greengates (1936)
The Hopkins Manuscript (1939)
Chedworth (1944)
Another Year (1946)
The White Carnation (1953)
King John's Treasure (1954)
The Wells of St Mary's (1961)

SHOLOKHOV, Mikhail (Alexandrovich)
(1905–84) Russian

And Quiet Flows the Don (1928-40) 4 vol
Virgin Soil Upturned (1931)

SHORTHOUSE, J(oseph) H(enry)
(1834–1903) English

John Inglesant (1881)

SHUTE, Nevil
(1899–1960) English
real name: Nevil Shute Norway

Marazan (1926)
The Lonely Road (1932)
An Old Captivity (1940)
The Pied Piper (1942)
Most Secret (1945)
The Chequer Board (1947)
No Highway (1948)
A Town Like Alice (1948)
Round the Bend (1951)
The Far Country (1952)
In the Wet (1953)
Requiem for a Wren (1955)
Behind the Black Stump (1956)
On the Beach (1957)
Trustee for the Toolroom (1960)

SIDNEY, Sir Philip
(1554–86) English

Arcadia (1590) 3 vol posth

SIENKIEWICZ, Henryk
(1846–1916) Polish

In Vain (1872)
With Fire and Sword (1884)
The Deluge (1886)
Without Dogma (1891)
Children of the Soil (1893)
Quo Vadis? (1896)
The Crusaders (1899-1900) 4 vol

SILLITOE, Alan
(1928–) English

Saturday Night and Sunday Morning (1958)
The Loneliness of the Long-Distance Runner (1959)
The Death of William Posters (1965)
A Tree on Fire (1967)
A Start in Life (1970)
The Widower's Son (1976)
Down from the Hill (1984)

SILONE, Ignazio (Secondo Tranquilli)
(1900–78) Italian

Fontamara (1930)
Pane e vino (1937)

SIMENON, Georges
(1903–89) Belgian

(crime)
Pietr-le-Letton (1931)
(plus many Maigret novels)

SIMMS, William Gilmore
(1806–70) American

Atalantis (1832)
Martin Faber (1833)
Guy Rivers (1834)
The Yemassee (1835)
The Partisan (1835)
Beauchampe (1842)
Charlemont (1856)

SIMON, Claude (Eugène Henri)
(1913–) French

Le Vent (1957)
L'Herbe (1958)
La Route de Flandres (1960)
Le Palace (1962)
Histoire (1967)
La Bataille de Pharsale (1969)
Triptyque (1973)

SINCLAIR, May (Mary Amelia)
(1863–1946) English

The Divine Fire (1904)
The Creators (1910)
The Three Sisters (1914)
The Tree of Heaven (1917)
The Life and Death of Harriet Frean (1922)
The Dark Night (1924)

SINCLAIR, Upton (Beall)
(1878–1968) American

The Jungle (1906)
The Metropolis (1908)
King Coal (1917)
The Brass Check (1919)
Oil! (1927)
Boston (1928)
The Way Out (1933)
World's End [1] (1940)
Dragon's Teeth [1] (1942)
Presidential Mission [1] (1947)
The Return of Lanny Budd [1] (1953)

[1] Lanny Budd novels

SINGER, Isaac Bashevis
(1904–91) Polish-Yiddish

The Family Moskat (1950)
Satan in Goray (1955)
Gimpel the Fool (1957) coll
The Magician of Lublin (1960)
The Slave (1962)
Zlateh the Goat [1] (1966) coll
The Manor (1967)
The Séance (1968) coll
The Estate (1969)
Enemies: a Love Story (1972)
Passions (1976) coll
Shosha (1978)
The Penitent (1984)

[1] children's

SITWELL, Dame Edith (Louisa)
(1887–1964) English
Sister of Osbert Sitwell

I Live Under a Black Sun (1937)

SITWELL, Sir (Francis) Osbert
(1892–1969) English
Brother of Edith Sitwell

Triple Fugue (1924) coll
Before the Bombardment (1926)
The Man Who Lost Himself (1929)
Miracle on Sinai (1933)

SLAUGHTER, Frank (Gill)
(1908–) American

(medical/thriller)
Spencer Brade MD (1942)
Air Surgeon (1943)
Battle Surgeon (1944)
Sangaree (1948)
The Healer (1955)
Sword and Scalpel (1957)
Epidemic (1961)
Surgeon, USA (1966)
Countdown (1970)
Life Blood (1974)
Plague Ship (1977)
Gospel Fever (1980)
Doctors at Risk (1983)
Transplant (1986)

SMITH, Betty
(1904–) American

A Tree Grows in Brooklyn (1943)
Tomorrow Will Be Better (1948)

SMITH, Charlotte
(1749–1806) English
née Turner

Emmeline (1788)
Celestina (1791)
The Old Manor House (1793)
Marchmont (1796)

SMITH, Dodie
(1896–) English

(children's)
I Capture the Castle [1] (1952)
The One Hundred and One Dalmatians (1956)
The Starlight Barking (1967)
The Midnight Kittens (1978)

[1] not children's

SMITH, E(dward) E(lmer) 'Doc'
(1890–1965) American

(science fiction)
The Skylarks of Space (1946)
Spacehounds of IBC (1947)
Triplanetary [1] (1948)
First Lensman [1] (1950)
Galactic Patrol [1] (1950)
Gray Lensman [1] (1951)
Second Stage [1] (1953)
Children of the Lens [1] (1954)
The Vortex Blaster (1960)
The Galaxy Primes (1965)
Skylark Duquesne (1966) posth
Masters of Space (1976) posth

[1] Lensman novels

SMITH, Martin Cruz
(1942–) American

(thriller)
Nightwing (1978)
Gorky Park (1981)
Stallion Gate (1986)
Polar Star (1989)

SMITH, Stevie (Florence Margaret)
(1902–71) English

Novel on Yellow Paper (1936)
Over the Frontier (1938)
The Holiday (1949)

SMITH, Wilbur (Addison)
(1933–) South African

(adventure/thriller)
When the Lion Feeds (1964)
Shout at the Devil (1966)
The Dark of the Sun (1968)
Gold Mine (1970)
The Diamond Hunters (1971)
The Sunbird (1972)

SMITH, Wilbur (cont.)
Eagle in the Sky (1974)
The Eye of the Tiger (1975)
Cry Wolf (1976)
A Sparrow Falls (1977)
Hungry as the Sea (1978)
Wild Justice (1979)
A Falcon Flies (1980)
Men of Men (1981)
The Angels Weep (1984)
The Leopard Hunts in Darkness (1984)
Power of the Sword (1986)
A Time to Die (1989)
Elephant Song (1991)

SMOLLETT, Tobias
(1721–71) Scottish

The Adventures of Roderick Random (1748)
The Adventures of Peregrine Pickle (1751)
The Adventures of Ferdinand Count Fathom (1753)
The Life and Adventures of Sir Launcelot Greaves (1762)
The Expedition of Humphry Clinker (1771)

SNOW, Baron C(harles) P(ercy)
(1905–80) English
Husband of Pamela Hansford-Johnson

Death Under Sail (1932)
New Lives for Old (1933)
The Search (1934)
George Pessant [1] (1940)
The Light and the Dark [1] (1947)
A Time of Hope [1] (1949)
The Masters [1] (1951)
The New Men [1] (1954)
Homecomings [1] (1956)
The Conscience of the Rich [1] (1958)
The Affair [1] (1959)
Corridors of Power [1] (1963)
The Sleep of Reason [1] (1968)
Last Things [1] (1970)
The Malcontents (1972)
In Their Wisdom (1974)

[1] Strangers and Brothers novels

SÖDERBERG, Hjalmar
(1869–1941) Swedish

Förvillelser (1895)
Martin Bircks Ungdom (1901)
Doktor Glas (1905)

SOLOGUB, Fedor
(1863–1927) Russian
real name: Fedor Kuzmich Teternikov

The Little Demon (1907)
The Created Legend (1908–12) 3 vol

SOLZHENITSYN, Alexander (Isayevich)
(1918–) Russian

One Day in the Life of Ivan Denisovich (1962)
Matrena's House (1963) coll
Cancer Ward (1968–9) 2 vol
The First Circle (1968)
August 1914 (1971)
The Gulag Archipelago (1973–5) 3 vol

SOMERVILLE, Edith (Oenone)
(1858–1949) Irish

An Irish Cousin (1889)
with Martin Ross[1]
The Real Charlotte (1894)
with Martin Ross[1]
The Silver Fox (1897)
with Martin Ross[1]
Some Experiences of an Irish RM (1899)
with Martin Ross[1]
Further Experiences of an Irish RM (1908)
with Martin Ross[1]
In Mr Knox's Country (1915)
with Martin Ross[1]
Mount Music (1919)
The Big House at Inver (1925)

[1] real name: Violet Martin

SOSEKI, Natsume
(1867–1916) Japanese

I Am a Cat (1905)

Young Master (1906)
The Three-Cornered World (1908)
The Heart (1914)
Star on the Wayside (1916)

SOUPAULT, Philippe
(1897–) French

Le Bon Apôtre (1923)
Les Frères Durandeau (1924)
Le Nègre (1927)
Les Dernières Nuits de Paris (1928)
Les Moribonds (1934)
Le Temps des Assassins (1945)

SOUTHERN, Terry
(1924–) American

Flash and Filigree (1958)
Candy [1] (1958)
The Magic Christian (1959)
Lollipop [2] (1962)
Blue Movie (1970)

[1] as Maxwell Kenton, with Mason Hoffenberg
[2] as Maxwell Kenton

SOYINKA, (Akinwande) Wole
(1934–) Nigerian

The Interpreters (1965)
Season of Anomy (1973)

SPARK, Muriel (Sarah)
(1918–) Scottish

The Comforters (1957)
Robinson (1958)
Memento Mori (1959)
The Bachelors (1960)
The Ballad of Peckham Rye (1960)
Voices at Play (1961)
The Prime of Miss Jean Brodie (1961)
The Girls of Slender Means (1963)
The Mandelbaum Gate (1965)
The Public Image (1968)
The Driver's Seat (1970)
Not to Disturb (1971)
The Hothouse by the East River (1972)
The Abbess of Crewe (1974)
The Takeover (1976)
Territorial Rights (1979)
Loitering with Intent (1981)
The Only Problem (1984)
A Far Cry from Kensington (1988)

SPENDER, Sir Stephen (Harold)
(1909–) English

The Burning Cactus (1936) coll
The Backward Son (1940)
The Fool and the Princess (1958)

SPILLANE, Mickey
(1918–) American
real name: Frank Morrison Spillane

(crime)
I, the Jury (1947)
My Gun Is Quick (1950)
Vengeance Is Mine! (1950)
The Big Kill (1951)
One Lonely Night (1951)
Kiss Me, Deadly (1952)
The Girl Hunters (1952)
The Deep (1961)
Me, Hood (1963) coll
Day of the Guns (1964)
The Snake (1964)
Bloody Sunrise (1965)
The Death Dealers (1965)
The By-Pass Control (1966)
The Twisted Thing (1966)
The Body Lovers (1967)
The Delta Factor (1967)
Survival... Zero! (1970)
The Erection Set (1972)
The Last Cop Out (1973)

SPRING, (Robert) Howard
(1889–1965) Welsh

Darkie & Co [1] (1932)
Shabby Tiger (1934)
Sampson's Circus [1] (1936)
My Son, My Son (1938)
Tumbledown Dick [1] (1939)
Fame Is the Spur (1940)
Dunkerleys (1946)
These Lovers Fled Away (1955)
Time and the Hour (1957)

[1] children's

SPYRI, Johanna
(1827–1901) Swiss
Heidi (1881)

STACPOOLE, Henry (de Vere)
(1863–1951) Irish
The Blue Lagoon (1908)
The Drums of War (1912)
The Pearl Fishers (1915)
The Starlit Garden (1918)
Men, Women and Beasts (1922)
Green Coral (1935)
Old Sailors Never Lie (1939)

STAËL, Madame de
(1766–1807) French
Baronne de Staël-Holstein
née Anne-Louise Germaine Necker,
Delphine (1802)
Corinne (1807)

STAPLEDON, Olaf
(1886–1950) English
(science fiction)
First and Last Men (1930)
Star Maker (1937)
Sirius (1944)

STEAD, Christina (Ellen)
(1902–83) Australian
The Salzburg Tales (1934) coll
The Beauties and Furies (1936)
The Man Who Loved Children (1940)
For Love Alone (1945)
Letty Fox: Her Luck (1946)
The People with the Dogs (1952)
Cotter's England (1967)
Miss Herbert (1976)

STEEL, Danielle
(1947–) American
Going Home (1973)
The Promise (1977)
Now and Forever (1978)
Season of Passion (1979)
Loving (1980)
Remembrance (1981)
Palomino (1982)
A Perfect Stranger (1982)
Full Circle (1984)
Thurston House (1986)
Changes (1987)
Noya (1988)
Daddy (1989)
Message from Nam (1990)

STEIN, Gertrude
(1874–1946) American
Three Lives (1909)
The Making of Americans (1925)

STEINBECK, John (Ernst)
(1902–68) American
Cup of Gold (1929)
The Pastures of Heaven (1932) coll
To a God Unknown (1933)
Tortilla Flat (1935)
In Dubious Battle (1936)
Of Mice and Men (1937)
The Long Valley (1938) coll
The Grapes of Wrath (1939)
The Moon Is Down (1942)
Cannery Row (1944)
The Wayward Bus (1947)
The Pearl (1947)
East of Eden (1952)
Sweet Thursday (1954)
The Short Reign of Pippin IV (1957)
The Winter of Our Discontent (1961)

STENDHAL
(1783–1842) French
real name: Henri Beyle
Armance (1827)
Le Rouge et le Noir (1830)
La Chartreuse de Parme (1839)
Lamiel (1889) posth unf
Lucien Leuwen (1894) posth unf

STEPHENS, James
(1882–1950) Irish
The Charwoman's Daughter (1911)

The Crock of Gold (1912)
The Demi-Gods (1914)
Deirdre (1923)

STERN, Daniel
(1805–76) French
real name: Comtesse d'Agoult, Marie de Flavigny
Nélida (1845)

STERNE, Laurence
(1713–68) Anglo-Irish
A Political Romance (1759)
Tristram Shandy (1760-1767) 9 vol
A Sentimental Journey (1768)

STEVENSON, Robert Louis
(1850–94) Scottish
(adventure)
Treasure Island (1883)
The Strange Case of Dr Jekyll and Mr Hyde (1886)
Kidnapped (1886)
The Black Arrow (1888)
The Master of Ballantrae (1889)
The Wrong Box (1889)
with Lloyd Osbourne
The Wrecker (1892)
with Lloyd Osbourne
Catriona (1893)
The Ebb-Tide (1894)
with Lloyd Osbourne
Weir of Hermiston (1896) posth unf

STEWART, J(ohn) I(nnes) M(ackintosh)
(1906–) English
Death at the President's Lodging (1936)
as Michael Innes
Hamlet's Revenge! (1937)
as Michael Innes
The Secret Vanguard (1941)
as Michael Innes
Appleby's End (1945)
as Michael Innes
The Hawk and the Handsaw (1948)
as Michael Innes
Mark Lambert's Supper (1954)
The Guardians (1955)
A Use of Riches (1957)
Silence Observed (1961)
as Michael Innes
The Man Who Won the Pools (1961)
A Connoisseur's Case (1962)
as Michael Innes
Money from Holme (1964)
as Michael Innes
An Acre of Grass (1965)
Death at the Chase (1970)
as Michael Innes
Mungo's dream (1973)
A Memorial Service (1976)
Andrew and Tobias (1980)
Sheiks and Adders (1982)
as Michael Innes
A Villa in France (1982)
The Gaudy (1983)
An Open Prison (1984)

STEWART, Lady Mary (Florence Elinor)
(1916–) English
Madame Will You Talk (1954)
The Ivy Tree (1961)
The Gabriel Hounds (1967)
The Crystal Cave (1970)
The Little Broomstick [1] (1971)
Ludo and the Star Horse [1] (1975)
Touch Not the Cat (1976)
A Walk in Wolf Wood (1980)
Thornyhold (1988)

[1] children's

STIFTER, Adalbert
(1805–68) Austrian
Der Condor (1840)
Der Hagestolz (1843)
Brigitta (1844)
Der Nachsommer (1857)
Witiko (1865–7) 3 vol

STOKER, Bram (Abraham)
(1847–1912) Irish
Dracula (1897)

STONE, Irving
(1903–) American
Lust for Life (1934)
Sailor on Horseback (1938)
Love Is Eternal (1954)
The Agony and the Ecstasy (1961)
The Passions of the Mind (1971)
The Origin (1980)

STOREY, David (Malcolm)
(1933–) English
This Sporting Life (1960)
Flight into Camden (1960)
Radcliffe (1963)
Pasmore (1972)
A Temporary Life (1973)
Saville (1976)
Present Times (1984)

STORM, Theodor (Woldsen)
(1817–88) German
Immensee (1851)
Im Schloss (1862)
Eekenhof (1879)
Hans und Heinz Kirch (1882)
Ein Doppelgänger (1887)

STOUT, Rex (Todhunter)
(1886–1975) American
(crime)
How Like a God [1] (1929)
Forest Fire [1] (1933)
Fer-de-Lance (1934)
(plus many Nero Wolfe novels)

[1] not crime

STOWE, Harriet (Elizabeth) Beecher
(1811–96) American
Uncle Tom's Cabin (1852)
Dred (1856)
The Minister's Wooing (1859)
The Pearl of Orr's Island (1862)
Oldtown Folks (1869)
Poganue People (1878)

STREATFEILD, Noel
(1895–1986) English
(children's)
The Whicharts [1] (1931)
Ballet Shoes (1936)
Tennis Shoes (1937)
The Circus Is Coming (1938)
Curtain Up (1944)
The Painted Garden (1949)
The Bell Family (1954)
New Town (1960)
Gemma (1968)

[1] not children's

STRIBLING, T(homas) S(igismund)
(1881–1965) American
Birthright (1921)
Fombombo (1922)
Red Sand (1923)
Teeftallow (1926)
Bright Metal (1928)
Strange Moon (1929)
The Forge [1] (1931)
The Store [1] (1932)
Cathedral [1] (1934)
These Bars of Flesh (1938)

[1] Alabama trilogy

STRINDBERG, (Johan) August
(1849–1912) Swedish
Röda Rummet (1879)
Hemsöborna (1887)

STRONG, L(eonard) A(lfred) G(eorge)
(1896–1958) English
Dewer Rides (1929)
The Brothers (1932)

Sea Wall (1933)
The Travellers (1945)
Deliverance (1955)

STUART, Ian
see **MACLEAN, Alistair**

STURGIS, Howard Overing
(1855–1920) American

Tim (1891)
Belchamber (1904)

STYRON, William (Clark)
(1925–) American

Lie Down in Darkness (1951)
The Long March (1953)
Set This House on Fire (1960)
The Confessions of Nat Turner (1967)
Sophie's Choice (1979)
This Quiet Dust (1982)

SURTEES, R(obert) S(mith)
(1805–64) English

Jorrocks's Jaunts and Jollities (1838) coll
Handley Cross (1843)
Hillingdon Hall (1845)
Hawbuck Grange (1847)
Mr Sponge's Sporting Tour (1853)
Ask Mamma (1858)
Plain or Ringlets? (1860)
Mr Facey Romford's Hounds (1865) posth

SUSANN, Jacqueline
(1925–76) American

Valley of the Dolls (1966)
The Love Machine (1969)
Dolores (1976)

SUTCLIFF, Rosemary
(1920–) English

(children's/historical)
The Armourer's House (1951)
The Eagle of the Ninth (1954)
The Silver Branch (1957)
The Lantern Bearers (1959)
The Mark of the Horse Lord (1965)
Blood Feud (1977)
Frontier Wolf (1980)

SVEVO, Italo
(1861–1928) Italian
real name: Ettore Schmitz

Una vita (1893)
Senelità (1898)
La conscienza di Zeno (1923)
La novella del buon vecchio e della bella fanciulla (1929) posth
Il vecchione (1967) posth unf

SWIFT, Graham (Colin)
(1949–) English

The Sweet-Shop Owner (1980)
Shuttlecock (1981)
Learning to Swim (1982) coll
Waterland (1983)
The Magic Wheel (1986)
Out of This World (1988)

SWIFT, Jonathan
(1667–1745) Irish

A Tale of a Tub (1704)
Gulliver's Travels(1726)

SWINBURNE, Algernon (Charles)
(1837–1909) English

Love's Cross Currents (1905)
Lesbia Brandon (1952) posth

SWINNERTON, Frank (Arthur)
(1884–1982) English

The Merry Heart (1909)
Nocturne (1917)
Young Felix (1923)
Tokefield Papers (1927)
Elizabeth (1934)
Harvest Comedy (1937)
The Two Wives (1939)
English Maiden (1946)

SWINNERTON, Frank (cont.)
Faithful Company (1948)
Master Jim Probity (1952)
A Tigress in Prothero (1959)
Death of a Highbrow (1961)
Quadrille (1965)
Rosalind Passes (1974)

SYMONS, Julian (Gustave)
(1912–) English

(crime)
The Immaterial Murder Case (1945)
Bland Beginning (1949)
The Broken Penny (1953)
The Paper Chase (1956)
The Gigantic Shadow (1958)
The Killing of Francie Lake (1962)
The End of Solomon Grundy (1964)
The Man Who Killed Himself (1967)
The Plot Against Roger Rider (1973)
The Blackheath Poisonings (1978)
Sweet Adelaide (1980)
The Detling Murders (1982)

T

TAGORE, Rabindranath
(1861–1941) Indian

Karuna (1881)
Binodini (1902)
Hungry Stones (1916) coll
The Home and the World (1919)
Gora (1924)

TAINE, Hippolyte
(1828–93) French

Etienne Mayran (1910) posth unf

TARKINGTON, (Newton) Booth
(1869–1946) American

The Gentleman from Indiana (1899)
Monsieur Beaucaire (1900)
The Conquest of Canaan (1905)
Guest of Quesnay (1908)
Penrod[1] (1914)
Seventeen[1] (1916)
The Magnificent Ambersons[2] (1918)
Alice Adams (1921)
The Midlander[2] (1923)
The Plutocrat[2] (1927)
Mirthful Haven (1930)
Little Orvie (1934)
Rumbin Galleries (1937)
The Heritage of Hatcher Ide (1940)
Kate Fennigate (1943)

[1] children's [2] Growth trilogy

TAYLOR, Elizabeth
(1912–75) English

At Mrs Lippincote's (1945)
A View of the Harbour (1947)
A Wreath of Roses (1950)
A Game of Hide-and-Seek (1951)
The Blush (1958) coll
In a Summer Season (1961)
The Wedding Group (1969)
Mrs Palfrey at the Claremont (1972)
Blaming (1976) posth

TAYLOR, Philip Meadows
(1808–76) Anglo-Indian

Confessions of a Thug (1839)
Tara: a Mahratta Tale (1843)
Ralph Darnell (1865)
Seeta (1872)

TENNANT, Emma
(1937–) English

The Crack (1973)
Hotel de Dream (1976)
The Bad Sister (1978)
Wild Nights (1979)
Alice Fell (1979)
Woman Beware Woman (1983)
The House of Hospitalities (1987)

TETERNIKOV, Fedor Kuzmich
see **SOLOGUB, Fedor**

TEY, Josephine
(1896–1952) Scottish
real name: Elizabeth Mackintosh
(crime)
Miss Pym Disposes (1946)
The Franchise Affair (1948)
Brat Farrar (1949)
To Love and Be Wise (1950)

THACKERAY, William Makepeace
(1811–63) English
Father of Lady Anna Isabella Ritchie
The Yellowplush Papers (1837–8) coll
Catherine (1839)
A Shabby Genteel Story (1840)
The Paris Sketch Book (1840) coll
as Michael Angelo Titmarsh
The Great Hoggarty Diamond (1841)
as Michael Angelo Titmarsh
Men's Wives (1843) coll
The Luck of Barry Lyndon (1844)
Vanity Fair (1848)
The History of Pendennis (1850)
The History of Henry Esmond Esquire (1852)
The Newcomes (1855)
The Rose and the Ring (1855)
as Michael Angelo Titmarsh
The Virginians (1859)
Lovel the Widower (1860)
The Adventures of Philip (1862)
Denis Duval (1864) posth unf

THEROUX, Paul (Edward)
(1941–) American
Waldo (1967)
Jungle Lovers (1971)
Saint Jack (1973)
The Family Arsenal (1976)
The London Embassy (1982)
Doctor Slaughter (1984)
O-Zone (1986)
Fong and the Indians (1990)

THIBAULT, Jacques-Anatole-François
see **FRANCE, Anatole**

THIONG'O, Ngugi Wa
(1938–) Kenyan
real name: James T Ngugi
Weep Not, Child (1964)
The River Between (1965)
A Grain of Wheat (1967)
Secret Lives (1974)
Devil on the Cross (1982)

THOMAS, Craig
(1942–) English
(thriller)
Rat Trap (1976)
Firefox (1977)
Wolfsbane (1978)
Snow Falcon (1980)
Emerald Decision (1984)
Winter Hawk (1987)
The Last Raven (1990)

THOMAS, D(onald) M(ichael)
(1935–) English
The Flute Player (1979)
Birthstone (1980)
The White Hotel (1981)
Ararat (1983)
Swallow (1984)
Summit (1987)

THOMAS, Leslie (John)
(1931–) Anglo-Welsh
The Virgin Soldiers (1966)
Orange Wednesday (1967)
Come to the War (1968)
His Lordship (1969)
Arthur McCann and All His Women (1970)
Onward Virgin Soldiers (1971)
The Man with the Power (1973)
Tropic of Ruislip (1974)
Stand Up Virgin Soldiers (1975)

THOMAS, Leslie (cont.)
Dangerous Davies (1976)
Ormerod's Landing (1979)
That Old Gang of Mine (1980)
The Magic Army (1981)
The Dearest and the Best (1984)
Orders for New York (1989)

TITMARSH, Michael Angelo
see **THACKERAY, William Makepeace**

TOLKIEN, J(ohn) R(onald) R(euel)
(1892–1973) English
(fantasy)
The Hobbit (1937)
The Lord of the Rings (1954–5) 3 vol
The Adventure of Tom Bombadil (1962)
Smith of Wootton Major (1967)
The Silmarillion (1977) posth

TOLSTOY, Count Leo (Nikolayevich)
(1828–1910) Russian
The Raid (1853)
War and Peace (1863–9) 4 vol
Anna Karenina (1875–8) 3 vol
The Death of Ivan Illich (1886)
The Kreutzer Sonata (1889)
Master and Man (1895)
Resurrection (1899)
Hadji Murad (1904)
The Devil (1911) posth

TOMLINSON, H(enry) M(ajor)
(1873–1958) English
Gallions Reach (1927)
All Our Yesterdays (1930)
All Hands (1937)
The Day Before (1939)

TOURGÉE, Albion W(inegar)
(1838–1905) American
'Toinette (1874)
A Fool's Errand (1879)
Bricks without Straw (1880)
John Eax and Mamelon (1882)
An Appeal to Caesar (1884)

TOYNBEE, (Theodore) Philip
(1916–81) English
The Savage Days (1937)
Tea with Mrs Goodman (1947)
The Garden to the Sea (1953)
Two Brothers (1964)

TRAVEN, B
(1890–1969) Polish-German
real name: Albert Otto Max Feige
Der Schatz der Sierra Madre (1927)
Das Totenschiff (1929)
Die Rebellion der Gehenkten (1936)

TRAVERS, P(amela) L(yndon)
(1906–) Anglo-Irish
(children's)
Mary Poppins (1934)
(plus many Mary Poppins books)
I Go by Sea, I Go by Land (1941)
The Fox and the Manger (1962)
Friend Monkey (1971)

TREECE, Henry
(1911–66) English
(children's)
The Dark Island[1] (1952)
Legions of the Eagle (1954)
Viking's Dawn[2] (1955)
Hunter Hunted (1957)
The Road to Miklagard[2] (1957)
Viking's Sunset[2] (1960)
The Dream-Time (1967) posth

[1] not children's [2] Viking trilogy

TRELAWNY, E(dward) J(ohn)
(1792–1881) English
The Adventures of a Younger Son (1831)

TRESSELL, Robert
(1868–1911) Irish
real name: Robert Noonan

The Ragged Trousered Philanthropist (1914) posth

TREVANIAN
(1925–) American
real name: Rodney Whitaker

The Eiger Sanction (1972)
The Loo Sanction (1973)
The Main (1976)
Shibumi (1979)
The Summer of Katya (1983)

TREVOR, Elleston
see **HALL, Adam**

TREVOR, William
(1928–) Irish
real name: William Trevor Cox

A Standard of Behaviour (1958)
The Old Boys (1964)
The Boarding House (1965)
Mrs Eckdorf in O'Neill's House (1969)
Elizabeth Alone (1973)
The Children of Dynmouth (1976)
Fools of Fortune (1983)

TRILLING, Lionel
(1905–75) American

The Middle of the Journey (1947)

TROLLOPE, Anthony
(1815–82) English

The Macdermots of Ballycloran (1847)
The Kellys and the O'Kellys (1848)
La Vendée (1850)
The Warden[1] (1855)
Barchester Towers[1] (1857)
The Three Clerks (1858)
Doctor Thorne[1] (1858)
The Bertrams (1859)
Castle Richmond (1860)
Framley Parsonage[1] (1861)
Orley Farm (1862)
The Small House at Allington[1] (1864)
Can You Forgive Her?[2] (1865)
The Belton Estate (1866)
Nina Balatka (1867)
The Last Chronicle of Barset[1] (1867)
The Claverings (1867)
Linda Tressel (1868)
He Knew He Was Right (1869)
Phineas Finn[2] (1869)
The Vicar of Bullhampton (1870)
The Eustace Diamonds[2] (1873)
Phineas Redux[2] (1874)
The Way We Live Now (1875)
The Prime Minister[2] (1876)
The American Senator (1877)
The Duke's Children[2] (1880)
Dr Wortle's School (1881)
Ayala's Angel (1881)
Mr Scarborough's Family (1883) posth

[1] Barsetshire novels [2] Palliser novels

TUOHY, (John) Frank
(1925–) English

The Animal Game (1957)
The Warm Nights of January (1960)
The Ice Saints (1964)

TUPPER, Martin (Farquhar)
(1810–89) English

The Crock of Gold (1844)
Stephen Langton (1858)

TURGENEV, Ivan (Sergeevich)
(1818–83) Russian

Rudin (1856)
A Nest of Gentlefolk (1858)
On the Eve (1860)
Fathers and Sons (1862)

TUTUOLA, Amos
(1920–) Nigerian

The Palm-Wine Drinkard (1952)
My Life in the Bush of Ghosts (1954)

TORTUOLA, Amos (cont.)
The Feather Woman of the Jungle (1962)
Abaiyi and His Inherited Poverty (1967)
The Witch Herbalist of the Remote Town (1980)
Pauper, Brawler and Slanderer (1987)

TWAIN, Mark
(1835–1910) American
real name: Samuel Langhorne Clemens
The Innocents Abroad (1869)
The Gilded Age (1873)
with CD Warner
The Adventures of Tom Sawyer (1876)
The Prince and the Pauper (1882)
The Adventures of Huckleberry Finn (1884)
A Connecticut Yankee in King Arthur's Court (1889)
The American Claimant (1892)
Pudd'nhead Wilson (1894)
Tom Sawyer Abroad (1894)
Tom Sawyer Detective (1896)
The Man That Corrupted Hadleyburg (1900) coll
The $30,000 Bequest (1906)
The Mysterious Stranger (1916) posth

TWEEDSMUIR, Baron
see **BUCHAN, John**

TYLER, Royall
(1757–1826) American
The Algerine Captive (1797)

U

UNAMUNO, Miguel de
(1864–1936) Spanish
Niebla (1914)

UNDSET, Sigrid
(1882–1949) Norwegian
Jenny (1911)
Kristin Lavransdatter (1920–2) 3 vol
Olav Audunssön (1925–7) 4 vol
Gymadenia (1929)
Den trofaste hustru (1936)

UPDIKE, John (Hoyer)
(1932–) American
The Poorhouse Fair (1959)
Rabbit, Run[1] (1960)
The Magic Flute[2] (1962)
The Centaur (1963)
Bech: a Book (1963)
Couples (1968)
Rabbit Redux[1] (1971)
Bech Is Back (1975)
Marry Me: A Romance (1976)
The Coup (1978)
Rabbit Is Rich[1] (1981)
The Witches of Eastwick (1984)
Roger's Version (1986)
5 (1988)
Just Looking (1989)
Rabbit at Rest[1] (1990)

[1] Rabbit tetralogy
[2] children's

UPWARD, Edward (Falaise)
(1903–) English
In the Thirties[1] (1962)
Rotten Elements[1] (1969)
No Home but the Struggle[1] (1977)

[1] Spiral Ascent trilogy

URIS, Leon (Marcus)
(1924–) American
Battle Cry (1953)
The Angry Hills (1955)
Exodus (1957)
Mila, 18 (1960)
Armageddon (1964)
Topaz (1967)
QB VII (1970)

Trinity (1976)
The Haj (1984)
Mitla Pass (1989)

UTTLEY, Alison
(1884–1976) English
(children's)
Little Grey Rabbit (1929)
(plus many Little Grey Rabbit books)
A Traveller in Time (1939)
Sam Pig (1940)
(plus many Sam Pig books)

V

VAN DER POST, Sir Laurens (Jan)
(1906–) South African
In a Province (1934)
A Bar of Shadow (1952)
The Face Beside the Fire (1953)
Flamingo Feather (1955)
The Hunter and the Whale (1967)
A Story Like the Wind (1972)
A Far-Off Place (1974)
A Mantis Carol (1975)

VAN DINE, SS
(1888–1939) American
real name: Willard Huntington Wright
(crime)
The Benson Murder Case (1926)
(plus many Philo Vance novels)

VANSITTART, Peter
(1920–) English
The Tournament (1959)
The Dark Tower (1965)
Pastimes of a Red Summer (1969)
Landlord (1970)
Quintet (1976)
Lancelot (1978)
Three Six Seven (1982)

VAN VOGT, A(lfred) E(lton)
(1912–) American
(science fiction)
Slan (1946)
The World of A (1948)
The Weapon Shops of Isher (1971)
Planets for Sale (1954)
Empire of the Atom (1957)
Triad (1959)
The Wizard of Linn (1962)
The Winged Man (1966)
The Silkie (1969)
The Darkness of Diamondia (1972)
Supermind (1977)
Renaissance (1979)
Computerworld (1983)

VARGAS LLOSA, (Jorge) Mario (Pedro)
(1936–) Peruvian
La cuidad y los perros (1963)
La casa verde (1966)
Conversación en la catedral (1969)
La Tia Julia y el escribidor (1977)
Alejandro Mayta (1984)

VERGA, Giovanni
(1840–1922) Italian
I Malavoglia (1881)
Cavalleria rusticana (1883)
Mastro-don Gesualdo (1889)

VERNE, Jules
(1828–1905) French
(science fiction)
Cinq Semaines en ballon (1863)
Voyage au centre de la terre (1864)
Les Aventures du Capitaine Hatteras (1866) 2 vol
Vingt Milles Lieues sous les mers (1869)
Le Tour du monde en quatre-vingts jours (1873)
L'Ile mystérieuse (1874–5) 3 vol
Michel Strogoff[1] (1876)

[1] not science fiction

VIAUD, Julien
see **LOTI, Pierre**

VIDAL, Gore
(1925–) American
Williwaw (1946)
In a Yellow Wood (1947)
The City and the Pillar (1948)
Dark Green, Bright Red (1950)
The Judgment of Paris (1952)
Julian (1964)
Myra Breckinridge (1968)
Myron (1974)
Creation (1981)
Lincoln (1984)
Empire (1987)

VIGNY, Alfred de
(1797–1863) French
(historical)
Cinq-Mars (1826)

VISCHER, Friedrich Theodor
(1807–87) German
Auch Einer (1879) 2 vol

VOLTAIRE
(1694–1778) French
real name: François-Marie Arouet
Zadig (1747)
Babouc (1749)
Candide (1759)
Jeannot et Colin (1764)
L'Ingénu (1767)

VON ARNIM, Elizabeth
(1866–1941) Australian
née Beauchamp
Elizabeth and Her German Garden (1898)
Pastor's Wife (1912)
Vera (1921)

VONNEGUT, Kurt
(1922–) American
(science fiction/fantasy)
Player Piano (1952)
The Sirens of Titan (1959)
Mother Night (1961)
Cat's Cradle (1963)
Breakfast of Champions (1964)
Slaughterhouse Five (1969)
Slapstick (1976)
Jailbird (1979)
Palm Sunday (1981)
Deadeye Dick (1982)
Galapagos (1985)
Bluebeard (1987)
Hocus Pocus (1990)

VOYNICH, Ethel Lillian
(1864–1960) Irish
née Boole
The Gadfly (1897)

WAIN, John (Barrington)
(1925–) English
Hurry on Down (1953)
Living in the Present (1955)
The Contenders (1958)
A Travelling Woman (1959)
Strike the Father Dead (1962)
The Young Visitors (1965)
The Smaller Sky (1967)
A Winter in the Hills (1970)
The Pardoner's Tale (1978)
Lizzie's Floating Shop (1981)
Young Shoulders (1982)
Where the Rivers Meet (1988)

WALKER, Alice (Malsenior)
(1944–) American
The Third Life of Grange Copeland (1970)
Meridian (1976)
The Color Purple (1983)

WALLACE, Lew(is)
(1827–1905) American

The Fair God (1873)
Ben-Hur (1880)

WALLACE, (Richard Horatio) Edgar
(1875–1932) American

(crime/adventure)
The Four Just Men (1905)
The Council of Justice (1908)
Sanders of the River (1911)
The Melody of Death (1915)
The Clue of the Twisted Candle (1916)
Down Under Donovan (1918)
The Daffodil Mystery (1920)
The Crimson Circle (1922)
Green Archer (1923)
Room 13 (1924)
The Black Abbot (1926)
The Forger (1927)
The Golden Hades (1929)
The Clue of the Silver Key (1930)
The Frightened Lady (1932)

WALLANT, Edward Lewis
(1926–62) American

The Human Season (1960)
The Pawnbroker (1961)
The Tenants of Moonbloom (1963) posth
The Children at the Gate (1964) posth

WALPOLE, Horace
(1717–97) English
Earl of Oxford

The Castle of Otranto (1764)

WALPOLE, Sir Hugh (Seymour)
(1884–1941) New Zealand

The Wooden Horse (1909)
Maradick at Forty (1910)
Mr Perrin and Mr Traill (1911)
Fortitude (1913)
The Duchess of Wrexe (1914)
The Dark Forest (1916)
The Secret City (1919)
Jeremy[1] (1919)
The Cathedral (1922)
Jeremy and Hamlet[1] (1923)
The Old Ladies (1924)
Portrait of a Man with Red Hair (1925)
Jeremy at Crale[1] (1927)
Farthing Hall (1929)
with JB Priestley
Rogue Herries[2] (1930)
Judith Paris[2] (1931)
The Fortress[2] (1932)
Vanessa[2] (1933)
The Youthful Delaneys (1938)
The Bright Pavilions[2] (1940)
Katherine Christian[2] (1943) posth unf

[1] children's [2] The Herries Chronicles

WAMBAUGH, Joseph
(1937–) American

(crime/thriller)
The Onion Field (1973)
The Choirboys (1975)
The Glitter Dome (1981)
The Delta Star (1983)
Lines and Shadows (1984)
The Secrets of Harry Bright (1985)
Echoes in the Darkness (1987)
The Blooding (1989)
The Golden Orange (1990)

WARD, Arthur Sarsfield
see **ROHMER, Sax**

WARD, Mary Augusta (Mrs Humphry)
(1851–1920) English
née Arnold

Miss Bretherton (1884)
Robert Elsmere (1888)
Marcella (1894)
Helbeck of Bannisdale (1898)
Lady Rose's Daughter (1903)
The Marriage of William Ashe (1905)

WARD, Plumer
(1765–1846) English
real name: Robert Ward

Tremaine (1825)
De Vere (1827)
De Clifford (1841)

WARNER, C(harles) D(udley)
(1829–1900) American

The Gilded Age (1873)
with Mark Twain
A Little Journey in the World (1889)
The Golden House (1895)
That Fortune (1899)

WARNER, Rex
(1905–86) English

(historical)
The Wild Goose Chase[1] (1937)
The Professor[1] (1938)
The Aerodrome[1] (1941)
The Vengeance of the Gods (1954)
The Young Caesar (1958)
Imperial Caesar (1960)
Pericles the Athenian (1963)
The Converts (1967)

[1] not historical

WARNER, Sylvia Townsend
(1893–1978) English

Lolly Willowes (1926)
Mr Fortune's Maggot (1927)
The True Heart (1929)
Summer Will Show (1936)
The Museum of Cheats (1947)
The Flint Anchor (1954)

WARREN, Robert Penn
(1905–89) American

Night Rider (1938)
At Heaven's Gate (1943)
All the King's Men (1946)
World Enough and Time (1950)
Band of Angels (1955)
The Cave (1959)
Wilderness (1961)
Flood (1964)
Meet Me in the Green Glen (1971)

WASSERMANN, Jakob
(1873–1934) German

Die Juden von Zirndorf (1897)
Caspar Hauser (1908)
Der goldene Spiegel (1911)
Der Wendekreis (1920) 3 vol
Der Fall Maurizius (1928)
Etzel Andergast (1931)
Joseph Kerkhovens dritte Existenz (1934)

WATERHOUSE, Keith (Spencer)
(1929–) English

There Is a Happy Land (1957)
Billy Liar (1959)
Jubb (1963)
The Bucket Shop (1968)
Billy Liar on the Moon (1975)
Office Life (1979)
Maggie Muggins (1981)
In the Wood (1983)
Thinks (1984)
Our Song (1988)
Bimbo (1990)

WATTS-DUNTON, (Walter) Theodore
(1832–1914) English

Aylwin (1898)

WAUGH, Alec (Alexander Raban)
(1898–1981) English
Brother of Evelyn Waugh

The Loom of Youth (1917)
Kept (1925)
So Lovers Dream (1931)
Wheels within Wheels (1933)
Going Their Own Ways (1938)
Unclouded Summer (1948)
Where the Clocks Chime Twice (1952)
Island in the Sun (1956)

Fuel for the Flame (1960)
The Fatal Gift (1973)

WAUGH, (Alexander) Auberon
(1939–) English
Son of Evelyn Waugh

The Foxglove Saga (1960)
Path of Dalliance (1963)
Where Are the Violets Now? (1965)
Consider the Lilies (1968)

WAUGH, Evelyn (Arthur St John)
(1903–66) English
Brother of Alec Waugh
Father of Auberon Waugh

Decline and Fall (1928)
Vile Bodies (1930)
Black Mischief (1932)
A Handful of Dust (1934)
Scoop (1938)
Put Out More Flags (1942)
Brideshead Revisited (1945)
The Loved One (1948)
Helena (1950)
Men at Arms[1] (1952)
Love Among the Ruins (1953)
Officers and Gentlemen[1] (1955)
The Ordeal of Gilbert Pinfold (1957)
Unconditional Surrender[1] (1961)
Basil Seal Rides Again (1963)

[1] Sword of Honour trilogy

WEBB, (Gladys) Mary
(1881–1927) English
née Meredith

Gone to Earth (1917)
The House in Dormer Forest (1920)
Seven for a Secret (1922)
Precious Bane (1924)
Armour Wherein He Trusted (1929) posth unf

WEINSTEIN, Nathan
see **WEST Nathanael**

WELCH, (Maurice) Denton
(1915–48) English

In Youth Is Pleasure (1944)
A Voice Through a Cloud (1950) posth unf

WELDON, Fay
(1931–) English
née Birkinshaw

The Fat Woman's Joke (1967)
Down Among the Women (1971)
Female Friends (1975)
Little Sister (1977)
Praxis (1978)
Puffball (1980)
Watching Me, Watching You (1981)
The President's Child (1982)
Life and Loves of a She-Devil (1984)
Sackcloth and Ashes (1989)

WELLS, H(erbert) G(eorge)
(1866–1946) English

(science fiction)
The Time Machine (1895)
The Wonderful Visit (1895)
The Island of Dr Moreau (1896)
The Wheels of Chance[1] (1896)
The Invisible Man (1897)
The War of the Worlds (1898)
When the Sleeper Wakes (1899)
Love and Mr Lewisham[1] (1900)
The First Men in the Moon (1901)
The Food of the Gods (1904)
A Modern Utopia (1905)
Kipps[1] (1905)
In the Days of the Comet (1906)
The War in the Air (1908)
Tono-Bungay[1] (1909)
Ann Veronica[1] (1909)
The History of Mr Polly[1] (1910)
The New Machiavelli[1] (1911)
The Passionate Friends[1] (1913)
The Research Magnificent[1] (1915)
Mr Britling Sees It Through[1] (1916)
Joan and Peter[1] (1918)
Men Like Gods (1923)
The World of William Clissold[1] (1926)

WELLS, HG (cont.)
Mr Blettsworthy on Rumpole Island[1] (1928)
The Shape of Things to Come (1933)
World Brain (1938)
Mind at the End of Its Tether (1945)

[1] not science fiction

WELTY, Eudora
(1909–) American
The Robber Bridegroom (1942)
Delta Wedding (1946)
The Ponder Heart (1954)
Losing Battles (1970)
The Optimist's Daughter (1972)

WESLEY, Mary
(1912–) English
née Farmar
Speaking Terms [1] (1969)
The Sixth Seal (1969)
Jumping the Queue (1983)
Haphazard House (1983)
The Camomile Lawn (1984)
Harnessing Peacocks (1985)
The Vacillations of Poppy Carew (1986)
Not That Sort of Girl (1987)
Second Fiddle (1988)
A Sensible Life (1990)

[1] children's

WEST, Morris (Langlo)
(1916–) Australian
Gallows on the Sand (1955)
The Big Story (1957)
The Devil's Advocate (1959)
Daughter of Silence (1961)
The Shoes of the Fisherman (1963)
The Ambassador (1965)
The Tower of Babel (1968)
Summer of the Red Wolf (1971)
The Salamander (1973)
Harlequin (1974)
The Navigator (1976)
Proteus (1979)
The Clowns of God (1981)
Cassidy (1986)
Masterclass (1988)

WEST, Nathanael
(1903–40) American
real name: Nathan Weinstein
The Dream Life of Balso Snell (1931)
Miss Lonelyhearts (1933)
A Cool Million (1934)
The Day of the Locust(1939)

WEST, Dame Rebecca
(1892–1983) English
real name: Cecily Isabel Fairfield
The Return of the Soldier (1918)
The Judge (1922)
The Strange Necessity (1928)
The Thinking Reed (1936)
The Fountain Overflows (1956)
The Birds Fall Down (1966)

WESTMACOTT, Mary
see **CHRISTIE, Agatha**

WEYMAN, Stanley John
(1855–1928) English
(historical)
The House of the Wolf (1889)
A Gentleman of France (1893)
Under the Red Robe (1894)
The Red Cockade (1895)
The Castle Inn (1898)
Count Hannibal (1901)
The Abbess of Vlaye (1904)
Chippinge (1906)
The Wild Geese (1908)

WHARTON, Edith (Newbold)
(1862–1937) American
née Jones
The Touchstone (1900)
The Valley of Decision (1902)
Sanctuary (1903)
The House of Mirth (1905)
The Fruit of the Tree (1907)

Madame de Treymes (1907)
Ethan Frome (1911)
The Reef (1912)
The Custom of the Country (1913)
Summer (1917)
The Marne (1918)
The Age of Innocence (1920)
The Glimpses of the Moon (1922)
A Son at the Front (1923)
The Old Maid (1924)
The Mother's Recompense (1925)
Twilight Sleep (1927)
The Children (1928)
Hudson River Bracketed (1929)
Certain People (1930)

WHARTON, William
(1925–) American
pseudonym
Birdy (1979)
Dad (1981)
A Midnight Clear (1982)
Scumbler (1984)
Pride (1986)
Tidings (1987)
Franky Furbo (1989)
Last Lovers (1991)

WHEATLEY, Dennis (Yates)
(1897–1977) English
(adventure/black magic)
The Forbidden Territory (1933)
The Devil Rides Out (1934)
The Eunuch of Stamboul (1935)
Contraband (1936)
The Quest of Julian Day (1939)
Three Inquisitive People (1940)
Faked Passports (1940)
The Black Baroness (1940)
Strange Conflict (1941)
V for Vengeance (1942)
Come into My Parlour (1946)
The Launching of Roger Brook (1947)
The Haunting of Toby Jugg (1948)
Star of Ill-Omen (1952)
To the Devil – a Daughter (1953)
The Island Where Time Stands Still (1954)
The Ka of Gifford Hilary (1956)
Traitors' Gate (1958)
The Rape of Venice (1959)
The Satanist (1960)
Mayhem in Greece (1962)
They Used Dark Forces (1964)
Unholy Crusade(1967)
Evil in a Mask (1969)
Gateway to Hell (1970)
The Strange Story of Linda Lee (1972)
The Irish Witch (1973)

WHITAKER, Rodney
see **TREVANIAN**

WHITE, Antonia
(1899–1979) English
Frost in May (1933)
The Lost Traveller (1950)
The Sugar House (1952)
Beyond the Glass (1954)

WHITE, Edmund (Valentine III)
(1940–) American
Forgetting Elena (1973)
Nocturnes for the King of Naples (1978)
A Boy's Own Storey (1982)
Caracole (1985)
The Beautiful Room is Empty (1988)

WHITE, Patrick (Victor Martindale)
(1912–) Australian
Happy Valley (1939)
The Living and the Dead (1941)
The Aunt's Story (1946)
The Tree of Man (1955)
Voss (1957)
Riders in the Chariot(1961)
The Solid Mandala (1966)
The Vivisector (1970)
The Eye of the Storm (1973)
A Fringe of Leaves (1976)
The Twyborn Affair (1979)
Memoirs of Many in One (1986)

WHITE, T(erence) H(anbury)
(1906–64) English
Loved Helen (1926)
Farewell Victoria (1933)
The Sword in the Stone [1] (1938)
The Witch in the Wood [1] (1940)
The Ill-Made Night [1] (1941)
Mistress Masham's Repose (1947)
Goshawk (1951)

[1] The Once and Future King trilogy

WHITE, William Hale
see **RUTHERFORD, Mark**

WHITEHEAD, Charles
(1804–62) English
Jack Ketch (1834)
Richard Savage (1842)

WIESEL, Elie
(1928–) Romanian-Yiddish
La nuit (1958)
L'aube (1960)
Les Portes de la forêt (1964)
Les Juifs du silence (1966)
Le mendiant de Jerusalem (1968)

WIGGIN, Kate (Douglas)
(1856–1923) American
née Smith
(children's)
The Story of Patsy (1883)
Polly Oliver's Problem (1893)
Rebecca of Sunnybrook Farm (1903)
Mother Carey's Chickens (1911)

WILDE, Oscar (Fingal O'Flahertie Wills)
(1854–1900) Irish
The Picture of Dorian Gray (1891)

WILDER, Laura Ingalls
(1867–1957) American
(children's)
Little House in the Big Woods (1932)
Little House on the Prairie (1935)
On the Banks of Plum Creek (1937)
By the Shores of Silver Lake (1939)
The Long Winter (1940)
Little Town on the Prairie (1941)
These Happy Golden Years (1943)

WILDER, Thornton (Niven)
(1897–1975) American
The Cabala (1926)
The Bridge on San Luis Rey (1927)
The Woman of Andros (1930)
Heaven's My Destination (1934)
The Ides of March (1948)
The Eighth Day (1967)
Theophilus North (1973)

WILLIAMS, Charles (Walter Stansby)
(1886–1945) English
War in Heaven (1930)
The Place of the Lion (1931)
Descent into Hell (1937)
All Hallows' Eve (1944)

WILLIAMS, Gwendolen
see **RHYS, Jean**

WILLIAMS, Raymond (Henry)
(1921–88) Welsh
Border Country (1960)
Second Generation (1964)
The Volunteers (1978)
The Fight for Manod (1979)
Loyalties (1985)

WILLIAMS, Tennessee
(1911–83) American
real name: Thomas Lanier Williams
The Roman Spring of Mrs Stone (1950)

WILLIAMS, William Carlos
(1883–1963) American
A Voyage to Pagany (1928)
The White Mule (1937)
In the Money (1940)
The Build-Up (1952)

WILLIAMSON, Henry
(1895–1977) English
The Beautiful Years [1] (1921)
Dandelion Days [1] (1922)
The Peregrine's Saga (1923)
A Dream of Fair Women [1] (1924)
The Old Stag (1926)
Tarka the Otter (1927)
The Pathway [1] (1928)
Salar the Salmon (1935)
The Phasian Bird (1948)
A Chronicle of Ancient Sunlight (1951–69) 15 vol

[1] The Flax of Dreams tetralogy

WILLIS, Baron Ted
(1918–) English (crime)
Death May Surprise Us (1974)
The Left-Handed Sleeper (1975)
Man Eater (1976)
The Buckingham Palace Connection (1978)
The Naked Sun (1980)
The Most Beautiful Girl in the World (1982)

WILSON, Sir Angus (Frank Johnstone)
(1913–91) English
The Wrong Set (1949) coll
Such Darling Dodos (1950) coll
Hemlock and After (1952)
Anglo-Saxon Attitudes (1956)
The Middle Age of Mrs Eliot (1958)
The Old Men at the Zoo (1961)
Late Call (1964)
No Laughing Matter (1967)
As If by Magic (1973)
Setting the World on Fire (1980)

WILSON, Colin (Henry)
(1931–) English
The Outsider (1956)
Ritual in the Dark (1960)
The Philosopher's Stone (1969)
The Killer (1970)
The Space Vampires (1976)

WILSON, Edmund
(1895–1972) American
I Thought of Daisy (1929)
Memoirs of Hecate County (1946) coll

WILSON, John Anthony Burgess
see **BURGESS, Anthony**

WINSOR, Kathleen
(1919–) American
(romance)
Forever Amber (1944)
The Lovers (1952)
America, with Love (1957)

WISTER, Owen
(1860–1938) American
The Virginian (1902)
Lady Baltimore (1906)

WODEHOUSE, Sir P(elham) G(renville)
(1881–1975) English
The Pothunters (1902)
Love Among the Chickens (1906)
The White Feather (1907)
Mike: a Public School Story (1909)
A Gentleman of Leisure (1910)
Psmith in the City (1910)
Psmith, Journalist (1915)
Something Fresh (1915)
Piccadilly Jim (1917)
A Damsel in Distress (1919)
My Man Jeeves (1919) coll
The Girl on the Boat (1922)
The Inimitable Jeeves (1923) coll

WODEHOUSE, PG (cont.)
Leave It to Psmith (1923)
Carry On, Jeeves! (1925) coll
Money for Nothing (1928)
Summer Lightning (1929)
Very Good, Jeeves! (1930) coll
If I Were You (1931)
Heavy Weather (1933)
Thank You, Jeeves (1934)
Right Ho, Jeeves (1934)
Laughing Gas (1936)
Summer Moonshine (1937)
The Code of the Woosters (1938)
Uncle Fred in the Springtime (1939)
Quick Service (1940)
Money in the Bank (1942)
Joy in the Morning (1946)
Full Moon (1947)
Uncle Dynamite (1948)
The Mating Season (1949)
The Old Reliable (1951)
Pigs Have Wings (1952)
Ring for Jeeves (1953)
Jeeves and the Feudal Spirit (1954)
French Leave (1956)
Cocktail Time (1958)
Jeeves in the Offing (1960)
Service with a Smile (1961)
Stiff Upper Lip, Jeeves (1963)
Frozen Assets (1964)
Galahad at Blandings (1965)
The World of Jeeves (1967) coll
A Pelican at Blandings (1969)
The Girl in Blue (1970)
Much Obliged, Jeeves (1971)
Pearls, Girls and Monty Bodkin (1972)
Bachelors Anonymous (1973)
Aunts Aren't Gentlemen (1974)
Sunset at Blandings (1977) posth

WOLFE, Thomas (Clayton)
(1900–38) American

Look Homeward, Angel (1929)
Of Time and the River (1935)
The Web and the Rock (1939) posth
You Can't Go Home Again (1940) posth
The Hills Beyond (1941) posth unf

WOLFE, Tom
(1930–) American
real name: Thomas Kennerly Wolfe, Jr.

The Bonfire of the Vanities (1987)

WOLLSTONECRAFT, Mary
(1759–97) English
Wife of Wiliam Godwin
Mother of Mary Shelley

Mary (1788)

WOOD, Ellen
(1814–87) English
née Price

East Lynne (1861)
The Channings (1862)
Lord Oakburn's Daughters (1864)
Elster's Folly (1866)
A Life's Secret (1867)
Roland Yorke (1869)

WOOD, Mrs Henry
see **WOOD, Ellen**

WOOLF, Leonard (Sidney)
(1880–1969) English
Husband of Virginia Woolf

The Village in the Jungle (1913)
The Wise Virgins (1914)

WOOLF, (Adeline) Virginia
(1882–1941) English
Wife of Leonard Woolf
née Stephen

The Voyage Out (1915)
Night and Day (1919)
Jacob's Room (1922)
Mrs Dalloway (1925)
To the Lighthouse (1927)
Orlando (1928)
The Waves (1931)
Flush (1933)
The Years (1937)
Between the Acts (1941) posth

WOOLSEY, Sarah Chauncy
see **COOLIDGE, Susan**

WOUK, Herman
(1915–) American
Aurora Dawn (1947)
The City Boy (1948)
The Caine Mutiny (1951)
Marjorie Morningstar (1955)
Slattery's Hurricanes (1956)
Youngblood Hawke (1962)
Don't Stop Stop the Carnival (1965)
The Lomokome Papers (1986)
The Winds of War (1971)
War and Remembrance (1975)
Inside, Outside (1985)

WREN, P(ercival) C(hristopher)
(1885–1941) English
The Wages of Virtue [1] (1916)
Beau Geste [1] (1924)
Beau Sabreur [1] (1926)
Beau Ideal [1] (1928)
Good Gestes [1] (1929)
Port o' Missing Men (1934)
Fort in the Jungle (1936)
None Are So Blind (1939)
Two Feet from Heaven (1940)

[1] Foreign Legion novels

WRIGHT, Richard
(1908–60) American
Native Son (1940)
The Outsider (1953)
The Long Dream (1958)
Land Today (1961) posth

WRIGHT, Willard Huntington
see **VAN DINE, SS**

WYLIE, Elinor (Morton Hoyt)
(1885–1928) American
(historical)
Jennifer Lorn (1923)
The Venetian Glass Nephew (1925)
The Orphan Angel (1926)
Mr Hodge and Mr Hazard (1927)

WYNDHAM, John
(1903–69) English
real name: John Wyndham Parkes Lucas Beynon Harris
(science fiction)
The Day of the Triffids (1951)
The Kraken Wakes (1953)
The Chrysalids (1955)
The Midwich Cuckoos (1957)
The Seeds of Time (1958)
The Outward Urge (1959)
Trouble with Lichen (1960)
Consider Her Ways (1964)
Chocky (1968)
Web (1979) posth

WYSS, Johann (David)
(1743–1818) Swiss
Der Schweizerische Robinson (1812–13) 2 vol

Y

YARMOLINSKY, Avrahm
see **DEUTSCH, Babette**

YATES, Dornford
(1885–1960) English
real name: Cecil William Mercer
The Brother of Daphne (1914)
Berry & Co (1920)
Jonah & Co (1922)
Blind Corner (1927)
The House That Berry Built (1945)

YERBY, Frank (Garvin)
(1916–) American

The Foxes of Harrow (1946)
The Golden Hawk (1948)
A Woman Called Fancy (1951)
Benton's Row (1954)
Captain Rebel (1956)
Jarrett's Jade (1959)
Griffin's Way (1962)
An Odour of Sanctity (1966)
Speak Now (1969)
The Dahomean (1971)
The Voyage Unplanned (1974)
Tobias and the Angel (1975)
A Darkness at Ingraham's Crest (1979)
Devilseed (1984)

YIN, Leslie Charles Bowyer
see **CHARTERIS, Leslie**

YONGE, Charlotte M(ary)
(1823–1901) English

The Heir of Redclyffe (1853)
The Little Duke (1854)
Heartsease (1854)
The Daisy Chain (1856)
Dynevor Terrace (1857)
Hopes and Fears (1860)
The Trial (1864)
The Prince and the Page (1865)
The Caged Lion (1870)
The Pillars of the House (1873)

YOUNG, Francis Brett
(1884–1954) English

Portrait of Clare (1927)
My Brother Jonathan (1928)
Jim Redlake (1930)
Dr Bradley Remembers (1935)
Far Forest (1936)
They Seek a Country (1937)
A Man About the House (1942)
Portrait of a Village (1951)

ZAMYATIN, Evgeny (Ivanovich)
(1884–1937) Russian

At the World's End (1914)
We (1920)
The Dragon (1966) coll posth

ZANGWILL, Israel
(1864–1926) Anglo-Yiddish

Children of the Ghetto (1892)
Ghetto Tragedies (1894)
Dreamers of the Ghetto (1898)
Ghetto Comedies (1907)

ZOLA, Émile
(1840–1902) French

La Confession de Claude (1865)
Thérèse Raquin (1867)
Madeleine Férat (1868)
Les Rougon-Macquart (1871–93) 20 vol
Les Trois Villes (1894–8) 3 vol
Fécondité (1899)
Travail (1901)
Vérité (1903) posth

Titles

A

Aaron's Rod (1922)
DH Lawrence
Aaron Sisson (flautist)

Abaiyi and His Inherited Poverty (1967)
Amos Tutuola

Abandoned Woman (1977)
Richard Condon

Abbess of Crewe, The (1974)
Muriel Spark

Abbess of Vlaye, The (1904)
Stanley John Weyman

Abbot, The (1820)
sequel to ***The Monastery***
Walter Scott
set: 16c; Lochleven Castle
Lady of Avenel
Edward Glendinning, or Father Ambrose
Magdalene Graeme (Roland's grandmother)
Roland Graeme (page)
Mary, Queen of Scots
Murray (regent)
Catherine Seyton (Roland's eventual wife)
Adam Woodcock (falconer)

Abbots Verney (1906)
Rose Macaulay

ABC Murders, The (1935)
Agatha Christie

Aberrations
see ***Förvillelser***

Abraxas (1938)
Jacques Audiberti

Absalom, Absalom! (1936)
William Faulkner
set: 19c Mississippi
house: Sutpen's Hundred
Clytie (Thomas' illegitimate daughter)
Charles Le Bon (Henry's friend)
Henry Sutpen (Thomas' son)
Judith Sutpen (Thomas' daughter)
Thomas (later Colonel) Sutpen (slave-owner)

Absentee, The (1812)
Maria Edgeworth
set: Ireland
Burke (land agent)
Lady Clonbrony (Clonbrony's wife)
Lord Clonbrony
Colambre, Lord (Clonbrony's son)
Garraghtys (brothers/land agents)
Grace (Colambre's cousin)

Absent in the Spring (1944)
Agatha Christie

Absolute Beginners (1959)
Colin MacInnes

Academic Question, An (1986) posth
Barbara Pym

Academic Year (1955)
DJ Enright

Accident (1964)
Nicholas Mosley

Accidental Man (1971)
Iris Murdoch

Ace Up My Sleeve, An (1971)
James Hadley Chase

Helga Rolfe

Acre of Grass, An (1965)
JIM Stewart

Acrobats, The (1954)
Mordecai Richler

Across Five Aprils (1964)
Irene Hunt

Across the Black Waters (1940)
Mulk Raj Anand

Across the River and into the Trees (1950)
Ernest Hemingway

Acté (1839)
Alexandre Dumas (père)

Action, The (1979)
Francis King

Action at Aquila (1938)
Hervey Allen

Active Service (1899)
Stephen Crane

Act of Will (1986)
Barbara Taylor Bradford

Ada (1969)
Vladimir Nabokov

Adalgisa (1944)
Carlo Emilio Gadda

Adam Bede (1859)
George Eliot

set: late 18c; Hall Farm, the Midlands
Adam Bede (carpenter)
Seth Bede (Adam's brother)
Arthur Donnithorne (Hetty's seducer)
Dinah Morris (Hetty's cousin)
Martin Poyser (Hetty's uncle)
Mrs Poyser (Poyser's wife)
Hetty Sorrel

Adam Johnstone's Son (1895)
F Marion Crawford

Adam's Rest (1922)
Sarah Gertrude Millin

Adèle (1858)
Julia Kavanagh

Adolescence
see ***Flegeljahre, Die***

Adolphe (1816)
Benjamin Constant

Adolphe
Ellénore (Adolphe's lover)

Adrienne Mesurat (1927)
Julien Green

Adultera, L' (1882)
Theodor Fontane

set: Berlin
Melanie
Ebenezer Rubehn (Melanie's 2nd husband)
Van der Straaten (financier/Melanie's 1st husband)

Adult Life of Toulouse Lautrec by Henri Toulouse Lautrec, The (1978)
Kathy Acker

Adventure of the Christmas Pudding, The (1960)
Agatha Christie
Miss Jane Marple (amateur sleuth)

Adventure of Tom Bombadil, The (1962)
JRR Tolkien

Adventurers, The (1966)
Harold Robbins

Adventures of a Brownie, The (1872)
Dinah Maria Craik

Adventures of Augie March, The (1953)
Saul Bellow
set: Chicago; Mexico; Paris
Augie March

Adventures of a Younger Son, The (1831)
EJ Trelawny

Adventures of a Young Man, The (1939)
John Dos Passos

Adventures of Baron Münchausen, The (1785) coll
RE Raspe
Baron Münchausen

Adventures of Captain Hatteras, The
see ***Aventures du Capitaine Hatteras, Les***

Adventures of David Simple, The (1744)
Sarah Fielding
Camilla (David's eventual wife)
David Simple

Adventures of Ferdinand Count Fathom, The (1753)
Tobias Smollett
Ferdinand, Count Fathom
Count de Melville

Adventures of God in His Search for the Black Girl, The (1973)
Brigid Brophy

Adventures of Hajji Baba in England, The (1828)
Adventures of Hajji Baba of Ispahan, The (1824)
James Justinian Morier

Adventures of Harry Richmond, The (1871)
George Meredith
Squire Beltham (Roy's sometime employer)
Janet Ilchester (Harry's eventual wife)
Princess Ottilia (Harry's sweetheart)
Harry Richmond (Roy's son)
Richmond Roy (singing teacher)

Adventures of Herr Baby, The (1881)
Mary Louisa Molesworth

Adventures of Huckleberry Finn, The (1884)
sequel to ***The Adventures of Tom Sawyer***
Mark Twain
set: Mississippi River
'Dauphin' (confidence trickster)
Widow Douglas (Huck's adoptive parent)
'Duke' (confidence trickster)

Adventures of Huckleberry Finn, The (cont.)
Huck(leberry) Finn
Grangerford family
Jim (slave)
Mrs Phelps (Phelps' wife)
Silas Phelps (plantation owner)
Tom Sawyer (Huck's friend)
Shepherdson family
Miss Watson (Jim's owner)

Adventures of Joseph Andrews, The (1742)
Henry Fielding

set: Booby Hall, Somerset
Parson Adams
Joseph Andrews
Lady Booby (Sir Thomas' wife)
Squire Booby (Sir Thomas' nephew)
Sir Thomas Booby
Fanny (milkmaid)
Mrs Slipshod (Lady Booby's chambermaid)
Parson Trulliber

Adventures of King Midas, The (1974)
Lynne Reid Banks

Adventures of Peregrine Pickle, The (1751)
Tobias Smollett

Emilia (Peregrine's eventual wife)
Gamaliel Pickle (Peregrine's father)
Peregrine Pickle
Commodore Hawser Trunnion

Adventures of Peter Wilkins, The (1751)
Robert Paltock

Adventures of Philip, The (1862)
William Makepeace Thackeray

Philip Firmin
Caroline Gann

Adventures of Robin Day, The (1839)
Robert Montgomery

Adventures of Roderick Random, The (1748)
Tobias Smollett

Tom Bowling (naval lieutenant/Roderick's uncle)
Narcissa (Roderick's eventual wife)
Roderick Random
Hugh Strap (Roderick's friend)
Miss Williams (Hugh's eventual wife)

Adventures of Sherlock Holmes, The (1892) coll
Sir Arthur Conan Doyle

set: 221b Baker Street, London
Mycroft Holmes (Holmes' brother)
Sherlock Holmes (detective)
Mrs Hudson (Holmes' housekeeper)
Inspector Lestrade (Scotland Yard officer)
Professor James Moriarty (Holmes' arch enemy)
Dr John Watson (Holmes' companion)

Adventures of the Wishing Chair, The (1937)
Enid Blyton

Adventures of Tom Sawyer, The (1876)
Mark Twain

set: Mississippi River; McDougal's Cave; Jackson's Island
Widow Douglas (Huck's adoptive parent)
Huck(leberry) Finn (Tom's friend)
Joe Harper (Tom's friend)
Injun Joe (murderer)
Aunt Polly (Tom's aunt)
Muff Potter (drunkard)
Sid Sawyer (Tom's brother)
Tom Sawyer
Becky Thatcher (Tom's sweetheart)

Aerodrome, The (1941)
Rex Warner

Affair, The (1959)
CP Snow
Lewis Eliot (narrator/barrister)

Affaire Clémenceau, L' (1864)
Alexandre Dumas (fils)

Affaire Lerouge, L' (1866)
Émile Gaboriau
Monsieur Lecoq (detective)

Afloat and Ashore (1844)
James Fenimore Cooper

A for Andromeda (1962)
Fred Hoyle

African Queen, The (1935)
CS Forester
set: Africa
boat: The African Queen
Charlie Allnutt (river-trader)
Peter Bull (captain of *The African Queen*)
Rose Sayer (missionary)

African Witch, The (1936)
Joyce Cary

After Candlemas (1974)
Ruth M Arthur

After Dark (1856)
Wilkie Collins

Afterglow and Nightfall (1977)
Ellis Peters

After Leaving Mr Mackenzie (1931)
Jean Rhys

After Many a Summer (1939)
Aldous Huxley

Aftermath (1896)
sequel to ***A Kentucky Cardinal***
James Lane Allen
Georgiana Cobb (Adam's beloved)
Adam Moss

Afternoon Men (1931)
Anthony Powell

Afternoon of an Autocrat (1956)
Norah Lofts

After the Banquet (1960)
Yukio Mishima

After the Funeral (1953)
Agatha Christie
Hercule Poirot (detective)

Against Nature
see ***À rebours***

Agents and Patients (1936)
Anthony Powell

Agents and Witnesses (1947)
PH Newby

Age of Assassins
see ***Temps des Assassins, Les***

Age of Innocence, The (1920)
Edith Wharton
set: 1870s New York
Dallas Archer (Newland's son)
Newland Archer (lawyer)
May (Ellen's cousin)
Mrs Mingott (Ellen's grandmother)
Ellen Olenska (née Welland)

Age of Longing, The (1951)
Arthur Koestler

Age of the Rainmakers, The (1971)
Wilson Harris

Agnes Grey (1847)
Anne Brontë

Bloomfield family
Agnes Grey (governess)
Murray family
Mr Weston (curate)

Agony and the Ecstasy, The (1961)
Irving Stone

Agony Column (1916)
Earl Derr Biggers

Agostino (1944)
(Two Adolescents)
Alberto Moravia

Ah, but Your Land Is Beautiful (1981)
Alan Paton

Ahnen, Die (1873–81) 6 vol
Gustav Freytag

Ahnung und Gegenwart (1815)
Joseph Freiherr von Eichendorff

Friedrich

Aimée (1922)
Jacques Rivière

Aimez-vous Brahms? (1959)
(Do You Like Brahms?)
Françoise Sagan

Air and Angels (1991)
Susan Hill

Air-Conditioned Nightmare, The (1945)
Henry Miller

Airport (1968)
Arthur Hailey

Air Surgeon (1943)
Frank Slaughter

Aissa Saved (1932)
Joyce Cary

AJ Wentworth, BA (1980)
HF Ellis

À la recherche du temps perdu (1913–27) 7 vol
(Remembrance of Things Past)
Marcel Proust

vols:
1 *Du Côté de chez Swann* (1913)
2 *A l'ombre des jeune filles en fleurs* (1919)
3 *Le Côté de Guermantes* (1921)
4 *Sodome et Gomorrhe* (1922)
5 *La Prisonnière* (1923)
6 *La Fugitive* (1925)
7 *Le Temps retrouvé* (1927)

set: 1880s–1900s Paris; Balbec
Bergotte (novelist)
Bloch (Jewish writer)
Charlus (Duc de Guermantes' brother)
Elstir (painter)
Françoise (servant)
Duc de Guermantes
Duchesse de Guermantes (Duc's wife)
Marcel (narrator)
Morel (violinist)
Marquis de Norpois (diplomat)
Odette (Swann's eventual wife)
Marquis de Saint-Loup (Duc de Guermantes' nephew)

Charles Swann
Gilberte Swann (Swann's daughter)
Madame Verdurin (Verdurin's wife)
Monsieur Verdurin
Madame de Villeparisis (Norpois' lover)
Vinteuil (composer)

Albatross (1982)
Evelyn Anthony

Albert Angelo (1964)
BS Johnson

Albigenses, The (1824)
Charles Maturin

Alec Forbes of Howglen (1865)
George MacDonald

Alejandro Mayta (1984)
Mario Vargas Llosa

Alexander's Bridge (1912)
Willa Cather

Alexandria Quartet, The
see **Durrell, Lawrence**

Algeria (1985)
Kathy Acker

Algerine Captive, The (1797)
Royall Tyler

set: USA; Africa
Dr Updike Underhill

Alice Adams (1921)
Booth Tarkington

Alice Fell (1979)
Emma Tennant

Alice Lorraine (1875)
RD Blackmore

Alice's Adventures in Wonderland (1865)
Lewis Carroll

Alice
Caterpillar
Cheshire Cat
Dinah (cat)
Dormouse
Gryphon
King of Hearts
Knave of Hearts
Queen of Hearts
Mad Hatter
March Hare
Mock Turtle
Ugly Duchess
White Rabbit

Alien Sky, The (1958)
Paul Scott

Allan Quatermain (1887)
H Rider Haggard

Allan Quatermain

All Day Saturday (1966)
Colin MacInnes

All Hallows' Eve (1944)
Charles Williams

All Hands (1937)
HM Tomlinson

All in the Family (1966)
Edwin O'Connor

All My Friends Are Going to Be Strangers (1972)
Larry McMurty

All or Nothing (1960)
John Cowper Powys

All Our Tomorrows (1982)
Ted Allbeury

All Our Yesterdays (1930)
HM Tomlinson

All-Out on the Road to Smolensk (1942)
Erskine Caldwell

All Passion Spent (1931)
Vita Sackville-West

Lady Slane

All Quiet on the Western Front
see ***Im Westen nichts Neues***

All Sorts and Conditions of Men (1882)
Walter Besant

All That Glitters (1941)
Frances Parkinson Keyes

All the Conspirators (1928)
Christopher Isherwood

All the King's Men (1946)
Robert Penn Warren

Willie Stark (state governor)

All the Young Men (1935)
Oliver La Farge

Almayer's Folly (1895)
Joseph Conrad

set: Malaya
Kaspar Almayer
Nina Almayer (Almayer's daughter)

Almond Tree, The (1923)
Walter De La Mare

Almond, White Almond (1933)
DK Broster

Alpha List, The (1979)
Ted Allbeury

Alroy (1835)
Benjamin Disraeli

Altenburg (1943)
André Malraux

Alte Nester (1880)
Wilhelm Raabe

Irene Everstein
Fritz Langreuter
Eva Sixtus (Ewald's sister)
Ewald Sixtus

Alteration, The (1974)
Kingsley Amis

Altiora Peto (1883)
Laurence Oliphant

Alton Locke (1850)
Charles Kingsley

set: London
Eleanor
Lillian (Alton's would-be sweetheart)
Alton Locke (apprentice tailor/poet)
Saunders Mackaye (bookseller)

Always Coming Home (1986)
Ursula Le Guin

Amant, L' (1984)
Amante anglaise, L' (1967)
Marguerite Duras

Amateur Cracksman, The (1899)
EW Hornung

AJ Raffles (gentleman burglar)
Bunny (Raffles' assistant)

Amazing Marriage, The (1895)
George Meredith

Lord Fleetwood (Carinthia's husband)
Captain Kirby (Carinthia's father)
Carinthia Kirby
Chillon Kirby (Carinthia's brother)
Lord Levellier (Carinthia's uncle)
Gower Woodseer (Carinthia's friend)
Minister Woodseer (Gower's father)

Ambassades, Les (1951)
(Diplomatic Diversions)
Roger Peyrefitte

Ambassador, The (1985)
André Brink

Ambassador, The (1965)
Morris West

Ambassadors, The (1903)
Henry James

set: Woollett, Massachusetts; Paris
Maria Gostrey (Strether's friend)
Chadwick Newsome
Mrs Newsome (Chadwick's mother)
Jim Pocock (Sarah's husband)
Sarah Pocock ('ambassador'/Mrs Newsome's daughter)
Lambert Strether ('ambassador')
Jeanne Vionnet (Chadwick's lover)
Madame de Vionnet (Jeanne's mother)
Waymarsh (Strether's friend)

Ambrose Holt and Family (1931)
Susan Glaspell

Amelia (1751)
Henry Fielding

set: London
prison: Newgate
Colonel Bath
Mrs Bennet (widow)
Amelia Booth
William Booth (Amelia's husband)
Mrs Ellison (Booths' landlady)
Colonel James (William's so-called friend)
Dr Harrison (parson)
Miss Matthews (William's cell-mate)
'My Lord' (enigmatic nobleman)
Justice Thrasher (judge)

American, The (1877)
Henry James

set: Paris
Mrs Bread (Marquise's maid)
Marquis De Bellegarde (Claire's brother)
Marquise De Bellegarde (Marquis' wife)
Valentin De Bellegarde (Claire's brother)
Claire De Cintre (widow/Christopher's wife)
Christopher Newman ('American')
Noémie Nioche (artist)
Mrs Tristram (Christopher's friend)

Americana (1971)
Don Delillo

American Beauty (1931)
Edna Ferber

American Claimant, The (1892)
Mark Twain

American Dream, An (1965)
Norman Mailer

American Earth (1931)
Erskine Caldwell

American Gothic (1974)
Robert Bloch

American Senator, The (1877)
Anthony Trollope

set: Mickewa (fictional US state); Dillsborough, England
Elias Gotobed (senator)
Mary Masters
John Morton (Reginald's cousin/Mary's suitor)
Reginald Morton (Mary's suitor)
Lord Rufford (Arabella's beloved)
Arabella Trefoil
Larry Twentyman (Mary's would-be suitor)

American Tragedy, An (1925)
Theodore Dreiser

basis: 1906 Chester Gilette murder case
Sondra Finchley (Clyde's would-be wife)
Clyde Griffiths ('accidental' killer)
Samuel Griffiths (Clyde's uncle)
Roberta (Clyde's tragic lover)

American Visitor, An (1933)
Joyce Cary

America, with Love (1957)
Kathleen Winsor

Amerika (1927) posth unf
Franz Kafka

Karl Rossmann

Aminadab (1942)
Maurice Blanchot

Amitiés particulières, Les (1944)
(Special Friendships)
Roger Peyrefitte

Among People (1915)
Maxim Gorky

Among the Believers (1981)
VS Naipaul

Amore conjugale, L' (1949)
(Conjugal Love)
Alberto Moravia

Amorous Death, The
see ***Morte amoreuse, La***

Amour, L' (1971)
Marguerite Duras

Amour impossible, L' (1841)
Jules-Amédée Barbey D'Aurevilly

Anatomy Lesson, The (1983)
Philip Roth

Nathaniel Zuckerman (novelist)

Ancient Evenings (1983)
Norman Mailer

set: Egypt

Andersonville (1955)
MacKinlay Kantor

And No Man's Wit (1940)
Rose Macaulay

And Quiet Flows the Don (1928–40) 4 vol
Mikhail Sholokhov

set: early 20c Russia

André Cornélis (1887)
Paul Bourget

Andrew and Tobias (1980)
JIM Stewart

Andromeda Strain, The (1969)
Michael Crichton

And the Crooked Shall Be Made Straight (1916)
SY Agnon

Angela Borgia (1891)
Conrad Ferdinand Meyer

Ángel guerra (1891)
(War Angel)
Benito Pérez Galdós

Angel Pavement (1930)
JB Priestley

Stanley Poole
Mr Smeeth
Mrs Smeeth (Smeeth's wife)

Angels Weep, The (1984)
Wilbur Smith

Ange Pitou (1853)
Alexandre Dumas (père)

Anges noirs, Les (1936)
(The Dark Angels)
François Mauriac

Anglo-Saxon Attitudes (1956)
Angus Wilson

Gerald Middleton (historian)

Angry Hills, The (1955)
Leon Uris

Angry Mountain, The (1950)
Hammond Innes

Angst des Tormanns beim Elfmeter, Die (1970)
(The Goalie's Anxiety at the Penalty Kick)
Peter Handke

Animal Farm (1945)
George Orwell

Boxer (horse)
Mr Jones (farmer)
Napoleon (pig)
Snowball (pig)

Animal Game, The (1957)
Frank Tuohy

Animals' Conference, The
see ***Konferenz der Tiere, Die***

Animal, the Vegetable and John D Jones, The (1982)
Betsy Byars

Anna Apparent (1972)
Nina Bawden

Anna Karenina (1873–7) 2 vol
Leo Tolstoy

Anna Karenina
Kitty Lévin (Lévin's wife)
Squire Lévin
Oblowski (Anna's brother)
Vronski (army officer/Anna's lover)

Annals of the Parish (1821)
John Galt

set: Dalmailing, Ayrshire
Rev Michael Balwhidder

Annaluise und Anton (1929)
Erich Kästner

Anna of the Five Towns (1902)
Arnold Bennett

Anna Tellwright

Année dernière à Marienbad, L' (1961)
(Last Year at Marienbad)
Alain Robbe-Grillet

Anne of Avonlea (1909)
LM Montgomery

Anne of Geierstein (1829)
Walter Scott

set: England; Switzerland; Burgundy
Margaret of Anjou
Arnold Biederman (Swiss magistrate)
Duke of Burgundy
Count Albert Geierstein (Anne's father)
Anne of Geierstein (Biederman's niece)
Arthur De Vere (Earl of Oxford's son)
Archibald of Hagenbach (governor of Burgundy)
Earl of Oxford

Anne of Green Gables (1908)
LM Montgomery

set: Green Gable Farm, Avonlea, Prince Edward Island
Marilla Cuthbert (Matthew's sister)
Matthew Cuthbert
Anne Shirley (orphan)

Anne of Ingleside (1939)
Anne of the Island (1919)
Anne of Windy Poplars (1936)
Anne's House of Dreams (1917)
LM Montgomery

Annette (1974)
Erskine Caldwell

Ann Veronica (1909)
HG Wells

Ann Vickers (1933)
Sinclair Lewis

Another Country (1962)
James Baldwin

Another Part of the Wood (1968)
Beryl Bainbridge

Another Roadside Attraction (1971)
Tom Robbins

Another World (1972)
James Hanley

Another Year (1946)
RC Sherriff

Ansichten eines Clowns, Die (1963)
(The Clowns)
Heinrich Böll

Answer Yes or No (1950)
John Mortimer

Anthony Adverse (1933)
Hervey Allen

set: Napoleonic Wars
Anthony Adverse
Captain Bittern (naval officer)
Dolores De La Fuente (Anthony's wife)
Captain Jorham (naval officer)
Neleta (Anthony's mistress)
Father Xavier (priest)

Antic Hay (1923)
Aldous Huxley

set: Bohemian London

Anti-Death League, The (1966)
Kingsley Amis

Antigua, Penny, Puce (1936)
Robert Graves

Antiquary, The (1816)
Walter Scott

Dousterswivel (charlatan)
Hector M'Intyre (Neville's duelling adversary)
Major Neville (army officer)
Jonathan Oldbuck (antiquary)
Jenny Rintherout (Oldbuck's servant)
Sir Arthur Wardour (Isabella's father)
Isabella Wardour (Neville's beloved)

Antonina (or the Fall of Rome) (1850)
Wilkie Collins

Anton Reiser (1785-1790) 5 vol
Karl Philipp Moritz

Any God Wil Do (1966)
Richard Condon

Any Old Iron (1988)
Anthony Burgess

Anything for Billy (1988)
Larry McMurty

Ape and Essence (1948)
Aldous Huxley

Apes of God, The (1930)
Wyndham Lewis

Aphrodite in Aulis (1930)
George Moore

Apostle, The (1943)
Sholem Asch

Apotheker Heinrich (1885)
Hermann Heiberg

Appeal to Caesar, An (1884)
Albion W Tourgée

Appel au soldat, L' (1900)
Maurice Barrès

Appleby's End (1945)
JIM Stewart

John Appleby (detective)

Apples Be Ripe (1930)
Llewellyn Powys

Appointment in Samarra (1934)
John O'Hara

Appointment with Death (1938)
Agatha Christie

Hercule Poirot (detective)

Apprenticeship of Duddy Kravitz, The (1959)
Mordecai Richler

Après-midi de M Andesmas, L' (1962)
Marguerite Duras

April, June and November (1972)
Frederic Raphael

Aquitaine Progression, The (1984)
Robert Ludlum

Arabella (1949)
Georgette Heyer

Ararat (1983)
DM Thomas

Arcadia (1590) 3 vol posth
Philip Sidney

Duke of Basilius (ruler of Arcadia)
Gynecia (Duke of Basilius' wife)

Archangel (1982)
Gerald Seymour

Ardath (1889)
Marie Corelli

À rebours (1884)
(Against Nature)
Joris-Karl Huysmans

Des Esseintes

Are You Listening, Rabbi Low? (1987)
JP Donleavy

Are You There, God? It's Me, Margaret (1970)
Judy Blume

Armadale (1866)
Wilkie Collins

Lydia Gwilt

Armageddon (1964)
Leon Uris

Armance (1827)
Stendhal

Armen, Die (1917)
(The Proletariat)
Heinrich Mann

Arme Spielmann, Der (1848)
Franz Grillparzer

Armies of the Night, The (1968)
Norman Mailer

Armourer's House, The (1951)
Rosemary Sutcliff

Armour Wherein He Trusted (1929) posth unf
Mary Webb

Around the World in Eighty Days
see ***Tour du monde en quatre-vingts jours, Le***

Arouse and Beware (1936)
MacKinlay Kantor

Arrêt de mort, L' (1948)
Maurice Blanchot

Arrival and Departure (1943)
Arthur Koestler

Arrow of God (1964)
Chinua Achebe

Arrow of Gold, The (1919)
Joseph Conrad

Arrowsmith (1924)
Sinclair Lewis

Arthur McCann and All His Women (1970)
Leslie Thomas

Arthur Mervyn (1799)
Charles Brockden Brown

Arthur Rex: A Legendary Novel (1979)
Thomas Berger

Artificial Princess, The (1934) posth
Ronald Firbank

Artist Among the Missing (1949)
Olivia Manning

Artist of the Floating World, An (1986)
Kazuo Ishiguro

Art of the Vieux Colombier, The (1918)
Waldo Frank

Ascanio (1843)
Alexandre Dumas (père)

Ascent to Omai (1970)
Wilson Harris

As Far As You Can Go (1963)
Julian Mitchell

Ashes
see ***Cenere***

Ashes and Diamonds (1948)
Jerzy Andrzejewski

As If By Magic (1973)
Angus Wilson

As I Lay Dying (1930)
William Faulkner

set: Jefferson, Mississippi
Addie Bundren (dying woman)
Anse Bundren (Addie's husband)
Darl Bundren (Addie's son)
Dewey Bundren (Addie's daughter)

Ask Mamma (1858)
RS Surtees

Ask Me Tomorrow (1962)
Stan Barstow

Ask Me Tomorrow (1940)
James Gould Cozzens

As Man Grows Older
see ***Senelità***

Aspern Papers, The (1888)
Henry James

set: Venice
Jeffrey Aspern (late poet)
Juliana Bordereau
Miss Tina Bordereau (Juliana's niece)
Prest, Mrs ([unnamed] US editor's friend)

Assassin (1973)
Evelyn Anthony

Assistant, The (1957)
Bernard Malamud

Astercote (1970)
Penelope Lively

As the Crow Flies (1991)
Jeffrey Archer

Atala (1801)
Chateaubriand

set: Louisiana
Atala (Chactas' beloved)
Père Aubry (missionary)
Chactas (Red Indian)
René

Atalantis (1832)
William Gilmore Simms

At Bertram's Hotel (1965)
Agatha Christie

Miss Jane Marple (amateur sleuth)

At Close Quarters (1987)
Gerald Seymour

At Fault (1890)
Kate Chopin

Athabasca (1980)
Alistair Maclean

At Heaven's Gate (1943)
Robert Penn Warren

Athelings, The (1857)
Margaret Oliphant

Atherton (1854)
Mary Russell Mitford

Atlantic Fury (1962)
Hammond Innes

Atlantis (1954)
John Cowper Powys

Atlas Shrugged (1957)
Ayn Rand

At Mrs Lippincote's (1945)
Elizabeth Taylor

Atómstöonin (1948)
(Atom Station)
Halldór Laxness

At Sunwich Point (1902)
WW Jacobs

At Swim-Two-Birds (1939)
Flann O'Brien

Attack Alarm (1941)
Hammond Innes

Attente, L'Oubli, L' (1961)
Maurice Blanchot

Attenzione, L' (1965)
(The Lie)
Alberto Moravia

At the Back of the North Wind (1871)
George MacDonald

Diamond (horse)
Diamond (boy named after the horse)
Jim (Nanny's friend)
Nanny ([boy] Diamond's friend)
North Wind (voice)

At the Mountain of Madness (1931)
HP Lovecraft

At the Villa Rose (1910)
AEW Mason

Inspector Hanaud (detective)

At the World's End (1914)
Evgeny Zamyatin

Aube, L' (1960)
(Dawn)
Elie Wiesel

Au bon soleil (1881)
Paul Arène

Auch Einer (1879) 2 vol
Friedrich Theodor Vischer

Auction Sale, The (1949)
CHB Kitchin

Auf den Marmorklippen (1939)
(On the Marble Cliffs)
Ernst Jünger

Auf der Höhe (1865) 3 vol
Berthold Auerbach

August Is a Wicked Month (1965)
Edna O'Brien

August 1914 (1971)
Alexander Solzhenitsyn

Augustus: The Memoirs of the Emperor (1986)
Allan Massie

Auld Licht Idylls (1888)
JM Barrie

set: Thrums (actual Kirriemuir)

Aunt Julia and the Scriptwriter
see ***Tia Julia y el escribidor, La***

Aunts Aren't Gentlemen (1974)
PG Wodehouse

Reginald Jeeves (Wooster's valet)
Bertie Wooster

Aunt's Story, The (1946)
Patrick White
Theodora Goodman (spinster)

Aura (1962)
Carlos Fuentes

Aurélien (1945)
Louis Aragon

Aurora Dawn (1947)
Herman Wouk

Aurora Floyd (1863)
Mary Elizabeth Braddon

Aus dem Leben eines Taugenichts (1826)
Joseph Freiherr von Eichendorff

Au service de L'Allemagne (1905)
Maurice Barrès

Ausgetobt (1883)
Hermann Heiberg

Au soleil de juillet (1903)
Paul Adam

Austin Ellott (1863)
Henry Kingsley

Australia Felix (1917)
Henry Handel Richardson
Richard Mahony

Autobiography of a Thief, The (1858)
Charles Reade

Autobiography of Mark Rutherford, The (1881)
Mark Rutherford

Autre, L' (1971)
(The Other)
Julien Green

Autumn Manoeuvres (1978)
Melvyn Bragg

Autumn of the Patriarch
see ***Otoño del patriarca, El***

Autumn People, The (1965)
Ray Bradbury

Avalon (1966)
Anya Seton

Avarice House
see ***Mont-Cinère***

À vau l'eau (1882)
Joris-Karl Huysmans
Monsieur Folantin

Aventures du Capitaine Hatteras, Les (1866) 2 vol
(The Adventures of Captain Hatteras)
Jules Verne

Aventures de dernier Abencérage, Les (1826)
Chateaubriand
Aben-Hamet
Bianca (Aben-Hamet's beloved)

Avenue of the Dead (1981)
Evelyn Anthony

Average Man, The (1913)
RH Benson

Awakening, The (1899)
Kate Chopin

set: Grand Isle; New Orleans
Arobin (amorist)
Madame Lebrun
Robert Lebrun (Madame Lebrun's son)
Edna Pontellier
Leonce Pontellier (Edna's husband)
Adèle Ratignolle (Edna's friend)
Mademoiselle Reisz (musician)

Awfully Big Adventure, An (1989)
Beryl Bainbridge

Awkward Age, The (1899)
Henry James

Aggie (Mitchett's eventual wife)
Mrs Brookenham (Nanda's mother)
Nanda Brookenham
Tishy Grendon (Nanda's friend)
Mr Longdon (Nanda's eventual lover)
Mitchett (Nanda's suitor)
Vanderbank (Nanda's suitor)

Ayala's Angel (1881)
Anthony Trollope

Captain Batsby (Ayala's would-be suitor)
Ayala Dormer
Egbert Dormer (Ayala's father)
Lucy Dormer (Ayala's sister)
Reginald Dosett
Isadore Hamel (artist/Lucy's lover)
Colonel Jonathan Stubbs (Ayala's eventual husband)
Emmeline Tringle (Sir Thomas' wife)
Sir Thomas Tringle
Tom Tringle (Sir Thomas' son)

Ayesha (1834)
James Justinian Morier

Ayesha (the Return of She) (1905)
H Rider Haggard

set: Africa
Ayesha (sorceress)

Aylwin (1898)
Theodore Watts-Dunton

Henry Aylwin
Sinfi Lovell (Aylwin's friend)
Winifred (Aylwin's beloved)

Ayrshire Legatees, The (1821)
John Galt
Dr Zachariah Pringle

Aziyadé (1879)
Pierre Loti

B

B (1972)
Eva Figes

Babbitt (1922)
Sinclair Lewis

set: Zenith (town), Mid-West USA
George Babbitt (businessman)

Baboo Jabberjee, BA (1897)
F Anstey

Babouac (1749)
Voltaire

Bachelor of Arts, The (1937)
RK Narayan

Bachelors, The (1960)
Muriel Spark

Bachelors, The
see ***Célibataires, Les***

Bachelors Anonymous (1973)
PG Wodehouse

Back (1946)
Henry Green

Backward Shadow, The (1970)
Lynne Reid Banks

Backward Son, The (1940)
Stephen Spender

Badgers, The (1924)
Leonid Leonov

Bad Man, A (1967)
Stanley Elkin

Bad Place, The (1990)
Dean R Koontz

Bad Sister, The (1978)
Emma Tennant

Bagatelles pour un massacre (1938)
Louis-Ferdinand Céline

Bagthorpes Unlimited (1978)
Bagthorpes v the World (1979)
Helen Cresswell

Bague d'Annibal, La (1843)
Jules-Amédée Barbey D'Aurevilly

Bahama Crisis (1980)
Desmond Bagley

Bahnwärter Thiel (1888)
(Signalman Thiel)
Gerhart Hauptmann

Baiser au lépreux, Le (1922)
(The Kiss to the Leper)
François Mauriac

Balisand (1924)
Joseph Hergesheimer

Balkan Trilogy, The
see **Manning, Olivia**

Ballad and the Source, The (1944)
Rosamund Lehmann

Ballad of Peckham Rye, The (1960)
Muriel Spark

Ballad of the Sad Café, The (1951) coll
Carson McCullers

Ballerina (1958)
Vicki Baum

Ballet Shoes (1936)
Noel Streatfeild

Pauline Fossil (Gum's adopted child)
Petrova Fossil (Gum's adopted child)
Posy Fossil (Gum's adopted child)
Great Uncle Matthew 'Gum'

Balthazar (1958)
Laurence Durrell

set: Alexandria, Egypt
Balthazar
Clea (artist)
LG Darley (narrator)
Justine
Melissa (Darley's mistress)
Mountolive (ambassador)
Nessim (Justine's husband)
Pursewarden (British agent)

Bambi (1923)
Bambis Kinder (1940)
(Bambi's Children)
Felix Salten

Bambi (deer)
Faline (deer)

Banana Bottom (1933)
Claude McKay

Bandicoot (1978)
Richard Condon

Bandits (1987)
Elmore Leonard

Band of Angels (1955)
Robert Penn Warren

Banjo (1929)
Claude McKay

Banker (1983)
Dick Francis

Banners (1919)
Babette Deutsch

Banquet, The (1934) coll
RH Mottram

Barabbas (1893)
Marie Corelli

Barabbas (1950)
Pär Lagerkvist

Barbarous Coast, The (1956)
Ross Macdonald

Barbary Shore (1951)
Norman Mailer

Barchester Towers (1857)
Anthony Trollope

set: Barsetshire
Dr Francis Arabin (dean)
Eleanor Bold
John Bold (surgeon)
Archdeacon Grantly
Rev Septimus Harding
Dr Proudie (Bishop of Barchester)
Mrs Proudie (Dr Proudie's wife)
Mr Quiverful (warden)
Obadiah Slope (chaplain)
Canon Stanhope
Signora Vesey-Neroni

Barfüssele (1856)
Berthold Auerbach

Amrei (orphan)

Barham Downs (1784)
Robert Bage

Barnaby Rudge (1841)
Charles Dickens

set: 1775–80 including Gordon Riots; Maypole Inn
Edward Chester (John's son) (later Sir) John Chester
Solomon Daisy (clerk)
Dennis (Newgate hangman)
Gashford (Lord Gordon's secretary)
Lord George Gordon (riot instigator)
Grip (Barnaby's raven)
John Grueby (Lord Gordon's servant)
Emma Haredale
Geoffrey Haredale (Emma's uncle)
Reuben Haredale (Emma's murdered brother)
Hugh (ostler)
Miggs (Mrs Varden's maid)
Rudge (Barnaby's father)
Barnaby Rudge
Mrs Rudge (Barnaby's mother)
Stagg (blind man)
Simon 'Sim' Tappertit (apprentice)
Dolly Varden
Gabriel Varden (locksmith/Dolly's father)
Mrs Varden (Dolly's mother)
Joe Willet
John Willet (landlord/Joe's father)

Bar of Shadow, A (1952)
Laurens Van Der Post

Barone rampante, Il (1957)
(Baron in the Trees)
Italo Calvino

Barren Ground (1925)
Ellen Glasgow

Jason Greylock
Dorinda Oakley
Nathan Pedlar (storekeeper)

Barrier, The (1973)
Robin Maugham

Barry Lyndon
see ***Luck of Barry Lyndon, The***

Bar Sinister, The (1903)
Richard Harding Davis

Basil (1852)
Wilkie Collins

Basil Seal Rides Again (1963)
Evelyn Waugh

Basil Seal

Bastard, The (1929)
Erskine Caldwell

Bataille de Pharsale, La (1969)
(The Battle of Pharsalus)
Claude Simon

Bath Tangle (1955)
Georgette Heyer

Battle Cry (1953)
Leon Uris

Battleground, The (1902)
Ellen Glasgow

Battle Lost and Won, The (1978)
Olivia Manning

set: Egypt
Guy Pringle
Harriet Pringle (Guy's wife)

Battle of Life, The (1846)
Charles Dickens

Arthur Heathfield (Marion's suitor/Grace's eventual husband)
Doctor Jeddler (philosopher)
Grace Jeddler (Jeddler's daughter)
Marion Jeddler (Jeddler's daughter)
Michael Warden (Marion's eventual husband)

Battle of Pharsalus, The
see ***Bataille de Pharsale, La***

Battle of the Villa Fiorita, The (1963)
Rumer Godden

Battle Surgeon (1944)
Frank Slaughter

Bauern, Bonzen und Bomben (1931)
Hans Fallada

Bauernspiegel, Der (1837)
Jeremias Gotthelf

Baumgartner's Bombay (1988)
Anita Desai

Bay of Noon, The (1970)
Shirley Hazzard

Beachcombers, The (1972)
Helen Cresswell

Béal Bocht, An (1941)
(The Poor Mouth)
Flann O'Brien

Beany-Eye (1935)
David Garnett

Bear Island (1971)
Alistair Maclean
set: Arctic

Bear Raid, The (1976)
Ken Follett

Beastly Beatitudes of Balthazar B, The (1968)
JP Donleavy

Beast Must Die, The (1938)
Nicholas Blake
Nigel Strangeways (detective)

Beasts and Super-Beasts (1914)
coll
Saki

Beauchampe (1842)
William Gilmore Simms

Beauchamp's Career (1876)
George Meredith
Nevil Beauchamp (naval officer)
Renée de Crosnel (Beauchamp's would-be partner)
Jenny Denham (Beauchamp's eventual wife)
Cecilia Halkett (Beauchamp's would-be partner)
Everard Romfrey (Beauchamp's uncle)
Doctor Shrapnel

Beau Geste (1924)
Beau Ideal (1928)
Beau Sabreur (1926)
PC Wren

Beauties and Furies, The (1936)
Christina Stead

Beautiful and Damned, The (1922)
F Scott Fitzgerald

Beautiful Room is Empty, The (1988)
Edmund White

Beautiful Summer, The
see ***Bella estate, La***

Beautiful Years, The (1921)
Henry Williamson

Beauvallet (1929)
Georgette Heyer

Beaux Draps, les (1941)
Louis-Ferdinand Céline

Beaux Quartiers, Les (1936)
Louis Aragon

Bech: a Book (1963)
Bech Is Back (1975)
John Updike

Beckoning Lady, The (1955)
Margery Allingham

Bedford Village (1945)
Hervey Allen

Bedrock (1990)
Lisa Alther

Beds in the East (1959)
Anthony Burgess

Bedtime for Frances (1960)
Russell Hoban

Bee in the Kitchen, A (1983)
HF Ellis

Beekeepers, The (1980)
Peter Redgrove

Beethoven Medal, The (1971)
KM Peyton

Before She Met Me (1982)
Julian Barnes

Before the Bombardment (1926)
Osbert Sitwell

Before the Fact (1932)
Francis Iles

Beggar in Jerusalem, A
see ***Mendiant de Jerusalem, Le***

Beggarman, Thief (1977)
Irwin Shaw

Behind the Mirror (1955)
Robin Maugham

Behold, Here's Poison (1936)
Georgette Heyer

Being Invisible (1997)
Thomas Berger

Being There (1971)
Jerzy Kosinski

Bel-Ami (1885)
Guy de Maupassant
set: Paris
Georges Duroy

Belchamber (1904)
Howard Overing Sturgis

Beleaguered City, A (1880)
Margaret Oliphant

Belinda (1928)
Hilaire Belloc

Belinda (1801)
Maria Edgeworth

Bell, The (1958)
Iris Murdoch
set: Gloucestershire Abbey

Bella (1976)
Jilly Cooper

Bella (1926)
Jean Giraudoux

Bella estate, La (1949)
(The Beautiful Summer)
Cesare Pavese

Bellarosa Connection, The (1989)
Saul Bellow

Belles Images, Les (1966)
Simone de Beauvoir

Bellezza e Unamità (1972)
Riccardo Bacchelli

Bell Family, The (1954)
Noel Streatfeild

Bell Jar, The (1963)
Sylvia Plath

Beloved (1987)
Toni Morrison

Belton Estate, The (1866)
Anthony Trollope
set: Somerset
Clara Amedroz (Amedroz' daughter)
Mr Amedroz (estate owner)
Captain Aylmer (Clara's beloved)
Lady Aylmer (Captain Aylmer's mother)
Will Belton (Clara's eventual husband)

Bend in the River, A (1979)
VS Naipaul

set: Central Africa
Metty
Salim

Bend Sinister (1947)
Vladimir Nabokov

Ben-Hur (a Tale of the Christ) (1880)
Lew Wallace

Judah Ben-Hur
Isas (Messala's wife)
Messala (Ben-Hur's sometime friend)

Benighted (1927)
JB Priestley

Benson Murder Case, The (1926)
SS Van Dine

Philo Vance (detective)

Benton's Row (1954)
Frank Yerby

Bent Twig, The (1915)
Dorothea Frances Fisher

Berge, Meere und Giganten (1924)
Alfred Döblin

Bergroman (1935)
Hermann Broch

Berlin Alexanderplatz (1929)
Alfred Döblin

Berlin Game (1984)
Len Deighton

Berlin Memorandum, The
see ***Quiller Memorandum, The***

Bernard Quesnay (1926)
André Maurois

Berry & Co (1920)
Dornford Yates

Bertie's Escapade (1946) posth
Kenneth Grahame

Bertram Cope's Year (1919)
Henry Blake Fuller

Bertrams, The (1859)
Anthony Trollope

George Bertram
Sir Henry Harcourt
Caroline Waddington (Harcourt's wife)

Bestiaires, Les (1926)
(The Gladiators)
Henry de Montherlant

Best Man to Die, The (1969)
Ruth Rendell

Inspector Reginald Wexford

Beth Book, The (1898)
Sarah Grand

Betrayal, The (1966)
LP Hartley

Betrothed, The (1825)
Walter Scott

set: 12c Welsh Marches
castle: Garde Douloreuse
Damian (Hugo's nephew/Eveline's eventual suitor)
Hugo De Lacy (Constable of Chester)
Eveline Berenger
Prince Gwenwyn

Betrothed, The
see ***Promessi sposi, I***

Betsy, The (1971)
Harold Robbins

Better Sort, The (1903) coll
Henry James

Better World of Reginald Perrin, The (1978)
David Nobbs
Reginald Perrin

Betty Zane (1903)
Zane Grey

Between Life and Death
see ***Entre la vie et la mort***

Between the Acts (1941) posth
Virginia Woolf
set: Poyntz Hall

Bevis, the Story of a Boy (1882)
Richard Jefferies

Beyond Desire (1932)
Sherwood Anderson

Beyond Land's End (1979)
DJ Enright

Beyond the Black Stump (1956)
Nevil Shute

Beyond the Blue Mountains (1948)
Jean Plaidy

Beyond the Glass (1954)
Antonia White

Beyond This Horizon (1948)
Robert A Heinlein

Beyond This Place (1953)
AJ Cronin
set: Tannochbrae (actual Callander)
Dr Cameron
Dr Finlay
Janet (doctors' housekeeper)

BFG, The (1982)
Roald Dahl

Bhowani Junction (1954)
John Masters

Bible in Spain, The (1843)
George Borrow

Bid Me to Live (1960)
Hilda Doolittle

Big as Life (1966)
EL Doctorow

Big Barn, The (1930)
Walter D Edmonds

Big Bounce, The (1969)
Elmore Leonard

Big Fisherman, The (1949)
Lloyd C Douglas

Big Footprints, The (1977)
Hammond Innes

Big Four, The (1927)
Agatha Christie
Hercule Poirot (detective)

Biggest Pig in Barbados, The (1965)
Wolf Mankowitz

Big House, The (1950)
Naomi Mitchison

Big House at Inver, The (1925)
Edith Somerville

Big Kill, The (1951)
Mickey Spillane

Mike Hammer (private eye)

Big Money, The (1936)
John Dos Passos

Big Six, The (1940)
Arthur Ransome

Big Sleep, The (1939)
Raymond Chandler

Philip Marlowe (detective)

Big Story, The (1957)
Morris West

Big Sur (1962)
Jack Kerouac

Big Town, The (1921)
Ring Lardner

Billard um halb zehn (1959)
(Billiards at Half-Past Nine)
Heinrich Böll

Billion-Dollar Brain (1966)
Len Deighton

Harry Palmer (spy)

Billy Bathgate (1989)
EL Doctorow

Billy Budd, Foretopman (1924)
posth
Herman Melville

ship: Indomitable

Billy Budd (sailor)
John Claggart (master-at-arms)
Captain Vere

Billy Bunter of Greyfriars School (1947)
Frank Richards

Johnny Bull (Bunter's school-chum)
Billy Bunter 'The Owl of the Remove'
Bob Cherry (Bunter's school-chum)
Frank Nugent (Bunter's school-chum)
Mr Quelch (schoolmaster)
Hurree Jamset Ram Singh (Bunter's school-chum)

Billy Liar (1959)
Billy Liar on the Moon (1975)
sequel to ***Billy Liar***
Keith Waterhouse

Billy Fisher

Bimbi (1882) coll
Ouida

Bimbo (1990)
Keith Waterhouse

Binodini (1902)
Rabindranath Tagore

Birchwood (1973)
John Banville

Bird Alone (1936)
Sean O'Faolain

Bird in the House, A (1970)
Margaret Laurence

Bird of Dawning, The (1933)
John Masefield

Bird of Night, The (1972)
Susan Hill

Birds, The (1952)
Daphne Du Maurier

Birds Fall Down, The (1966)
Rebecca West

Birds of America (1971)
Mary McCarthy

Birds of the Air, The (1980)
Alice Thomas Ellis

Birds on the Trees, The (1970)
Nina Bawden

Birdy (1979)
William Wharton

Birthday Party, The (1938)
CHB Kitchin

Birth of a Hero (1951)
Herbert Gold

Birthright (1921)
TS Stribling

Birthstone (1980)
DM Thomas

Bitch, The (1979)
Jackie Collins

Bit of a Do, A (1986)
David Nobbs

Bitter Creek (1939)
James Boyd

Bitter Lotus (1945)
Louis Bromfield

Black Abbot, The (1926)
Edgar Wallace

Black Arrow, The (1888)
RL Stevenson
set: The Wars of the Roses

Black As He's Painted (1974)
Ngaio Marsh
Inspector Roderick Alleyn

Black Baroness, The (1940)
Dennis Wheatley
Gregory Sallust (agent)

Black Beauty (1877)
Anna Sewell
Black Beauty (horse)
Squire Gordon (Black Beauty's sometime owner)
Justice (horse)

Blackboard Jungle, The (1954)
Ed McBain

Black Book: an Agon, The (1938)
Laurence Durrell

Black Bryony (1923)
TF Powys

Black Cauldron, The (1965)
Lloyd Alexander
set: Prydain
Taran

Black Cloud, The (1957)
Fred Hoyle

Black Diamonds (1870)
Mór Jókai

Black Dwarf, The (1816)
Walter Scott

Elshender the Recluse (later revealed as Sir Edward Manley)

Black Easter of Faust Aleph Null (1968)
James Blish

Blackerchief Dick (1921)
Margery Allingham

Black Hearts in Battersea (1964)
Joan Aiken

Blackheath Poisonings, The (1978)
Julian Symons

Black Ivory (1873)
RM Ballantyne

Black Marsden (1972)
Wilson Harris

Black Mischief (1932)
Evelyn Waugh

Black Moth, The (1921)
Georgette Heyer

Black Narcissus (1939)
Rumer Godden

set: Himalayas

Black-Out in Gretley (1942)
JB Priestley

Black Oxen, The (1923)
Gertrude Atherton

Black Pearl, The (1988)
Ian McEwan

Black Prince, The (1972)
Iris Murdoch

Black Robe, The (1985)
Brian Moore

Black Snow (1937)
Mikhail Bulgakov

Black Sparta (1928) coll
Naomi Mitchison

Black Spring (1936)
Henry Miller

Black Sunday (1975)
Thomas Harris

Black Tide, The (1982)
Hammond Innes

Black Tower, The (1975)
PD James

Adam Dalgliesh (detective)

Black Tulip, The
see ***Tulipe noire, La***

Blame the Dead (1973)
Gavin Lyall

Blaming (1976) posth
Elizabeth Taylor

Blanche, ou L'Oubli (1967)
Louis Aragon

Blancs et les bleus, les (1868)
(The Whites and the Blues)
Alexandre Dumas (père)

Bland Beginning (1949)
Julian Symons

Bleak House (1853)
Charles Dickens

set: Court of Chancery, London (Jarndyce v Jarndyce)
Malta Bagnet (Bagnet's daughter)
Matthew Bagnet (bassoonist)
Mrs Bagnet (Bagnet's wife)
Quebec Bagnet (Bagnet's daughter)
Woolwich Bagnet (Bagnet's son)
Inspector Bucket (detective)
Richard Carstone (Ada's cousin)
Rev Chadband (clergyman)
Ada Clare (Richard's eventual wife)
Lady Dedlock (Dedlock's wife)
Sir Leicester Dedlock
Miss Flite (eccentric/bird-owner)
Guppy (lawyer's clerk)
Guster (Snagsby's maidservant)
Captain Hawdon (scrivener)
Hortense (Lady Dedlock's maid)
John Jarndyce (Richard & Ada's guardian)
Jellyby
Mrs Jellyby (Jellyby's wife)
Jo (crossing-sweeper)
Krook (rag-and-bone man)
Mr Pardiggle (philanthropist)
Mrs Pardiggle (Pardiggle's wife)
Harold Skimpole
Mrs Skimpole (Skimpole's wife)
Snagsby (law stationer)
Mrs Snagsby (Snagsby's wife)
Esther Summerson (part-narrator)
Tulkinghorn (lawyer)
Turveydrop (dance-school proprietor)
Prince Turveydrop (Turveydrop's son)
Vholes (Richard carstone's solicitor)
Dr Allan Woodcourt (Esther's eventual husband)

Blechtrommel, Die (1959)
(The Tin Drum)
Günther Grass

Bleeding heart, The (1980)
Marilyn French

Blé en herbe, Le (1923)
Colette

Blendung, Die (1935)
Elias Canetti

Peter Kien

Blessing, The (1951)
Nancy Mitford

Radlett family

Bless This House (1968)
Norah Lofts

Blind Corner (1927)
Dornford Yates

Blind Date (1977)
Jerzy Kosinski

Blinder, The (1966)
Barry Hines

Blind Love (1890) posth
Wilkie Collins

Blindness (1926)
Henry Green

Bliss (1981)
Peter Carey

Bliss (1920)
Katherine Mansfield

Blithedale Romance, The (1852)
Nathaniel Hawthorne

set: Concord; Boston (USA)
Miles Coverdale (narrator)
Silas Forster (farmer)
Zenobia Forster (Forster's wife)
Hollingsworth (ex-blacksmit

Blizzard, The (1854)
Sergei Timofeevich Aksakov

Blood and Guts in High School (1984)
Kathy Acker

Blood and Sand (1908)
Vicente Blasco Ibañez

Blood Feud (1977)
Rosemary Sutcliff

Bloodhunt (1952)
Neil Gunn

Blooding, The (1989)
Joseph Wambaugh

Bloodline (1977)
Sidney Sheldon

Blood of the Martyrs, The (1939)
Naomi Mitchison

Bloodshed (1976)
Cynthia Ozick

Bloodsmoor Romance, A (1982)
Joyce Carol Oates

Bloody Chasm, The (1881)
John William De Forest

Bloody Sunrise (1965)
Mickey Spillane

Tiger Mann

Blossom Like the Rose (1970)
Norah Lofts

Blott on the Landscape (1975)
Tom Sharpe

Blubber (1974)
Judy Blume

Bluebeard (1987)
Kurt Vonnegut

Blue Camellia (1957)
Frances Parkinson Keyes

Blue Hammer, The (1976)
Ross MacDonald

Blue Hawk, The (1976)
Peter Dickinson

Blue Lagoon, The (1908)
Henry Stacpoole

set: tropical island
Dick
Emmeline (Dick's cousin)

Blue Movie (1970)
Terry Southern

Bluest Eye, The (1970)
Toni Morrison

Blue Voyage (1927)
Conrad Aiken

Blush, The (1958) coll
Elizabeth Taylor

Boarding House, The (1965)
William Trevor

Boat, The (1949)
LP Hartley

Bobbsey Twins (1904)
Laura Lee Hope
Bert and Nan Bobbsey (twins)
Freddie and Flossie Bobbsey (twins)

Bödeln (1933)
(The Hangman)
Pär Lagerkvist

Bodily Harm (1982)
Margaret Atwood

Body, The (1949)
William Sansom

Body in the Library, The (1942)
Agatha Christie
Miss Jane Marple (amateur sleuth)

Body Lovers, The (1967)
Mickey Spillane
Mike Hammer (private eye)

Body's Rapture, The
see ***Dieu des corps, Les***

Bolt (1986)
Dick Francis

Bon Apotre, Le (1923)
(The Good Apostle)
Philippe Soupault

Bonaventure (1888)
George Washington Cable

Bondman, The (1890)
Hall Caine

Bone Crack (1971)
Dick Francis

Bone People, The (1984)
Keri Hulme

Bones of Contention (1936) coll
Frank O'Connor

Bonfire (1933)
Dorothea Frances Fisher

Bonfire of the Vanities, The (1987)
Tom Wolfe

Bonheur et le salut, Le (1961)
Luc Estang

Bonjour Tristesse (1954)
Françoise Sagan

Book and the Brotherhood, The (1987)
Iris Murdoch

Book Class, The (1984)
Louis Auchinloss

Book of Common Prayer, A (1977)
Joan Didion
Charlotte Douglas

Book of Daniel, The (1971)
EL Doctorow

Book of Evidence, The (1989)
John Banville

Book of Three, The (1964)
Lloyd Alexander
set: Prydain
Hen Wen (pig)
Taran

Book of Wonder, The (1912)
Edward Dunsany

Boon Companions, The (1974)
June Drummond

Border and Bastille (1863)
George Alfred Lawrence

Border Country (1960)
Raymond Williams

Born in Exile (1892)
George Gissing

Borrowers, The (1952)
Borrowers Afield, The (1955)
Borrowers Afloat, The (1959)
Borrowers Aloft, The (1961)
Borrowers Avenged, The (1982)
Mary Norton
Arrietty ('being')
Homily ('being')
Pod ('being')

Bosnian Story (1945)
Ivo Andric

Boston (1928)
Upton Sinclair

Bostonians, The (1886)
Henry James
set: Boston, USA
Miss Birdseye (philanthropist)
Olive Chancellor (Basil's cousin)
Mrs Luna (Olive's sister)
Matthias Pardon (reporter)
Dr Prance (physician)
Basil Ransom (lawyer)
Selah Tarrant (charlatan)
Verena Tarrant (Selah's daughter)

Boswell (1964)
Stanley Elkin

Bottle Factory Outing, The (1974)
Beryl Bainbridge

Boule-de-Suif (1880)
Guy de Maupassant
Boule-de-Suif (prostitute)

Bounty Hunters, The (1953)
Elmore Leonard

Bouquet of Barbed Wire, A (1969)
Andrea Newman

Bourgeois, The
see ***Untertan, Der***

Bourne Identity, The (1980)
Bourne Supremacy, The (1986)
Bourne Ultimatum, The (1990)
Robert Ludlum

Bouvard et Pécuchet (1881) posth unf
Gustave Flaubert

Box of Delights, The (1935)
John Masefield
Kay Harker (orphan)
Cole Hawlings
Nibbins (cat)
Sir Theopompus (Kay's guardian)

Boy (1984)
Roald Dahl

Boy (1931)
James Hanley

Boyds of Black River, The (1953)
Walter D Edmonds

Boy Hunters, The (1852)
Mayne Reid

Boys, The
see ***Garçons, Les***

Boys and Girls Come Out to Play (1949)
Nigel Dennis

Boys and Girls Together (1964)
William Goldman

Boy's Own Story, A (1982)
Edmund White

Boy Tar (1859)
Mayne Reid

Bracebridge Hall (1822) coll
Washington Irving

Brain (1981)
Robin Cook

Brass Bottle, The (1900)
F Anstey

Professor Anthony Futvoye (archaeologist)
Sylvia Futvoye (Futvoye's daughter)

Brass Check, The (1919)
Upton Sinclair

Brass Cupcake, The (1950)
John D MacDonald

Brat Farrar (1949)
Josephine Tey

Brave New World (1932)
Aldous Huxley

Lenina Crowne
Bernard Marx
Mustapha Mond (world controller)

Brave New World Revisited (1958)
Aldous Huxley

Bravest of the Brave (1887)
GA Henty

Bravo, The (1831)
James Fenimore Cooper

Brazen Head, The (1956)
John Cowper Powys

Brazzaville Beach (1990)
William Boyd

Bread and Play
see ***Brot und Spiele***

Bread and Wine
see ***Pane e vino***

Bread upon the Waters (1981)
Irwin Shaw

Bread-Winners, The (1884)
John Hay

Breakfast at Tiffany's (1958)
Truman Capote

Holly Golightly

Breakfast of Champions (1964)
Kurt Vonnegut

Breakheart Pass (1974)
Alistair Maclean
set: late 19c USA

Breaking Point, The (1959)
Daphne Du Maurier

Breaking Strain, The (1967)
John Masters

Breakthrough, The (1966)
Daphne Du Maurier

Breast, The (1972)
Philip Roth

Breast Stroke (1983)
Molly Parkin

Breath of Air, A (1950)
Rumer Godden

Brekkukotsannáll (1957)
(The Fish Can Sing)
Halldór Laxness

Brickfield, The (1964)
LP Hartley

Bricks without Straw (1880)
Albion W Tourgée

Bridal Canopy, The (1922)
SY Agnon
set: 19c Galicia

Bride of Lammermoor, The (1819)
Walter Scott
set: 17c; Wolf's Crag (ruined tower)
Lady Ashton (Sir William's wife)
Lucy Ashton (Sir William's daughter)
Sir William Ashton (lawyer)
Caleb Balderstone (Ravenswood's butler)
Laird of Bucklaw (Lucy's [brief] husband)
Lord Ravenswood

Bride of Pendorric (1963)
Jean Plaidy

Brideshead Revisited (1945)
Evelyn Waugh
house: Brideshead
Sebastian Flyte
Lady Marchmain
Lord Marchmain
Charles Ryder (narrator)

Bridge, The (1986)
Iain Banks

Bridge of San Luis Rey, The (1927)
Thornton Wilder
set: Peru

Bridge on the Drina, The (1945)
Ivo Andric

Bridge over the River Kwai, The (1952)
Pierre Boulle

Bridges at Toko-Ri, The (1953)
James A Michener

Briefing for a Descent into Hell (1971)
Doris Lessing

Brigadier Gerard
see ***Exploits of Brigadier Gerard, The***

Bright Day (1946)
JB Priestley

Brightfount Diaries, The (1955)
Brian W Aldiss

Bright Metal (1928)
TS Stribling

Brighton Belle, The (1968)
Francis King

Brighton Rock (1938)
Graham Greene

set: Brighton
Colleoni (gang leader)
Ida (Pinkie's acquaintance)
Pinkie (teenage criminal)
Rose (waitress)

Bright Pavilions (1940)
Hugh Walpole

Brigitta (1844)
Adalbert Stifter

Brimming Cup, The (1921)
Dorothea Frances Fisher

Bring Larks and Heroes (1967)
Thomas Keneally

British Museum Is Falling Down, The (1965)
David Lodge

Brittle Glass, The (1942)
Norah Lofts

Broken Journey (1932)
Morley Callaghan

Broken Penny, The (1953)
Julian Symons

Brolga (1948) posth
Joseph Furphy

Brook Evans (1928)
Susan Glaspell

Brook Kerith, The (A Syrian Story) (1916)
George Moore

set: Biblical times
Joseph of Arimathea

Broom Square, The (1896)
Sabine Baring-Gould

Brot der frühen Jahre, Das (1955)
Heinrich Böll

Brother of Daphne, The (1914)
Dornford Yates

Brothers (1986)
William Goldman

Brothers, The (1932)
LAG Strong

Brothers and Sisters (1929)
Ivy Compton-Burnett

Brothers Karamazov, The (1880)
Fyodor Dostoevsky

Karamazov (brothers' father)
Alyosha Karamazov (brother)
Dmitri Karamazov (brother)
Ivan Karamazov (brother)
Smerdyakov Karamazov (half-brother)

Brother's Tale (1980)
Stan Barstow

Brot und Spiele (1959)
(Bread and Play)
Siegfried Lenz

Brown on Resolution (1929)
CS Forester

Bruder Lucifer (1932)
Stefan Andres

Bruno's Dream (1969)
Iris Murdoch

Bucket Shop, The (1968)
Keith Waterhouse

Buckingham Palace Connection, The (1978)
Ted Willis

Buddenbrooks (1901)
Thomas Mann

set: North German city (actual Lübeck)
Buddenbrook family
Hanno family

Buffalo Girls (1990)
Larry McMurty

Bug-Jargal (1826)
Victor Hugo

Build-Up, The (1952)
William Carlos Williams

Bulldog Drummond (1920)
Sapper

Hugh 'Bulldog' Drummond (army officer)
Carl Peterson (Drummond's arch-enemy)

Bullet Park (1969)
John Cheever

Bull from the Sea, The (1962)
Mary Renault

Bunduki (1975)
JT Edson

Burger's Daughter (1979)
Nadine Gordimer

Burmese Days (1934)
Geworge Orwell

Burn, The (1991) coll
James Kelman

Burning Cactus, The (1936) coll
Stephen Spender

Burning Daylight (1910)
Jack London

Burnt Child, A (1948)
Stig Dagerman

Burnt-Out Case, A (1961)
Graham Greene

set: Belgian Congo
Doctor Colin (leper doctor)
Monsieur Querry (architect)

Busconductor Hines, The (1984)
James Kelman

Busman's Honeymoon (1937)
Dorothy L Sayers

Bunter (Wimsey's servant)
Lord Peter Wimsey (amateur detective)

Butcher's Broom (1934)
Neil Gunn

But Gentlemen Marry Brunettes (1928)
Anita Loos

Butt, Der (1977)
(The Flounder)
Günther Grass

Butterfield 8 (1935)
John O'Hara

Butterfly House (1912)
Mary E Freeman

But Who Wakes the Burglar? (1940)
Peter De Vries

By Celia's Arbour (1878)
Walter Besant

Bye-Bye, Blackbird (1971)
Anita Desai

By Love Possessed (1957)
James Gould Cozzens

Bylow Hill (1902)
George Washington Cable

By-Pass Control, The (1966)
Mickey Spillane

Tiger Mann

By the Green of the Spring (1981)
John Masters

By the Pricking of My Thumbs (1968)
Agatha Christie

By the Shores of Silver Lake (1939)
Laura Ingalls Wilder

C

Cabala (1926)
Thornton Wilder

Cabanis (1832)
Willibald Alexis

Cabbages and Kings (1904) coll
O Henry

Cabin, The (1898)
Vicente Blasco Ibañez

Cadillac Jack (1982)
Larry McMurty

Caesar's Column (1891)
Ignatius Donnelly

Caged Lion, The (1870)
Charlotte M Yonge

Caine Mutiny, The (1951)
Herman Wouk

set: World War II
ship: Caine (minesweeper)
Captain Queeg

Cakes and Ale (1930)
W Somerset Maugham

Edward Driffield
Rosie Driffield (barmaid/Edward's 1st wife)
Alroy Kear (novelist)

Cal (1983)
Bernard MacLaverty

Calabrian Summer (1980)
Ian McEwan

Caleb Field (1851)
Margaret Oliphant

Caleb Williams (1794)
William Godwin

Californians, The (1935)
Gertrude Atherton

Call of the Wild (1903)
Jack London

set: Klondike
Buck (dog)
Spitz (dog)
John Thornton (prospector)

Camberwell Beauty, The (1974) coll
VS Pritchett

Cambio de piel (1967)
(A Change of Skin)
Carlos Fuentes

Came a Cavalier (1948)
Frances Parkinson Keyes

Camels Are Coming, The (1932)
WE Johns

Major James 'Biggles' Bigglesworth
Flying-officer Ginger Hebblethwaite
Captain Algernon 'Algy' Lacy

Camilla (or a Picture of Youth) (1796)
Fanny Burney

Camilla Tyrold

Camomile Lawn, The (1984)
Mary Wesley

Campbell's Kingdom (1952)
Hammond Innes

set: Rocky Mountains, USA
Bruce Campbell Wetheral

Canal Dreams (1989)
Iain Banks

Cancer Ward (1968–9) 2 vol
Alexander Solzhenitsyn

Candide (1759)
Voltaire

set: 1755 during & after Lisbon earthquake
Candide
Cunégonde (Baron's daughter/Candide's lover)
Dr Pangloss (philosopher)
Baron Thunder-Ten-Tronckh

Candle for St Jude (1980)
Rumer Godden

Candy (1958)
Terry Southern

Canes in the Wind
see ***Canne al vento***

Canne al vento (1913)
(Canes in the Wind)
Grazia Deledda

Cannery Row (1944)
John Steinbeck

Doc

Cannibal Galaxy, The (1983)
Cynthia Ozick

Cannibals and Missionaries (1980)
Mary McCarthy

Canticle for Leibowitz, A (1960)
Walter Miller

Can You Forgive her? (1865)
Anthony Trollope

Burgo Fitzgerald (Glencora's former sweetheart)
Lady Glencora (Alice's friend)
Mrs Greenow (Alice's aunt)
John Grey (Alice's husband)
Plantagent Palliser (Glencora's husband)
Alice Vavasor
George Vavasor (Alice's cousin)

Capel Sion (1916) coll
Caradoc Evans

Capital (1975)
Maureen Duffy

Caprice (1917)
Ronald Firbank

Captain and the Enemy, The (1988)
Grahame Greene

Captain Bottell (1933)
James Hanley

Captain Hornblower RN (1939)
CS Forester

Horatio Hornblower

Captain Macklin (1902)
Richard Harding Davis

Captain Margaret (1908)
John Masefield

Captain of the Gray-Horse Troop, The (1902)
Hamlin Garland

Captain Rebel (1956)
Frank Yerby

Captains Courageous (or Story of the Grand Banks) (1897)
Rudyard Kipling

set: off Massachusetts, USA
Harvey Cheyne

Captain Singleton (1720)
Daniel Defoe

Captain's Lady (1947)
DK Broster

Captive and the Free, The (1959) posth unf
Joyce Cary

Caracole (1985)
Edmund White

Caravans (1963)
James A Michener

Caravan to Vaccares (1970)
Alistair Maclean

set: Camargue, France

Card, The (1911)
Arnold Bennett

Cardinal of the Kremlin, The (1988)
Tom Clancy

Cardinal's Snuff-Box, The (1900)
Henry Harland

Cards of Identity (1955)
Nigel Dennis

Cards on the Table (1936)
Agatha Christie

Career in C Major (1943)
James M Cain

Career of David Noble, The (1921)
Frances Parkinson Keyes

Caribbean (1979)
James A Michener

Caribbean Mystery, A (1964)
Agatha Christie

Miss Jane Marple (amateur sleuth)

Carnal Island, The (1970)
Roy Fuller

Carnival (1912)
Compton MacKenzie

Carpenter's Gothic (1985)
William Gaddis

Carpetbaggers, The (1961)
Harold Robbins

Jonas Cord (tycoon)

Carr (1929)
Phyllis Bentley

Carrie (1973)
Stephen King

Carrie's War (1973)
Nina Bawden
set: 1940s Wales

Carry On, Jeeves! (1925) coll
PG Wodehouse

Reginald Jeeves (Wooster's valet)
Bertie Wooster

Carved Lions, The (1895)
Mary Louisa Molesworth

Casanova (1976)
John Masters

Casa verde, La (1966)
(The Green House)
Mario Vargas Llosa

Case Book of Sherlock Holmes, The (1927) coll
Arthur Conan Doyle

set: 221b Baker Street, London
Mycroft Holmes (Holmes' brother)
Sherlock Holmes (detective)
Mrs Hudson (Holmes' housekeeper)
Inspector Lestrade (Scotland Yard officer)
Professor James Moriarty (Holmes' arch-enemy)
Dr John Watson (Holmes' companion)

Case Is Altered, The (1932)
William Plomer

Case of Charles Dexter Ward, The (1928)
HP Lovecraft

Case of Conscience, A (1958)
James Blish

Case of the Abominable Snowman, The (1941)
Nicholas Blake

Nigel Strangeways (detective)

Case of the Late Pig, The (1958)
Margery Allingham

Albert Campion (detective)

Case of the Poisoned Éclairs, The (1979)
Howard Fast

Case of the Velvet Claws, The (1933)
Erle Stanley Gardner

Paul Drake (private detective)
Perry Mason (trial lawyer)
Della Street (Mason's secretary)

Cashel Byron's Profession (1886)
GB Shaw

Cashelmara (1974)
Susan Howatch

Casino Royale (1953)
Ian Fleming

James Bond '007' (spy)
M (Bond's boss)
Miss Moneypenny (M's secretary)

Cask of Amontillado, The (1846)
Edgar Allan Poe

Caspar Hauser (1908)
Jakob Wassermann

Cassidy (1986)
Morris West

Cass Timberlane (1945)
Sinclair Lewis

Castello di Udine, Il (1934)
(The Castle of Udine)
Carlo Emilio Gadda

Castle, The
see ***Schloss, Das***

Castle Corner (1938)
Joyce Cary

Castle Dangerous (1831)
Walter Scott

set: 1306; Douglas Castle
Sir John De Walton

Castle Gay (1926)
John Buchan

Dick MacCunn

Castle Inn, The (1898)
Stanley John Weyman

Castle of Llyr, The (1966)
Lloyd Alexander

set: Prydain
Taran

Castle of Otranto, The (A Gothic Story) (1764)
Horace Walpole

set: 13c
Hippolita (Manfred's wife)
Prince Manfred

Castle of Udine, The
see ***Castello di Udine, Il***

Castle Rackrent (1800)
Maria Edgeworth

set: 18c Ireland
Sir Condy Rackrent (Sir Murtagh's son)
Sir Kit Rackrent (Sir Murtagh's son)
Sir Murtagh Rackrent (Sir Patrick's son)
Sir Patrick Rackrent
Jason Quirk (Thady's son)
Thady Quirk (narrator)

Castle Richmond (1860)
Anthony Trollope

set: Ireland
Herbert Fitzgerald
Owen Fitzgerald (Herbert's brother)

Castles of Athlin and Dunbayne, The (1789)
Ann Radcliffe

Casualties of Peace (1966)
Edna O'Brien

Cat Among the Pigeons (1959)
Agatha Christie

Hercule Poirot (detective)

Cat and Mouse
see ***Katz und Maus***

Cat and Shakespeare, The (1965)
Raja Rao

Cat Chaser (1982)
Elmore Leonard

Catcher in the Rye, The (1951)
JD Salinger

Holden Caulfield
Phoebe Caulfield (Holden's sister)

Catch-22 (1961)
Joseph Heller

set: World War II Mediterranean
Doc Daneeka
Orr (pilot)
Yossarian (pilot)

Cathedral (1934)
TS Stribling

Cathedral, The (1922)
Hugh Walpole

Cathédrale, La (1898)
Joris-Karl Huysmans

Durtal

Catherine (1839)
William Makepeace Thackeray

basis: real life murderess
Catherine Hayes (executed 1726)

Catherine Herself (1920)
James Hilton

Catholics (1972)
Brian Moore

Catmint (1961)
Compton MacKenzie

Catriona (1893)
sequel to ***Kidnapped***
RL Stevenson

David Balfour
Alan Breck (Balfour's companion)
Catriona Drummond (Balfour's beloved)

Cats' Arabian Nights, The (1881)
Abby Morton Diaz

Cat's Cradle (1963)
Kurt Vonnegut

Cat's Eye (1989)
Margaret Atwood

Caught (1943)
Henry Green

Cavaliere inesistente (1959)
(The Non-Existent Knight)
Italo Calvino

Cavalleria rusticana (1883)
(Rustic Chivalry)
Giovanni Verga

Cavanagh, Forest Ranger (1910)
Hamlin Garland

Cave, The (1950)
Richard Church

Cave, The (1959)
Robert Penn Warren

Caves du Vatican, Les (1914)
André Gide

Caves of Steel, The (1954)
Isaac Asimov

Cécile (1844)
Alexandre Dumas (père)

Cécile (1887)
Theodor Fontane

Cecilia (or Memoirs of an Heiress) (1782)
Fanny Burney

Cecilia Beverley

Celebrity, The (1898)
Winston Churchill

Celestina (1791)
Charlotte Smith

Célibataires, Les (1934)
(The Bachelors)
Henry de Montherlant

Celui qui ne m'accompagnait pas (1953)
Maurice Blanchot

Cement Garden, The (1978)
Ian McEwan

Cenere (1903)
(Ashes)
Grazia Deledda

Centaur, The (1963)
John Updike

Centennial (1974)
James A Michener

Cent Jours (1947)
(A Hundred Days)
Jacques Audiberti

Ce qui ne meurt pas (1884)
Jules-Amédée Barbey D'Aurevilly

Cercle de Famille, Le (1932)
(The Family Circle)
André Maurois

Certain People (1930)
Edith Wharton

Certain Smile, A
see ***Certain Sourire, Un***

Certain Sourire, Un (1956)
(A Certain Smile)
Françoise Sagan

Chad Hanna (1940)
Walter D Edmonds

set: circus

Chainbearer, The (1845)
James Fenimore Cooper

Andries Coejemans (surveyor, known as Chainbearer)
Anneke Littlepage (Cornelius' wife)
Cornelius Littlepage
Mordaunt Littlepage (Cornelius' son)

Chain of Voices, A (1982)
André Brink

Chair Molle (1885)
Paul Adam

Chalk Face (1924)
Waldo Frank

Challenge, The (1923)
Vita Sackville-West

Chamade, La (1966)
Françoise Sagan

Champion of Virtue, The (1777)
Clara Reeve

Chance (1914)
Joseph Conrad
Flora De Barral (heiress)
Marlow (narrator)

Chancer, A (1985)
James Kelman

Chances (1981)
Jackie Collins

Change (1987)
Maureen Duffy

Change and Decay in All Around I See (1978)
Allan Massie

Change for the Better, A (1969)
Susan Hill

Change Here for Babylon (1956)
Nina Bawden

Change of Skin, A
see ***Cambio de piel***

Changes (1987)
Danielle Steel

Changing Places (1975)
David Lodge
Philip Swallow (professor)
Morris Zapp (US academic)

Changeing the Past (1989)
Thomas Berger

Channings, The (1862)
Ellen Wood

Chant of Jimmy Blacksmith, The (1972)
Thomas Keneally

Chaos et la nuit, Le (1965)
(The Chaos and the Night)
Henry de Montherlant

Chaplain of the Fleet, The (1881)
Walter Besant

Chapter House Dune (1985)
Frank Herbert

Chaque homme dans sa nuit (1960)
(Every Man in His Night)
Julien Green

Charade (1947)
John Mortimer

Charioteer, The (1953)
Mary Renault

Charlemont (1856)
William Gilmore Simms

Charles O'Malley (1841)
Charles Lever

Charley Is My Darling (1940)
Joyce Cary

Charlie and the Chocolate Factory (1964)
Roald Dahl

Charlie Buckett
Willy Wonka (factory owner)

Charlie and the Great Glass Elevator (1972)
Roald Dahl

Charlie Buckett

Charlotte (1972)
Norah Lofts

Charmed Life, A (1955)
Mary McCarthy

Charterhouse of Parma, The
see ***Chartreuse de Parme, Le***

Chartreuse de Parme, Le (1839)
(The Charterhouse of Parma)
Stendhal

set: Italy
Fabrice Del Dongo

Charwoman's Daughter, The (1911)
James Stephens

Chatterton (1987)
Peter Ackroyd

Checkmate (1871)
Sheridan Le Fanu

Chedworth (1944)
RC Sherriff

Chelkash (1895)
Maxim Gorky

Chelkash (smuggler)

Chelsea Murders, The (1978)
Lionel Davidson

Chemins de la Liberté, Les (1947–50) 3 vol
(The Roads to Freedom)
Jean-Paul Sartre

set: World War II
Mathieu Delarue (teacher)

Chequer Board, The (1947)
Nevil Shute

Chéri (1920)
Colette

Chess Players, The (1961)
Frances Parkinson Keyes

Chevalier des Touches, Le (1864)
Jules-Amédée Barbey D'Aurevilly

Chevalier d'Harmenthal, Le (1843)
Alexandre Dumas (père)

Chiendent, Le (1933)
(The Obstacle)
Raymond Queneau

Chike and the River (1966)
Chinua Achebe

Childermass, The (1928)
Wyndham Lewis

Childhood (1913)
Maxim Gorky

Childhood's End (1953)
Arthur C Clarke

Childhood Years of Bagrov Grandson, The (1858)
Sergei Timofeevich Aksakov

Child in the House, The (1878)
Walter Pater

Childlike Life of the Black tarantula: Some Lives of Murderesses, The (1975)
Kathy Acker

Child of the Jago, A (1896)
Arthur Morrison

set: London's East End
Dicky Perrot (street urchin)

Child Possessed, A (1964)
RC Hutchinson

Child prodigy, The
see ***Wunderkind, Das***

Children, The (1935)
Howard Fast

Children, The (1928)
Edith Wharton

Children and Others (1965)
James Gould Cozzens

Children at the Gate, The (1964)
posth
Edward Lewis Wallant

Children of Ananse, The (1968)
Peggy Appiah

Ananse (spider)

Children of Dune (1976)
Frank Herbert

Baron Vladimir Harkonnen

Children of Dynmouth, The (1976)
William Trevor

Children of Filth, The
see ***Enfants du limon, Les***

Children of Gibeon (1886)
Walter Besant

Children of Kaywana (1952)
Edgar Mittelholzer

Children of Primrose Lane, The (1941)
Noel Streatfeild

Children of Tender Years (1985)
Ted Allbeury

Children of the Castle, The (1890)
Mary Louisa Molesworth

Children of the Ghetto (1892)
Israel Zangwill

Children of the Lens (1954)
EE 'Doc' Smith

Children of the Mist (1898)
Eden Phillpotts

Children of the New Forest (1847)
Frederick Marryat

set: English Civil War
Jacob Armitage (forester)
Alice Beverley (orphan/Edward's sister)
Edith Beverley (orphan/Edward's sister)
Edward Beverley (orphan)

Humphrey Beverley (orphan/Edward's brother)
Patience Heatherstone (Edward's eventual wife)
Pablo (gipsy)

Children of the Rose, The (1975)
Elaine Feinstein

Child Royal (1937)
DK Broster

Child Wife, The (1853)
Mayne Reid

Chimera (1974)
John Barth

Chimes, The (1844)
Charles Dickens

Alderman Cute
Richard (Meg's fiancé)
Meg Veck (Toby's daughter)
Toby Veck (porter)

China Court (1961)
Rumer Godden

China Governess, The (1963)
Margery Allingham
Albert Campion (detective)

Chinese Love Pavilion, The (1960)
Paul Scott

Chinese Puzzle (1935)
Rumer Godden

Chinese Widow, The (1975)
James Leasor

Chippinge (1906)
Stanley John Weyman

Chita (1889)
Lafcadio Hearn

Chitty-Chitty-Bang-Bang (1964)
Ian Fleming

Caractacus Potts (eccentric inventor)

Chocky (1968)
John Wyndham

Choice of Enemies, A (1971)
Ted Allbeury

Choice of Enemies, A (1984)
George V Higgins

Choice of Enemies, A (1957)
Mordecai Richler

Choirboys, The (1975)
Joseph Wambaugh

Choir Invisible, The (1897)
James Lane Allen

John Gray (schoolmaster)

Chouans, Les (1829)
Honoré de Balzac

Christian, The (1897)
Hall Caine

Christianity at the Glacier
see ***Kristnihald undir Jökli***

Christie Johnstone (1853)
Charles Reade

Christine (1983)
Stephen King

Christmas Carol, A (1843)
Charles Dickens
Bob Cratchit (Scrooge's clerk)
'Tiny' Tim Cratchit (Bob's son)
Marley (ghost/Scrooge's deceased partner)
Ebenezer Scrooge (miser)

Christmas Mouse, The (1973)
Miss Read

Christmas Pudding (1932)
Nancy Mitford

Christ Recrucified (1954)
Nikos Kazantzakis

Christy Malry's Own Double-Entry (1973)
BS Johnson

Chronicle of a Death Foretold
see ***Crónica de una muerte anunciada***

Chronicle of Ancient Sunlight, A (1951–69) 15 vol
Henry Williamson
Phillip Maddison (writer)

Chronicles of Clovis, The (1911) coll
Saki

Chronicles of Count Antonio, The (1895)
Anthony Hope

Chronique des Pasquier (1933–45) 10 vol
(The Pasquier Chronicles)
Georges Duhamel
Raymond Pasquier

Chronique du règne de Charles IX (1829)
Prosper Mérimée

Chrysalids, The (1955)
John Wyndham

Chthon (1967)
Piers Anthony

Chute, La (1956)
(The Fall)
Albert Camus

Cider House Rules, The (1985)
John Irving
Wilbur Larch (doctor)
Homer Wells (orphan)

Cider with Rosie (1959)
Laurie Lee
set: 1920s Cotswolds

Cien años de soledad (1967)
(One Hundred Years of Solitude)
Gabriel García Márquez
set: Macondo [village]
Buendía family

Cimarron 91929)
Edna Ferber

Cinq-Mars (1826)
Alfred de Vigny
Marquis de Cinq-Mars
Marion Delorme (Cinq-Mars' mistress)
Cardinal de Richelieu

Cinq Semains en ballon (1863)
(Five Weeks in a Balloon)
Jules Verne

Ciociara, La (1957)
(Two Women)
Alberto Moravia

Circle, The (1970)
Elaine Feinstein

Circle of Friends (1990)
Maeve Binchy

Circles of Deceit (1987)
Nina Bawden

Circuit Rider, The (1874)
Edward Eggleston

Circus (1975)
Alistair Maclean

Circus Is Coming, The (1938)
Noel Streatfeild

Citadel, The (1937)
AJ Cronin

Cities of the Interior (1959)
Anaïs Nin

Cities of the Red Night (1981)
William Burroughs

Citizens (1940)
Meyer Levin

Città invisibili, Le (1972)
(Invisible Cities)
Italo Calvino

City and the Pillar, The (1948)
Gore Vidal

City and the Stars, The (1956)
Arthur C Clarke

City Block (1922)
Waldo Frank

City Boy, The (1948)
Herman Wouk

City Conversation
see ***Stadtgespräch***

City of Illusions (1967)
Ursula Le Guin

City of Spades (1957)
Colin MacInnes

City of the Discreet, The (1905)
Pia Baroja

City on a Hill, A (1975)
George V Higgins

City Primeval (1980)
Elmore Leonard

Civil to Strangers (1987) posth
Barbara Pym

Claire Drummer (1929)
VS Pritchett

Clan of the Cave Bear, The (1980)
Jean M Auel

Clara Howard (1801)
Charles Brockden Brown

Clara Vaughan (1864)
RD Blackmore

Clare Lennox (1797)
Harriet lee

Clarissa (or The History of a Young Lady) (1747–8) 8 vol
Samuel Richardson

John Belford (Lovelace's friend)
Arabella Harlowe (Clarissa's sister)
Clarissa Harlowe
Anne Howe (Clarissa's correspondent)
Robert Lovelace (Clarissa's admirer)
Mr Solmes (Clarissa's would-be suitor)

Clark's Field (1914)
Robert Herrick

Class, The (1985)
Erich Segal

Claude Geuex (1834)
Victor Hugo

Claude's Confession
see ***Confession de Claude, La***

Claudine à l'école (1900)
Colette

Claudine

Claudius the God (1934)
sequel to ***I, Claudius***
Robert Graves

Claverings, The (1867)
Anthony Trollope

Julie Brabazon (Ongar's eventual wife)
Florence Burton (Clavering's eventual wife)
Harry Clavering
Lord Ongar

Claw, The (1981)
Norah Lofts

Clayhanger (1910)
Arnold Bennett

Edwin Clayhanger
Auntie Hamps
Hilda Lessways (Clayhanger's eventual wife)

Clea (1960)
Laurence Durrell

set: Alexandria, Egypt
Balthazar
Clea (artist)
LG Darley (narrator)
Justine
Melissa (Darley's mistress)
Mountolive (ambassador)
Nessim (Justine's husband)
Pursewarden (British agent)

Clear and Present Danger (1989)
Tom Clancy

Clear Light of Day (1980)
Anita Desai

Clementina (1901)
AEW Mason

Clérambault (1920)
Romain Rolland

Clergyman's Daughter, A (1935)
George Orwell

Clés de Saint Pierre, Les (1955)
(The Keys of St Peter)
Roger Peyrefitte

Cliff Dwellers, The (1893)
Henry Blake Fuller

set: Chicago skyscraper

Cliffs of Fall (1963)
Shirley Hazzard

Climates (1928)
André Maurois

Clio, The (1925)
LH Myers

yacht: Clio

Clochemerle (1934)
Clochemerle Babylon (1954)
Gabriel Chevallier

set: Beaujolais village

Cloches de Bâle, Les (1933)
Louis Aragon

Clock, The (1908)
Alexei Remizov

Clocks, The (1963)
Agatha Christie

Hercule Poirot (detective)

Clock without Hands (1961)
Carson McCullers

Clockwork Orange, A (1962)
Anthony Burgess

Alex (narrator)

Clockwork Testament, The (1974)
Anthony Burgess

Cloister and the Hearth, The (A Tale of the Middle Ages) (1861)
Charles Reade

set: 15c Tergou, Holland
Erasmus (Gerard's son)
Gerard
Margaret (Gerard's beloved)

Closed at Dusk (1990)
Monica Dickens

Closed Eye, A (1991)
Anita Brookner

Closed Harbour, The (1952)
James Hanley

Close Quarters (1987)
William Golding

Close to Home (1962)
Erskine Caldwell

Clothes in the Wardrobe, The (1987)
Alice Thomas Ellis

Cloud Cuckoo Land (1925)
Naomi Mitchison

Cloudesley (1830)
William Godwin

Cloud Howe (1933)
Lewis Grassic Gibbon

Chris Guthrie

Cloud Nine (1984) posth
James M Cain

Clouds of Witness (1927)
Dorothy L Sayers

Bunter (Wimsey's servant)
Lord Peter Wimsey (amateur detective)

Clover (1888)
Susan Coolidge

Clownen Jac (1930)
Hjalmar Bergman

Clowns of God, The (1981)
Morris West

Club of Queer Trades, The (1905)
GK Chesterton

Clue of the Silver Key, The (1930)
Clue of the Twisted Candle, The (1916)
Edgar Wallace

Clutch of Constables (1968)
Ngaio Marsh
Inspector Roderick Alleyn

Cock-a-Hoop (1985)
Molly Parkin

Cock and Anchor, The (1845)
Sheridan Le Fanu

Cockatrice (1963)
Wolf Mankowitz

Cock House at Fellsgarth (1891)
Talbot Baines Reed

Cocksure (1968)
Mordecai Richler

Cocktail Time (1958)
PG Wodehouse
Earl of Ickenham, 'Uncle Fred'

Code of the Woosters, The (1938)
PG Wodehouse
Reginald Jeeves (Wooster's valet)
Bertie Wooster

Coeur simple, Un (1877)
(A Simple Heart)
Gustave Flaubert

Coffer Dams, The (1969)
Kamala Markandaya

Cogan's Trade (1974)
George V Higgins

Cognisance of Sorrow, The
see ***Cognizione del dolore***

Cognizione del dolore (1963) unf
(The Cognisance of Sorrow)
Carlo Emilio Gadda

Cold Comfort Farm (1932)
Stella Gibbons
set: Sussex
Flora Poste
Starkadder family (Flora's rural relatives)

Cold Heaven (1983)
Brian Moore

Colette Baudoche (1909)
Maurice Barrès

Collages (1964)
Anaïs Nin

Collector, The (1963)
John Fowles

Collegians, The (1829)
Gerald Griffin
Cregan

Collier de la Reine, Le (1849)
Alexandre Dumas (père)

Colline inspirée, La (1913)
Maurice Barrès

Colmena, La (1951)
(The Hive)
Camilo José Cela

Colomba (1841) coll
Prosper Mérimée

Colonel Jack (1722)
Daniel Defoe

Colonel Sun (1968)
Kingsley Amis

Colorado (1947)
Louis Bromfield

Color Purple (1983)
Alice Walker

Colossus of Maroussi, The (1941)
Henry Miller

Colour of Blood, The (1987)
Brian Moore

Colour of Light, The (1984)
William Goldman

Colours Aloft! (1986)
Alexander Kent

Richard Bolitho (sailor)

Coma (1977)
Robin Cook

Come and Get It (1935)
Edna Ferber

Comeback (1991)
Dick Francis

Come Back, Dr Caligari (1964)
Donald Barthelme

Come Back to Erin (1940)
Sean O'Faolain

Comedians, The (1966)
Graham Greene

set: Haiti
Mr Brown (narrator/businessman)
'Major' Jones
Doctor Magiot
Pineda (ambassador)
Angel Pineda (Pineda's son)
Madame Pineda (Pineda's wife/Brown's mistress)
Mr Smith (ex-presidential candidate)

Comédie humaine, La (1842–8)
17 vol
(The Human Comedy)
Honoré de Balzac

parts:
1 *Études de Moeurs* (comprising 58 separate novels)
2 *Études Philosophiques* (comprising 20 separate novels)
3 *Études Analytiques* (comprising 40 essays/sketches)

Comédienne, The (1896)
WS Reymont

Come into My Parlour (1946)
Dennis Wheatley

Gregory Sallust (agent)

Come Rack! Come Rope! (1912)
RH Benson

Comet Halley (1985)
Fred Hoyle

Come to the War (1968)
Leslie Thomas

Comforters, The (1957)
Muriel Spark

Georgina Hogg (buxom 'witch')
Louisa Jepp (Manders' grandmother)
Laurence Manders (Caroline's sometime lover)
Caroline Rose

Coming Race, The (1871)
Edward Bulwer-Lytton

Coming Up for Air (1939)
George Orwell

George Bowling (insurance man)
Hilda Bowling (Bowling's wife)

Common Lot, The (1904)
Robert Herrick

Communistes, Les (1949–51) 6 vol
Louis Aragon

Compagno, Il (1947)
(The Comrade)
Cesare Pavese

Companions de Jehu, Les (1857)
Alexandre Dumas (père)

Company of Saints, The (1983)
Evelyn Anthony

Company She Keeps, The (1942)
Mary McCarthy

Compass Error, A (1968)
Sybille Bedford

Compulsion (1956)
Meyer Levin

Computer Connection, The (1974)
Alfred Bester

Computerworld (1983)
AE Van Vogt

Comrade, The
see ***Compagno, Il***

Comte de Monte-Cristo, Le (1845)
(The Count of Monte Cristo)
Alexandre Dumas (père)
set: isle of Monte-Cristo
prison: Château d'If
Edmond Dantès (imprisoned sea-captain)
Abbé Faria (Dantès' cell-mate)

Comtesse de Charny, La (1855)
(The Countess of Charny)
Alexandre Dumas (père)

Comtesse de Rudolstadt, La (1845)
(The Countess of Rudolstadt)
sequel to ***Consuelo***
George Sand

Concerning the Eccentricities of Cardinal Pirelli (1926)
posth
Ronald Firbank

Concluding (1948)
Henry Green

Concrete Island (1972)
JG Ballard

Concubine, The (1964)
Norah Lofts

Condition Black (1991)
Gerald Seymour

Condition humaine, Le (1933)
(Man's Fate)
André Malraux
set: Shanghai

Condition of Muzak, The (1977)
Michael Moorcock

Condor, Der (1840)
Adalbert Stifter

Conduct of Major Maxim, The (1983)
Gavin Lyall

Conference at Cold Comfort Farm (1949)
Stella Gibbons

Confession de Claude, La (1865)
(Claude's Confession)
Émile Zola

Confessions of a Mask (1949)
Yukio Mishima

Confessions of a Thug (1839)
Philip Meadows Taylor

Confessions of Nat Turner, The (1967)
William Styron

Confessions of Zeno
see ***Coscienza di Zeno, La***

Confidence (1880)
Henry James

Confidence Man: His Masquerade, The (1857) unf
Herman Melville

set: Mississippi
steamboat: Fidèle

Confidential Agent, The (1939)
Graham Greene

Conformista, Il (1951)
Alberto Moravia

Confusion (1924)
James Gould Cozzens

Coningsby (or The New Generation) (1844)
Benjamin Disraeli

set: Eton; Cambridge
Harry Coningsby
Edith Millbank (Oswald's sister)
Oswald Millbank (Harry's friend)

Coniston (1906)
Winston Churchill

Conjugal Love
see ***Amore conjugale, L'***

Connecticut Yankee in King Arthur's Court, A (1889)
Mark Twain

set: 6c Camelot
Hank Morgan (Yankee)

Connoisseur, The (1974)
ES Connell

Connoisseur's Case, A (1962)
JIM Stewart

John Appleby (detective)

Conquérants, Les (1928)'André Malraux

Conquered, The (1923)
Naomi Mitchison

Conqueror, The (1922)
Gertrude Atherton

Conquest of Canaan, The (1905)
Booth Tarkington

Conquistadors, The (1969)
Hammond Innes

Conscience of the Rich, The (1958)
CP Snow

Lewis Eliot (narrator/barrister)

Consenting Adults (1980)
Peter De Vries

Consequence of Fear (1980)
Ted Allbeury

Conservationist, The (1974)
Nadine Gordimer

Consider Her Ways (1964)
John Wyndham

Consider the Lilies (1968)
Auberon Waugh

Constance (1982)
Laurence Durrell

Constant Nymph, The (1924)
Margaret Kennedy

Albert Sanger (musician)
Tessy Sanger (Albert's wife)

Consuelo (1843)
George Sand

set: Austria; Bohemia
Consuelo (singer)

Contarini Fleming (1832)
Benjamin Disraeli

Contenders, The (1958)
John Wain

Contes Drolatiques (1832–7) 3 vol
Honoré de Balzac

Contes du chat perché, Les (1939)
(Wonderful Farm Series)
Marcel Aymé

Delphine
Marinette

Contraband (1936)
Dennis Wheatley

Gregory Sallust (agent)

Contract, The (1980)
Gerald Seymour

Contradictions (1847)
Mikhail Saltykov

Control (1982)
William Goldman

Conversación en la catedral (1969)
Mario Vargas Llosa

Conversations with My Uncle (1936) coll
Frank Sargeson

Converts, The (1967)
Rex Warner

Coolie, The (1936)
Mulk Raj Anand

Cool Million, A (1934)
Nathanael West

Coonardoo (1929)
Katharine Susannah Prichard

Coot Club (1934)
Arthur Ransome

Cop Hater (1956)
Ed McBain

set: 87th Precinct, New York

Copper Pot, The (1942)
Oliver La Farge

Coral (1925)
Compton MacKenzie

Coral Island, The (1858)
RM Ballantyne
set: South Seas, Pacific Ocean
Bloody Bill (pirate)
Peterkin Gay
Jack Martin
Ralph Rover

Corde au cou, La (1873)
Émile Gaboriau
Monsieur Lecoq (detective)

Corentyne Thunder (1941)
Edgar Mittelholzer

Corinne (1807)
Anne-Louise Staël

Corker's Freedom (1964)
John Berger

Cornish Trilogy
see **Davies, Robertson**

Corn King and Spring Queen (1931)
Naomi Mitchison

Coronel no tiene quien le escriba (1961)
(No One Writes to the Colonel)
Gabriel García Márquez

Coroner's Pidgin (1945)
Margery Allingham
Albert Campion (detective)

Corridors of Power (1963)
CP Snow
Lewis Eliot (narrator/barrister)

Coscienza di Zeno, La (1923)
(Confessions of Zeno)
Italo Svevo

Cosima (1937)
Grazia Deledda

Cosmopolis (1893)
Paul Bourget

Cotter's England (1967)
Christina Stead

Council of Justice, The (1908)
Edgar Wallace
sequel to ***The Four Just Men***

Count Belsarius (1938)
Robert Graves

Countdown (1970)
Frank Slaughter

Counterfeiters, The
see ***Faux-Monnayeurs, Les***

Counterlife, The (1986)
Philip Roth

Countess of Charny, The
see ***Comtesse de Charny, La***

Countess of Rudolstadt, The
see ***Comtesse de Rudolstadt, La***

Count Hannibal (1901)
Stanley John Weyman

Count of Monte Cristo, The
see ***Comte de Monte-Cristo, Le***

Count Robert of Paris (1831)
Walter Scott

Country Doctor, A (1884)
Sarah Orne Jewett

Country Girls, The (1960)
Edna O'Brien

set: Ireland
Caithleen 'Cait' Brady
Bridget 'Baba' Brennan

Country of the Pointed Firs, The (1896)
Sarah Orne Jewett
set: Maine, USA

Coup, The (1978)
John Updike

Coup de grâce, Le (1931)
Joseph Kessel

Couples (1968)
John Updike
set: Tarbox, Massachusetts

Courrier-Sud (1928)
(Southern Mail)
Antoine de Saint-Exupéry

Course of True Love, The (1857)
Charles Reade

Courthouse Square (1936)
Hamilton Basso

Courts of the Morning, The (1929)
John Buchan

Sandy Arbuthnot (Hannay's friend)
Richard Hannay

Cousin Phillis (1864)
Elizabeth Gaskell
set: Hope Farm
Betty (Holmans' maidservant)
Holdsworth (Paul's work superior)
Phillis Holman (Paul's cousin)
Minister Holman (farmer/churchman)
Paul Manning (narrator)

Covenant, The (1980)
James A Michener

Cover Her Face (1962)
PD James

Adam Dalgliesh (detective)

Crab Apple Jelly (1944) coll
Frank O'Connor

Crack, The (1973)
Emma Tennant

Cradock Nowell (1866)
RD Blackmore

Cranford (1853)
Elizabeth Gaskell

set: Cranford (actual Knutsford)
Captain Brown
Lady Glenmire (Hoggins' eventual wife)
Mr Hoggins (surgeon)
Deborah Jenkyns
Matty Jenkyns (Deborah's sister)

Crash (1972)
JG Ballard

Craven House (1926)
Patrick Hamilton

Crazy in Berlin (1958)
Thomas Berger

Created Legend, The (1908–12) 3 vol
Fedor Sologub

Creation (1981)
Gore Vidal

Creators, The (1910)
May Sinclair

Creed (1990)
James Herbert

Cretan Lover, The (1980)
Jack Higgins

Crewe Train (1926)
Rose Macaulay

Cricket on the Hearth, The (1845)
Charles Dickens

May Fielding (Tackleton's fiancée)
Dot Peerybingle (John's wife)
John Peerybingle
Tackleton (toy merchant)

Crime, Un (1935)
Georges Bernanos

Crime and Punishment (1866)
Fyodor Dostoevsky

Raskolnikov

Crime at Black Dudley (1928)
Margery Allingham

Albert Campion (detective)

Crime at Christmas (1934)
CHB Kitchin

Crime de Sylvestre Bonnard, Le (1881)
Anatole France

Crime d'Orcival, Le (1867)
Émile Gaboriau

Monsieur Lecoq (detective)

Crime of Vanderlynden's, The (1926)
RH Mottram

Crimson Circle, The (1922)
Edgar Wallace

Crimson Witch, The (1971)
Dean R Koontz

Crisis, The (1901)
Winston Churchill

Crock of Gold, The (1912)
James Stephens

Crock of Gold, The (1844)
Martin Tupper

Crome Yellow (1921)
Aldous Huxley

Crónica de una muerte anunciada (1981)
(Chronicle of a Death Foretold)
Gabriel García Márquez

Croquis parisiens (1880)
Joris-Karl Huysmans

Cross Creek (1942)
Marjorie Kinnan Rawlings

Crossing, The (1987)
Ted Allbeury

Crossing, The (1904)
Winston Churchill

Crotchet Castle (1831)
Thomas Love Peacock

Dr Folliott (reverend)
Mr MacQuedy (economist)

Crown of Life, The (1899)
George Gissing

Cruelle Énigme (1885)
Paul Bourget

Cruel Sea, The (1945)
Nicholas Monsarrat
set: World War II

Cruise of the Dazzler, The (1902)
Jack London

Crusader's Tomb (1956)
AJ Cronin

Crying of Lot 49, The (1966)
Thomas Pynchon

Crying Out Loud (1976)
Jackie Gillott

Crystal Age, A (1887)
WH Hudson

Crystal Cave, The (1970)
Mary Stewart

Crystal World, The (1966)
JG Ballard

Cry, the Beloved Country (1948)
Alan Paton
set: Natal; Johannesburg
Stephen Kumalo (reverend)

Cry, the Peacock (1963)
Anita Desai

Cry Wolf (1976)
Wilbur Smith

Cuchilo (1969)
JT Edson

Cuckoo Clock, The (1877)
Mary Louisa Molesworth Griselda

Cuckoo Tree, The (1971)
Joan Aiken

Cuidad y los perros, La (1963)
(The Time of the Hero)
Mario Vargas Llosa

Cujo (1981)
Stephen King

Cunning Murrell (1900)
Arthur Morrison

Cuore, Il (1878)
Edmondo De Amicis

Cup of Gold (1929)
John Steinbeck

Cure for Cancer, A (1971)
Michael Moorcock
Jerry Cornelius

Curse of the King, The (1986)
Evelyn Anthony

Curse of the Viking Grave (1974)
Farley Mowat

Curse of the Wise Women, The (1933)
Edward Dunsany

Curtain (1975)
Agatha Christie
Hercule Poirot (detective)

Curtain Up (1944)
Noel Streatfeild

Custom House, The (1961)
Francis King

Custom of the Country, The (1913)
Edith Wharton

Cuts (1987)
Malcolm Bradbury

Cutting Edge (1978)
Penelope Gilliat

Cyclone, The (1950)
Miguel Asturias

Cyclops (1986)
Clive Cussler

Cytherea (1922)
Joseph Hergesheimer

D

Daddy (1989)
Danielle Steel

Daddy Darwin's Dovecote (1884)
Juliana Horatia Ewing

Daddy's Gone A-Hunting (1958)
Penelope Mortimer

Daffodil Mystery, The (1920)
Edgar Wallace

Dahomean, The (1971)
Frank Yerby

Dain Curse, The (1929)
Dashiell Hammett

Daisy Chain, The (1856)
Charlotte M Yonge

Dr May

Daisy Miller (1879)
Henry James

set: Switzerland

Daisy Miller

Dalkey Archives, The (1965)
Flann O'Brien

Dame aux camélias, La (1848)
Alexandre Dumas (fils)

Armand Duval (Marguerite's lover)
Marguerite Gautier

Dame de Monsoreau, La (1848)
Alexandre Dumas (père)

Damsel in Distress, A (1919)
PG Wodehouse

Dance of Death, The (1927)
Algernon Blackwood

Dance of the Dwarfs (1968)
Geoffrey Household

Dancer of Izu Province, The (1925)
Yasunari Kawabata

Dance to the Music of Time, A (1951–75) 12 vol
Anthony Powell

vols: 1 *A Question of Upbringing* (1951)
2 *A Buyer's Market* (1932)
3 *The Acceptance World* (1955)
4 *At Lady Molly's* (1957)
5 *Casanova's Chinese Restaurant* (1960)
6 *The Kindly Ones* (1962)
7 *The Valley of Bones* (1964)
8 *The Soldier's Art* (1966)
9 *The Military Philosophers* (1968)
10 *Books Do Furnish a Room* (1971)
11 *Temporary Kings* (1973)
12 *Hearing Secret Harmonies* (1975)

Lord Erridge
Nicholas Jenkins (narrator)
Kenneth Widmerpool

Dancing Bear, The (1972)
Peter Dickinson

Dancing Floor, The (1926)
John Buchan

Edward Leithen

Dandelion Days (1922)
Henry Williamson

Dandelion Wine (1957)
Ray Bradbury

Dangerous Ages (1921)
Rose Macaulay

Dangerous Davies (1976)
Leslie Thomas

Danger Tree, The (1977)
Olivia Manning

set: Egypt
Guy Pringle
Harriet Pringle (Pringle's wife)

Dangling Man (1944)
Saul Bellow

Daniel Deronda (1876)
George Eliot

Daniel Deronda (Gwendolen's would-be 2nd husband)
Lydia Glasher
Henleigh Grandcourt (Gwendolen's husband)
Gwendolen Harleth

Daniele Cortis (1885)
Antonio Fogazzaro

Daniel Martin (1977)
John Fowles

Daniel Martin (screenwriter)

Danny, the Champion of the World (1975)
Roald Dahl

Danse Macabre (1981)
Stephen King

Dans le labyrinthe (1959)
(In the Labyrinth)
Alain Robbe-Grillet

Darfsteller, The (1955)
Walter Miller

Daring Young Man on the Flying Trapeze, The (1934) coll
William Saroyan

Dark, The (1980)
James Herbert

Dark Angels, The
see ***Anges noirs, Les***

Dark Arena, The (1955)
Mario Puzo

Dark As the Grave Wherein My Friend Is Laid (1968) coll posth
Malcolm Lowry

Dark Crusader, The (1961)
Alistair Maclean

Dark Flower, The (1913)
John Galsworthy

Dark Forest, The (1916)
Hugh Walpole

Dark Frontier, The (1936)
Eric Ambler

Dark Green, Bright Red (1950)
Gore Vidal

Dark Half, The (1989)
Stephen King

Dark Horse, The (1981)
Rumer Godden

Darkie & Co (1932)
Howard Spring

Dark Island, The (1952)
Henry Treece

Dark Laughter (1925)
Sherwood Anderson

Dark Mile, The (1929)
DK Broster

Darkness and Day (1951)
Ivy Compton-Burnett

Darkness at Ingraham's Crest, A (1979)
Frank Yerby

Darkness at Noon (1940)
Arthur Koestler

NS Rubashov (political prisoner)

Darkness Comes (1984)
Dean R Koontz

Darkness of Diamondia, The (1972)
AE Van Vogt

Darkness Visible (1979)
William Golding

Dark Night, The (1924)
May Sinclair

Dark of the Sun, The (1968)
Wilbur Smith

Dark Princess, The (1928)
William EB DuBois

Dark Quartet (1976)
Lynne Reid Banks

Dark River, The (1919)
Sarah Gertrude Millin

Dark Room, The (1938)
RK Narayan

Dark Tower, The (1965)
Peter Vansittart

Dark Tunnel, The (1944)
Ross Macdonald

Darling Buds of May, The (1958)
HE Bates

Ma Larkin
Pa Larkin

Date with Darkness (1947)
Donald Hamilton

Daughter Buffalo (1972)
Janet Frame

Daughter of Heth, A (1871)
William Black

Daughter of Silence (1961)
Morris West

Daughters and Sons (1937)
Ivy Compton-Burnett

David Copperfield (1850)
Charles Dickens

set: Salem House School; London; Dover
Barkis (Clara's eventual husband)
David Copperfield
Mrs Copperfield (David's mother)
Creakle (headmaster)
Sophy Crewler (Traddles' eventual wife)
Mr Dick (Betsey's eccentric lodger)
Mrs Heep (Uriah's mother)
Uriah Heep (Wickfield's clerk)
Little Em'ly (Ham's fiancée)
Mrs Micawber (Micawber's wife)
Wilkins Micawber (David's 'optimistic' friend)
Edward Murdstone (wine merchant/Mrs Copperfield's 2nd husband)
Jane Murdstone (Murdstone's brother)
Clara Peggotty (David's nurse)
Daniel Peggotty (fisherman/Clara's brother)
Ham Peggotty (Daniel's nephew)
Dora Spenlow (David's 1st wife)
James Steerforth (David's school-friend)
Thomas Traddles (David's school-friend)
Betsey Trotwood (David's aunt)
Wickfield (lawyer)
Agnes Wickfield (Wickfield's daughter/David's 2nd wife)

David Elginbrod (1863)
George MacDonald

David Simple
see ***Adventures of David Simple, The***

Dawn (1884)
H Rider Haggard

Dawn
see ***Aube, L'***

Dawn in Russia (1932)
Waldo Frank

Dawn O'Hara (1911)
Edna Ferber

Day Before, The (1939)
HM Tomlinson

Day in the Dark, A (1965)
Elizabeth Bowen

Day of Glory, The (1919)
Dorothea Frances Fisher

Day of the Butterfly (1979)
Norah Lofts

Day of the Guns (1964)
Mickey Spillane

Tiger Mann

Day of the Jackal, The (1971)
Frederick Forsyth

set: France

Day of the Locust, The (1939)
Nathanael West

Day of the Scorpion, The (1968)
Paul Scott

set: 1940s India
Hari Kumar
Daphne Manners
Ronald Merrick (police superintendent)

Day of the Triffids, The (1951)
John Wyndham

Day of Wrath, The (1850)
Mór Jókai

Days (1974)
Eva Figes

Days of Hope, The
see ***Espoir, L'***

Dazzled (1990)
Judith Krantz

Dead and Alive (1946)
Hammond Innes

Dead Babies (1975)
Martin Amis

Dead Cert (1962)
Dick Francis

Deadeye Dick (1982)
Kurt Vonnegut

Dead Father, The (1975)
Donald Barthelme

Dead Fingers Talk (1963)
William Burroughs

Deadlier Than the Male (1981)
Jessica Mann

Deadly Percheron, The (1946)
John Franklin Bardin

Dead Man Leading (1937)
VS Pritchett

Dead Man's Rock (1887)
Arthur Quiller-Couch

Dead Ned (1938)
John Masefield

Dead of Jericho, The (1981)
Colin Dexter

Inspector Morse

Dead Secret, The (1857)
Wilkie Collins

Dead Souls (1842)
Nikolai Vasilevich Gogol

Chichikov

Dead Water (1964)
Ngaio Marsh

Inspector Roderick Alleyn

Dead Zone, The (1979)
Stephen King

Dean's December, The (1982)
Saul Bellow

set: Chicago; Bucharest
Albert Corde

Dearest and the Best, The (1984)
Leslie Thomas

Dear Fred (1981)
KM Peyton

Dear Shrink (1982)
Helen Cresswell

Death and the Visiting Fireman (1959)
HRF Keating

Death at the Chase (1970)

Death at the President's Lodging (1936)
JIM Stewart
John Appleby (detective)

Death Be Not Proud (1949)
John Gunther

Death Comes for the Archbishop (1927)
Willa Cather

Death Dealers, The (1965)
Mickey Spillane
Tiger Mann

Death in the Afternoon (1932)
Ernest Hemingway
set: Spain

Death in the Family, A (1957)
James Agee

Death in the Stocks (1935)
Georgette Heyer

Death in Venice
see ***Tod in Venedig, Der***

Death Is a Lonely Business (1985)
Ray Bradbury

Death Mask (1959)
Ellis Peters

Death May Surprise Us (1974)
Ted Willis

Death of a Citizen (1960)
Donald Hamilton
Matt Helm (private eye)

Death of a Ghost (1934)
Margery Allingham
Albert Campion (detective)

Death of a Hero (1929)
Richard Aldington
George Winterbourne

Death of a Highbrow (1961)
Frank Swinnerton

Death of an Expert Witness (1977)
PD James
Adam Dalgliesh (detective)

Death of a Nobody
see ***Mort de quelqu'un***

Death of a Politician (1979)
Richard Condon

Death of Ivan Illich, The (1886)
Leo Tolstoy

Death of Men, The (1981)
Allan Massie

Death of My Aunt (1929)
CHB Kitchin

Death of Reginald Perrin, The (1975)
David Nobbs
Reginald Perrin

Death of the Heart, The (1938)
Elizabeth Bowen

Death of William Posters, The (1965)
Alan Sillitoe

Death on the Nile (1937)
Agatha Christie
Hercule Poirot (detective)

Death Ship, The
see ***Totenschiff, Das***

Death to the Landlords! (1972)
Ellis Peters

Death Under Sail (1932)
CP Snow

Death Walks in Berlin (1955)
Death Walks in Cyprus (1956)
Death Walks in Kashmir (1953)
MM Kaye

Debbie Go Home (1961) coll
Alan Paton

Debits and Credits (1926) coll
Rudyard Kipling

Defence, The (1930)
Vladimir Nabokov

Defy the Foul Fiend (1934)
John Collier

Degrés (1960)
Michel Butor

Deirdre (1923)
James Stephens

Delectable Duchy, The (1893)
Arthur Quiller-Couch

Delia Delaney (1898)
Amanda Ros

Delicate Fire, The (1933) coll
Naomi Mitchison

Delicate Prey, The (1950)
(also titled ***A Little Stone***)
Paul Bowles

Deliverance (1955)
LAG Strong

Deliverance, The (1904)
Ellen Glasgow

Deloraine (1833)
William Godwin

Delphine (1802)
Anne-Louise Staël

Delta Factor, The (1967)
Mickey Spillane

Delta Star, The (1983)
Joseph Wambaugh

Delta Wedding (1946)
Eudora Welty

Deluge, The (1886)
Henryk Sienkiewicz

Demian (1919)
Hermann Hesse
Max Demian
Emil Sinclair (Demian's friend)

Demi-Gods, The (1914)
James Stephens

Democracy (1880)
Henry Brooks Adams

Democracy (1984)
Joan Didion

Demolished Man, The (1953)
Alfred Bester

Demon, The (1977)
Hubert Selby

Demon Box (1986) coll
Ken Kesey

Démon de midi, Le (1914)
Paul Bourget

Demon in My View, A (1976)
Ruth Rendell

Demos (1886)
George Gissing

Denis Duval (1864) posth unf
William Makepeace Thackeray
set: Rye
Denis Duval (narrator)

Deptford Trilogy, The (1983) 3 vol
Robertson Davies
vols:
1 *Fifth Business* (1970)
2 *The Manticore* (1972)
3 *World of Wonders* (1975)

Déracinés, Les (1897)
Maurice Barrès

Derelict, The (1928)
Charles Nordhoff

Dernier Homme, Le (1957)
(The Last Man)
Maurice Blanchot

Dernières Nouvelles (1873) coll posth
Prosper Mérimée

Dernières Nuits de Paris, Les (1928)
(The Last Nights of Paris)
Philippe Soupault

Descendant, The (1897)
Ellen Glasgow

Descent from Xanadu (1984)
Harold Robbins

Descent into Hell (1937)
Charles Williams

Desert Rose, The (1983)
Larry McMurty

Desire and Pursuit of the Whole, The (1934) posth
Frederick William Rolfe

Desolation Angels (1965)
Jack Kerouac

Despair (1936)
Vladimir Nabokov

Desperate Remedies (1871)
Thomas Hardy

Miss Aldclyffe (Cytherea's employer)
Cytherea Gray (lady's maid)
Aeneas Manston (Miss Aldclyffe's illegitimate son)
Edward Springrove (Cytherea's beloved)

Destination (1799)
Clara Reeve

Destinies of Darcy Dancer, Gentleman, The (1977)
JP Donleavy

Destiny (1831)
Susan Ferrier

Detling Murders, The (1982)
Julian Symons

Détruire dit-elle (1969)
Marguerite Duras

Deutschstunde (1968)
Siegfried Lenz

Devenir (1909)
Roger Martin du Gard

De Vere (1827)
Plumer Ward

Devices and Desires (1989)
PD James

Adam Dalgliesh (detective)

Devil, The (1911) posth
Leo Tolstoy

Evgeniy Irtyenev (magistrate)
Stepanida (Irtyenev's mistress)

Devil and Daniel Webster, The (1937)
Stephen Vincent Benét

set: New Hampshire
Jabez Stone (farmer)
Daniel Webster (lawyer)

Devil at Long Bridge, The
see ***Il diavolo al Pontelungo***

Devil by the Sea (1957)
Nina Bawden

Devil on Horseback, The (1977)
Jean Plaidy

Devil on the Cross (1982)
Ngugi Wa Thiong'o

Devil Rides Out, The (1934)
Dennis Wheatley

Duke de Richleau

Devils, The (1872)
(also titled ***The Possessed***)
Fyodor Dostoevsky

Kirilov (Radical)
Shatov (Radical)
Nikolai Stavrogin (aristocrat)
Pyotr Verkhovensky (Stepan's son)
Stepan Verkhovensky (Liberal)

Devil's Advocate, The (1959)
Morris West

Devil's Alternative, The (1979)
Frederick Forsyth

Devil's Children, The (1970)
Peter Dickinson

Devil's Cub (1934)
Georgette Heyer

Devil's Die, The (1888)
Grant Allen

Devilseed (1984)
Frank Yerby

Devil's Elixir, The
see ***Elixier des Teufels, Die***

Devil's Lake, The
see ***Mare au Diable, La***

Devil's Mode, The (1990)
Anthony Burgess

Devil's Motor, The (1910)
Marie Corelli

Devil Take the Blue-Tail Fly (1948)
John Franklin Bardin

Devil Water (1962)
Anya Seton

Dewer Rides (1929)
LAG Strong

Dharma Bums, The (1958)
Jack Kerouac

Diable boiteux, Le (1707)
Alain-René Lesage

Diaboliques, Les (1874) coll
Jules-Amédée Barbey D'Aurevilly

Dialstone Lane (1904)
WW Jacobs

Diamond Hunters, The (1971)
Wilbur Smith

Diamonds Are Forever (1956)
Ian Fleming

James Bond '007' (spy)
M (Bond's boss)
Miss Moneypenny (M's secretary)

Diana of the Crossways (1885)
George Meredith

basis: Lord Melbourne/Caroline Norton case
Lord Dannisburgh (successful defendant against Mr Warwick)
Thomas Redworth (Diana's 2nd husband)
Diana Warwick (née Merion) (Warwick's wife)
Mr Warwick

Diary of a Drug Fiend, The (1932)
Aleister Crowley

Diary of a Nobody, The (1892)
George & Weedon Grossmith

set: Brickfield Terrace, Holloway
Daisy Mutlar (Lupin's girlfriend)
Mr Perkupp (Mr Pooter's boss)
Carrie Pooter (Mr Pooter's wife)
Mr Charles Pooter (hapless diarist)
Lupin Pooter (Mr Pooter's son)

Diary of a Rapist, The (1966)
ES Connell

Diary of a Yuppie (1986)
Louis Auchinloss

Diavolo al Pontelungo, Il (1927)
(The Devil at Long Bridge)
Riccardo Bacchelli

Dichter und ihre Gesellen (1834)
Joseph Freiherr von Eichendorff

Dichter und Kaufmann (1840)
Berthold Auerbach

Dick Gibson Show, The (1971)
Stanley Elkin

Did She? (1934)
Elinor Glyn

Died in the Wool (1945)
Ngaio Marsh
Inspector Roderick Alleyn

Dieu des corps, Le (1928)
(The Body's Rapture)
Jules Romains

Dieux ont soif, Les (1912)
(The Gods Are A-Thirst)
Anatole France

Different Face, A (1953)
Olivia Manning

Difficulties with Girls (1988)
Kingsley Amis

Digger's Game, The (1973)
George V Higgins

Dinner at Antoine's (1949)
Frances Parkinson Keyes

Diplomat, The (1949)
James Aldridge

Diplomatic Diversions
see ***Ambassades, Les***

Dirk Gently's Holistic Detective Agency (1987)
Douglas Adams

Dirty Story (1967)
Eric Ambler

Disaffection, A (1989)
James Kelman

Disciple, Le (1889)
Paul Bourget

Disentanglers, The (1902)
Andrew Lang

Disowned and Devereux, The (1829)
Edward Bulwer-Lytton

Dispossessed, The (1974)
Ursula Le Guin

Disquiet and Peace (1956)
William Cooper

Distant Trumpet, A (1960)
Paul Horgan

Ditte (1917–21) 4 vol
Martin Nexø

Diversey (1928)
MacKinlay Kantor

Dividing Line, The (1979)
Robin Maugham

Dividing Stream, The (1951)
Francis King

Divine Fire (1904)
May Sinclair

Diviners, The (1974)
Margaret Laurence

Division of the Spoils, A (1975)
Paul Scott
set: 1940s India

Division of the Spoils, A (cont.)
Hari Kumar
Daphne Manners
Ronald Merrick (police superintendent)

Divorce, Un (1904)
Paul Bourget

For **DOCTOR** also see **DR**

Doctor Copernicus (1976)
John Banville

Doctor Dolittle
see ***Story of Doctor Dolittle, The***

Doctor Faustus
see ***Doktor Faustus***

Doctor Fischer of Geneva (or The Bomb Party) (1980)
Graham Greene
Doctor Fischer (toothpaste millionaire)

Doctor Glas
see ***Doktor Glas***

Doctor in the House (1952)
Richard Gordon

Doctor is Sick, The (1960)
Anthony Burgess

Doctors (1988)
Erich Segal

Doctors at Risk (1983)
Frank Slaughter

Doctor Slaughter (1984)
Paul Theroux

Doctor's Wife, The (1864)
Mary Elizabeth Braddon

Doctor's Wife, The (1976)
Brian Moore

Doctor Thorne (1858)
Anthony Trollope

set: Greshambury, Barsetshire
Miss Dunstable (heiress)
Frank Gresham
Sir Roger Scatcherd (stonemason/railway contractor)
Doctor Thorne
Mary Thorne (Doctor Thorne's adopted daughter/Gresham's eventual wife)

Doctor Zhivago (1957)
Boris Pasternak

set: World War I
Lara (Zhivago's beloved)
Doctor Yuri Zhivago

Documents in the Case, The (1930)
Dorothy L Sayers

Documents Relating to the Sentimental Agents in the Volyen Empire (1983)
Doris Lessing

Dodd Family Abroad, The (1854)
Charles Lever

Dodo (1893)
EF Benson

Dodsworth (1929)
Sinclair Lewis

Dog Crusoe, The (1861)
RM Ballantyne

Dog of Flanders, A (1872)
Ouida

Dogs of War, The (1974)
Frederick Forsyth

Dog Who Wouldn't Be, The (1957)
Farley Mowat

Dog Years
see Hundejahre

Doktor Faustus (1947)
(Doctor Faustus)
Thomas Mann

set: Germany
Esmerelda (prostitute)
Doktor Faustus
Adrian Leverkühn (composer)
Serenus Zeitblom (Leverkühn's friend)

Doktor Glas (1905)
(Doctor Glas)
Hjalmar Söderberg

Dolina Issy (1955)
Czeslaw Milosz

Dolly Dialogues, The (1894)
Anthony Hope

Samuel Carter (Dolly's sweetheart)
Dolly Foster

Dolores (1911)
Ivy Compton-Burnett

Dolores (1976)
Jacqueline Susann

Domain (1984)
James Herbert

Dombey and Son (Dealings with the Firm of) (1848)
Charles Dickens

set: London
Doctor Blimber (school principal)
James Carker (Paul Snr's assistant)
Captain Cuttle (Gills' friend)
Edith Dombey (Paul Snr's 2nd wife)
Fanny Dombey (Paul Snr's 1st wife)
Florence Dombey (Paul Snr's daughter)
Paul Dombey Jnr (Paul Snr's son)
Paul Dombey Snr (shipping-house owner)
Walter Gay (clerk)
Solomon Gills (Gay's uncle)
Mrs MacStinger (Cuttle's landlady)
Susan Nipper (Florence's servant)
Mrs Pipchin (boarding-house keeper)
Hon Mrs Skewton (Edith's mother)
Toodle (engine-driver)
Polly Toodle (Toodle's wife)
Robin Toodle (Toodle's son)
Toots (Florence's admirer/Susan's eventual husband)
Lucretia Tox (Paul Snr's housekeeper)

Do Me a favour (1963)
Susan Hill

Domestic Relations (1957) coll
Frank O'Connor

Dominique (1863)
Eugène Fromentin

Dominique De Bray (narrator)

Doña perfecta (1876)
(Perfect Lady)
Benito Pérez Galdós

Don Juan (1813)
Ernst Theodor Amadeus Hoffmann

Donovan (1882)
Edna Lyall

Don Quixote (1605–15) 2 vol

Manuel de Cervantes

set: La Mancha, Spain
Camacho (farmer)
Samson Carrasco (Quixote's friend)
Dapple (Panza's horse)
Don Quixote (cont.)
Dulcinea (Quixote's mistress)
Sancho Panza (Quixote's companion)
Don Quixote ('dreamer')
Rosinante (Quixote's horse)

Don Quixote: Which was a Dream (1986)
Kathy Acker

Don Sebastian (1809)
Anne Maria Porter

Don Tarquinio (1905)
Frederick William Rolfe

Don't Let Him Die (1978)
Chinua Achebe

Don't Look Now (1970)
Daphne Du Maurier

Don't Stop the Carnival (1965)
Herman Wouk

Don't Tell Alfred (1960)
Nancy Mitford

Radlett family

Doom Castle (1901)
Neil Munro

Doomed Oasis, The (1960)
Hammond Innes

Doomsters, The (1958)
Ross Macdonald

Doppelgänger, Ein (1887)
Theodor Storm

Doreen (1895)
Edna Lyall

Dorothy and the Wizard of Oz (1908)
L Frank Baum

Dossier 113, Le (1867)
Émile Gaboriau

Monsieur Lecoq (detective)

Doting (1952)
Henry Green

Double, The (1846)
Fyodor Dostoevsky

Double Event, The (1891)
Nat Gould

Double Honeymoon (1976)
ES Connell

Double Indemnity (1943)
James M Cain

Double Star (1956)
Robert A Heinlein

Doubtfire (1967)
Robert Nye

Douleur, La (1945)
Marguerite Duras

Dove's Nest, The (1923) coll posth
Katherine Mansfield

Doves of Venus, The (1955)
Olivia Manning

Do With Me What You Will (1973)
Joyce Carol Oates

Down Among the Women (1971)
Fay Weldon

Down-Easters, The (1833)
John Neal

Down from the Hill (1984)
Alan Sillitoe

Down There on a Visit (1962)
Christopher Isherwood

Down Under Donovan (1918)
Edgar Wallace

Do You Hear Them?
see ***Vous les entendez?***

Do You Like Brahms?
see ***Aimez-vous Brahms?***

Dracula (1897)
Bram Stoker

set: Transylvania; Essex; Carfax Estate; Whitby
Count Dracula ('vampire')
Jonathan Harker (narrator/solicitor)
Mina (Harker's fiancée)
Doctor Seward (asylum superintendent)
Professor Van Helsing (Seward's old teacher)
Lucy Westenra (Mina's friend)

Dragon (1990)
Clive Cussler

Dragon, The (1966) coll posth
Evgeny Zamyatin

Dragon in the Sea, The (1956)
Frank Herbert

Dragon Seed (1942)
Pearl Buck

Dragon's Teeth (1942)
Upton Sinclair

Lanny Budd

Dragon Summer (1962)
Ruth M Arthur

Dragonwyck (1944)
Anya Seton

Drama in Muslin, A (1886)
George Moore

Dr Bradley Remembers (1935)
Francis Brett Young

Dr Dumanany's Wife (1891)
Mór Jókai

Dreadful Hollow, The (1953)
Nicholas Blake

Nigel Strangeways (detective)

Dream, The
see ***Songe, Le***

Dream Days (1898) coll
Kenneth Grahame

Dreamers of the Ghetto (1898)
Israel Zangwill

Dreamland (1977)
George V Higgins

Dream Life of Balso Snell, The (1931)
Nathanael West

Dream Merchants, The (1949)
Harold Robbins

Dream of Fair Women, A (1924)
Henry Williamson

Dream of John Ball, The (1888)
William Morris

Dreams and Fancies (1962) coll posth
HP Lovecraft

Dreams Die Fast (1977)
Harold Robbins

Dream-Time, The (1967) posth
Henry Treece

Dred (A Tale of the Great Dismal Swamp) (1856)
Harriet Beecher Stowe

set: North Carolina, USA; Canada
Edward Clayton (Nina's fiancé)
John Cripps (trader)
Dred (coloured religious fanatic)
Harry Gordon (Nina's half-brother)
Nina Gordon
Tom Gordon (Nina's brother)

Drei Federn (1865)
(Three Feathers)
Wilhelm Raabe

Drei Kameraden (1938)
(Three Comrades)
Erich Maria Remarque

Drei Männer im Schnee (1934)
(Three Men in the Snow)
Erich Kästner

Dressmaker, The (1973)
Beryl Bainbridge

Dr Fu Manchu (1913)
Sax Rohmer

Dr Fu Manchu (oriental villain)

Dr Hudson's Secret Journal (1939)
Lloyd C Douglas

Drift (1930)
James Hanley

Drifters, The (1971)
James A Michener

Driftway, The (1972)
Penelope Lively

Driver's Seat, The (1970)
Muriel Spark

Dr Jekyll and Mr Hyde
see ***Strange Case of Dr Jekyll and Mr Hyde, The***

Dr No (1958)
Ian Fleming

James Bond '007' (spy)
M (Bond's boss)
Miss Moneypenny (M's secretary)

Drought, The (1965)
Drowned World, The (1962)
JG Ballard

Drowning Pool, The (1950)
Ross Macdonald

Dr Sevier (1885)
George Washington Cable

Drum (1962)
Kyle Onstott

set: 1860s New Orleans

Drums (1925)
James Boyd

Drums Along the Mohawk (1936)
Walter D Edmonds

Drums of War, The (1912)
Henry Stacpoole

Dr Wortle's School (1881)
Anthony Trollope

Lord Carstairs (Mary's lover)
Mr Peacocke (teacher)
Mrs Peacocke (Peacocke's wife)
Dr Wortle (school owner)
Mary Wortle (Wortle's daughter)

Dry White Season, A (1979)
André Brink

Dubin's Lives (1979)
Bernard Malamud

Dubliners, The (1914) coll
James Joyce

Ducdame (1925)
John Cowper Powys

Duchess of Wrexe, The (1914)
Hugh Walpole

Duke's Children, The (1880)
Anthony Trollope

Lady Glencora
Plantagenet Palliser (Glencora's husband)

D'un château l'autre (1957)
(Castle to Castle)
Louis-Ferdinand Céline

Dune (1965)
Dune Messiah (1969)
Frank Herbert

Paul Atreides
Baron Vladimir Harkonnen

Dunkerleys (1946)
Howard Spring

Durandeau Brothers
see ***Frères Durandeau, Les***

Dusklands (1974)
John Michael Coetzee

Dust on the Sea (1972)
Edward Beach

Dusty Answer (1927)
Rosamund Lehmann

Judith Earle

Dutch Interior (1940)
Frank O'Connor

Dutiful Daughter, A (1971)
Thomas Keneally

Dvärgen (1944)
(The Dwarf)
Pär Lagerkvist

Dwarf, The
see ***Dvärgen***

Dwelling Place of Light, The
(1917)

Winston Churchill

Dying, The
see ***Moribonds, Les***

Dynevor Terrace (1857)
Charlotte M Yonge

E

Eagle Has Landed, The (1975)
Jack Higgins
set: World War II

Eagle in the Sky (1974)
Wilbur Smith

Eagle of the Ninth, The (1954)
Rosemary Sutcliff
set: Roman Britain
Esca (ex-slave)
Marcus (the 'Eagle')

Eagle's Shadow, The (1904)
James Branch Cabell

Early Autumn (1926)
Louis Bromfield

Earthly Powers (1980)
Anthony Burgess
Kenneth Toomey (narrator)

Earthman Come Home (1955)
James Blish

East Lynne (1861)
Ellen Wood
Lady Isabel Vane

East of Eden (1952)
John Steinbeck
Hamilton family
Trask family

East River (1946)
Sholem Asch
set: New York

East Wind, West Wind (1930)
Pearl Buck

Eating People Is Wrong (1959)
Malcolm Bradbury
Professor Treece

Ebb-Tide, The (1894)
RL Stevenson

Eberhard im Kontrapunkt (1933)
Stefan Andres

Ebony Tower, The (1974) coll
John Fowles

Échéance, L' (1921)
Paul Bourget

Echoes (1953)
Compton MacKenzie

Echoes (1985)
Maeve Binchy

Echoes in the Darkness (1987)
Joseph Wambaugh

Echoing Grove, The (1953)
Rosamund Lehmann

Ecstasy Business (1967)
Richard Condon

Edge of the Cloud, The (1969)
KM Peyton

Christina

Edible Woman, The (1969)
Margaret Atwood

Education Sentimentale, L' (1869)
(The Sentimental Education)
Gustave Flaubert

set: Paris
Madame Arnoux (Moreau's would-be lover)
Frédéric Moreau

Edward (1796)
John Moore

Edwardians, The (1930)
Vita Sackville-West

Edwin Drood
see ***Mystery of Edwin Drood, The***

Eekenhof (1879)
Theodor Storm

Effi Briest (1895)
Theodor Fontane

Effie Ogilvie (1886)
Margaret Oliphant

Egoist, The (1879)
George Meredith

Laetitia Dale (Sir Willoughby's eventual wife)
Constantia Durham (Sir Willoughby's sometime fiancée)
Clara Middleton (Sir Willoughby's sometime fiancée)
Sir Willoughby Patterne (the `Egoist')
Harry Oxford (army officer)

Eiger Sanction, The (1972)
Trevanian

Jonathan Hemlock (spy)

Eight Cousins (or The Aunt-Hill) (1875)
Louisa M Alcott

Rose

Eighteenth Emergency, The (1973)
Betsy Byars

Eighth Day, The (1967)
Thornton Wilder

Eighth Deadly Sin, The (1976)
Jessica Mann

Einstein's Monsters (1987)
Martin Amis

Elders and Betters (1944)
Ivy Compton-Burnett

Elective Affinities
see ***Wahlverwandtschaften, Die***

Elephant & Castle (1949)
RC Hutchinson

Elephants Can Remember (1972)
Agatha Christie

Hercule Poirot (detective)

Elephant Song (1991)
Wilbur Smith

Elephant War, The (1960)
Gillian Avery

set: London Zoo

Elias Portolu (1900)
Grazia Deledda

Elidor (1965)
Alan Garner

Elixiere des Teufels, Die (1816)
(The Devil's Elixir)
Ernst Theodor Amadeus Hoffmann

Elizabeth (1934)
Frank Swinnerton

Elizabeth Alone (1973)
William Trevor

Elizabeth and Her German Garden (1898)
Elizabeth Von Arnim

Ellen Rogers (1941)
James T Farrell

Elmer Gantry (1927)
Sinclair Lewis

set: Mid-West USA
Elmer Gantry (evangelist)

Elsie Venner (1861)
Oliver Wendell Holmes

set: New England
Helen Darley (schoolteacher)
Bernard Langdon (Elsie's beloved)
Elsie Venner

Elster's Folly (1866)
Ellen Wood

Emancipated, The (1890)
George Gissing

Emerald City of Oz, The (1910)
L Frank Baum

Emerald Decision (1984)
Craig Thomas

Emigrants, The (1793)
Gilbert Imlay

Emigrants, The (1954)
George Lamming

Émigré, L' (1907)
Paul Bourget

Emil and the Detectives
see ***Emil und die Detektiv***

Emilia in England
see ***Sandra Belloni***

Émile (1762)
Jean-Jacques Rousseau

Emil und die Detektiv (1929)
Erich Kästner

set: Neustadt; Berlin
Emil Tischbein

Emily (1975)
Jilly Cooper

Emily (1948)
James Hanley

Emily of New Moon (1923)
LM Montgomery

Emma (1816)
Jane Austen

set: Highbury (village); Donwell Abbey (George Knightley's home); Box Hill
Miss Bates (Jane's aunt)
Frank Churchill (Weston's son by a former marriage)
Mr Elton (vicar)

Jane Fairfax (Frank's fiancée)
Mrs Goddard (headmistress)
George Knightley (Emma's eventual husband)
John Knightley (George's brother/Isabella's husband)
Robert Martin (farmer/Harriet's eventual husband)
Harriet Smith (Emma's protégée)
Anne Taylor (Emma's friend)
Mr Weston (Anne's soon-to-be husband)
Emma Woodhouse
Isabella Woodhouse (Emma's sister)
Mr Woodhouse (Emma's hypochondriac father)

Emma (1855) unf
Charlotte Brontë

Emma McChesney & Co (1915)
Edna Ferber

Emmanuel Burden, Merchant (1904)
Hilaire Belloc

Emmeline (1788)
Charlotte Smith

Emperor of Ice Cream, The (1965)
Brian Moore

Emperor's Candlesticks, The (1899)
Baroness Orczy

Empire (1987)
Gore Vidal

Empire of the Atom (1957)
AE Van Vogt

Empire of the Sun (1984)
JG Ballard
set: Shanghai

Empire of the Senseless (1988)
Kathy Acker

Emploi du temps, L' (1956)
(Passing Time)
Michel Butor
set: Manchester

Empty Canvas, The
see ***Noia, La***

Empty House, The (1906)
Algernon Blackwood

En arrière (1950)
Marcel Aymé

Enchanted Castle, The (1907)
E Nesbit

Enchanted Isle, The (1985) posth
James M Cain

Enchanter, The (1986) posth
Vladimir Nabokov

Enclosure, The (1961)
Susan Hill

En décor (1891)
Paul Adam

Enderby Outside (1968)
Enderby's Dark Lady (1984)
Anthony Burgess
Enderby (slovenly poet)

Ending Up (1974)
Kingsley Amis

Endless Night (1967)
Agatha Christie

Ending Up (1974)
Kingsley Amis

Endless Night (1967)
Agatha Christie

End of Chapter (1957)
Nicholas Blake

Nigel Strangeways (detective)

End of Desire, The (1931)
Robert Herrick

End of Solomon Grundy, The (1964)
Julian Symons

End of the Affair, The (1951)
Graham Greene

End of the Chapter (1931–3) 3 vol
John Galsworthy

vols:
2 *Maid in Waiting* (1931)
2 *Flowering Wilderness* (1932)
3 *Over the River* (1933)

End of the Night, The
see ***Fin de la nuit, La***

End of the Road, The (1958)
John Barth

End of the World, The (1872)
Edward Eggleston

End of the World News, The (1982)
Anthony Burgess

Endymion (1880)
Benjamin Disraeli

Endymion Ferrars (Pitt Ferrars' son)
Myra Ferrars (Endymion's twin-sister)
Pitt Ferrars (politician)
Lady Montfort (Endymion's eventual wife)
Lord Roehampton (Myra's 1st husband)
Job Thornberry (politician)

End Zone (1972)
Don Delillo

Enemies: a Love Story (1972)
Isaac Bashevis Singer

Enemies of the System (1978)
Brian W Aldiss

Enemy, The (1978)
Desmond Bagley

Enemy in Sight! (1970)
Alexander Kent

Richard Bolitho (sailor)

Enemy in the Blanket, The (1958)
Anthony Burgess

Enfant chargé de chaînes, L' (1913)
(Young Man in Chains)
François Mauriac

Enfant d'Austerlitz, L' (1902)
Paul Adam

Enfants du limon, Les (1938)
(The Children of Filth)
Raymond Queneau

Enfants terribles, Les (1929)
Jean Cocteau

England Made Me (1935)
Graham Greene

English Assassin, The (1972)
Michael Moorcock

Jerry Cornelius

English Maiden (1946)
Frank Swinnerton

English Teacher, The (1945)
RK Narayan

Enigma of Arrival, The (1987)
VS Naipaul

En ménage (1881)
Joris-Karl Huysmans

En 1851 (1851)
(In 1851)
Edmond & Jules de Goncourt

Enormous Crocodile, The (1978)
Roald Dahl

Enormous Room, The (1922)
ee cummings

En route (1895)
Joris-Karl Huysmans
Durtal

Ensorcelée, L' (1854)
(Bewitched)
Jules-Amédée Barbey D'Aurevilly

Entail, The (1823)
John Galt
Claude Walkinshaw (packman)

Enter a Murderer (1935)
Ngaio Marsh
Inspector Roderick Alleyn

Entrave, L' (1913)
Colette

Entre la vie et la mort (1968)
(Between Life and Death)
Nathalie Sarraute

Entretiens avec le professeur Y (1959)
Louis-Ferdinand Céline

Entropy Tango, The (1981)
Michael Moorcock

Entwining, The (1981)
Richard Condon

Epidemic (1961)
Frank Slaughter

Episode of Sparrows, An (1955)
Rumer Godden

Epitaph for a Spy (1938)
Eric Ambler

Équipage, L' (1923)
Joseph Kessel

Erasers, The
see ***Gommes, Les***

Erection Set, The (1972)
Mickey Spillane

Erewhon (or Over the Range) (1872)
Samuel Butler
set: Erewhon (anagram of nowhere)
Higgs (narrator)
Arowhena Nosnibor (Nosnibor's daughter/Higgs' eventual wife)
Mr Nosnibor
Yram (lady gaoler)

Erewhon Revisited (1901)
Samuel Butler

Erfolg, Der (1930)
Lion Feuchtwanger

Eric Brighteyes (1891)
H Rider Haggard

Eric Dorn (1921)
Ben Hecht

Eric, or Little by Little (A Tale of Roslyn School) (1858)
Frederick William Farrar

set: Roslyn School
Edwin Russell (Eric's schoolfriend)
Eric Williams (schoolboy)
Vernon Williams (Eric's younger brother)

Erie Water (1933)
Walter D Edmonds

Ernest Maltravers (1837)
Edward Bulwer-Lytton

Ernstes Leben, Ein (1930)
(A Serious Life)
Heinrich Mann

Errors of Innocence (1786)
Harriet Lee

Erwählte, Der (1951)
Thomas Mann

Escape from Five Shadows (1956)
Elmore Leonard

Esclaves de Paris, Les (1869)
Émile Gaboriau

Monsieur Lecoq (detective)

Esclusa, L' (1901)
(The Outcast)
Luigi Pirandello

Esmond in India (1957)
Ruth Prawer Jhabvala

Espoir, L' (1937)
(The Days of Hope)
André Malraux

Estate, The (1969)
sequel to ***The Manor***
Isaac Bashevis Singer

Esther (1884)
Henry Brooks Adams

Esther (1950)
Norah Lofts

Esthers Ehe (1886)
Hermann Heiberg

Esther Waters (1894)
George Moore

house: Woodview
Mr Barfield (owner of Woodview)
Mrs Barfield (Barfield's wife)
William Latch (Esther's seducer)
Esther Waters (Barfields' servant)

Étape, L' (1902)
Paul Bourget

Eternal City, The (1901)
Hall Caine

Ethan Frome (1911)
Edith Wharton

set: Massachusetts
Ethan Frome (farmer)
Zenobia Frome (Frome's wife)

Ethel Churchill (1837)
Letitia Elizabeth Landon

Étienne Mayran (1910) posth unf
Hippolyte Taine

Étranger, L' (1942)
(The Outsider)
Albert Camus

Meursault (murderer/pariah)

Être, ou les Feux du sabbat (1888)
Paul Adam

Etzel Andergast (1931)
Jakob Wassermann

Eugene Aram (1832)
Edward Bulwer-Lytton
basis: Knaresborough schoolmaster
Eugene Aram (schoolmaster)

Eugene Onegin (1831)
Alexander Pushkin

Eugene Onegin
Lensky (poet)
Olga (Tatyana's sister/Lensky's beloved)
Tatyana (Onegin's beloved)

Eunuch of Stamboul, The (1935)
Dennis Wheatley

Euphemia (1790)
Charlotte Lennox

Euphues (1579–80) 2 vol
John Lyly

Euphues (Athenian)
Lucilla (sweetheart of both Euphues & Philautus)
Philautus (Euphues' Italian friend)

Europeans, The (1878)
Henry James

Wentworth family
Eugenia Young, Baroness Münster
Felix Young (Eugenia's brother)

Eustace and Hilda (1947)
LP Hartley

Eustace Diamonds, The (1873)
Anthony Trollope

Lady Lizzie Eustace

Évangéliste, L' (1883)
Alphonse Daudet

Evan Harrington (1861)
George Meredith
set: Lymport; Lisbon
Evan Harrington (tailor's son)
Rose Jocelyn (Harrington's fiancée)

Eva Trout (1969)
Elizabeth Bowen

Evelina (or The History of a Young Lady's Entrance into the World) (1778)
Fanny Burney

Evelina Belmont
Sir John Belmont (Evelina's father)
Lord Orville (Evelina's eventual husband)
Mr Villars (Evelina's guardian)

Evelyn Innes (1898)
George Moore

Even Cowgirls Get the Blues (1976)
Tom Robbins

Evening in Byzantium (1973)
Irwin Shaw

Evening News, The (1990)
Arthur Hailey

Eve of St Venus, The (1965)
Anthony Burgess

Every Man in His Night
see ***Chaque homme dans sa nuit***

Everything to Live For (1968)
Paul Horgan

Evil Hour, The
see ***Mala hora, La***

Evil in a Mask (1969)
Dennis Wheatley

Evil Streak, An (1977)
Andrea Newman

Evil Under the Sun (1941)
Agatha Christie

Hercule Poirot (detective)

Excellent Women (1952)
Barbara Pym

Except the Lord (1953)
Joyce Cary

Chester Nimmo (politician)

Exil (1940)
Lion Feuchtwanger

Exile, The (1936)
Pearl Buck

Exiles (1950)
Warwick Deeping

Exiles, The (1788)
Clara Reeve

Exit Lady Masham (1984)
Louis Auchinloss

Exocet (1983)
Jack Higgins

Exodus (1957)
Leon Uris

Exorcist, The (1971)
William Peter Blatty

Regan MacNeil (possessed girl)

Expedition of Humphry Clinker, The (1771)
Tobias Smollett

set: Wales; Scotland; London
Matthew Bramble (Welsh squire)
Tabitha Bramble (Bramble's sister)
Humphry Clinker (Bramble's servant)
Winifred Jenkins (Tabitha's maid)
Lt Obadiah Lismahago (soldier)

Experimentor, The (1960)
William Burroughs

Exploits of Brigadier Gerard, The (1896)
Arthur Conan Doyle

Brigadier Gerard

Explorer, The (1965)
Frances Parkinson Keyes

Exterminator! (1973)
William Burroughs

Extraordinary Women (1928)
Extremes Meet (1928)
Compton MacKenzie

Eye, The (1930)
Vladimir Nabokov

Eyebright (1879)
Susan Coolidge

Eyeless In Gaza (1936)
Aldous Huxley

Anthony Beavis

Eye of the Needle (1978)
Ken Follett

Eye of the Storm, The (1973)
Patrick White

Eye of the Tiger, The (1975)
Wilbur Smith

Eyes of the Sea, The (1917)
Marie Corelli

F

Fabian (1931)
Erich Kästner

Fable, A (1954)
William Faulkner

Face, The (1929)
EF Benson

Face Beside the Fire, The (1953)
Laurens Van Der Post

Face of Time, The (1953)
James T Farrell

Face of Trespass, The (1974)
Ruth Rendell

Faces in the Water (1962)
Janet Frame

Facial Justice (1960)
LP Hartley

Factotum (1975)
Charles Bukowski

Fahrenheit 451 (1953)
Ray Bradbury

Fairacre Festival, The (1969)
Miss Read

Fair Do's (1990)
David Nobbs

Fair God, The (1873)
Lew Wallace

Fair Haven, The (1873)
Samuel Butler

Fairly Honourable Defeat, A (1970)
Iris Murdoch

Fair Maid of Perth, The (1828)
Walter Scott

set: 14c
Catharine Glover (Glover's daughter/the 'Fair Maid')
Simon Glover (burgher)
Oliver Proudfute (bonnet-maker)
Sir John Ramorny (Master of the Horse)
Henry Smith (armourer)

Fair Stood the Wind for France (1944)
HE Bates

Fair Syrian, The (1787)
Robert Bage

Fairy Tale of New York, A (1960)
JP Donleavy

Faith Doctor, The (1891)
Edward Eggleston

Faithful Company (1948)
Frank Swinnerton

Faked Passports (1940)
Dennis Wheatley
Gregory Sallust (agent)

Falconer (1977)
John Cheever

Falconet (1927) posth unf
Benjamin Disraeli
Joseph Falconet (politician)

Falcon Flies, A (1980)
Wilbur Smith

Falkland (1827)
Edward Bulwer-Lytton

Falkner (1837)
Mary Shelley

Fallen into the Pit (1951)
Ellis Peters

Falling Star (1934)
Vicki Baum

Fall Maurizius, Der (1928)
(The Maurizius Case)
Jakob Wassermann

Fall of Kelvin Walker: A Fable of the Sixties, The (1985)
Alasdair Gray

Fall of the House of Usher, The (1840)
Edgar Allan Poe
Madeline Usher (Usher's sister)
Roderick Usher

Fallow Land, The (1932)
HE Bates

False Scent (1960)
Ngaio Marsh
Inspector Roderick Alleyn

Falstaff (1976)
Robert Nye

Fame Is the Spur (1940)
Howard Spring

Familiar Letters Between the Principal Characters in David Simple (1747)
Sarah Fielding
David Simple

Familiar Passions (1979)
Nina Bawden

Family and a Fortune, A (1939)
Ivy Compton-Burnett

Family and Friends (1985)
Anita Brookner

Family Arsenal, The (1976)
Paul Theroux

Family Chronicle, A (1856)
Sergei Timofeevich Aksakov

Family Circle, The
see ***Cercle de Famille, Le***

Family from One End Street, The (1937)
Eve Garnett
set: Otwell (imaginary Midlands town)
Ruggles family

Family Madness, A (1985)
Thomas Keneally

Family Moskat, The (1950)
Isaac Bashevis Singer

Family of Pascual Duarte, The (1942)
Camilo José Cela

Famine (1937)
Liam O'Flaherty

Famished Road, The (1991)
Ben Okri

Fan (1892)
WH Hudson

Fanatic, The (1964)
Meyer Levin

Fanny Herself (1917)
Edna Ferber

Fanny Hill (Memoirs of a Woman of Pleasure) (1748–9)
John Cleland

Fanny's Sister (1977)
Penelope Lively

Fanshawe (1828)
Nathaniel Hawthorne

Fantastic Mr Fox (1970)
Roald Dahl

Fantastic Voyage (1966)
Fantastic Voyage II (1987)
Isaac Asimov

Fantôme de l'Opéra, Le (1911)
(The Phantom of the Opera)
Gaston Leroux

Faraway (1932)
JB Priestley

Far Barbarian, A (1881)
Frances Hodgson Burnett

Far Country, A (1915)
Winston Churchill

Far Country, The (1952)
Nevil Shute

Far Cry from Kensington, A (1988)
Muriel Spark

Farewell My Lovely (1940)
Raymond Chandler
Philip Marlowe (detective)

Farewell Party, The (1976)
Milan Kundera

Farewell to Arms, A (1929)
Ernest Hemingway
set: World War I
Catherine Barkley (nurse)
Frederic Henry (lieutenant)

Farewell Victoria (1933)
TH White

Far Forest (1936)
Francis Brett Young

Far from Cibola (1938)
Paul Horgan

Far from the Madding Crowd (1874)
Thomas Hardy

set: Wessex
Farmer Boldwood (Bathsheba's suitor)
Bathsheba Everdene (Oak's eventual wife)
Gabriel Oak (shepherd)
Fanny Robin (servant)
Sergeant Troy (Bathsheba's 1st husband)

Far Journey of Oudin, The (1961)
Wilson Harris

Far-Off Place, A (1974)
Laurens Van Der Post

Faro's Daughter (1941)
Georgette Heyer

Far Pavilions, The (1978)
MM Kaye

set: India

Farther Adventures of Robinson Crusoe (1719)
Daniel Defoe

Robinson Crusoe
Friday (Crusoe's helper)

Farthest Shore, The (1972)
Ursula Le Guin

Farthing Hall (1929)
JB Priestley

Far Tortuga (1975)
Peter Matthiessen

Fasching (1888)
Gerhart Hauptmann

Fatal Gift, The (1973)
Alec Waugh

Fatal Revenge, The (1807)
Charles Maturin

Father and His Fate, A (1957)
Ivy Compton-Burnett

Father and Son (1940)
James T Farrell

Fathers, The (1967)
Herbert Gold

Fathers and Sons (1862)
Ivan Turgenev

Father's Comedy, The (1961)
Roy Fuller

Fat Woman's Joke, The (1967)
Fay Weldon

Fault of Angels, The (1933)
Paul Horgan

Faust (1980)
Robert Nye

Faux-Monnayeurs, Les (1926)
(The Counterfeiters)
André Gide

Favourite of the Gods, A (1962)
Sybille Bedford

Fear, The (1965)
Thomas Keneally

Fearful Joy, A (1949)
Joyce Cary

Fearful Responsibility, A (1881)
William Dean Howells

Fear Is the Key (1961)
Alistair Maclean

set: Florida

Fear of Flying (1974)
Erica Jong
Isadora Wing

Feast, The (1950)
Margaret Kennedy

Feast of Lupercal, The (1957)
Brian Moore

Feathers In the Fire (1971)
Catherine Cookson

Feather Woman of the Jungle, The (1962)
Amos Tutuola

February Doll Murders, The (1966)
Michael Avallone

Ed Noon (private eye)

Fécondité (1899)
Émile Zola

Federigo (1954)
Howard Nemerov

Feelings Have Changed (1981)
PH Newby

Felix and Felicitas (1881) unf
Marcus Clarke

Felix Holt (The Radical) (1866)
George Eliot

set: Loamshire
Esther
Felix Holt (Esther's eventual husband)
Harold Transome (Esther's suitor)
Lady Wyvern (Lord Wyvern's wife)
Lord Wyvern

Felix Krull (1954)
Thomas Mann

Female friends (1975)
Fay Weldon

Female Quixote, The (or The Adventures of Arabella) (1752)
Charlotte Lennox

Fer-de-Lance (1934)
Rex Stout

Archie Godwin (Wolfe's assistant)
Nero Wolfe (private eye)

Ferdinand Count Fathom
see ***Adventures of Ferdinand Count Fathom, The***

Festival at Farbridge (1951)
JB Priestley

Feud, The (1983)
Thomas Berger

Fictions (1944) coll
Jorge Luis Borges

Fiddle City (1983)
Julian barnes

Fidelity (1915)
Susan Glaspell

Field of Blood (1985)
Gerald Seymour

Fields, The (1946)
Conrad Richter

Fifth Child, The (1988)
Doris Lessing

Fifth Form at St Dominic's, The (1887)
Talbot Baines Reed

Fifth Pestilence, The (1911)
Alexei Remizov

Fifth Queen and How She Came to Court, The (1906)
Fifth Queen Crowned (1908)
Ford Madox Ford

Fifty-Two Pickup (1974)
Elmore Leonard

Fight for Manod, The (1979)
Raymond Williams

Fighting the Flames (1867)
RM Ballantyne

Figure of Eight (1936)
Compton MacKenzie

Figures of Earth (1915)
James Branch Cabell

Figures of Speech (1965)
DJ Enright

Fille du Régent, La (1845)
Alexandre Dumas (père)

Filthy Lucre (1986)
Beryl Bainbridge

Final Curtain (1947)
Ngaio Marsh

Inspector Roderick Alleyn

Final Diagnosis, The (1959)
Arthur Hailey

Final Problem, The (1893)
Arthur Conan Doyle

set: Reichenbach Falls
Sherlock Holmes (detective)
Professor James Moriarty (Holmes' arch-enemy)

Final Programme, The (1968)
Michael Moorcock

Jerry Cornelius

Financial Expert, The (1952)
RK Narayan

Financier, The (1912)
Theodore Dreiser

Fin de Chéri, La (1926)
Colette

Fin de la nuit, La (1935)
(The End of the Night)
François Mauriac

sequel to *Thérèse Desqueyroux*

Finding, The (1985)
Nina Bawden

Fine and Private Place, A (1975)
Morley Callaghan

Finger of Fire (1977)
John Braine

Finishing Touch, The (1963)
Brigid Brophy

Finnegans Wake (1939)
James Joyce

set: Dublin

Anna Livia Earwicker (née Plurabelle) (Humphrey's wife)
Humphrey Chimpden Earwicker (innkeeper)
Isabel Earwicker (Humphrey's daughter)
Shaun Earwicker (Humphrey's son)
Shem Earwicker (Humphrey's son)

Firebug (1961)
Robert Bloch

Fire Down Below (1989)
William Golding

Fire-Dwellers, The (1969)
Margaret Laurence

Firefly Gadroon (1982)
Jonathan Gash

Lovejoy (dodgy antiques dealer)

Firefly Summer (1987)
Maeve Binchy

Firefox (1977)
Craig Thomas

Fireman Flower (1944) coll
William Sansom

Fire on the Mountain (1977)
Anita Desai

Fires of Spring, The (1972)
James A Michener

Fires over England (1936)
AEW Mason

Firestarter (1980)
Stephen King

First Among Equals (1984)
Jeffrey Archer

First and Last Men (1930)
Olaf Stapledon

First Circle, The (1968)
Alexander Solzhenitsyn

First Lensman (1950)
EE 'Doc' Smith

First Light (1989)
Peter Ackroyd

First Love, Last Rites (1975) coll
Ian McEwan

First Men in the Moon, The (1901)
HG Wells

First Two Lives of Lukas-Kasha, The (1978)
Lloyd C Alexander

Fish Can Sing, The
see ***Brekkukotsannáll***

Fisher King, The (1986)
Anthony Powell

Five Children and It (1902)
E Nesbit

Five of Us and Madeline (1925) coll posth
E Nesbit

Five on a Treasure Island (1942)
Enid Blyton

Anne
Dick
George (Georgina)
Julian
Uncle Quentin
Timmy (dog)

Five Pieces of Jade (1972)
John Ball

Five Red Herrings, The (1931)
Dorothy L Sayers

Bunter (Wimsey's servant)
Lord Peter Wimsey (amateur detective)

Five Weeks in a Balloon
see ***Cinq Semaines en ballon***

Fixer, The (1967)
Bernard Malamud

Flag Is Born, A (1946)
Ben Hecht

Flambards (1967)
Flambards Divided (1982)
Flambards in Summer (1969)
KM Peyton

Christina

Flame of Hercules, The (1957)
Richard Llewellyn

Flamingo Feather (1955)
Laurens Van Der Post

Flash and Filigree (1958)
Terry Southern

Flashman (1969)
George Macdonald Fraser

Sir Harry Flashman (soldier)

Flat Iron for a Farthing, A (1872)
Juliana Horatia Ewing

Flaubert's Parrot (1984)
Julian Barnes

Flaunting Extravagant Queen (1957)
Jean Plaidy

Flax of Dreams, The
see Henry Williamson

Fledgling, The (1919)
Charles Nordhoff

Fleetwood (1805)
William Godwin

Flegeljahre, Die (1804–5) 4 vol unf
(Adolescence)
Jean Paul

Flesh (1962)
Brigid Brophy

Fliegende Klassenzimmer, Die (1933)
(The Flying Classroom)
Erich Kästner

Flight from the Enchanter, The (1956)
Iris Murdoch

Flight into Camden (1960)
David Storey

Flight of Chariots, A (1973)
Jon Cleary

Flight of the Falcon, The (1965)
Daphne Du Maurier

Flight of the Heron, The (1925)
DK Broster

Flights (1973)
Francis King

Flight to Arras
see ***Pilote de guerre***

Flint Anchor, The (1954)
Sylvia Townsend Warner

Floating Opera, The (1956)
John Barth

Flood (1964)
Robert Penn Warren

Floodgate (1983)
Alistair Maclean

Florence (1935) posth unf
Jacques Rivière

Flounder, The
see ***Butt, Der***

Flower Beneath the Foot, The (1923)
Ronald Firbank

Flowering Judas (1930) coll
Kathleen Anne Porter

Flowers and Shadows (1980)
Ben Okri

Flowers for Mrs Harris (1958)
Paul Gallico

Flowers for the Judge (1936)
Margery Allingham
Albert Campion (detective)

Fluke (1977)
James Herbert

Flush (A Biography) (1933)
Virginia Woolf

Flute, The (1977)
Chinua Achebe

Flute-Player, The (1979)
DM Thomas

Flyaway (1979)
Desmond Bagley

Flying Classroom, The
see ***Fliegende Klassenzimmer, Die***

Flying Inn, The (1914)
GK Chesterton

Flying to Nowhere (1983)
John Fuller

Fly in the Ointment, The (1989)
sequel to ***The Skeleton in the Cupboard***
Alice Thomas Ellis

Focus (1945)
Arthur Miller

Foe (1986)
John Michael Coetzee

Foe-Farrell (1918)
Arthur Quiller-Couch

Fog, The (1978)
James Herbert

Folks That Live on the Hill, The (1990)
Kingsley Amis

Folle-Farine (1871)
Ouida

Following Darkness (1912)
Forrest Reid

Follow the Drum (1972)
James Leasor

Foma Gordeyev (1899)
Maxim Gorky

set: town on the Volga
Gordeyev family

Fombombo (1922)
TS Stribling

Fong and the Indians (1990)
Paul Theroux

Fontamara (1930)
Ignazio Silone

Food of the Gods, The (1904)
HG Wells

Fool and the Princess, The (1958)
Stephen Spender

Fool of Quality, The (1770)
Henry Brooke

Harry Clinton ('fool')

Foolscap Rose, The (1934)
Joseph Hergesheimer

Fools Die (1978)
Mario Puzo

Fool's Errnad, A (1879)
Albion W Tourgée

Fools of Fortune (1983)
William Trevor

Foot of Clive, The (1962)
John Berger

Forbidden Territory, The (1933)
Dennis Wheatley

Force, La (1899)
Force du mal, La (1896)
Paul Adam

Force 10 from Navarone (1968)
Alistair Maclean

set: World War II Yugoslavia

Forest and the Fort, The (1943)
Hervey Allen

Forest Fire (1933)
Rex Stout

Forest Lovers, The (1898)
Maurice Hewlett

Forests of the Night (1963)
Jon Cleary

Forever (1975)
Judy Blume

Forever Amber (1944)
Kathleen Winsor

set: 17c

Forever England (1986)
Beryl Bainbridge

Forfeit (1969)
Dick Francis

Forge, The (1931)
TS Stribling

Forger, The (1927)
Edgar Wallace

Forgetting Elena (1973)
Edmund White

Forgotten Life (1988)
Brian W Aldiss

Forgotten Smile, The (1961)
Margaret Kennedy

Forjaettede Land, Det (1891–5) 2 vol
(The Promised Land)
Henrik Pontoppidan

For Kicks (1967)
Dick Francis

For Love Alone (1945)
Christina Stead

Forstmeister, Der (1879) 2 vol
Berthold Auerbach

Forsyte Saga, The (1906–21) 3 vol
John Galsworthy

vols:
1 *The Man of Property* (1906)
2 *In Chancery* (1920)
3 *To Let* (1921)

see also: A Modern Comedy (1924–8) 3 vol; *End of the Chapter* (1931–3) 3 vol; in which some of the characters below also appear

set: London; Robin Hill (house)
Philip Bosinney (architect)
Fleur Forsyte (Soames and Annette's daughter)
Irene Forsyte (Soames' 1st wife)
Jon Forsyte ('Young' Jolyon and Irene's son)
'Old' Jolyon Forsyte (Soames' uncle)
Soames Forsyte (solicitor/Irene's 1st husband)
'Young' Jolyon Forsyte (Soames' cousin/Irene's 2nd husband)
Annette Lamotte (Soames' 2nd wife)
Michael Mont (Fleur's eventual husband)

Fort Amity (1904)
Arthur Quiller-Couch

Fort comme la mort (1889)
(Strong as the Dead)
Guy de Maupassant

For the Term of His Natural Life (1872)
Marcus Clarke

Fort in the Jungle (1936)
PC Wren

Fortitude (1913)
Hugh Walpole

Fortnight in September, The (1931)
RC Sherriff

Fortress, The (1932)
Hugh Walpole

Fortunata y Jacinta (1887)
Benito Péres Galdós

Fortune Pilgrim, The (1965)
Mario Puzo

Fortunes of Glencore, The (1857)
Charles Lever

Fortunes of Nigel, The (1822)
Walter Scott

Lord Dalgarno
Nigel Olifaunt
Margaret Ramsey (Olifaunt's admirer)
Dame Ursula Suddlechop (milliner/secret agent)

Fortunio (1837)
Théophile Gautier

Forty Lashes Less One (1837)
Elmore Leonard

42nd Parallel, The (1930)
John Dos Passos

Förvillelser (1895)
(Aberrations)
Hjalmar Sóderberg

For Want of a Nail (1965)
Melvyn Bragg

For Whom the Bell Tolls (1940)
Ernest Hemingway

set: Spanish Civil War
Robert Jordan
Maria (Jordan's lover)

For Your Eyes Only (1960)
Ian Fleming

James Bond '007' (spy)
M (Bond's boss)
Miss Moneypenny (M's secretary)

Foucault's Pendulum (1988)
Umberto Eco

Colonel Ardenti
Jacopo Belpo (Casaubon's friend)
Casaubon

Foul Play (1869)
Charles Reade

Foundation (1951)
Foundation and Empire (1952)
Isaac Asimov

Found in the Street (1986)
Patricia Highsmith

Fountain, The (1932)
Charles Morgan

Fountainhead, The (1943)
Ayn Rand

Fountain of Bakhchisarai, The (1826)
Alexander Pushkin

Fountains of Paradise, The (1979)
Arthur C Clarke

Fountain Overflows, The (1956)
Rebecca West

Four-Chambered Heart, The (1950)
Anaïs Nin

Four Feathers, The (1902)
AEW Mason

Harry Feversham

4.50 from Paddington (1957)
Agatha Christie

Miss Jane Marple (amateur sleuth)

Four-Gated City, The (1969)
Doris Lessing

Martha Quest

Four Horsemen of the Apocalypse, The (1916)
Vicente Blasco Ibañez

Four Just Men, The (1905)
Edgar Wallace

Four Past Midnight (1990)
Stephen King

Four Portraits (1954)
Jocelyn Brooke

Fourteenth of October, The (1942)
Bryher

Fourth of June (1962)
David Benedictus

Fourth Protocol, The (1984)
Frederick Forsyth

Four Winds of Love, The (1937–45)
4 vol
Compton MacKenzie

John Ogilvie

Fox and the Manger, The (1962)
PL Travers

Foxes of Harrow, The (1946)
Frank Yerby

Fox Fire (1951)
Anya Seton

Foxglove Saga, The (1960)
Auberon Waugh

Fox in the Attic, The (1961)
Richard Hughes

Framley Parsonage (1861)
Anthony Trollope

set: Framley, Barsetshire
Josiah Crawley (curate)
Archdeacon Grantly
Lady Lufton
Lord Ludovic Lufton (Lady Lufton's son)
Lucy Robarts (Mark's sister)
Mark Robarts (clergyman)

Franchise Affair, The (1948)
Josephine Tey

Franchiser, The (1976)
Stanley Elkin

Frankenstein (or A Modern Prometheus) (1818)
Mary Shelley

set: Geneva; Arctic
Dr Victor Frankenstein
Walton (Frankenstein's friend)

Frankenstein Unbound (1973)
Brian W Aldiss

Frank Mildmay (1829)
Frederick Marryat

Franky Furbo (1989)
William Wharton

Franny and Zooey (1961)
JD Salinger

Glass family

Fraternity (1909)
John Galsworthy

Frau Jennt Treibel (1892)
Theodor Fontane

Frau Professorin, Die (1846)
Berthold Auerbach

Freaky Deaky (1988)
Elmore Leonard

Freedom Road (1944)
Howard Fast

Freedom Trap, The (1971)
Desmond Bagley

Free Fall (1959)
William Golding

Free Frenchman, The (1986)
Piers Paul Read

Free Joe (1887)
Joel Chandler Harris

French Bride, The (1976)
Evelyn Anthony

French Leave (1956)
PG Wodehouse

French Lieutenant's Woman, The (1969)
John Fowles

set: 19c Lyme Regis
Ernestine Freeman (Smithson's fiancée)
Charles Smithson (palaeontologist)
Sarah Woodruff (Smithson's sometime lover)

Frenchman's Creek (1942)
Daphne Du Maurier

Jean-Bénoit Aubéry (pirate)
Dona St Columb (Sir Henry's wife)
Henrietta St Columb (Sir Henry's daughter)
James St Columb (Sir Henry's son)
Sir Henry St Columb
William (St Columbs' servant)

Frères Durandeau, Les (1924)
(The Durandeau Brothers)
Philippe Soupault

Friday (1982)
Robert A Heinlein

Friend from England, A (1987)
Anita Brookner

Friend Monkey (1971)
PL Travers

Friends and Heroes (1965)
Olivia Manning

set: Romania
Guy Pringle
Harriet Pringle (Pringle's wife)

Friends and Relations (1931)
Elizabeth Bowen

Friends of Eddie Coyle, The (1972)
George V Higgins

Frightened Lady, The (1932)
Edgar Wallace

Fringe of Leaves, A (1976)
Patrick White

From a View to a Death (1933)
Anthony Powell

From Doon with Death (1964)
Ruth Rendell

Inspector Reg Wexford

From Here to Eternity (1951)
James Jones

From Man to Man (1926) posth
Olive Schreiner

Fromont jeune et Risler aîné (1874)
Alphonse Daudet

From Russia with Love (1957)
Ian Fleming

James Bond '007' (spy)
M (Bond's boss)
Miss Moneypenny (M's secretary)

Frontier Wolf (1980)
Rosemary Sutcliff

Frost in May (1933)
Antonia White

Frozen Assets (1964)
PG Wodehouse

Frühling, Ein (1857)
(A Spring)
Wilhelm Raabe

Fruit of the Tree, The (1907)
Edith Wharton

Fruits d'or, Les (1963)
(The Golden Fruits)
Nathalie Sarraute

Fuel for the Flame (1960)
Alec Waugh

Fugitive's Return, The (1929)
Susan Glaspell

Fugue in Time (1945)
Rumer Godden

Full Circle (1984)
Danielle Steel

Full Moon (1947)
PG Wodehouse
set: Blandings Castle, Shropshire
Empress of Blandings (pig)
Lord Emsworth
Lady Constance Keeble (Lord Emsworth's sister)
Freddie Threepwood (Lord Emsworth's son)
Galahad Threepwood (Lord Emsworth's brother)

Fu Mattia Pascal, Il (1904)
(The Late Mattia Pascal)
Luigi Pirandello

Funeral in Berlin (1965)
Len Deighton
Harry Palmer (spy)

Fuoco, Il (1900)
(The Flame of Life)
Gabriele D'Annunzio

Fürsorgliche belagerung (1979)
(The Safety Net)
Heinrich Böll

Further Adventures of the Family from One End Street (1956)
Eve Garnett
set: Otwell (imaginary Midlands town)
Ruggles family

Further Experiences of an Irish RM (1908)
Edith Somerville
set: Shreelane (manor house), Ireland
Flurry Knox (Yeates' landlord)
Major Yeates (narrator/resident magistrate)
Philippa Yeates (Yeates' wife)

Furys, The (1935)
James Hanley

Futility (A Novel on Russian Themes) (1922)
William Gerhardie

G

G (1972)
John Berger

Gabriel Hounds, The (1967)
Mary Stewart

Gabriella, Clove and Cinnamon (1958)
Jorge Amado

Gabriel Tolliver (1902)
Joel Chandler Harris

Gadfly, The (1897)
Ethel Lillian Voynich

Gad's Hall (1977)
Norah Lofts

Galactic Patrol (1950)
EE 'Doc' Smith

Galahad at Blandings (1965)
PG Wodehouse

set: Blandings Castle, Shropshire
Beach (Lord Emsworth's butler)
Empress of Blandings (pig)
Lord Emsworth
Galahad Threepwood (Lord Emsworth's brother)

Galapagos (1985)
Kurt Vonnegut

Galatea, La (1585)
Manuel de Cervantes

Galaxy Primes, The (1965)
EE 'Doc' Smith

Gallions Reach (1927)
HM Tomlinson

Gallows on the Sand (1955)
Morris West

Galton Case, The (1959)
Ross Macdonald

Game, The (1967)
AS Byatt

Gamekeeper, The (1975)
Barry Hines

Game of Hide-and-Seek, A (1951)
Elizabeth Taylor

Games of Night, The (1947)
Stig Dagerman

Gap in the Curtain (1927)
John Buchan

Edward Leithen

Garçons, Les (1969)
(The Boys)
Henry de Montherlant

Garden God, The (1905)
Forrest Reid

Garden of Allah, The (1904)
Robert Smythe Hichens

set: North Africa desert

Garden of Earthly Delights, A (1967)
Joyce Carol Oates

Garden of the Finzi-Continis, The (1962)
Giorgio Bassani

Garden Party, The (1922)
Katherine Mansfield

Garden to the Sea, The (1953)
Philip Toynbee

Gargantua and Pantagruel (1532–52) 5 vol
François Rabelais

Gargantua (giant)
Pantagruel (Gargantua's son)
Panurge (rogue)

Gargoyles (1922)
Ben Hecht

Garrick Year, The (1964)
Margaret Drabble

Gas-House McGinty (1933)
James T Farrell

Gates of the Forest, The
see ***Portes de la Forêt, Les***

Gates of Wrath, The (1903)
Arnold Bennett

Gatewell to Hell (1970)
Dennis Wheatley

Duke de Richleau

Gattopardo, Il (1958) posth
(The Leopard)
Giuseppe Lampedusa

set: 19c Sicily

Gaudy, The (1983)
JIM Stewart

Gaudy Night (1934)
Dorothy L Sayers

Bunter (Wimsey's servant)
Lord Peter Wimsey (amateur detective)

Gaverocks, The (1888)
Sabine Baring-Gould

Geisterseher, Der (1789) unf
Johann Schiller

Geld und Geist (1844)
Jeremias Gotthelf

Gemini Contenders, The (1976)
Robert Ludlum

Gemma (1968)
Noel Streatfeild

General, The (1936)
CS Forester

Genesis of the Clowns (1975)
Wilson Harris

Génie du Piev, Le (1960)
Michel Butor

Génie du Rhin, Le (1921)
Maurice Barrès

Genius, The (1915)
Theodore Dreiser

Genius and the Goddess, The (1955)
Aldous Huxley

Gentle Annie (1942)
MacKinlay Kantor

Gentleman and Ladies (1968)
Susan Hill

Gentleman from Indiana, The (1899)
Booth Tarkington

Gentleman from San Francisco, The (1914)
Ivan Bunin

Gentleman of France, A (1893)
Stanley John Weyman

Gentleman of Leisure, A (1910)
PG Wodehouse

Gentlemen Prefer Blondes (1925)
Anita Loos

Geoffrey Hamlyn (1859)
Henry Kingsley

George Mills (1982)
Stanley Elkin

George Pessant (1940)
(also titled ***Strangers and Brothers***)
CP Snow
Lewis Eliot (narrator/barrister)

George's Marvellous Medicine (1981)
Roald Dahl

Gerald's Party (1986)
Robert Coover

Germinie Lacerteux (1864)
Edmond & Jules de Goncourt

Gerpla (1952)
Halldór Laxness

Gertrud (1910)
Hermann Hesse

Geschichten Jaakobs, Die (1933)
Thomas Mann

Geschwister Oppenheim, Die (1933)
Lion Feuchtwanger

Get Ready for Battle (1962)
Ruth Prawer Jhabvala

Get Shorty (1990)
Elmore Leonard

Getting of Wisdom, The (1910)
Henry Handel Richardson

Ghetto Comedies (1907)
Ghetto Tragedies (1894)
Israel Zangwill

Ghosts (1988)
Eva Figes

Ghost Stories of an Antiquary (1904) coll
MR James

Ghost Writer, The (1979)
Philip Roth
Nathaniel Zuckerman (novelist)

Giant (1950)
Edna Ferber
set: Texas

Giants' Bread (1930)
Agatha Christie

Gideon Planish (1943)
Sinclair Lewis

Gideon's Day (1955)
John Creasey
Inspector Gideon (CID officer)

Gift, The (1938)
Vladimir Nabokov

Gigantic Shadow, The (1958)
Julian Symons

Gigi (1943)
Colette

Gigolo (1922)
Edna Ferber

Gil Blas (de Santillane) (1715–35) 4 vol
Alain-René Lesage
set: Spain
Gil Blas

Gilded Age, The (1873)
Mark Twain & CD Warner

Giles Corey (1893)
Mary E Freeman

Giles Goat-Boy (1966)
John Barth

Gillyvors, The (1990)
Catherine Cookson

Gimlet Goes Again (1944)
WE Johns
Gimlet (commando)

Gimpel the Fool (1957) coll
Isaac Bashevis Singer

Ginger Man, The (1955)
JP Donleavy
set: Dublin
Sebastian Dangerfield (law student)

Ginger You're Barmy (1962)
David Lodge

Giovanni's Room (1956)
James Baldwin

Gipsy Baron, The (1885)
Mór Jókai

Girl from Addis, The (1984)
Ted Allbeury

Girl Hunters, The (1952)
Mickey Spillane

Girl in a Swing, The (1980)
Richard Adams

Girl in Blue, The (1970)
PG Wodehouse

Girl in Winter, A (1947)
Philip Larkin

Girl of the Sea of Cortez, The (1982)
Peter Benchley

Girl on the Boat, The (1922)
PG Wodehouse

Girls, The (1921)
Edna Ferber

Girls at War (1972)
Chinua Achebe

Girls in Their Married Bliss (1964)
Edna O'Brien
set: Ireland
Caithleen 'Cait' Brady
Bridget 'Baba' Brennan

Girls of Slender Means, The (1963)
Muriel Spark

Girl 20 (1971)
Kingsley Amis

Girl with Green Eyes
see ***Lonely Girl, The***

Girondin, The (1911)
Hilaire Belloc

Gladiators, The (1939)
Arthur Koestler

Gladiators, The
see ***Bestiaires, Les***

Glamorous Powers (1988)
Susan Howatch

Gläserne Bienen (1957)
(The Glass Bees)
Ernst Jünger

Glasperlenspiel, Das (1943)
(The Glass Bead Game)
Hermann Hesse

set: 23c
Josef Knecht

Glass Alembic, The (1973)
Elaine Feinstein

Glass Bead Game, The
see *Glasperlenspiel, Das*

Glass Bees, The
see *Gläserne Bienen*

Glass-Blowers, The (1963)
Daphne Du Maurier

set: France

Glass Key, The (1931)
Dashiell Hammett

Glass of Blessings, A (1958)
Barbara Pym

Glastonbury Romance, A (1932)
John Cowper Powys

Gleam in the North, The (1927)
DK Broster

Gli indifferenti (1929)
(The Time of Indifference)
Alberto Moravia

Glimpses of the Moon, The (1922)
Edith Wharton

Glitter Dome, The (1981)
Joseph Wambaugh

Glittering Images (1986)
Susan Howatch

Glittering Prizes, The (1976)
Frederic Raphael

set: 1950s Cambridge University

Glitz (1985)
Elmre Leonard

Gloriana (1978)
Michael Moorcock

Glory (1932)
Vladimir Nabokov

Glory Boys, The (1976)
Gerald Seymour

Glory of the Conquered, The (1909)
Susan Glaspell

Glory of the Hummingbird, The (1975)
Peter De Vries

Goalie's Anxiety at the Penalty Kick, The
see ***Angst des Tormanns beim Elfmeter, Die***

Go-Between, The (1953)
LP Hartley
set: Edwardian Norfolk
Leo Colston (lovers' go-between)
Ted Burgess (farmer/Marian's lover)
Marcus Winlow (Marian's brother)
Marian Winlow

God and His Gifts, A (1963)
Ivy Compton-Burnett

God Emperor of Dune (1980)
Frank Herbert

Godfather, The (1969)
Mario Puzo
Don Corleone ('Godfather')
Michael Corleone (Corleone's son)

God Is One (1877)
Mór Jókai

God Knows (1984)
Joseph Heller

Godolphin (1833)
Edward Bulwer-Lytton

Godplayer (1983)
Robin Cook

Gods Are A-Thirst, The
see ***Dieux ont soif, Les***

God's Good Man (1904)
Marie Corelli

God's Grace (1982)
Bernard Malamud

God's Little Acre (1933)
Erskine Caldwell
set: Georgia, USA
Dave Dawson (albino)
Rosamund Thompson, née Walden (Will's wife)
Will Thompson

Gods of Pegana, The (1905)
Edward Dunsany

God's Stepchildren (1924)
Sarah Gertrude Millin

Going Home (1973)
Danielle Steel

Going Their Own Ways (1938)
Alec Waugh

Gold and Iron (1918)
Joseph Hergesheimer

Gold Bug, The (1843)
Edgar Allan Poe
Jupiter (Legrand's companion)
Legrand (impoverished gentleman)

Gold Coast (1980)
Elmore Leonard

Golden Age, The (1895) coll
Kenneth Grahame

Golden Apples (1935)
Marjorie Kinnan Rawlings

Golden Arrow, The (1916)
Mary Webb

Golden Bowl, The (1904)
Henry James

set: Europe; Fawns (the Ververs' home)
Prince Amerigo (impoverished Italian)
Fanny Assingham (Maggie's acquaintance)
Charlotte Stant (Maggie's friend/Adam's eventual wife)
Adam Verver (art collector)
Maggie Verver (Adam's daughter)

Golden Butterfly, The (1876)
Walter Besant

Goldene Spiegel, Der (1911)
(The Golden Mirror)
Jakob Wassermann

Golden Fleece, The (1944)
Robert Graves

Golden Fruits, The
see ***Fruits d'or, Les***

Golden Gate, The (1976)
Alistair Maclean

Golden Hades, The (1929)
Edgar Wallace

Golden Hawk, The (1948)
Frank Yerby

Golden Honeycomb (1979)
Kamala Markandaya

Golden House, The (1895)
CD Warner

Golden Keel, The (1963)
Desmond Bagley

Golden Miles (1948)
Katharine Susannah Prichard

Golden Mirror, The
see ***Goldene Spiegel, Der***

Golden Notebook, The (1962)
Doris Lessing

Anna Wulf

Golden Orange, The (1990)
Joseph Wambaugh

Golden Pot, The
Goldene Topf, Der

Golden Sabre, The (1981)
Jon Cleary

Goldfinger (1959)
Ian Fleming

James Bond '007' (spy)
Auric Goldfinger (villain)
M (Bond's boss)
Miss Moneypenny (M's secretary)
Oddjob (Goldfinger's Korean guardian)

Gold from Gemini (1978)
Jonathan Gash

Lovejoy (dodgy antiques dealer)

Gold Mine (1970)
Wilbur Smith

Goldene Topf, Der (1814)
(The Golden Pot)
Ernst Theodor Amadeus Hoffmann

Gold Rimmed Spectacles, The (1958)
Giorgio Bassani

Golovlyov Family, The (1876)
Mikhail Saltykov

Gommes, Les (1953)
(The Erasers)
Alain Robbe-Grillet

Gondola Scam, The (1984)
Jonathan Gash

Lovejoy (dodgy antiques dealer)

Gone to Earth (1917)
Mary Webb

Gone with the Wind (1936)
Margaret Mitchell

set: American Civil War;
Tara (house/plantation)
Rhett Butler (Scarlett's 3rd husband)
Melanie Hamilton (Wilkes' fiancée)
Gerald O'Hara (plantation owner/ Scarlett's father)
Scarlett O'Hara (twice married woman)
Ashley Wilkes (Scarlett's real love)

Good Apostle, The
see ***Bon Apôtre, Le***

Good Apprentice, The (1985)
Iris Murdoch

Good As Gold (1979)
Joseph Heller

Goodbye California (1978)
Alistair Maclean

Goodbye, Chicken Little (1979)
Betsy Byars

Goodbye, Columbus (1959) coll
Philip Roth

Goodbye Janette (1981)
Harold Robbins

Goodbye Look, The (1969)
Ross Macdonald

Goodbye Mr Chips (1934)
James Hilton

set: Brookfield School
Mr Chipping, 'Chips' (schoolmaster)

Goodbye to All That (1929)
Robert Graves

set: World War I

Goodbye to Berlin (1939)
Christopher Isherwood

set: 1930s Berlin
Sally Bowles (cabaret artist)
Mr Isherwood (narrator)
Fräulein Schroeder (Isherwood's landlady)

Goodbye Un-America (1979)
James Aldridge

Good Companions, The (1929)
JB Priestley

set: 1920s England;
troupe: Dinky Doos
Susie Dean (actress)
Inigo Jollifant (actor)
Jimmy Nunn (actor)
Jess Oakroyd (stage manager)
Elizabeth Trant (sponsor)

Good Earth, The (1931)
Pearl Buck

Ching (Wang's steward)
Cuckoo (brothel-keeper)
Wang Lung (farmer)
O-Lan (Wang's wife)

Good Gestes (1929)
PC Wren

Good Man in Africa, A (1981)
William Boyd

Good Man Is Hard to Find, A (1955) coll
Flannery O'Connor

Good Morning Midnight (1939)
Jean Rhys

set: Paris
Sasha Jensen

Good Soldier, The (A Tale of Passion) (1915)
Ford Madox Ford

Captain Ashburnham
Leonora Ashburnham (Ashburnham's wife)
Florence Dowell (Dowell's wife)
John Dowell (narrator)
Nancy Rufford (Ashburnhams' ward)

Good Terrorist, The (1985)
Doris Lessing

Good Wives (or Little Women II) (1869)
Louisa M Alcott

Professor Bhaer (Jo's husband)
John Brooke (Meg's husband)
Old Mr Laurence (Laurie's grandfather)
Theodore Laurence, 'Laurie' (Amy's husband)
Amy March
Beth March (Amy's sister)
Jo March (Amy's sister)
Meg March (Amy's sister)
Mr March (Amy's father)
Mrs March, 'Marmee' (Amy's mother)

Good Woman, A (1927)
Louis Bromfield

Goose Cathedral, The (1950)
Jocelyn Brooke

Gora (1924)
Rabindranath Tagore

Gorilla Hunters, The (1861)
sequel to ***The Coral Island***
RM Ballantyne

Gorky Park (1981)
Martin Cruz Smith

set: Moscow

Gormenghast (1950)
Mervyn Peake

Goshawk (1951)
TH White

Gospel Fever (1980)
Frank Slaughter

Gospel of Freedom, The (1898)
Robert Herrick

Gosta Berlings saga (1891)
(The Story of Gosta Berling)
Selma Lagerlöf

Go Tell It on the Mountain (1953)
James Baldwin

set: Harlem, New York

Go to the Widow-Maker (1967)
James Jones

Governess, The (or The Little Female Academy (1749)
Sarah Fielding

Governing Class, The
see ***Kopf, Der***

Graf Petöfy (1884)
Theodor Fontane

Grail Tree, The (1979)
Jonathan Gash

Lovejoy (dodgy antiques dealer)

Grain of Wheat, A (1967)
Ngugi Wa Thiong'o

Grand Babylon Hotel (1902)
Arnold Bennett

Grand Design, The (1949)
John Dos Passos

Grand Écart (1923)
Jean Cocteau

Grand Hotel (1930)
Vicki Baum

Grandissimes, The (1880)
George Washington Cable

De Grapion family

Grand Meaulnes, Le (1913)
Alain-Fournier

Frantz De Galais (Yvonne's brother)
Yvonne De Galais (Meaulnes' eventual wife)
Augustin Meaulnes
François Seurel (Meaulnes' friend)

Grand Old Man, The
see ***Vecchione, Il***

Grand Sophy, The (1950)
Georgette Heyer

Grapes of Wrath, The (1939)
John Steinbeck

set: 1930s Oklahoma; California
Joad family

Grass, The
see ***Herbe, L'***

Grass Harp, The (1951)
Truman Capote

Grass Is Singing, The (1950)
Doris Lessing

Grass Widow's Tale, The (1968)
Ellis Peters

Grave Goods (1984)
Jessica Mann

Grave Mistake (1978)
Ngaio Marsh

Inspector Roderick Alleyn

Grave of Truth, The (1980)
Evelyn Anthony

Graveyard for Lunatics, A (1990)
Ray Bradbury

Gravity's Rainbow (1973)
Thomas Pynchon

Gray Lensman (1951)
EE 'Doc' Smith

Graysons, The (1888)
Edward Eggleston

Great Circle (1933)
Conrad Aiken

Great Emergency, A (1877)
Juliana Horatia Ewing

Greatest Gresham, The (1962)
Gillian Avery

Julia Gresham

Great Expectations (1861)
Charles Dickens

set: London; Satis House, Rochester
Compeyson (Miss Havisham's absconded fiancé)
Bentley Drummle (Estella's sometime husband)
Estella (Miss Havisham's adoptee)
Georgiana Gargery (Joe's wife/Pip's sister)
Joe Gargery (blacksmith)
Miss Havisham (recluse)
Jaggers (lawyer)
Abel Magwitch (escaped convict/Pip's benefactor)
Philip Pirrip, 'Pip'
Herbert Pocket (Pip's friend)
Uncle Pumblechook (Joe's uncle)
John Wemmick (Jaggers' clerk)
Mr Wopsle (parish clerk)

Great Expectations (1982)
Kathy Acker

Great Fortune, The (1960)
Olivia Manning

Romania
Guy Pringle

Harriet Pringle (Pringle's wife)
Prince Yakimov

Great Gatsby, The (1925)
F Scott Fitzgerald

set: West Egg (village), Long Island
Daisy Buchanan (Gatsby's lover)
Tom Buchanan (Daisy's husband)
Nick Carraway (narrator)
Jay Gatsby (financier)
Myrtle Wilson (Tom's lover)

Great God Pan, The (1894)
Arthur Machen

Great Hoggarty Diamond, The (1841)
William Makepeace Thackeray

Samuel Titmarsh (clerk)

Great Jones Street (1973)
Don Delillo

Great Northern? (1947)
Arthur Ransome

Great Pursuit, The (1977)
Tom Sharpe

Great Shadow, The (1892)
Arthur Conan Doyle

Great World and Timothy Colt, The (1956)
Louis Auchinloss

Green Archer (1923)
Edgar Wallace

Green Bay Tree, The (1924)
Louis Bromfield

Green Carnation, The (1894)
Robert Smythe Hichens

Green Coral (1935)
Henry Stacpoole

Green Darkness (1972)
Anya Seton

Greengage Summer, The (1958)
Rumer Godden

Greengates (1936)
RC Sherriff

Green Grass of Wyoming (1946)
Mary O'Hara

Flicka (colt)
Ken McLaughlin (Flicka's boy-owner)

Green, Green My Valley Now (1975)
Richard Llewellyn

Green Hat, The (1924)
Michael Arlen

Green Henry
see ***Grüne Heinrich, Der***

Green Hills of Africa, The (1935)
Ernest Hemingway

Green House, The
see Casa verde, La

Green Light (1935)
Lloyd C Douglas

Green Mansions (1904)
WH Hudson

set: Venezuelan jungle
Abel
Nuflo (tribesman)
Rima (Nuflo's granddaughter)

Greenmantle (1916)
John Buchan

Richard Hannay

Green Overcoat, The (1912)
Hilaire Belloc

Green Shade, The (1968)
Robin Maugham

Greenvoe (1972)
George Mackay Brown

Green Years, The (1944)
AJ Cronin

Grete Minde (1879)
Theodor Fontane

Greybeard (1964)
Brian W Aldiss

Grey Coast (1926)
Neil Gunn

Grey Granite (1934)
Lewis Grassic Gibbon

Chris Guthrie

Greyhound for Breakfast (1987) coll
James Kelman

Grey Roses (1895)
Henry Harland

Greyslaer (A Romance of the Mohawk) (1840)
Charles Fenno Hoffman

Max Greyslaer (lawyer)

Griffin's Way (1962)
Frank Yerby

Griffith Gaunt (or Jealousy) (1866)
Charles Reade

Grimus (1975)
Salman Rushdie

Group, The (1963)
Mary McCarthy

Group of Noble Dames, A (1891)
coll
Thomas Hardy

Group Portrait with Lady
see ***Gruppenbild mit Dame***

Groves of Academe, The (1952)
Mary McCarthy

Growth of the Soil
see ***Markens gro de***

Grüne Heinrich, Der (1854)
(Green Henry)
Gottfried Keller

Gruppenbild mit Dame (1971)
(Group Portrait with Lady)
Heinrich Böll

Leni Pfeiffer, née Gruytens

Gryll Grange (1861)
Thomas Love Peacock

set: Wales
Mr Falconer (classicist)
Mr Gryll (house-owner)
Miss Ilex (confirmed spinster)
Reverend Opimian

Guardian Angel, The (1867)
Oliver Wendell Holmes

Guardians, The (1955)
JIM Stewart

Guard of Honour (1948)
James Gould Cozzens

Guernsey Lily, A (1880)
Susan Coolidge

Guerre des Femmes, La (1846)
Alexandrer Dumas (père)

Guerrillas (1975)
VS Naipaul

Guest for the Night, A (1968)
SY Agnon

Guest of Honour, A (1970)
Nadine Gordimer

Guest of Quesnay (1908)
Booth Tarkington

Gueuse parfumé, récits provençaux, La (1876)
Paul Aréne

Guide, The (1958)
RK Narayan

Guilty River, The (1886)
Wilkie Collins

Guilty Thing Surprised, A (1970)
Ruth Rendell

Inspector Reg Wexford

Gulag Archipelago, The (1973-1975) 3 vol
Alexander Solzhenitsyn

set: Soviet labour camps

Gulliver's Travels (1726)
Jonathan Swift

set: Lilliput; Brobdingnag; Laputa (flying island); Glubbdubrib (island); Luggnagg, capital Lagado; Balnibarbi; Blefuscu (isle off Lilliput)
Brobdingnagians (giants)
Glumdalclitch (Brobdingnagian farmer's daughter)

Lemuel Gulliver (ship's surgeon, later captain)
Houyhnhnms (reasoning horses)
Lilliputians (midgets)
Struldbrugs (immortals)
Yahoos (brutal humans)

Gun for Sale, A (1936)
Graham Greene

Gunhild (1907)
Dorothea Frances Fisher

Gunsights (1979)
Elmore Leonard

Gunslinger, The (1982)
Stephen King

Guns of Navarone, The (1957)
Alistair Maclean

set: 1943 Turkish island

Gutta Percha Willie (1873)
George MacDonald

Guy and Pauline (1915)
Compton MacKenzie

Guy Deverell (1865)
Sheridan Le Fanu

Guy Fawkes (1841)
William Harrison Ainsworth

Guy Livingstone (1857)
George Alfred Lawrence

Guy Mannering (1815)
Walter Scott

set: Ellangowan, Dumfries; India
Harry Bertram
Dandie Dinmont (farmer)
Glossin (lawyer)
Dirk Hatteraick (smuggler)
Colonel Guy Mannering (army officer)
Julia Mannering (Mannering's daughter/Bertram's eventual wife)
Meg Merrilies (gypsy)
Dominie Sampson (Bertram's tutor)

Guy Rivers (1834)
William Gilmore Simms

Guzmón de Alfarache (1604)
Mateo Alemón

Gymadenia (1929)
Sigrid Undset

H

Habit of Empire, The (1941)
Paul Horgan

Hacienda (1934)
Kathleen Anne Porter

Hackenfeller's Ape (1953)
Brigid Brophy

Hadrian the Seventh (1904)
Frederick William Rolfe

Hagestolz, Der (1843)
Adalbert Stifter

Haj, The (1984)
Leon Uris

Hallowe'en Party (1969)
Agatha Christie

Hamlet, The (1940)
William Faulkner

set: Yoknapatawpha County, Mississippi
Snopes family

Hamlet's Revenge! (1937)
JIM Stewart

John Appleby (detective)

Ham on Rye (1982)
Charles Bukowski

Handful of Dust, A (1934)
Evelyn Waugh

set: Hetton (Lasts' country home), Brighton
John Beaver (Brenda's lover)
Lady Brenda Last (Last's wife)
Tony Last

Handful of Rice, A (1966)
Kamala Markandaya

Handful of Thieves, A (1967)
Nina Bawden

Handley Cross (1843)
RS Surtees

Mr Jorrocks (huntsman/grocer)

Handmaid's Tale, The (1985)
Margaret Atwood

Hand of Ethelberta, The (1876)
Thomas Hardy

Chickerel (butler)
Ethelberta Chickerel (Chickerel's daughter)
Picotee Chickerel (Chickerel's daughter)
Christopher Julian (musician/Ethelberta's admirer/Picotee's eventual husband)

Hand of Mary Constable, The (1964)
Paul Gallico

Hand-Reared Boy, The (1970)
Brian W Aldiss

Handy Andy (A Tale of Irish Life) (1842)
Samuel Lover

Andy Rooney

Handyman, The (1983)
Penelope Mortimer

Hanging On (1974)
Dean R Koontz

Hangman, The
see ***Bödeln***

Hangman's Holiday (1933)
Dorothy L Sayers

Bunter (Wimsey's servant)
Lord Peter Wimsey (amateur detective)

Hangover, The (1967)
Frank Sargeson

Hangover Square (1941)
Patrick Hamilton

set: Earl's Court
George Harvey Bone

Hans und Heinz Kirch (1882)
Theodor Storm

Haphazard House (1983)
Mary Wesley

Happy Land (1943)
MacKinlay Kantor

Happy Return, The (1937)
CS Forester

Horatio Hornblower

Happy Valley (1939)
Patrick White

Hard Cash (1863)
Charles Reade

David Dodd (sea captain)

Hard Feelings (1976)
Francis King

Harding's Luck (1909)
E Nesbit

Dickie Harding
Mouldiwarp (mole)

Hard Times (1854)
Charles Dickens

set: Coketown (actual Preston)
Stephen Blackpool (weaver)
Josiah Bounderby (Louisa's soon-to-be husband)
Louisa Gradgrind (Gradgrind's daughter)
Thomas Gradgrind (retired merchant)
Tom Gradgrind (Gradgrind's son)
Signor Jupe (clown)
Sissy Jupe (Jupe's daughter)
Sleary (circus owner)

Harlequin (1974)
Morris West

Harmful Intent (1990)
Robin Cook

Harnessing Peacocks (1985)
Mary Wesley

Harold (1848)
Edward Bulwer-Lytton

Haroun and the Sea of Stories (1990) coll
Salman Rushdie

Harriet (1977)
Jilly Cooper

Harriet Said (1972)
Beryl Bainbridge

Harrington (1817)
Maria Edgeworth

Harrowing of Hubertus, The (1954)
Edgar Mittelholzer

Harry Lorrequer (1839)
Charles Lever

Harry Richmond
see ***Adventures of Harry Richmond, The***

Harry's Game (1975)
Gerald Seymour

Harvest, The (1978)
Meyer Levin

Harvest Comedy (1937)
Frank Swinnerton

Hässliche Herzogin, Die (1923)
(The Ugly Duchess)
Lion Feuchtwanger

Hastenbeck (1898)
Wilhelm Raabe

Hatter's Castle (1931)
AJ Cronin

Haunted (1988)
James Herbert

Haunted Hotel, The (1879)
Wilkie Collins

Haunted House (1978)
Norah Lofts

Haunted Man and the Ghost's Bargain, The (1848)
Charles Dickens

Redlaw (chemist/'haunted' man)
Milly Swidger (Swidger's wife)
William Swidger (Redlaw's manservant)
Adolphus Tetterby (newsagent)

Haunting of Bellamy Four, The (1988)
Monica Dickens

Haunting of Toby Jugg, The (1948)
Dennis Wheatley

Haus Düsterweg (1835)
Willibald Alexis

Haus ohne Hüter (1954)
(The Unguarded House)
Heinrich Böll

Have His Carcase (1932)
Dorothy L Sayers

Bunter (Wimsey's servant)
Lord Peter Wimsey (amateur detective)

Hawaii (1959)
James A Michener

Hawbuck Grange (1847)
RS Surtees

Thomas Scott (huntsman)

Hawk and the Handsaw, The (1948)
JIM Stewart

John Appleby (detective)

Hawksmoor (1985)
Peter Ackroyd

Haxby's Circus (1930)
Katharine Susannah Prichard

Hazard of New Fortunes, A (1890)
William Dean Howells

set: New York
Dryfoos (farmer/businessman)

Head Birth, The
see ***Kopfgeburten***

Head Case, The (1979)
Jackie Gillott

Headless Angel (1948)
Vicki Baum

Headless Horseman, The (1866)
Mayne Reid

Headlong Hall (1816)
Thomas Love Peacock

Mr Escot (pessimist)
Mr Foster (optimist)

Headsman, The (1833)
James Fenimore Cooper

Healer, The (1911)
Robert Herrick

Healer, The (1955)
Frank Slaughter

Heart, The (1914)
Natsume Soseki

Heart for the Gods of Mexico, A (1939)
Conrad Aiken

Hearth and the Eagle, The (1948)
Anya Seton

Heart Is a Lonely Hunter, The (1940)
Carson McCullers

Heart of Darkness (1902)
Joseph Conrad

Kurtz (ivory-trader)

Heart of Midlothian, The (1818)
Walter Scott

set: 18c Heart of Midlothian (Edinburgh prison)
basis: Porteous Riot
Duke of Argyle
Reuben Butler (minister/Jeanie's husband)
Effie Deans
Jeanie Deans (Effie's half-sister)
Captain John Porteous City Guard commander)

Heart of the Matter, The (1948)
Graham Greene

set: Sierra Leone, West Africa
Ali (Scobie's servant)
Helen (Scobie's mistress)
Louise (Scobie's wife)
Scobie (deputy police commissioner)
Mr Wilson (intelligence agent)

Heart of War (1980)
John Masters

Heartsease (1854)
Charlotte M Yonge

Heat and Dust (1975)
Ruth Prawer Jhabvala

Heathen Chinee, The (1870)
Bret Harte

Heat of the Day, The (1949)
Elizabeth Bowen

Heaven and Earth (1985)
Frederic Raphael

Heaven Knows Where (1957)
DJ Enright

Heavenly Twins, The (1893)
Sarah Grand

Heaven's My Destination (1934)
Thornton Wilder

Heavy Weather (1933)
PG Wodehouse

set: Blandings Castle, Shropshire
Beach (Lord Emsworth's butler)
Empress of Blandings (pig)
Lord Emsworth
Lady Constance Keeble (Lord Emsworth's sister)
Galahad Threepwood (Lord Emsworth's brother)

He Cometh Leaping on the Mountain (1963)
Jerzy Andrzejewski

Hedgehog, The (1936)
Hedylus (1928)
Hilda Doolittle

Heidenmauer, The (1832)
James Fenimore Cooper

Heidi (1881)
Johanna Spyri
set: Switzerland; Frankfurt
Alm-Uncle (Heidi's grandfather)
Dete (Heidi's cousin)
Heidi (Adalheid) (orphan)
Peter (goatherd)
Fräulein Rottenmeier (Sesemanns' housekeeper)
Sesemann family

Heilige, Der (1880)
(The Saint)
Conrad Ferdinand Meyer

Heimsljós (1937–40) 4 vol
(World Light)
Halldór Laxness

Heiress, The (1987)
Evelyn Anthony

Heir of Redclyffe, The (1853)
Charlotte M Yonge
Amy (Guy's soon-to-be wife)
Guy Morville
Philip Morville (Guy's cousin)

He Knew He Was Right (1869)
Anthony Trollope
Bozzle (private detective)
Colonel Osborne (philanderer)
Emily Trevelyan, née Rowley (Trevelyan's wife)
Louis Trevelyan

Helbeck of Bannisdale (1898)
Mary Augusta Ward

Held in Bondage (1863)
Ouida

Helen (1834)
Maria Edgeworth

Helena (1950)
Evelyn Waugh

Helga's Web (1971)
Jon Cleary
Scobie Malone (detective)

Heliopolis (1949)
Ernst Jünger

Helliconia Spring (1982)
Helliconia Summer (1983)
Helliconia Winter (1985)
Brian W Aldiss

Hello, I'm Erica Long (1984)
Kathy Acker

Hell! Said the Duchess (1934)
Michael Arlen

Héloise and Abelard (1921)
George Moore

Hemlock and After (1952)
Angus Wilson
Bernard Sands (novelist)

Hemsöborna (1887)
(The People of Hemsö)
August Strindberg

Henderson the Rain King (1959)
Saul Bellow
set: Africa
Gene Henderson

Henrietta (1758)
Charlotte Lennox

Henrietta Temple (1837)
Benjamin Disraeli

Ferdinand Armine (soldier)
Katherine Grandison (Armine's sometime fiancée)
Lord Montfort
Henrietta Temple (Armine's sometime fiancée)

Henry and Cato (1977)
Iris Murdoch

Henry Brocken (1904)
Walter De La Mare

Henry Dunbar (1864)
Mary Elizabeth Braddon

Henry Esmond Esquire
see ***History of Henry Esmond Esquire, The***

Henry's Letters to His Grandmother (1870)
Abby Morton Diaz

Herbe, L' (1958)
(The Grass)
Claude Simon

Heretic of Soana, The
see ***Ketzer von Soana, Der***

Heretics of Dune (1982)
Frank Herbert

Hereward the Wake (1866)
Charles Kingsley

set: 11c
Hereward
Torfrida (Hereward's wife)

Heritage (1919)
Vita Sackville-West

Heritage and Its History, A (1959)
Ivy Compton-Burnett

Heritage of Hatcher Ide, The (1940)
Booth Tarkington

Her Mother's Daughter (1987)
Marilyn French

Hermsprong, or, Man As He Is Not (1796)
Robert Bage

Hero and a Martyr, A (1874)
Charles Reade

Hérodias (1877)
Gustave Flaubert

Heroes and Villains (1969)
Angela Carter

Heroes of Clone, The (1957)
Margaret Kennedy

Heron, The (1968)
Giorgio Bassani

Hero of Our Time, A (1840)
Mikhail Lermontov

Herself Surprised (1941)
Joyce Cary

Gulley Jimson (artist)

Her Son's Wife (1926)
Dorothea Frances Fisher

Herzog (1964)
Saul Bellow

Moses Herzog

Hesperus (1795)
Jean Paul

Hester (1883)
Margaret Oliphant

Hetty Wesley (1903)
Arthur Quiller-Couch

Hickory Dickory Death (1953)
Agatha Christie

Hercule Poirot (detective)

Hide and Tallow Man, The (1974)
JT Edson

Hide My Eyes (1958)
Margery Allingham

Albert Campion (detective)

High Citadel (1965)
Desmond Bagley

High Commissioner, The (1970)
Jon Cleary

Scobie Malone (detective)

High King, The (1968)
Lloyd Alexander

set: Prydain
Princess Eilonwy
Taran

Highland Fling (1931)
Nancy Mitford

Highland River (1937)
Neil Gunn

Highland Widow, The (1827)
Walter Scott

High Place, The (1923)
James Branch Cabell

High Rise (1975)
JG Ballard

High Stakes (1976)
Dick Francis

High Stand (1985)
Hammond Innes

High Wind in Jamaica (1929)
Richard Hughes

set: early 19c

High Window, The (1942)
Raymond Chandler

Philip Marlowe (detective)

High World (1954)
Ludwig Bemelmans

Hilda Lessways (1911)
Arnold Bennett

Edwin Clayhanger (Hilda's soon-to-be husband)
Hilda Lessways

Hillingdon hall (1845)
RS Surtees

Mr Jorrocks (huntsman/grocer)

Hill of Dreams, The (1907)
Arthur Machen

Hills Beyond, The (1941) posth unf
Thomas Wolfe

Hillsboro People (1915)
Dorothea Frances Fisher

Hillyers and the Burtons, The (1865)
Henry Kingsley

Hind Let Loose, A (1910) coll
CE Montague

Hired Man, The (1968)
Melvyn Bragg

Tallentire family

Hireling, The (1957)
LP Hartley

Lady Franklin

His Lordship (1969)
Leslie Thomas

His Monkey Wife (1930)
John Collier

Histoire (1967)
(History)
Claude Simon

Histoire Contemporaine, L' (1896–1901) 4 vol
Anatole France

vols:
1 *L'Orme du mail* (1896)
2 *Le Mannequin d'osier* (1897)
3 *L'Anneau d'améthyste* (1899)
4 *M Bergeret à Paris* (1901)

Monsieur Bergeret (provincial professor)

Histoire sans nom, Une (1882)
Jules-Amédée Barbey D'Aurevilly

History
see ***Histoire***

History Man, The (1975)
Malcolm Bradbury

set: Watermouth University
Howard Kirk (professor)

History of Henry Esmond Esquire, The (1852)
William Makepeace Thackeray

Lady Castlewood (Castlewood's wife)
Lord Castlewood
Henry Esmond (narrator)
Father Holt (Jesuit priest/Henry's tutor)

History of Mr Polly, The (1910)
HG Wells

Alfred Polly (tradesman)
Miriam Polly (Polly's wife)

History of Ophelia, The (1760)
Sarah Fielding

History of Pendennis, The (1850)
William Makepeace Thackeray

Laura Bell (Arthur's eventual wife)
Arthur Pendennis
Helen Pendennis (Arthur's mother)
Major Pendennis (Arthur's uncle)
Captain Shandon (journalist)
Mr Wagg (journalist)

History of Sir Charles Grandison, The (1753–4) 7 vol
Samuel Richardson

Harriet Byron (Sir Charles' eventual wife)
Sir Charles Grandison

History of the Countess of Delwyn, The (1759)
Sarah Fielding

History of the World in 10½ Chapters, A (1989)
Julian Barnes

History of Tom Jones, A Foundling, The (1749)
Henry Fielding

set: Somerset; Bristol
Bridget Allworthy (Allworthy's sister)
Squire Allworthy (widower)
Captain Blifil (Sophie's fiancé)
Jenny Jones Mrs Partridge's maidservant)
Tom Jones (foundling)
Mr Partridge (schoolmaster)
Mrs Partridge (Partridge's wife)
George Seagrim (Allworthy's gamekeeper)
Mollie Seagrim (Seagrim's daughter)
Square (philosopher)
Thwackum (tutor)
Sophie Western (Western's daughter)
Squire Western (fox-hunter)

Hitch-Hiker's Guide to the Galaxy, The (1978)
Douglas Adams

Arthur Dent (unwitting space traveller)
Marvin (paranoid android)
Ford Prefect

HM Pulham Esq (1941)
John Marquand

HMS Ulysses (1955)
Alistair Maclean

Hobbit, The (or There and Back Again) (1937)
JRR Tolkien

set: Middle Earth; Misty Mountains; Rivendell
Bilbo Baggins (Hobbit [or dwarf])
Frodo Baggins (Hobbit/Bilbo's nephew)
Beorn (half-man, half-bear)
Gandalf (wizard)
Gollum ('slimy creature')
Shadowfax (horse)
Smaug (dragon)

Hocus Pocus (1990)
Kurt Vonnegut

Hojarasca, La (1955)
(Leaf Storm)
Gabriel García Márquez

Holcroft Covenant, The (1977)
Robert Ludlum

Hold the Dream (1985)
Barbara Taylor Bradford

Hole in the Wall, The (1902)
Arthur Morrison

Holiday, The (1949)
Stevie Smith

Holiday at Dew Drop Inn (1962)
Eve Garnett

Hollow, The (1946)
Agatha Christie

Hercule Poirot (detective)

Hollywood (1989)
Charles Bukowski

Hollywood Husbands (1986)
Hollywood Wives (1983)
Jackie Collins

Holy Deadlock (1934)
AP Herbert

Holy War, The (1682)
John Bunyan

set: Mansoul (metropolis of the universe)
Diabolus
Emmanuel (Shaddai's son)
King Shaddai

Hombre (1961)
Elmore Leonard

Home and the World, The (1919)
Rabindranath Tagore

Home as Found (1838)
James Fenimore Cooper

Homecomings (1956)
CP Snow

Lewis Eliot (narrator/barrister)

Homely Lilla (1923)
Robert Herrick

Home to Harlem (1928)
Claude McKay

Home Town (1940)
Sherwood Anderson

Homeward Bound (1838)
James Fenimore Cooper

Homme de neige, L' (1856)
(The Snowman)
George Sand

Homme libre, Un (1889)
Maurice Barrès

Homme qui rit, L' (1869)
(The Laughing Man)
Victor Hugo

Homo (Ursus' trained wolf)
Ursus (vagabond)

Hommes de bonne volonté, Les (1932–47) 27 vol
(Men of Good Will)
Jules Romains

Homo Faber (1957)
Max Frisch

Hondo (1953)
Louis L'Amour

Honest John Vane (1875)
John William De Forest

Honey for the Bears (1963)
Anthony Burgess

Honey out of the Rock (1925)
Babette Deutsch

Honorary Consul, The (1973)
Graham Greene

set: Argentina

Honor Bright (1936)
Frances Parkinson Keyes

Honourable Schoolboy, The (1977)
John Le Carré

Karla (Smiley's adversary)
George Smiley (secret agent)

Honour This Day (1987)
Alexander Kent

Richard Bolitho (sailor)

Hoosier Schoolboy, The (1883)
Hoosier Schoolmaster, The (1871)
Edward Eggleston

Hopes and Fears (1860)
Charlotte M Yonge

Hopkins Manuscript, The (1939)
RC Sherriff

Horacker (1876)
Wilhelm Raabe

Hordubal (1933)
Karel Capek

Horloger du Cherche-Midi, L' (1959)
Luc Estang

Hornblower and the Atropos (1953)
Hornblower and the Hotspur (1962)
Hornblower in the West Indies (1958)
CS Forester

Horatio Hornblower

Hornets, The
see ***Hornissen, Die***

Hornissen, Die (1966)
(The Hornets)
Peter Handke

Horn of Roland, The (1974)
Ellis Peters

Horse and His Boy, The (1954)
CS Lewis

set: Narnia
Bree (talking horse)
Shasta

Horseman, Pass By (1961)
Larry McMurty

Horse's Mouth, The (1944)
Joyce Cary

Gulley Jimson (artist)

Hosen des Herrn von Bredow, Die
(1846-1848) 2 vol
Willibald Alexis

Hosts of Extras (1973)
James Leasor

Dr Jason Love

Hotel (1965)
Arthur Hailey

set: New Orleans

Hotel, The (1927)
Elizabeth Bowen

Hotel de Dream (1976)
Emma Tennant

Hotel du Lac (1984)
Anita Brookner

set: Switzerland
Edith Hope (novelist)

Hotel New Hampshire, The (1981)
John Irving

Hotel Splendide (1941)
Ludwig Bemelmans

Hothouse (1962)
Brian W Aldiss

Hothouse by the East River, The (1972)
Muriel Spark

Hot Money (1987)
Dick Francis

Hound of the Baskervilles, The (1902)
Arthur Conan Doyle

set: London; Devon
Sherlock Holmes (detective)
Dr John Watson (Holmes' companion)

House, The (1971)
Penelope Mortimer

House and Its Head, A (1935)
Ivy Compton-Burnett

House at Old Vine, The (1961)
Norah Lofts

House at Pooh Corner, The (1928) coll
AA Milne

Eeyore (donkey)
Kanga
Owl
Piglet
Rabbit
Christopher Robin
Roo
Tigger
Winnie-the-Pooh, or Pooh Bear

House at Sunset, The (1963)
Norah Lofts

House by the Churchyard, The (1863)
Sheridan Le Fanu

House by the Medlar Tree, The
see ***Malavoglia, I***

House Divided, A (1935)
Pearl Buck

House for Mr Biswas, A (1961)
VS Naipaul

set: Trinidad
Mr Biswas

Houseguest, The (1988)
Thomas Berger

Householder, The (1960)
Ruth Prawer Jhabvala

House in Dormer Forest, The (1920)
Mary Webb

House in Norham Gardens, The (1974)
Penelope Lively

House in Order, A (1966)
Nigel Dennis

House in Paris, The (1935)
Elizabeth Bowen

House Inside Out, A (1987)
Penelope Lively

House Mother Normal (1971)
BS Johnson

House of Arden, The (1908)
E Nesbit

Edred Arden
Elfrida Arden (Edred's sister)
Mouldiwarp (mole)

House of Children, The (1941)
Joyce Cary

House of Fear, The (1927)
Robert William Service

House of Gair, The (1953)
Eric Linklater

House of Hospitalities, The (1987)
Emma Tennant

House of Mirth, The (1905)
Edith Wharton

Lily Bart
Lawrence Selden (Lily's would-be suitor)

House of the Dead, The (1861)
Fyodor Dostoevsky

House of the Four Winds (1934)
John Buchan

Dick MacCunn

House of the Seven Gables, The (1851)
Nathaniel Hawthorne

Pyncheon family

House of the Sleeping Beauty (1969)
Yasunari Kawabata

House of the Wolf, The (1889)
Stanley John Weyman

House on the Strand, The (1969)
Daphne Du Maurier

House That Berry Built, The (1945)
Dornford Yates

House without a Key, The (1925)
Earl Derr Biggers

Charlie Chan (detective)

House with the Green Shutters, The (1901)
George Douglas

set: Barbie (Scottish burgh)
John Gourlay (businessman)

Howards End (1910)
EM Forster

house: Howards End
Helen Schlegel (Margaret's sister)
Margaret Schlegel (Henry's 2nd wife)
Tibby Schlegel (Margaret's brother)
Charles Wilcox (Henry's son)
Evie Wilcox (Henry's daughter)
Henry Wilcox
Paul Wilcox (Henry's son)

How Far Can You Go? (1980)
David Lodge

How Green Was My Valley (1939)
Richard Llewellyn

set: Welsh village
Huw Morgan (narrator)

How It Is (1961)
Samuel Beckett

How Like a God (1929)
Rex Stout

How the Leopard Got His Claws (1972)
Chinua Achebe

How the West Was Won (1962)
Louis L'Amour

How to Save Your Own Life (1978)
Erica Jong

Isadora Wing

Huck and Her Time Machine (1977)
Gillian Avery

Huckleberry Finn
see ***Adventures of Huckleberry Finn, The***

Hudson River Bracketed (1929)
Edith Wharton

Human Boy, The (1899)
Eden Phillpotts

Human Chord, The (1910)
Algernon Blackwood

Human Comedy, The (1943)
William Saroyan

Human Comedy, The
see ***Comédie humaine, La***

Human Factor, The (1978)
Graham Greene

Human Season, The (1960)
Edward Lewis Wallant

Humble Romance, A (1887)
Mary E Freeman

Humboldt's Gift (1975)
Saul Bellow
Charlie Citrine (narrator/playwright)

Humphry Clinker
see ***Expedition of Humphry Clinker, The***

Hundejahre (1963)
(Dog Years)
Günter Grass

158-Pound Marriage, The (1974)
John Irving

Hundred Days, A
see ***Cent Jours***

Hungarian Brothers, The (1807)
Anne Maria Porter

Hunger
see ***Sult***

Hungry As the Sea (1978)
Wilbur Smith

Hungry Hill (1943)
Daphne Du Maurier

Hungry Stones (1916) coll
Rabindranath Tagore

Hunt, The (1971)
Melvyn Bragg

Hunted, The (1977)
Elmore Leonard

Hunter and the Whale, The (1967)
Laurens Van Der Post

Hunter Hunted (1957)
Henry Treece

Hunt for Red October, The (1984)
Tom Clancy

Huntingtower (1922)
John Buchan
Dick MacCunn

Hurry on Down (1953)
John Wain

Hypatia (or New Foes with Old Faces) (1853)
Charles Kingsley

set: 5c Alexandria
Hypatia (Theon's daughter)
Orestes (city leader)
Philammon (monk)
Theon (mathematician)

Hyperion (1799)
Friedrich Hölderlin

I

I Am a Cat (1905)
Natsume Soseki

I Am Mary Dunne (1968)
Brian Moore

Iberia (1968)
James A Michener

Icarus Agenda, The (1988)
Robert Ludlum

I Capture the Castle (1952)
Dodie Smith

Ice Age, The (1977)
Margaret Drabble

Ice-Cream War, An (1982)
William Boyd

Ice House, The (1983)
Nina Bawden

Icelandic Fisherman
see ***Pêcheur d'Islande***

Iceland's Bell
see ***Íslandsklukkan***

Ice Palace (1958)
Edna Ferber

Ice Saints, The (1964)
Frank Tuohy

Ice Station Zebra (1963)
Alistair Maclean

set: Arctic

I, Claudius (1934)
Robert Graves

Ides of march, The (1948)
Thornton Wilder

Idiot, The (1868)
Fyodor Dostoevsky

Prince Myshkin

If Beale Street Could Talk (1974)
James Baldwin

If Ever I Cease to Love (1943)
Frances Parkinson Keyes

set: Louisiana

If I Were You (1931)
PG Wodehouse

If I Were You
see ***Si j'étais vous ...***

I For One (1956)
Frank Sargeson

If Tomorrow Comes (1985)
Sidney Sheldon

Iggie's House (1970)
Judy Blume

I Go by Sea, I Go by Land (1941)
PL Travers

I Hold Four Aces (1977)
James Hadley Chase
Helga Rolfe

Île des pingouins, L' (1908)
(Penguin Island)
Anatole France

Île mystérieuse, L' (1874–5) 3 vol
(The Mysterious Island)
Jules Verne

I Like It Here (1958)
Kingsley Amis

I Live Under a Black Sun (1937)
Edith Sitwell

Ill-Made Night, The (1941)
TH White

I'll Take Manhattan (1986)
Judith Krantz

I'll Tell Them I Remember You (1974)
William Peter Blatty

Illustrated Man, The (1951)
Ray Bradbury

Illywhacker (1985)
Peter Carey

Ilona (1960)
Hans Habe

Image Men, The (1968)
JB Priestley

Image of a Drawn Sword, The (1950)
Jocelyn Brooke

Image of a Society (1956)
Roy Fuller

Imaginary Friends (1967)
Alison Lurie

Imaginary Toys (1961)
Julian Mitchell

I Met a Gypsy (1935)
Norah Lofts

I'm King of the Castle (1970)
Susan Hill

Immaterial Murder Case, The (1945)
Julian Symons

Immensee (1851)
Theodor Storm

Immigrants, The (1971)
Howard Fast

Immoraliste, L' (1902)
André Gide

Immortel, L' (1888)
Alphonse Daudet

Imogen (1978)
Jilly Cooper

Imperative Duty, An (1893)
William Dean Howells

Imperial Caesar (1960)
Rex Warner

Imperial City (1937)
Elmer Rice

Imperial Palace (1930)
Arnold Bennett

Imperial Women (1956)
Pearl Buck

Impossible Object (1968)
Nicholas Mosley

Imposters (1986)
George V Higgins

Improvisatore, The (1835)
Hans Christian Andersen

Impudents, Les (1942)
Marguerite Duras

Im Schlaraffenland (1900)
Heinrich Mann

Im Schloss (1862)
(To the Castle)
Theodor Storm

Im Westen nichts Neues (1929)
(All Quiet on the Western Front)
Erich Maria Remarque

set: World War I

In a German Pension (1911) coll
Katherine Mansfield

In a Glass Darkly (1872) coll
Sheridan Le Fanu

Dr Martin Hesselius

In a Province (1934)
Laurens Van Der Post

In a Summer Season (1961)
Elizabeth Taylor

In a Yellow Wood (1947)
Gore Vidal

In Brief Authority (1915)
F Anstey

Inclinations (1916)
Ronald Firbank

In Cold Blood (1966)
Truman Capote

Incomparable Auk, The (1963)
Mordecai Richler

Incurable, The (1971)
Nell Dunn

In Custody (1980)
Anita Desai

Inde, L' (1903)
(India)
Pierre Loti

Indecent Exposure (1973)
Tom Sharpe

India
see ***Inde, L'***

Indiana (1832)
George Sand

set: Île Bourbon (actual Réunion, Indian Ocean)

Indiana (Creole beauty)

Indian Summer (1886)
William Dean Howells

Indifferent Children, The (1947)
Louis Auchinloss

In Dubious Battle (1936)
John Steinbeck

In 1851
see ***En 1851***

In einer Familie (1894)
Heinrich Mann

Infernal Desire Machines of Dr Hoffman, The (1972)
Angela Carter

Infinity of Mirrors, An (1964)
Richard Condon

Informer, The (1925)
Liam O'Flaherty

In Freedom's Cause (1885)
GA Henty

Ingénu, L' (1767)
Voltaire

Ingénue (1854)
Alexandre Dumas (père)

Ingénue libertine, L' (1909)
Colette

In Hazard (A Sea Story) (1938)
Richard Hughes

Inheritance (1932)
Phyllis Bentley

Inheritance, The (1824)
Susan Ferrier

Inheritors, The (1901)
Joseph Conrad & Ford Madox Ford

Inheritors, The (1955)
William Golding

In High Places (1962)
Arthur Hailey

In Honour Bound (1984)
Gerald Seymour

Inimitable Jeeves, The (1923) coll
PG Wodehouse

Reginald Jeeves (Wooster's valet)
Bertie Wooster

Injury Time (1977)
Beryl Bainbridge

In Maremma (1882)
Ouida

Inmates, The (1952)
John Cowper Powys

In Memoriam to Identity (1990)
Kathy Acker

In Mr Knox's Country (1915)
Edith Somerville

set: Shreelane (manor house), Ireland
Flurry Knox (Yeates' landlord)
Major Yeates (narrator/resident magistrate)
Philippa Yeates (Yeates' wife)

Inn at the Edge of the World, The (1990)
Alice Thomas Ellis

Innocence of Father Brown, The (1911)
GK Chesterton

Father Brown (priest/detective)
Flambeau (reformed criminal/Father Brown's assistant)

Innocent Birds (1926)
TF Powys

Innocent Blood (1982)
PD James

Innocente, L' (1892)
Gabriele D'Annunzio

Innocents Abroad, The (1869)
Mark Twain

set: Mediterranean
ship: Quaker City

In Ole Virginia (1887) coll
Thomas Nelson Page

Inquisitors, The (1957)
Jerzy Andrzejewski

In Search of Love and Beauty (1983)
Ruth Prawer Jhabvala

Insel Felsenburg, Die (1731–43) 4 vol
(The Island of Felsenburg)
Johann Gottfried Schnabel

Inshore Squadron, The (1979)
Alexander Kent

Richard Bolitho (sailor)

Inside Mr Enderby (1963)
Anthony Burgess

Enderby (slovenly poet)

Inside of the Cup, The (1913)
Winston Churchill

Inside, Outside (1985)
Herman Wouk

Instant in the Wind, An (1976)
André Brink

In Such a Night (1927)
Babette Deutsch

Insular Possession, An (1986)
Timothy Mo

Insurrection (1950)
Liam O'Flaherty

Integral Trees, The (1983)
Larry Niven

Intensive Care (1970)
Janet Frame

Intercom Conspiracy, The (1970)
Eric Ambler

International Episode, An (1879)
Henry James

Interpreters, The (1965)
Wole Soyinka

Interrogataire, L' (1957)
Luc Estang

Intervalle (1973)
Michel Butor

In the Absence of Mrs Petersen (1966)
Nigel Balchin

In the American Jungle (1937)
Waldo Frank

In the Beginning (1928)
Norman Douglas

In the Castle of My Skin (1953)
George Lamming

In the Country of Last Things (1987)
Paul Auster

In the Country of the Skin (1973)
Peter Redgrove

In the Days of the Comet (1906)
HG Wells

In the Golden Days (1885)
Edna Lyall

In the Heart of the Country (1977)
John Michael Coetzee

In the Heart of the Seas (1948)
SY Agnon

In the Heat of the Night (1965)
John Ball

Virgil Tibbs (detective)

In the High Valley (1890)
Susan Coolidge

In the House of Brede (1970)
Rumer Godden

In Their Wisdom (1974)
CP Snow

In the Labyrinth
see ***Dans le labyrinthe***

In the Money (1940)
William Carlos Williams

In the Springtime of the Year (1974)
Susan Hill

In the Teeth of the Evidence (1940)
Dorothy L Sayers

Bunter (Wimsey's servant)
Lord Peter Wimsey (amateur detective)

In the Thirties (1962)
Edward Upward

In the Wet (1953)
Nevil Shute

In the Wood (1983)
Keith Waterhouse

In This Our Life (1941)
Ellen Glasgow

Intimate Relations (1980)
Jackie Gillott

Intimate Strangers (1937)
Katharine Susannah Prichard

In Transit (1969)
Brigid Brophy

Introducing the Toff (1938)
John Creasey

The Toff (adventurer)

Intruder in the Dust (1948)
William Faulkner

Intrusions of Peggy, The (1902)
Anthony Hope

Invaders, The (1934)
William Plomer

In Vain (1872)
Henryk Sienkiewicz

Invisible Man (1952)
Ralph Ellison

Invisible Man, The (1897)
HG Wells

Griffin (scientist)

Invitation to a Beheading (1938)
Vladimir Nabokov

Invitation to Live (1940)
Lloyd C Douglas

Invitation to the Waltz (1932)
Rosamund Lehmann

Invitée, L' (1943)
(She Came to Stay)
Simone de Beauvoir

In Youth Is Pleasure (1944)
Denton Welch

Ipcress File, The (1962)
Len Deighton

Harry Palmer (spy)

Irene Iddesleigh (1897)
Amanda Ros

Irish Cousin, An (1889)
Edith Somerville

Irish Witch, The (1973)
Dennis Wheatley

I, Robot (1950)
Isaac Asimov

Iron-Bound (1936)
Ellis Peters

Iron Heel, The (1907)
Jack London

set: 1930s
Avis (agitator/Everhard's wife)
Everhard

Iron Horse, The (1871)
RM Ballantyne

Ironing Board, The (1949)
Christopher Morley

Irréparable, L' (1884)
Paul Bourget

Irrungen Wirrungen (1888)
Theodor Fontane

Isabel Clarendon (1886)
George Gissing

Isabelle de Bavière (1836)
Alexandre Dumas (père)

I Saw In My Dream (1949)
Frank Sargeson

I Saw Three Ships (1892)
Arthur Quiller-Couch

I Say No (1881)
Wilkie Collins

Isegrimm (1854)
Willibald Alexis

Ishmael (1884)
Mary Elizabeth Braddon

Island (1962)
Aldous Huxley
set: Pala (imaginary Far East island)
Will Farnaby (journalist)

Island, The (1979)
Peter Benchley

Island in the Sun (1956)
Alec Waugh

Island of Dr Moreau, The (1896)
HG Wells

Island of Felsenburg, The
see ***Insel Felsenburg, Die***

Island of Sheep, The (1936)
John Buchan
Sandy Arbuthnot (Hannay's friend)
Richard Hannay

Island Pharisees, The (1904)
John Galsworthy

Islands in the Stream (1970) posth
Ernest Hemingway

Íslandsklukkan (1943–9)
(Iceland's Bell)
Halldór Laxness

Island Where Time Stands Still, The (1954)
Dennis Wheatley
Gregory Sallust (agent)

Israel Potter (His Fifty Years in Exile) (1855)
Herman Melville
Israel Potter

I Stand on a Quiet Shore (1982)
Richard Llewellyn

Isvik (1991)
Hammond Innes

It (1986)
Stephen King

Italian, The (1797)
Ann Radcliffe

Italian Girl, The (1964)
Iris Murdoch

Italian Spring, The (1964)
Gillian Avery

Italian Woman (1952)
Jean Plaidy

It Can't Happen Here (1935)
Sinclair Lewis

I, the Jury (1947)
Mickey Spillane
Mike Hammer (private eye)

I Thought of Daisy (1929)
Edmund Wilson

It Is Never Too Late to Mend (1856)
Charles Reade

It's a Battlefield (1934)
Graham Greene

It's Never Over (1930)
Morley Callaghan

It's Not the End of the World (1972)
Judy Blume

It Was Like This (1940)
Hervey Allen

Ivanhoe (1819)
Walter Scott

set: late 12c Ashby-de-la-Zouch; Torquilstone Castle
Bois-Guilbert (Templar)
Cedric (Ivanhoe's father)
Gurth (swineherd)
Robin Hood ('outlaw')
Isaac (Rebecca's father)
Ivanhoe
Rebecca (Jewess)
Richard I (King of England)
Rowena (Ivanhoe's beloved)
Friar Tuck
Ulrica (crone)
Wamba (Cedric's servant)

Ivory Tower, The (1917) posth unf
Henry James

Ivy Tree, The (1961)
Mary Stewart

I Want It Now (1968)
Kingsley Amis

I Want to Go to Moscow (1986)
Maureen Duffy

I Was Dancing (1964)
Edna O'Connor

I Will Fear No Evil (1971)
Robert A Heinlein

I Wish He Would Not Die (1957)
James Aldridge

I Would Be Private (1937)
Rose Macaulay

J

Jacaranda Tree, The (1949)
HE Bates

Jack (1876)
Alphonse Daudet

Jackanapes (1879)
Juliana Horatia Ewing

Jack and Jill (1880)
Louisa M Alcott

Jack Hinton the Guardsman (1843)
Charles Lever

Jack Ketch (1834)
Charles Whitehead

Jack Sheppard (1839)
William Harrison Ainsworth

Jack Sheppard (highwayman)

Jacob Faithful (1834)
Frederick Marryat

Tom Beazley (Jacob's friend)
Dominic Dobbs (schoolmaster)
Jacob Faithful (orphan/lighterman)

Jacob's Room (1922)
Virginia Woolf

set: World War I
Jacob Flanders

Jacques (1834)
George Sand

Jacques le fataliste (1796) posth
Denis Diderot

Jade Gate (1976)
James Leasor

Jailbird (1979)
Kurt Vonnegut

Jake Baldwin's Vow (1948)
Morley Callaghan

Jake's Thing (1978)
Kingsley Amis

Jalna (1927)
Mazo De La Roche
Whiteoak family

Jalousie, La (1957)
(Jealousy)
Alain Robbe-Grillet

Jamaica (1957)
Peter Abrahams

Jamaica Inn (1936)
Daphne Du Maurier
set: Bodmin Moor
Jem Merlyn (Joss' brother)
Joss Merlyn (Jamaica Inn landlord/Mary's uncle)
Mary Yellan

James and the Giant Peach (1961)
Roald Dahl

James Wallace (1788)
Robert Bage

James without Thomas (1959)
Gillian Avery

Jane Eyre (1847)
Charlotte Brontë
set: Lowood Institution (school); Thornfield Hall
Helen Burns (orphan)
Jane Eyre (orphan/governess)
Richard Mason (Bertha's brother)
Mrs Read (Jane's aunt)
Diana Rivers (St John's sister)
Mary Rivers (St John's sister)
Rev St John Rivers
Adèle Rochester (Rochester's illegitimate daughter)
Bertha Rochester (Rochester's wife)
Edward Fairfax Rochester
Miss Temple (school superintendent)

Jane Field (1893)
Mary E Freeman

Jane Talbot (1801)
Charles Brockden Brown

Jan of the Windmill (1876)
Juliana Horatia Ewing

Japhet in Search of a Father (1836)
Frederick Marryat

Jardin de Bérénice, Le (1891)
Jardin sur l'Oronte, Un (1922)
Maurice Barrès

Jarrett's Jade (1959)
Frank Yerby

Jason Edwards: an Average Man (1892)
Henry Garland

Jassy (1944)
Norah Lofts

Jaunty Jock (1918)
Neil Munro

Java Head (1919)
Joseph Hergesheimer

Jaws (1974)
Peter Benchley

set: off Long Island
Jaws (shark)

Jealous God, The (1964)
John Braine

Jealousy
see ***Jalousie, La***

Jean Barois (1913)
Roger Martin du Gard

Jean-Christophe (1905–1912) 10 vol
Romain Rolland

Jean des figues (1868)
Paul Arène

Jean Huguenot (1923)
Stephen Vincent Benét

Jeannot et Colin (1764)
Voltaire

Jeeves and the Feudal Spirit (1954)
Jeeves in the Offing (1960)
PG Wodehouse

Reginald Jeeves (Wooster's valet)
Bertie Wooster

Jennie (1950)
Paul Gallico

Jennie Gerhardt (1911)
Theodore Dreiser

set: Ohio
Senator Brander (Jennie's seducer)
Letty Gerald (Kane's eventual wife)
Jennie Gerhardt
Vesta Gerhardt (Jennie's daughter)
Lester Kane (manufacturer)

Jennifer Lorn (1923)
Elinor Wylie

Jennings Goes to School (1950)
Anthony Buckeridge

set: Linbury Court Preparatory School
Mr Carter (schoolmaster)
Darbishire (Jennings' schoolfriend)
Jennings (schoolboy)
Mr Wilkins (schoolmaster)

Jenny (1911)
Sigrid Undset

Jenny by Nature (1961)
Erskine Caldwell

Jenny Villiers (1947)
JB Priestley

Jeremy (1919)
Jeremy and Hamlet (1923)
Jeremy at Crale (1927)
Hugh Walpole

Jerome, a Poor Man (1897)
Mary E Freeman

Jerusalem (1902)
Selma Lagerlöf

Jerusalem the Golden (1967)
Margaret Drabble

Jest of God, A (1966)
Margaret Laurence

Jewel in the Crown, The (1966)
Paul Scott

set: 1940s India
Edwina Crane (missionary)
Hari Kumar
Daphne Manners
Ronald Merrick (police superintendent)

Jew in Love, A (1930)
Ben Hecht

Maxwell Bodenheim

Jews of Silence, The
see ***Juif du silence, Les***

Jews of Zirndorf, Die
see ***Juden von Zirndorf, Die***

Jew Süss
see ***Jud Süss***

Jill (1946)
Philip Larkin

Jim Davies (1911)
John Masefield

Jim Redlake (1930)
Francis Brett Young

Jitterbug Perfume (1984)
Tom Robbins

Joan and Peter (1918)
HG Wells

Job (1930)
Joseph Roth

Job, The (1917)
Sinclair Lewis

Joby (1964)
Stan Barstow

Jocelyn (1898)
John Galsworthy

Johanna (1947)
Penelope Mortimer

John Barleycorn (1913)
Jack London

John Eax and Mamelon (1882)
Albion W Tourgée

John Halifax, Gentleman (1856)
Dinah Maria Craik

set: Tewkesbury
Abel Fletcher (tanner)
Phineas Fletcher (Abel's son)
John Halifax
Ursula March (John's eventual wife)

John Inglesant (1881)
JH Shorthouse

set: early 17c

John Macnab (1925)
John Buchan

Edward Leithen

John March, Southerner (1894)
Johnnie Sahib (1952)
Paul Scott

Johnny I Hardly Knew You (1977)
Edna O'Brien

John Silence (1908)
Algernon Blackwood

John Splendid (1898)
Neil Munro

Joie, La (1929)
Georges Bernanos

Joke, The (1967)
Milan Kundera

Joker in the Pack, The (1975)
James Hadley Chase

Helga Rolfe

Joke Shop, The (1976)
DJ Enright

Jonah, The (1981)
James Herbert

Jonah & Co (1922)
Dornford Yates

Jonathan Wild the Great
see ***Life of Jonathan Wild the Great, The***

Jorrocks's Jaunts and Jollities (1838) coll
RS Surtees

Mr Jorrocks (huntsman/grocer)

Jo's Boys (1886)
Louisa M Alcott

set: Plumfield School
Professor Bhaer (Jo's husband)
John Brooke (Meg's husband)
Old Mr Laurence (Laurie's grandfather)
Theodore Laurence, `Laurie' (Amy's husband)
Amy March
Jo March (Amy's sister)
Meg March (Amy's sister)

Joseph Andrews
see ***Adventures of Joseph Andrews, The***

Joseph der Ernährer (1942)
Thomas Mann

Joseph im Schnee (1860)
Berthold Auerbach

Joseph in Ägypten (1936)
Thomas Mann

Joseph Kerkhovens dritte Existenz (1934)
Jakob Wassermann

Josh Lawton (1972)
Melvyn Bragg

Joshua Then and Now (1980)
Mordecai Richler

Journal d'un curé de campagne, Le (1936)
Giorgio Bernanos

Journal of the Fictive Life (1965)
Howard Nemerov

Journal of the Plague Year (1720)
Daniel Defoe

Journey (1988)
James A Michener

Journeyman (1935)
Erskine Caldwell

Journey to the Centre of the Earth
see ***Voyage au centre de la terre***

Journey to the Interior (1946)
PH Newby

Joy and Josephine (1948)
Monica Dickens

Joy in the Morning (1946)
PG Wodehouse

Reginald Jeeves (Wooster's valet)
Bertie Wooster

Joy of the Worm (1969)
Frank Sargeson

Joy Street (1951)
Frances Parkinson Keyes

JR (1976)
William Gaddis

Juan in America (1931)
Juan in China (1937)
Eric Linklater

Jubb (1963)
Keith Waterhouse

Judas Country (1975)
Gavin Lyall

Judas Pair, The (1977)
Jonathan Gash

Lovejoy (dodgy antiques dealer)

Juden von Zirndorf, Die (1897)
(The Jews of Zirndorf)
Jakob Wassermann

Jude the Obscure (1895)
Thomas Hardy

set: Christminster (actual Oxford)
Sue Bridehead (Jude's cousin & lover; Phillotson's wife)
Arabella Donn (barmaid/Jude's soon-to-be wife)
Jude Fawley
Richard Phillotson (schoolteacher)

Judge, The (1922)
Rebecca West

Judgement Day (1981)
Penelope Lively

Judgement in Stone, A (1977)
Ruth Rendell

Judge Not (1938)
Sholem Asch

Judge's Story, The (1947)
Charles Morgan

Judgment Day (1935)
James T Farrell

Judgment of Deke Hunter, The (1976)
George V Higgins

Judgment of Paris, The (1952)
Gore Vidal

Judith Hearne (1955)
Brian Moore

Judith Paris (1931)
Hugh Walpole

Jud Süss (1925)
(Jew Süss)
Lion Feuchtwanger

Juifs du silence, Les (1966)
(The Jews of Silence)
Elie Wiesel

Julia de Roubigné (1777)
Henry Mackenzie

Julian (1964)
Gore Vidal

Julian Home: a Tale of College Life (1859)
Frederick William Farrar

Julie, ou la Nouvelle Héloïse (1761)
Jean-Jacques Rousseau

Juliet Grenville (1774)
Henry Brooke

Juliette (1798)
Marquis de Sade

Juliette au pays des hommes (1924)
Jean Giraudoux

July's People (1981)
Nadine Gordimer

Jumbo Spencer (1963)
Helen Cresswell

Jument verte, La (1933)
(The Green Mare)
Marcel Aymé

Jumping Joan (1954)
CHB Kitchin

Jumping the Queue (1983)
Mary Wesley

Junge Joseph, Der (1934)
(The Young Joseph)
Thomas Mann

Jungle, The (1906)
Upton Sinclair

set: Chicago

Jungle Books, The (1894–5) 2 vol
Rudyard Kipling

set: (mainly) India
Akela (chief wolf)
Bagheera (black panther)
Baloo (brown bear)
Bandar-Log (monkey-people)
Buldeo (hunter)
Chil (kite)
Chuchundra (musk-rat)
Darzee (tailor-bird)
Ferao (woodpecker)
Hathi (elephant)
Ikki (porcupine)
Kaa (python)
Kadlu (eskimo)
Kala Nag (elephant)
Ko (crow)
Limmershin (wren)
Mang (bat)
Mao (peacock)
Matkah (seal)
Mowgli (wolf-boy)
Mugger-Ghaut (crocodile)
Nag (cobra)
Nagaina (cobra)
Purun Bhagat (hermit)
Quiquern (sledge-dog)
Rama (bull)
Rikki-Tikki-Tavi (mongoose)
Sea Catch (seal)
Seeonee (wolf-pack)
Shere Khan (tiger)
Slow-Solid (tortoise)
Tabaqui (jackal)
Tha (elephant)
Toomai (boy)
Won-Tolla (lone wolf)

Jungle Lovers (1971)
Paul Theroux

Junkers, The (1966)
Piers Paul Read

Junkie (1953)
William Burroughs

Jurgen (1919)
James Branch Cabell
set: Kingdom of Poictesme
Jurgen (pawnbroker)
Lisa Jurgen's wife

Jürg Jenatsch (1876)
Conrad Ferdinand Meyer

Just Above My Head (1979)
James Baldwin

Just and the Unjust, The (1942)
James Gould Cozzens

Just Another Sucker (1961)
James Hadley Chase

Justicier, Le (1919)
Paul Bourget

Justine (1957)
Laurence Durrell
set: Alexandria, Egypt
Balthazar
Clea (artist)
LG Darley (narrator)
Justine
Melissa (Darley's mistress)
Mountolive (ambassador)
Nessim (Justine's husband)
Pursewarden (British agent)

Justine (1791)
Marquis de Sade

Just Like a Lady (1960)
Nina Bawden

Just Looking (1989)
John Updike

Just So Stories (1902) coll
Rudyard Kipling

Just You Wait and See (1986)
Stan Barstow

K

Kane and Abel (1979)
Jeffrey Archer

Kangaroo (1923)
DH Lawrence
set: Australia
Jack Calcott (Somers' neighbour)
'Kangaroo' Ben Cooley (lawyer)
Harriet Somers (Richard's wife)
Richard Lovat Somers (writer)

Kanthapura (1938)
Raja Rao

Ka of Gifford Hillary, The (1956)
Dennis Wheatley

Kapillan of malta, The (1973)
Nicholas Monsarrat

Karl und Rosa (1950)
Alfred Döblin

Karpathy (1854)
Mór Jókai

Karuna (1881)
Rabindranath Tagore

Kate and Emma (1964)
Monica Dickens

Kate Fennigate (1943)
Booth Tarkington

Kate Hannigan (1947)
Catherine Cookson

Katherine (1954)
Anya Seton

Katherine Christian (1943) posth unf
Hugh Walpole

Käthi (1847)
Jeremias Gotthelf

Kathleen (1920)
Christopher Morley

Kathy Goes to Haiti (1978)
Kathy Acker

Katie Mulholland (1967)
Catherine Cookson

Katz und Maus (1961)
(Cat and Mouse)
Günter Grass

Kaywana Blood (1958)
Edgar Mittelholzer

Keeping Henry (1988)
Nina Bawden

Keeping Up Appearances (1928)
Rose Macaulay

Keep the Aspidistra Flying (1936)
George Orwell

Gordon Comstock (bookseller's assistant)

Kellys and the O'Kellys, The (1848)
Anthony Trollope

Kenelm Chillingly (1873)
Edward Bulwer-Lytton

Kenilworth (1821)
Walter Scott

set: 16c Kenilworth Castle; Cumnor Place (house), near Oxford
Queen Elizabeth
Earl of Leicester (Amy's soon-to-be husband/Varney's patron)
Amy Robsart
Dickie 'Flibbertigibbet' Sludge (Smith's friend)
Wayland Smith (farrier/physician)
Edmund Tressilian (Amy's Cornish suitor)
Richard Varney (Amy's villainous guardian)

Kennedy for the Defense (1980)
George V Higgins

Kentucky Cardinal, A (1894)
James Lane Allen

Georgiana Cobb (Adam's beloved)
Adam Moss

Képi, Le (1943)
Colette

Kepler (1981)
John Banville

Kept (1925)
Alec Waugh

Kept in the Dark (1982)
Nina Bawden

Kes
see ***Kestrel for a Knave, A***

Kestrel for a Knave, A (1968)
(also titled ***Kes***)
Barry Hines

Kes (kestrel)

Ketzer von Soana, Der (1918)
(The Heretic of Soana)
Gerhart Hauptmann

Keys of St Peter, The
see ***Clés de Saint Pierre, Les***

Keys of the Kingdom, The (1941)
AJ Cronin

Key to Rebecca, The (1980)
Ken Follett

Kid for Two Farthings, A (1953)
Wolf Mankowitz

set: London's East End

Kidnapped (1886)
RL Stevenson

set: Mull; Highlands
David Balfour
Alan Breck (Balfour's companion)
Colin Campbell (murder victim)

Kidnapper, The (1954)
Robert Bloch

Killer, The (1970)
Colin Wilson

Killer Mine (1947)
Hammond Innes

Killing Bottle, The (1932) coll
LP Hartley

Killing Doll, The (1984)
Ruth Rendell

Killing Mister Watson (1990)
Peter Matthiessen

Killing of Francie Lake, The (1962)
Julian Symons

Killing Time (1967)
Thomas Berger

Killshot (1989)
Elmore Leonard

Kim (1901)
Rudyard Kipling

set: India
Colonel Creighton (military surveyor)
Kimball 'Kim' O'Hara (orphan)

Kind of Healthy Game, A (1986)
Jessica Mann

Kind of Loving, A (1960)
Stan Barstow

set: Yorkshire
Ingrid Brown (Vic's wife)
Vic Brown

Kinflicks (1976)
Lisa Alther

King Coal (1917)
Upton Sinclair

King Coffin (1935)
Conrad Aiken

Kingdom, A (1978)
James Hanley

Kingdom and the Cave, The (1960)
Joan Aiken

Kingdom Come (1980)
Melvyn Bragg

Tallentire family

Kingdom of the Wicked, The (1985)
Anthony Burgess

Kingdom of Twilight, The (1904)
Forrest Reid

Kingfisher (1977)
Gerald Seymour

King Jesus (1946)
Robert Graves

King John's Treasure (1954)
RC Sherriff

King Must Die, The (1958)
Mary Renault

King of Alsander, The (1914)
James Elroy Flecker

King of a Rainy Country, The (1956)
Brigid Brophy

King, Queen, Knave (1928)
Vladimir Nabokov

King Rat (1962)
James Clavell

Kingsblood Royal (1947)
Sinclair Lewis

King's General, The (1946)
Daphne Du Maurier

King's Jackal, The (1898)
Richard Harding Davis

King Solomon's Mines (1885)
H Rider Haggard

set: South Africa
Sir Henry Curtis (Quatermain's companion)
Gagool (Kukuanas' tribal witch)
Captain John Good (Quatermain's companion)
Allan Quatermain

Kipps (1905)
HG Wells

set: Folkestone
Arthur 'Arty' Kipps (draper)
Ann Pornick (Kipps' 1st love)
Helen Walsingham (Kipps' fiancée)

Kirsteen (1890)
Margaret Oliphant

Kiss Me, Deadly (1952)
Mickey Spillane

Mike Hammer (private eye)

Kiss, Kiss (1960)
Roald Dahl

Kiss to the Leper, The
see ***Baiser au lépreux, Le***

Kit Brandon (1936)
Sherwood Anderson

Kith (1977)
PH Newby

Kitty Foyle (1939)
Christopher Morley

Kleine Herr Friedemann, Der (1898) coll
(Little Herr Friedemann)
Thoman Mann

Kleiner Mann – was nun? (1932)
(Little Man What Now?)
Hans Fallada

Kleine Stadt, Die (1909)
(The Small Town)
Heinrich Mann
set: Italy

Kloster bei Sendomir, Das (1828)
Franz Grillparzer

Knight of Gwynne, The (1847)
Charles Lever

Knight's Acre (1975)
Norah Lofts

Knight without Armour (1933)
James Hilton

Knulp (1915)
Hermann Hesse

Konferenz der Tiere, Die (1949)
(The Animals' Conference)
Erich Kästner

Königliche Hoheit (1909)
Thomas Mann

Konovalov (1903)
Maxim Gorky

Kopf, Der (1925)
(The Governing Class)
Heinrich Mann

Kopfgeburten (1980)
(The Head Birth)
Günter Grass

Kotik Letaev (1915–16) 2 vol
Andrei Bely

Kraken Wakes, The (1953)
John Wyndham

Kreutzer Sonata, The (1889)
Leo Tolstoy

Kristin Lavransdatter (1920–2) 3 vol
Sigrid Undset

Kristnihald undir Jökli (1968)
(Christianity at the Glacier)
Halldór Laxness

Kroniki (1987)
Czeslaw Milosz

Kyoto (1962)
Yasunari Kawabata

L

Là-bas (1891)
(Over There)
Joris-Karl Huysmans
Durtal

Labours of Hercules, The (1947)
Agatha Christie
Hercule Poirot (detective)

LaBravo (1983)
Elmore Leonard

Labyrinth, Das (1922)
Ina Seidel

Labyrinths (1953) coll
Jorge Luis Borges

Ladders to Fire (1946)
Anaïs Nin

Ladies of Lyndon, The (1923)
Margaret Kennedy

Lady, The (1957)
Conrad Richter

Lady and Unicorn (1937)
Rumer Godden

Lady Audley's Secret (1862)
Mary Elizabeth Braddon

Lady Baltimore (1906)
Owen Wister

Lady Boss (1990)
Jackie Collins

Lady Chatterley's Lover (1928)
DH Lawrence

set: Wragby Hall, the Midlands
Sir Clifford Chatterley
Lady Constance Chatterley (Sir Clifford's wife)
Hilda (Lady Chatterley's sister)
Oliver Mellors (gamekeeper/Lady Chatterley's lover)
Michaelis (playwright/Lady Chatterley's previous lover)

Lady Good-for-Nothing (1910)
Arthur Quiller-Couch

Lady in the Lake, The (1943)
Raymond Chandler

Philip Marlowe (detective)

Lady in the Tower (1986)
Jean Plaidy

Lady into Fox (1922)
David Garnett

Lady Judge, The
see ***Richterin, Die***

Lady of the Aroostook, The (1879)
William Dean Howells

Lady Oracle (1976)
Margaret Atwood

Lady Rose's Daughter (1903)
Mary Augusta Ward

Lady Susan (1871) posth
Jane Austen

set: Churchill (Vernons' house)
Lady De Courcy
Mrs Johnson (Lady Susan's friend)
Lady Susan
Mr Vernon
Mrs Vernon (Vernon's wife/Lady De Courcy's daughter)

Lair (1979)
James Herbert

Lake of Darkness, The (1980)
Ruth Rendell

Lamb (1980)
Bernard MacLaverty

Lamiel (1889) posth unf
Stendhal

Lamp for Nightfall, A (1952)
Erskine Caldwell

Lanark: A Life in Four Books (1981)
Alasdair Gray

Lancashire Witches, The (1848)
William Harrison Ainsworth
set: Pendle Forest

Lancelot (1977)
Walker Percy

Lancelot (1978)
Peter Vansittart

Landhaus am Rhein, Das (1869)
Berthold Auerbach

Land Leviathan, The (1974)
Michael Moorcock

Landlocked (1965)
Doris Lessing
Martha Quest

Landlord (1970)
Peter Vansittart

Land of Mist, The (1926)
Arthur Conan Doyle

Land of Plenty, The (1934)
Robert Cantwell

Landscapes Within, The (1981)
Ben Okri

Landslide (1967)
Desmond Bagley

Land Today (1961) posth
Richard Wright

Lange Rejse, Den (1908–22) 3 vol
(The Long Journey)
Johannes Vilhelm Jensen

Lantern Bearers, The (1959)
Rosemary Sutcliff

Lantern Network, The (1978)
Ted Allbeury

Laodicean, A (1881)
Thomas Hardy
Paula Power

Last and the First, The (1971) posth
Ivy Compton-Burnett

Last Bus to Woodstock (1975)
Colin Dexter
Inspector Morse

Last Chronicle of Barset, The (1867)
Anthony Trollope
set: Barsetshire
Dr Francis Arabin (dean)
Grace Crawley (Crawley's daughter)
Josiah Crawley (curate)
Archdeacon Grantly
Major Grantly (Grantly's son)
Rev Septimus Harding
Dr Proudie (Bishop of Barchester)
Mrs Proudie (Proudie's wife)

Last Cop Out, The (1973)
Mickey Spillane

Last Days of Pompeii, The (1834)
Edward Bulwer-Lytton
set: 1c

Last Ditch (1977)
Ngaio Marsh
Inspector Roderick Alleyn

Last Exit to Brooklyn (1964)
Hubert Selby
set: 1950s Brooklyn

Last Frontier (1941)
Howard Fast

Last Frontier, The (1959)
Alistair Maclean

Last Gentleman, The (1966)
Walker Percy

Last Hurrah, The (1956)
Edwin O'Connor

Last Lovers (1991)
William Wharton

Last Man, The (1826)
Mary Shelley
Lionel Verney (narrator)

Last Man, The
see ***Dernier Homme, Le***

Last Night of Summer, The (1963)
Erskine Caldwell

Last Nights of Paris
see ***Dernières Nuits de Paris, Les***

Last of Philip Banter, The (1947)
John Franklin Bardin

Last of the Barons, The (1843)
Edward Bulwer-Lytton

Last of the Mohicans, The (1826)
James Fenimore Cooper
Natty Bumppo, called Hawkeye
Chingachgook (Mohican)
Uncas (Chingachgook's son)

Last of the Wine, The (1956)
Mary Renault

Last One Left, The (1967)
John D MacDonald

Last Peacock, The (1980)
Allan Massie

Last Picture Show, The (1966)
Larry McMurty

Last Post, The (1928)
Ford Madox Ford
Christopher Tietjens

Last Puritan, The (1935)
George Santayana
Oliver Alden

Last Raven, The (1990)
Craig Thomas

Last Refuge, The (1900)
Henry Blake Fuller

Last Seen Wearing (1976)
Colin Dexter
Inspector Morse

Last September, The (1929)
Elizabeth Bowen

Last Stand at Sober River (1959)
Elmore Leonard

Last Tales (1957) coll
Karen Blixen

Last Testament of Oscar Wilde, The (1983)
Peter Ackroyd

Launching of Roger Brook, The (1947)
Dennis Wheatley

Lavengro (1951)
George Borrow

Belle Berners (Jasper's lover)
Jasper Petulengro (gypsy)

Law and the Lady, The (1875)
Wilkie Collins

Law at Randado, The (1955)
Elmore Leonard

Law of the Gun, The (1966)
JT Edson

Laxdale hall (1933)
Eric Linklater

Lay Anthony, The (1914)
Joseph Hergesheimer

Lay Brother, The
see ***Oblat, L'***

Leader of the Band (1988)
Fay Weldon

Leaf Storm
see ***Hojarasca, La***

Leaning in the Wind (1986)
PH Newby

Learning to Swim (1982) coll
Graham Swift

Leatherwood God (1916)
William Dean Howells

Leave It to Psmith (1923)
PG Wodehouse

set: Blandings Castle, Shropshire
Rupert 'the efficient' Baxter (Lord Emsworth's secretary)
Beach (Lord Emsworth's butler)
Lord Emsworth
Lady Constance Keeble (Lord Emsworth's sister)
Psmith
Freddie Threepwood (Lord Emsworth's son)

Leaving Cheyenne (1963)
Larry McMurty

Lee Shore, The (1920)
Rose Macaulay

Left-Handed Sleeper, The (1975)
Ted Willis

Legacy, The (1982)
Desmond Bagley

Legacy, The (1956)
Sybille Bedford

Légende de Saint Julien l'Hospitalier (1877)
Gustave Flaubert

Legend of Montrose, A (1819)
Walter Scott

set: 17c Highlands
Marquess of Argyle
Annot Lyle
Allan M'Aulay (Annot's suitor)
Earl of Menteith (Annot's suitor)
Earl of Montrose

Legion (1983)
William Peter Blatty

Legions of the Eagle (1954)
Henry Treece

Leiden des jungen Werthers, Die (1774)
(The Sorrows of Young Werther)
Johann Goethe

Leila (1983)
JP Donleavy

Leila (1910)
Antonio Fogazzaro

Lélia (1833)
George Sand

Leonora (1806)
Maria Edgeworth

Leopard, The
see ***Gattopardo, Il***

Leopard Hunts in Darkness, The (1985)
Wilbur Smith

Lesbia Brandon (1952) posth
Algernon Swinburne

Less Than Angels (1955)
Barbara Pym

Let It Come Down (1952)
Paul Bowles

Letters (1979)
John Barth

Let the People Sing (1939)
JB Priestley

Letting Go (1962)
Philip Roth

Letty Fox: Her Luck (1946)
Christina Stead

Leurs figures (1902)
Maurice Barrès

Levanter, The (1972)
Eric Ambler

Léviathan (1929)
Julien Green

Levine (1956)
James Hanley

Levitation (1982)
Cynthia Ozick

Levkas Man (1971)
Hammond Innes

Libra (1988)
Don Delillo

Lie, The
see ***Attenzione, L'***

Lie Down in Darkness (1951)
William Styron

Lie Down with Lions (1985)
Ken Follett

Lies of Silence (1990)
Brian Moore

Life, A
see 1 ***Vie, Une***
2 ***Vita, Una***

Life and Adventures of Mr Duncan Campbell, The (1720)
Daniel Defoe

Life and Adventures of Sir Launcelot Greaves, The (1762)
Tobias Smollett

Aurelia (Sir Launcelot's beloved)
Bronzomarte (Sir Launcelot's horse)
Crabshaw (Sir Launcelot's companion)
Darnel Aurelia's uncle)
Ferret (charlatan)
Sir Launcelot Greaves

Life and Death of Harriet Frean, The (1922)
May Sinclair

Life and Death of Mr Badman, The (1680)
John Bunyan

Mr Attentive
Mr Badman
Mr Wiseman

Life and Death of Sylvia, The (1953)
Edgar Mittelholzer

Life and Gabriella (1916)
Ellen Glasgow

Life and Loves of a She-Devil (1984)
Fay Weldon

Life and Times of Michael K (1983)
John Michael Coetzee

Life at the Top (1962)
sequel to ***Room at the Top***
John Braine

Susan Browne
Joe Lampton

Life Before Man (1979)
Margaret Atwood

Life Blood (1974)
Frank Slaughter

Lifeboat, The (1864)
RM Ballantyne

Life Is Elsewhere (1973)
Milan Kundera

Life of Arsenev, The (1927)
Ivan Bunin

Life of a Useless Man, The (1917)
Maxim Gorky

Life of Harriot Stuart, The (1750)
Charlotte Lennox

Life of Jonathan Wild the Great, The (1743)
Henry Fielding

basis: Jonathan Wild, a thief, hanged in 1725
Jonathan Wild

Life of Klim Samgin, The (1925–36) 4 vol unf
Maxim Gorky

Life's Little Ironies (1894)
Thomas Hardy

Life's Morning, A (1888)
George Gissing

Life's Secret, A (1867)
Ellen Wood

Life, the Universe and Everything (1982)
Douglas Adams

Light (1983)
Eva Figes

Light a Penny Candle (1982)
Maeve Binchy

Light and the Dark, The (1947)
CP Snow

Lewis Eliot (narrator/barrister)

Lighthouse, The (1865)
RM Ballantyne

Light in August (1932)
William Faulkner

set: Jefferson, Mississippi
Lucas Burch (Lena's lover)
Joanna Burden
Joe Christmas (murderer/Joanna's lover)
Lena Grove

Light in the Forest, The (1953)
Conrad Richter

Lightning (1988)
Dean R Koontz

Light That Failed, The (1890)
Rudyard Kipling

Light Thickens (1982)
Ngaio Marsh

Inspector Roderick Alleyn

Likely Lad, A (1971)
Gillian Avery

Like Men Betrayed (1954)
John Mortimer

Like Men Betrayed (1970)
Frederic Raphael

Lilith (1895)
George MacDonald

Limestone Tree, The (1931)
Joseph Hergesheimer

Limits (1985) coll
Larry Niven

Limits of Love, The (1960)
Frederic Raphael

Lincoln (1984)
Gore Vidal

Linda Condon (1919)
Joseph Hergesheimer

Linda Tressel (1868)
Anthony Trollope

set: Nuremberg
Madame Stanbach (Linda's aunt & guardian)
Peter Steinmarc (Linda's eventual husband)
Linda Tressel

Lindmann (1963)
Frederic Raphael

Line of Fire (1955)
Donald Hamilton

Lines and Shadows (1984)
Joseph Wambaugh

Lingo (1990)
Penelope Gilliat

Lionel Lincoln (1825)
James Fenimore Cooper

Lion of Boaz-Jachin and Jachin-Boaz, The (1972)
Russell Hoban

Lion of St Mark's, The (1889)
GA Henty

Lisa & Co (1981)
Jilly Cooper

Lit défait, Le (1977)
(The Unmade Bed)
Françoise Sagan

Litle Big Man (1964)
Thomas Berger

Little Birds (1979) posth
Anaïs Nin

Little Broomstick, The (1971)
Mary Stewart

Little Demon, The (1907)
Fedor Sologub

Little Dorrit (1857)
Charles Dickens

set: Marshalsea (prison), London
Christopher Casby (Pancks' employer)
John Chivery (jailer)
Young John Chivery (Chivery's son)
Arthur Clennam (Amy's eventual husband)
Mrs Clennam (Arthur's adoptive mother)
Amy 'Little' Dorrit (Dorrit's daughter)
Fanny Dorrit (dancer/Dorrit's daughter)
Tim Dorrit (Dorrit's son)
William Dorrit (debtor)
Jeremiah Flintwinch (Mrs Clennam's partner)
Mrs General (Dorrits' etiquette tutor)
Henry Gowan (painter)
Meagles (retired banker)
Merdle (crooked financier)
Pancks (rent-collector)
Rigaud (French prisoner)
Tattycoram (foundling)
Miss Wade (Meagles' friend)

Little Drummer Girl, The (1983)
John Le Carré

Little Duke, The (1854)
Charlotte M Yonge

Little Fadette
see ***Petite Fadette, La***

Little Girls, The (1964)
Elizabeth Bowen

Little Grey Rabbit (1929)
Alison Uttley

Little Guest, The (1907)
Mary Louisa Molesworth

Little Herr Friedemann
see ***Kleine Herr Friedemann, Der***

Little House in the Big Woods (1932)
Little House on the Prairie (1935)
Laura Ingalls Wilder

Little Journey in the World, A (1889)
CD Warner

Little Lame Prince, The (1875)
Dinah Maria Craik

Little Lord Fauntleroy (1886)
Frances Hodgson Burnett

Lord Cedric Fauntleroy

Little Man What Now?
see ***Kleiner Mann – was nun?***

Little Match Girl, The (1848)
Hans Christian Andersen

Little Men (1871)
Louisa M Alcott

set: Plumfield School
Professor Bhaer (Jo's husband)
John Brooke (Meg's husband)
Old Mr Laurence (Laurie's grandfather)
Theodore Laurence, 'Laurie' (Amy's husband)
Amy March
Jo March (Amy's sister)
Meg March (Amy's sister)

Little Minister, The (1889)
JM Barrie

set: Thrums (actual Kirriemuir)

Little Misery, The
see ***Sagouin, Le***

Little Noddy Goes to Toyland (1949)
Enid Blyton

Big Ears (Noddy's friend)
Noddy

Little Orvie (1934)
Booth Tarkington

Littlepage Manuscripts (1845)
James Fenimore Cooper

Little Pilgrim, A (1882)
Margaret Oliphant

Little Prince, The
see ***Petit Prince, Le***

Little Princess, The (1905)
Frances Hodgson Burnett

Little Sister (1977)
Fay Weldon

Little Sister, The (1949)
Raymond Chandler

Philip Marlowe (detective)

Little Tiger (1925)
Anthony Hope

Little Town on the Prairie (1941)
Laura Ingalls Wilder

Little Women (1868)
Louisa M Alcott

John Brooke (Meg's eventual husband)
Theodore Laurence, 'Laurie' (Amy's eventual husband)
Old Mr Laurence (Laurie's grandfather)
Amy March
Beth March (Amy's sister)
Jo March (Amy's sister)
Meg March (Amy's sister)
Mr March (Amy's father)
Mrs March, 'Marmee' (Amy's mother)

Little Wooden Doll, The (1925)
Margery Williams Bianco

Little World, The (1925)
Stella Benson

Little World of the Past, The
see ***Piccolo mondo antico***

Live and Kicking Ned (1939)
John Masefield

Live and Let Die (1954)
Ian Fleming

James Bond '007' (spy)
M (Bond's boss)
Miss Moneypenny (M's secretary)

Lively Dead, The (1975)
Peter Dickinson

Lives of Girls and Women (1971)
Alice Munro

Lives of Wives (1939)
Laura Riding

Livia (1978)
Laurence Durrell

Living (1929)
Henry Green

Living and the Dead, The (1941)
Patrick White

Living Daylights, The (1966) posth
Ian Fleming

James Bond '007' (spy)
M (Bond's boss)
Miss Moneypenny (M's secretary)

Living End, The (1979) coll
Stanley Elkin

Living in the Maniototo (1979)
Janet Frame

Living in the Present (1955)
John Wain

Liza of Lambeth (1897)
W Somerset Maugham

set: London slums

Lizzie Dripping (1973)
Helen Cresswell

Lizzie's Floating Shop (1981)
John Wain

Lob-Lie-by-the-Fire (1873)
Juliana Horatia Ewing

Local Anaesthetic
see ***Örtlich betäubt***

Lodore (1835)
Mary Shelley

Loitering with Intent (1981)
Muriel Spark

Lolita (1958)
Vladimir Nabokov

Humbert Humbert (professor/Lolita's much-older lover)
Lolita ('nymphet')

Lollipop (1962)
Terry Southern

Lolly Willowes (1926)
Sylvia Townsend Warner

Lomokone Papers, The (1968)
Herman Wouk

London Embassy, The (1982)
Paul Theroux

Londoners (1983)
Maureen Duffy

London Fields (1989)
Martin Amis

London Match (1986)
Len Deighton

Loneliness of the Long-Distance Runner, The (1959)
Alan Sillitoe

Lonely, The (1947)
Paul Gallico

Lonely Girl, The (1962)
(also titled *Girl with Green Eyes*)
Edna O'Brien

set: Ireland
Caithleen 'Cait' Brady
Bridget 'Baba' Brennan

Lonely Lady, The (1976)
Harold Robbins

Lonely Road, The (1932)
Nevil Shute

Lonesome Dove (1985)
Larry McMurty

Long After Midnight (1976)
Ray Bradbury

Long Arm of Gil Hamilton, The (1976)
Larry Niven

Long Dark Tea-Time of the Soul (1988)
Douglas Adams

Long Distance (1974)
Penelope Mortimer

Long Dream, The (1958)
Richard Wright

Longest Journey, The (1907)
EM Forster

Stewart Ansell (Elliott's friend)
Rickie Elliott (disabled orphan)
Agnes Pembroke (Elliott's eventual wife)

Long Goodbye, The (1953)
Raymond Chandler

Philip Marlowe (detective)

Long Journey, The
see ***Lange Rejse, Den***

Long March, The (1953)
William Styron

Long Odds (1868)
Marcus Clarke

Long Remember (1934)
MacKinlay Kantor

Long Time Ago, A (1932)
Margaret Kennedy

Long Valley, The (1938) coll
John Steinbeck

Long Way to Shiloh, A (1966)
Lionel Davidson

Long Winter, The (1940)
Laura Ingalls Wilder

Look At Me (1983)
Anita Brookner

Look At the Harlequins! (1974)
Vladimir Nabokov

Look Homeward, Angel (1929)
Thomas Wolfe

Eugene Gant

Looking Backward: 2000–1887 (1888)
Edward Bellamy

Julian West

Looking Glass War, The (1965)
John Le Carré

Looking on Darkness (1974)
André Brink

Loom of Youth, The (1917)
Alec Waugh

Looney, The (1987)
Spike Milligan

Loon Lake (1980)
EL Doctorow

Loo Sanction, The (1973)
Trevanian

Jonathan Hemlock (spy)

Lord Edgware Dies (1933)
Agatha Christie

Hercule Poirot (detective)

Lord Hornblower (1946)
CS Forester

Horatio Hornblower

Lord Jim (1900)
Joseph Conrad

ship: Patna
Jim
Captain Marlow

Lord Kilgobbin (1872)
Charles Lever

Lord Oakburn's Daughters (1864)
Ellen Wood

Lord of the Far Island (1975)
Jean Plaidy

Lord of the Flies (1954)
William Golding

set: desert island
Jack Merridew (boys' leader)
Piggy
Ralph

Lord of the Rings, The (1954–5) 3 vol
JRR Tolkien

set: Middle Earth; Mordor

vols:
1 *The Fellowship of the Ring* (1954)
2 *The Two Towers* (1954)
3 *The Return of the King* (1955)

Bilbo Baggins (Hobbit [or dwarf])
Frodo Baggins (Hobbit/Bilbo's nephew)
Beorn (half-man, half-bear)
Gandalf (wizard)
Gollum ('slimy creature')
Sauron (evil ruler)
Shadowfax (horse)
Smaug (dragon)

Lord of the World, The (1907)
RH Benson

Lord Ormont and His Aminta (1894)
George Meredith

Aminta Farrell
Lord Ormont (cavalry commander)

Lord Peter Views the Body (1929)
Dorothy L Sayers

Bunter (Wimsey's servant)
Lord Peter Wimsey (amateur detective)

Lorna Doone (or A Romance of Exmoor) (1869)
RD Blackmore

set: late 17c Exmoor (including the Monmouth Rebellion)
Carver Doone (Doones' evil leader)
Lorna Doone
Tom Faggus (highwayman)
Judge Jeffreys
Annie Ridd (John's sister)
John Ridd (Lorna's eventual husband)

Loser Takes All (1955)
Graham Greene
set: London; Monte Carlo
Cary Bertrand (Bertrand's wife)
Mr Bertrand (narrator/accountant)

Losing Battles (1970)
Eudora Welty

Lost City, The (1964)
John Gunther

Lost Empires (1965)
JB Priestley

Lost Endeavour (1910)
John Masefield

Lost Glen, The (1928)
Neil Gunn

Lost Horizon, The (1933)
James Hilton
set: 'Shangri-La', Himalayas

Lost in the Barrens (1965)
Farley Mowat

Lost Lady, A (1923)
Willa Cather

Lost Name, A (1868)
Sheridan Le Fanu

Lost Possessions (1985)
Keri Hulme

Lost Prince, The (1915)
Frances Hodgson Burnett

Lost Princess, The (1875)
George MacDonald

Lost Profile
see ***Profil perdu, Un***

Lost Railway, The (1980)
Gillian Avery

Lost Traveller, The (1950)
Antonia White

Lost World, The (1912)
Arthur Conan Doyle
Professor Challenger

Lothair (1870)
Benjamin Disraeli
set: Scotland
Clare Arundel (Lothair's admirer)
Lady Corisande (Lothair's eventual wife)
Lord Culloden (Lothair's co-guardian)
Cardinal Grandison (Lothair's co-guardian)
Lothair (orphaned nobleman)
Theodora (Lothair's admirer)

Lotte in Weimar (1939)
Thomas Mann

Lot to Ask, A (1975)
PH Newby

Louvres de Machecoul, Les (1859)
Alexandre Dumas (père)

Love-Adept, The (1969)
LP Hartley

Love-All (1971)
James Leasor

Love All (1974)
Molly Parkin

Love Among the Artists (1900)
GB Shaw

Love Among the Chickens (1906)
PG Wodehouse
Stanley Featherstonehaugh Ukridge

Love Among the Ruins (1904)
Warwick Deeping

Love Among the Ruins (1953)
Evelyn Waugh

Love and Death (An Imaginary Biography) (1939)
Llewellyn Powys

Love and Desire and Hate (1990)
Joan Collins

Love and Friendship (1922) posth
Jane Austen

Love and Friendship (1962)
Alison Lurie

Love and Glory (1983)
Melvyn Bragg

Love and Mary Ann (1961)
Catherine Cookson

Love and Money (1954)
Erskine Caldwell

Love and Mr Lewisham (1900)
HG Wells
Mr Lewisham (science teacher)

Love Bites (1982)
Molly Parkin

Loved and the Envied, The (1951)
Enid Bagnold

Loved and the Lost, The (1951)
Morley Callaghan

Loved Helen (1926)
TH White

Loved One, The (1948)
Evelyn Waugh
set: California

Love for Lydia (1952)
HE Bates

Lovehead (1974)
Jackie Collins

Love in a Cold Climate (1949)
Nancy Mitford
Radlett Family

Love in Amsterdam (1962)
Nicholas Freeling
Piet Van Der Valk (inspector)

Love in the Ruins (1971)
Walker Percy

Love Is Eternal (1954)
Irving Stone

Lovel the Widower (1860)
William Makepeace Thackeray

Lovely Beasts, The (1948) coll
Liam O'Flaherty

Love Machine, The (1969)
Jacqueline Susann

Love Me Little, Love Me Long (1859)
Charles Reade

Love of Parson Lord, The (1900)
Mary E Freeman

Love on the Dole (1933)
Walter Greenwood

set: 1930s Lancashire

Lovers, The (1952)
Kathleen Winsor

Lovers and Gamblers (1977)
Jackie Collins

Lover's Revolt, A (1889)
John William De Forest

Love's Cross Currents (1905)
Algernon Swinburne

Love's Lovely Counterfeit (1942)
James M Cain

Love Story (1970)
Erich Segal

Loving (1945)
Henry Green

set: Ireland
Edith (housemaid)
Raunce (butler)

Loving (1980)
Danielle Steel

Loving Spirit, The (1931)
Daphne Du Maurier

Loyalties (1985)
Raymond Williams

L-Shaped Room, The (1960)
Lynne Reid Banks

set: London boarding-house

Luciano's Luck (1981)
Jack Higgins

Lucien Leuwen (1894) posth unf
Stendhal

Luck and Pluck (or John Oakley's Inheritance) (1869)
Horatio Alger

Luck of Barry Lyndon, The (1844)
William Makepeace Thackeray

Cornelius Barry (Redmond's uncle)
Redmond Barry, later Barry Lyndon (Irish adventurer)
Viscount Bullington (Countess of Lyndon's son)
Countess of Lyndon (Redmond's soon-to-be wife)

Luck of Ginger Coffey, The (1960)
Brian Moore

Luck of Roaring Camp, The (1868)
Bret Harte

Cherokee Sal (prostitute)
Kentuck (gold-miner)
Thomas Luck (Cherokee Sal's son)

Lucky (1985)
Jackie Collins

Lucky Jim (1954)
Kingsley Amis

set: Welsh university
Jim Dixon (history lecturer)

Lucy Crown (1956)
Irwin Shaw

Lucy Gayheart (1935)
Willa Cather

Ludmila (1955)
Paul Gallico

Ludo and the Star Horse (1975)
Mary Stewart

Luna e i falò, La (1950)
(The Moon and the Bonfires)
Cesare Pavese

Lunar Caustic (1963) posth
Malcolm Lowry

Lust for Life (1934)
Irving Stone

Luteplayer, The (1951)
Norah Lofts

Luttrel of Arran (1865)
Charles Lever

Lying Days, The (1953)
Nadine Gordimer

Lying Prophets (1896)
Eden Phillpotts

Lykke-Per (1898–1904) 3 vol
Henrik Pontoppidan

Lyre of Orpheus, The (1988)
Robertson Davies

Lys Rouge, Le (1894)
(The Red Lily)
Anatole France

M

Macdermots of Ballycloran, The (1847)
Anthony Trollope

Mackenzie (1980)
Andrea Newman

Macleod of Dare (1879)
William Black

Madame Bovary (1857)
Gustave Flaubert

set: Yonville (imaginary town), near Rouen
Charles Bovary (doctor)
Madame Emma Bovary (Bovary's wife)

Madame Delphine (1881)
George Washington Cable

Delphine Carraze

Madame de Treymes (1907)
Edith Wharton

Madame Gervaisais (1869)
Edmond & Jules de Goncourt

Madame Serpent (1951)
Jean Plaidy

Madame Will You Talk (1954)
Mary Stewart

Madcap Violet (1876)
William Black

Madeleine (1848)
Julia Kavanagh

Madeleine Férat (1868)
Émile Zola

Madeline (1938)
Ludwig Bemelmans

set: Parisian convent school
Miss Clavell (teacher)
Madeline (schoolgirl)

Mademoiselle de Maupin (1835)
Théophile Gautier

Mademoiselle de Quintinie (1863)
George Sand

Mademoiselle Fifi (1882) coll
Guy de Maupassant

Mademoiselle Loulou (1888)
Gyp

Maggie: a Girl of the Streets (1893)
Stephen Crane

Maggie Muggins (1981)
Keith Waterhouse

Maggot, A (1985)
John Fowles
set: 1730s South of England

Magic Army, The (1981)
Leslie Thomas

Magic Christian, The (1959)
Terry Southern

Magic City, The (1910)
E Nesbit

Magic Cottage, The (1986)
James Herbert

Magic Finger, The (1966)
Roald Dahl

Magic Flute, The (1962)
John Updike

Magic Goes Away, The (1978)
Larry Niven

Magician of Lublin, The (1960)
Isaac Bashevis Singer

Magicians, The (1954)
JB Priestley

Magic Kingdom, The (1985)
Stanley Elkin

Magic Mountain, The
see ***Zauberberg, Der***

Magic Ring, The
see ***Zauberring, Der***

Magic Wheel, The (1986)
Graham Swift

Magnificent Ambersons, The (1918)
Booth Tarkington

Magnificent Obsession (1929)
Lloyd C Douglas

Magnus (1973)
George Mackay Brown

Magnus Merriman (1934)
Eric Linklater

Magus, The (1966)
John Fowles
set: Phraxos (imaginary isle), Greece
Nicholas D'Urfe

Magyar Nabob, The (1853)
Mór Jókai

Maiden Castle (1936)
John Cowper Powys

Maiden's Progress, The (1894)
Violent Hunt

Maid Marian (1822)
Thomas Love Peacock

Robin Hood
Maid Marian
Friar Tuck

Maid of Buttermere, The (1987)
Melvyn Bragg

Maid of Sker, The (1872)
RD Blackmore

Maigret and the Enigmatic Lett
see ***Pietr-le-Letton***

Main, The (1976)
Trevanian

Main Street (1920)
Sinclair Lewis

set: Minnesota

Main-Travelled Roads (1891) coll
Henry Garland

Maison de Claudine, La (1922)
Colette

Maison Rouge (1846)
Alexandre Dumas (père)

Maîtres Sonneurs, Les (1852)
(The Master Bell-Ringers)
George Sand

Makar Chudra (1892)
Maxim Gorky

Make Death Love Me (1979)
Ruth Rendell

Make Me an Offer (1952)
Wolf Mankowitz

Making Good Again (1968)
Lionel Davidson

Making of Americans, The (1925)
Gertrude Stein

Making of the Representative for Planet 8, The (1982)
Doris Lessing

Mala hora, La (1966)
(The Evil Hour)
Gabriel García Márquez

Malavoglia, I (1881)
(The House by the Medlar Tree)
Giovanni Verga

Malcontents, The (1972)
CP Snow

Malice Aforethought (1931)
Francis Iles

Malice in Wonderland (1940)
Nicholas Blake

Nigel Strangeways (detective)

Malign Fiesta (1955)
Wyndham Lewis

Mallen Girl, The (1973)
Mallen Lot, The (1974)
Mallen Streak, The (1973)
Catherine Cookson

Mallory (1950)
James Hadley Chase

Malone Dies (1956)
Samuel Beckett

Malory Towers (1946)
Enid Blyton

Maltese Falcon, The (1930)
Dashiell Hammett

Sam Spade (private eye)

Mamista (1991)
Len Deighton

Mammoth Hunters, The (1985)
Jean M Auel

Man About the House, A (1942)
Francis Brett Young

Man and His Wife, A (1940) coll
Frank Sargeson

Man and Maid (1922)
Elinor Glyn

Man and Wife (1870)
Wilkie Collins

Man As He Is (1792)
Robert Bage

Manchurian Candidate, The (1959)
Richard Condon

set: USA; Korea

Sergeant Raymond Shaw (brainwashed soldier)

Man Could Stand Up, A (1926)
Ford Madox Ford

Christopher Tietjens

Mandarin Gold (1973)
James Leasor

set: Chinese coast

Robert Gunn (ship's surgeon)

Mandarins, Les (1954)
Simone de Beauvoir

Mandelbaum Gate, The (1965)
Muriel Spark

Mandeville (1817)
William Godwin

Mandingo (1957)
Kyle Onstott

set: 1840s Louisiana

Man Eater (1976)
Ted Willis

Man-Eater of Malgudi, The (1961)
RK Narayan

Man from St Petersburg, The (1982)
Ken Follett

Man from the North, A (1898)
Arnold Bennett

Mangan Inheritance, The (1979)
Brian Moore

Manhattan Transfer (1925)
John Dos Passos

Man in the Zoo, A (1924)
David Garnett

Man Lay Dead, A (1934)
Ngaio Marsh

Inspector Roderick Alleyn

Mann im Strom, Der (1957)
Siegfried Lenz

Mann ohne Eigenschaften, Der (1930–43) 3 vol; 1 vol posth unf
(The Man without Qualities)
Robert Musil

Mann von Asteri, Der (1939)
Stefan Andres

Man of Devon (1901) coll
John Galsworthy

Man of England Now (1972)
Frank Sargeson

Man of Feeling, The (1771)
Henry Mackenzie

Man of Mark, A (1890)
Anthony Hope

Man of the People, A (1966)
Chinua Achebe

Man of the World, The (1773)
Henry Mackenzie

Manon Lescaut (1731)
Abbé Antoine-François Prévost

Chevalier Des Grieux
Manon Lescaut (Des Grieux' beloved)

Manor, The (1967)
Isaac Bashevis Singer

Manservant and Maidservant (1947)
Ivy Compton-Burnett

Man's Fate
see ***Condition humaine, Le***

Mansfield Park (1814)
Jane Austen

set: Mansfield Park (Bertrams' home)
Edmund Bertram (Sir Thomas' son/Fanny's eventual husband)
Julia Bertram (Sir Thomas' daughter)
Lady Bertram (Sir Thomas' wife)
Maria Bertram (Sir Thomas' daughter)
Sir Thomas Bertram
Tom Bertram (Sir Thomas' son)
Henry Crawford (Maria's sometime sweetheart)
Mary Crawford (Henry's sister/Edmund's sometime sweetheart)
Mrs Norris (Lady Bertram's sister)
Fanny Price (Mrs Brice's daughter)
Mrs Price (Lady Bertram's sister)
Mr Rushworth (Maria's fiancé)
Mr Yates (Julia's illicit lover)

Mansie Wauch, Tailor in Dalkeith (1828)
David Macbeth Moir

Mansion, The (1959)
William Faulkner

Man That Corrupted Hadleyburg, The (1900) coll
Mark Twain

Mantis Carol, A (1975)
Laurens Van Der Post

Mantissa (1982)
John Fowles

Mantrap (1926)
Sinclair Lewis

Manufacture of the Absolute, The (1923)
Karel Capek

Man Who Killed Himself, The (1967)
Julian Symons

Man Who Knew Coolidge, The (1928)
Sinclair Lewis

Man Who Lost Himself, The (1929)
Osbert Sitwell

Man Who Loved Children, The (1940)
Christina Stead

Man Who Sold the Moon, The (1970)
Robert A Heinlein

Man Who Was Not With It, The (1956)
Herbert Gold

Man Who Was Thursday, The (1908)
GK Chesterton

Gabriel Syme

Man Who Wins, The (1897) coll
Robert Herrick

Man Who Won the Pools, The (1961)
JIM Stewart

Man Within, The (1929)
Graham Greene

Man without Qualities, The
see ***Mann ohne Eigenschaften, Der***

Man with the Coat, The (1955)
Morley Callaghan

Man with the Golden Arm, The (1949)
Nelson Algren

Man with the Golden Gun, The (1965) posth
Ian Fleming

James Bond '007' (spy)
M (Bond's boss)
Miss Moneypenny (M's secretary)

Man with the Power, The (1973)
Leslie Thomas

Man with the President's Mind, The (1977)
Ted Allbeury

Man with Two Shadows, The (1958)
Robin Maugham

Manxman (1891)
Hall Caine

Many Colored Coat, The (1960)
Morley Callaghan

Many Cargoes (1896) coll
WW Jacobs

Many Marriages (1922)
Sherwood Anderson

Mao II (1991)
Don Delillo

Maplin Bird, The (1964)
KM Peyton

Maracot Deep, The (1929)
Arthur Conan Doyle

Professor Challenger

Maradick at Forty (1910)
Hugh Walpole

Marathon Man (1974)
William Goldman

set: New York
Thomas Levy

Marazan (1926)
Nevil Shute

Marble Faun, The (1860)
Nathaniel Hawthorne

set: Rome
Count Donatello
Miriam (Donatello's beloved)

Marcella (1894)
Mary Augusta Ward

March Has Horse's Ears (1966)
Robert Nye

Marching Men (1917)
Sherwood Anderson

Marching On (1927)
James Boyd

Marchmont (1796)
Charlotte Smith

Mardi (and A Voyage Thither) (1849)
Herman Melville

set: Polynesia (Mardi islands)
brigantine: Parki
Jarl (seaman)
Taji (narrator)

Mare au diable, La (1846)
(The Devil's Lake)
George Sand

Mariage de Chiffon (1894)
Gyp

Mariner Dances (1948)
PH Newby

Marionette, The (1927)
Edwin Muir

Mario und der Zauberer (1930)
Thomas Mann

Marius the Epicurean (1885)
Walter Pater

Marjorie Morningstar (1955)
Herman Wouk

Markens grøde (1917)
(Growth of the Soil)
Knut Hamsun

Mark Lambert's Supper (1954)
JIM Stewart

Mark of Cain, The (1886)
Andrew Lang

Mark of the Horse Lord, The (1965)
Rosemary Sutcliff

Mark One – the Dummy (1974)
John Ball

Mark Rutherford's Deliverance (1885)
Mark Rutherford

Marmorbild, Das (1819)
Joseph Freiherr von Eichendorff

Marne, The (1918)
Edith Wharton

Marquis de Villemer, Le (1861)
George Sand

Marriage (1818)
Susan Ferrier

Marriage of William Ashe, The (1905)
Mary Augusta Ward

Marriages between Zones Three, Four and Five, The (1980)
Doris Lessing

Married Man, A (1979)
Piers Paul Read

Marry Me (1976)
John Updike

Marsh Island, A (1885)
Sarah Orne Jewett

Marston (1846)
George Croly

Martereau (1953)
Nathalie Sarraute

Martha Quest (1952)
Doris Lessing

Martha Quest

Martian, The (1897) posth
George Du Maurier

Martian Chronicles, The (1950)
(also titled ***The Silver Locusts***)
Ray Bradbury

Martin Bircks Ungdom (1901)
Hjalmar Söderberg

Martin Chuzzlewit (1844)
Charles Dickens

set: London; America
Anthony Chuzzlewit (Martin Snr's brother/Jonas' father)
Jonas Chuzzlewit (Mercy's eventual husband)
Martin Chuzzlewit Jnr
Martin Chuzzlewit Snr (Martin Jnr's grandfather)
Sarah Gamp (Anthony's nurse)
Mary Graham (orphan/Martin Jnr's eventual wife)
Charity Pecksniff (Pecksniff's daughter)
Mercy Pecksniff (Pecksniff's daughter)
Seth Pecksniff (architect/hypocrite)
Ruth Pinch (Tom's sister)
Tom Pinch (Pecksniff's assistant)
Mark Tapley (Martin Jnr's servant)
Montague Tigg (shady dealer)
Mrs Todgers (landlady)

Martin Eden (1909)
Jack London

Russ Brissenden (Eden's friend)
Martin Eden (labourer, later writer)
Ruth Morse (Eden's would-be friend)

Martin Faber (1833)
William Gilmore Simms

Constance Claiborne (Faber's soon-to-be wife)
Emily (village girl)
Martin Faber

Martin Rattler (1858)
RM Ballantyne

Martin Salander (1886)
Gottfried Keller

Marvellous Misadventures of Sebastian, The (1970)
Lloyd Alexander

Marvelous Land of Oz, The (1905)
L Frank Baum

Mary (1926)
Vladimir Nabokov

Mary (1788)
Mary Wollstonecraft

Mary Anne (1954)
Daphne Du Maurier

Mary Barton (A Tale of Manchester Life) (1848)
Elizabeth Gaskell

set: Manchester
John Barton (trade-unionist)
Mary Barton (Barton's daughter)
Jem Wilson (Mary's admirer)

Mary Deare, The (1956)
Hammond Innes

Mary Glenn (1925)
Sarah Gertrude Millin

Mary Poppins (1934)
PL Travers

Mask, The (1981)
Dean R Koontz

Mask of Dimitrios, The (1939)
Eric Ambler

Masqueraders, The (1928)
Georgette Heyer

Master and Man (1895)
Leo Tolstoy

Master Bell-Ringers, The
see ***Maîtres Sonneurs, Les***

Master Christian, The (1900)
Marie Corelli

Masterclass (1988)
Morris West

Master Jim Probity (1952)
Frank Swinnerton

Masterman Ready (1841)
Frederick Marryat

set: desert island
Masterman Ready
Seagrave family

Master Mariner, The (1979–80)
2 vol; 1 vol posth
Nicholas Monsarrat

Master of Ballantrae, The (A Winter's Tale) (1889)
RL Stevenson

set: 1740s
Henry Durrisdeer (Lord Durrisdeer's younger son)
Lord Durrisdeer
Ephraim Mackellar (narrator)
'The Master of Ballantrae' (Lord Durrisdeer's older son)
Teach (pirate captain)

Master of Falconhurst (1964)
Kyle Onstott

Master of the Game, The (1982)
Sidney Sheldon

Master of the Inn, The (1908)
Robert Herrick

Master of the Moor (1982)
Ruth Rendell

Masters, The (1951)
CP Snow

Lewis Eliot (narrator/barrister)

Masters of Space (1976) posth
EE 'Doc' Smith

Mastro-don Gesualdo (1889)
Giovanni Verga

Matarese Circle, The (1978)
Robert Ludlum

Matchlock Gun, The (1941)
Walter D Edmonds

Matelot (1893)
Pierre Loti

Mathilde Möhring (1906) posth unf
Theodor Fontane

Matilda (1988)
Roald Dahl

Mating Season, The (1949)
PG Wodehouse

Reginald Jeeves (Wooster's valet)
Bertie Wooster

Matrena's House (1963) coll
Alexander Solzhenitsyn

Matter of Honour, A (1985)
Jeffrey Archer

Matthew Wald (1824)
John Gibson Lockhart

Mauprat (1837)
George Sand

Tristan de Mauprat

Maurice (1971) posth
EM Forster

Maurice Guest (1908)
Henry Handel Richardson

Maurizius Case, The
see ***Fall Maurizius, Der***

Maximum Bob (1991)
Elmore Leonard

Mayhem in Greece (1962)
Dennis Wheatley

Mayor of Casterbridge, The (1886)
Thomas Hardy

set: Casterbridge (actual Dorchester); Egdon Heath
Donald Farfrae (Henchard's rival)
Michael Henchard (eventual disgraced Mayor of Casterbridge)
Mrs Henchard (Henchard's 'sold' wife)
Newson (sailor)

McGrotty and Ludmilla; or, The Harbinger Report (1990)
Alasdair Gray

McTeague (1899)
Frank Norris

set: San Francisco

Mea Culpa (1891)
Henry Harland

Mediterranean Caper, The (1973)
Clive Cussler

Medusa (1988)
Hammond Innes

Meeting by the River (1967)
Christopher Isherwood

Meeting in Telgte, The
see ***Treffen in Telgte, Das***

Meet Me in the Green Glen (1971)
Robert Penn Warren

Meet the Baron (1937)
John Creasey

The Baron (antiques dealer/spy)

Meet the Tiger (1928)
Leslie Charteris

Simon Templar, 'The Saint'

Mefisto (1986)
John Banville

Mehalah (1880)
Sabine Baring-Gould

Me, Hood (1963) coll
Mickey Spillane

Mein Name sei Gantenbein (1964)
Max Frisch

Melincourt (or Sir Oran Haut-ton) (1817)
Thomas Love Peacock

Sylvan Forester (Haut-ton's `educator')
Sir Oran Haut-ton (orang-utan)
Anthelia Melincourt

Melmoth the Wanderer (1820)
Charles Maturin

Melmoth
Isadora (Melmoth's wife)

Melodramatists, The (1949)
Howard Nemerov

Melody of Death, The (1915)
Edgar Wallace

Member, The (1832)
John Galt

Member of the Wedding, The (1946)
Carson McCullers

Memento Mori (1959)
Muriel Spark

Mémoires d'un honnête homme (1745)
Abbé Antoine-Françoise Prévost

Memoirs of a Cavalier (1724)
Daniel Defoe

Memoirs of a Coxcomb (1751)
John Cleland

Memoirs of a Fox-Hunting Man (1928)
Siegfried Sassoon

George Sherston

Memoirs of a Midget (1921)
Walter De La Mare

Memoirs of an Infantry Officer (1930)
Siegfried Sassoon

George Sherston

Memoirs of a Shy Pornographer (1945)
Kenneth Patchen

Memoirs of a Spacewoman (1962)
Naomi Mitchison

Memoirs of a Survivor (1975)
Doris Lessing

Memoirs of Hecate County (1946) coll
Edmund Wilson

Memoirs of Lord Bron, The (1989)
Robert Nye

Memoirs of Many In One (1986)
Patrick White

Memoirs of Sherlock Holmes, The (1894) coll
Arthur Conan Doyle

set: 221b Baker Street, London
Mycroft Holmes (Holmes' brother)
Sherlock Holmes (detective)
Mrs Hudson (Holmes' housekeeper)
Inspector Lestrade (Scotland Yard officer)
Professor James Moriarty (Holmes' arch-enemy)
Dr John Watson (Holmes' companion)

Memoirs of Sir Roger de Clarendon (1793)
Clara Reeve

Memorial, The (1932)
Christopher Isherwood

Memorial Service, A (1976)
JIM Stewart

Memories of Another day (1979)
Harold Robbins

Menace from the Earth, The (1968)
Robert A Heinlein

Men Against the Sea (1934)
Charles Nordhoff

Men and Brethren (1936)
James Gould Cozzens

Men and Wives (1931)
Ivy Compton-Burnett

Men at Arms (1952)
Evelyn Waugh

set: World War II
Apthorpe (Crouchback's fellow-officer)
Guy Crouchback (army officer)
Brigadier Ritchie-Hook
Virginia Troy (Crouchback's ex-wife)

Mendiant de Jerusalem, Le (1968)
(A Beggar in Jerusalem)
Elie Wiesel

Menfreya (1966)
Jean Plaidy

Men Like Gods (1923)
HG Wells

Men of Good Will
see ***Hommes de bonne volonté, Les***

Men of Maize (1949)
Miguel Asturias

Men of Men (1981)
Wilbur Smith

Men of Ness, The (1932)
Eric Linklater

Men's Wives (1843) coll
William Makepeace Thackeray

Men without Women (1927) coll
Ernest Hemingway

Men, Women and Beasts (1922)
Henry Stacpoole

Mere Accident, A (1887)
George Moore

Meridian (1976)
Alice Walker

Merlin (1978)
Robert Nye

Merry Heart, The (1909)
Frank Swinnerton

Merry Month of May, The (1971)
James Jones

Mervyn Clithero (1857)
William Harrison Ainsworth

Mes Apprentissages (1936)
Colette

Message from Nam (1990)
Danielle Steel

Message to the Planet, The (1989)
Iris Murdoch

Messiah of Stockholm, The (1987)
Cynthia Ozick

Metamorphosis
see ***Verwandlung, Die***

Meteor, The (1933)
Karel Capek

Methuselah's Children (1958)
Robert A Heinlein

Metroland (1980)
Julian Barnes

Metropolis, The (1908)
Upton Sinclair

Mexico Bay (1982)
Paul Horgan

Mexico Set (1985)
Len Deighton

MF (1971)
Anthony Burgess
Miles Faber

Miami and the Siege of Chicago (1969)
Norman Mailer

Miau (1888)
Benito Pérez Galdós

Micah Clarke (1889)
Arthur Conan Doyle

Michaela (1959)
Ina Seidel

Michel Strogoff (1876)
Jules Verne

Microcosm, The (1966)
Maureen Duffy

Midas Touch, The (1938)
Margaret Kennedy

Middle Age of Mrs Eliot, The (1958)
Angus Wilson

Middle Ground(1980)
Margaret Drabble

Middlemarch (A Study of Provincial Life) (1872)
George Eliot

set: Middlemarch, Loamshire
Celia Brooke (Dorothea's sister)
Dorothea Brooke (Casaubon's wife/Ladislaw's eventual wife)
Mr Bulstrode (Vincy's brother-in-law)
Mrs Bulstrode (Bulstrode's wife)
Mrs Cadwallader (Cadwallader's wife)
Rev Cadwallader (rector)
Edward Casaubon
Sir James Chettam (Celia's eventual husband)
Caleb Garth (land agent)
Mary Garth (Garth's daughter)
Will Ladislaw (Casaubon's cousin)
Tertius Lydgate (doctor/Rosamund's eventual husband)
Fred Vincy (Vincy's son)
Rosamund Vincy (Vincy's daughter)
Walter Vincy (Mayor of Middlemarch)

Middle of the Journey, The (1947)
Lionel Trilling

Midi rouge, Le (1895)
Paul Arène

Midlander, The (1923)
Booth Tarkington

Midnight (1989)
Dean R Koontz

Midnight
see ***Minuit***

Midnight Bell, The (1929)
Patrick Hamilton

Midnight Clear, A (1982)
William Wharton

Midnight Folk, The (1927)
John Masefield

Kay Harker (orphan)
Nibbins (cat)
Sir Theopompus (Kay's guardian)

Midnight Kittens, The (1978)
Dodie Smith

Midnight Plus One (1965)
Gavin Lyall

Midnight's Children (1981)
Salman Rushdie

set: late 1940s India
Saleem Sinai

Midshipman Easy
see ***Mr Midshipman Easy***

Midwich Cuckoos, The (1957)
John Wyndham

Mighty and Their Fall, The (1961)
Ivy Compton-Burnett

Mighty Atom, The (1896)
Marie Corelli

Miguel Street (1959) coll
VS Naipaul

Mike: a Public School Story (1909)
PG Wodehouse

Mike Jackson
Psmith

Mike Fletcher (1889)
George Moore

Mila, 18 (1960)
Leon Uris

Mildred Pierce (1941)
James M Cain

Mile High (1969)
Richard Condon

Milesian Chief, The (1811)
Charles Maturin

Miles Wallingford (1844)
James Fenimore Cooper

Military Orchid, The (1948)
Jocelyn Brooke

Mill on the Floss, The (1860)
George Eliot

set: Dorlcote Mill; St Ogg's
Lucy Deane (Tom & Maggie's cousin)
Mrs Glegg (Mrs Tulliver's sister)
Stephen Guest (Lucy's fiancé)
Bob Jakin (packman)
Doctor Kenn (clergyman)
Mrs Pullett (Mrs Tulliver's sister)
Maggie Tulliver (Tulliver's daughter)
Mr Tulliver
Mrs Tulliver (Tulliver's wife)
Tom Tulliver (Tulliver's son)
Philip Wakem (Wakem's son)
Mr Wakem (lawyer)

Mill on the Po, The
see ***Mulino del Po, Il***

Millstone, The (1965)
Margaret Drabble

Mimic Men, The (1967)
VS Naipaul

Ralph Singh (narrator)

Mind at the End of Its Tether (1945)
HG Wells

Mindbend (1985)
Robin Cook

Mind Readers, The (1965)
Margery Allingham

Albert Campion (detective)

Mind to Murder, A (1963)
PD James

Adam Dalgliesh (detective)

Mine Boy (1946)
Peter Abrahams

Mine of Serpents, A (1949)
Jocelyn Brooke

Mine Own Executioner (1945)
Nigel Balchin

Mingo (1884)
Joel Chandler Harris

Mingo (Negro servant)

Minister's Charge, The (1887)
William Dean Howells

Minister's Wooing, The (1859)
Harriet Beecher Stowe

Ministry of Fear, The (1943)
Graham Greene

Minuit (1936)
(Midnight)
Julien Green

Minute for Murder (1947)
Nicholas Blake

Nigel Strangeways (detective)

Miracle de la rose (1946)
(Miracle of the Rose)
Jean Genet

Miracle of St Bruno's, The (1972)
Jean Plaidy

Miracle on Sinai (1933)
Osbert Sitwell

Mirage (1924)
Edgar Lee Masters

Mirror Crack'd from Side to Side, The (1962)
Agatha Christie

Miss Jane Marple (amateur sleuth)

Mirror of the Sea, The (1906)
Joseph Conrad

Mirthful Heaven (1930)
Booth Tarkington

Misalliance, A (1986)
Anita Brookner

Misérables, Les (1862)
Victor Hugo

set: Paris; Waterloo
Cosette (Fantine's illegitimate child)
Fantine
Javert (police officer)
Monseigneur Myriel
Thénardier (innkeeper)
Jean Valjean (sometime prisoner)

Misery (1987)
Stephen King

Misfortunes of Elphin, The (1829)
Thomas Love Peacock

Elphin (ancient Welsh king)

Miss Bretherton (1884)
Mary Augusta Ward

Missee Lee (1941)
Arthur Ransome

Miss Herbert (1976)
Christina Stead

Missing Millionaire, The (1893)
Hal Meredith

Sexton Blake (detective)

Mission, Die (1965)
Hans Habe

Miss Linsey and Pa (1936)
Stella Gibbons

Miss Lonelyhearts (1933)
Nathanael West

Miss Marjoribanks (1866)
Margaret Oliphant

Miss Pym Disposes (1946)
Josephine Tey

Miss Ravenel's Conversion (1866)
John William De Forest

Mist
see ***Niebla***

For **MISTER** also see **MR**

Mister Johnson (1939)
Joyce Cary

Mistral's Daughter (1982)
Judith Krantz

For **MISTRESS** also see **MRS**

Mistress Masham's Repose (1947)
TH White

Mitch Miller (1920)
Edgar Lee Masters

Mitla Pass (1989)
Leon Uris

Moby-Dick (1851)
Herman Melville

whaler: Pequod
Captain Ahab
Daggoo (harpooner)
Flask (3rd mate)
Ishmael (narrator)
Moby-Dick (white whale)
Pip (cabin-boy)
Queequeg (harpooner)
Starbuck (1st mate)
Stubb (2nd mate)
Tashtego (harpooner)

Model, The
see ***Vorbild, Das***

Moderato cantabile (1958)
Marguerite Duras

Modern Chronicle, A (1910)
Winston Churchill

Modern Comedy, A (1924–8) 3 vol
John Galsworthy

vols:
1 *The White Monkey* (1924)
2 *The Silver Spoon* (1926)
3 *Swan Song* (1928)

Modern Instance, A (1882)
William Dean Howells

Modern Lover, A (1883)
George Moore

Modern Mephistopheles, A (1877)
Louisa M Alcott

Modern Midas, The (1875)
Mór Jókai

Modern Tragedy, A (1934)
Phyllis Bentley

Modern Utopia, A (1905)
HG Wells

Modification, La (1957)
Michel Butor

Moïra (1950)
Julien Green

Moll Flanders (1722)
Daniel Defoe

set: Virginia, USA; Colchester
Moll Flanders (reformed thief)

Molloy(1951)
Samuel Beckett

Moment of Eclipse, The (1971)
Brian W Aldiss

Monastery, The (1820)
Walter Scott

set: Kennaquhair (monastery)
Mary Avenel (Halbert's eventual wife)
Edward Glendinning (Simon's son)
Halbert Glendinning (Simon's son)
Simon Glendinning (monastery tenant)

Money (1984)
Martin Amis

Money-Changers, The (1975)
Arthur Hailey

Money for Nothing (1928)
PG Wodehouse

Money from Holme (1964)
JIM Stewart

Money in the Bank (1942)
PG Wodehouse

Money Is Love (1975)
Richard Condon

Mon frère Yves (1883)
(My Brother Yves)
Pierre Loti

Monk, The (1796)
MG Lewis

Ambrosio (Capuchin monk)

Monk Dawson (1969)
Piers Paul Read

Monkey King, The (1978)
Timothy Mo

Monkey's Paw, The (1902)
WW Jacobs

Monsieur (1974)
Laurence Durrell

Monsieur Beaucaire (1900)
Booth Tarkington

set: 18c Bath

Monsieur Lecoq (1869)
Émile Gaboriau

Monsieur Lecoq (detective)

Monsieur Ouine (1946)
Georges Bernanos

Monsieur Parent (1886) coll
Guy de Maupassant

Monsignor Quixote (1982)
Graham Greene

Monster, The (1899)
Stephen Crane

Monstre Gai (1955)
Wyndham Lewis

Mont-Cinère (1925)
(Avarice House)
Julien Green

Montezuma's Daughter (1893)
H Rider Haggard

Mont-Oriol (1887)
Guy de Maupassant

Moods (1864)
Louisa M Alcott

Moon (1985)
James Herbert

Moon and Sixpence, The (1919)
W Somerset Maugham

set: Tahiti
basis: Gauguin's life
Charles Strickland

Moon and the Bonfires, The
see ***Luna e i falò, La***

Moon Is Down, The (1942)
John Steinbeck

Moonlight, The (1946)
Joyce Cary

Moon of Gomrath, The (1963)
Alan Garner

Moon Palace (1989)
Paul Auster

Moonraker (1955)
Ian Fleming

James Bond `007' (spy)
M (Bond's boss)
Miss Moneypenny (M's secretary)

Moonshine (1969)
Elmore Leonard

Moonspender (1987)
Jonathan Gash

Lovejoy (dodgy antiques dealer)

Moonstone, The (1868)
Wilkie Collins

Godfrey Ablewhite (Rachel's suitor)
Gabriel Betteredge (main narrator/ steward)
Franklin Blake (Rachel's cousin/suitor)
Sergeant Cuff (detective)
Rosanna Spearman (housemaid)
Lady Verinder (Rachel's mother)
Rachel Verinder

Moon Tiger (1986)
Penelope Lively

Moran of the Lady Letty (1898)
Frank Norris

Morbid Taste for Bones, A (1977)
Ellis Peters

set: 12c Shrewsbury Abbey
Brother Cadfael (monk)

Mordaunt (1800)
John Moore

More Die of Heartbreak (1987)
Saul Bellow

More Joy in Heaven (1937)
Morley Callaghan

More Women Than Men (1933)
Ivy Compton-Burnett

More Work for the Undertaker (1948)
Margery Allingham

Albert Campion (detective)

Morgenlandfahrt (1932)
Hermann Hesse

Moribonds, Les (1934)
(The Dying)
Philippe Soupault

Morning After Death, The (1966)
Nicholas Blake

Nigel Strangeways (detective)

Morning at the Office, A (1950)
Edgar Mittelholzer

Morning Face (1968)
Mulk Raj Anand

Morning , Noon and Night (1968)
James Gould Cozzens

Morning Tide (1931)
Neil Gunn

Morning Watch, The (1954)
James Agee

Mort à crédit (1936)
Louis-Ferdinand Céline

Mortal Antipathy, A (1884)
Oliver Wendell Holmes

Mortal Coils (1922) coll
Aldous Huxley

Mortal Fear (1988)
Robin Cook

Mortal Matters (1983)
Penelope Gilliat

Mortal Strife (1941)
John Cowper Powys

Mort de quelqu'un (1911)
(Death of a Nobody)
Jules Romains

Morte amoreuse, La (1836)
(The Amorous Death)
Théophile Gautier

Morwyn (1937)
John Cowper Powys

Mosaïque (1833) coll
Prosper Mérimée

Mosquitos (1927)
William Faulkner

Mosses from the Old Manse (1846) coll
Nathaniel Hawthorne

Most Beautiful Girl in the World, The (1982)
Ted Willis

Most Dangerous Game, The (1963)
Gavin Lyall

Most Likely to Succeed (1954)
John Dos Passos

Mostly Canallers (1934)
Walter D Edmonds

Most Secret (1945)
Nevil Shute

Mother, The (1930)
Sholem Asch

Mother, The (1907)
Maxim Gorky

Mother and Son (1955)
Ivy Compton-Burnett

Mother Carey's Chickens (1911)
(also titled ***Mother Carey***)
Kate Wiggin

Mother Night (1961)
Kurt Vonnegut

Mother's Recompense, The (1925)
Edith Wharton

Anne Clephane
Kate Clephane (Anne's mother)

Moths (1880)
Ouida

Mountain Blood (1915)
Joseph Hergesheimer

Mount Henneth (1781)
Robert Bage

Mount Music (1919)
Edith Somerville

Mountolive (1958)
Laurence Durrell

set: Alexandria, Egypt
Balthazar
Clea (artist)
LG Darley (narrator)
Justine
Melissa (Darley's mistress)
Mountolive (ambassador)
Nessim (Justine's husband)
Pursewarden (British agent)

Mouse and His Child, The (1967)
Russell Hoban

Moviegoer, The (1961)
Walker Percy

Moving Finger, The (1943)
Agatha Christie

Miss Jane Marple (amateur sleuth)

Moving On (1970)
Larry McMurty

Moving Target, The (1949)
Ross Macdonald

Mr Balcony (1927)
CHB Kitchin

Mr Beluncle (1951)
VS Pritchett

Mr Blake's Walking-Stick (1870)
Edward Eggleston

Mr Blettsworthy on Rumpole Island (1928)
HG Wells

Mr Bridge (1969)
ES Connell

Mr Britling Sees It Through (1916)
HG Wells

Hugh Britling

Mr Clutterbuck's Election (1908)
Hilaire Belloc

Mr Crewe's Career (1908)
Winston Churchill

Mr Facey Romford's Hounds (1865) posth
RS Surtees

Facey Romford (hunstman)

Mr Fortune's maggot (1927)
Sylvia Townsend Warner

Mr Galliano's Circus (1938)
Enid Blyton

Mr Galliano (circus-owner)

Mr Hodge and Mr Hazard (1927)
Elinor Wylie

Mr Isaacs (A Tale of Modern India) (1882)
F Marion Crawford

Mr Majestik (1974)
Elmore Leonard

Mr Midshipman Easy (1836)
Frederick Marryat

Mr Biggs (bosun)
Jack Easy (midshipman)
Mesty (Easy's fellow-midshipman)
Mr Pottifar (lieutenant)

Mr Midshipman Hornblower (1950)
CS Forester

Horatio Hornblower

Mr Norris Changes Trains (1935)
Christopher Isherwood

Arthur Norris (Nazi collaborator)

Mr Perrin and Mr Traill (1911)
Hugh Walpole

Mr Prohack (1922)
Arnold Bennett

Mr Rabbit at Home (1895) coll
Joel Chandler Harris

Mr Rowl (1924)
DK Broster

Mr Sammler's Planet (1969)
Saul Bellow

Mr Sampath (1949)
RK Narayan

Mrs Bridge (1958)
ES Connell

Mr Scarborough's Family (1883) posth
Anthony Trollope

John Scarborough

Mrs Craddock (1902)
W Somerset Maugham

Mrs Dalloway (1925)
Virginia Woolf

set: one June day only, London
Clarissa Dalloway (Dalloway's wife)
Richard Dalloway (MP)

Mrs Dymond (1885)
Anna Isabella Ritchie

Mrs Eckdorf in O'Neill's Hotel (1969)
William Trevor

Mrs Knox's Profession (1972)
Jessica Mann

Mrs Maxon Protests (1911)
Anthony Hope

Mrs McGinty's Dead (1952)
Agatha Christie

Miss Jane Marple (amateur sleuth)

Mr Smith (1951)
Louis Bromfield

Mrs Overtheway's Remembrances (1869)
Juliana Horatia Ewing

Mrs Palfrey at the Claremont (1972)
Elizabeth Taylor

Mr Sponge's Sporting Tour (1853)
RS Surtees

Soapey Sponge (huntsman)

Mrs Skaggs's Husbands (1873)
Bret Harte

Mr Standfast (1918)
John Buchan

Richard Hannay

Mr Stone and the Knights Companion (1963)
VS Naipaul

Mr Weston's Good Wine (1927)
TF Powys

Much Obliged, Jeeves (1971)
PG Wodehouse

Reginald Jeeves (Wooster's valet)
Bertie Wooster

Mulatta and Mr Fly, The (1960)
Miguel Asturias

Mulino del Po, Il (1938–40) 2 vol
(The Mill on the Po)
Riccardo Bacchelli

Multitude and Solitude (1909)
John Masefield

Mum and Mr Armitage (1985)
Beryl Bainbridge

Mummer's Wife, A (1885)
George Moore

Mungo's Dream (1973)
JIM Stewart

Murder at the Vicarage, The (1930)
Agatha Christie

Miss Jane Marple (amateur sleuth)

Murder Being Done Once (1972)
Ruth Rendell

Inspector Reg Wexford

Murder in Mesopotamia (1936)
Agatha Christie

Hercule Poirot (detective)

Murder Is Announced, A (1950)
Agatha Christie

Miss Jane Marple (amateur sleuth)

Murder Is Easy (1939)
Agatha Christie

Murder Must Advertise (1933)
Dorothy L Sayers

Bunter (Wimsey's servant)
Lord Peter Wimsey (amateur detective)

Murder of Quality, A (1962)
John Le Carré

Murder of Roger Ackroyd, The (1926)
Murder on the Links, The (1923)
Murder on the Orient Express (1934)
Agatha Christie

Hercule Poirot (detective)

Murders in the Rue Morgue, The (1841)
Edgar Allan Poe

C Auguste Dupin (detective)

Murder Twice Told (1950)
Donald Hamilton

Murther and Walking Spirits (1991)
Robertson Davies

Murphy (1938)
Samuel Beckett

Museum of Cheats, The (1947)
Sylvia Townsend Warner

Museum Pieces (1952)
William Plomer

Music from Behind the Moon, The (1926)
James Branch Cabell

Music of Chance, The (1990)
Paul Auster

Mustard Seed, The (1953)
Vicki Baum

Mutation (1989)
Robin Cook

Mutiny on the Bounty (1932)
Charles Nordhoff

My Antonia (1918)
Willa Cather

My Bones and My Flute (1955)
Edgar Mittelholzer

My Brother Jonathan (1928)
Francis Brett Young

set: West Midlands

My Brother Yves
see ***Mon frère Yves***

My Child, My Sister (1965)
Roy Fuller

My Cousin Rachel (1951)
Daphne Du Maurier

Philip Ashley (narrator)
Rachel Coryn (widow)

My Days of Anger (1943)
James T Farrell

My Dog Tulip (1956)
JR Ackerley

My Fellow Devils (1951)
LP Hartley

My Friend Flicka (1941)
Mary O'Hara

Flicka (colt)
Ken McLaughlin (Flicka's boy-owner)

My Friend Prospero (1904)
Henry Harland

My Gun Is Quick (1950)
Mickey Spillane

Mike Hammer (private eye)

My Life As a Man (1974)
Philip Roth

Nathaniel Zuckerman (novelist)

My Life in the Bush of Ghosts (1954)
Amos Tutuola

My Love and Justice (1960)
Colin MacInnes

My Man Jeeves (1919) coll
PG Wodehouse

Reginald Jeeves (Wooster's valet)
Bertie Wooster

My Mortal Enemy (1926)
Willa Cather

My Neighbours (1919) coll
Caradoc Evans

My Novel (1853)
Edward Bulwer-Lytton

My Old Man's a Dustman (1956)
Wolf Mankowitz

My People (1915)
Caradoc Evans

Myra Breckinridge (1968)
Myron (1974)
sequel to ***Myra Breckinridge***
Gore Vidal

My Son, My Son (1938)
(also titled ***O Absalom!***)
Howard Spring

Mystère de la Chambre jaune, Le (1907)
(The Mystery of the Yellow Room)
Gaston Leroux

Mystère des Foules, Le (1895)
(The Mystery of the Crowds)
Paul Adam

Mysterier (1892)
Knut Hamsun

Mysteries of Udolpho, The (1794)
Ann Radcliffe

set: 16c Gascony; Apennines

Mysterious Affair at Styles, The (1920)
Agatha Christie

Hercule Poirot (detective)

Mysterious Island, The
see ***Île mystérieuse, L'***

Mysterious Stranger, The (1916) posth
Mark Twain

Mystery of Edwin Drood, The (1870) unf
Charles Dickens

set: London; Cloisterham (actual Rochester); Twinkleton's School
Rosa Bud (Edwin's betrothed)
Canon Septimus Crisparkle
Dick Datchery (investigator)
Edwin Drood
Hiram Grewgious (Rosa's guardian)
Luke Honeythunder (philanthropist/Landless twins' guardian)
John Jasper (Edwin's uncle)
Helena Landless (orphan)
Neville Landless (orphan/Helen's twin)
Mr Sapsea (Mayor of Cloisterham)
Lieutenant Tartar (Crisparkle's former schoolfellow)
Miss Twinkleton (school principal)

Mystery of Metropolisville, The (1873)
Edward Eggleston

Mystery of the Blue train, The (1928)
Agatha Christie

Hercule Poirot (detective)

Mystery of the Crowds, The
see ***Mystère des Foules, Le***

Mystery of the Yellow Room, The
see ***Mystère de la Chambre jaune, Le***

Mystic Masseur, The (1957)
VS Naipaul

My Theodosia (1941)
Anya Seton

My Uncle Oswald (1979)
Roald Dahl

My Universities (1923)
Maxim Gorky

N

Nabab, Le (1877)
Alphonse Daudet

Nachsommer, Der (1857)
Adalbert Stifter

Nada the Lily (1892)
H Rider Haggard

Naissance du jour, La (1928)
Colette

Naive and Sentimental Lover, The (1971)
John Le Carré

Naked and the Dead, The (1948)
Norman Mailer
set: World War II, Pacific Ocean

Naked Face, The (1970)
Sidney Sheldon

Naked Lunch, The (1959)
William Burroughs

Naked Sun, The (1957)
Isaac Asimov

Naked Sun, The (1980)
Ted Willis

Name of Action, The (1930)
Graham Greene

Name of the Rose, The
see *Nome della rosa, Il*

Names, The (1982)
Don Delillo

Napoleon of Notting Hill, The (1904)
GK Chesterton

Narcissus and Goldmund
see ***Narziss und Goldmund***

Narrowing Stream, The (1952)
John Mortimer

Narziss und Goldmund (1930)
(Narcissus and Goldmund)
Hermann Hesse

Natalia, the Boyar's Daughter (1792)
Nikolai Mikhailovich Karamzin

Natalie Natalia (1971)
Nicholas Mosley

Nathalie (1850)
Julia Kavanagh

National Velvet (1935)
Enid Bagnold
Velvet Brown
The Piebald (horse)

Native Argosy (1929)
Morley Callaghan

Natives of My Person (1972)
George Lamming

Native Son (1940)

Richard Wright

Bigger Thomas (criminal)

Natural, The (1952)
Bernard Malamud

Natural Curiosity, A (1989)
Margaret Drabble

Nature and Art (1796)
Elizabeth Inchbald

Naughty Amelia Jane (1939)
Enid Blyton

Amelia Jane (doll)

Nausea
see ***Nausée, La***

Nausée, La (1938)
(Nausea)
Jean-Paul Sartre

Navigator, The (1976)
Morris West

Nazarene, The (1939)
Sholem Asch

Near and the Far, The (1929)
LH Myers

set: 16c India

Nectar in a Sieve (1954)
Kamala Markandaya

Needful Things (1991)
Stephen King

Needle's Eye, The (1972)
Margaret Drabble

Negotiator, The (1989)
Frederick Forsyth

Nègre, Le (1927)
(The Negro)
Philippe Soupault

Negro, The
see ***Nègre, Le***

Neighbors (1980)
Thomas Berger

Neighbour's Wife, The (1923)
Liam O'Flaherty

Nélida (1845)
Daniel Stern

Nelly's Version (1977)
Eva Figes

Nemesis (1971)
Agatha Christie

Miss Jane Marple (amateur sleuth)

Nemesis of Faith, The (1849)
JA Froude

Nerve (1964)
Dick Francis

Nerve, The (1971)
Melvyn Bragg

Nest of Gentlefolk, A (1858)
Ivan Turgenev

Nest of Simple Folk, A (1933)
Sean O'Faolain

Neues Leben (1852) 3 vol
Berthold Auerbach

Never Come Morning (1942)
Nelson Algren

Never Had a Spanner on Her (1970)
James Leasor

Never Love a Stranger (1948)
Harold Robbins

Neveu de Rameau, Le (1823) posth
Denis Diderot

Newcomes, The (1855)
William Makepeace Thackeray

Mrs Mackenzie (widow)
Rosie Mackenzie (Mrs Mackenzie's daughter/Clive's soon-to-be wife)
Brian Newcome (Thomas' half-brother)
Clive Newcome (Thomas' son)
Ethel Newcome (Brian's daughter)
Hobson Newcome (Thomas' half-brother)
Colonel Thomas Newcome

New Confessions, The (1987)
William Boyd

New England Nun, A (1891)
Mary E Freeman

New Grub Street (1891)
George Gissing

Harold Biffen (author)
Jasper Milvain (reviewer)
Amy Reardon (Reardon's wife/Milvain's eventual wife)
Edwin Reardon (author)
Alfred Yule (academic)
Marian Yule (Yule's daughter/Milvain's fiancée)

New June, The (1909)
Henry Newbolt

New Landlord, The (1862)
Mór Jókai

New Leaf Mills (1913)
William Dean Howells

New Lease of Death, A (1967)
Ruth Rendell

Inspector Reg Wexford

New Life, A (1961)
Bernard Malamud

New Lives for Old (1933)
CP Snow

New Machiavelli, The (1911)
HG Wells

New Men, The (1954)
CP Snow

Lewis Eliot (narrator/barrister)

New Road, The (1914)
Neil Munro

News from Nowhere (1891)
William Morris

Newton Letter, The (1982)
John Banville

New Town (1960)
Noel Streatfeild

New Treasure-Seekers, The (1903) coll
E Nesbit

Bastable family

New Year's Eve, 1929 (1967)
James T Farrell

New York Trilogy, The (1990) 3 vol
Paul Auster

vols: 1 *City of Glass* (1985)
2 *Ghosts* (1986)
3 *The Locked Room* (1987)

Nexus (1960)
Henry Miller

Nice and the Good, The (1968)
Iris Murdoch

Nice Work (1988)
David Lodge

set: Rummidge (imaginary Midlands town)
Robyn Penrose (lecturer)
Vic Wilcox (engineering manager)

Nicholas Nickleby (1839)
Charles Dickens

set: London; Yorkshire
school: Dotheboys Hall
Madeline Bray (Nicholas' eventual wife)
Walter Bray (Madeline's father)
Charles Cheeryble (merchant)
Edwin Cheeryble (merchant/Charles' twin)
Frank Cheeryble (Charles & Edwin's nephew/Kate's eventual husband)
Vincent Crummles (actor-manager)
Arthur Gride (Bray's co-creditor)
Mr Kenwigs
Mrs Kenwigs (Kenwigs' wife)
Mr Lillyvick (Mrs Kenwigs' uncle)
Tim Linkinwater (Cheerybles' clerk)
Alfred Mantalini
Madame Mantalini (Mantalini's wife/dressmaker)
Kate Nickleby (Nicholas' sister)
Mrs Nickleby (Nicholas' widowed mother)
Nicholas Nickleby
Ralph Nickleby (Nicholas' uncle/Bray's co-creditor)
Newman Noggs (Ralph's clerk)
Henrietta Petowker (Lillyvick's eventual wife)
Smike (Nicholas' friend)
Snevellicci family (actors)
Wackford Squeers (school owner)
Henry Wititterly
Julia Wititterly (Wititterly's wife/Kate's sometime companion)

Nick of the Woods (1837)
Robert Montgomery Bird

Niebla (1914)
(Mist)
Miguel de Unamuno

Nigger of the Narcissus, The (1897)
Joseph Conrad

ship: Narcissus
James Wait

Night (1972)
Edna O'Brien

Mary Hooligan

Night, The
see ***Nuit, La***

Night and Day (1919)
Virginia Woolf

set: London
Katherine Hilbery

Night Birds of Nantucket (1966)
Joan Aiken

Night Chills (1977)
Dean R Koontz

Night-Comers, The (1956)
Eric Ambler

Nightfall (1941)
Isaac Asimov

Night Fears (1924) coll
LP Hartley

Night Flight
see ***Vol de nuit***

Nightingale Wood (1946)
Stella Gibbons

Nightmare, The (1954)
CS Forester

Nightmare Abbey (1818)
Thomas Love Peacock

Mr Cypress (as Byron)
Mr Flosky (as Coleridge)
Mr Scythrop (as Shelley)

Nightmare in Pink (1964)
John D MacDonald

Travis McGhee (shady dealer)

Night of Bright Stars, A (1979)
Richard Llewellyn

Night of Error (1984) posth
Desmond Bagley

Night of the Fox (1986)
Jack Higgins

Night of Their Own (1965)
Peter Abrahams

Night of the Ripper (1984)
Robert Bloch

Night of Wenceslas, The (1960)
Lionel Davidson

set: Prague
Nicholas Whistler

Night on the Island (1960)
MM Kaye

Night Over Water (1991)
Ken Follett

Night Probe (1981)
Clive Cussler

Night Rider (1938)
Robert Penn Warren

Nightrunners of Bengal (1951)
John Masters

Nights at the Circus (1984)
Angela Carter

Night Shift (1976)
Stephen King

Nightspawn (1971)
John Banville

Night Swimmers, The (1980)
Betsy Byars

Nights with Uncle Remus (1883) coll
Joel Chandler Harris

Night Walker (1954)
Donald Hamilton

Night-Watchmen, The (1969)
Helen Cresswell

Nightwing (1978)
Martin Cruz Smith

Night without End (1960)
Alistair Maclean

set: Greenland

Nightwood (1936)
Djuna Barnes

Nightwork (1975)
Irwin Shaw

Night-World (1972)
Robert Bloch

Nils Holgerssons underbara resa genom Sverige (1907)
(The Wonderful Adventures of Nils)
Selma Lagerlöf

Nina Balatka (1867)
Anthony Trollope

set: Prague
Nina Balatka (Trendellsohn's admirer)
Rebecca Loth (Trendellsohn's intended wife)
Anton Trendellsohn

Nine Billion Names of God, The (1967)
Arthur C Clarke

Nine Stories (1953) coll
(also titled ***For Esmé – with Love and Squalor***)
JD Salinger

Glass family

Nine Tailors, The (1934)
Dorothy L Sayers

set: Fenchurch St Paul, East Anglia
Bunter (Wimsey's servant)
Lord Peter Wimsey (amateur detective)

1985 (1978)
Anthony Burgess

Nineteen Eighty-Four (1949)
George Orwell

'Big Brother' (party head)
Winston Smith

1982, Janine (1984)
Alasdair Gray

1919 (1932)
John Dos Passos

1962: a Model Kit
see ***62: modelo para armar***

Ninety-Three
see ***Quatre-vingt-treize***

No Adam in Eden (1963)
Grace Metalious

Noble House (1981)
James Clavell

Nocturne (1917)
Frank Swinnerton

Nocturnes for the King of Naples (1978)
Edmund White

No Fond Return of Love (1961)
Barbara Pym

No Highway (1948)
Nevil Shute

No Holly for Miss Quin (1976)
Miss Read

No Home but the Struggle (1977)
Edward Upward

Noia, La (1952)
(The Empty Canvas)
Alberto Moravia

Noise of Their Wings, The (1938)
MacKinlay Kantor

No Laughing Matter (1967)
Angus Wilson

Matthews family

No Longer at Ease (1960)
Chinua Achebe

No Longer Human (1948)
Osamu Dazai

No Man's Island (1983)
Jessica Mann

Nome della rosa, Il (1980)
(The Name of the Rose)
Umberto Eco

set: medieval abbey
Adso of Melk (novice monk)
William of Baskerville (monk)

No More Dying Then (1971)
Ruth Rendell

Inspector Reg Wexford

No More Parades (1925)
Ford Madox Ford

Christopher Tietjens

No Mother to Guide Her (1961)
Anita Loos

No Name (1862)
Wilkie Collins

Magdalen Vanstone

None Are So Blind (1939)
PC Wren

None but the Lonely Heart (1943)
Richard Llewellyn

Non-Stop (1958)
Brian W Aldiss

No One Writes to the Colonel
see ***Coronel no tiene quien le escriba***

Noon Wine (1937)
Kathleen Anne Porter

No Orchids for Miss Blandish (1939)
James Hadley Chase

No Promises in the Wind (1970)
Irene Hunt

No Quarter Given (1935)
Paul Horgan

Nord (1960)
(North)
Louis-Ferdinand Céline

N or M? (1941)
Agatha Christie

Norma Ashe (1942)
Susan Glaspell

North
see ***Nord***

North and South (1855)
Elizabeth Gaskell

set: North & South of England
Margaret Hale
Reverend Hale (Margaret's father)
John Thornton (Margaret's eventual husband)

Northanger Abbey (1818) posth
Jane Austen

set: Bath; Northanger Abbey (Tilneys' home)
Mr Allen (Catherine's friend)
Mrs Allen (Allen's wife/Catherine's friend)
Catherine Morland (clergyman's daughter)

Isabella Thorpe (Catherine's friend)
John Thorpe (Isabella's brother)
Captain Tilney (Henry's brother)
Eleanor Tilney (Henry's sister)
General Tilney (Henry's father)
Henry Tilney (Catherine's fiancé)

North Star (1974)
Hammond Innes

No Signposts in the Sea (1961)
Vita Sackville-West

Nostalgia (1905)
Grazia Deledda

No Star Is Lost (1938)
James T Farrell

Nostromo (A Tale of the Seaboard) (1904)
Joseph Conrad

set: Costaguana (imaginary South American country)
Charles Gould
Emilia Gould (Gould's wife)
Nostromo (Italian sailor)

Not a Penny More, Not a Penny Less (1976)
Jeffrey Archer

Note in Music, A (1930)
Rosamund Lehmann

Notes from Underground (1864)
coll
Fyodor Dostoevsky

Not Heaven (1953)
Waldo Frank

Nothing (1950)
Henry Green

Nothing Like Leather (1935)
VS Pritchett

Nothing Like the Sun (1964)
Anthony Burgess

Not Honour More (1955)
Joyce Cary

Chester Nimmo (politician)

Not in the Calendar (1964)
Margaret Kennedy

Notre coeur (1890)
(Our Heart)
Guy de Maupassant

Notre-Dame de Paris (1831)
Victor Hugo

set: 15c Paris
Esmerelda (gypsy dancer)
Claude Frollo (archdeacon)
Quasimodo (hunchbacked bell-ringer)

Notre-Dame des Fleurs (1944)
(Our Lady of the Flowers)
Jean Genet

Not Such a Bad Day (1946)
James Leasor

Not That Sort of Girl (1987)
Mary Wesley

Not to Disturb (1971)
Muriel Spark

Noughts and Crosses (1891)
Arthur Quiller-Couch

Nouvelle Histoire de Mouchette (1937)
Georges Bernanos

Nouvelles (1852) coll
(including *Carmen*)
Prosper Mérimée

Nova Express (1964)
William Burroughs

Novella del buon vecchio e della bella fanciulla, La (1929) posth
(The Tale of the Good Old Man and the Lovely Young Girl)
Italo Svevo

Novel on Yellow Paper (1936)
Stevie Smith

November Reef (1962)
Robin Maugham

Now and Forever (1978)
Danielle Steel

Now, God Be Thanked (1979)
John Masters

Nowhere (1985)
Thomas Berger

Nowhere Man (1972)
Kamala Markandaya

NTR: Nothing to Report (1955)
James Leasor

Nuit, La (1958)
(The Night)
Elie Wiesel

Nuits des princes (1928)
(Princes' Nights)
Joseph Kessel

Numa Roumestan (1881)
Alphonse Daudet

Number of the Beast, The (1980)
Robert A Heinlein

Number One (1943)
John Dos Passos

Nun, The
see ***Religieuse, La***

Nunquam (1970)
Laurence Durrell

Nuns and Soldiers (1980)
Iris Murdoch

Nylon Pirates (1960)
Nicholas Monsarrat

O

O Absalom!
see ***My Son, My Son***

Oasis, The (1949)
Mary McCarthy

Obermann (1804)
Étienne Senancour

Oblat, L' (1903)
(The Lay Brother)
Joris-Karl Huysmans

Durtal

Oblómov (1859)
Ivan Goncharov

Oblómov (lethargic Russian)

Obstacle, The
see ***Chiendent, Le***

Ob Tausend fallen (1943)
(A Thousand Shall Fall)
Hans Habe

Ocalenie (1945)
Czeslaw Milosz

Occasion for Loving (1963)
Nadine Gordimer

Occupying Power, The (1973)
Evelyn Anthony

Ocean, The (1941)
James Hanley

Octavia (1977)
Jilly Cooper

October the First Is Too Late (1966)
Fred Hoyle

Octopus, The (1901)
Frank Norris

set: Pacific & Southwest railroad

Octopussy (1966) posth
Ian Fleming

James Bond '007' (spy)
M (Bond's boss)
Miss Moneypenny (M's secretary)

Odd Flamingo (1954)
Nina Bawden

Odds Against (1965)
Dick Francis

Odd Women, The (1893)
George Gissing

Madden sisters

Odessa File, The (1972)
Frederick Forsyth

Odour of Sanctity, An (1966)
Frank Yerby

Odtaa (1926)
John Masefield

Of Age and Innocence (1958)
George Lamming

Office Life (1979)
Keith Waterhouse

Officers and Gentlemen (1955)
Evelyn Waugh

set: World War II
Guy Crouchback (army officer)
Trimmer (Virginia's lover)
Virginia Troy (Crouchback's ex-wife)

Off Limits (1955)
Hans Habe

Off the Deep End (1928)
Christopher Morley

Off with His head (1957)
Ngaio Marsh

Inspector Roderick Alleyn

Of Human Bondage (1915)
W Somerset Maugham

set: Blackstable (actual Whitstable); Tercanbury (actual Canterbury)
Philip Carey
Mildred Rodgers (waitress)

Of Mice and Men (1937)
John Steinbeck

George (itinerant worker)
Lennie (slow-witted itinerant worker)

Of Mortal Love (1936)
William Gerhardie

Of Time and the River (1935)
sequel to ***Look Homeward, Angel***
Thomas Wolfe

Eugene Gant

Of Trees and the Sea (1956)
Edgar Mittelholzer

Ogilvies, The (1846)
Dinah Maria Craik

O, How the Wheel Becomes It! (1983)
Anthony Powell

Oh What a Paradise It Seems (1982)
John Cheever

Oil! (1927)
Upton Sinclair

Olav Audunssön (1925-1927) 4 vol
Sigrid Undset

Old and the Young, The
see ***Vecchi e i giovani, I***

Old Boys, The (1964)
William Trevor

Old Bunch, The (1937)
Meyer Levin

Old Captivity, An (1940)
Nevil Shute

Old Country, The (1906)
Henry Newbolt

Old Curiosity Shop, The (1841)
Charles Dickens

set: London; Midlands
Sampson Brass (attorney)
Codlin (Punch & Judy man)
Mr Garland (Nubbles' friend)
Mrs Garland (Garland's wife)
'The Marchioness' (maidservant/Dick's eventual wife)
Kit Nubbles (Nell's friend)
Daniel Quilp (deformed money-lender)
Short, alias Harris (Codlin's partner)
Dick Swiveller (Brass' clerk)
Trent (Nell's grandfather/shopkeeper)
Fred Trent (Nell's brother)
Nell Trent, 'Little Nell'
Vuffin (travelling showman)
Mrs Wackles (school proprietress)

Old Devils, The (1986)
Kingsley Amis

Oldest Confession, The (1958)
Richard Condon

Old-Fashioned Girl, An (1870)
Louisa M Alcott

Polly Milton

Old Gray Homestead, The (1919)
Frances Parkinson Keyes

Old Kensington (1873)
Anna Isabella Ritchie

Old Ladies, The (1924)
Hugh Walpole

Old Lamps for New (1965)
Harold Acton

Old Maid, The (1924)
Edith Wharton

Charlotte Lovell
Delia Lovell (Charlotte's cousin)

Old Man and the Sea, The (1952)
Ernest Hemingway
set: Cuba

Old Manor House, The (1793)
Charlotte Smith

Old Men at the Zoo, The (1961)
Angus Wilson

Old Mortality (1816)
Walter Scott
set: late18c Scotland
John Balfour (Covenanter)
Edith Bellenden
Lord Evandale (Edith's would-be husband)
Reverend Kettledrummle (Covenanter)
Henry Morton (Edith's would-be husband)
Robert Paterson, 'Old Mortality' (Covenanter)
Reverend Poundtext (Presbyterian)

Old Pybus (1928)
Warwick Deeping

Old Reliable, The (1951)
PG Wodehouse

Old Sailors Never Lie (1939)
Henry Stacpoole

Old Stag, The (1926)
Henry Williamson

Old St Paul's (1841)
William Harrison Ainsworth

Oldtown Folks (1869)
Harriet Beecher Stowe

Old Wives' Tale, The (1908)
Arnold Bennett
set: Bursley (actual Burslem)
Constance Baines
Sophia Baines (Constance's sister)
Samuel Povey (Constance's husband)
Gerald Scales (Sophia's husband)

Olga Frohmut (1910)
Felix Salten

Olive (1850)
Dinah Maria Craik

Oliver's Story (1977)
Erich Segal
sequel to *Love Story*

Oliver Twist (or The Parish Boy's Progress) (1838)
Charles Dickens
set: workhouse; London
Mr Brownlow (Oliver's befriender)
Bull's Eye (Sikes' dog)
Bumble (parish beadle)
Mrs Bumble, née Corney (Bumble's wife/matron)
Noah Claypole, alias Morris Bolter (Sowerberry's apprentice)
John Dawkins, alias The Artful Dodger (pick-pocket)
Fagin (thieves' leader)
Edward Leeford, alias Monks (Oliver's half-brother)
Mrs Maylie
Rose Maylie (Mrs Maylie's adopted niece)
Nancy (Sikes' mistress)
Bill Sikes (burglar)
Sowerberry (undertaker)
Oliver Twist (orphan)

Omoo (1847)
Herman Melville
set: Tahiti
ship: Julia
Tom (seaman)

On a Field Azure (1927) coll
Alexei Remizov

Once and Future King, The (1938–41)
TH White

One Across, Two Down (1972)
Ruth Rendell

One and Last Love (1981)
John Braine

One Bright Summer's Morning (1963)
James Hadley Chase

One by One (1965)
Penelope Gilliat

One Day in the Afternoon of the World (1964)
William Saroyan

One Day in the Life of Ivan Denisovich (1962)
Alexander Solzhenitsyn

One Fat Englishman (1963)
Kingsley Amis

One Flew over the Cuckoo's Nest (1962)
Ken Kesey

set: mental hospital

One Hand Clapping (1961)
Anthony Burgess

One Hundred and One Dalmatians, The (1956)
Dodie Smith

Cruella De Vil (puppy-stealer)
Missis (Pongo's mate)
Pongo (Dalmatian dog)

One Hundred Years of Solitude
see ***Cien años de soledad***

One Lonely Night (1951)
Mickey Spillane

Mike Hammer (private eye)

One Man's Initiation (1917)
John Dos Passos

One Night in Winter (1984)
Allan Massie

One of Our Conquerors (1891)
George Meredith

Natalie Dreighton (Victor's lover)
Nesta (Victor & Natalie's illegitimate daughter)
Victor Radnor

One of Ours (1922)
Willa Cather

One Woman's Life (1913)
Robert Herrick

On Her Majesty's Secret Service (1963)
Ian Fleming

James Bond '007' (spy)
M (Bond's boss)
Miss Moneypenny (M's secretary)

Onion Eaters, The (1971)
JP Donleavy

Onion Field, The (1973)
Joseph Wambaugh

Onlookers (1983)
Gillian Avery

Only a Fiddler (1837)
Hans Christian Andersen

Only Afterwards (1947)
SY Agnon

Only Child, The (1978)
Nell Dunn

Only Children (1979)
Alison Lurie

Only Problem, The (1984)
Muriel Spark

Only Toys! (1903)
F Anstey

Only When I Larf (1968)
Len Deighton

On Newfound River (1891)
Thomas Nelson Page

On the Banks of Plum Creek (1937)
Laura Ingalls Wilder

On the Beach (1957)
Nevil Shute
set: Australia

On the Eve (1860)
Ivan Turgenev

On the Marble Cliffs
see ***Auf den Marmorklippen***

On the Road (1957)
Jack Kerouac
Dean Moriarty (Sal's friend)
Sal Paradise (writer)

On the Run (1964)
Nina Bawden

Onward Virgin Soldiers (1971)
Leslie Thomas

On Wings of Eagles (1984)
Ken Follett

Open Boat, The (1898)
Stephen Crane

Opening Night (1951)
Ngaio Marsh
Inspector Roderick Alleyn

Open Prison, An (1984)
JIM Stewart

Open Secret (1982)
James Leasor

O Pioneers! (1913)
Willa Cather

Optimist's Daughter, The (1972)
Eudora Welty

Oracle, The (1955)
Margaret Kennedy

Oracle, The (1951)
Edwin O'Connor

Orage immobile, Un (1983)
(The Still Storm)
Françoise Sagan

Orange Wednesday (1967)
Leslie Thomas

Ordeal by Innocence (1958)
Agatha Christie

Ordeal of Gilbert Pinfold, The (1957)
Evelyn Waugh

Gilbert Pinfold (novelist)

Ordeal of Richard Feverel, The (1859)
George Meredith

Lucy Desborough (Richard's eventual wife)
Sir Austin Feverel
Richard Feverel (Sir Austin's son)
Bella Mount (Richard's sometime lover)
Lord Mountfalcon (Lucy's would-be lover)

Orders for New York (1989)
Leslie Thomas

Ordinary Jack (1977)
Helen Cresswell

Ordinary Life, An (1934)
Karel Capek

Ordinary Princess, The (1980)
MM Kaye

Ordinary Story, An (1847)
Ivan Goncharov

Origin, The (1980)
Irving Stone

Origin of the Brunists, The (1966)
Robert Coover

Orissers, The (1922)
LH Myers

Orlando (1928)
Virginia Woolf

Orlando (twin-charactered aristocrat)

Orley Farm (1862)
Anthony Trollope

set: Groby Park; Orley Farm
Mr Chaffanbrass (lawyer)
Joseph Mason
Lady Mason (Lucius' mother)
Lucius Mason (Joseph's step-brother)

Ormerod's Landing (1979)
Leslie Thomas

Ormond (1799)
Charles Brockden Brown

Ormond (1817)
Maria Edgeworth

Oroonoko (or The History of the Royal Slave) (1688)
Aphra Benn

set: Surinam
Imoinda (Oroonoko's beloved)
Oroonoko (African king's grandson)

Orphan Angel, The (1926)
Elinor Wylie

Orphan Island (1924)
Rose Macaulay

Orrie's (1990)
Thomas Berger

Örtlich betäubt (1969)
(Local Anaesthetic)
Günter Grass

Oscar and Lucinda (1989)
Peter Carey

Ossian's Ride (1959)
Fred Hoyle

Osterman Weekend, The (1973)
Robert Ludlum

OT (1836)
Hans Christian Andersen

Other, The
see ***Autre, L'***

Other Gods (1940)
Pearl Buck

Other House, The (1896)
Henry James

Other Landscape, The (1954)
Neil Gunn

Other Side of Midnight, The (1974)
Sidney Sheldon

Other Side of the Fire, The (1983)
Alice Thomas Ellis

Other Voices, Other Rooms (1948)
Truman Capote

Othon l'Archer (1840)
Alexandre Dumas (père)

Otoño del patriarca, El (1975)
(The Autumn of the Patriarch)
Gabriel García Márquez

Our America (1919)
Waldo Frank

Our Friend the Charlatan (1901)
George Gissing

Our Heart
see ***Notre coeur***

Our Lady of the Flowers
see ***Notre-Dame des Fleurs***

Our Man in Havana (1958)
Graham Greene

set: Cuba

Our Mr Wrenn (1914)
Sinclair Lewis

Our Mutual Friend (1865)
Charles Dickens

set: London
Henrietta Boffin (Boffin's wife)
Nicodemus Boffin (Harmon's foreman)
Fledgeby (moneylender)
Harmon (John Harmon's deceased father)
John Harmon, alias John Rokesmith
Bradley Headstone (headmaster)
Jesse Hexam (shady boatman)
Lizzie Hexam (Hexam's daughter/Wrayburn's eventual wife)
Betty Higden (child-minder/laundress)
John Podsnap (businessman)
Riah (Fledgeby's Jewish employee)
Roger 'Rogue' Riderhood (waterman)
Anastasia Veneering (Veneering's wife)
Hamilton Veneering (druggist)
Mr Venus (taxidermist)
Silas Wegg (one-legged balladmonger/fruiterer)
Bella Wilfer (John Harmon's eventual wife)
Eugene Wrayburn (barrister)

Ourselves to Know (1960)
John O'Hara

Our Song (1988)
Keith Waterhouse

Our Time Is Gone (1940)
James Hanley

Outbreak (1987)
Robin Cook

Outcast, The
see ***Esclusa, L'***

Outcast of the Islands, An (1896)
Joseph Conrad

Outcasts of Poker Flat, The (1869)
Bret Harte

Out in the Pampas (1871)
GA Henty

Outlanders, The (1970)
Helen Cresswell

Outlaws (1987)
George V Higgins

Outlaws, The (1922)
Richmal Crompton
Violet Elizabeth Bott
Robert Brown (William's elder brother)
William Brown

Out of Africa (1938)
Karen Blixen

Out of the Shelter (1970)
David Lodge

Out of the Silent Planet (1938)
CS Lewis

Out of This Nettle (1939)
Norah Lofts

Out of This World (1988)
Graham Swift

Outsider, The (1956)
Colin Wilson

Outsider, The (1953)
Richard Wright

Outsider, The
see ***Étranger, L'***

Outward Urge, The (1959)
John Wyndham

Overload (1979)
Arthur Hailey

Over the Frontier (1938)
Stevie Smith

Over There
see ***Là-bas***

Over to You (1946) coll
Roald Dahl

Overture to Death (1939)
Ngaio Marsh
Inspector Roderick Alleyn

Owen Glendower (1940)
John Cowper Powys

Owls Do Cry (1957)
Janet Frame

Owl Service, The (1967)
Alan Garner

Owls in the Family (1961)
Farley Mowat

Ozma of Oz (1907)
L Frank Baum

O-Zone (1986)
Paul Theroux

P

Pacific Vortex (1983)
Clive Cussler

Pagan Place, A (1970)
Edna O'Brien

Pagan Rabbit, The (1971)
Cynthia Ozick

Page d'histoire, Une (1886)
Jules-Amédée Barbey D'Aurevilly

Painted Bird, The (1965)
Jerzy Kosinski

Painted Garden, The (1949)
Noel Streatfeild

Painted Veil, The (1925)
W Somerset Maugham

Painter of Our Time, A (1958)
John Berger

Painter of Signs, The (1977)
RK Narayan

Pair of Blue Eyes, A (1873)
Thomas Hardy

set: Cornwall
Henry Knight (Elfride's suitor)
Stephen Smith (architect/Elfride's suitor)
Elfride Swancourt

Palace, Le (1962)
Claude Simon

Palace of the Peacock (1960)
Wilson Harris

Pale Fire (1962)
Vladimir Nabokov

Pale Gray for Guilt (1968)
John D MacDonald
Travis McGhee (shady dealer)

Pale Horse, The (1961)
Agatha Christie

Pale View of Hills, A (1982)
Kazuo Ishiguro

Palimpsest (1926)
Hilda Doolittle

Pal Joey (1940)
John O'Hara

Palm Sunday (1981)
Kurt Vonnegut

Palm-Wine Drinkard, The (1952)
Amos Tutuola

Palomar (1983)
Italo Calvino

Palomino (1982)
Danielle Steel

Pamela (or Virtue Rewarded) (1740–1) 2 vol
Samuel Richardson

Pamela Andrews
Lady B
Mr B (Lady B's son/Pamela's eventual husband)
Lady Davers (Mr B's sister)
Mrs Jervis (housekeeper)
Mrs Jewkes (Mr B's servant)
Mr Longman (steward)
Mr Williams (chaplain)

Pan (1894)
Knut Hamsun

Pane e vino (1937)
(Bread and Wine)
Ignazio Silone

Panic Spring (1937)
Laurence Durrell

Paper Chase, The (1956)
Julian Symons

Paper Men, The (1984)
William Golding

Wilfred Barclay (author)
Rick L Turner (academic)

Paradine Case, The (1933)
Robert Smythe Hichens

Paradisarheimt (1960)
(Paradise Reclaimed)
Halldór Laxness

Paradise (1986)
Donald Barthelme

Paradise News (1991)
David Lodge

Paradise Postponed (1985)
John Mortimer

Simeon Simcox (rector)

Paradise Reclaimed
see ***Paradisarheimt***

Paradox King (1906)
Pia Baroja

Paradox Players, The (1967)
Maureen Duffy

Para Handy (1931) coll posth
Neil Munro

Parasites, The (1949)
Daphne Du Maurier

Pardoner's Tale, The (1978)
John Wain

Parents and Children (1941)
Ivy Compton-Burnett

Parfum de la dame en noir, Le (1909)
(The Perfume of the Lady in Black)
Gaston Leroux

Parisians, The (1873) unf
Edward Bulwer-Lytton

Paris Sketch Book, The (1840) coll
William Makepeace Thackeray

Parnassus on Wheels (1917)
Christopher Morley

Parsifal Mosaic, The (1982)
Robert Ludlum

Partisan, The (1835)
William Gilmore Simms

Partisans (1982)
Alistair Maclean

Partisans, The (1955)
Peter Matthiessen

Partners in Crime (1929) coll
Agatha Christie

Party Going (1939)
Henry Green

Pasmore (1972)
David Storey

Pas perdidos, Los (1953)
(The Lost Steps)
Alejo Carpentier

Pasquier Chronicles, The
see ***Chronique des Pasquier***

Passage de Milan (1954)
Michel Butor

Passage of Arms (1959)
Eric Ambler

Passage to India, A (1924)
EM Forster
set: Chandrapore; Marabar Caves, India
Dr Aziz (surgeon's assistant)
Cyril Fielding (college principal)
Professor Godbole
Mrs Moore (Adele's companion)
Ronny Moore (Mrs Moore's son/magistrate)
Adele Quested

Passage to Mutiny (1976)
Alexander Kent
Richard Bolitho (seaman)

Passe-Muraille, Le (1943)
Marcel Aymé

Passenger (1979)
Thomas Keneally

Passenger to Frankfurt (1970)
Agatha Christie

Passing On (1989)
Penelope Lively

Passionate Elopement, The (1911)
Compton MacKenzie

Passionate Friends, The (1913)
HG Wells

Passion Play (1979)
Jerzy Kosinski

Passions (1976) coll
Isaac Bashevis Singer

Passions of the Mind, The (1971)
Irving Stone

Passport for a Pilgrim (1968)
Passport in Suspense (1967)
Passport to Oblivion (1964)
Passport to Peril (1966)
James Leasor
Dr Jason Love

Pastimes of a Red Summer (1969)
Peter Vansittart

Pastoral Symphony, The
see ***Symphonie pastorale, La***

Pastors and Masters (1925)
Ivy Compton-Burnett

Pastor's Fireside, The (1815)
Jane Porter

Pastor's Wife (1912)
Elizabeth Von Arnim

Pastures of Heaven, The (1932) coll
John Steinbeck

Patchwork Girl, The (1980)
Larry Niven

Patchwork Girl of Oz, The (1913)
L Frank Baum

Pathfinder, The (1840)
James Fenimore Cooper
Natty Bumppo, called Pathfinder
Chingachgook (Mohican)

Path of Dalliance (1963)
Auberon Waugh

Path of Thunder (1948)
Peter Abrahams

Path to the Silent Country (1977)
Lynne Reid Banks

Pathway, The (1928)
Henry Williamson

Patriot, The (1939)
Pearl Buck

Patriot, The (1960)
ES Connell

Patriot Games (1987)
Tom Clancy

Patriot Game, The (1982)
George V Higgins

Patriots, The (1979)
June Drummond

Patronage (1814)
Maria Edgeworth

Paul Clifford (1830)
Edward Bulwer-Lytton

Pauline (1838)
Alexandre Dumas (père)

Paul Klever (1902)
Jerome K Jerome

Pauper, Brawler and Slanderer (1987)
Amos Tutuola

Pawnbroker, The (1961)
Edward Lewis Wallant

Payment Deferred (1926)
CS Forester

Paysan de Paris, Le (1926)
Louis Aragon

Peach Stone, The (1967) coll
Paul Horgan

Peacock House, The (1963)
Gillian Avery

Pearl, The (1947)
John Steinbeck

Pearl Fishers, The (1915)
Henry Stacpoole

Pearl Lagoon, The (1924)
Charles Nordhoff

Pearl Maiden, The (1903)
H Rider Haggard

Pearl of Orr's Island, The (1862)
Harriet Beecher Stowe

Pearls, Girls and Monty Bodkin (1972)
PG Wodehouse

Peasants, The (1902–9) 4 vol
WS Reymont

Pêcheur d'Islande (1886)
(Icelandic Fisherman)
Pierre Loti

Peckham's Marbles (1986)
Peter De Vries

Peg Woffington (1853)
Charles Reade

Ernest Vane
Mabel Vane (Vane's wife)
Margaret 'Peg' Woffington (actress)

Pélerin d'Angkor, Un (1912)
(A Pilgrim of Angkor)
Pierre Loti

Pelham (1828)
Edward Bulwer-Lytton

Pelican at Blandings, A (1969)
PG Wodehouse

set: Blandings Castle, Shropshire
Beach (Lord Emsworth's butler)
Empress of Blandings (pig)
Lord Emsworth
Lady Constance Keeble (Lord Emsworth's sister)
Galahad Threepwood (Lord Emsworth's brother)

Pelle (1906-1910) 4 vol
Martin Nexø

Pembroke (1894)
Mary E Freeman

Pennance for Jerry Kennedy (1985)
George V Higgins

Pendennis
see ***History of Pendennis, The***

Pending Heaven (1930)
William Gerhardie

Penguin Island
see ***Île des pingouins, L'***

Penitent, The (1984)
Isaac Bashevis Singer

Penmarric (1964)
Susan Howatch

Pennington's Heir (1973)
Pennington's Seventeenth Summer (1970)
KM Peyton

Penrod (1914)
Booth Tarkington

Peonies and Ponies (1941)
Harold Acton

set: Peking

People in Glass Houses (1967)
Shirley Hazzard

People of Hemsö, The
see ***Hemsöborna***

People with the Dogs, The (1952)
Christina Stead

Peppermint Pig, The (1975)
Nina Bawden

Peregrine Pickle
see ***Adventures of Peregrine Pickle, The***

Peregrine's Saga, The (1923)
Henry Williamson

Perelandra (1943)
CS Lewis

Perfect Lady
see ***Doña perfecta***

Perfect Murder, The (1964)
HRF Keating

set: Bombay
Inspector Ganesh Ghote (CID officer)

Perfect Spy, A (1986)
John Le Carré

Magnus Pym (secret agent)

Perfect Stranger, A (1982)
Danielle Steel

Perfect Woman, A (1955)
LP Hartley

Perfume of the Lady in Black, The
see ***Parfum de la dame en noir, Le***

Pericles the Athenian (1963)
Rex Warner

Peril at End House (1932)
Agatha Christie

Hercule Poirot (detective)

Perpetual Curate, The (1864)
Margaret Oliphant

Persian Boy, The (1972)
Mary Renault

Persiles y Sigismunda (1617) posth
Manuel de Cervantes

Persuasion (1818) posth
Jane Austen

set: Bath; Lyme Regis; Kellynch Hall (Elliots' seat)
Captain Benwick (Louisa's fiancé)
Mrs Clay (Sir Walter's would-be wife)
Admiral Croft (Wentworth's brother-in-law)
Mrs Croft (Croft's wife/Wentworth's sister)
Anne Elliot (Sir Walter's daughter)
Elizabeth Elliot (Sir Walter's daughter)
Mary Elliot (Sir Walter's daughter)
Sir Walter Elliot
William Elliot (Anne's cousin)
Charles Musgrove (Mary's soon-to-be husband)
Henrietta Musgrove (Charles' sister)
Louisa Musgrove (Charles' sister)
Lady Russell (Anne's godmother)
Captain Frederick Wentworth (naval officer/Anne's eventual husband)

Peste, La (1947)
(The Plague)
Albert Camus

Peter and Wendy (1911)
JM Barrie

Peter Camenzind (1904)
Hermann Hesse

Peter Duck (1932)
Arthur Ransome

Peter Ibbetson (1891)
George Du Maurier

Peterkin (1902)
Mary Louisa Molesworth

Petersburg (1913)
Andrei Bely

Peter Schlemihl (1813)
Adelbert von Chamisso

Peter Schlemihl

Peter Simple (1834)
Frederick Marryat

Mr Chucks (bosun)
Peter (seaman)
Captain Savage

Peter's Pence (1974)
Jon Cleary

Peter Wilkins
see ***Adventures of Peter Wilkins, The***

Petit Bob (1882)
Gyp

Petit Chose, Le (1868)
Alphonse Daudet

set: Paris
Camille (Daniel's eventual wife)
Daniel Eysette
Jacques Eysette (Daniel's brother)

Petite Fadette, La (1848)
(Little Fadette)
George Sand

Petit Prince, Le (1943)
(The Little Prince)
Antoine de Saint-Exupéry

Peur, La (1930)
Gabriel Chevallier

Peveril of the Peak (1822)
Walter Scott

set: English Civil War, Derbyshire
Alice Bridgenorth (Bridgenorth's daughter)
Major Bridgenorth (Puritan)
Sir Geoffrey Peveril (Cavalier)
Julian Peveril (Peveril's son)

Peyton Place (1956)
Grace Metalious

Phantastes (1858)
George MacDonald

Phantom, Der (1923)
Gerhart Hauptmann

Phantom of the Opera, The
see ***Fantôme de l'Opéra, Le***

Phantoms (1983)
Dean R Koontz

Phantom Ship, The (1839)
Frederick Marryat

Phasian Bird, The (1948)
Henry Williamson

Philista (1884)
Grant Allen

Philosopher's Pupil, The (1983)
Iris Murdoch

Philosopher's Stone (1969)
Colin Wilson

Phil the Fiddler (or The Story of a Young Street Musician) (1872)
Horatio Alger

Phineas Finn (The Irish Member) (1869)
Anthony Trollope

Lord Chiltern
Violet Effingham (Lord Chiltern's eventual wife)
Phineas Finn (barrister/politician)
Madame Max Goesler, 'Marie'
Mr Kennedy
Lady Laura Standish (Kennedy's sometime wife)

Phineas Redux (1874)
Anthony Trollope

Mr Chaffanbrass (lawyer)
Phineas Finn (politician)
Madame Max Goesler, 'Marie' (Finn's eventual wife)
Mr Kennedy

Phoenix and the Carpet, The (1904)
E Nesbit

Photo-Finish (1980)
Ngaio Marsh

Inspector Roderick Alleyn

Phroso (1897)
Anthony Hope

Piacere, Il (1889)
(The Child of Pleasure)
Gabriele D'Annunzio

Piano Players, The (1986)
Anthony Burgess

Piazza Tales, The (1856) coll
Herman Melville

Piccadilly (1870)
Laurence Oliphant

Piccolo mondo antico (1895)
(The Little World of the Past)
Antonio Fogazzaro

Pickwick Papers (or The Posthumous Papers of the Pickwick Club) (1837)
Charles Dickens

set: Rochester; Manor Farm, Dingley Dell; Eatanswill; Bury St Edmunds; Ipswich; Fleet Prison
Arabella Allen (Winkle's eventual wife)
Benjamin Allen (Arabella's brother/medical student)
Martha Bardell (Pickwick's sometime lady)
Serjeant Buzfuz (counsel)
Captain Dowler (army officer)
Mrs Leo Hunter (poetess)
Alfred Jingle (Rachael's seducer)
Peter Magnus (Pickwick's fellow-traveller)
Mary (Nupkins' maid)
George Nupkins (Mayor of Ipswich)
Solomon Pell (attorney)
Samuel Pickwick (Pickwick Club chairman)
Pott (editor)
Bob Sawyer (medical student)
Skimpin (junior counsel)
Hon Samuel Slumkey (parliamentary candidate)
Count Smorltork (Mrs Hunter's guest)
Augustus Snodgrass (Pickwick Club member)
Mr Stareleigh (judge)
Reverend Stiggins (drunken churchman)
Job Trotter (Jingle's servant)
Tracy Tupman (Pickwick Club member)
Mr Wardle (Manor Farm owner)
Rachael Wardle (Wardle's sister)
Sam Weller (Pickwick's servant)
Tony Weller (Sam's father)
Nathanial Winkle (Pickwick Club member)
Miss Witherfield (Magnus' fiancée)

Picnic at Sakhara, The (1955)
PH Newby

Picts and the Martyrs, The (1943)
Arthur Ransome

Picturegoers, The (1960)
David Lodge

Picture of Dorian Gray, The (1891)
Oscar Wilde

Dorian Gray (dandy)
Basil Hallward (artist)
Sybil Vane (Gray's sometime lover)
Lord Henry Wotton (aesthete)

Pictures from an Institution (1954)
Randall Jarrell

Picture This (1988)
Joseph Heller

Piece of the Sky Is Missing, A (1965)
David Nobbs

Pied Piper, The (1942)
Nevil Shute

Pied Piper of Lovers (1935)
Laurence Durrell

Piemakers, The (1967)
Helen Cresswell

Pierre (1852)
Herman Melville

Pierre et Jean (1888)
Guy de Maupassant

set: Le Havre
Jean Roland (lawyer)
Pierre Roland (Jean's brother)
Madame Rosémilly (Jean's fiancée)

Pietr-le-Letton (1931)
(Maigret and the Enigmatic Lett)
Georges Simenon

set: Paris
Chief Inspector Jules Maigret
Janvier (detective)
Lukas (detective)

Pigeon Pie (1945)
Nancy Mitford

Pigeon Post (1936)
Arthur Ransome

Pigs Have Wings (1952)
PG Wodehouse

set: Blandings Castle, Shropshire
Beach (Lord Emsworth's butler)
Empress of Blandings (pig)
Lord Emsworth
Lady Constance Keeble (Lord Emsworth's sister)
Galahad Threepwood (Lord Emsworth's brother)

Pilgrimage (1915–38, 1967) 12 vol; 1 vol posth
Dorothy M Richardson

Miriam

Pilgrim of Angkor, A
see ***Pélerin d'Angkor, Un***

Pilgrim's Progress, The (1678-84) 2 vol
John Bunyan

set: City of Destruction; Slough of Despond; Valley of Humiliation; Valley of the Shadow of Death; Vanity Fair; Doubting Castle; Delectable Mountains; Beulah; Celestial City
Apollyon (fiend)
Christian ('pilgrim')
Christiana (Christian's wife)
Giant Despair (Doubting Castle's owner)
Faithful (Christian's companion)
Great-Heart (Christiana's escort)
Hopeful (Christian's companion)
Mercy (Christiana's companion)
Mr Worldly Wiseman

Pillars of the Earth, The (1989)
Ken Follett

Pillars of the House, The (1873)
Charlotte M Yonge

Pilot, The (1823)
James Fenimore Cooper

Pilote de guerre (1942)
(Flight to Arras)
Antoine de Saint-Exupéry

Pincher Martin (1956)
William Golding

Pioneers, The (1823)
James Fenimore Cooper

Natty Bumppo, called Leather-Stocking
Chingachgook (Mohican)

Pioneers, The (1915)
Katharine Susannah Prichard

Piracy (1922)
Michael Arlen

Piranhas, The (1991)
Pirate, The (1974)
Harold Robbins

Pirate, The (1821)
Walter Scott

set: 17c Shetland
Cleveland (pirate)
Basil Mertoun
Mordaunt Mertoun (Mertoun's son)
Bryce Snailsfoot (pedlar)
Brenda Troil (Troil's daughter)
Magnus Troil (landlord)
Minna Troil (Troil's daughter)

Pirate City (1874)
RM Ballantyne

Pirates in the Deep Green Sea, The (1949)
Eric Linklater

Pit, The (1903) posth
Frank Norris

set: Chicago stock exchange (the 'Pit')

Pit and the Pendulum, The (1845)
Edgar Allan Poe

Place at Whitton, The (1964)
Thomas Keneally

Place in England, A (1970)
Melvyn Bragg

Tallentire family

Place of the Lion, The (1931)
Charles Williams

Place without Chairs (1978)
Brigid Brophy

Plague, The
see ***Peste, La***

Plague Dogs, The (1977)
Richard Adams

Plague Ship (1977)
Frank Slaughter

Plain Murder (1930)
CS Forester

Plain or Ringlets? (1860)
RS Surtees

Plains of Cement, The (1934)
Patrick Hamilton

Plains of Passage, The (1990)
Jean M Auel

Plain Tales from the Hills (1888) coll
Rudyard Kipling

Planétarium, Le (1959)
Nathalie Sarraute

Planet of Exile (1966)
Ursula Le Guin

Planet of the Apes, The (1961)
Pierre Boulle

Planets for Sale (1954)
AE Van Vogt

Playback (1958)
Raymond Chandler

Philip Marlowe (detective)

Player Piano (1952)
Kurt Vonnegut

Players (1977)
Don Delillo

Playfellow, The (1841) coll
Harriet Martineau

Play It As It Lays (1970)
Joan Didion

Play in the Fields, A (1965)
Peter Matthiessen

Playmaker, The (1987)
Thomas Keneally

Play Room, The (1969)
Olivia Manning

Pleasure City (1982)
Kamala Markandaya

Plexus (1953)
Henry Miller

Plot Against Roger Rider, The (1973)
Julian Symons

Plough over the Bones (1973)
David Garnett

Plumed Serpent, The (1926)
DH Lawrence

set: Mexico
Kate Leslie (widow)

Plum Tree, The (1905)
David Graham Phillips

Plutocrat, The (1927)
Booth Tarkington

Pnin (1957)
Vladimir Nabokov

Pocket Full of Rye, A (1953)
Agatha Christie

Pocket Full of Rye, A (1969)
AJ Cronin

Poet's Pub (1929)
Eric Linklater

Poganue People (1878)
Harriet Beecher Stowe

Point Counter Point (1928)
Aldous Huxley

Walter Bidlake
Burlap
Philip Quarles
Rampion
Lucy Tantamount

Point of No Return (1949)
John Marquand

Poirot Investigates (1924) coll
Agatha Christie

Hercule Poirot (detective)

Poison Belt, The (1913)
Arthur Conan Doyle

Professor Challenger

Poisoned Chocolates Case, The (1929)
Francis Iles

Roger Sheringham (journalist/detective)

Poisoned Kiss, The (1975)
Joyce Carol Oates

Poisoned Stream, The (1969)
Hans Habe

Poison Island (1907)
Arthur Quiller-Couch

Poison Oracle, The (1974)
Peter Dickinson

Poland (1983)
James A Michener

Polar Star (1989)
sequel to ***Gorky Park***
Martin Cruz Smith

Police at the Funeral (1931)
Margery Allingham

Albert Campion (detective)

Political Romance, A (1759)
Laurence Sterne

Polly Oliver's Problem (1893)
Kate Wiggin

Polo (1991)
Jilly Cooper

Polyglots, The (1925)
William Gerhardie

set: Far East
George Diabologh

Pond, The (1906)
Alexei Remizov

Ponder Heart, The (1954)
Eudora Welty

Pool of Vishnu, The (1940)
LH Myers

set: 16c India

Poor Cecco (1925)
Margery Williams Bianco

Poor Clare (1968)
LP Hartley

Poor Cow (1967)
Nell Dunn

Poor Folk (1846)
Fyodor Dostoevsky

Poor Fool (1930)
Erskine Caldwell

Poorhouse Fair, The (1959)
John Updike

Poor Jack (1840)
Frederick Marryat

Poor Liza (1792)
Nikolai Mikhailovich Karamzin

Poor Mouth, The
see ***Béal Bocht, An***

Poor Pumpkin (1971)
Robert Nye

Poor Tom (1932)
Edwin Muir

Poor White (1920)
Sherwood Anderson

Popanilla (1827)
Benjamin Disraeli

Porch, The (1937)
Richard Church

Porius (1951)
John Cowper Powys

Porterhouse Blue (1974)
Tom Sharpe

Portes de la Forêt, Les (1964)
(The Gates of the Forest)
Elie Wiesel

Port étroite, La (1909)
(Strait Is the Gate)
André Gide

Portion of Labor, The (1901)
Mary E Freeman

Portnoy's Complaint (1969)
Philip Roth

Alexander Portnoy

Port o' Missing Men (1934)
PC Wren

Portrait d'un inconnu (1947)
(Portrait of a Man Unknown)
Nathalie Sarraute

Portrait in a Mirror (1929)
Charles Morgan

Portrait in Brownstone (1962)
Louis Auchinloss

Portrait of a Lady, The (1881)
Henry James

set: mainly Italy
Isabel Archer (the lady)
Caspar Goodwood (Isabel's would-be suitor)
Madame Merle (Mrs Touchett's friend)
Gilbert Osmond (Isabel's soon-to-be husband)
Pansy Osmond (Osmond's daughter from 1st marriage)
Henrietta Stackpole (journalist)
Mr Touchett (Isabel's uncle/banker)
Mrs Touchett (Touchett's wife)
Ralph Touchett (Touchett's son)
Lord Warburton (Isabel's would-be suitor)

Portrait of a Man Unknown
see ***Portrait d'un inconnu***

Portrait of a Man with Red Hair (1925)
Hugh Walpole

Portrait of a Village (1951)
Portrait of Clare (1927)
Francis Brett Young

Portrait of Margarita (1968)
Ruth M Arthur

Portrait of the Artist As a Young Man, A (1916)
James Joyce

Father Arnall
Stephen Dedalus

Poseidon Adventure, The (1969)
Paul Gallico

Possessed, The
see ***Devils, The***

Possession (1925)
Louis Bromfield

Possession (1990)
AS Byatt

Possession (1963)
Kamala Markandaya

Postern of Fate (1973)
Agatha Christie

Post Haste (1880)
RM Ballantyne

Postman Always Rings Twice, The (1934)
James M Cain

Post Office (1971)
Charles Bukowski

Pothunters, The (1902)
PG Wodehouse

Potomak, Le (1913)
Jean Cocteau

Potterism (1920)
Rose Macaulay

Mr Potter (newspaper proprietor)

Power and the Glory, The (1940)
Graham Greene

set: Mexico
Padre José
Mr Tench (dentist)
'Whisky Priest'

Power House, The (1910)
John Buchan

Edward Leithen

Power of the Sword (1986)
Wilbur Smith

Prague Orgy, The (1985)
Philip Roth

Nathaniel Zuckerman (novelist)

Prairie, The (1827)
James Fenimore Cooper

Natty Bumppo, called Trapper

Prancing Nigger (1924)
(also titled ***Sorrow in Sunlight***)
Ronald Firbank

set: West Indies
Mouth family

Prater Violet (1945)
Christopher Isherwood

Pratt of the Argus (1988)
David Nobbs

Praxis (1978)
Fay Weldon

Prayer for Owen Meany, A (1989)
John Irving

Owen Meany

Precaution (1820)
James Fenimore Cooper

Precious Bane (1924)
Mary Webb

Prudence Sarn (narrator)

Prelude (1918)
Katherine Mansfield

Prelude to Foundation (1988)
Isaac Asimov

Premature Burial, The (1845)
Edgar Allan Poe

Premios, Los (1960)
(The Winners)
Julio Cortázar

Present and the Past, The (1953)
Ivy Compton-Burnett

Present Times (1984)
David Storey

President, The (1946)
Miguel Asturias

Presidential Mission (1947)
Upton Sinclair

Lanny Budd

President's Child, The (1982)
Fay Weldon

Prester John (1910)
John Buchan

set: Africa

Pretender, The (1915)
Robert Wiliam Service

Prêtre marié, Un (1865)
Jules-Amédée Barbey D'Aurevilly

Prick of Noon, The (1985)
Peter De Vries

Pride (1986)
William Wharton

Pride and Prejudice (1813)
Jane Austen

set: Hertfordshire
houses: Longbourn (Bennet's); Netherfield (Bingley's); Pemberley (Darcy's)
Catherine Bennet (Bennet's daughter)
Elizabeth Bennet (Bennet's daughter)
Jane Bennet (Bennet's eldest daughter)
Lydia Bennet (Bennet's youngest daughter)
Mary Bennet (Bennet's daughter)
Mr Bennet
Mrs Bennet (Bennet's wife)
Charles Bingley (Jane's eventual husband)
William Collins (rector)
Fitzwilliam Darcy (Elizabeth's eventual husband)
Georgiana Darcy (Darcy's sister)
Lady Catherine De Bourgh (patroness)
Mr Gardiner (Bennet girls' uncle)
Mrs Gardiner (Gardiner's wife)
Charlotte Lucas (Collins' soon-to-be wife)
George Wickham (officer-adventurer/Lydia's eventual husband)

Prima Donna, The (1908)
F Marion Crawford

Primal Urge, The (1961)
Brian W Aldiss

Prime Minister, The (1876)
Anthony Trollope

Ferdinand Lopez
Duke of Omnium
Duchess of Omnium (Omnium's wife)
Emily Wharton (Lopez's wife)

Prime of Miss Jean Brodie, The (1961)
Muriel Spark

set: 1930s Marcia Blaine School, Edinburgh
Jean Brodie (teacher)

Prime Time (1988)
Joan Collins

Prince Albert (1963)
Richard Church

Prince and the Page, The (1865)
Charlotte M Yonge

Prince and the Pauper, The (1882)
Mark Twain

set: 1540s London
Tom Canty (pauper boy)
Prince Edward

Prince Caspian: the Return to Narnia (1951)
CS Lewis

set: Narnia
Aslan (lion)
Prince Caspian
Edmund
Lucy
Peter
Susan

Prince Jali (1931)
LH Myers

set: 16c India

Princes' Nights
see ***Nuits des princes***

Princess and Curdie, The (1883)
Princess and the Goblin, The (1872)
George MacDonald

Princess Casamassima, The (1886)
Henry James

Princess Daisy (1980)
Judith Krantz

Princesse de Clèves, La (1678)
Princesse de Montpensier, La (1662)
Marie-Madeleine La Fayette

Princess of Thule, A (1873)
William Black

Prisoner of Grace (1952)
Joyce Cary

Chester Nimmo (politician)

Prisoner of Sex, The (1971)
Norman Mailer

Prisoner of the Caucasus, The (1821)
Alexander Pushkin

Prisoner of Zenda, The (1894)
Anthony Hope

set: Ruritania
Black Michael (usurper)
Princess Flavia
Rudolf Rassendyll (the prisoner)
Rupert of Hentzau (usurper)

Prison of Ice (1976)
Dean R Koontz

Private Angelo (1946)
Eric Linklater

set: World War II Italy

Private Life of an Indian Prince (1953)
Mulk Raj Anand

Private Memoirs and Confessions of a Justified Sinner, The (1824)
James Hogg

Private Papers of Henry Ryecroft, The (1903) George Gissing

Privy Seal: His Last Venture (1907)
Ford Madox Ford

Prizzi's Family (1986)
Prizzi's Honor (1982)
Richard Condon

Proceed Sergeant Lamb (1941)
sequel to ***Sergeant Lamb of the Ninth***
Robert Graves

Prodigal Daughter, The (1982)
Jeffrey Archer

Prodigal Parents (1938)
Sinclair Lewis

Prodigal Son, The (1904)
Hall Caine

Professor, The (1857)
Charlotte Brontë
set: North of England; Brussels
William Crimsworth (teacher)
Frances Henri (student/lace-mender)
M Pelet (headmaster)
Zoraide Reuter (headmistress)

Professor, The (1938)
Rex Warner

Professor's Daughter, The (1975)
Piers Paul Read

Professor's House, The (1925)
Willa Cather

Professor Unrat (1905)
Heinrich Mann

Profil perdu, Un (1974)
(Lost Profile)
Françoise Sagan

Progress of Julius, The (1933)
Daphne Du Maurier

Proletariat, The
see ***Armen, Die***

Promessi sposi, I (1825–7) 2 vol
(The Betrothed)
Alessandro Manzoni
set: 17c Lombardy

Promise, The (1977)
Danielle Steel

Promised Land, The (1899)
WS Reymont

Promised Land, The
see ***Forjaettede Land, Det***

Proof (1984)
Dick Francis

Proper Marriage, A (1954)
Doris Lessing
Martha Quest

Prophet, The (1955)
Sholem Asch

Prophet's Mantle, The (1885)
E Nesbit

Protector (1973)
Larry Niven

Proteus (1979)
Morris West

Prove Yourself a Hero (1977)
KM Peyton

Providence (1982)
Anita Brookner

Provost, The (1822)
John Galt

Mr Pawkie

Prozess, Der (1925) posth
(The Trial)
Franz Kafka

Josef K (bank official)

Prudence (1978)
Jilly Cooper

Psmith in the City (1910)
Psmith, Journalist (1915)
PG Wodehouse

Psmith

Psycho (1959)
Psycho II (1982)
Robert Bloch

Norman Bates

Public Burning, The (1977)
Robert Coover

Public Faces (1932)
Harold Nicolson

Public Image, The (1968)
Muriel Spark

Puck of Pook's Hill (1906)
Rudyard Kipling

set: Pook's Hill, near Burwash, Sussex
Dan
Puck (fairy)
Una (Dan's sister)

Puckoon (1963)
Spike Milligan

set: Ireland

Pudd'nhead Wilson (1894)
Mark Twain

Chambers (slave)
Percy Driscoll (slave-owner)
Tom Driscoll (Driscoll's son)
Roxy (slave)
David `Pudd'nhead' Wilson (lawyer)

Puffball (1980)
Fay Weldon

Pumpkin Eater, The (1962)
Penelope Mortimer

Pünktchen und Anton (1931)
Erich Kästner

Puppet Masters, The (1951)
Robert A Heinlein

Puppet on a Chain (1969)
Alistair Maclean

set: Netherlands

Pursuit of Love, The (1945)
Nancy Mitford

Radlett family

Pussy Owl (1976)
Brigid Brophy

Put on by Cunning (1981)
Ruth Rendell

Inspector Reg Wexford

Put Out More Flags (1942)
Evelyn Waugh

Basil Seal

Putting the Boot In (1985)
Julian Barnes

Put Yourself in His Place (1870)
Charles Reade

Puzzled America (1935)
Sherwood Anderson

Pylon (1935)
William Faulkner

Pyramid, The (1967)
William Golding

Q

QB VII (1970)
Leon Uris

Q Clearance (1986)
Peter Benchley

Quadrille (1965)
Frank Swinnerton

Quadroon, The (1856)
Mayne Reid

Quality of Mercy, The (1892)
William Dean Howells

Quartet (1928)
Jean Rhys

Quartet in Autumn (1977)
Barbara Pym

Quatre-vingt-treize (1873)
(Ninety-Three)
Victor Hugo

Que ces mots répondent (1964)
Luc Estang

Queen Anne's Lace (1930)
Frances Parkinson Keyes

Queen Jezebel (1953)
Jean Plaidy

Queen Lucia (1920)
EF Benson

Queen of a Distant Country, The (1972)
John Braine

Queen of Spades, The (1834)
Alexander Pushkin

Queen Sheba's Ring (1910)
H Rider Haggard

Queen's Quair, The (1904)
Maurice Hewlett

Queen Zixi of Ix (1905)
L Frank Baum

Quentin Durward (1823)
Walter Scott

set: 15c France
Charles the Bold (Duke of Burgundy)
Lord Crawford (Commander of the Archers)
Countess Isabelle de Croye
William De La Marck (Louis XI's companion)
Quentin Durward (archer)
Louis XI (King of France)

Querelle de Brest (1947)
Jean Genet

Quer pasticciaccio brutto de via Merulana (1957) unf
(That Awful Mess on the Via Merulana)
Carlo Emilio Gadda

Question of Loyalties, A (1989)
Allan Massie

Question of Proof, A (1935)
Nicholas Blake

Nigel Strangeways (detective)

Quest of Julian Day, The (1939)
Dennis Wheatley

Quick Service (1940)
PG Wodehouse

Quiet American, The (1955)
Graham Greene

set: Vietnam
Alben Pyle

Quiet As a Nun (1977)
Antonia Fraser

Jemima Shore (detective)

Quiet Gentleman, The (1951)
Georgette Heyer

Quiet Life, A (1976)
Beryl Bainbridge

Quiller Memorandum, The (1965)
(also titled ***The Berlin Memorandum***)
Adam Hall

Quintet (1976)
Peter Vansittart

Quintus Fixlein (1796)
Jean Paul

Quinx (1985)
Laurence Durrell

Quito Express (1938)
Ludwig Bemelmans

Quo Vadis? (1896)
Henryk Sienkiewicz

set: 1c Rome
Nero (emperor)
Petronius
Poppaea (Nero's wife)

R

Rabbit at Rest (1990)
Rabbit is Rich (1981)
Rabbit Redux (1971)
Rabbit, Run (1960)
John Updike

Harry Angstrom, 'Rabbit' (car salesman)
Janice Angstrom (Rabbit's wife)

Race Rock (1954)
Peter Matthiessen

Rachel Dyer (1828)
John Neal

Rachel Papers, The (1973)
Martin Amis

Raconti Romani (1954)
(Roman Tales)
Alberto Moravia

Radcliffe (1963)
David Storey

Radetzskymarsch (1932)
(The Radetzky March)
Joseph Roth

Radiant Way, The (1987)
Margaret Drabble

Raditzer (1961)
Peter Matthiessen

Ragazzi di vita (1955)
Pier Paolo Pasolini

Ragged Dick (or Street Life in New York) (1868)
Horatio Alger

Ragged Trousered Philanthropist, The (1914) posth
Robert Tressell

set: Mugsborough (imaginary South of England town)
Mr Barrington (wealthy socialist)
Easton family
Frank Owen (craftsman)

Rage to Live, A (1949)
John O'Hara

Raging Calm, A (1968)
Stan Barstow

Ragtime (1975)
EL Doctorow

Rahab (1922)
Waldo Frank

Raid, The (1853)
Leo Tolstoy

Railway Children, The (1906)
E Nesbit

'Old Gentleman'
Perks (railway porter)
Peter (Bobbie's brother)
Phyllis (Bobbie's sister)
Roberta, 'Bobbie'

Rain (1932)
W Somerset Maugham

Sadie Thompson

Rainbow, The (1915)
DH Lawrence

set: March Farm, Derbyshire/Nottinghamshire border
Anna Brangwen (Will's wife)
Gudrun Brangwen (Will's daughter)
Mrs Brangwen (Tom's wife)
Tom Brangwen (colliery manager)
Ursula Brangwen (Will's daughter)
Will Brangwen (draughtsman/Tom's nephew)
Anton Skrebensky (Ursula's sometime fiancé)

Rainbow's End (1975)
James M Cain

Rain Forest, The (1974)
Olivia Manning

Rains Came, The (1937)
Louis Bromfield

Raise High the Roof Beam, Carpenters (1963)
JD Salinger

Glass family

Raise the Titanic (1976)
Clive Cussler

Raj Quartet, The
see **Scott, Paul**

Ralph Darnell (1865)
Philip Meadows Taylor

Rameau's Nephew
see ***Neveu de Rameau, Le***

Ramuntcho (1897)
Pierre Loti

Randall and the River of Time (1951)
CS Forester

Randolph (1823)
John Neal

Random Harvest (1941)
James Hilton

Ransom (1972)
Jon Cleary

Scobie Malone (detective)

Rape of Venice, The (1959)
Dennis Wheatley

Raspberry Reich (1979)
Wolf Mankowitz

Rasselas (Prince of Abyssinia) (1759)
Samuel Johnson

set: Abyssinia; Egypt
Imlac (philosopher)
Nekayah (Rasselas' sister)
Pekuah (Nekayah's attendant)
Prince Rasselas

Rat, The
see ***Ratte, Die***

Rates of Exchange (1983)
Malcolm Bradbury

Doctor Petworth

Ratner's Star (1976)
Don Delillo

Rat on Fire, The (1981)
George V Higgins

Rat Race (1973)
Dick Francis

Rats, The (1974)
James Herbert

Ratte, Die (1987)
(The Rat)
Günter Grass

Rat Trap (1976)
Craig Thomas

Ravenshoe (1862)
Henry Kingsley

Ravi Lancers, The (1985) posth
John Masters

Ravine, The (1869)
Ivan Goncharov

Raw Material (1923)
Dorothea Frances Fisher

Raw Youth, A (1875)
Fyodor Dostoevsky

Arkady Dolgoruky

Rayuila (1963)
Julio Cortázar

Razor's Edge, The (1944)
W Somerset Maugham

set: USA; India
Larry Darrell

Ready-Money Mortiboy (1872)
Walter Besant

Real Charlotte, The (1894)
Edith Somerville

Real Life of Sebastian Knight, The (1941)
Vladimir Nabokov

Realms of Gold, The (1975)
Margaret Drabble

Real World, The (1901)
Robert Herrick

Rebecca (1938)
Daphne Du Maurier

set: Manderley (house), Cornwall
Mrs Danvers (housekeeper)
Max De Winter
Rebecca De Winter (De Winter's 1st wife)
Beatrice Lacy (Giles' wife/De Winter's sister)
Giles Lacy

Rebecca of Sunnybrook Farm (1903)
Kate Wiggin

Rebecca Randall

Rebel Angels, The (1981)
Robertson Davies

Rebellion der Gehenkten, Die (1936)
(The Rebellion of the Hanged)
B Traven

Rebel on a Rock (1978)
sequel to ***Carrie's War***
Nina Bawden

Recognitions, The (1955)
William Gaddis

Re: Colonised Planet 5, Shikasta (1979)
Doris Lessing

Rector of Justin, The (1965)
Louis Auchinloss

Red and the Black, The
see ***Rouge et le Noir, Le***

Red and the Green, The (1965)
Iris Murdoch

set: Ireland

Red Badge of Courage, The (1895)
Stephen Crane

set: American Civil War
Henry Fleming

Redburn (1849)
Herman Melville

set: Liverpool
ship: Highlander
Wellingborough Redburn (seaman)
Captain Riga

Red Cavalry (1926)
Isaak babel

Red Cockade, The (1895)
Stanley John Weyman

Red Fox (1979)
Gerald Seymour

Redgauntlet (1824)
Walter Scott

set: 1740s
Herries of Birrenswork, alias Sir Edward Redgauntlet
Darise Latimer, alias Sir Arthur Darsie Redgauntlet (Sir Edward's nephew)

Red Dragon (1981)
Thomas Harris

Red Group of Asakusa (1930)
Yasunari Kawabata

Red Harvest (1929)
Dashiell Hammett

Rediscovery of America, The (1929)
Waldo Frank

Red Lily, The
see ***Lys rouge, Le***

Red Planet, The (1966)
Robert A Heinlein

Red Rock (1898)
Thomas Nelson Page

Red Room, The
see ***Röda Rummet***

Red Rover, The (1827)
James Fenimore Cooper

Red Sand (1923)
TS Stribling

Red Shift (1973)
Alan Garner

Redskin and Cowboy (1892)
GA Henty

Redskins, The (1846)
James Fenimore Cooper

Red Sky at Morning (1927)
Margaret Kennedy

Red Storm Rising (1986)
Tom Clancy

Reef, The (1912)
Edith Wharton

Reflections in a Golden Eye (1941)
Carson McCullers

Reflex (1981)
Dick Francis

Refugees, The (1891)
Arthur Conan Doyle

Regency Buck (1935)
Georgette Heyer

Regiment of Women (1973)
Thomas Berger

Reginald (1904) coll
Saki

Reginald Dalton (1823)
John Gibson Lockhart

Reginald in Russia (1910) coll
Saki

Reine Margot, La (1845)
Alexandre Dumas (père)

Reinhart in Love (1962)
Reinhart's Women (1981)
Thomas Berger

Reino de este mundo, El (1949)
(The Kingdom of the World)
Alejo Carpentier

Reise nach Portiuncula, Die (1954)
Stefan Andres

Reivers, The (1962)
William Faulkner

Rejected Guest (1939)
Richard Aldington

Religieuse, La (1760) posth
(The Nun)
Denis Diderot

Reluctant Odyssey (1946)
Ellis Peters

Reluctant Widow, The (1946)
Georgette Heyer

Remains of the Day, The (1989)
Kazuo Ishiguro

Remember (1991)
Barbara Taylor Bradford

Remember to Remember (1947)
Henry Miller

Remembrance (1981)
Danielle Steel

Remembrance of Things Past
see ***A la recherche du temps perdu***

Renaissance (1979)
AE Van Vogt

Rendezvous, The (1980)
Daphne Du Maurier

Rendezvous with Rama (1973)
Arthur C Clarke

René (1802)
Chateaubriand

Amélie (René's sister)
Atala
Chactas (Red Indian)
René
Père Souël (missionary)

Renegade (1978)
JT Edson

Reporter (1929)
Meyer Levin

Report on Probability A (1968)
Brian W Aldiss

Requiem for a Dream (1979)
Hubert Selby

Requiem for a Nun (1951)
William Faulkner

Temple Drake

Requiem for a Wren (1955)
Nevil Shute

Rescue, The (1920)
Joseph Conrad

Research Magnificent, The (1915)
HG Wells

Restaurant at the End of the Universe, The (1980)
Douglas Adams

Resurrection (1934)
William Gerhardie

Resurrection (1899)
Leo Tolstoy

Katusha Maslova (prostitute)
Prince Dmitri Nekhludov (judge)

Retreat, The (1933)
Forrest Reid

Return, The (1910)
Walter De La Mare

Return I Dare Not (1931)
Margaret Kennedy

Return of Lanny Budd, The (1953)
Upton Sinclair

Lanny Budd

Return of Reginald Perrin, The (1977)
David Nobbs

Reginald Perrin

Return of Sherlock Holmes, The (1905) coll
Arthur Conan Doyle

set: 221b Baker Street, London
Mycroft Holmes (Holmes' brother)
Sherlock Holmes (detective)
Mrs Hudson (Holmes' housekeeper)
Inspector Lestrade (Scotland Yard officer)
Professor James Moriarty (Holmes' arch-enemy)
Dr John Watson (Holmes' companion)

Return of the Native, The (1878)
Thomas Hardy

set: Egdon Heath, Wessex
Diggory Venn (Thomasin's 2nd husband)
Eustacia Vye (Clym's wife)
Damon Wildeve (publican/Thomasin's 1st husband)
Clym Yeobright ('the native'/Thomasin's cousin)
Thomasin Yeobright

Return of the Soldier, The (1918)
Rebecca West

Revenge for Love, The (1937)
Wyndham Lewis

Revenge of Samuel Stokes, The (1981)
Penelope Lively

Revolution in Tanner's Lane (1887)
Mark Rutherford

Rewards and Fairies (1910)
Rudyard Kipling

Rhinemann Exchange, The (1975)
Robert Ludlum

Rhoda Fleming (1865)
George Meredith

set: Kent
Edward Blancove (Dahlia's seducer)
Robert Eccles (Rhoda's eventual husband)
Dahlia Fleming (Rhoda's sister)
Rhoda Fleming

Riceyman Steps (1923)
Arnold Bennett

set: Clerkenwell, London

Richard Bolitho – Midshipman (1975)
Alexander Kent

Richard Bolitho (seaman)

Richard Carvel (1899)
Winston Churchill

Richard Savage (1842)
Charles Whitehead

Richard Yea-and-Nay (1900)
Maurice Hewlett

Rich Are Different, The (1977)
Susan Howatch

Rich Man, Poor Man (1970)
Irwin Shaw

Richterin, Die (1885)
(The Lady Judge)
Conrad Ferdinand Meyer

Riddle of the Sands, The (1903)
Erskine Childers

Riddle of the Third Mile, The (1983)
Colin Dexter

Inspector Morse

Riddley Walker (1980)
Russell Hoban

Riders (1984)
Jilly Cooper

Riders in the Chariot (1961)
Patrick White

Riders of the Purple Sage (1912)
Zane Grey

Rienzi (1835)
Edward Bulwer-Lytton

Rifle Rangers, The (1850)
Mayne Reid

Rigby's Romance (1946) posth
Joseph Furphy

Right Ho, Jeeves (1934)
PG Wodehouse

Reginald Jeeves (Wooster's valet)
Bertie Wooster

Right True End (1976)
Stan Barstow

Ingrid Brown (Vic's wife)
Vic Brown

Rigodon (1969) posth
Louis-Ferdinand Céline

Rilla of Ingleside (1921)
LM Montgomery

Ring for Jeeves (1953)
PG Wodehouse

Reginald Jeeves (Wooster's valet)

Ringworld (1970)
Larry Niven

Riotous Assembly (1971)
Tom Sharpe

Ripley's Game (1974)
Ripley Under Ground (1971)
Ripley Under Water (1991)
Patricia Highsmith

Tom Ripley (crook)

Ripple from the Storm, A (1958)
Doris Lessing

Martha Quest

Rise of Silas Lapham, The (1885)
William Dean Howells

set: Vermont; Boston
Colonel Silas Lapham (businessman)
Persis Lapham (Lapham's wife)

Rising (1976) posth
RC Hutchinson

Risk (1978)
Dick Francis

Rites of Passage (1980)
William Golding
set: 19c voyage
Edmund Talbot (narrator)

Ritter Gluck (1809)
Ernst Theodor Amadeus Hoffmann

Ritual in the Dark (1960)
Colin Wilson

Rivals (1988)
Jilly Cooper

River, The (1946)
Rumer Godden
set: River Ganges

River Between, The (1965)
Ngugi Wa Thiong'o

River Line, The (1949)
Charles Morgan

River of Death (1981)
Alistair Maclean

Riverside Villas Murder, The (1973)
Kingsley Amis

River Sot, The (1929)
Leonid Leonov

Road Back, The
see ***Weg zurück, Der***

Roads to Freedom, The
see ***Chemins de la Liberté, Les***

Road to Flanders
see ***Route de Flandres, La***

Road to Klockrike, The
see ***Vägen till Klockrike***

Road to Lichfield, The (1979)
Penelope Lively

Road to Miklagard, The (1957)
Henry Treece

Road to Oz, The (1909)
L Frank Baum

Road to the Ocean, The (1935)
Leonid Leonov

Road to the Open, The
see ***Weg ins Freie, Der***

Roaring Nineties, The (1946)
Katharine Susannah Prichard

Robber Bridegroom, The (1942)
Eudora Welty

Robbers, The (1979)
Nina Bawden

Robbery Under Arms (1888)
Rolf Boldrewood

Robe, The (1942)
Lloyd C Douglas

Robert (1930)
André Gide

Robert Elsmere (1888)
Mary Augusta Ward

Robert Falconer (1868)
George MacDonald

Robes rouges (1891)
Paul Adam

Robin (1922)
Frances Hodgson Burnett

Robinson (1958)
Muriel Spark

Robinson Crusoe (1719)
Daniel Defoe

set: desert island (actual Juan Fernandez, off Chile)
Robinson Crusoe
Friday (Crusoe's helper)

Robots and Empire (1985)
Robots of Dawn, The (1983)
Isaac Asimov

Rob Roy (1817)
Walter Scott

set: Osbaldistone Hall, North of England; Highlands
Andrew Fairservice (Francis' servant)
Nicol Jarvie (bailie)
Rob Roy Macgregor (outlaw)
Francis Osbaldistone
Sir Hildebrand Osbaldistone (Francis' uncle)
Rashleigh Osbaldistone (Sir Hildebrand's son)
Diana Vernon (Sir Hildebrand's niece)

Rocannon's World (1966)
Ursula Le Guin

Rock, The (1970)
John Masters

Rockets Galore (1957)
Compton MacKenzie

Rock Pool, The (1936)
Cyril Connolly

Röda Rummet (1879)
(The Red Room)
August Strindberg

Roderick Hudson (1876)
Henry James

set: Massachusetts; Rome
Roderick Hudson (sculptor)
Christina Light (Hudson's would-be lover)
Rowland Mallet (art connoisseur)

Roderick Random
see ***Adventures of Roderick Random, The***

Rodmoor (1916)
John Cowper Powys

Rodney Stone (1896)
Arthur Conan Doyle

Roger's Version (1986)
John Updike

Rogue Herries (1930)
Hugh Walpole

Rogue Male (1939)
Geoffrey Household

set: Dorset

Rogue's Legacy (1942)
Babette Deutsch

Rois en exil, Les (1879)
Alphonse Daudet

Roland Cashel (1850)
Charles Lever

Roland Yorke (1869)
Ellen Wood

Roll Call, The (1918)
Arnold Bennett

Roll of Honour (1961)
Eric Linklater

Romana, La (1947)
(The Woman of Rome)
Alberto Moravia

Romance (1903)
Joseph Conrad & Ford Madox Ford

Romance and reality (1831)
Letitia Elizabeth

Romance of the Forest, The (1791)
Ann Radcliffe

Romance of Two Worlds, A (1886)
Marie Corelli

Romance of Westdale, A (1895)
AEW Mason

Roman Hat Mystery, The (1929)
Ellery Queen

Ellery Queen (detective)

Roman Spring of Mrs Stone, The (1950)
Tennessee Williams

Roman Tales
see ***Raconti Romani***

Romantic Comedians, The (1926)
Ellen Glasgow

Romany Rye, The (1857)
George Borrow

Belle Berners (Jasper's lover)
Jasper Petulengro (gypsy)

Rome Haul (1929)
Walter D Edmonds

Romola (1862)
George Eliot

set: 15c France
Tito Melema (Romola's husband)
Romola

Rookwood (1834)
William Harrison Ainsworth

set: London; York
Black Bess (Turpin's horse)
Dick Turpin (highwayman)

Room, The (1971)
Hubert Selby

Room at the Top (1957)
John Braine

set: Bradford
Susan Browne
Joe Lampton

Room 13 (1924)
Edgar Wallace

Room Upstairs, The (1966)
Monica Dickens

Room with a View, A (1908)
EM Forster

set: Pensione Bertolini, Italy; Summer Street, Surrey
Miss Bartlett (Lucy's chaperone)
Mr Beebe (vicar)
George Emerson (Lucy's eventual husband)
Mr Emerson (George's father)

Lucy Honeychurch
Cecil Vyse (Lucy's fiancé)

Root and the Flower, The (1935)
LH Myers

set: 16c India

Roper's Row (1928)
Warwick Deeping

Rory O'Moore (1836)
Samuel Lover

Rosalind passes (1974)
Frank Swinnerton

Rose and the Key, The (1871)
Sheridan Le Fanu

Rose and the Ring, The (1855)
William Makepeace Thackeray

Blackstick (fairy)
Prince Giglio
Princess Rosalba

Rose and the Yew Tree, The (1948)
Agatha Christie

Rose in Bloom (1876)
sequel to ***Eight Cousins***
Louisa M Alcott

Rose

Rose of Dutcher's Coolly (1895)
Hamlin Garland

Rose Dutcher

Rose of Tibet, The (1962)
Lionel Davidson

Rosshalde (1914)
Hermann Hesse

Ross Poldark (1945)
Winston Graham

set: 18c Cornwall
Ross Poldark

Rôtisserie de la Reine Pédauque, La (1893)
Anatole France

Rotten Elements (1969)
Edward Upward

Rouge et le Noir, Le (1830)
(The Red and the Black)
Stendhal

Julien Sorel

Rough Justice (1982)
Geoffrey Household

Rough Justice (1926)
CE Montague

Roughneck, The (1923)
Robert William Service

Rough Shaking, A (1891)
George MacDonald

Rougon-Macquart, Les (1871–93) 20 vol
Émile Zola

vols:
1 *La Fortune des Rougon* (1871)
2 *La Curée* (1872)
3 *Le Ventre de Paris* (1873)
4 *La Conquête de Plassans* (1874)
5 *La Faute de l'abbé Mouret* (1875)
6 *Son Excellence Eugène Rougon* (1876)
7 *L'Assommoir* (1877)
8 *Une Page d'amour* (1878)
9 *Nana* (1880)
10 *Pot-Bouille* (1882)
11 *Au bonheur des dames* (1883)

Rougon-Maccquart, Les (cont.)
12 *La Joie de Vivre* (1884)
13 *Germinal* (1885)
14 *L'Oeuvre* (1886)
15 *La Terre* (1887)
16 *Le Rêve* (1888)
17 *La Bête humaine* (1890)
18 *L'Argent* (1891)
19 *Le Débâcle* (1892)
20 *Le Docteur Pascal* (1893)

Coupeau (Gervaise's eventual husband)
Gundermann (banker)
Auguste Lantier (Gervaise's lover)
Claude Lantier (artist)
Étienne Lantier (machinist)
Jacques Lantier (maniac/engine-driver)
Antoine Macquart
Gervaise Macquart (Antoine's daughter)
Nana Macquart (actress/Gervaise's daughter)
Octave Mouret
Félicité Rougon
Pierre Rougon (Félicité's brother/Antoine's half-brother)
Aristide Saccard

Round the Bend (1951)
Nevil Shute

Route de Flandres, La (1960)
(The Road to Flanders)
Claude Simon

Rover, The (1923)
Joseph Conrad

Roving Commission, A (1900)
GA Henty

Roxana (or The Fortunate Mistress) (1724)
Daniel Defoe

set: England; France; Holland
Amy (Roxana's maid)
Roxana Beleau

Roxy (1878)
Edward Eggleston

Royal Box, The (1954)
Frances Parkinson Keyes

Royal Route, The
see ***Voie royale, La***

Rudin (1856)
Ivan Turgenev

Ruined Boys, The (1959)
Roy Fuller

Ruins (1986)
Brian W Aldiss

Rumbin Galleries (1937)
Booth Tarkington

Rumming Park (1948)
John Mortimer

Rumour at Nightfall (1931)
Graham Greene

Rumours of Rain (1978)
André Brink

Rumpole of the Bailey (1978) coll
John Mortimer

Hilda Rumpole (Rumpole's wife)
Horace Rumpole (barrister)

Runaway Soul, The (1991)
Hariold Brodkey

Runaway Summer, The (1969)
Nina Bawden

Running Blind (1970)
Desmond Bagley

Running Dog (1978)
Don Delillo

Run River (1963)
Joan Didion

Run Silent, Run Deep (1955)
Edward Beach

Rupert of Hentzau (1898)
sequel to ***The Prisoner of Zenda***
Anthony Hope
set: Ruritania
Queen Flavia
Rudolf Rassendyll
Rupert of Hentzau (usurper)

Ruse, La (1903)
Paul Adam

Russia House, The (1989)
John Le Carré

Russian Forest, The (1953)
Leonid Leonov

Russian Hide and Seek (1980)
Kingsley Amis

Russian Interpreter, The (1966)
Michael Frayn

Rustic Chivalry
see ***Cavalleria rusticana***

Ruth (1853)
Elizabeth Gaskell
Henry Bellingham (Ruth's seducer)
Thurston Benson (minister)
Ruth Benson (orphan)

Ryder (1928)
Djuna Barnes

S

S (1988)
John Updike

Sabbatical (1982)
John Barth

Sackcloth and Ashes (1989)
Fay Weldon

Sackett (1961)
Louis L'Amour

Sacred and Profane Love Machine, The (1974)
Iris Murdoch

Sacred Fount (1901)
Henry James

Sacrificial Egg, The (1962)
Chinua Achebe

Sad Cypress (1940)
Agatha Christie

Sadness (1972)
Donald Barthelme

Sado (1931)
William Plomer

Sad Variety, The (1964)
Nicholas Blake
Nigel Strangeways (detective)

Safe Brigade, The (1934)
Frances Parkinson Keyes

Safe House, The (1975)
Jon Cleary

Sagouin, Le (1950)
(The Little Misery)
François Mauriac

Sailor on Horseback (1938)
Irving Stone

Sailor's Return, The (1925)
David Garnett

Sailor Who Fell from Grace with the Sea, The (1963)
Yukio Mishima

For **SAINT** also see **ST**

Saint, The
see ***Heilige, Der***

Saint Glinglin (1948)
Raymond Queneau

Saint Jack (1973)
Paul Theroux

Salamander, The (1973)
Morris West

Salammbô(1862)
Gustave Flaubert
set: ancient Carthage

Salar the Salmon (1935)
Henry Williamson
Salar (salmon)

Salathiel (1829)
George Croly

Salavin (1920–32) 5 vol
Georges Duhamel
Louis Salavin

Salem Chapel (1863)
Margaret Oliphant

Salem's Lot (1975)
Stephen King

Saliva Tree, The (1966)
Brain W Aldiss

Salka Valka (1931–2) 2 vol
Halldór Laxness

Salome and the head (1909)
E Nesbit

Salt (1963)
Herbert Gold

Salterton Trilogy, The (1986) 3 vol
Robertson Davies
vols:
1 *Tempest Tost* (1951)
2 *Leaven of Malice* (1954)
3 *A Mixture of Frailties* (1958)

Salvage (1968)
Jackie Gillott

Salvos (1924)
Waldo Frank

Salzburg Tales, The (1934) coll
Christina Stead

Sam Pig (1940)
Alison Uttley

Sampson's Circus (1936)
Howard Spring

San Andreas (1984)
Alistair Maclean

San Camilo (1936)
Camilo José Cela

Sanctuary (1931)
William Faulkner

Temple Drake

Sanctuary (1903)
Edith Wharton

Sandalmagernes gade (1931)
(The Street of the Sandal-Makers)
Nils Petersen

Sandcastle, The (1957)
Iris Murdoch

Sanders of the River (1911)
Edgar Wallace

Sanditon (1925) posth
Jane Austen

set: Sanditon (South Coast village)
Clara Brereton (Sir Edward's would-be sweetheart)
Sir Edward Denham (Lady Denham's nephew)
Miss Denham (Lady Denham's niece)
Lady Denham (local dignitary)
Mrs Griffiths (West Indian chaperone)
Charlotte Heywood (Parkers' guest)
Arthur Parker (Parker's brother)
Diana Parker (Parker's sister)
Mr Parker
Mrs Parker (Parker's wife)
Susan Parker (Parker's sister)

Sandra Belloni (1864)
(also titled ***Emilia in England***)
George Meredith

Emilia Sandra Belloni
Pole family

Sands of Time, The (1988)
Sidney Sheldon

Sangaree (1948)
Frank Slaughter

Sang des autres, Le (1944)
(The Blood of Others)
Simone de Beauvoir

San Marco (1963)
Michel Butor

Santal (1921)
Ronald Firbank

set: North Africa

Santo, Il (1905)
Antonio Fogazzaro

Santorini (1986)
Alistair Maclean

Sapho (1884)
Alphonse Daudet

Sapphira and the Slave Girl (1940)
Willa Cather

Sara Crewe (1888)
Frances Hodgson Burnett

Sara Crewe (schoolgirl)

Saratoga Trunk (1941)
Edna Ferber

Sard Harker (1924)
John Masefield

Sartoris (1929)
William Faulkner

set: Mississippi
Sartoris family

Satan Bug, The (1962)
Alistair Maclean

Satanic Verses, The (1988)
Salman Rushdie

Satan in Goray (1955)
Isaac Bashevis Singer

Satanist, The (1960)
Dennis Wheatley

Saturday Night and Sunday Morning (1958)
Alan Sillitoe

set: Nottingham
Arthur Seaton (lathe operator)

Saturday Night at the Crown (1959)
Walter Greenwood

Savage Day, The (1972)
Jack Higgins

Savage Days, The (1937)
Philip Toynbee

Saville (1976)
David Storey

Savrola (1900)
Winston Spencer Churchill

Say Nothing (1962)
James Hanley

Sayonara (1954)
James A Michener

set: Tokyo

Scales of Justice (1954)
Ngaio Marsh

Inspector Roderick Alleyn

Scalp Hunters, The (1851)
Mayne Reid

Scandalous Risks (1991)
Susan Howatch

Scapegoat, The (1948)
Jocelyn Brooke

Scapegoat, The (1891)
Hall Caine

Scapegoat, The (1957)
Daphne Du Maurier

Scarecrow of Oz, The (1915)
L Frank Baum

Scarf, The (1947)
Robert Bloch

Scarlatti Inheritance, The (1971)
Robert Ludlum

Scarlet Letter, The (1850)
Nathaniel Hawthorne

set: Puritan New England
Arthur Dimmesdale (minister/Hester's lover)
Prynne (Hester's husband)
Hester Prynne

Scarlet Pimpernel, The (1905)
Baroness Orczy

set: Napoleonic Wars
Sir Percy Blakeney, alias 'the Scarlet Pimpernel'

Scarlet Ruse, The (1973)
John D MacDonald

Travis McGhee (shady dealer)

Scarlet Seed, The (1963)
Ellis Peters

Scarlet Thread, The (1989)
Evelyn Anthony

Scenes from Later Life (1983)
Scenes from Married Life (1961)
Scenes from Metropolitan Life (1982)
Scenes from Provincial Life (1950)
William Cooper

Joe Lunn

Scenes of Clerical Life (1858) coll
George Eliot

Scented Gardens for the Blind (1963)
Janet Frame

Scent of Cloves (1958)
Norah Lofts

Schandfleck, Der (1877)
Ludwig Anzengrüber

Schatz der Sierra Madre, Der (1927)
(The Treasure of the Sierra Madre)
B Traven

Schindler's Ark (1982)
Thomas Keneally

Schlafwandler, Die (1930–2) 3 vol
(The Sleepwalkers)
Hermann Broch

Schloss, Das (1926) posth unf
(The Castle)
Franz Kafka

Frieda (K's sometime lover)
K

Schloss Avignon (1827)
Willibald Alexis

School for Love (1951)
Olivia Manning

School for Widows, The (1791)
Clara Reeve

Schultz (1980)
JP Donleavy

Schwarzwälder Dorfgeschichten (1843–53) 4 vol
Berthold Auerbach

Schweizerische Robinson, Der (1812–13) 2 vol
(The Swiss Family Robinson)
Johann Wyss

set: tropical island
Robinson family

Scoop (1938)
Evelyn Waugh

John Boot (novelist)
William Boot (columnist)
Lord Copper (owner of *The Beast* newspaper)

Scottish Chiefs, The (1810)
Jane Porter

Scouring of the White Horse, The (1859)
Thomas Hughes

Scruffy (1962)
Paul Gallico

Scruples (1978)
Judith Krantz

Scumbler (1984)
William Wharton

Scum of the Earth (1941)
Arthur Koestler

Sea-Grape Tree, A (1970)
Rosamund Lehmann

Séance, The (1968) coll
Isaac Bashevis Singer

Sea of Fertility (1965–70) 4 vol
Yukio Mishima

Sea of Grass, The (1937)
Conrad Richter

Search, The (1934)
CP Snow

Seasoned Timber (1939)
Dorothea Frances Fisher

Season in Hell, A (1989)
Jack Higgins

Season of Adventure (1960)
George Lamming

Season of Anomy (1973)
Wole Soyinka

Season of Passion (1979)
Danielle Steel

Sea, the Sea, The (1978)
Iris Murdoch

Sea Wall (1933)
LAG Strong

Sea Witch (1977)
Alistair Maclean

Sea without a Haven, The (1941)
DK Broster

Sea-Wolf, The (1904)
Jack London
ship: Ghost
Wolf Larsen (captain)

Sebastian (1983)
Laurence Durrell

Second Coming, The (1980)
Walker Percy

Second Curtain, The (1953)
Roy Fuller

Second Fiddle (1988)
Mary Wesley

Second Foundation (1953)
Isaac Asimov

Second from Last in the Sack Race (1983)
David Nobbs

Second Generation (1964)
Raymond Williams

Second Inheritance, The (1966)
Melvyn Bragg

Second Son, The (1888)
Margaret Oliphant

Second Stage (1953)
EE 'Doc' Smith

Secret Agent, The (1907)
Joseph Conrad
Verloc (spy)

Secret Battle, The (1919)
AP Herbert

Secret City, The (1919)
Hugh Walpole

Secret Garden, The (1910)
Frances Hodgson Burnett
set: Misselthwaite Manor, Yorkshire
Mary Lennox

Secret House of Death, The (1968)
Ruth Rendell

Secret Island, The (1938)
Enid Blyton

Secret Journey, The (1936)
James Hanley

Secret Kingdom, The (1938)
Walter Greenwood

Secret Ladder, The (1963)
Wilson Harris

Secret Lives (1974)
Ngugi Wa Thiong'o

Secret of Annexe 3, The (1986)
Colin Dexter
Inspector Morse

Secret Passage, The (1963)
Nina Bawden

Secret Pilgrim, The (1991)
John Le Carré

Secret Power, The (1921)
Marie Corelli

Secret River, The (1956)
CHB Kitchin

Secret Servant, The (1980)
Gavin Lyall

Secrets of Harry Bright, The (1985)
Joseph Wambaugh

Secret Vanguard, The (1941)
JIM Stewart
John Appleby (detective)

Secret Water (1939)
Arthur Ransome

Seeds of Time, The (1958)
John Wyndham

Seeds of Treason (1988)
Ted Allbeury

Seeta (1872)
Philip Meadows Taylor

See the Old Lady Decently (1975) posth
BS Johnson

See You in the Morning (1948)
Kenneth Patchen

Seize the Day (1956)
Saul Bellow

Self Condemned (1957)
Wyndham Lewis

Semaine sainte, La (1958)
Louis Aragon
basis: artist Theodore Géricault

Semi-Detached Couple, The (1860)
Semi-Detached House, The (1859)
Emily Eden

Senelità (1898)
(As Man Grows Older)
Italo Svevo

Sense and Sensibility (1811)
Jane Austen
set: Norland park, Sussex; London; Devonshire
Colonel Brandon (Mariane's eventual husband)
Elinor Dashwood (Henry's daughter/'sense')
Henry Dashwood
John Dashwood (Henry's stepson)
Margaret Dashwood (Henry's daughter)
Marianne Dashwood (Henry's daughter/'sensibility')
Mrs Dashwood (Henry's wife)
Edward Ferrars (Mrs Ferrar's son/Elinor's eventual husband)
Mrs Ferrars (John's mother-in-law)
Robert Ferrars (Mrs Ferrar's son/Lucy's eventual husband)
Mrs Jennings (Elinor & Marianne's old friend)
Lucy Steele (Edward's sometime fiancée)
John Willoughby (Marianne's sometime beloved)

Sense of Guilt, A (1988)
Andrea Newman

Sense of the Past, The (1917) posth unf
Henry James

Sensible Life, A (1990)
Mary Wesley

Sentiero dei nidi di ragno, Il (1947)
(The Path to the Nest of Spiders)
Italo Calvino

Sentimental Education, The
see ***Education Sentimentale, L'***

Sentimental Journey, A (Through France and Italy) (1768)
Laurence Sterne
La Fleur (Yorick's servant)
Mundungus (author)
Smelfungus (author)
Parson Yorick (narrator)

Sentimental Tommy (1896)
JM Barrie

Separate Peace, A (1959)
John Knowles

Sepulchre (1987)
James Herbert

Serena Blandish (1925)
Enid Bagnold

Serenade (1937)
James M Cain

Sergeant Lamb of the Ninth (1940)
Robert Graves

Serious Life, A
see ***Ernstes Leben, Ein***

Serpent and the Rope, The (1960)
Raja Rao

Servant, The (1948)
Robin Maugham

Service of All the Dead (1979)
Colin Dexter

Inspector Morse

Service with a Smile (1961)
PG Wodehouse

set: Blandings Castle, Shropshire
Beach (Lord Emsworth's butler)
Empress of Blandings (pig)
Lord Emsworth

Set This House on Fire (1960)
William Styron

Setting Free the Bears (1968)
John Irving

set: Vienna

Setting Sun, The (1947)
Osamu Dazai

Setting the World on Fire (1980)
Angus Wilson

Settlers, The (1972)
Meyer Levin

Settlers in Canada, The (1844)
Frederick Marryat

set: Lake Ontario
Campbell family

Seven Ages, The (1983)
Eva Figes

Seven Dials Mystery, The (1929)
Agatha Christie

Seven for a Secret (1922)
Mary Webb

Seven Keys to Baldpate (1913)
Earl Derr Biggers

Seventeen (1916)
Booth Tarkington

Seventh Raven, The (1981)
Peter Dickinson

79 Park Avenue (1955)
Harold Robbins

Severed Head, A (1961)
Iris Murdoch

Honor Klein

Sexus (1949)
Henry Miller

Seymour: an Introduction (1963)
JD Salinger

Glass family

Shabby Genteel Story, A (1840)
William Makepeace Thackeray

Philip Firmin, alias George Brandon
Caroline Gann

Shabby Tiger (1934)
Howard Spring

Shadow Dance (1966)
Angela Carter

Shadow Guests, The (1980)
Joan Aiken

Shadow Line, The (1917)
Joseph Conrad

Shadow master, The (1979)
Elaine Feinstein

Shadow of a Crime, The (1885)
Hall Caine

Shadow of a Sun (1964)
AS Byatt

Shadow of the Lynx, The (1971)
Jean Plaidy

Shadow of the Moon (1957)
MM Kaye

Shadow of the Sorcerer, The (1955)
Stella Gibbons

Shadow over Innsmouth, The (1936) coll
HP Lovecraft

Shadows Move Among Them (1951)
Edgar Mittelholzer

Shadows of the Rock (1931)
Willa Cather

Shake Hands For Ever (1975)
Ruth Rendell

Inspector Reg Wexford

Shall We Tell the President? (1977)
Jeffrey Archer

Shame (1983)
Salman Rushdie

Shamela Andrews (1741)
Henry Fielding

parody of ***Pamela***
Shamela (Pamela) Andrews
Mr Booby
Parson Oliver
Parson Tickletext
Parson Williams

Shandygaff (1918)
Christopher Morley

Shannon's Way (1948)
AJ Cronin

Shape of Things to Come, The (1933)
HG Wells

Shardik (1974)
Richard Adams

Shardik (bear)

Share of the World, A (1964)
Andrea Newman

Shaving of Shagpat, The (1856) coll
George Meredith

She (1887)
H Rider Haggard

set: Africa
Ayesha (sorceress)

She Came to Stay
see ***Invitée, L'***

She Goes to War (1942)
Ellis Peters

Sheiks and Adders (1982)
JIM Stewart

Sheltered Life, The (1932)
Ellen Glasgow

Sheltering Sky, The (1949)
Paul Bowles

set: Morocco

Shepherd, The (1975)
Frederick Forsyth

Shepherd's Life, A (1910)
WH Hudson

set: Wiltshire
Caleb Bawcombe (shepherd)

Sheppard Lee (1836)
Robert Montgomery Bird

Sherston's Progress (1936)
Siegfried Sassoon

George Sherston

Shibumi (1979)
Trevanian

Shifting of the Fire, The (1892)
Ford Madox Ford

Shining, The (1976)
Stephen King

Shining Scabbard (1936)
RC Hutchinson

Ship, The (1943)
CS Forester

Ship of Fools (1962)
Kathleen Anne Porter

set: Mexico-to-Germany voyage

Ship of Stars, The (1899)
Arthur Quiller-Couch

Ship of the Line (1938)
CS Forester

Horatio Hornblower

Ships in the Bay! (1931)
DK Broster

Ship That Died of Shame, The (1959)
Nicholas Monsarrat

Shirley (1849)
Charlotte Brontë

set: Luddite Riots, Yorkshire
Caroline Helstone (Robert's cousin)
Shirley Keeldar
Louis Moore (Robert's brother)
Robert Gérard Moore (mill-owner)
Mrs Pryor (Shirley's companion)
Sam Wynne (magistrate)

Shock-Headed Peter
see ***Struwwelpeter***

Shocks (1935)
Algernon Blackwood

Shoes of the Fisherman, The (1963)
Morris West

Shogun (1975)
James Clavell

Shooting Star (1958)
Robert Bloch

Shoot It Again, Sam (1972)
Michael Avallone

Ed Noon (private eye)

Short Reign of Pippin IV, The (1957)
John Steinbeck

Shosha (1978)
Isaac Bashevis Singer

Shout at the Devil (1966)
Wilbur Smith

Show Boat (1926)
Edna Ferber
set: Mississippi River

Shrimp and the Anemone, The (1944)
LP Hartley

Shrine (1983)
James Herbert

Shrouded Walls (1972)
Susan Howatch

Shroud for a Nightingale (1971)
PD James
Adam Dalgliesh (detective)

Shuddering Fall (1964)
Joyce Carol Oates

Shuttlecock (1981)
Graham Swift

Sicilian, The (1984)
Mario Puzo

Sicilian Romance, A (1790)
Ann Radcliffe

Sick Heart Pass (1941) posth
John Buchan
Edward Leithen

Siddharta (1922)
Hermann Hesse
Siddharta (Brahmin)

Sido (1929)
Colette

Siege of London, The (1883) coll
Henry James

Siege of Pleasure, The (1932)
Patrick Hamilton

Siegfried et le Limousin (1922)
Jean Giraudoux

Siglo de las luces, El (1962)
(Explosion in the Cathedral)
Alejo Carpentier

Signalman Thiel
see ***Bahnwärter Thiel***

Signed with Their Honour (1942)
James Aldridge

Sign of Four, The (1890)
Arthur Conan Doyle
set: 221b Baker Street, London
Sherlock Holmes (detective)
Dr John Watson (Holmes' companion)

Signposters, The (1967)
Helen Cresswell

Si j'étais vous ... (1947)
(If I Were You)
Julien Green

Silas Marner (1861)
George Eliot
set: Raveloe (village)
Dunstan Cass
Eppie Cass (Marner's 'adopted' girl)
Godfrey Cass (Dunstan's elder brother)
Molly Farren (Godfrey's 1st, secret wife)
Nancy Lammeter (Godfrey's 2nd wife)
Silas Marner (weaver)
Dolly Winthrop (Marner's friend)

Silence (1898)
Mary E Freeman

Silence Among the Weapons (1982)
John Arden

Silence Observed (1961)
JIM Stewart

John Appleby (detective)

Silence of Desire, A (1960)
Kamala Markandaya

Silence of the Lambs, The (1989)
Thomas Harris

Silent World of Nicholas Quinn, The (1977)
Colin Dexter

Inspector Morse

Silken Net, The (1974)
Melvyn Bragg

Silkie, The (1969)
AE Van Vogt

Silmarillion, The (1977) posth
JRR Tolkien

Silver Branch, The (1957)
Rosemary Sutcliff

Silver Chair, The (1953)
CS Lewis

set: Narnia
Aslan (lion)
Eustace
Jill

Silver Darlings, The (1941)
Neil Gunn

Silver Dove, The (1909)
Andrei Bely

Silver Fox, The (1897)
Edith Somerville

Silver Nutmeg (1947)
Norah Lofts

Silver Stallion, The (1917)
James Branch Cabell

Simon Dale (1898)
Anthony Hope

Simone (1944)
Lion Feuchtwanger

Simonetta Perkins (1925)
LP Hartley

Simon le pathétique (1918)
Jean Giraudoux

Simple Heart, A
see ***Coeur simple, Un***

Simple Story, A (1791)
Elizabeth Inchbald

Simplicissimus (1669)
Johann Grimmelshausen

Sincerely Willis Wayde (1955)
John Marquand

Sin Eater, The (1977)
Alice Thomas Ellis

Single Eye, The (1964)
Maureen Duffy

Single Man, A (1964)
Christopher Isherwood

Singular Man, A (1963)
JP Donleavy

Sinister Street (1913–14) 2 vol
Compton MacKenzie

Michael Fane

Sinners
see ***Sunday Simmons and Charlie Brick***

Sins of the Fathers (1980)
Susan Howatch

Sir Charles Grandison
see ***History of Sir Charles Grandison, The***

Sirens of Titan, The (1959)
Kurt Vonnegut

Sirian Experiments, The (1981)
Doris Lessing

Sir Isumbras at the Ford (1918)
DK Broster

Sirius (1944)
Olaf Stapledon

Sir Jasper Carew (1855)
Charles Lever

Sir Launcelot Greaves
see ***Life and Adventures of Sir Launcelot Greaves, The***

Sir Nigel (1906)
Arthur Conan Doyle

Sir Quixote of the Moors (1895)
John Buchan

Sir Robert's Fortune (1895)
Margaret Oliphant

Sister Carrie (1900)
Theodore Dreiser

set: Chicago; New York
Charles Drouet (salesman)
George Hurstwood (Drouet's friend/Carrie's sometime lover)
Carrie Meeber (Drouet's mistress)

Sister Jane (1896)
Joel Chandler Harris

Sister Philomène
see ***Soeur Philomène***

Sister Theresa (1901)
sequel to ***Evelyn Innes***
George Moore

Six Bars at Seven (1940)
MM Kaye

Sixth Heaven, The (1946)
LP Hartley

Sixth Seal, The (1969)
Mary Wesley

Six to Sixteen (1875)
Juliana Horatia Ewing

Sixty-Four, Ninety-Four (1925)
RH Mottram

set: North France

62: modelo para armar (1962)
(1962: a Model Kit)
Julio Cortázar

Skeeters Kirby (1923)
Edgar Lee Masters

Skeleton Crew (1985)
Stephen King

Skeleton in the Cupboard, The (1988)
sequel to ***The Clothes in the Wardrobe***
Alice Thomas Ellis

Sketch Book, The (1820) coll
Washington Irving

set: Sleepy Hollow; Catskill Mountains
Ichabod Crane (schoolmaster)
Rip Van Winkle ('20-year sleeper')

Skin Deep (1968)
Peter Dickinson

Skinny Legs and All (1990)
Tom Robbins

Skull Beneath the Skin, The (1982)
PD James

Cordelia Gray (private eye)

Skutarevsky (1932)
Leonid Leonov

Skylark Duquesne (1966) posth
Skylark of Space, The (1946)
EE 'Doc' Smith

Slan (1946)
AE Van Vogt

Slapstick (1976)
Slaughterhouse Five (or The Children's Crusade) (1969)
Kurt Vonnegut

Slattery's Hurricane (1956)
Herman Wouk

Slave, The (1962)
Isaac Bashevis Singer

Slaves of Solitude, The (1947)
Patrick Hamilton

Slaves of Timbuktu, The (1961)
Robin Maugham

Slay-Ride (1974)
Dick Francis

Sleep and His Brother (1972)
Peter Dickinson

Sleepers Awake (1946)
Kenneth Patchen

Sleepers of Erin, The (1983)
Jonathan Gash

Lovejoy (dodgy antiques dealer)

Sleeping Beauty (1973)
Ross Macdonald

Sleeping Fires (1895)
George Gissing

Sleeping Life, A (1978)
Ruth Rendell

Inspector Reg Wexford

Sleeping Murder (1976)
Agatha Christie

Miss Jane Marple (amateur sleuth)

Sleeping Tiger (1982)
Ian McEwan

Sleep It Off, Lady (1976) coll
Jean Rhys

Sleep of Reason, The (1968)
CP Snow
Lewis Eliot (narrator/barrister)

Sleeps Six (1979)
Frederic Raphael

Sleepwalkers, The
see ***Schlafwandler, Die***

Sloop of War (1972)
Alexander Kent
Richard Bolitho (seaman)

Slower Learner (1984) coll
Thomas Pynchon

Small Back Room, The (1943)
Nigel Balchin
Sammy Rice

Smaller Sky, The (1967)
John Wain
Arthur Geary (scientist)

Small House at Allington, The (1864)
Anthony Trollope
Adolphus Crosbie (civil servant)
Bell Dale (Lily's sister)
Lily Dale (Crosbie's sometime fiancée)
Lady Alexandria De Courcy (Crosbie's sometime wife)
Johnny Eames (Lily's admirer)

Small Miracle, The (1952)
Paul Gallico

Small Town, The
see ***Kleine Stadt, Die***

Small Town in Germany, A (1968)
John Le Carré

Small World (1984)
David Lodge
Philip Swallow (professor)
Morris Zapp (US academic)

Smiler with the Knife, The (1939)
Nicholas Blake
Nigel Strangeways (detective)

Smiley's People (1980)
John Le Carré
Karla (Smiley's adversary)
George Smiley (secret agent)

Smith of Wootton Major (1967)
JRR Tolkien

Smith's Gazelle (1971)
Lionel Davidson

Smoke (1867)
Ivan Turgenev

Smoke Bellew (1912)
Jack London

Smoke Ring, The (1987)
Larry Niven

Snake, The (1964)
Mickey Spillane
Mike Hammer (private eye)

Sneaky People (1975)
Thomas Berger

Snow Ball, The (1964)
Brigid Brophy

Snow Country (1935–47)
Yasunari Kawabata

Snow Falcon (1980)
Craig Thomas

Snow Goose, The (1941)
Paul Gallico
set: Essex marshes
Philip Rhayader

Snowman, The
see ***Homme de neige, L'***

Snow Tiger, The (1975)
Desmond Bagley

Snow White (1967)
Donald Barthelme

Snow Woman, The (1969)
Stella Gibbons

So Big (1924)
Edna Ferber

Soeur Philomène (1861)
(Sister Philomène)
Edmond & Jules de Goncourt

Soft Machine, the (1961)
William Burroughs

Sojourners, The (1953)
Marjorie Kinnan Rawlings

Soldier Erect, The (1971)
Brian W Aldiss

Soldiers of Fortune (1897)
Richard Harding Davis

Soldier's Pay (1926)
William Faulkner

Solid Mandala, The (1966)
Patrick White

Soll und Haben (1855) 3 vol
Gustav Freytag

Solo (1980)
Jack Higgins

Solomon's Seal (1980)
Hammond Innes

So Long and Thanks for the Fish (1985)
Douglas Adams

So Lovers Dream (1931)
Alec Waugh

Solstice (1985)
Joyce Carol Oates

Sombrero de tres picos, El (1874)
(The Three-Cornered Hat)
Pedro Antonio de Alarcón

Some Adventures of Captain Simon Suggs (1846)
JJ Hooper

Some American People (1935)
Erskine Caldwell

Some Angry Angel (1960)
Richard Condon

Somebody in Boots (1935)
Nelson Algren

Some Can Whistle (1989)
Somebody's Darling (1978)
Larry McMurty

Some Do Not (1924)
Ford Madox Ford

Christopher Tietjens

Some Experiences of an Irish RM (1899)
Edith Somerville

set: Shreelane (manor house), Ireland
Flurry Knox (Yeates' landlord)
Major Yeates (narrator/resident magistrate)
Philippa Yeates (Yeates' wife)

Some Live and Some Die (1973)
Ruth Rendell

Someone Like You (1954)
Roald Dahl

Some Passages in the Life of Adam Blair (1822)
John Gibson Lockhart

Some Tame Gazelle (1950)
Barbara Pym

Something About Cats (1949) posth
HP Lovecraft

Something Childish (1924) coll posth
Katherine Mansfield

Something Fresh (1915)
PG Wodehouse

set: Blandings Castle, Shropshire
Rupert 'the efficient' Baxter (Lord Emsworth's secretary)
Beach (Lord Emsworth's butler)
Lord Emsworth
Freddie Threepwood (Lord Emsworth's son)

Something Happened (1974)
Joseph Heller

Something Leather (1990)
Alasdair Gray

Something to Answer for (1968)
PH Newby

Something Wicked This Way Comes (1962)
Ray Bradbury

Sometime (1933)
Robert Herrick

Sometime Never (1948)
Roald Dahl

Sometimes a Great Notion (1964)
Ken Kesey

Son at the Front, A (1923)
Edith Wharton

Songe, Le (1922)
(The Dream)
Henry de Montherlant

Song in the Morning, A (1986)
Gerald Seymour

Song of Sixpence, A (1964)
AJ Cronin

Song of Solomon (1977)
Toni Morrison

Song of the City (1945)
Peter Abrahams

Song of the Lark, The (1915)
Willa Cather

Son of a Smaller Hero (1955)
Mordecai Richler

Son of Royal Langbirth, The (1904)
William Dean Howells

Son of the Morning (1979)
Joyce Carol Oates

Son of the Wolf, The (1900) coll
Jack London

Sons (1932)
Pearl Buck

Sons and Lovers (1913)
DH Lawrence

set: Bestwood (village), Nottinghamshire
Baxter Dawes
Clara Dawes (Dawes' wife/Paul's sometime lover)
Miriam Leivers (Paul's eventual lover)
Annie Morel (Morel's daughter)
Paul Morel (Morel's son)
Mrs Morel (Morel's wife)
Walter Morel
William Morel (Morel's son)

Sons of Mrs Aab, The (1931)
Sarah Gertrude Millin

Sophia (1762)
Charlotte Lennox

Sophie's Choice (1979)
William Styron

set: late 1940s

Sophy of Kravonia (1906)
Anthony Hope

Sorrell and Son (1925)
Warwick Deeping

Sorrow in Sunlight
see ***Prancing Nigger***

Sorrows of Satan, The (1895)
Marie Corelli

Sorrows of Young Werther, The
see ***Leiden des jungen Werthers, Die***

Sot-Weed Factor, The (1960)
John Barth

Soul of Melicent, The (1913)
James Branch Cabell

Sound and the Fury, The (1929)
William Faulkner

set: Yoknapatawpha County, Mississippi
Compson family

Sound of the Mountain, The (1949–54)
Yasunari Kawabata

Sound of Waves, The (1954)
Yukio Mishima

Source, The (1965)
James A Michener

Sour Sweet (1982)
Timothy Mo

Sous le soleil de Satan (1926)
(Under Satan's Sun)
Georges Bernanos

Sous l'oeil des barbares (1888)
Maurice Barrès

South by Java Head (1958)
Alistair Maclean

set: China Sea

Southern Mail
see ***Courrier-Sud***

South Moon Under (1933)
Marjorie Kinnan Rawlings

South Wind (1917)
Norman Douglas

Space (1982)
James A Michener

Spacehounds of IBC (1947)
EE 'Doc' Smith

Space Vampires, The (1976)
Colin Wilson

Spanish Farm, The (1924)
RH Mottram
set: North France

Spanking The Maid (1982)
Robert Coover

Sparkenbroke (1936)
Charles Morgan

Sparkling Cyanide (1945)
Agatha Christie

Sparks Fly Upward (1931)
Oliver La Farge

Sparrow Falls, A (1977)
Wilbur Smith

Spartacus (1951)
Howard Fast

Speaker of Mandarin, The (1983)
Ruth Rendell
Inspector Reg Wexford

Speaking Terms (1969)
Mary Wesley

Speak Now (1969)
Frank Yerby

Special Friendships
see ***Amitiés particulières, Les***

Spellbinder (1982)
Harold Robbins

Spell for Chameleon, A (1977)
Piers Anthony

Spencer Brade MD (1942)
Frank Slaughter

Spend Game (1980)
Jonathan Gash
Lovejoy (dodgy antiques dealer)

Sphinx (1979)
Robin Cook

Spider's House, The (1955)
Paul Bowles

Spinoza (1837)
Berthold Auerbach

Spinster (1958)
Sylvia Ashton-Warner

Spiral Ascent, The
see ***Upward, Edward***

Spire, The (1964)
William Golding

Spiridion (1838)
George Sand

Splendid Spur, The (1889)
Arthur Quiller-Couch

Split Images (1982)
Elmore Leonard

Spoilers, The (1969)
Desmond Bagley

Spoils of Poynton, The (1897)
Henry James

house: Poynton Park
Gereth family

Spoilt City, The (1962)
Olivia Manning

set: Bucharest
Guy Pringle
Harriet Pringle (Guy's wife)

Sport of Nature, A (1987)
Nadine Gordimer

Spreading Fires (1974)
John Knowles

Spring, A
see ***Frühling, Ein***

Spring Days (1888)
George Moore

Springhaven (1877)
RD Blackmore

Spring of the Tiger (1979)
Jean Plaidy

Spring Sowing (1924) coll
Liam O'Flaherty

Spy, The (1821)
James Fenimore Cooper

Spy in the House of Love, A (1954)
Anaïs Nin

Spy Story (1974)
Len Deighton

Spy Who Came In from the Cold (1963)
John Le Carré

set: cold-war Berlin

Spy Who Loved Me, The (1962)
Ian Fleming

James Bond '007' (spy)
M (Bond's boss)
Miss Moneypenny (M's secretary)

Square, Le (1955)
Marguerite Duras

Square Egg, The (1924) coll posth
Saki

Squeeze Play (1982)
Paul Auster

Squib (1971)
Nina Bawden

Squirrel-Cage, The (1912)
Dorothea Frances Fisher

SS-GB (1978)
Len Deighton

SS San Pedro (1931)
James Gould Cozzens

Stadtgespräch (1963)
(City Conversation)
Siegfried Lenz

Stained Radiance (1930)
Lewis Grassic Gibbon

Stalky & Co (1899)
Rudyard Kipling

set: Devon school
Bates (Stalky's schoolfriend)
Beetle (Stalky's schoolfriend)
M'Turk (Stalky's schoolfriend)
Stalky, surnamed Corkran

Stallion Gate (1986)
Martin Cruz Smith

Stamboul Train (1932)
Graham Greene

set: on the Orient Express

Stand, The (1978)
Stephen King

Standard of Behaviour, A (1958)
William Trevor

Stand into Danger (1981)
Alexander Kent

Richard Bolitho (seaman)

Stand Up Virgin Soldiers (1975)
Leslie Thomas

Stanley and the Women (1984)
Kingsley Amis

Staring at the Sun (1986)
Julian Barnes

Starlight Barking, The (1967)
Dodie Smith

Starlit Garden, The (1918)
Henry Stacpoole

Star Maker (1937)
Olaf Stapledon

Star of Ill-Omen (1952)
Dennis Wheatley

Star of Randevi (1984)
Ian McEwan

Star on the Wayside (1916)
Natsume Soseki

Star Quest (1968)
Dean R Koontz

Stars Look Down, The (1935)
AJ Cronin

Stars and Bars (1984)
William Boyd

Stars My Destination, The (1956)
Alfred Bester

Star Stalker, The (1968)
Robert Bloch

Start in Life, A (1981)
Anita Brookner

Start in Life, A (1970)
Alan Sillitoe

State of Siege, A (1966)
Janet Frame

States of Emergency (1988)
André Brink

Staying On (1977)
Paul Scott

Stay With Me Till Morning (1968)
John Braine

St Clare's (1943)
Enid Blyton

Steaming (1981)
Nell Dunn

Steamy Side, The (1881)
Walter Besant

Steel Tsar, The (1982)
Michael Moorcock

Stephen Hero (1944) posth
James Joyce

Stephen Langton (1858)
Martin Tupper

Stepmother, The (1955)
RC Hutchinson

Steppenwolf, Der (1927)
Hermann Hesse

Harry Haller

Stepping Westward (1965)
Malcolm Bradbury

Steps (1968)
Jerzy Kosinski

Sternsteinhof, Der (1885)
Ludwig Anzengrüber

Stick (1983)
Elmore Leonard

Stiff Upper Lip, Jeeves (1963)
PG Wodehouse

Reginald Jeeves (Wooster's valet)
Bertie Wooster

Stiller (1954)
Max Frisch

Still Life (1985)
AS Byatt

Still Life with Woodpecker (1980)
Tom Robbins

Still Storm, The
see ***Orage immobile, Un***

Stillwater Tragedy, The (1880)
Thomas Bailey Aldrich

Sting of Death, The (1978)
Jessica Mann

Stin Kapradiny (1930)
Josef Capek

Stitch in Time, A (1976)
Penelope Lively

St Leon (1799)
William Godwin

Stoic, The (1947) posth
Theodore Dreiser

Stolen Lake, The (1981)
Joan Aiken

Stone Angel, The (1964)
Margaret Laurence

Stone Book, The (1976)
Alan Garner

Stone for Danny Fisher, A (1952)
Harold Robbins

Store, The (1932)
TS Stribling

Stories Toto Told Me (1898)
Frederick William

Storm Island (1978)
Ken Follett

Story Like the Wind, A (1972)
Laurens Van Der Post

Story of a Bad Boy, The (1870)
Thomas Bailey Aldrich

set: Portsmouth, New Hampshire

Story of a Country Town, The (1883)
EW Howe

set: Midwest USA

Story of an African Farm, The (1883)
Olive Schreiner

Em (Lyndall's cousin)
Lyndall

Story of a Year, The (1910)
Mary Louisa Molesworth

Story of Babar, The (1931)
Jean de Brunhoff

Arthur (elephant)
Babar (elephant)
Celeste (elephant)

Story of Doctor Dolittle, The (1920)
Hugh Lofting

set: Puddleby-on-the-Marsh
Dab-Dab (duck)
Dr John Dolittle
Chee-Chee (monkey)
Gub-Gub (pig)
Polynesia (parrot)
Pushmi-Pullyu (two-headed beast)
Too-Too (owl)

Story of Esther Costello, The (1953)
Nicholas Monsarrat

Story of Gosta Berling, The
see ***Gosta Berlings saga***

Story of Patsy, The (1883)
Kate Wiggin

Story of San Michele, The (1929)
Axel Munthe

set: Paris; Rome; Capri

Story of the Treasure-Seekers, The (1899)
E Nesbit

Bastable family

Storyteller, The (1986)
Harold Robbins

Straight (1989)
Dick Francis

Strait Is the Gate
see ***Porte étroite, La***

Strange Adventures of a Phaeton, The (1872)
William Black

Strange Case of Dr Jekyll and Mr Hyde, The (1886)
RL Stevenson

Doctor Jekyll
Mr Hyde (Jekyll's alter ego)

Strange Case of Miss Annie Spragge, The (1928)
Louis Bromfield

Strange Conflict (1941)
Dennis Wheatley

Duke de Richleau

Strange Fugitive (1928)
Morley Callaghan

Strange Glory (1936)
LH Myers

Strange Land, The (1954)
Hammond Innes

Strange Meeting (1971)
Susan Hill

Strange Moon (1929)
TS Stribling

Strange Necessity, The (1928)
Rebecca West

Stranger in a Strange Land (1961)
Robert A Heinlein

Stranger in the Mirror, A (1976)
Sidney Sheldon

Strangers (1986)
Dean R Koontz

Strangers and Brothers
see 1 **Snow, CP**
2 **George Pessant**

Strangers on a Train (1950)
Patricia Highsmith

Strange Story, A (1862)
Edward Bulwer-Lytton

Strange Story of Linda Lee, The (1972)
Dennis Wheatley

Strathmore (1865)
Ouida

Streamers Waving (1925)
CHB Kitchin

Streamlines (1937)
Christopher Morley

Street of Today, The (1911)
John Masefield

Street of the Sandal-Makers, The
see ***Sandalmagernes gade***

Street Where the Heart Lies, The (1963)
Ludwig Bemelmans

Striding Folly (1973) posth
Dorothy L Sayers

Bunter (Wimsey's servant)
Lord Peter Wimsey (amateur detective)

Strike the Father Dead (1962)
John Wain

Strode Venturer, The (1965)
Hammond Innes

St Ronan's Well (1823)
Walter Scott

Meg Dods (landlady)
Earl of Etherington (Francis' half-brother)
Clara Mowbray
Mr Touchstone (nabob)
Francis Tyrrel

Strong as the Dead
see ***Fort comme la mort***

Strong Delusion, The (1951)
James Leasor

Strong Medicine (1984)
Arthur Hailey

Strong Poison (1930)
Dorothy L Sayers

Bunter (Wimsey's servant)
Lord Peter Wimsey (amateur detective)

Struggling Upward (or Luke Larkin's Luck) (1890)
Horatio Alger

Struwwelpeter (1847)
(Shock-Headed Peter)
Heinrich Hoffmann

Stud, The (1970)
Jackie Collins

Study in Scarlet, A (1887)
Arthur Conan Doyle

set: 221b Baker Street, London
Sherlock Holmes (detective)
Dr John Watson (Holmes' companion)

Stumps (1873)
Stella Austin

St Urbain's Horsemen (1971)
Mordecai Richler

St Winifred's, or the World of School (1862)
Frederick William Farrar

Subterraneans, The (1958)
Jack Kerouac

Success (1978)
Martin Amis

Success to the Brave (1983)
Alexander Kent

Richard Bolitho (seaman)

Such Darling Dodos (1950) coll
Angus Wilson

Such Is Life (1903)
Joseph Furphy

Such Is My Beloved (1934)
Morley Callaghan

Sudden View, The (1953)
Sybille Bedford

Suffrage of Elvira, The (1958)
VS Naipaul

Sugar House, The (1952) Antonia White

Sukhodol (1911)
Ivan Bunin

Sula (1974)
Toni Morrison

Sult (1890)
(Hunger)
Knut Hamsun

Summer (1917)
Edith Wharton

Summer Birdcage, A (1963)
Margaret Drabble

Summer Lightning (1929)
PG Wodehouse

set: Blandings Castle, Shropshire
Rupert 'the efficient' Baxter (Lord Emsworth's sometime secretary)
Beach (Lord Emsworth's butler)
Empress of Blandings (pig)
Lord Emsworth
Lady Constance Keeble (Lord Emsworth's sister)
Galahad Threepwood (Lord Emsworth's brother)

Summer Moonshine (1937)
PG Wodehouse

Summer Never Ends (1941)
Waldo Frank

Summer of Katya, The (1983)
Trevanian

Summer of the Red Wolf (1971)
Morris West

Summer of the Swans, The (1970)
Betsy Byars

Summer's Lease (1988)
John Mortimer

Summertime Island (1969)
Erskine Caldwell

Summer Will Show (1936)
Sylvia Townsend Warner

Summit (1987)
DM Thomas

Sum of All Fears, The (1991)
Tom Clancy

Sum of Things, The (1980)
Olivia Manning

set: Egypt
Guy Pringle
Harriet Pringle (Guy's wife)

Sun Also Rises, The (1926)
Ernest Hemingway

Lady Brett Ashley (Barnes' lover)
Jake Barnes

Sunbird, The (1972)
Wilbur Smith

Sun Chemist, The (1976)
Lionel Davidson

Sun Circle (1933)
Neil Gunn

Sunday Bloody Sunday (1972)
Penelope Gilliat

Sunday Simmons and Charlie Brick (1972)
(also titled Sinners)
Jackie Collins

Sun in Capricorn (1942)
Hamilton Basso

Sunset at Blandings (1977) posth
PG Wodehouse

set: Blandings Castle, Shropshire
Beach (Lord Emsworth's butler)
Empress of Blandings (pig)
Lord Emsworth
Freddie Threepwood (Lord Emsworth's son)
Galahad Threepwood (Lord Emsworth's brother)

Sunset Song (1932)
Lewis Grassic Gibbon

Chris Guthrie

Sunset Village (1973)
Frank Sargeson

Superfudge (1980)
Judy Blume

Supermind (1977)
AE Van Vogt

Sure Hand of God (1947)
Erskine Caldwell

Surfacing (1972)
Margaret Atwood

Surfeit of Lampreys (1941)
Ngaio Marsh

Inspector Roderick Alleyn

Surgeon's Daughter, The (1827)
Walter Scott

Surgeon, USA (1966)
Frank Slaughter

Surprises of Love, The (1764)
John Cleland

Survival ... Zero! (1970)
Mickey Spillane

Mike Hammer (private eye)

Survivor, The (1976)
James Herbert

Survivor, The (1969)
Thomas Keneally

Survivors, The (1982)
Elaine Feinstein

Susan Lennox (1917)
David Graham Phillips

Suzanne et le Pacifique (1921)
Jean Giraudoux

Swag (1976)
Elmore Leonard

Swallow (1984)
DM Thomas

Swallow and the Tom Cat, The (1982)
Jorge Amado

Swallowdale (1931)
Arthur Ransome

Swallows and Amazons (1930)
Arthur Ransome

set: Lake District
dinghies: Swallow; Amazon
Nancy Blackett ('Amazon')
Peggy Blackett ('Amazon')
John Walker ('Swallow')
Roger Walker ('Swallow')
Susan Walker ('Swallow')
Titty Walker ('Swallow')
Vicky Walker ('Swallow')

Swami and Friends (1935)
RK Narayan

Swan Song of AJ Wentworth BA (1982)
HF Ellis

Swan's Road (1954)
Naomi Mitchison

Sweet Adelaide (1980)
Julian Symons

Sweet Dove Died, The (1979)
Barbara Pym

Sweet Dreams (1973)
Michael Frayn

Sweet-Shop Owner, The (1980)
Graham Swift

Sweet Thursday (1954)
John Steinbeck

Doc

Sweet Waters (1921)
Harold Nicolson

Sweet William (1975)
Beryl Bainbridge

Swing, Brother, Swing (1949)
Ngaio Marsh

Inspector Roderick Alleyn

Swiss Family Manhattan (1932)
Christopher Morley

Swiss Family Robinson
see ***Schweizerische Robinson, Der***

Switchback (1978)
Molly Parkin

Switch, The (1978)
Elmore Leonard

Switch Bitch (1974)
Roald Dahl

Sword and Gown (1859)
George Alfred Lawrence

Sword and Scalpel (1957)
Frank Slaughter

Sword and the Sickle, The (1942)
Mulk Raj Anand

Sword in the Stone, The (1938)
TH White

Sword of Honour
see Waugh, Evelyn

Sword of Welleran, The (1908)
Edward Dunsany

Swords and Roses (1929)
Joseph Hergesheimer

Sybil (or The Two Nations) (1845)
Benjamin Disraeli

set: Marney Abbey; Mowbray
Sybil Gerard (Gerard's daughter)
Walter Gerard (Chartist)
Lord Marney

Sylvia Scarlett (1918)
Compton MacKenzie

Sylvia's Lovers (1863)
Elizabeth Gaskell

set: Monkshaven (actual Whitby)
Philip Hepburn (Sylvia's sometime husband)
Charley Kinraid (harpooner/Sylvia's lover)
Daniel Robson (farmer/Sylvia's father)
Sylvia Robson

Sylvie and Bruno (1889)
Lewis Carroll

Bruno (fairy)
Sylvie (fairy)

Symphonie pastorale, La (1919)
(The Pastoral Symphony)
André Gide

System of Dante's Hell, The (1965)
LeRoi Jones

T

Tai Pan (1966)
James Clavell

Take a Girl Like You (1960)
Kingsley Amis

Taken at the Flood (1948)
Agatha Christie

Hercule Poirot (detective)

Taken from the Enemy (1892)
Henry Newbolt

Takeover, The (1976)
Muriel Spark

Taking of Helen, The (1923)
John Masefield

Talented Mr Ripley, The (1955)
Patricia Highsmith

Tom Ripley (crook)

Talent for Loving, A (1961)
Richard Condon

Tale of a Tub, A (1704)
Jonathan Swift

Jack (Peter's brother/Calvinist)
Martin (Peter's brother/Anglican)
Peter (Catholic)

Tale of Chloe, The (1879)
George Meredith

Tale of Peter Rabbit, The (1901)
Beatrix Potter

Tale of the Good Old Man and the Lovely Young Girl, The
see ***Novella del buon vecchio e della bella fanciulla, La***

Tale of Three Places, A (1957)
Edgar Mittelholzer

Tale of Two Cities, A (1859)
Charles Dickens

set: French Revolution London; Paris
Sydney Carton (barrister)
Roger Cly (Charles St Évremonde's villainous ex-servant)
Jerry Cruncher (bank messenger)
Ernest Defarge (wine-shop keeper)
Madame Defarge (Defarge's wife)
Jarvis Lorry (bank agent)
Doctor Manette (ex-Bastille inmate)
Lucie Manette (Manette's daughter)
Miss Pross (Lucie's companion)
Solomon Pross, alias John Barsad (Miss Pross' brother/informer)
Charles St Évremonde, alias Charles Darnay (Marquis' son)
Marquis St Évremonde
Stryver (barrister)

Tales of a Fourth Grade Nothing (1972)
Judy Blume

Tales of Horror and the Supernatural (1948) coll posth
Arthur Machen

Tales of Mean Streets (1894) coll
Arthur Morrison

Tales of the Argonauts (1875)
Bret Harte

Tales of the South Pacific (1947)
James A Michener

Talisman, The (1825)
Walter Scott

set: late 12c
Berengaria (Richard I's queen)
Sir Kenneth (Scottish Crusader)
Nectabanus (dwarf)
Richard I (King of England)
Saladin (Richard I's adversary)

Talisman Ring, The (1936)
Georgette Heyer

Talking It Over (1991)
Julian Barnes

Talking to Strange Men (1987)
Ruth Rendell

Tall Dolores, The (1956)
Michael Avallone

Ed Noon (private eye)

Tamarind Seed, The (1971)
Evelyn Anthony

Tampico (1926)
Joseph Hergesheimer

Tancred (or The New Crusade) (1847)
Benjamin Disraeli

set: London; Sinai
Eva (Tancred's Jewish beloved)
Lady Montacute (Lord Montacute's wife)
Lord Montacute
Tancred Montacute (Lord Montacute's son)

Tapestry Room, The (1879)
Mary Louisa Molesworth

Tara: a Mahratta Tale (1843)
Philip Meadows Taylor

Tarabas (1935)
Joseph Roth

Tar, a Midwest Childhood (1926)
Sherwood Anderson

Taran Wanderer (1968)
Lloyd Alexander

Taran

Tar Baby (1981)
Toni Morrison

Tar-Baby, The (1904) coll
Joel Chandler Harris

Tarka the Otter (1927)
Henry Williamson

Tarka (otter)

Tarr (1918)
Wyndham Lewis

Tarry Flynn (1948)
Patrick Kavanagh

Tartan Ringers, The (1986)
Jonathan Gash

Lovejoy (dodgy antiques dealer)

Tarzan of the Apes (1914)
Edgar Rice Burroughs

Chita (monkey)
Jane (Tarzan's girlfriend)
Tarzan ('ape-man')

Taste for Death, A (1986)
PD James
Adam Dalgliesh (detective)

Tattered Tom (or The Story of a Street Arab) (1871)
Horatio Alger

Tax Inspector, The (1991)
Peter Carey

Tears His Head Off His Shoulders (1974)
Nell Dunn

Tea with Mrs Goodman (1947)
Philip Toynbee

Teeftallow (1926)
TS Stribling

Tell Freedom: Men of Africa (1954)
Peter Abrahams

Tell Me How Long the Train's Been Gone (1968)
James Baldwin

Tell-Tale Heart, The (1845)
Edgar Allan Poe

Temple Bells (1985)
Ian McEwan

Temple of the Golden Pavilion, The (1956)
Yukio Mishima

Temporal Power (1902)
Marie Corelli

Temporary Life, A (1973)
David Storey

Temps des Assassins, Les (1945)
(Age of Assassins)
Philippe Soupault

Temptation of Eileen Hughes, The (1981)
Brian Moore

Temptation of St Anthony, The
see ***Tentation de Saint Antoine, La***

Tenant of Wildfell Hall, The (1848)
Anne Brontë

set: Wildfell Hall
Arthur Graham (Helen's son)
Helen Graham (widow/'tenant')
Arthur Huntingdon (Helen's drunken 1st husband)
Frederick Lawrence (landlord/Helen's brother)
Gilbert Markham (narrator/Helen's eventual 2nd husband)

Tenants, The (1971)
Bernard Malamud

Tenants of Malory, The (1867)
Sheridan Le Fanu

Tenants of Moonbloom, The (1963) posth
Ewdard Lewis Wallant

Tender Is the Night (1934)
F Scott Fitzgerald

Dick Diver (psychiatrist)
Nicole Warren (patient/Diver's eventual wife)

Ten Little Indians
see ***Ten Little Niggers***

Ten Little Niggers (1939)
(also titled ***Ten Little Indians***)
Agatha Christie

Tennis Shoes (1937)
Noel Streatfeild

Ten North Frederick (1955)
John O'Hara

Ten Pollitt Place (1957)
CHB Kitchin

Tent, The (1926) coll
Liam O'Flaherty

Tentation de Saint Antoine, La (1874)
(The Temptation of Saint Anthony)
Gustave Flaubert

Tenth Man, The (1985)
Graham Greene

Tents of Wickedness, The (1959)
Peter De Vries

Terminal Man, The (1972)
Michael Crichton

Terms of Endearment (1975)
Larry McMurty

Terra nostra (1975)
Carlos Fuentes

Terre des hommes (1939)
(Wind, Sand and Stars)
Antoine de Saint-Exupéry

Terrible Temptation, A (1871)
Charles Reade

Sir Charles Bassett (Richard's cousin)
Lady Bassett (Sir Charles' wife)
Richard Bassett

Territorial Rights (1979)
Muriel Spark

Terror (1962)
Robert Bloch

Tess of the D'Urbervilles (1891)
Thomas Hardy

set: Blackmoor Vale; Sandbourne, Wessex
Angel Clare (Tess' eventual husband)
Alec D'Urberville (Tess' seducer)
Tess Durbeyfield

Testament (1938)
RC Hutchinson

Texas (1985)
James A Michener

Texasville (1987)
Larry McMurty

Thaddeus of Warsaw (1803)
Jane Porter

Thaïs (1890)
Anatole France

set: 4c Egypt
Thaïs

Thanatos Syndrome, The (1987)
Walker Percy

Thanksgiving Visitor (1968)
Truman Capote

Thank You, Jeeves (1934)
PG Wodehouse

Reginald Jeeves (Wooster's valet)
Bertie Wooster

That Awful Mess on the Via Merulana
see ***Quer pasticciaccio brutto de via Merulana***

That Fortune (1899)
CD Warner

That Hideous Strength (1945)
CS Lewis

That Lass O'Lowrie's (1877)
Frances Hodgson Burnett

That Old Gang of Mine (1980)
Leslie Thomas

That's How It Was (1962)
Maureen Duffy

That Summer in Paris (1963)
Morley Callaghan

That Uncertain Feeling (1955)
Kingsley Amis

That Which Is Hidden (1939)
Robert Smythe Hichens

Theatre (1937)
W Somerset Maugham

Their Wedding Journey (1872)
William Dean Howells

Thelma (1887)
Marie Corelli

Them (1969)
Joyce Carol Oates

Then Again, Maybe I Won't (1971)
Judy Blume

Theophilus North (1973)
Thornton Wilder

There Is a Happy Land (1957)
Keith Waterhouse

There Is a Serpent in Eden (1979)
Robert Bloch

Thérèse (1928)
Arthur Schnitzler

Thérèse Desqueyroux (1927)
François Mauriac

Thérèse Raquin (1867)
Émile Zola

Camille Raquin(Thérèse's husband)
Laurent (Thérèse's lover)
Thérèse Raquin

There's Trouble Brewing (1937)
Nicholas Blake

Nigel Strangeways (detective)

These Bars of Flesh (1938)
TS Stribling

These Happy Golden Years (1943)
Laura Ingalls Wilder

These Lovers Fled Away (1955)
Howard Spring

These Old Shades (1926)
Georgette Heyer

These Twain (1915)
Arnold Bennett

Edwin Clayhanger
George Lessways (Hilda's son by 1st marriage)
Hilda Lessways

They Do It with Mirrors (1952)
Agatha Christie
Miss Jane Marple (amateur sleuth)

They Seek a Country (1937)
Francis Brett Young

They Shall Inherit the Earth (1935)
Morley Callaghan

They Stooped to Folly (1929)
Ellen Glasgow

They Used Dark Forces (1964)
Dennis Wheatley
Gregory Sallust (agent)

They Went (1920)
Norman Douglas

They Were Defeated (1932)
Rose Macaulay

Thibault, Les (1922–40) 8 vol
Roger Martin du Gard
vols: 1 *Le Cahier gris* (1922)
2 *Le Pénitencier* (1922)
3 *La Belle Saison* (1923)
4 *La Consultation* (1928)
5 *La Sorellina* (1928)
6 *La Mort du père* (1929)
7 *L'Été 1914* (1936)
8 *Épilogue* (1940)
Antoine Thibault
Jacques Thibault (Antoine's brother)

Thief, The (1927)
Leonid Leonov

Things As They Are (1965)
Paul Horgan

Things Fall Apart (1958)
Chinua Achebe
set: Africa
Okonkwo

Thin Ice (1956)
Compton MacKenzie

Thinking Reed, The (1936)
Rebecca West

Thinks (1984)
Keith Waterhouse

Thin Man, The (1932)
Dashiell Hammett
set: New York
Nick Charles (detective)

Thin Mountain Air, The (1977)
Paul Horgan

Third Eye, The (1940)
Elinor Glyn

Third Girl (1966)
Agatha Christie
Hercule Poirot (detective)

Third Life of Grange Copeland, The (1970)
Alice Walker

Third Man, The (1950)
Graham Greene
set: Vienna
Harry Lime ('third man')
Rollo Martins (writer/Lime's old friend)
Anna Schmidt (actress)

Third Policeman, The (1967) posth
Flann O'Brien

Third Violet, The (1897)
Stephen Crane

Thirst for Love (1950)
Yukio Mishima

Thirty-Nine Steps, The (1915)
John Buchan
set: London; Scotland
Sandy Arbuthnott (Hannay's friend)
Richard Hannay
Paddock (Hannay's servant)

$30,000 Bequest, The (1906)
Mark Twain

This Bed My Centre (1936)
Pamela Hansford-Johnson

This Is for Real (1965)
James Hadley Chase

This Island Now (1966)
Peter Abrahams

This Man and His Woman (1951)
James T Farrell

This Quiet Dust (1982)
William Styron

This Side of Jordan (1960)
Margaret Laurence

This Side of Paradise (1920)
F Scott Fitzgerald

This Sporting Life (1960)
David Storey
Arthur Machin (rugby-player)

Thistledown (1981)
MM Kaye

Thomas l'Imposteur (1923)
(Thomas the Impostor)
Jean Cocteau

Thomas l'Obscur (1941)
(Thomas the Obscure)
Maurice Blanchot

Thornyhold (1988)
Mary Stewart

Thorofare (1942)
Christopher Morley

Those Barren Leaves (1925)
Aldous Huxley
set: Italy

Thousand Cranes, A (1948)
Yasunari Kawabata

Thousand Shall Fall, A
see ***Ob Tausend fallen***

Thou Shell of Death (1936)
Nicholas Blake
Nigel Strangeways (detective)

Three (1970)
Sylvia Ashton-Warner

Three Black Pennys, The (1917)
Joseph Hergesheimer

Three Brothers, The (1931)
Edwin Muir

Three Cheers for a Paraclete (1968)
Thomas Keneally

Three Cities (1933)
Sholem Asch

Three Clerks, The (1858)
Anthony Trollope

Harry Norman (clerk)
Alaric Tudor (clerk)
Charley Tudor (clerk/Alaric's cousin)
Mrs Woodward (widow)

Three Comrades
see ***Drei Kameraden***

Three-Cornered Hat, The
see ***Sombrero de tres picos, El***

Three-Cornered World, The (1908)
Natsume Soseki

Three Corvettes (1945)
Nicholas Monsarrat

Three Daughters of Madame Liang, The (1969)
Pearl Buck

Three Feathers
see ***Drei Federn***

Three Homes: a Tale for Fathers (1865)
Frederick William Farrar

Three Hostages, The (1924)
John Buchan

Richard Hannay

Three Inquisitive People (1940)
Dennis Wheatley

Duke de Richleau

Three Lives (1909)
Gertrude Stein

Three Men in a Boat (1889)
Jerome K Jerome

set: River Thames
George
Harris
'I' (narrator)
Montmorency (dog)

Three Men in the Snow
see ***Drei Männer im Schnee***

Three Men on the Bummel (1900)
Jerome K Jerome

set: Germany

Three Mulla-Mulgars, The (1910)
Walter De La Mare

Three Musketeers, The
see ***Trois Mousquetaires, Les***

Three Sisters, The (1914)
May Sinclair

Three Six Seven (1982)
Peter Vansittart

Three Soldiers (1921)
John Dos Passos

Three Towns, The
see ***Trois Villes, Les***

Three Ways of Love (1964)
Frances Parkinson Keyes

Three Weeks (1907)
Elinor Glyn

Through Fire and Flame (1868)
Sabine Baring-Gould

Through the Field of Clover (1961)
Peter De Vries

Through the Looking-Glass (1871)
Lewis Carroll

Alice
Dinah (cat)
Fawn
Humpty Dumpty
Red King
Red Queen
Tweedledee
Tweedledum
White Knight
White Queen

Thrush Green (1959)
Miss Read

Thunder at Sunset (1975)
John Masters

Thunderball (1961)
Ian Fleming

James Bond '007' (spy)
M (Bond's boss)
Miss Moneypenny (M's secretary)

Thunderhead (1943)
Mary O'Hara

Flicka (colt)
Ken McLaughlin (Flicka's boy-owner)

Thunder in the Sky (1966)
KM Peyton

Thunder on the Left (1925)
Christopher Morley

Thunder Returning (1961)
Edgar Mittelholzer

Thursday's Children (1984)
Rumer Godden

Thurston House (1986)
Danielle Steel

Thyrza (1887)
George Gissing

Tia Julia y el escribidor, La (1977)
(Aunt Julia and the Scriptwriter)
Mario Vargas Llosa

Tiberius (1990)
Allan Massie

Ticket That Exploded, The (1962)
William Burroughs

Tidewater Tales (1988)
John Barth

Tidings (1987)
William Wharton

Tieta (1978)
Jorge Amado

Tiger for Malgudi, The (1983)
RK Narayan

Tiger in the Smoke, The (1952)
Margery Allingham

Albert Campion (detective)

Tigers Are Better Looking (1968)
coll
Jean Rhys

Tightrope Men, The (1973)
Desmond Bagley

Tight White Collar (1960)
Grace Metalious

Tigress in Prothero, A (1959)
Frank Swinnerton

Tik-Tok of Oz (1914)
L Frank Baum

Till We Meet Again (1988)
Judith Krantz

Tilly Trotter (1980)
Tilly Trotter Wed (1981)
Tilly Trotter Widowed (1982)
Catherine Cookson

Tilly Trotter

Tim (1891)
Howard Overing Sturgis

Time and the Gods (1906)
Edward Dunsany

Time and the Hour (1957)
Howard Spring

Time Cat (1963)
Lloyd Alexander

Time Enough for Love (1973)
Robert A Heinlein

Time for a Tiger (1956)
Anthony Burgess

Time for Judas, A (1983)
Morley Callaghan

Time Machine, The (1895)
HG Wells

set: year 802701
Eloi (decadent people)
Morlocks (underground workers)

Time Must Have a Stop (1944)
Aldous Huxley

Time of Desecration
see ***Vita interiore, La***

Time of Hope, A (1949)
CP Snow

Lewis Eliot (narrator/barrister)

Time of Indifference, The
see ***Gli indifferenti***

Time of the Angels, The (1966)
Iris Murdoch

Time of the Hero, The
see ***Cuidad y los perros, La***

Time's Arrow (1991)
Martin Amis

Time to Dance, A (1989)
Melvyn Bragg

Time to Die, A (1989)
Wilbur Smith

Time without Shadows, A (1990)
Ted Allbeury

Tin Drum, The
see ***Blechtrommel, Die***

Tinker, Tailor, Soldier, Spy (1974)
John Le Carré

Karla (Smiley's adversary)
George Smiley (secret agent)

Tinkling in the Twilight, A (1959)
Edgar Mittelholzer

Tin Man, The (1965)
Michael Frayn

Tinted Venus, The (1885)
F Anstey

Titan (1800-1803) 6 vol
Jean Paul

Titan, The (1914)
Theodore Dreiser

Tit for Tat (1972) coll
Harolfd Acton

Titmuss Regained (1989)
John Mortimer

Titus Alone (1959)
Titus Groan (1946)
Mervyn Peake

To a God Unknown (1933)
John Steinbeck

Tobacco Road (1932)
Erskine Caldwell

set: Georgia, USA

To Be a Pilgrim (1942)
Joyce Cary

Gulley Jimson (artist)

To Be the Best (1988)
Barbara Taylor Bradford

Tobias and the Angel (1975)
Frank Yerby

Tobit Transplanted (1931)
Stella Benson

Toda Raba (1929)
Nikos Kazantzakis

Todd Dossier, The (1969)
Robert Bloch

Tod des Virgil, Der (1945)
(The Death of Virgil)
Hermann Broch

Tod in Venedig, Der (1912)
(Death in Venice)
Thomas Mann

Gustav Von Aschenbach (author)

To Fear a Painted Devil (1965)
Ruth Rendell

Together (1908)
Robert Herrick

Together and Apart (1936)
Margaret Kennedy

To Glory We Steer (1968)
Alexander Kent

Richard Bolitho (seaman)

To Have and Have Not (1937)
Ernest Hemingway

set: Martinique

'Toinette (1874)
Albion W Tourgée

Tokefield Papers (1927)
Frank Swinnerton

To Kill a Mockingbird (1960)
Harper Lee

set: Alabama

Told by an Idiot (1923)
Rose Macaulay

Toll for the Brave (1971)
Jack Higgins

Toll-Gate, The (1954)
Georgette Heyer

To Love and Be Wise (1950)
Josephine Tey

Tom Brown at Oxford (1861)
sequel to ***Tom Brown's Schooldays***
Thomas Hughes

Tom Brown

Tom Brown's Schooldays (1857)
Thomas Hughes

set: Rugby School
Dr Arnold (headmaster)
George Arthur (Tom's room-mate)
Tom Brown (schoolboy)
Harry 'Scud' East (Tom's school-mate)
Harry Flashman (bully)

Tombs of Atuan, The (1971)
Ursula Le Guin

Tom Jones
see ***History of Tom Jones, The***

Tommy and Grizel (1900)
sequel to ***Sentimental Tommy***
JM Barrie

Tommy Gallagher's Crusade (1937)
James T Farrell

Tommyknockers, The (1988)
Stephen King

Tommy Upmore (1884)
RD Blackmore

Tomorrow Night (1966)
Ray Bradbury

Tomorrow Will Be Better (1948)
Betty Smith

Tom Sawyer
see ***Adventures of Tom Sawyer, The***

Tom Sawyer Abroad (1894)
Tom Sawyer Detective (1896)
Mark Twain

Tom Sawyer

Tongues of Fire (1924)
Algernon Blackwood

Tonio Kröger (1903)
Thomas Mann

Tono-Bungay (1909)
HG Wells

Edward Ponderevo charlaten/George's uncle)
George Ponderevo

Too Dear for My Possessing (1940)
Pamela Hansford-Johnson

Too Late?
see ***Zu spät?***

Too Late the Phalarope (1953)
Alan Paton

Too Many Ghosts (1961)
Paul Gallico

Topaz (1967)
Leon Uris

Top of the Hill, The (1979)
Irwin Shaw

Torlogh O'Brien (1847)
Sheridan Le Fanu

Torquemada (1966)
Howard Fast

Torrents of Spring (1926)
Ernest Hemingway

Tortilla Flat (1933)
John Steinbeck
set: around Monterey, California

Tortoise by Candlelight (1963)
Nina Bawden

To Sing Strange Songs (1979)
Ray Bradbury

To Tame a Sister (1961)
Gillian Avery

Totenschiff, Das (1929)
(The Death Ship)
B Traven

To the Castle
see ***Im Schloss***

To the Coral Strand (1962)
John Masters

To the Dark Tower (1946)
Francis King

To the Devil – a Daughter (1953)
Dennis Wheatley

To the Lighthouse (1927)
Virginia Woolf
set: Hebridean island
Ramsay family

To the North (1932)
Elizabeth Bowen

Touch (1987)
Elmore Leonard

Touch Not the Cat (1976)
Mary Stewart

Touch the Devil (1982)
Jack Higgins

Tough Guys Don't Dance (1984)
Norman Mailer

Tour de monde en quatre-vingts jours, Le (1873)
(Around the World in Eighty Days)
Jules Verne
Phileas Fogg
Passepartout (Fogg's valet)

Tourmalin's Time Cheques (1891)
F Anstey

Tournament, The (1959)
Peter Vansittart

Tous les hommes sont mortels (1946)
(All Men Are Mortal)
Simone de Beauvoir

Towards the End of the Morning (1967)
Michael Frayn

Tower of Babel, The (1968)
Morris West

Tower of London, The (1840)
William Harrison Ainsworth

Towers of Silence, The (1971)
Paul Scott

set: 1940s India
Hari Kumar
Daphne Manners
Ronald Merrick (police superintendent)

Towers of Trebizond, The (1956)
Rose Macaulay

To Whom She Will Marry (1955)
Ruth Prawer Jhabvala

Town, The (1950)
Conrad Richter

Town, The (1957)
William Faulkner

Town House, The (1959)
Norah Lofts

Town in the City, The (1950)
Jack Kerouac

set: Lowell, Massachusetts

Town Like Alice, A (1949)
Nevil Shute

set: Alice Springs, Australia
Jean Paget

Toys of Peace, The (1919) coll posth
Saki

Trade Wind (1963)
MM Kaye

Tradition and Dream (1964)
James T Farrell

Tragic Comedians, The (1880)
George Meredith

Alvin (Clotilde's lover)
Clotilde
Marko (Clotilde's eventual husband)

Tragic Muse, The (1890)
Henry James

Lady Agnes Dormer

Trail Boss (1961)
JT Edson

Trail of '98, The (1910)
Robert William Service

Trail of the Serpent (1861)
Mary Elizabeth Braddon

Traitors' Gate (1958)
Dennis Wheatley

Gregory Sallust (agent)

Transit of Venus, The (1980)
Shirley Hazzard

Transparent Things (1972)
Vladimir Nabokov

Transplant (1986)
Frank Slaughter

Travail (1901)
(Work)
Émile Zola

Travailleurs de la mer, Les (1866)
(The Workers of the Sea)
Victor Hugo

Monsieur Lethierry

Traveller from Atlanta, A (1894)
William Dean Howells

Traveller in Time, A (1939)
Alison Uttley

Travellers, The (1945)
LAG Strong

Traveller's Samples (1950) coll
Frank O'Connor

Travelling People (1963)
BS Johnson

Travelling Woman, A (1959)
John Wain

Travels with My Aunt (1969)
Graham Greene

Aunt Augusta (Henry's aunt)
Henry Pulling (bank manager)

Travel Tales of Mr Jorkens, The (1931)
Edward Dunsany

Trawl (1966)
BS Johnson

Treasure (1988)
Clive Cussler

Treasure Island
RL Stevenson

set: late 18c West Country
inn: Admiral Benbow
schooner: Hispaniola
Billy Bones (pirate)
Captain Flint (treasure-map leaver) (parrot)
Ben Gunn (pirate)
Jim Hawkins (narrator)
Mrs Hawkins (Jim's mother/innkeeper)
Dr Livesey (Trelawney's friend)
'Blind' Pew (pirate)
Long John Silver (one-legged pirate)
Captain Smollett (Hispaniola's commander)

Treasure of the Sierra Madre, The
see ***Schatz der Sierra Madre, Der***

Tree Grows in Brooklyn, A (1943)
Betty Smith

set: 1900s New York

Tree of Hands, The (1984)
Ruth Rendell

Tree of Heaven, The (1917)
May Sinclair

Tree of Knowledge, The (1911)
Pia Baroja

Tree of Knowledge, The (1990)
Eva Figes

Tree of Man, The (1955)
Patrick White

set: early 20c Australia
Stan Parker (farmer)

Tree of the Sun, The (1978)
Wilson Harris

Tree on Fire, A (1967)
Alan Sillitoe

Trees, The (1940)
Conrad Richter

Treffen in Telgte, Das (1979)
(The Meeting in Telgte)
Günter Grass

Tremaine (1825)
Plumer Ward

Trembling upon Rome, A (1983)
Richard Condon

Tremor of Intent (1966)
Anthony Burgess

Trent's Last Case (1913)
EC Bentley

Philip Trent (detective)

Trespasser, The (1912)
DH Lawrence

Trespassers at Charlecote (1958)
Gillian Avery

Triad (1959)
AE Van Vogt

Trial, The (1864)
Charlotte M Yonge

Trial, The
see ***Prozess, Der***

Trial at Monomoy (1964)
John Masters

Trial Run (1979)
Dick Francis

Triangles (1990)
Andrea Newman

Tribe That Lost Its Head, The (1956)
Nicholas Monsarrat

set: imaginary island off SW Africa

Trilby (1894)
George Du Maurier

set: Paris
Trilby O'Ferrall (model/singer)
Svengali (scheming musician)

Trimblerigg (1924)
Laurence Housman

Trinity (1976)
Leon Uris

Trionfo della morte, Il (1894)
(Triumph of Death)
Gabriele D'Annunzio

Triplanetary (1948)
EE 'Doc' Smith

Triple Fugue (1924) coll
Osbert Sitwell

Triptyque (1973)
(Triptych)
Claude Simon

Tristan (1903)
Thomas Mann

Tristessa (1960)
Jack Kerouac

Tristram Shandy (1760–7) 9 vol
Laurence Sterne

Obadiah (Shandys' servant)
Mrs Shandy (Tristram's mother)
Tristram Shandy (narrator)
Uncle Toby Shandy (Tristram's uncle)
Walter Shandy (Tristram's father)
Dr Slop (quack physician)
Corporal Trim (Toby's servant)
Mrs Wadman (Shandys' neighbour)
Parson Yorick

Triumph of Death
see ***Trionfo della morte, Il***

Trofaste hustru, Den (1936)
(The Unfaithful Wife)
Sigrid Undset

Trois Mousquetaires, Les (1844)
(The Three Musketeers)
Alexandre Dumas (père)

set: 17c Paris
Aramis
Athos
D'Artagnan (Gascon)
Porthos

Trois Villes, Les (1894–8) 3 vol
(The Three Towns)
Émile Zola

vols:
1 *Lourdes* 1894)
2 *Rome* (1896)
3 *Paris* (1898)

Trojan Ending, A (1937)
Laura Riding

Troll Gardens, The (1905)
Willa Cather

Trooper Peter Halket of Mashonaland (1897)
Olive Schreiner

Tropical Winter (1933)
Joseph Hergesheimer

Tropic of Cancer (1934)
Tropic of Capricorn (1939)
Henry Miller

Tropic of Ruislip (1974)
Leslie Thomas

Tropics, The
see ***Wendekreis, Der***

Tropismes (1939)
Nathalie Sarraute

Troubled Air, The (1950)
Irwin Shaw

Trouble with England, The (1962)
Frederic Raphael

Trouble with Lichen (1960)
John Wyndham

Trouble with Tigers, The (1938) coll
William Saroyan

Trou de l'enfer, Le (1850)
Alexandre Dumas (père)

Troy Chimneys (1953)
Margaret Kennedy

Troy Town (1888)
Arthur Quiller-Couch

set: Fowey, Cornwall

True Heart (1929)
Sylvia Townsend Warner

Trumpet-Major, The (1880)
Thomas Hardy

set: Napoleonic Wars, Overcombe Mill, Wessex
Festus Derriman (yeoman/Anne's suitor)
Anne Garland
Bob Loveday (John's brother/sailor/Anne's eventually successful suitor)
John Loveday (trumpet-major/Anne's suitor)

Trust (1989)
George V Higgins

Trust (1966)
Cynthia Ozick

Trustee for the Toolroom (1960)
Nevil Shute

Truth
see ***Vérité***

Truth About Lorin Jones, The (1988)
Alison Lurie

Trzy Zimy (1936)
Czeslaw Milosz

Tsotsi (1980)
Athol Fugard

Tulipe noire, La (1850)
(The Black Tulip)
Alexandre Dumas (père)

Cornelius Van Baerle (tulip-grower)

Tulku (1979)
Peter Dickinson

Tumbledown Dick (1939)
Howard Spring

Tunc (1968)
Laurence Durrell

Tunnel of Love, The (1954)
Peter De Vries

Turbott Wolfe (1926)
William Plomer

Turks in Hungary, The (1852)
Mór Jókai

Turn in the South, A (1989)
VS Naipaul

Turn of the Screw, The (1898)
Henry James

house: Bly
Flora (Miles' sister)
Mrs Grose (housekeeper)
Miss Jessel ('ghost')
Miles
Peter Quint ('ghost')

Turquoise, The (1946)
Anya Seton

Turtle Diary (1976)
Russell Hoban

Twentieth-Century Man (1978)
David Benedictus

27th Kingdom, The (1982)
Alice Thomas Ellis

Twenty-Six Men and a Girl (1899)
Maxim Gorky

20,000 Leagues under the Sea
see ***Vingt Mille Lieues sous les mers***

Twenty Years After
see ***Vingt Ans après***

Twice Shy (1981)
Dick Francis

Twice-Told Tales (1837) coll
Nathaniel Hawthorne

Twilight Eyes (1987)
Dean R Koontz

Twilight Sleep (1927)
Edith Wharton

Twisted Thing, The (1966)
Mickey Spillane

Mike Hammer (private eye)

Twits, The (1980)
Roald Dahl

Two Adolescents
see ***Agostino***

Two Brothers (1964)
Philip Toynbee

Two Drovers, The (1827)
Walter Scott

Two Feet from Heaven (1940)
PC Wren

Two Is Lonely (1974)
Lynne Reid Banks

Two Leaves and a Bud (1937)
Mulk Raj Anand

Two Little Pilgrims' Progress (1895)
Frances Hodgson Burnett

Two Little Wooden Shoes (1874)
Ouida

Two Mentors, The (1783)
Clara Reeve

Two on a Tower (1882)
Thomas Hardy

Lady Constantine (St Cleeve's lover)
Swithin St Cleeve (astronomer)

Two Sisters, The (1926)
HE Bates

2001: a Space Odyssey (1968)
Arthur C Clarke

Hal 9000 (on-board computer)

Two Virgins (1973)
Kamala Markandaya

Two Weeks in Another Time (1960)
Irwin Shaw

Two Wives, The (1939)
Frank Swinnerton

Two Women
see ***Ciociara, La***

Two Worlds and Their Ways (1949)
Ivy Compton-Burnett

Two Years Ago (1857)
Charles Kingsley

set: Aberalva (West Country village)

Twyborn Affair, The (1979)
Patrick White

Tylney Hall (1834)
Thomas Hood

Typee (A Peep at Polynesian Life) (1846)
Herman Melville

Fayaway (Tom's Polynesian friend)
Toby (seaman)
Tom (seaman)

Typhoon (1903)
Joseph Conrad

steamer: Nan-Shan
Captain MacWhirr

U

Ugly Duchess, The
see ***Hässliche Herzogin, Die***

Ultimate Prizes (1990)
Susan Howatch

Ultimate Viking, The (1955)
Eric Linklater

Ultima Thule (1929)
Henry Handel Richardson

Richard Mahony

Ultramarine (1933)
Malcolm Lowry

Ulysses (1922)
James Joyce

set: June 16, 1904 Dublin
Molly Bloom (Bloom's unfaithful wife)
Leopold Bloom (Jewish advertisement salesman)
Stephen Dedalus

Unbearable Bassington, The (1912)
Saki

Unbearable Lightness of Being, The (1984)
Milan Kundera

Unbekannte Grösse, Die (1933)
(The Unknown Quantity)
Hermann Broch

Unclassed, The (1884)
George Gissing

Unclay (1931)
TF Powys

Uncle Bernac (1897)
Arthur Conan Doyle

Uncle Dynamite (1948)
PG Wodehouse

Earl of Ickenham, 'Uncle Fred'

Uncle Fred in the Springtime (1939)
PG Wodehouse

set: Blandings Castle, Shropshire
Rupert 'the efficient' Baxter (Lord Emsworth's secretary)
Empress of Blandings (pig)
Lord Emsworth
Earl of Ickenham, 'Uncle Fred'
Lady Constance Keeble (Lord Emsworth's sister)

Uncle Moses (1938)
Sholem Asch

Uncle Remus (His Songs and Sayings) (1880) coll
Uncle Remus and Brer Rabbit (1906) coll
Uncle Remus and His Friends (1892) coll
Uncle Remus and the Little Boy (1910) coll posth
Joel Chandler Harris

Brer Fox
Brer Rabbit
Uncle Remus (narrator)

Uncle Silas (1864)
Sheridan Le Fanu

Uncle Stephen (1931)
Forrest Reid

Uncle Tom's Cabin (or Life Among the Lowly) (1852)
Harriet Beecher Stowe

set: Kentucky; New Orleans
Aunt Chloe (slave/Uncle Tom's wife)
Eliza (slave)
Simon Legree (plantation owner)
George Shelby (Shelby's son)
Mr Shelby (slave-owner)
Augustine St Clair
Little Eva St Clair (Augustine's daughter)
Uncle Tom (slave)
Topsy (slave)

Unclouded Summer (1948)
Alec Waugh

Uncommercial Traveller, The (1860) coll
Charles Dickens

Unconditional Surrender (1961)
Evelyn Waugh
set: World War II
Guy Crouchback (army officer)
Virginia Troy (Crouchback's wife, briefly, 2nd time around)

Under Drake's Flag (1883)
GA Henty

Underground Man, The (1971)
Ross Macdonald

Under Plum Lake (1980)
Lionel Davidson

Under Satan's Sun
see ***Sous le soleil de Satan***

Under the Greenwood Tree (1872)
Thomas Hardy

set: Mellstock, Wessex
Fancy Day (Dewy's sweetheart)
Dick Dewy

Under the Lilacs (1877)
Louisa M Alcott

Under the Net (1954)
Iris Murdoch

Under the Red Robe (1894)
Stanley John Weyman

Under the Sangre de Cristo (1985)
Paul Horgan

Under the Volcano (1947)
Malcolm Lowry

set: 1939 Mexico
Geoffrey Firmin (ex-consul/alcoholic)
Yvonne Firmin (Firmin's wife)
Jacques Laruelle (film-maker)

Under the Waves (1876)
RM Ballantyne

Under Two Flags (1867)
Ouida

set: French Foreign Legion
Hon Bertie Cecil (military guard)

Under Western Eyes (1911)
Joseph Conrad

set: Geneva; St Petersburg
Kirylo Sidorovitch Razumov

Undine (1811)
Friedrich Fouqué

Bertalda (Huldbrand's would-be wife)
Huldbrand (knight/Undine's 'husband')
Kühleborn (water spirit)
Undine (nymph)

Undine (1929) posth
Olive Schreiner

Undiscovered Country, The (1880)
William Dean Howells

Undiscovered Country, The (1966)
Julian Mitchell

Und sagte kein einziges Wort (1953)
(And Never Said a Word)
Heinrich Böll

Unexplained Laughter (1985)
Alice Thomas Ellis

Unfaithful Wife, The
see ***Trofaste hustru, Die***

Unfinished Portrait (1934)
Agatha Christie

Unforgotten Prisoner, The (1933)
RC Hutchinson

Unfortunates, The (1969)
BS Johnson

Ungava (1857)
RM Ballantyne

Unholy Crusade (1967)
Dennis Wheatley

Unholy Trinity (1986)
Robert Bloch

Unicorn, The (1963)
Iris Murdoch

Universal baseball Association, Inc., J. Henry Waugh prop., The (1968)
Robert Coover

Unkindness of Ravens, An (1985)
Ruth Rendell

Inspector Reg Wexford

Unknown Ajax, The (1959)
Georgette Heyer

Unknown Man No 89 (1977)
Elmore Leonard

Unknown Quantity, The
see ***Unbekannte Grösse, Die***

Unknown Warrior, The (1980)
James Leasor

Unmade Bed, The
see ***Lit défait, Le***

Unnamable, The (1958)
Samuel Beckett

Unnatural Causes (1967)
PD James

Adam Dalgliesh (detective)

Unnatural Death (1928)
Dorothy L Sayers

Bunter (Wimsey's servant)
Lord Peter Wimsey (amateur detective)

Unofficial Rose, An (1962)
Iris Murdoch

Unpleasantness at the Bellona Club, The (1928)
Dorothy L Sayers
Bunter (Wimsey's servant)
Lord Peter Wimsey (amateur detective)

Unsichtbare Mauer, Die (1934)
Stefan Andres

Unsocial Socialist, An (1887)
GB Shaw

Unspeakable Skipton, The (1959)
Pamela Hansford-Johnson

Unsuitable Job for a Woman, An (1972)
PD James
Cordelia Gray (private eye)

Unterm Rad (1906)
Hermann Hesse

Untertan, Der (1918)
(The Bourgeois)
Heinrich Mann

Until the Daybreak (1942)
Louis Bromfield

Untouchable (1935)
Mulk Raj Anand

Unvanquished, The (1938)
William Faulkner

Unwelcome Man, The (1917)
Waldo Frank

Up and Coming (1980)
Molly Parkin

Up a Road Slowly (1966)
Irene Hunt

Up into the Singing Mountain (1963)
Richard Llewellyn

Upstart, The (1973)
Piers Paul Read

Up the Junction (1966)
Nell Dunn

Uptight (1975)
Molly Parkin

Use of Riches, A (1957)
JIM Stewart

Utopia (1516)
Thomas More
Raphael Hythloday (traveller)

V

V (1963)
Thomas Pynchon
set: New York sewers

Vaccilations of Poppy Carew, The (1986)
Mary Wesley

Vagabonde, La (1910)
Colette

Vägen till Klockrike (1948)
(The Road to Klockrike)

Vägen ut (1936)
(The Way Out)
Harry Edmund Martinson

Vainglory (1915)
Ronald Firbank

Valdez is Coming (1969)
Elmore Leonard

Valentine (1832)
George Sand

Valley Forge (1975)
MacKinlay Kantor

Valley of Decision, The (1902)
Edith Wharton

set: 18c Lombardy
Odo Valsecca (heir to a dukedom)
Fulvia Vivaldi (Vivaldi's daughter)
Orazio Vivaldi (philosopher)

Valley of Horses, The (1983)
Jean M Auel

Valley of the Dolls (1966)
Jacqueline Susann

Valley of the Moon, The (1913)
Jack London

Valmouth (1919)
Ronald Firbank

Mrs Yajñavalka (masseuse)

Valperga (1823)
Mary Shelley

set: 14c Italy

Van Bibber (1892)
Richard Harding Davis

Vanderlyn (1837) unf
Charles Fenno Hoffman

Vandover and the Brute (1914) posth
Frank Norris

Vanessa (1933)
Hugh Walpole

Vanity Dies Hard (1965)
Ruth Rendell

Vanity Fair (1848)
William Makepeace Thackeray

set: Napoleonic Wars
Sir Pitt Crawley
Rawdon Crawley (Crawley's son/Becky's soon-to-be husband)
Colonel William Dobbin (Osborne's friend/Amelia's 2nd husband)
George Osborne (Amelia's 1st husband)
Miss Pinkerton (school owner)
Amelia Sedley
Jos Sedley (Amelia's brother)
Becky (Rebecca) Sharp
Lord Steyne (Becky's secret sponsor)
Mr Wagg (journalist)

Vathek (1787)
William Beckford

Vatican Rip, The (1981)
Jonathan Gash

Lovejoy (dodgy antiques dealer)

Vecchi e i giovani, I (1909)
(The Old and the Young)
Luigi Pirandello

Vecchione, Il (1967) posth unf
(The Grand Old Man)
Italo Svevo

Vendor of Sweets, The (1967)
RK Narayan

Venetia (1837)
Benjamin Disraeli

Ventian Glass Nephew, The (1925)
Elinor Wylie

Vengeance Is Mine! (1950)
Mickey Spillane

Mike Hammer (private eye)

Vengeance of the Gods, The (1954)
Rex Warner

Vent, Le (1957)
(The Wind)
Claude Simon

Venusberg (1932)
Anthony Powell

Venus with Pistol (1969)
Gavin Lyall

Vera (1921)
Elizabeth Von Arnim

Veranilda (1904) Posth
George Gissing

Vera the Medium (1908)
Richard Harding Davis

Vérité (1903) posth
(The Truth)
Émile Zola

Verlorene Ehre der Katharina Blüm, Die (1974)
(The Lost Honour of Katharina Blüm)
Heinrich Böll

Verlorene Handschrift, Die (1864)
Gustav Freytag

Versuchung des Synesios, Der (1971) posth
Stefan Andres

Vertical Smile (1971)
Richard Condon

Verwandlung, Die (1915)
(Metamorphosis)
Franz Kafka

Gregor Samsa

Very Good, Jeeves (1930) coll
PG Wodehouse

Reginald Jeeves (Wooster's valet)
Bertie Wooster

Very Heaven (1937)
Richard Aldington

Very Last Gambado, The (1989)
Jonathan Gash

Lovejoy (dodgy antiques dealer)

Very Private Life, A (1968)
Michael Frayn

Very Private War, A (1980)
Jon Cleary

Vestal Fire (1927)
Compton MacKenzie

V for Vengeance (1942)
Dennis Wheatley

Gregory Sallust (agent)

Via Crucis (1898)
F Marion Crawford

Viaje a la Alcarria (1948)
(Journey to the Alcarria)
Camilo José Cela

Vicar of Bullhampton, The (1870)
Anthony Trollope

Carry Brattle
Sam Brattle (Carry's brother)
Frank Fenwick (vicar)
Marquis of Trowbridge
Mr Trumble (farmer)

Vicar of Wakefield, The (1766)
Oliver Goldsmith

Deborah Primrose (Primrose's wife)
Dr Primrose (vicar)

Vice-Consul, Le (1966)
Marguerite Duras

Vice filial, Le (1891)
Paul Adam

Vice Versa (or A Lesson to Fathers) (1882)
F Anstey

Dick Bultitude (Paul's son)
Paul Bultitude

Vicomte de Bragelonne, Le (1850)
sequel to ***Vingt Ans après***
Alexandre Dumas (père)

Aramis
Athos
D'Artagnan (Gascon)
Porthos

Victim, The (1947)
Saul Bellow

Victories (1990)
George V Higgins

Victory (1915)
Joseph Conrad

set: Timor; Samburan
Axel Heyst

Vie, Une (1883)
(A Life)
Guy de Maupassant

set: Normandy
Jeanne

Vieille Maîtresse, Une (1851)
Jules-Amédée Barbey D'Aurevilly

View from Coyoba, The (1985)
Peter Abrahams

View from Pompey's Head, The (1954)
Hamilton Basso

View of the Harbour, A (1947)
Elizabeth Taylor

Views and Vagabonds (1912)
Rose Macaulay

Viking's Dawn (1955)
Viking's Sunset (1960)
Henry Treece

Vile Bodies (1930)
Evelyn Waugh

Village, The (1939)
Mulk Raj Anand

Village, The (1910)
Ivan Bunin

Village by the Sea, The (1982)
Anita Desai

Village Commune, A (1881)
Ouida

Village in the Jungle, The (1913)
Leonard Woolf

Village School (1955)
Miss Read

Villa in France, A (1982)
JIM Stewart

Villa in Summer, A (1954)
Penelope Mortimer

Ville inconnue, La (1911)
Paul Adam

Villette (1853)
Charlotte Brontë

set: Villette (actual Brussels)
Madame Beck (headmistress)
John Bretton (doctor)
Paul Emmanuel (Lucy's beloved)
Ginevra Fanshawe (John's sometime beloved)
Pauline Home (John's sometime beloved)
Lucy Snowe (teacher)

Vingt Ans après (1845)
(Twenty Years After)
sequel to ***Les Trois Mousquetaires***
Alexandre Dumas (père)

Aramis
Athos
D'Artagnan (Gascon)
Porthos

Vingt Mille Lieues sous les mers (1869)
(20,000 Leagues under the Sea)
Jules Verne

set: Nautilus (submarine)
Captain Nemo

Vintage Murder (1937)
Ngaio Marsh

Inspector Roderick Alleyn

Vintage Stuff (1982)
Tom Sharpe

Violent Bear It Away, The (1960)
Flannery O'Connor

Violent Land, The (1945)
Jorge Amado

Violent Life, A
see ***Vita violenta, Una***

Virginia (1913)
Ellen Glasgow

Virginian, The (A Horseman of the Plains) (1902)
Owen Wister

Virginians, The (1859)
Anthony Trollope

George Warrington
Harry Warrington (George's twin)
Rachel Warrington (George & Harry's mother)

Virgin in the Garden, The (1978)
AS Byatt

Virgin Soil (1877)
Ivan Turgenev

Virgin Soil Upturned (1931)
Mikhail Sholokhov

Virgin Soldiers, The(1966)
Leslie Thomas

Visconte dimezzato, Il (1952)
Italo Calvino

Visioning, The (1911)
Susan Glaspell

Visits of Elizabeth, The (1900)
Elinor Glyn

Vita, Una (1893)
(A Life)
Italo Svevo

Vita interiore, La (1978)
(Time of Desecration)
Alberto Moravia

Vital Parts (1970)
Thomas Berger

Vital Signs (1991)
Robin Cook

Vital Spark, The (1906)
Neil Munro

Vita militare, La (1868)
Edmondo De Amicis

Vita violenta, Una (1958)
(A Violent Life)
Pier Paolo Pasolini

Vittoria (1867)
sequel to ***Sandra Belloni***
George Meredith

Emilia Sandra Belloni (singer, as Vittoria)
Pole family

Vivero Letter, The (1968)
Desmond Bagley

Vivian Grey (1826)
Benjamin Disraeli

Marquis of Carabas (politician)
Vivian Grey (politician)

Vivisector, The (1970)
Patrick White

Vixen 03 (1977)
Clive Cussler

Vodi, The (1959)
John Braine

Voice of the Heart, The (1983)
Barbara Taylor Bradford

Voice of the People, The (1900)
Ellen Glasgow

Voices at Play (1961)
Muriel Spark

Voices of a Summer Day (1965)
Irwin Shaw

Voice Through a Cloud, A (1950)
posth unf
Denton Welch

Voie royale, La (1930)
(The Royal Route)
André Malraux

Vol de nuit (1931)
(Night Flight)
Antoine de Saint-Exupéry

Volume the Last (1753)
Sarah Fielding

David Simple

Volunteers, The (1978)
Raymond Williams

Volupté (1834)
Charles-Augustin Sainte-Beuve

Amaury (narrator/priest)

Vorbild, Das (1973)
(The Model)
Siegfried Lenz

Vortex (1977)
Jon Cleary

Vortex Blaster, The (1960)
EE 'Doc' Smith

Voss (1957)
Patrick White

set: 1845 Australia
Laura Trevelyan (Voss' mystic companion)
Johann Voss (expedition leader)

Vous les entendez? (1972)
(Do You Hear Them?)
Nathalie Sarraute

Voyage, The (1940)
Charles Morgan

Voyage au bout de la nuit (1932)
(Journey to the End of the Night)
Louis-Ferdinand Céline

Voyage au centre de la terre (1864)
(Journey to the Centre of the Earth)
Jules Verne

Professor Lidenbrock

Voyage in the Dark (1934)
Jean Rhys

set: London
Anna Morgan

Voyage of QV66, The (1978)
Penelope Lively

Voyage of the Challenger, The (1972)
Eric Linklater

Voyage of the Dawn Treader, The (1952)
CS Lewis

set: Narnia
Aslan (lion)
Edmund
Eustace
Lucy

Voyage of the Destiny, The (1982)
Robert Nye

Voyage Out, The (1915)
Virginia Woolf

set: en route to South America
Terence Hewet
Rachel Vinrace (Hewet's fiancée)

Voyage to Pagany, A (1928)
William Carlos Williams

Voyage to Purilia, A (1930)
Elmer Rice

Voyage Unplanned, The (1974)
Frank Yerby

Voyageurs de l'imperiale (1942)
Louis Aragon

Voyeur, Le (1955)
Alain Robbe-Grillet

W

Waco's Debt (1964)
JT Edson

Wages of Virtue, The (1916)
PC Wren

Wahlverwandtschaften, Die (1809)
(Elective Affinities)
Johann Goethe

Waiting for the Barbarians (1980)
John Michael Coetzee

Waiting Room, The (1967)
Wilson Harris

Waking (1981)
Eva Figes

Waldfried (1874)
Berthold Auerbach

Waldo (1967)
Paul Theroux

Walking Dead (1977)
Peter Dickinson

Walk in the Wilderness, (1950)
James Hanley

Walk in Wolf Wood, A (1980)
Mary Stewart

Walk on the Wild Side, A (1956)
Nelson Algren

Walladmor (1824)
Willibald Alexis

Wall of the Plague, The (1984)
André Brink

Wanda (1928)
Gerhart Hauptmann

Wanderer, The (or Female Difficulties) (1814)
Fanny Burney

Wanderer's Necklace, The (1914)
H Rider Haggard

Wanting Seed, The (1962)
Anthony Burgess

Wapshot Chronicle, The (1957)
Wapshot Scandal, The (1964)
John Cheever

War and Peace (1863–9) 4 vol
Leo Tolstoy

vols:
1 *Before Tilsit*
2 *The Invasion*
3 *The French at Moscow*
4 *Epilogue*

set: Russia, Napoleonic Wars 1805–20
Pierre Bezushov
Prince André Bolkonski
Princess Marie
Natasha

War and Remembrance (1975)
Herman Wouk

War Angel
see ***Angel guerra***

War Baby (1971)
Jackie Gillott

War between the Tates, The (1974)
Alison Lurie

Warden, The (1855)
Anthony Trollope

set: Barsetshire
John Bold (surgeon)
Archdeacon Grantly (Harding's son-in-law)
Eleanor Harding (Harding's daughter/Bold's eventual wife)
Rev Septimus Harding (warden)

Warden's Niece, The (1957)
Gillian Avery

Reverend Copplestone (warden)

War Goes On, The (1936)
Sholem Asch

War in Heaven (1930)
Charles Williams

War in the Air, The (1908)
HG Wells

Bert Smallways

Warm Nights of January, The (1960)
Frank Tuohy

War of the Worlds, The (1898)
HG Wells

set: Woking, Martian invasion

Warsaw Document, The (1971)
Adam Hall

War to the Knife (1899)
Rolf Boldrewood

War Trail (1857)
Mayne Reid

War with the Newts (1936)
Karel Capek

Wärwolf, Der (1848)
Willibald Alexis

Washington Square (1881)
Henry James

Lavinia Penniman (Catherine's aunt)
Doctor Sloper (physician)
Catherine Sloper (Sloper's daughter)
Morris Townsend (Catherine's sometime fiancé)

Wasp Factory, The (1984)
Iain Banks

Waste (1924)
Robert Herrick

Watch and Ward (1871)
Henry James

Nora Lambert (Roger's ward & eventual wife)
Hubert Lawrence (Roger's brother/clergyman)
Roger Lawrence

Watcher in the Shadows (1960)
Geoffrey Household

Watchers (1987)
Dean R Koontz

Watchers on the Shore, The (1966)
Stan Barstow

Ingrid Brown (Vic's wife)
Vic Brown

Watching Me, Watching You (1981)
Fay Weldon

Water-Babies, The (1863)
Charles Kingsley

set: Harthover (mansion); St Brandan's Isle (magic land)
Mrs Bedonebyasyoudid ('moral guardian')
Mother Carey ('maker of the sea creatures')
Mrs Doasyouwouldbedoneby ('moral guardian')
Ellie (Tom's friend)
Mr Grimes (Tom's employer)
Tom (chimney-sweep)

Waterfall, The (1969)
Margaret Drabble

Water Gipsies, The (1930)
AP Herbert

Waterland (1983)
Graham Swift

Water-Method Man, The (1972)
John Irving

Watership Down (1972)
Richard Adams

set: Berkshire/Hampshire border
Bigwig (rabbit)
Fiver (rabbit)
Hazel (rabbit)

Water-Witch, The (1830)
James Fenimore-Cooper

Water with Berries (1971)
George Lamming

Watsons, The (1927) posth
Jane Austen

Mr Howard (clergyman)
Tom Musgrave
Lady Osborne
Lord Osborne (Lady Osborne's son)
Elizabeth Watson
Emma Watson (Elizabeth's sister)
Margaret Watson (Elizabeth's sister)
Penelope Watson (Elizabeth's sister)

Watson's Apology (1984)
Beryl Bainbridge

Watt (1953)
Samuel Beckett

Wave, The (1916)
Algernon Blackwood

Waverley (1814)
Walter Scott

set: 1740s
Rose Bradwardine
Prince Charles Edward, the Young Pretender
Fergus Mac-Ivor
Flora Mac-Ivor (Fergus' sister)
Duncan Macwheeble (bailie)
Colonel Talbot
Edward Waverley
Sir Everard Waverley (Waverley's uncle)

Waves, The (1931)
Virginia Woolf

Way Home, The (1925)
Henry Handel Richardson

Richard Mahony

Way of All Flesh, The (1903) posth
Samuel Butler

Aunt Alethea (Ernest's aunt)
Ellen (maidservant)
Mr Overton (narrator)
Ernest Pontifex (Theo's son)
George Pontifex (John's son)
John Pontifex (carpenter)
Theo Pontifex (George's son)
Doctor Skinner (headmaster)

Way Out, The (1933)
Upton Sinclair

Way Out, The
see ***Vägen ut***

Way to Dusty Death, The (1973)
Alistair Maclean

Wayward Bus, The (1947)
John Steinbeck

Way We Live Now, The (1875)
Anthony Trollope
Augustus Melmotte (financier)

We (1920)
Evgeny Zamyatin
set: 26c

Weapon Shops of Isher, The (1951)
AE Van Vogt

We Are Not Alone (1937)
James Hilton

Weather in the Streets, The (1936)
Rosamund Lehmann

Weathermonger, The (1968)
Peter Dickinson

Weather Shelter, The (1970)
Erskine Caldwell

Web (1979) posth
John Wyndham

Web and the Rock, The (1939) posth
Thomas Wolfe

Web of Life, The (1900)
Robert Herrick

Wedding Group, The (1969)
Elizabeth Taylor

We Didn't Mean to Go to Sea (1937)
Arthur Ransome

Weekend with Claude, A (1967)
Beryl Bainbridge

Weep Not, Child (1964)
Ngugi Wa Thiong'o

Weg ins Freie, Der (1908)
(The Road to the Open)
Arthur Schnitzler

Weg zurück, Der (1931)
(The Road Back)
sequel to ***Im Westen nichts Neues***
Erich Maria Remarque

Weirdstone of Brisingamen, The (1960)
Alan Garner

Weir of Hermiston (18960 posth unf
RL Stevenson
set: Scottish Lowlands
Christina Elliott (Archie's beloved)
Kirstie (Archie's housekeeper)
Adam Weir (Lord Hermiston/justice)
Archie Weir (Weir's son)

Welcome to Hard Times (1960)
EL Doctorow

Well at the World's End, The (1951)
Neil Gunn

Well at the World's End, The (1896)
William Morris

Well-Beloved, The (1897)
Thomas Hardy
set: Isle of Slingers (actual Portland Island)
Jocelyn Pierston (sculptor)

Well of Days, The (1933)
Ivan Bunin

Wells of St Mary's, The (1961)
RC Sherriff

Wench Is Dead, The (1989)
Colin Dexter

Inspector Morse

Wendekreis, Der (1920) 3 vol
(The Tropics)
Jakob Wassermann

Wept of Wish-Ton-Wish, The (1829)
James Fenimore Cooper

Wer Einmal aus dem Blechnapf Frisst (1934)
(Who Once Eats out of the Tin Bowl)
Hans Fallada

Wessex Tales (1888) coll
Thomas Hardy

Westcotes, The (1902)
Arthur Quiller-Couch

Westward Ho! (1855)
Charles Kingsley

set: 16c
Don Guzman (Spanish captain)
Amyas Leigh (seaman)
Frank Leigh (Amyas' brother)
Rose Salterne (Guzman's eventual wife)

Westward to Laughter (1970)
Colin MacInnes

We the Living (1959)
Ayn Rand

Wetherel Affair, The (1873)
John William De Forest

We Think the World of You (1960)
JR Ackerley

Wet Magic (1913)
E Nesbit

We Two (1884)
sequel to ***Donovan***
Edna Lyall

Weymouth Sands (1934)
John Cowper Powys

What Farrar Saw (1946)
James Hanley

What Katy Did (1872)
What Katy Did at School (1873)
What Katy Did Next (1886)
Susan Coolidge

Doctor Carr (Katy's father)
Katy Carr
Cecy Hall (Katy's friend)
Aunt Izzie (Katy's aunt)

What Maisie Knew (1898)
Henry James

Sir Claude (Ida's sometime fiancé)
Beale Farrange Ida Farrange (Farrange's estranged wife)
Maisie Farrange (Farranges' daughter)
Miss Overmore (governess/Farrange's soon-to-be 2nd wife)
Mrs Wix (governess)

What's Become of Waring (1939)
Anthony Powell

What's Bred in the Bone (1985)
Robertson Davies

What's It Like Out? (1968)
Penelope Gilliat

What Will He Do with It? (1858)
Edward Bulwer-Lytton

Wheel of Fortune (1984)
Susan Howatch

Wheels (1971)
Arthur Hailey

Wheels of Chance, The (1896)
HG Wells

Wheels within Wheels (1933)
Alec Waugh

When Eight Bells Toll (1966)
Alistair Maclean

set: Scotland

When in Rome (1970)
Ngaio Marsh

Inspector Roderick Alleyn

When My Girl Comes Home (1961) coll
VS Pritchett

When She Was Good (1967)
Philip Roth

When the Bough Breaks (1924) coll
Naomi Mitchison

When the Lion Feeds (1964)
Wilbur Smith

When the Sleeper Wakes (1899)
HG Wells

When the Wicked Man (1932)
Ford Madox Ford

When William Came (1913)
Saki

Where Angels Fear to Tread (1905)
EM Forster

set: England; Italy
Gino Carella (Lilia's 2nd husband)
Harriet Herriton (Lilia's sister-in-law)
Irma Herriton (Lilia's daughter)
Lilia Herriton (widow)
Philip Herriton ((Lilia's cousin)

Where Are the Violets Now? (1965)
Auberon Waugh

Where Eagles Dare (1967)
Alistair Maclean

set: World war II, Bavarian Alps

Where Shall We Go This Summer? (1975)
Anita Desai

Where the Blue Begins (1922)
Christopher Morley

Where the Clocks Chime Twice (1952)
Alec Waugh

Where the Rivers Meet (1988)
John Wain

Where the Wind Blows (1966)
Helen Cresswell

Whicharts, The (1931)
Noel Streatfeild

Which Way to Mecca, Jack? (1961)
William Peter Blatty

Whip Hand (1980)
Dick Francis

Whirlpool, The (1897)
George Gissing

Whisky Galore (1947)
Compton MacKenzie

set: 1943 Hebrides
ship: Cabinet Minister
Sergeant Odd
Captain Waggett

Whispering Mountain, The (1968)
Joan Aiken

Whisper in the Gloom, The (1954)
Nicholas Blake

Nigel Strangeways (detective)

Whisper of the Axe (1976)
Richard Condon

Whispers (1980)
Dean R Koontz

White Banners (1936)
Lloyd C Douglas

White Carnation, The (1953)
RC Sherriff

White Company, The (1891)
Arthur Conan Doyle

White Fang (1906)
Jack London

set: North Canada
Grey Beaver (Indian chief/White Fang's master)
Matt (dog-handler)
Scott (mining engineer)
Smith (White Fang's later master)
White Fang (wolf-dog)

White Father, The (1964)
Julian Mitchell

set: Africa

White Feather, The (1907)
PG Wodehouse

White Goddess, The (1947)
Robert Graves

White Guard, The (1925)
Mikhail Bulgakov

White Horse Gang, The (1966)
Nina Bawden

White Hotel, The (1981)
DM Thomas

White Indian (1981)
JT Edson

White-Jacket (1850)
Herman Melville

set: en route from Peru to Virginia
frigate: Neversink
Jack Chase (seaman) Captain Claret
Mr Cuticle (surgeon)

White Man's Saga (1928)
Eric Linklater

White Mice, The (1909)
Richard Harding Davis

White Mule, The (1937)
William Carlos Williams

White Nights (1848)
Fyodor Dostoevsky

White Noise (1985)
Don Delillo

White Peacock, The (1911)
DH Lawrence

White Prophet, The (1909)
Hall Caine

White Rose of Weary Leaf (1908)
Violet Hunt

Whites and the Blues, The
see ***Blancs et les bleus, Les***

White Sister, The (1909)
F Marion Crawford

White South, The (1949)
Hammond Innes

Whitewater (1970)
Paul Horgan

White Woman of Leutschau, The (1884)
Mór Jókai

Who Is Teddy Villanova? (1977)
Thomas Berger

Whole Armour, The (1962)
Wilson Harris

Whom God Hath Sundered (1912–13) 2 vol
Oliver Onions

Who Once Eats out of the Tin Bowl
see ***Wer Einmal aus dem Blechnapf Frisst***

Whose Body? (1923)
Dorothy L Sayers

Bunter (Wimsey's servant)
Lord Peter Wimsey (amateur detective)

Why Are We in Vietnam? (1967)
Norman Mailer

Why Come to Slaka? (1986)
Malcolm Bradbury

Why Didn't They Ask Evans? (1934)
Agatha Christie

Why Pick on Me? (1951)
James Hadley Chase

Wickford Point (1939)
John Marquand

Widdershins (1911) coll
Oliver Onions

Wide Sargasso Sea (1966)
Jean Rhys

set: Dominica; Jamaica
Antoinette Cosway (actress)

Widow, The (1957)
Francis King

Widow Rugby's Husband, The (1851)
JJ Hooper

Widow's Cruise, The (1959)
Nicholas Blake

Nigel Strangeways (detective)

Wieland (1798)
Charles Brockden Brown

Wife to Mr Milton (1943)
Robert Graves

Mr Milton (poet)
Mrs Milton (Milton's wife)

Wifey (1978)
Judy Blume

Wigs on the Green (1935)
Nancy Mitford

Wild Boys, The (1971)
William Burroughs

Wild Conquest (1951)
Peter Abrahams

Wilderness (1961)
Robert Penn Warren

Wild Geese, The (1908)
Stanley John Weyman

Wild Geese Overhead (1939)
Neil Gunn

Wild Ghost Chase (1978)
DJ Enright

Wild Goose Chase, The (1937)
Rex Warner

Wild Hunt of Hagworthy, The (1971)
Penelope Lively

Wild Irish Boy, The (1808)
Charles Maturin

Wild Is the River (1941)
Louis Bromfield

Wild Justice (1979)
Wilbur Smith

Wild Man of the West, The (1863)
RM Ballantyne

Wild Nights (1979)
Emma Tennant

Wild Palms (1939)
William Faulkner

set: Mississippi

Wild Wales (1862)
George Borrow

Wilhelm Meisters Lehrjahre (1796)
(Wilhelm Meister's Apprenticeship)
Johann Goethe

William Conrad (1950)
Pierre Boulle

Williwaw (1946)
Gore Vidal

Will Warburton (1905) posth
George Gissing

Wilt (1976)
Wilt Alternative, The (1979)
Wilt on High (1984)
Tom Sharpe

Henry Wilt

Wind, The
see ***Vent, Le***

Wind Changes, The (1937)
Olivia Manning

set: Dublin

Windfall (1982)
Desmond Bagley

Windfall (1962)
KM Peyton

Wind in the Willows, The (1908)
Kenneth Grahame
set: riverbank; Toad Hall
Mr Badger
Mr Mole
Mr Rat
Mr Toad

Windlestraws, Working Bullocks (1926)
Katharine Susannah Prichard

Wind on the Moon, The (1944)
Eric Linklater

Window in Thrums, A (1889)
JM Barrie
set: Thrums (actual Kirriemuir)

Wind, Sand and Stars
see ***Terre des hommes***

Winds of War, The (1971)
Herman Wouk

Windsor Castle (1843)
William Harrison Ainsworth

Windy McPherson's Son (1916)
Winesburg, Ohio (1919)
Sherwood Anderson

Winged Man, The (1966)
AE Van Vogt

Winged Seeds (1950)
Katharine Susannah Prichard

Wings of the Dove, The (1902)
Henry James
Kate Croy
Merton Densher (Kate's sometime lover)
Maud Lowder (Kate's aunt)

Winners, The
see ***Premios, Los***

Winnie-the-Pooh (1926) coll
AA Milne
Christopher Robin
Eeyore (donkey)
Kanga
Owl
Piglet
Rabbit
Roo
Winnie-the-Pooh, or Pooh (bear)

Winter Garden (1980)
Beryl Bainbridge

Winter Hawk (1987)
Craig Thomas

Winter Holiday (1933)
Arthur Ransome

Winter in the Hills, A (1970)
John Wain

Winter Journey (1967)
Eva Figes

Winter Kills (1974)
Richard Condon

Winter of Our Discontent, The (1961)
John Steinbeck

Winter of the Birds, The (1975)
Helen Cresswell

Winters of Artifice (1939)
Anaïs Nin

Winter's Tales (1942) coll
Karen Blixen

Winthrop Woman, The (1958)
Anya Seton

Wise Blood (1952)
Flannery O'Connor

Wise Children, The (1966)
Robert Graves

Wise Virgins, The (1914)
Leonard Woolf

Wishing Gold (1970)
Robert Nye

Witch Herbalist of the Remote Town, The (1980)
Amos Tutuola

Witch in the Wood, The (1940)
TH White

Witches of Eastwick, The (1984)
John Updike

Witch's Daughter, The (1966)
Nina Bawden

Witch's Head, The (1885)
H Rider Haggard

Witch Wood (1927)
John Buchan

With Clive in India (1884)
GA Henty

With Fire and Sword (1884)
Henryk Sienkiewicz

Without a City Wall (1968)
Melvyn Bragg

Without Dogma (1891)
Henryk Sienkiewicz

With Roberts to Pretoria (1902)
GA Henty

With the Procession (1895)
Henry Blake Fuller

Witiko (1865-1867) 3 vol
Adalbert stifter

Wives and Daughters (1866) posth unf
Elizabeth Gaskell

set: Hollingford (actual Knutsford)
Lady Cumnor (Cumnor's wife)
Lord Cumnor (local magnate)
Molly Gibson (Gibson's daughter)
Mr Gibson (surgeon)
Osborne Hamley (Hamley's son)
Roger Hamley (Hamley's son)
Squire Hamley
Clare Kirkpatrick (Gibson's 2nd wife-to-be)
Cynthia Kirkpatrick (Clare's daughter)

Wizard of Earthsea, A (1968)
Ursula Le Guin

Wizard of Linn, The (1962)
AE Van Vogt

Wolfsbane (1978)
Craig Thomas

Wolf Solent (1929)
John Cowper Powys

set: West Country

Wolf to the Slaughter (1967)
Ruth Rendell

Inspector Reg Wexford

Wolves of Willoughby Chase, The (1962)
Joan Aiken

Woman Beware Woman (1983)
Emma Tennant

Woman Called Fancy, A (1951)
Frank Yerby

Woman from Sarajevo, The (1946)
Ivo Andric

Woman in Black: A Ghost Story, The (1983)
Susan Hill

Woman in the Sky, A (1973)
James Hanley

Woman in White, The (1860)
Wilkie Collins

set: Hampstead, London; Cumberland
Anne Catherick ('the woman in white')
Laura Fairlie (Sir Percival's soon-to-be wife/Walter's eventual wife)
Mr Fairlie (Laura's uncle)
Count Fosco (Sir Percival's co-conspirator)
Sir Percival Glyde
Marian Halcombe (Laura's half-sister)
Walter Hartright (main narrator)

Woman of Andros, The (1930)
Thornton Wilder

Woman of Rome, The
see ***Romana, La***

Woman of Substance, A (1980)
Barbara Taylor Bradford

Woman Thou Gavest Me, The (1913)
Hall Caine

Woman Who Did, The (1895)
Grant Allen

Women (1978)
Charles Bukowski

Women in His Life, The (1990)
Barbara Taylor Bradford

Women in Love (1920)
DH Lawrence

set: Beldover, the Midlands; Alps
Rupert Birkin (Ursula's eventual husband)
Gudrun Brangwen
Ursula Brangwen (Gudrun's sister)
Gerald Crich (Gudrun's lover)
Loerke (sculptor)

Women, or pour et contre (1818)
Charles Maturin

Women's Room, The (1977)
Marilyn French

Wonderful Adventures of Nils, The
see ***Nils Holgerssons underbara resa genom Sverige***

Wonderful Garden, The (1911)
E Nesbit

Wonderful Visit, The (1895)
HG Wells

Wonderful Wizard of Oz, The (1900)
L Frank Baum

set: Land of Oz; Emerald City
Cowardly Lion
Dorothy
Scarecrow
Tin Woodman
Toto (Dorothy's dog)
Wizard of Oz

Wonderful Years, Wonderful Years (1988)
George V Higgins

Wonderland (1971)
Joyce Carol Oates

Wood and Stone (1915)
John Cowper Powys

Wooden Horse, The (1909)
Hugh Walpole

Wooden Shepherdess, The (1973)
Richard Hughes

Woodlanders, The (1887)
Thomas Hardy

set: Little Hintock, Wessex
Edred Fitzpiers (doctor)
Grace Melbury (Fitzpiers' eventual wife)
Marty South (Giles' admirer)
Giles Winterbourne (ciderman)

Wood Magic (1881)
Richard Jefferies

Woods in Winter, The (1970)
Stella Gibbons

Woodstock (or The Cavalier) (1826)
Walter Scott

set: 1651 (English Civil War) Oxfordshire
Charles II (king-in-exile)
Oliver Cromwell (Lord Protector)
Colonel Mark Everard (Lee's nephew)
Alice Lee (Lee's daughter)
Colonel Albert Lee (Lee's son)
Sir Henry Lee (park ranger)
Roger Wildrake (Cavalier)

Word Child, A (1975)
Iris Murdoch

Word for World Is Forest, The (1977)
Ursula Le Guin

Work (1873)
Louisa M Alcott

Work
see ***Travail***

Workers in the Dawn (1880)
George Gissing

Workers of the Sea, The
see ***Travailleurs de la mer, Les***

World According to Garp, The (1976)
John Irving

Garp

World Brain (1938)
HG Wells

World Decision, The (1916)
Robert Herrick

World Enough and Time (1950)
Robert Penn Warren

World I Never Made, A (1936)
James T Farrell

World in the Evening, The (1954)
Christopher Isherwood

World Is Full of Divorced Women, The (1975)
World Is Full of Married Women, The (1968)
Jackie Collins

World Light
see ***Heimsljós***

World My Wilderness, The (1950)
Rose Macaulay

World of A, The (1948)
(also titled ***The World of Null-A***)
AE Van Vogt

World of Apples, The (1973)
John Cheever

World of Ice, The (1860)
RM Ballantyne

World of Jeeves, The (1967) coll
PG Wodehouse

Reginald Jeeves (Wooster's valet)
Bertie Wooster

World of Love, A (1955)
Elizabeth Bowen

World of Profit, A (1968)
Louis Auchinloss

World of Strangers, A (1958)
Nadine Gordimer

World of William Clissold, The (1926)
HG Wells

World of Windows (1971)
David Benedictus

World's Desire, The (1890)
H Rider Haggard

World's End (1940)
Upton Sinclair

Lanny Budd

World's Fair (1985)
EL Doctorow

Worm of Death, The (1961)
Nicholas Blake

Nigel Strangeways (detective)

Wouldbegoods, The (1901)
E Nesbit

Bastable family

Wounded Name, The (1922)
DK Broster

Wounds (1969)
Maureen Duffy

Wreath for Odomo, A (1956)
Peter Abrahams

Wreath of Roses, A (1950)
Elizabeth Taylor

Camilla Hill (secretary)

Wrecker, The (1892)
RL Stevenson

Wreckers Must Breathe (1940)
Hammond Innes

Wrong Box, The (1889)
RL Stevenson

Wrong Set, The (1949) coll
Angus Wilson

Wunderkind, Das (1914)
(The Child Prodigy)
Thomas Mann

Wunnigel (1879)
Wilhelm Raabe

Wunschfind, Das (1930)
(The Wish Child)
Ina Seidel

Wuthering Heights (1847)
Emily Brontë

set: Thrushcross Grange (Lintons); Wuthering Heights (Earnshaws)
Nelly Dean (Earnshaws' housekeeper)
Catherine Earnshaw (Mr Earnshaw's daughter/Edgar's eventual wife)
Hareton Earnshaw (Hindley's son)
Hindley Earnshaw (Mr Earnshaw's son)
Mr Earnshaw
Heathcliff (orphan, later landlord)
Linton Heathcliff (Heathcliff's son)
Cathy Linton (Edgar's daughter)
Edgar Linton
Isabella Linton (Heathcliff's eventual wife)
Lockwood (narrator/Grange tenant)
Zillah (Heathcliff's servant)

Wyatt's Hurricane (1966)
Desmond Bagley

Wycherley Woman, The (1961)
Ross Macdonald

Wyvern Mystery, The (1869)
Sheridan Le Fanu

Yearling, The (1938)
Marjorie Kinnan Rawlings

Yera or So with Edgar, A (1979)
George V Higgins

Years, The (1937)
Virginia Woolf

Year 1794, The (1913-1918) 3 vol
WS Reymont

Yeast (A Problem) (1850)
Charles Kingsley

Lancelot Smith

Yehuda (1931)
Meyer Levin

Yellowplush Papers, The (1837–8) coll
William Makepeace Thackeray

Yellow Poppy, The (1920)
DK Broster

Yemassee, The (1835)
William Gilmore Simms

set: 18c South Carolina
Occonestoga (Sanutee's son)
Sanutee (Yemassee Indian chief)

You Can't Go Home Again (1940) posth
Thomas Wolfe

You Can't See Around Corners (1947)
Jon Cleary

Youma (1890)
Lafcadio Hearn

Young Adolf (1978)
Beryl Bainbridge

Youngblood Hawke (1962)
Herman Wouk

Young Buglers, The (1880)
GA Henty

Young Caesar (1958)
Rex Warner

Young Cosima, The (1939)
Henry Handel Richardson

Young Diana, The (1918)
Marie Corelli

Young Duke, The (1831)
Benjamin Disraeli

Young Felix (1923)
Frank Swinnerton

Young Franc-Tireurs, The (1872)
GA Henty

Young Fur-Traders, The (1856)
RM Ballantyne

Young Joseph
see ***Junge Joseph, Der***

Young Lions, The (1948)
Irwin Shaw

Young Lonigan (1932)
Young Manhood of Studs Lonigan, The (1934)
James T Farrell

Young Man in Chains
see ***Enfant chargé de chaînes, L'***

Young Master (1906)
Natsume Soseki

Young Shoulders (1982)
John Wain

Young Tom (1944)
Forrest Reid

Young Visiters, The (1919)
Daisy Ashford

Bernard Clark (Ethel's eventual husband)
Ethel Monticue
Mr Salteena (Ethel's admirer)

Young Visitors, The (1965)
John Wain

Young Wife's Tale, A (1974)
William Sansom

You Only Live Twice (1964)
Ian Fleming

James Bond '007' (spy)
M (Bond's boss)
Miss Moneypenny (M's secretary)

Youthful Delaneys, The (1938)
Hugh Walpole

You Want the Right Frame of Reference (1970)
William Cooper

Yvette (1885)
Guy de Maupassant

Z

Zadig (1747)
Voltaire

set: Middle East
Zadig

Zanoni (1842)
Edward Bulwer-Lytton

Zauberberg, Der (1924)
(The Magic Mountain)
Thomas Mann

Zauberring, Der (1813)
(The Magic Ring)
Friedrich Fouqué

Zaÿde (1670)
Marie-Madeleine La Fayette

Zazie dans le Métro (1959)
(Zazie in the Metro)
Raymond Queneau

Zeluco (1786)
John Moore

Ziemia ulro (1977)
Czeslaw Milosz

Zincali, The (or An Account of the Gypsies in Spain) (1841)
George Borrow

Zisha (1897)
Marie Corelli

Zlateh the Goat (1966) coll
Isaac Bashevis Singer

Zniewolony umysl (1953)
Czeslaw Milosz

Zorba the Greek (1946)
Nikos Kazantzakis

set: Crete
Zorba (Greek peasant)

Zuckerman Unbound (1981)
Philip Roth

Nathaniel Zuckerman (novelist)

Zug war pünktlich, Der (1949)
(The Train Was on Time)
Heinrich Böll

Zuleika Dobson (1911)
Max Beerbohm

set: Judas College, Oxford
Zuleika Dobson (frivolous beauty)

Züricher Novellen (1878) coll
(Zürich Novels)
Gottfried Keller

Zu spät? (1940)
(Too Late?)
Hans Habe

Zwölf Nächte (1838)
(Twelfth Night)
Willibald Alexis

Characters

A

Aben-Hamet
Les Aventures du dernier Abencérage
Chateaubriand

Ablewhite, Godfrey
The Moonstone
Collins

Adams, Parson
The Adventures of Joseph Andrews
Fielding

Adolphe
Adolphe
Constant

Adso of Melk
Il nome della rosa
Eco

Adverse, Anthony
Anthony Adverse
Allen

Aggie
The Awkward Age
James

Ahab, Captain
Moby-Dick
Melville

Akela
The Jungle Books
Kipling

Aldclyffe, Miss
Desperate Remedies
Hardy

Alden, Oliver
The Last Puritan
Santayana

Alethea, Aunt
The Way of All Flesh
Butler

Alex
A Clockwork Orange
Burgess

Ali
The Heart of the Matter
Greene

Alice
Alice's Adventures in Wonderland; Through the Looking-Glass
Carroll

Allen, Arabella
Allen, Benjamin
Pickwick Papers
Dickens

Allen, Mr
Allen, Mrs
Northanger Abbey
Austen

Alleyn, Inspector Roderick
A Man Lay Dead; Enter A Murderer; Vintage Murder; Overture to Death; Surfeit of Lampreys; Died in the Wool; Final Curtain; Swing, Brother, Swing; Opening Night; Scales of Justice; Off with His Head; False Scent; Dead Water; Clutch of Constables; When in Rome; Black As He's Painted; Last Ditch; Grave Mistake; Photo-Finish; Light Thickens
Marsh

Allnutt, Charlie
The African Queen
Forester

Allworthy, Bridget
Allworthy, Squire
The History of Tom Jones
Fielding

Almayer, Kaspar
Almayer, Nina
Almayer's Folly
Conrad

Alm-Uncle
Heidi
Spyri

Alvin
The Tragic Comedians
Meredith

Amaury
Volupté
Sainte-Beuve

Ambrosio
The Monk
Lewis

Amedroz, Clara
Amedroz, Mr
The Belton Estate
Trollope

Amelia Jane
Naughty Amelia Jane & others
Blyton

Amélie
René
Chateaubriand

Amerigo, Prince
The Golden Bowl
James

Amrei
Barfüssele
Auerbach

Amy
The Heir of Redclyffe
Yonge

Amy
Roxana
Defoe

Ananse
The Children of Ananse
Appiah

Andrews, Joseph
The Adventures of Joseph Andrews
Fielding

Andrews, Pamela
Pamela
Richardson

Andrews, Shamela (Pamela)
Shamela Andrews
Fielding

Angstrom, Harry
Angstrom, Janice
Rabbit, Run; Rabbit Redux; Rabbit is Rich; Rabbit at Rest
Updike

Anjou, Margaret of
Anne of Geierstein
Scott

Anne
Five on a Treasure Island & others
Blyton

Ansell, Stewart
The Longest Journey
Forster

Apollyon
The Pilgrim's Progress
Bunyan

Appleby, John
Death at the President's Lodging; Hamlet's Revenge!; The Hawk and the Hacksaw; The Secret Vanguard; Appleby's End; Silence Observed; A Connoisseur's Case; Death at the Chase; Sheiks and Adders
Stewart

Apthorpe
Men at Arms
Waugh

Arabin, Dr Francis
Barchester Towers; The Last Chronicle of Barset
Trollope

Aram, Eugene
Eugene Aram
Bulwer-Lytton

Aramis
Les Trois Mousquetaires; Vingt Ans après; Le Vicomte de Bragelonne
Dumas

Arbuthnott, Sandy
The Thirty-Nine Steps; The Courts of the Morning; The Island of Sheep
Buchan

Archer, Dallas
Archer, Newland
The Age of Innocence
Wharton

Archer, Isabel
The Portrait of a Lady
James

Arden, Edred
Arden, Elfrida
The House of Arden
Nesbit

Ardenti, Colonel
Foucault's Pendulum
Eco

Argyle, Duke of
The Heart of Midlothian
Scott

Argyle, Marquess of
A Legend of Montrose
Scott

Armine, Ferdinand
Henrietta Temple
Disraeli

Armitage, Jacob
Children of the New Forest
Marryat

Arnall, Father
A Portrait of the Artist as a Young Man
Joyce

Arnold, Dr
Tom Brown's Schooldays
Hughes

Arnoux, Madame
L'Education sentimentale
Flaubert

Arobin
The Awakening
Chopin

Arrietty
The Borrowers; The Borrowers Afield; The Borrowers Afloat; The Borrowers Aloft; The Borrowers Avenged
Norton

Artful Dodger, The
see **Dawkins, John**

Arthur
The Story of Babar & others
Brunhoff

Arthur, George
Tom Brown's Schooldays
Hughes

Arundel, Clare
Lothair
Disraeli

Ashburnham, Captain
Ashburnham, Leonora
The Good Soldier
Ford

Ashley, Lady Brett
The Sun Also Rises
Hemingway

Ashley, Philip
My Cousin Rachel
Du Maurier

Ashton, Lady
Ashton, Lord
Ashton, Lucy
The Bride of Lammermoor
Scott

Aspern, Jeffrey
The Aspern Papers
James

Assingham, Fanny
The Golden Bowl
James

Atala
Atala; René
Chateaubriand

Athos
Les Trois Mousquetaires; Vingt Ans après; Le Vicomte de Bragelonne
Dumas

Atreides, Paul
Dune; Dune Messiah
Herbert

Attentive, Mr
The Life and Death of Mr Badman
Bunyan

Aubéry, Jean-Benoît
Frenchman's Creek
Du Maurier

Aubry, Père
Atala
Chateaubriand

Augusta, Aunt
Travels with My Aunt
Greene

Aurelia
The Life and Adventures of Sir Launcelot Greaves
Smollett

Avenel, Mary (Lady of)
The Monastery; The Abbot
Scott

Avis
The Iron Heel
London

Ayesha
She; Ayesha
Haggard

Aylmer, Captain
Aylmer, Lady
The Belton Estate
Trollope

Aylwin, Henry
Aylwin
Watts-Dunton

Aziz, Dr
A Passage to India
Forster

B

B, Lady
B, Mr
Pamela
Richardson

Babar
The Story of Babar & others
Brunhoff

Babbitt, George
Babbitt
Lewis

Badger, Mr
The Wind in the Willows
Grahame

Badman, Mr
The Life and Death of Mr Badman
Bunyan

Baggins, Bilbo
Baggins, Frodo
The Hobbit; The Lord of the Rings
Tolkien

Bagheera
The Jungle Books
Kipling

Bagnet, Malta
Bagnet, Matthew
Bagnet, Mrs
Bagnet, Quebec
Bagnet, Woolwich
Bleak House
Dickens

Baines, Constance
Baines, Sophia
The Old Wives' Tale
Bennett

Balatka, Nina
Nina Balatka
Trollope

Balderstone, Caleb
The Bride of Lammermoor
Scott

Balfour, David
Kidnapped; Catriona
Stevenson

Balfour, John
Old Mortality
Scott

Baloo
The Jungle Books
Kipling

Balthazar
Justine; Balthazar; Mountolive; Clea
Durrell

Balwhidder, Rev Michael
Annals of the Parish
Galt

Bambi
Bambi; Bambis Kinder
Salten

Bandar-Log
The Jungle Books
Kipling

Barclay, Wilfred
The Paper Men
Golding

Bardell, Martha
Pickwick Papers
Dickens

Barfield, Mr
Barfield, Mrs
Esther Waters
Moore

Barkis
David Copperfield
Dickens

Barkley, Catherine
A Farewell to Arms
Hemingway

Barnes, Jake
The Sun Also Rises
Hemingway

Baron, The
Meet the Baron & others
Creasey

Barrington, Mr
The Ragged Trousered Philanthropist
Tressell

Barry, Cornelius
Barry, Redmond
The Luck of Barry Lyndon
Thackeray

Barsad, John
see **Pross, Solomon**

Bart, Lily
The House of Mirth
Wharton

Bartlett, Miss
A Room with a View
Forster

Barton, John
Barton, Mary
Mary Barton
Gaskell

Basilius, Duke of
Arcadia
Sidney

Bassett, Sir Charles
Bassett, Lady
Bassett, Richard
A Terrible Temptation
Reade

Bastable family
The Story of the Treasure-Seekers; The Wouldbegoods; The New Treasure-Seekers
Nesbit

Bates
Stalky & Co
Kipling

Bates, Miss
Emma
Austen

Bates, Norman
Psycho; Psycho II
Bloch

Bath, Colonel
Amelia
Fielding

Batsby, Captain
Ayala's Angel
Trollope

Bawcombe, Caleb
A Shepherd's Life
Hudson

Baxter, Rupert 'the efficient'
Something Fresh; Leave It to Psmith; Summer Lightning; Uncle Fred in the Springtime
Wodehouse

Beach
Something Fresh; Leave It to Psmith; Summer Lightning; Heavy Weather; Pigs Have Wings; Service with a Smile; Galahad at Blandings; A Pelican at Blandings; Sunset at Blandings
Wodehouse

Beauchamp, Nevil
Beauchamp's Career
Meredith

Beaver, John
A Handful of Dust
Waugh

Beavis, Anthony
Eyeless in Gaza
Huxley

Beazley, Tom
Jacob Faithful
Marryat

Beck, Madame
Villette
Brontë

Bede, Adam
Bede, Seth
Adam Bede
Eliot

Bedonebyasyoudid, Mrs
The Water-Babies
Kingsley

Beebe, Mr
A Room with a View
Forster

Beetle
Stalky & Co
Kipling

Belbo, Jacopo
Foucault's Pendulum
Eco

Beleau, Roxana
Roxana
Defoe

Belford, John
Clarissa
Richardson

Bell, Laura
The History of Pendennis
Thackeray

Bellenden, Edith
Old Mortality
Scott

Bellingham, Henry
Ruth
Gaskell

Belloni, Emilia Sandra
Sandra Belloni; Vittoria
Meredith

Belmont, Evelina
Belmont, Sir John
Evelina
Burney

Beltham, Squire
The Adventures of Harry Richmond
Meredith

Belton, Will
The Belton Estate
Thackeray

Ben-Hur, Judah
Ben-Hur
Wallace

Bennet, Catherine
Bennet, Elizabeth
Bennet, Jane
Bennet, Lydia
Bennet, Mary
Bennet, Mr
Bennet, Mrs
Pride and Prejudice
Austen

Bennet, Mrs
Amelia
Fielding

Benson, Thurston
Ruth
Gaskell

Benwick, Captain
Persuasion
Austen

Beorn
The Hobbit; The Lord of the Rings
Tolkien

Berengaria
The Talisman
Scott

Berenger, Eveline
The Betrothed
Scott

Bergeret, Monsieur
L'Histoire contemporaine
France

Bergotte
À la recherche du temps perdu
Proust

Berners, Belle
Lavengro; The Romany Rye
Borrow

Bertalda
Undine
Fouqué

Bertram, Edmund
Bertram, Julia
Bertram, Lady
Bertram, Maria
Bertram, Sir Thomas
Bertram, Tom
Mansfield Park
Austen

Bertram, George
The Bertrams
Trollope

Bertram, Harry
Guy Mannering
Scott

Bertrand, Cary
Bertrand, Mr
Loser Takes All
Greene

Betteredge, Gabriel
The Moonstone
Collins

Betty
Cousin Phillis
Gaskell

Beverley, Alice
Beverley, Edith
Beverley, Edward
Beverley, Humphrey
Children of the New Forest
Marryat

Beverley, Cecilia
Cecilia
Burney

Bezushov, Pierre
War and Peace
Tolstoy

Bhaer, Professor
Good Wives; Little Men; Jo's Boys
Alcott

Bianca
Les Aventures du dernier Abencérage
Chateaubriand

Bidlake, Walter
Point Counter Point
Huxley

Biederman, Arnold
Anne of Geierstein
Scott

Biffen, Harold
New Grub Street
Gissing

'Big Brother'
Nineteen Eighty-Four
Orwell

Big Ears
Little Noddy Goes to Toyland & others
Blyton

Biggles
see **Bigglesworth**

Bigglesworth, Major James 'Biggles'
The Camels Are Coming & others
Johns

Biggs, Mr
Mr Midshipman Easy
Marryat

Bigwig
Watership Down
Adams

Bingley, Charles
Pride and Prejudice
Austen

Birdseye, Miss
The Bostonians
James

Birkin, Rupert
Women in Love
Lawrence

Biswas, Mr
A House for Mr Biswas
Naipaul

Bittern, Captain
Anthony Adverse
Allen

Black Beauty
Black Beauty
Sewell

Black Bess
Rookwood
Ainsworth

Blackett, Nancy
Blackett, Peggy
Swallows and Amazons & others
Ransome

Black Michael
The Prisoner of Zenda
Hope

Blackpool, Stephen
Hard Times
Dickens

Blackstick
The Rose and the Ring
Thackeray

Blake, Franklin
The Moonstone
Collins

Blake, Sexton
The Missing Millionaire & others
Meredith
(plus later by many authors)

Blakeney, Sir Percy
The Scarlet Pimpernel & others
Orczy

Blancove, Edward
Rhoda Fleming
Meredith

Blandings, Empress of
Summer Lightning; Heavy Weather; Uncle Fred in the Springtime; Full Moon; Pigs Have Wings; Service with a Smile; Galahad at Blandings; A Pelican at Blandings; Sunset at Blandings
Wodehouse

Blas, Gil
Gil Blas
Lesage

Blifil, Captain
The History of Tom Jones
Fielding

Blimber, Doctor
Dombey and Son
Dickens

Bloch
À la recherche du temps perdu
Proust

Bloody Bill
The Coral Island
Ballantyne

Bloomfield family
Agnes Grey
Brontë

Bobbsey, Bert and Nan
Bobbsey, Freddie and Flossie
Bobbsey Twins & others
Hope

Bodenheim, Maxwell
A Jew in Love
Hecht

Boffin, Henrietta
Boffin, Nicodemus
Our Mutual Friend
Dickens

Bois-Guilbert
Ivanhoe
Scott

Bold, Eleanor (née Harding)
Bold, John
The Warden; Barchester Towers
Trollope

Boldwood, Farmer
Far from the Madding Crowd
Hardy

Bolitho, Richard
To Glory We Steer; Enemy in Sight!; Sloop of War; Richard Bolitho – Midshipman; Passage to Mutiny; The Inshore Squadron; Stand into Danger; Success to the Brave; Colours Aloft!; Honour This Day
Kent

Bolkonski, Prince André
War and Peace
Tolstoy

Bond, James
Casino Royale; Live and Let Die; Moonraker; Diamonds Are Forever; From Russia, with Love; Dr No; Goldfinger; For Your Eyes Only; Thunderball; The Spy Who Loved Me; On Her Majesty's Secret Service; You Only Live Twice; The Man with the Golden Gun; Octopussy; The Living Daylights
Fleming

Bone, George Harvey
Hangover Square
Hamilton

Bones, Billy
Treasure Island
Stevenson

Booby, Lady
Booby, Squire
Booby, Sir Thomas
The Adventures of Joseph Andrews
Fielding

Booby, Mr
Shamela Andrews
Fielding

Boot, John
Boot, William
Scoop
Waugh

Booth, Amelia
Booth, William
Amelia
Fielding

Bordereau, Julia
Bordereau, Miss Tina
The Aspern Papers
James

Bosinney, Philip
The Forsyte Saga
Galsworthy

Bott, Violet Elizabeth
The Outlaws & others
Crompton

Boule-de-Suif
Boule-de-Suif
Maupassant

Bounderby, Josiah
Hard Times
Dickens

Bovary, Charles
Bovary, Madame Emma
Madame Bovary
Flaubert

Bowles, Sally
Goodbye to Berlin
Isherwood

Bowling, George
Bowling, Hilda
Coming Up for Air
Orwell

Bowling, Tom
The Adventures of Roderick Random
Smollett

Boxer
Animal farm
Orwell

Bozzle
He Knew He Was Right
Trollope

Brabazon, Julie
The Claverings
Bennett

Bradwardine, Rose
Waverley
Scott

Brady, Caithleen 'Cait'
The Country Girls; The Lonely Girl; Girls in Their Married Bliss
O'Brien

Bramble, Matthew
Bramble, Tabitha
The Expedition of Humphry Clinker
Smollett

Brander, Senator
Jennie Gerhardt
Dreiser

Brandon, Colonel
Sense and Sensibility
Austen

Brangwen, Anna
Brangwen, Gudrun
Brangwen, Mrs
Brangwen, Tom
Brangwen, Ursula
Brangwen, Will
The Rainbow; Women in Love (Gudrun and Ursula only)
Lawrence

Brass, Sampson
The Old Curiosity Shop
Dickens

Brattle, Carry
Brattle, Sam
The Vicar of Bullhampton
Trollope

Bray, Madeline
Bray, Walter
Nicholas Nickleby
Dickens

Bread, Mrs
The American
James

Breck, Alan
Kidnapped; Catriona
Stevenson

Brennan, Bridget 'Baba'
The Country Girls; The Lonely Girl; Girls in Their Married Bliss
O'Brien

Brereton, Clara
Sanditon
Austen

Brer Fox
Brer Rabbit
Uncle Remus; Nights with Uncle Remus; Uncle Remus and His Friends; Uncle Remus and Brer Rabbit; Uncle Remus and the Little Boy
Harris

Bretton, John
Villette
Brontë

Bridehead, Sue
Jude the Obscure
Hardy

Bridgenorth, Alice
Bridgenorth, Major
Peveril of the Peak
Scott

Brissenden, Russ
Martin Eden
London

Britling, Hugh
Mr Britling Sees It Through
Wells

Brobdingnagians
Gulliver's Travels
Swift

Brodie, Jean
The Prime of Miss Jean Brodie
Spark

Bronzomarte
The Life and Adventures of Sir Launcelot Greaves
Smollett

Brooke, Celia
Brooke, Dorothea
Middlemarch
Eliot

Brooke, John
Little Women; Good Wives; Little Men; Jo's Boys
Alcott

Brookenham, Mrs
Brookenham, Nanda
The Awkward Age
James

Brown, Captain
Cranford
Gaskell

Brown, Father
The Innocence of Father Brown & others
Chesterton

Brown, Ingrid
Brown, Vic
A Kind of Loving; The Watchers on the Shore; Right True End
Barstow

Brown, Mr
The Comedians
Greene

Brown, Robert
Brown, William
The Outlaws & others
Crompton

Brown, Tom
Tom Brown's Schooldays; Tom Brown at Oxford
Hughes

Brown, Velvet
National Velvet
Bagnold

Browne, Susan
Room at the Top; Life at the Top
Braine

Brownlow, Mr
Oliver Twist
Dickens

Bruno
Sylvie and Bruno
Carroll

Buchanan, Daisy
Buchanan, Tom
The Great Gatsby
Fitzgerald

Buck
The Call of the Wild
London

Bucket, Inspector
Bleak House
Dickens

Buckett, Charlie
Charlie and the Chocolate Factory; Charlie and the Great Glass Elevator
Dahl

Bucklaw, Laird of
The Bride of Lammermoor
Scott

Bud, Rosa
The Mystery of Edwin Drood
Dickens

Budd, Billy
Billy Budd, Foretopman
Melville

Budd, Lanny
World's End; Dragon's Teeth; Presidential Mission; The Return of Lanny Budd
Sinclair

Buddenbrook family
Buddenbrooks
Mann

Buendía family
Cien años de soledad
García Márquez

Buldeo
The Jungle Books
Kipling

Bull, Johnny
Billy Bunter of Greyfriars School & others
Richards

Bull, Peter
The African Queen
Forester

Bullingdon, Viscount
The Luck of Barry Lyndon
Thackeray

Bull's Eye
Oliver Twist
Dickens

Bulstrode, Mr
Bulstrode, Mrs
Middlemarch
Eliot

Bultitude, Dick
Bultitude, Paul
Vice Versa
Anstey

Bumble
Bumble, Mrs
Oliver Twist
Dickens

Bumppo, Natty
The Pioneer; The Last of the Mohicans; The Prairie; The Pathfinder; The Deerslayer
Cooper

Bundren, Addie
Bundren, Anse
Bundren, Darl
Bundren, Dewey
As I Lay Dying
Faulkner

Bunny
The Amateur Cracksman & others
Hornung

Bunter
Whose Body?; Clouds of Witness; Unnatural Death; The Unpleasantness at the Bellona Club; Lord Peter Views the Body; Strong Poison; The Five Red Herrings; Have His Carcase; Murder Must Advertise; Hangman's Holiday; The Nine Tailors; Gaudy Night; Busman's Honeymoon; In the Teeth of the Evidence; Striding Folly
Sayers

Bunter, Billy
Billy Bunter of Greyfriars School & others
Richards

Burch, Lucas
Burden, Joanna
Light in August
Faulkner

Burgess, Ted
The Go-Between
LP Hartley

Burgundy, Duke of
Anne of Geierstein
Scott

Burke
The Absentee
Edgeworth

Burlap
Point Counter Point
Huxley

Burns, Helen
Jane Eyre
Brontë

Burton, Florence
The Claverings
Trollope

Butler, Reuben
The Heart of Midlothian
Scott

Butler, Rhett
Gone with the Wind
Mitchell

Buzfuz, Serjeant
Pickwick Papers
Dickens

Byron, Harriet
The History of Sir Charles Grandison
Richardson

C

Cadfael, Brother
A Morbid Taste for Bones & others
Peters

Cadwallader, Mrs
Cadwallader, Rev
Middlemarch
Eliot

Calcott, Jack
Kangaroo
Lawrence

Camacho
Don Quixote
Cervantes

Cameron, Dr
Beyond This Place
Cronin

Camilla
The Adventures of David Simple
Fielding

Camille
Le Petit Chose
Daudet

Campbell family
The Settlers in Canada
Marryat

Campbell, Colin
Kidnapped
Stevenson

Campion, Albert
Crime at Black Dudley; Police at the Funeral; Death of a Ghost; Flowers for the Judge; Coroner's Pidgin; More Work for the Undertaker; The Tiger in the Smoke; The Beckoning Lady; The China Governess; The Mind Readers
Allingham

Candide
Candide
Voltaire

Canty, Tom
The Prince and the Pauper
Twain

Carabas, Marquis of
Vivian Grey
Disraeli

Carella, Gino
Where Angels Fear to Tread
Forster

Carey, Mother
The Water-Babies
Kingsley

Carey, Philip
Of Human Bondage
Maugham

Carker, James
Dombey and Son
Dickens

Carr, Doctor
Carr, Katy
What Katy Did; What Katy Did at School; What Katy Did Next
Coolidge

Carrasco, Samson
Don Quixote
Cervantes

Carraway, Nick
The Great Gatsby
Fitzgerald

Carraze, Delphine
Madame Delphine
Cable

Carstairs, Lord
Dr Wortle's School
Trollope

Carstone, Richard
Bleak House
Dickens

Carter, Mr
Jennings Goes to School & others
Buckeridge

Carter, Samuel
The Dolly Dialogues
Hope

Carton, Sydney
A Tale of Two Cities
Dickens

Casaubon
Foucault's Pendulum
Eco

Casaubon, Edward
Middlemarch
Eliot

Casby, Christopher
Little Dorrit
Dickens

Cass, Dunstan
Cass, Eppie
Cass, Godfrey
Silas Marner
Eliot

Castlewood, Lady
Castlewood, Lord
The History of Henry Esmond Esquire
Thackeray

Caterpillar
Alice's Adventures in Wonderland
Carroll

Catherick, Anne
The Woman in White
Collins

Caulfield, Holden
Caulfield, Phoebe
The Catcher in the Rye
Salinger

Cecil, Hon Bertie
Under Two Flags
Ouida

Cedric
Ivanhoe
Scott

Celeste
The Story of Babar & others
Brunhoff

Chactas
Atala; René
Chateaubriand

Chadband, Rev
Bleak House
Dickens

Chaffanbrass, Mr
Orley Farm; Phineas Redux
Trollope

Challenger, Professor
The Lost World; The Poison Belt; The Land of Mist; The Maracot Deep
Doyle

Chambers
Pudd'nhead Wilson
Twain

Chan, Charlie
The House without a Key & others
Biggers

Chancellor, Olive
The Bostonians
James

Charles II
Woodstock
Scott

Charles Edward, Prince
Waverley
Scott

Charles, Nick
The Thin Man
Hammett

Charles the Bold
Quentin Durward
Scott

Charlus
À la recherche du temps perdu
Proust

Chase, Jack
White-Jacket
Melville

Chatterley, Sir Clifford
Chatterley, Lady Constance
Lady Chatterley's Lover
Lawrence

Chee-Chee
The Story of Dr Dolittle & others
Lofting

Cheeryble, Charles
Cheeryble, Edwin
Cheeryble, Frank
Nicholas Nickleby
Dickens

Chelkash
Chelkash
Gorky

Cherokee Sal
The Luck of Roaring Camp
Harte

Cherry, Bob
Billy Bunter of Greyfriars School & others
Richards

Cheshire Cat
Alice's Adventures in Wonderland
Carroll

Chester, Edward
Chester, John
Barnaby Rudge
Dickens

Chettam, Sir James
Middlemarch
Eliot

Cheyne, Harvey
Captains Courageous
Kipling

Chichikov
Dead Souls
Gogol

Chickerel
Chickerel, Ethelberta
Chickerel, Picotee
The Hand of Ethelberta
Hardy

Chil
The Jungle Books
Kipling

Chiltern, Lord
Phineas Finn
Trollope

Ching
The Good Earth
Buck

Chingachgook
The Pioneers; The Last of the Mohicans; The Pathfinder; The Deerslayer
Cooper

Chipping, Mr
Goodbye Mr Chips
Hilton

Chita
Tarzan of the Apes & others
Burroughs

Chivery, John
Chivery, Young John
Little Dorrit
Dickens

Chloe, Aunt
Uncle Tom's Cabin
Stowe

Christian
Christiana
The Pilgrim's Progress
Bunyan

Christina
Flambards; The Edge of the Cloud; Flambards in Summer; Flambards Divided
Peyton

Christmas, Joe
Light in August
Faulkner

Christopher Robin
Winnie-the-Pooh; The House at Pooh Corner
Milne

Chuchundra
The Jungle Books
Kipling

Chucks, Mr
Peter Simple
Marryat

Churchill, Frank
Emma
Austen

Chuzzlewit, Anthony
Chuzzlewit, Jonas
Chuzzlewit, Martin Jnr
Chuzzlewit, Martin Snr
Martin Chuzzlewit
Dickens

Cinq-Mars, Marquis de
Cinq-Mars
Vigny

Citrine, Charlie
Humboldt's Gift
Bellow

Claggart, John
Billy Budd, Foretopman
Melville

Claiborne, Constance
Martin Faber
Simms

Clare, Ada
Bleak House
Dickens

Clare, Angel
Tess of the D'Urbervilles
Hardy

Claret, Captain
White-Jacket
Melville

Clark, Bernard
The Young Visiters
Ashford

Claude, Sir
What Maisie Knew
James

Claudine
Claudine à l'école & others
Colette

Clavell, Miss
Madeline
Bemelmans

Clavering, Henry
The Claverings
Trollope

Clay, Mrs
Persuasion
Austen

Clayhanger, Edwin
Clayhanger; Hilda Lessways; These Twain
Bennett

Claypole, Noah
Oliver Twist
Dickens

Clayton, Edward
Dred
Stowe

Clea
Justine; Balthazar; Mountolive; Clea
Durrell

Clennam, Arthur
Clennam, Mrs
Little Dorrit
Dickens

Clephane, Anne
Clephane, Kate
The Mother's Recompense
Wharton

Cleveland
The Pirate
Scott

Clinker, Humphry
The Expedition of Humphry Clinker
Smollett

Clinton, Harry
The Fool of Quality
Brooke

Clonbrony, Lady
Clonbrony, Lord
The Absentee
Edgeworth

Clotilde
The Tragic Comedians
Meredith

Cly, Roger
A Tale of two Cities
Dickens

Clytie
Absalom, Absalom!
Faulkner

Cobb, Georgiana
A Kentucky Cardinal; Aftermath
Allen

Codlin
The Old Curiosity Shop
Dickens

Coejemans, Andries
The Chainbearer
Cooper

Colambre, Lord
The Absentee
Edgeworth

Colin, Doctor
A Burnt-Out Case
Greene

Colleoni
Brighton Rock
Greene

Collins, William
Pride and Prejudice
Austen

Colston, Leo
The Go-Between
Hartley

Compeyson
Great Expectations
Dickens

Compson family
The Sound and the Fury
Faulkner

Coningsby, Harry
Coningsby
Disraeli

Constantine, Lady
Two on a Tower
Hardy

Cooley, 'Kangaroo' Ben
Kangaroo
Lawrence

Copper, Lord
Scoop
Waugh

Copperfield, David
Copperfield, Mrs
David Copperfield
Dickens

Copplestone, Reverend
The Warden's Niece
Avery

Cord, Jonas
The Carpetbaggers
Robbins

Corde, Albert
The Dean's December
Bellow

Corisande, Lady
Lothair
Disraeli

Corleone, Don
Corleone, Michael
The Godfather
Puzo

Cornelius, Jerry
The Final Programme; A Cure for Cancer; The English Assassin
Moorcock

Coryn, Rachel
My Cousin Rachel
Du Maurier

Cosette
Les Misérables
Hugo

Cosway, Antoinette
Wide Sargasso Sea
Rhys

Coupeau
Les Rougon-Macquart
Zola

Coverdale, Miles
The Blithedale Romance
Hawthorne

Cowardly Lion
The Wonderful Wizard of Oz
Baum

Crabshaw
The Life and Adventures of Sir Launcelot Greaves
Smollett

Crane, Edwina
The Jewel in the Crown
Scott

Crane, Ichabod
The Sketch Book
Irving

Cratchit, Bob
Cratchit, `Tiny' Tim
A Christmas Carol
Dickens

Crawford, Henry
Crawford, Mary
Mansfield Park
Austen

Crawford, Lord
Quentin Durward
Scott

Crawley, Grace
The Last Chronicle of Barset
Trollope

Crawley, Josiah
Framley Parsonage; The Last Chronicle of Barset
Trollope

Crawley, Sir Pitt
Crawley, Rawdon
Vanity Fair
Thackeray

Creakle
David Copperfield
Dickens

Cregan
The Collegians
Griffin

Creighton, Colonel
Kim
Kipling

Crewe, Sara
Sara Crewe
Burnett

Crewler, Sophy
David Copperfield
Dickens

Crich, Gerald
Women in Love
Lawrence

Crimsworth, William
The Professor
Brontë

Crisparkle, Canon Septimus
The Mystery of Edwin Drood
Dickens

Cripps, John
Dred
Stowe

Croft, Admiral
Croft, Mrs
Persuasion
Austen

Cromwell, Oliver
Woodstock
Scott

Crosbie, Adolphus
The Small House at Allington
Trollope

Crosnel, Renée de
Beauchamp's Career
Meredith

Crouchback, Guy
Men at Arms; Officers and Gentlemen; Unconditional Surrender
Waugh

Crowne, Lenina
Brave New World
Huxley

Croy, Kate
The Wings of the Dove
James

Croye, Countess Isabelle de
Quentin Durward
Scott

Crummles, Vincent
Nicholas Nickleby
Dickens

Cruncher, Jerry
A Tale of Two Cities
Dickens

Crusoe, Robinson
Robinson Crusoe
Defoe

Cuckoo
The Good Earth
Buck

Cuff, Sergeant
The Moonstone
Collins

Culloden, Lord
Lothair
Disraeli

Cumnor, Lady
Cumnor, Lord
Wives and Daughters
Gaskell

Cunégonde
Candide
Voltaire

Curtis, Sir Harry
King Solomon's Mines
Haggard

Cute, Alderman
The Chimes
Dickens

Cuthbert, Marilla
Cuthbert, Matthew
Anne of Green Gables
Montgomery

Cuticle, Mr
White-Jacket
Melville

Cuttle, Captain
Dombey and Son
Dickens

Cypress, Mr
Nightmare Abbey
Peacock

D

Dab-Dab
The Story of Dr Dolittle & others
Lofting

Daggoo
Moby-Dick
Melville

Daisy, Solomon
Barnaby Rudge
Dickens

Dale, Bell
Dale, Lily
The Small House at Allington
Trollope

Dale, Laetitia
The Egoist
Meredith

Dalgarno, Lord
The Fortunes of Nigel
Scott

Dalgliesh, Adam
Cover Her Face; A Mind to Murder; Unnatural Causes; Shroud for a Nightingale; The Black Tower; Death of an Expert Witness; A Taste for Death; Devices and Desires
James

Dalloway, Clarissa
Dalloway, Richard
Mrs Dalloway
Woolf

Damian
The Betrothed
Scott

Dan
Puck of Pook's Hill
Kipling

Daneeka, Doc
Catch-22
Heller

Dangerfield, Sebastian
The Ginger Man
Donleavy

Dannisburgh, Lord
Diana of the Crossways
Meredith

Dantès, Edmond
Le Comte de Monte-Cristo
Dumas

Danvers, Mrs
Rebecca
Du Maurier

Dapple
Don Quixote
Cervantes

Darbishire
Jennings Goes to School & others
Buckeridge

Darcy, Fitzwilliam
Darcy, Georgiana
Pride and Prejudice
Austen

Darley, Helen
Elsie Venner
Holmes

Darley, LG
Justine; Balthazar; Mountolive; Clea
Durrell

Darnay, Charles
see **St Évrémonde, Charles**

Darnel
The Life and Adventures of Sir Launcelot Greaves
Smollett

Darrell, Larry
The Razor's Edge
Maugham

D'Artagnan
Les Trois Mousquetaires; Vingt Ans après; Le Vicomte de Bragelonne
Dumas

Darzee
The Jungle Books
Kipling

Dashwood, Elinor
Dashwood, Henry
Dashwood, John
Dashwood, Margaret
Dashwood, Marianne
Dashwood, Mrs
Sense and Sensibility
Austen

Datchery, Dick
The Mystery of Edwin Drood
Dickens

'Dauphin'
The Adventures of Huckleberry Finn
Twain

Davers, Lady
Pamela
Richardson

Dawes, Baxter
Dawes, Clara
Sons and Lovers
Lawrence

Dawkins, John
Oliver Twist
Dickens

Dawson, Dave
God's Little Acre
Caldwell

Day, Fancy
Under the Greenwood Tree
Hardy

Dean, Nelly
Wuthering Heights
Brontë

Dean, Susie
The Good Companions
Priestley

Deane, Lucy
The Mill on the Floss
Eliot

Deans, Effie
Deans, Jeanie
The Heart of Midlothian
Scott

De Barral, Flora
Chance
Conrad

De Bellegarde, Marquis
De Bellegarde, Marquise
De Bellegarde, Valentin
The American
James

De Bourgh, Lady Catherine
Pride and Prejudice
Austen

De Bray, Dominique
Dominique
Fromentin

De Cintre, Claire
The American
James

De Courcy, Lady
Lady Susan
Austen

De Courcy, Lady Alexandrina
The Small House at Allington
Trollope

Dedalus, Stephen
A Portrait of the Artist as a Young Man; Ulysses
Joyce

Dedlock, Lady
Dedlock, Sir Leicester
Bleak House
Dickens

Defarge, Ernest
Defarge, Madame
A Tale of Two Cities
Dickens

De Galais, Frantz
De Galais, Yvonne
Le Grand Meaulnes
Alain-Fournier

De Grapion family
The Grandissimes
Cable

De Lacy, Hugo
The Betrothed
Scott

De La Fuente, Dolores
Anthony Adverse
Allen

De La Marck, William
Quentin Durward
Scott

Delarue, Mathieu
Les Chemins de la Liberté
Sartre

Del Dongo, Fabrice
Le Chartreuse de Parme
Stendhal

Delorme, Marion
Cinq-Mars
Vigny

Delphine
Les Contes du chat perché
Aymé

De Melville, Count
The Adventures of Ferdinand Count Fathom
Smollett

Demian, Max
Demian
Hesse

Denham, Sir Edward
Denham, Miss
Sanditon
Austen

Denham, Jenny
Beauchamp's Career
Meredith

Dennis
Barnaby Rudge
Dickens

Densher, Merton
The Wings of the Dove
James

Dent, Arthur
The Hitch-Hiker's Guide to the Galaxy
Adams

Deronda, Daniel
Daniel Deronda
Eliot

Derriman, Festus
The Trumpet-Major
Hardy

Desborough, Lucy
The Ordeal of Richard Feverel
Meredith

Des Esseintes
À rebours
Huysmans

Des Grieux, Chevalier
Manon Lescaut
Prévost

Despair, Giant
The Pilgrim's Progress
Bunyan

Dete
Heidi
Spyri

De Vere, Arthur
Anne of Geierstein
Scott

De Vil, Cruella
The One Hundred and One Dalmatians
Smith

De Walton, Sir John
Castle Dangerous
Scott

De Winter, Max
De Winter, Rebecca
Rebecca
Du Maurier

Dewy, Dickh)
Under the Greenwood Tree
Hardy

Diabologh, George
The Polyglots
Gerhardie

Diabolus
The Holy War
Bunyan

Diamond
At the Back of the North Wind
MacDonald

Dick
The Blue Lagoon
Stacpoole

Dick
Five on a Treasure Island & others
Blyton

Dick, Mr
David Copperfield
Dickens

Dimmesdale, Arthur
The Scarlet Letter
Hawthorne

Dinah
Alice's Adventures in Wonderland; Through the Looking-Glass
Carroll

Dinmont, Dandie
Guy Mannering
Scott

Diver, Dick
Tender Is the Night
Fitzgerald

Dixon, Jim
Lucky Jim
Amis

Doasyouwouldbedoneby, Mrs
The Water-Babies
Kingsley

Dobbin, Colonel William
Vanity Fair
Thackeray

Dobbs, Dominic
Jacob Faithful
Marryat

Dobson, Zuleika
Zuleika Dobson
Beerbohm

Doc
Cannery Row; Sweet Thursday
Steinbeck

Dodd, David
Hard Cash
Reade

Dods, Meg
St Ronan's Well
Scott

Dolgoruky, Arkady
A Raw Youth
Dostoevsky

Dolittle, Dr John
The Story of Dr Dolittle & others
Lofting

Dombey, Edith
Dombey, Fanny
Dombey, Florence
Dombey, Paul Jnr
Dombey, Paul Snr
Dombey and Son
Dickens

Donatello, Count
The Marble Faun
Hawthorne

Donn, Arabella
Jude the Obscure
Hardy

Donnithorne, Arthur
Adam Bede
Eliot

Doone, Carver
Doone, Lorna
Lorna Doone
Blackmore

Dormer, Lady Agnesh)
The Tragic Muse
James

Dormer, Ayala
Dormer, Egbert
Dormer, Lucy

Ayala's Angel
Trollope

Dormouse
Alice's Adventures in Wonderland
Carroll

Dorothy
The Wonderful Wizard of Oz
Baum

Dorrit, Amy 'Little'
Dorrit, Fanny
Dorrit, Tim
Dorrit, William
Little Dorrit
Dickens

Dosett, Reginald
Ayala's Angel
Trollope

Douglas, Charlotte
A Book of Common Prayer
Didion

Douglas, Widow
The Adventures of Tom Sawyer; The Adventures of Huckleberry Finn
Twain

Dousterswivel
The Antiquary
Scott

Dowell, Florence
Dowell, John
The Good Soldier
Ford

Dowler, Captain
Pickwick Papers
Dickens

Dracula, Count
Dracula
Stoker

Drake, Paul
The Case of the Velvet Claws & others
Gardner

Drake, Temple
Sanctuary; Requiem for a Nun
Faulkner

Dred
Dred
Stowe

Dreighton, Natalie
One of Our Conquerors
Meredith

Driffield, Edward
Driffield, Rosie
Cakes and Ale
Maugham

Driscoll, Percy
Driscoll, Tom
Pudd'nhead Wilson
Twain

Drood, Edwin
The Mystery of Edwin Drood
Dickens

Drouet, Charles
Sister Carrie
Dreiser

Drummle, Bentley
Great Expectations
Dickens

Drummond, Catriona
Catriona
Stevenson

Drummond, Hugh 'Bulldog'
Bulldog Drummond & others
Sapper

Dryfoos
A Hazard of New Fortunes
Howells

'Duke'
The Adventures of Huckleberry Finn
Twain

Dulcineah
Don Quixote
Cervantes

Dunstable, Miss
Doctor Thorne
Trollope

Dupin, C Auguste
The Murders in the Rue Morgue
Poe

D'Urberville, Alec
Durbeyfield, Tess
Tess of the D'Urbervilles
Hardy

D'Urfe, Nicholas
The Magus
Fowles

Durham, Constantia
The Egoist
Meredith

Duroy, Georges
Bel-Ami
Maupassant

Durrisdeer, Henry
Durrisdeer, Lord
The Master of Ballantrae
Stevenson

Durtal
Là-bas; En route; La Cathédrale; L'Oblat
Huysmans

Durward, Quentin
Quentin Durward
Scott

Dutcher, Rose
Rose of Dutcher's Coolly
Garland

Duval, Armand
La Dame aux camélias
Dumas

Duval, Denis
Denis Duval
Thackeray

E

Eames, Johnny
The Small House at Allington
Trollope

Earle, Judith
Dusty Answer
Lehmann

Earnshaw, Catherine
Earnshaw, Hareton
Earnshaw, Hindley
Earnshaw, Mr
Wuthering Heights
Brontë

Earwicker, Anna Livia (née Plurabelle)
Earwicker, Humphrey Chimpden
Earwicker, Isabel
Earwicker, Shaun
Earwicker, Shem
Finnegans Wake
Joyce

East, Harry 'Scud'
Tom Brown's Schooldays
Hughes

Easton family
The Ragged Trousered Philanthropist
Tressell

Easy, Jack
Mr Midshipman Easy
Marryat

Eccles, Robert
Rhoda Fleming
Meredith

Eden, Martin
Martin Eden
London

Edith
Loving
Green

Edward, Prince
The Prince and the Pauper
Twain

Eeyore
Winnie-the-Pooh; The House at Pooh Corner
Milne

Effingham, Violet
Phineas Finn
Trollope

Eilonwy, Princess
The High King
Alexander

Eleanor
Alton Locke
Kingsley

Eliot, Lewis
George Pessant; The Light and the Dark; A Time of Hope; The Masters; The New Men; Homecomings; The Conscience of the Rich; The Affair; Corridors of Power; The Sleep of Reason; Last Things
Snow

Eliza
Uncle Tom's Cabin
Stowe

Elizabeth, Queen
Kenilworth
Scott

Ellen
The Way of All Flesh
Butler

Ellénore
Adolphe
Constant

Ellie
The Water-Babies
Kingsley

Elliot, Anne
Elliot, Elizabeth
Elliot, Mary
Elliot, Sir Walter
Elliot, William
Persuasion
Austen

Elliott, Christina
Weir of Hermiston
Stevenson

Elliott, Rick
The Longest Journey
Forster

Ellison, Mrs
Amelia
Fielding

Eloi
The Time Machine
Wells

Elphin
The Misfortunes of Elphin
Peacock

Elshender the Recluse
The Black Dwarf
Scott

Elstir
À la recherche du temps perdu
Proust

Elton, Mr
Emma
Austen

Em
The Story of an African Farm
Schreiner

Emerson, George
Emerson, Mr
A Room with a View
Forster

Emilia
The Adventures of Peregrine Pickle
Smollett

Emily
Martin Faber
Simms

Emmanuel
The Holy War
Bunyan

Emmanuel, Paul
Villette
Brontë

Emmeline
The Blue Lagoon
Stacpoole

Emsworth, Lord
Something Fresh; Leave It to Psmith; Summer Lightning; Heavy Weather; Uncle Fred in the Springtime; Full Moon; Pigs Have Wings; Service with a Smile; Galahad at Blandings; A Pelican at Blandings; Sunset at Blandings
Wodehouse

Enderby
Inside Mr Enderby; Enderby Outside; Enderby's Dark Lady
Burgess

Erasmus
The Cloister and the Hearth
Reade

Erridge, Lord
A Dance to the Music of Time
Powell

Esca
The Eagle of the Ninth
Sutcliff

Escot, Mr
Headlong Hall
Peacock

Esmerelda
Doktor Faustus
Mann

Esmerelda
Notre-Dame de Paris
Hugo

Esmond, Henry
The History of Henry Esmond Esquire
Thackeray

Estella
Great Expectations
Dickens

Esther
Felix Holt
Eliot

Etherington, Earl of
St Ronan's Well
Scott

Euphues
Euphues
Lyly

Eustace, Lady Lizzie
The Eustace Diamonds
Trollope

Eva
Tancred
Disraeli

Evandale, Lord
Old Mortality
Scott

Everard, Colonel Mark
Woodstock
Scott

Everdene, Bathsheba
Far from the Madding Crowd
Hardy

Everhard
The Iron Heel
London

Everstein, Irene
Alte Nester
Raabe

Eyre, Jane
Jane Eyre
Brontë

Eysette, Daniel
Eysette, Jacques
Le Petit Chose
Daudet

F

Faber, Martin
Martin Faber
Simms

Faber, Miles
MF
Burgess

Faggus, Tom
Lorna Doone
Blackmore

Fagin
Oliver Twist
Dickens

Fairfax, Jane
Emma
Austen

Fairlie, Laura
Fairlie, Mr
The Woman in White
Collins

Fairservice, Andrew
Rob Roy
Scott

Faithful
The Pilgrim's Progress
Bunyan

Faithful, Jacob
Jacob Faithful
Marryat

Falconer, Mr
Gryll Grange
Peacock

Falconet, Joseph
Falconet
Disraeli

Faline
Bambi; Bambis Kinder
Salten

Fane, Michael
Sinister Street
MacKenzie

Fanny
The Adventures of Joseph Andrews
Fielding

Fanshawe, Ginevra
Villette
Brontë

Fantine
Les Misérables
Hugo

Farfrae, Donald
The Mayor of Casterbridge
Hardy

Faria, Abbé
Le Comte de Monte-Cristo
Dumas

Farnaby, Will
Island
Huxley

Farrange, Beale
Farrange, Ida
Farrange, Maisie
What Maisie Knew
James

Farrell, Aminta
Lord Ormont and His Aminta
Meredith

Farren, Molly
Silas Marner
Eliot

Fauntleroy, Lord Cedric
Little Lord Fauntleroy
Burnett

Faustus, Doktor
Doktor Faustus
Mann

Fawley, Jude
Jude the Obscure
Hardy

Fawn
Through the Looking-Glass
Carroll

Fayaway
Typee
Melville

Fenwick, Frank
The Vicar of Bullhampton
Trollope

Ferao
The Jungle Books
Kipling

Ferdinand, Count Fathom
The Adventures of Ferdinand Count Fathom
Smollett

Ferrars, Edward
Ferrars, Mrs
Ferrars, Robert
Sense and Sensibility
Austen

Ferrars, Endymion
Ferrars, Myra
Ferrars, Pitt
Endymion
Disraeli

Ferret
The Life and Adventures of Sir Launcelot Greaves
Smollett

Feverel, Sir Austin
Feverel, Richard
The Ordeal of Richard Feverel
Meredith

Feversham, Harry
The Four Feathers
Mason

Fielding, Cyril
A Passage to India
Forster

Fielding, May
The Cricket on the Hearth
Dickens

Fincastle, Ada
Vein of Iron
Glasgow

Finchley, Sondra
An American Tragedy
Dreiser

Finlay, Dr
Beyond This Place
Cronin

Finn, Huck(leberry)
The Adventures of Tom Sawyer; The Adventures of Huckleberry Finn
Twain

Finn, Phineas
Phineas Finn; Phineas Redux
Trollope

Firmin, Geoffrey
Firmin, Yvonne
Under the Volcano
Lowry

Firmin, Philip
A Shabby Genteel Story; The Adventures of Philip
Thacheray

Fischer, Doctor
Doctor Fischer of Geneva
Greene

Fisher, Billy
Billy Liar; Billy Liar on the Moon
Waterhouse

Fitzgerald, Burgo
Can You Forgive Her?
Trollope

Fitzgerald, Herbert
Fitzgerald, Owen
Castle Richmond
Trollope

Fitzpiers, Edred
The Woodlanders
Hardy

Fiver
Watership Down
Adams

Flambeau
The Innocence of Father Brown & others
Chesterton

Flanders, Jacob
Jacob's Room
Woolf

Flanders, Moll
Moll Flanders
Defoe

Flashman
Flashman & others
Fraser

Tom Brown's Schooldays
Hughes

Flask
Moby-Dick
Melville

Flavia, Princess
The Prisoner of Zenda
Hope

Flavia, Queen
Rupert of Hentzau
Hope

Fledgeby
Our Mutual Friend
Dickens

Fleetwood, Lord
The Amazing Marriage
Meredith

Fleming, Dahlia
Fleming, Rhoda
Rhoda Fleming
Meredith

Fleming, Henry
The Red Badge of Courage
Crane

Fletcher, Abel
Fletcher, Phineas
John Halifax, Gentleman
Craik

Flicka
My Friend Flicka; Thunderhead; Green Grass of Wyoming
O'Hara

Flint, Captain
Treasure Island
Stevenson

Flintwinch, Jeremiah
Little Dorrit
Dickens

Flite, Miss
Bleak House
Dickens

Flora
The Turn of the Screw
James

Flosky, Mr
Nightmare Abbey
Peacock

Flyte, Sebastian
Brideshead Revisited
Waugh

Fogg, Phileas
Le Tour du monde en quatre-vingt jours
Verne

Folantin, Monsieur
À vau l'eau
Huysmans

Folliott, Dr
Crotchet Castle
Peacock

Forester, Sylvan
Melincourt
Peacock

Forster, Silas
Forster, Zenobia
The Blithedale Romance
Hawthorne

Forsyte, Fleur
Forsyte, Irene
Forsyte, Jon
Forsyte, `Old' Jolyon
Forsyte, Soames
Forsyte, `Young' Jolyon
The Forsyte Saga
Galsworthy

Fosco, Count
The Woman in White
Collins

Fossil, Pauline
Fossil, Petrova
Fossil, Posy
Ballet Shoes
Streatfeild

Foster, Dolly
The Dolly Dialogues
Hope

Foster, Mr
Headlong Hall
Peacock

Françoise
À la recherche du temps perdu
Proust

Frankenstein, Dr Victor
Frankenstein
Shelley

Franklin, Lady
The Hireling
Hartley

Freeman, Ernestina
The French Lieutenant's Woman
Fowles

Friday
Robinson Crusoe
Defoe

Frieda
Das Schloss
Kafka

Friedrich
Ahnung und Gegenwart
Eichendorff

Frollo, Claude
Notre-Dame de Paris
Hugo

Frome, Ethan
Frome, Zenobia
Ethan Frome
Wharton

Fu Manchu, Dr
Dr Fu Manchu & others
Rohmer

Futvoye, Professor Anthony
Futvoye, Sylvia
The Brass Bottle
Anstey

G

Gagool
King Solomon's Mines
Haggard

Galliano, Mr
Mr Galliano's Circus & others
Blyton

Gamp, Sarah
Martin Chuzzlewit
Dickens

Gandalf
The Hobbit; The Lord of the Rings
Tolkien

Gann, Caroline
A Shabby Genteel Story; The Adventures of Philip
Thackeray

Gant, Eugene
Look Homeward, Angel; Of Time and the River
Wolfe

Gantry, Elmer
Elmer Gantry
Lewis

Gardiner, Mr
Gardiner, Mrs
Pride and Prejudice
Austen

Gargantua
Gargantua and Pantagruel
Rabelais

Gargery, Georgiana
Gargery, Joe
Great Expectations
Dickens

Garland, Anne
The Trumpet-Major
Hardy

Garland, Mr
Garland, Mrs
The Old Curiosity Shop
Dickens

Garp
The World According to Garp
Irving

Garraghtys
The Absentee
Edgeworth

Garth, Caleb
Garth, Mary
Middlemarch
Eliot

Gashford
Barnaby Rudge
Dickens

Gatsby, Jay
The Great Gatsby
Fitzgerald

Gautier, Marguerite
La Dame aux camélias
Dumas

Gay, Peterkin
The Coral Island
Ballantyne

Gay, Walter
Dombey and Son
Dickens

Geary, Arthur
The Smaller Sky
Wain

Geierstein, Count Albert
Geierstein, Anne of
Anne of Geierstein
Scott

General, Mrs
Little Dorrit
Dickens

'George'
Five on a Treasure Island & others
Blyton

George
Of Mice and Men
Steinbeck

George
Three Men in a Boat
Jerome

Gerald, Letty
Jennie Gerhardt
Dreiser

Gerard
The Cloister and the Hearth
Reade

Gerard, Brigadier
The Exploits of Brigadier Gerard
Doyle

Gerard, Sybil
Gerard, Walter
Sybil
Disraeli

Gereth family
The Spoils of Poynton
James

Gerhardt, Jennie
Gerhardt, Vesta
Jennie Gerhardt
Dreiser

Ghote, Inspector Ganesh
The Perfect Murder & others
Keating

Gibson, Mr
Gibson, Molly
Wives and Daughters
Gaskell

Gideon, Inspector
Gideon's Day & others
Creasey

Giglio, Prince
The Rose and the Ring
Thackeray

Gills, Solomon
Dombey and Son
Dickens

Gimlet
Gimlet Goes Again & others
Johns

Glasher, Lydia
Daniel Deronda
Eliot

Glass family
Nine Stories; Franny and Zooey; Raise High the Roof Beam, Carpenters; Seymour: an Introduction
Salinger

Glegg, Mrs
The Mill on the Floss
Eliot

Glencora, Lady
see **Palliser, Lady Glencora**

Glendinning, Edward
Glendinning, Halbert
Glendinning, Simon
The Monastery; The Abbot
Scott

Glenmire, Lady
Cranford
Gaskell

Glossin
Guy Mannering
Scott

Glover, Catharine
Glover, Simon
The Fair Maid of Perth
Scott

Glumdalglitch
Gulliver's Travels
Swift

Glyde, Sir Percival
The Woman in White
Collins

Godbole, Professor
A Room with a View
Forster

Goddard, Mrs
Emma
Austen

Goesler, Madame Max 'Marie'
Phineas Finn; Phineas Redux
Trollope

Goldfinger, Auric
Goldfinger
Fleming

Golightly, Holly
Breakfast at Tiffany's
Capote

Gollum
The Hobbit; The Lord of the Rings
Tolkien

Good, Captain John
King Solomon's Mines
Haggard

Goodman, Theodora
The Aunt's Story
White

Goodwin, Archie
Fer-de-Lance & others
Stout

Goodwood, Caspar
The Portrait of a Lady
James

Gordeyev family
Foma Gordeyev
Gorky

Gordon, Harry
Gordon, Nina
Gordon, Tom
Dred
Stowe

Gordon, Lord George
Barnaby Rudge
Dickens

Gordon, Squire
Black Beauty
Sewell

Gostrey, Maria
The Ambassadors
James

Gotobed, Elias
The American Senator
Trollope

Gould, Charles

Gould, Emilia
Nostromo
Conrad

Gourlay, John
The House with the Green Shutters
Douglas

Gowan, Henry
Little Dorrit
Dickens

Grace
The Absentee
Edgeworth

Gradgrind, Louisa
Gradgrind, Thomas
Gradgrind, Tom
Hard Times
Dickens

Graeme, Magdalene
Graeme, Roland
The Abbot
Scott

Graham, Helen
Graham, Arthur
The Tenant of Wildfell Hall
Brontë

Graham, Mary
Martin Chuzzlewit
Dickens

Grandcourt, Henleigh
Daniel Deronda
Eliot

Grandison, Cardinal
Lothair
Disraeli

Grandison, Sir Charles
The History of Sir Charles Grandison
Richardson

Grandison, Katherine
Henrietta Temple
Disraeli

Grangerford family
The Adventures of Huckleberry Finn
Twain

Grantly, Archdeacon
The Warden; Barchester Towers; Framley Parsonage; The Last Chronicle of Barset
Trollope

Grantly, Major
The Last Chronicle of Barset
Trollope

Gray, Cordelia
An Unsuitable Job for a Woman; The Skull Beneath the Skin
James

Gray, Cytherea
Desperate Remedies
Hardy

Gray, Dorian
The Picture of Dorian Gray
Wilde

Gray, John
The Choir Invisible
Allen

Great-Heart
The Pilgrim's Progress
Bunyan

Greaves, Sir Launcelot
The Life and Adventures of Sir Launcelot Greaves
Smollett

Greenow, Mrs
Can You Forgive Her?
Trollope

Grendon, Tishy
The Awkward Age
James

Gresham, Frank
Doctor Thorne
Trollope

Gresham, Julia
The Greatest Gresham
Avery

Grewgious, Hiram
The Mystery of Edwin Drood
Dickens

Grey, Agnes
Agnes Grey
Brontë

Grey, John
Can You Forgive Her?
Trollope

Grey, Vivian
Vivian Grey
Disraeli

Grey Beaver
White Fang
London

Greylock, Jason
Barren Ground
Glasgow

Greyslaer, Max
Greyslaer
Hoffman

Gride, Arthur
Nicholas Nickleby
Dickens

Griffin
The Invisible Man
Wells

Griffiths, Clyde
Griffiths, Samuel
An American Tragedy
Dreiser

Griffiths, Mrs
Sanditon
Austen

Grimes, Mr
The Water-Babies
Kingsley

Grip
Barnaby Rudge
Dickens

Griselda
The Cuckoo Clock
Molesworth

Grose, Mrs
The Turn of the Screw
James

Grove, Lena
Light in August
Faulkner

Grueby, John
Barnaby Rudge
Dickens

Gryll, Mr
Gryll Grange
Peacock

Gryphon
Alice's Adventures in Wonderland
Carroll

Gub-Gub
The Story of Dr Dolittle & others
Lofting

Guermantes, Duc de
Guermantes, Duchesse de
À la recherche du temps perdu
Proust

Guest, Stephen
The Mill on the Floss
Eliot

Gulliver, Lemuel
Gulliver's Travels
Swift

Gum
Ballet Shoes
Streatfeild

Gundermann
Les Rougon-Macquart
Zola

Gunn, Ben
Treasure Island
Stevenson

Gunn, Robert
Mandarin Gold
Leasor

Guppy
Bleak House
Dickens

Gurth
Ivanhoe
Scott

Guster
Bleak house
Dickens

Guthrie, Chris
Sunset Song; Cloud Howe; Grey Granite
Gibbon

Guzman, Don
Westward Ho!
Kingsley

Gwenwyn, Prince
The Betrothed
Scott

Gwilt, Lydia
Armadale
Collins

Gynecia
Arcadia
Sidney

H

Hagenbach, Archibald of
Anne of Geierstein
Scott

Halcombe, Marian
The Woman in White
Collins

Hale, Margaret
Hale, Reverend
North and South
Gaskell

Halifax, John
John Halifax, Gentleman
Craik

Halkett, Cecilia
Beauchamp's Career
Meredith

Hall, Cecy
What Katy Did; What Katy Did at School; What Katy Did Next
Coolidge

Haller, Harry
Der Steppenwolf
Hesse

Hallward, Basil
The Picture of Dorian Gray
Wilde

Hal 9000
2001: a Space Odyssey
Clarke

Hamel, Isadore
Ayala's Angel
Trollope

Hamilton, Melanie
Gone with the Wind
Mitchell

Hamilton family
East of Eden
Steinbeck

Hamley, Osborne
Hamley, Roger
Hamley, Squire
Wives and Daughters
Gaskell

Hammer, Mike
I, the Jury; My Gun Is Quick; Vengeance Is Mine!; The Big Kill; One Lonely Night; Kiss Me, Deadly; The Girl Hunters; The Snake; The Twisted Thing; The Body Lovers; Survival ... Zero!
Spillane

Hamps, Auntie
Clayhanger
Bennett

Hanaud, Inspector
At the Villa Rose & others
Mason

Hannay, Richard
The Thirty-Nine Steps; Greenmantle; Mr Standfast; The Three Hostages; The Courts of the Morning; The Island of Sheep
Buchan

Hanno family
Buddenbrooks
Mann

Harcourt, Sir Henry
The Bertrams
Trollope

Harding, Dickie
Harding's Luck
Nesbit

Harding, Eleanor
see **Bold, Eleanor**

Harding, Rev Septimus
The Warden; The Last Chronicle of Barset
Trollope

Haredale, Emma
Haredale, Geoffrey
Haredale, Reuben
Barnaby Rudge
Dickens

Harker, Jonathan
Dracula
Stoker

Harker, Kay
The Midnight Folk; The Box of Delights
Masefield

Harkonnen, Baron Vladimir
Dune; Dune Messiah; Children of Dune
Herbert

Harleth, Gwendolen
Daniel Deronda
Eliot

Harlowe, Arabella
Harlowe, Clarissa
Clarissa
Richardson

Harmon
Harmon, John
Our Mutual Friend
Dickens

Harper, Joe
The Adventures of Tom Sawyer
Twain

Harrington, Evan
Evan Harrington
Meredith

Harris
Three Men in a Boat
Jerome

Harrison, Dr
Amelia
Fielding

Hartright, Walter
The Woman in White
Collins

Hathi
The Jungle Books
Kipling

Hatteraik, Dirk
Guy Mannering
Scott

Haut-Ton, Sir Oran
Melincourt
Peacock

Havisham, Miss
Great Expectations
Dickens

Hawdon, Captain
Bleak House
Dickens

Hawkeye
see **Bumppo, Natty**

Hawkins, Jim
Hawkins, Mrs
Treasure Island
Stevenson

Hazel
Watership Down
Adams

Headstone, Bradley
Our Mutual Friend
Dickens

Heathcliff
Heathcliff, Linton
Wuthering Heights
Brontë

Heatherstone, Patience
Children of the New Forest
Marryat

Heathfield, Arthur
The Battle of Life
Dickens

Hebblethwaite, Flying-officer Ginger
The Camels Are Coming & others
Johns

Heep, Mrs
Heep, Uriah
David Copperfield
Dickens

Heidi
Heidi
Spyri

Helen
The Heart of the Matter
Greene

Helm, Matt
Death of a Citizen & others
Hamilton

Helstone, Caroline
Shirley
Brontë

Hemlock, Jonathan
The Eiger Sanction; The Loo Sanction
Trevanian

Henchard, Michael
Henchard, Mrs
The Mayor of Casterbridge
Hardy

Henderson, Gene
Henderson the Rain King
Bellow

Henri, Frances
The Professor
Brontë

Henry, Frederic
A Farewell to Arms
Hemingway

Hen Wen
The Book of Three
Alexander

Hepburn, Philip
Sylvia's Lovers
Gaskell

Hereward
Hereward the Wake
Kingsley

Herries of Birrenswork
Redgauntlet
Scott

Herriton, Harriet
Herriton, Irma
Herriton, Lilia
Herriton, Philip
Where Angels Fear to Tread
Forster

Herzog, Moses
Herzog
Bellow

Hesselius, Doctor Martin
In a Glass Darkly
Le Fanu

Hewet, Terence
The Voyage Out
Woolf

Hexam, Jesse
Hexam, Lizzie
Our Mutual Friend
Dickens

Heyst, Axel
Victory
Conrad

Heywood, Charlotte
Sanditon
Austen

Higden, Betty
Our Mutual Friend
Dickens

Higgs
Erewhon
Butler

Hilbery, Katherine
Night and Day
Woolf

Hilda
Lady Chatterley's Lover
Lawrence

Hill, Camilla
A Wreath of Roses
Taylor

Hilton, Ruth
Ruth
Gaskell

Hippolita
The Castle of Otranto
Walpole

Hogg, Georgina
The Comforters
Spark

Hoggins, Mr
Cranford
Gaskell

Holdsworth
Cousin Phillis
Gaskell

Hollingsworth
The Blithedale Romance
Hawthorne

Holman, Minister
Holman, Phillis
Cousin Phillis
Gaskell

Holmes, Mycroft
The Adventures of Sherlock Holmes; The Memoirs of Sherlock Holmes; The Return of Sherlock Holmes; The Case Book of Sherlock Holmes
Doyle

Holmes, Sherlock
A Study in Scarlet; The Sign of Four; The Adventures of Sherlock Holmes; The Final Problem; The Memoirs of Sherlock Holmes; The Hound of the Baskervilles; The Return of Sherlock Holmes; The Case Book of Sherlock Holmes
Doyle

Holt, Father
The History of Henry Esmond Esquire
Thackeray

Holt, Felix
Felix Holt
Eliot

Home, Pauline
Villette
Brontë

Homily
The Borrowers; The Borrowers Afield; The Borrowers Afloat; The Borrowers Aloft; The Borrowers Avenged
Norton

Homo
L'Homme qui rit
Hugo

Honeychurch, Lucy
A Room with a View
Forster

Honeythunder, Luke
The Mystery of Edwin Drood
Dickens

Honour
The History of Tom Jones
Fielding

Hood, Robin
Ivanhoe
Scott

Hood, Robin
Maid Marian
Peacock

Hooligan, Mary
Night
O'Brien

Hope, Edith
Hotel du Lac
Brookner

Hopeful
The Pilgrim's Progress
Bunyan

Hornblower, Horatio
The Happy Return; Ship of the Line; Captain Hornblower RN; Lord Hornblower; Mr Midshipman Hornblower; Hornblower and the Atropos; Hornblower in the West Indies; Hornblower and the Hotspur
Forester

Hortense
Bleak House
Dickens

Houyhnhnms
Gulliver's Travels
Swift

Howard, Mr
The Watsons
Austen

Howe, Anne
Clarissa
Richardson

Hudson, Mrs
The Adventures of Sherlock Holmes; The Memoirs of Sherlock Holmes; The Return of Sherlock Holmes; The Case Book of Sherlock Holmes
Doyle

Hudson, Roderick
Roderick Hudson
James

Hugh
Barnaby Rudge
Dickens

Huldbrand
Undine
Fouqué

Humbert, Humbert
Lolita
Nabokov

Humpty Dumpty
Through the Looking-Glass
Carroll

Hunter, Mrs Leo
Pickwick Papers
Dickens

Huntingdon, Arthur
The Tenant of Wildfell Hall
Brontë

Hurstwood, George
Sister Carrie
Dreiser

Hyde, Mr
The Strange Case of Dr Jekyll and Mr Hyde
Stevenson

Hypatia
Hypatia
Kingsley

Hythloday, Raphael
Utopia
More

I

'I'
Three Men in a Boat
Jerome

Ickenham, Earl of, 'Uncle Fred'
Uncle Fred in the Springtime; Uncle Dynamite; Cocktail Time
Wodehouse

Ida
Brighton Rock
Greene

Ikki
The Jungle Books
Kipling

Ilchester, Janet
The Adventures of Harry Richmond
Meredith

Ilex, Miss
Gryll Grange
Peacock

Imlac
Rasselas
Johnson

Imoinda
Oroonoko
Behn

Indiana
Indiana
Sand

Injun Joe
The Adventures of Tom Sawyer
Twain

Irtyenev, Evgeniy
The Devil
Tolstoy

Isaac
Ivanhoe
Scott

Isadora
Melmoth the Wanderer
Maturin

Isas
Ben-Hur
Wallace

Isherwood, Mr
Goodbye to Berlin
Isherwood, Christopher

Ishmael
Moby-Dick
Melville

Ivanhoe
Ivanhoe
Scott

Izzie, Aunt
What Katy Did; What Katy Did at School; What Katy Did Next
Coolidge

J

Jack
A Tale of a Tub
Swift

Jackson, Mike
Mike: a Public School Story
Wodehouse

Jaggers
Great Expectations
Dickens

Jakin, Bob
The Mill on the Floss
Eliot

James, Colonel
Amelia
Fielding

Jane
Tarzan of the Apes & others
Burroughs

Janet
Beyond This Place
Cronin

Janvier
Pietr-le-Letton & others
Simenon

Jarl
Mardi
Melville

Jarndyce, John
Bleak House
Dickens

Jarvie, Nicol
Rob Roy
Scott

Jasper, John
The Mystery of Edwin Drood
Dickens

Javert
Les Misérables
Scott

Jaws
Jaws
Benchley

Jeanne
Une Vie
Maupassant

Jeddler, Doctor
Jeddler, Grace
Jeddler, Marion
The Battle of Life
Dickens

Jeeves, Reginald
My Man Jeeves; The Inimitable Jeeves; Carry On, Jeeves!; Very Good, Jeeves!; Thank You, Jeeves; Right Ho, Jeeves; The Code of the Woosters; Joy in the Morning; The Mating Season; Ring for Jeeves; Jeeves and the Feudal Spirit; Jeeves in the Offing; Stiff Upper Lip, Jeeves; The World of Jeeves; Much Obliged, Jeeves; Aunts Aren't Gentlemen
Wodehouse

Jeffreys, Judge
Lorna Doone
Blackmore

Jekyll, Doctor
The Strange Case of Dr Jekyll and Mr Hyde
Stevenson

Jellyby
Jellyby, Mrs
Bleak House
Dickens

Jenkins, Nicholas
A Dance to the Music of Time
Powell

Jenkins, Winifred
The Expedition of Humphry Clinker
Smollett

Jenkyns, Deborah
Jenkyns, Matty
Cranford
Gaskell

Jennings
Jennings Goes to School & others
Buckeridge

Jennings, Mrs
Sense and Sensibility
Austen

Jensen, Sasha
Good Morning Midnight
Rhys

Jepp, Louisa
The Comforters
Spark

Jervis, Mrs
Pamela
Richardson

Jessel, Miss
The Turn of the Screw
James

Jewkes, Mrs
Pamela
Richardson

Jim
The Adventures of Huckleberry Finn
Twain

Jim
At the Back of the North Wind
MacDonald

Jim
Lord Jim
Conrad

Jimson, Gulley
Herself Surprised; To Be a Pilgrim; The Horse's Mouth
Cary

Jingle, Alfred
Pickwick Papers
Dickens

Jo
Bleak House
Dickens

Joad family
The Grapes of Wrath
Steinbeck

Jocelyn, Rose
Evan Harrington
Meredith

Johnson, Mrs
Lady Susan
Austen

Jollifant, Inigo
The Good Companions
Priestley

Jones, Jenny
Jones, Tom
The History of Tom Jones
Fielding

Jones, 'Major'
The Comedians
Greene

Jones, Mr
Animal Farm
Orwell

Jordan, Robert
For Whom the Bell Tolls
Hemingway

Jorham, Captain
Anthony Adverse
Hope

Jorrocks, Mr
Jorrocks's Jaunts and Jollities; Handley Cross; Hillingdon Hall
Surtees

José, Padre
The Power and the Glory
Greene

Joseph of Arimathea
The Brook Kerith
Moore

Julian
Five on a Treasure Island & others
Blyton

Julian, Christopher
The Hand of Ethelberta
Hardy

Jupe, Signor
Jupe, Sissy
Hard Times
Dickens

Jupiter
The Gold Bug
Poe

Jurgen
Jurgen
Cabell

Justice
Black Beauty
Sewell

Justine
Justine; Balthazar; Mountolive; Clea
Durrell

K

K
Das Schloss
Kafka

K, Josef
Der Prozess
Kafka

Kaa
Kadlu
Kala Nag
The Jungle Books
Kipling

Kane, Lester
Jennie Gerhardt
Dreiser

Kanga
Winnie-the-Pooh; The House at Pooh Corner
Milne

Karamazov
Karamazov, Alyosha
Karamazov, Dmitri
Karamazov, Ivan
Karamazov, Smerdyakov
The Brothers Karamazov
Dostoevsky

Karenina, Anna
Anna Karenina
Tolstoy

Karla
Tinker, Tailor, Soldier, Spy; The Honourable Schoolboy; Smiley's People
Le Carré

Kear, Alroy
Cakes and Ale
Maugham

Keeble, Lady Constance
Leave It to Psmith; Summer Lightning; Heavy Weather; Uncle Fred in the Springtime; Full Moon; Pigs Have Wings; A Pelican at Blandings
Wodehouse

Keeldar, Shirley
Shirley
Brontë

Kenn, Doctor
The Mill on the Floss
Eliot

Kennedy, Mr
Phineas Finn; Phineas Redux
Trollope

Kenneth, Sir
The Talisman
Scott

Kentuck
The Luck of Roaring Camp
Harte

Kenwigs, Mr
Kenwigs, Mrs
Nicholas Nickleby
Dickens

Kes
A Kestrel for a Knave
Hines

Kettledrummle, Reverend
Old Mortality
Scott

Kien, Peter
Die Blendung
Canetti

Kim
see **O'Hara, Kimball**

Kinraid, Charley
Sylvia's Lovers
Gaskell

Kipps, Arthur `Arty'
Kipps
Wells

Kirby, Captain
Kirby, Carinthia
Kirby, Chillon
The Amazing Marriage
Meredith

Kirilov
The Devils
Dostoevsky

Kirk, Howard
The History Man
Bradbury

Kirkpatrick, Clare
Kirkpatrick, Cynthia
Wives and Daughters
Gaskell

Kirstie
Weir of Hermiston
Stevenson

Klein, Honor
A Severed Head
Murdoch

Knecht, Josef
Das Glasperlenspiel
Hesse

Knight, Henry
A Pair of Blue Eyes
Hardy

Knightley, George
Knightley, John
Emma
Austen

Knox, Flurry
Some Experiences of an Irish RM; Further Experiences of an Irish RM; In Mr Knox's Country
Somerville

Ko
The Jungle Books
Kipling

Krook
Bleak House
Dickens

Kühleborn
Undine
Fouqué

Kumalo, Stephen
Cry, the Beloved Country
Paton

Kumar, Hari
The Jewel in the Crown; The Day of the Scorpion; The Towers of Silence; A Division of the Spoils
Scott

Kurtz
Heart of Darkness
Conrad

L

Lacy, Captain Algernon 'Algy'
The Camels Are Coming & others
Johns

Lacy, Beatrice
Lacy, Giles
Rebecca
Du Maurier

Ladislaw, Will
Middlemarch
Eliot

La Fleur
A Sentimental Journey
Sterne

Lambert, Nora
Watch and Ward
James

Lammeter, Nancy
Silas Marner
Eliot

Lamotte, Annette
The Forsyte Saga
Galsworthy

Lampton, Joe
Room at the Top; Life at the Top
Braine

Landless, Helena
Landless, Neville
The Mystery of Edwin Drood
Dickens

Langdon, Bernard
Elsie Venner
Holmes

Langreuter, Fritz
Alte Nester
Raabe

Lantier, Auguste
Lantier, Claude
Lantier, Étienne
Lantier, Jacques
Les Rougon-Macquart
Zola

Lapham, Persis
Lapham, Colonel Silas
The Rise of Silas Lapham
Howells

Lara
Doctor Zhivago
Pasternak

Larch, Wilbur
The Cider House Rules
Irving

Larkin, Ma
Larkin, Pa
The Darling Buds of May
Bates

Larsen, Wolf
The Sea-Wolf
London

Laruelle, Jacques
Under the Volcano
Lowry

Last, Lady Brenda
Last, Tony
A Handful of Dust
Waugh

Latch, William
Esther Waters
Moore

Latimer, Darsie
Redgauntlet
Scott

Laurence, Old Mr
Laurence, Theodore `Laurie'
Little Women; Good Wives; Little Men; Jo's Boys
Alcott

Laurent
Thérèse Raquin
Zola

Lawrence, Frederick
The Tenant of Wildfell Hall
Brontë

Lawrence, Hubert
Lawrence, Robert
Watch and Ward
James

Le Bon, Charles
Absalom, Absalom!
Faulkner

Lebrun, Madame
Lebrun, Robert
The Awakening
Chopin

Lecoq, Monsieur
L'Affaire Lerouge; Le Crime d'Orcival; Le Dossier 113; Monsieur Lecoq; Les Esclaves de Paris; La Corde au cou
Gaboriau

Lee, Colonel Albert
Lee, Alice
Lee, Sir Henry
Woodstock
Scott

Leeford, Edward
Oliver Twist
Dickens

Legrand
The Gold Bug
Poe

Legree, Simon
Uncle Tom's Cabin
Stowe

Leicester, Earl of
Kenilworth
Scott

Leigh, Amyas
Leigh, Frank
Westward Ho!
Kingsley

Leithen, Edward
The Power House; John Macnab; The Dancing Floor; Gap in the Curtain; Sick Heart River
Buchan

Leivers, Miriam
Sons and Lovers
Lawrence

Lennie
Of Mice and Men
Steinbeck

Lennox, Mary
The Secret Garden
Burnett

Lensky
Eugene Onegin
Pushkin

Lescaut, Manon
Manon Lescaut
Prévost

Leslie, Kate
The Plumed Serpent
Lawrence

Lessways, Hilda
Clayhanger; Hilda Lessways; These Twain
Bennett

Lessways, George
Hilda Lessways; These Twain
Bennett

Lestrade, Inspector
The Adventures of Sherlock Holmes; The Memoirs of Sherlock Holmes; The Return of Sherlock Holmes; The Case Book of Sherlock Holmes
Doyle

Lethierry, Monsieur
Les Travailleurs de la mer
Hugo

Levellier, Lord
The Amazing Marriage
Meredith

Leverkühn, Adrian
Doktor Faustus
Mann

Lévin, Kitty
Lévin, Squire
Anna Karenina
Tolstoy

Levy, Thomas
The Marathon Man
Goldman

Lewisham, Mr
Love and Mr Lewisham
Wells

Lidenbrock, Professor
Voyage au centre de la terre
Verne

Light, Christina
Roderick Hudson
James

Lillian
Alton Locke
Kingsley

Lilliputians
Gulliver's Travels
Swift

Lillyvick, Mr
Nicholas Nickleby
Dickens

Lime, Harry
The Third Man
Greene

Limmershin
The Jungle Books
Kipling

Linkinwater, Tim
Nicholas Nickleby
Dickens

Linton, Cathy
Linton, Edgar
Linton, Isabella
Wuthering Heights
Brontë

Lisa
Jurgen
Cabell

Lismahago, Lt Obadiah
The Expedition of Humphry Clinker
Smollett

Little Em'ly
David Copperfield
Dickens

Little Nell
see **Trent, Nell**

Littlepage, Anneke
Littlepage, Cornelius
Littlepage, Mordaunt
The Chainbearer
Cooper

Livesey, Dr
Treasure Island
Stevenson

Locke, Alton
Alton Locke
Kingsley

Lockwood
Wuthering Heights
Brontë

Loerke
Women in Love
Lawrence

Lolita
Lolita
Nabokov

Longdon, Mr
The Awkward Age
James

Longman, Mr
Pamela
Richardson

Lopez, Ferdinand
The Prime Minister
Trollope

Lorry, Jarvis
A Tale of Two Cities
Dickens

Loth, Rebecca
Nina Balatka
Trollope

Lothair
Lothair
Disraeli

Louis XI
Quentin Durward
Scott

Louise
The Heart of the Matter
Greene

Love, Dr Jason
Passport to Oblivion; Passport to Peril; Passport in Suspense; Passport for a Pilgrim; Hosts of Extras
Leasor

Loveday, Bob
Loveday, John
The Trumpet-Major
Hardy

Lovejoy
The Judas Pair; Gold from Gemini; The Grail Tree; Spend Game; The Vatican Rip; Firefly Gadroon; The Sleepers of Erin; The Gondola Scam; The Tartan Ringers; Moonspender; The Very Last Gambado
Gash

Lovelace, Robert
Clarissa
Richardson

Lovell, Charlotte
Lovell, Delia
The Old Maid
Wharton

Lovell, Sinfi
Aylwin
Watts-Dunton

Lowder, Maud

The Wings of the Dove
James

Lucas
Pietr-le-Letton & others
Simenon

Lucas, Charlotte
Pride and Prejudice
Austen

Lucilla
Euphues
Lyly

Luck, Thomas
The Luck of Roaring Camp
Harte

Lufton, Lady
Lufton, Lord Ludovic
Framley Parsonage
Trollope

Luna, Mrs
The Bostonians
James

Lung, Wang
The Good Earth
Buck

Lunn, Joe
Scenes from Provincial Life; Scenes from Married Life; Scenes from Metropolitan Life; Scenes from Later Life
Cooper

Lydgate, Tertius
Middlemarch
Eliot

Lyle, Annot
A Legend of Montrose
Scott

Lyndall
The Story of an African Farm
Schreiner

Lyndon, barry
see **Barry, Redmond**

Lyndon, Countess of
The Luck of Barry Lyndon
Thackeray

M

M
Casino Royale; Live and Let Die; Moonraker; Diamonds Are Forever; From Russia, with Love; Dr No; Goldfinger; For Your Eyes Only; Thunderball; The Spy Who Loved Me; On Her Majesty's Secret Service; You Only Live Twice; The Man with the Golden Gun; Octopussy; The Living Daylights
Fleming

MacCunn, Dick
Huntingtower; Castle Gay; House of the Four Winds
Buchan

Macgregor, Rob Roy
Rob Roy
Scott

Machin, Arthur
This Sporting Life
Storey

Mac-Ivor, Fergus
Mac-Ivor, Flora
Waverley
Scott

Mackaye, Saunders
Alton Locke
Kingsley

Mackellar, Ephraim
The Master of Ballantrae
Stevenson

Mackenzie, Mrs
Mackenzie, Rosie
The Newcomes
Thackeray

MacNeil, Regan
The Exorcist
Blatty

Macquart, Antoine
Macquart, Gervaise
Macquart, Nana
Les Rougon-Macquart
Zola

MacQuedy, Mr
Crotchet castle
Peacock

MacStinger, Mrs
Dombey and Son
Dickens

Macwheeble, Duncan
Waverley
Scott

MacWhirr, Captain
Typhoon
Conrad

Madden sisters
The Odd Women
Gissing

Maddison, Phillip
A Chronicle of Ancient Sunlight
Williamson

Madeline
Madeline
Bemelmans

Mad Hatter
Alice's Adventures in Wonderland
Carroll

Magiot, Doctor
The Comedians
Greene

Magwitch, Abel
Great Expectations
Dickens

Mahony, Richard
Australia Felix; The Way Home; Ultima Thule
Richardson

Maid Marian
Maid Marian
Peacock

Maigret, Chief Inspector Jules
Pietr-le-Letton & others
Simenon

Mallet, Rowland
Roderick Hudson
James

Malone, Scobie
High Commissioner; Helga's Web; Ransom
Cleary

Manders, Laurence
The Comforters
Spark

Manette, Doctor
Manette, Lucy
A Tale of Two Cities
Dickens

Manfred, Prince
The Castle of Otranto
Walpole

Mang
The Jungle Books
Kipling

Mann, Tiger
Day of the Guns; Bloody Sunrise; The Death Dealers; The By-Pass Control
Spillane

Mannering, Colonel Guy
Mannering, Julia
Guy Mannering
Scott

Manners, Daphne
The Jewel in the Crown; The Day of the Scorpion; The Towers of Silence; A Division of the Spoils
Scott

Manning, Paul
Cousin Phillis
Gaskell

Manston, Aeneas
Desperate Remedies
Hardy

Mantalini, Alfred
Mantalini, Madame
Nicholas Nickleby
Dickens

Mao
The Jungle books
Kipling

Marcel
À la recherche du temps perdu
Proust

March, Amy
March, Beth (1st two books only)
March, Jo
March, Meg
March, Mr (1st two books only)

March, Mrs, 'Marmee' (1st two books only)
Little Women; Good Wives; Little Men; Jo's Boys
Alcott

March, Augie
The Adventures of Augie March
Bellow

March, Ursula
John Halifax, Gentleman
Craik

March Hare
Alice's Adventures in Wonderland
Carroll

Marchioness, The
The Old Curiosity Shop
Dickens

Marchmain, Lady
Marchmain, Lord
Brideshead Revisited
Waugh

Marcus
The Eagle of the Ninth
Sutcliff

Margaret
The Cloister and the Hearth
Reade

Maria
For Whom the Bell Tolls
Hemingway

Marian, Maid
see **Maid Marian**

Marie, Princess
War and Peace
Tolstoy

Marinette
Les Contes du chat perché
Aymé

Markham, Gilbert
The Tenant of Wildfell Hall
Brontë

Marko
The Tragic Comedians
Meredith

Marley, Jacob
A Christmas Carol
Dickens

Marlow
Chance
Conrad

Marlow, Captain
Lord Jim
Conrad

Marlowe, Philip
The Big Sleep; Farewell, My Lovely; The High Window; The Lady in the Lake; The Little Sister; The Long Goodbye; Playback
Chandler

'Marmee'
see **March, Mrs**

Marner, Silas
Silas Marner
Eliot

Marney, Lord
Sybil
Eliot

Marple, Miss Jane
The Murder at the Vicarage; The Body in the Library; The Moving Finger; A Murder Is Announced; Mrs McGinty's Dead; They Do It with Mirrors; 4.50 from Paddington; The Adventure of the Christmas Pudding; The Mirror Crack'd from Side to Side; A Caribbean Mystery; At Bertram's Hotel; Nemesis; Sleeping Murder
Christie

Martin
A Tale of a Tub
Swift

Martin, Daniel
Daniel Martin
Fowles

Martin, Jack
The Coral Island
Ballantyne

Martin, Robert
Emma
Austen

Martins, Rollo
The Third Man
Greene

Marvin
The Hitch-Hiker's Guide to the Galaxy
Adams

Marx, Bernard
Brave New World
Huxley

Mary
The Adventures of Tom Sawyer
Twain

Mary
Pickwick Papers
Dickens

Mary, Queen of Scots
The Abbot
Scott

Maslova, Katusha
Resurrection
Tolstoy

Mason, Joseph
Mason, Lady
Mason, Lucius
Orley Farm
Trollope

Mason, Perry
The Case of the Velvet Claws & others
Gardner

Mason, Richard
Jane Eyre
Brontë

Master of Ballantrae, The
The Master of Ballantrae
Stevenson

Masters, Mary
The American Senator
Trollope

Matkah
The Jungle Books
Kipling

Matt
White Fang
London

Matthews family
No Laughing Matter
Wilson

Matthews, Miss
Amelia
Fielding

M'Aulay
A Legend of Montrose
Scott

Mauprat, Tristan de
Mauprat
Sand

May
The Age of Innocence
Wharton

May, Dr
The Daisy Chain
Yonge

Maylie, Mrs
Maylie, Rose
Oliver Twist
Dickens

McGhee, Travis
Nightmare in Pink; Pale Gray for Guilt; The Scarlet Ruse
MacDonald

McLaughlin, Ken
My Friend Flicka; Thunderhead; Green Grass of Wyoming
O'Hara

Meagles
Little Dorrit
Dickens

Meany, Owen
A Prayer for Owen Meany
Irving

Meaulnes, Augustin
Le Grand Meaulnes
Alain-Fournier

Meeber, Carrie
Sister Carrie
Dreiser

Melanie
L'Adultera
Fontane

Melbury, Grace
The Woodlanders
Hardy

Melema, Tito
Romola
Eliot

Melincourt, Anthelia
Melincourt
Peacock

Melissa
Justine; Balthazar; Mountolive; Clea
Durrell

Mellors, Olive
Lady Chatterley's Lover
Lawrence

Melmoth
Melmoth the Wanderer
Maturin

Melmotte, Augustus
The Way We Live Now
Trollope

Menteith, Earl of
A Legend of Montrose
Scott

Mercy
The Pilgrim's Progress
Bunyan

Merdle
Little Dorrit
Dickens

Merle, Madame
The Portrait of a Lady
James

Merlyn, Jem
Merlyn, Joss
Jamaica Inn
Du Maurier

Merrick, Ronald
The Jewel in the Crown; The Day of the Scorpion; The Towers of Silence; A Division of the Spoils
Scott

Merridew, Jack
Lord of the Flies
Golding

Merrilies, Meg
Guy Mannering
Scott

Mertoun, Basil
Mertoun, Mordaunt
The Pirate
Scott

Messala
Ben-Hur
Wallace

Mesty
Mr Midshipman Easy
Marryat

Metty
A Bend in the River
Naipaul

Meursault
L'Étranger
Camus

Micawber, Mrs
Micawber, Wilkins
David Copperfield
Dickens

Michaelis
Lady Chatterley's Lover
Lawrence

Middleton, Clara
The Egoist
Meredith

Middleton, Gerald
Anglo-Saxon Attitudes
Wilson

Miggs
Barnaby Rudge
Dickens

Miles
The Turn of the Screw
James

Millbank, Edith
Millbank, Oswald
Coningsby
Disraeli

Miller, Daisy
Daisy Miller
James

Milton, Mr
Milton, Mrs
Wife to Mr Milton
Graves

Milton, Polly
An Old-Fashioned Girl
Alcott

Milvain, Jasper
New Grub Street
Gissing

Mina
Dracula
Stoker

Mingo
Mingo
Harris

Mingott, Mrs
The Age of Innocence
Wharton

M'Intyre, Hector
The Antiquary
Scott

Miriam
The Marble Faun
Hawthorne

Miriam
Pilgrimage
Richardson

Missis
The One Hundred and One Dalmatians
Smith

Mitchett
The Awkward Age
James

Moby-Dick
Moby-Dick
Melville

Mock Turtle
Alice's Adventures in Wonderland
Carroll

Mole, Mr
The Wind in the Willows
Grahame

Mond, Mustapha
Brave New World
Huxley

Moneypenny, Miss
Casino Royale; Live and Let Die; Moonraker; Diamonds Are Forever; From Russia, with Love; Dr No; Goldfinger; For Your Eyes Only; Thunderball; The Spy Who Loved Me; On Her Majesty's Secret Service; You Only Live Twice; The Man with the Golden Gun; Octopussy; The Living Daylights
Fleming

Monks
see **Leeford, Edward**

Mont, Michael
The Forsyte Saga
Galsworthy

Montacute, Lady
Montacute, Lord
Montacute, Tancred
Tancred
Disraeli

Montfort, Lady
Endymion
Disraeli

Montfort, Lord
Henrietta Temple
Disraeli

Monticue, Ethel
The Young Visiters
Ashford

Montmorency
Three Men in a Boat
Jerome

Montrose, Earl of
A Legend of Montrose
Scott

Moore, Louis
Moore, Robert Gérard
Shirley
Brontë

Moore, Mrs
Moore, Ronny
A Passage to India
Forster

Moreau, Frédéric
L'Education sentimentale
Flaubert

Morel
À la recherche du temps perdu
Proust

Morel, Annie
Morel, Mrs
Morel, Paul
Morel, Walter
Morel, William
Sons and Lovers
Lawrence

Morgan, Anna
Voyage in the Dark
Rhys

Morgan, Hank
A Connecticut Yankee in King Arthur's Court
Twain

Morgan, Huw
How Green Was My Valley
Llewellyn

Moriarty, Dean
On the Road
Kerouac

Moriarty, Professor James
The Adventures of Sherlock Holmes; The Final Problem; The Memoirs of Sherlock Holmes; The Return of Sherlock Holmes; The Case Book of Sherlock Holmes
Doyle

Morland, Catherine
Northanger Abbey
Austen

Morlocks
The Time Machine
Wells

Morris, Dinah
Adam Bede
Eliot

Morse, Inspector
Last Bus to Woodstock; Last Seen Wearing; The Silent World of Nicholas Quinn; Service of All the Dead; The Dead of Jericho; The Riddle of the Third Mile; The Secret of Annexe 3; The Wench Is Dead
Dexter

Morse, Ruth
Martin Eden
London

Morton, Harry
Old Mortality
Scott

Morton, John
Morton, Reginald
The American Senator
Trollope

Morville, Guy
Morville, Philip
The Heir of Redclyffe
Yonge

Moss, Adam
A Kentucky Cardinal; Aftermath
Allen

Mouldiwarp
The House of Arden; Harding's Luck
Nesbit

Mount, Bella
Mountfalcon, Lord
The Ordeal of Richard Feverel
Meredith

Mountolive
Justine; Balthazar; Mountolive; Clea
Durrell

Mouret, Octave
Les Rougon-Macquart
Zola

Mouth family
Prancing Nigger
Firbank

Mowbray, Clara
St Ronan's Well
Scott

Mowgli
The Jungle Books
Kipling

M'Turk
Stalky & Co
Kipling

Mugger-Ghaut
The Jungle books
Kipling

Münchausen, Baron
The Adventures of Baron Münchausen
Raspe

Mundungus
A Sentimental Journey
Sterne

Murdstone, Edward
Murdstone, Jane
David Copperfield
Dickens

Murray
The Abbot
Scott

Murray family
Agnes Grey
Brontë

Musgrave, Tom
The Watsons
Austen

Musgrove, Charles

Musgrove, Henry
Musgrove, Louisa
Persuasion
Austen

Mutlar, Daisy
The Diary of a Nobody
Grossmith

'My Lord'
Amelia
Fielding

Myra
Endymion
Disraeli

Myriel, Monseigneur
Les Misérables
Hugo

Myshkin, Prince
The Idiot
Dostoevsky

N

Nag
Nagaina
The Jungle Books
Kipling

Nana
see **Macquart, Nana**

Nancy
Oliver Twist
Dickens

Nanny
At the Back of the North Wind
MacDonald

Napoleon
Animal farm
Orwell

Narcissa
The Adventures of Roderick Random
Smollett

Natasha
War and Peace
Tolstoy

Nectabanus
The Talisman
Scott

Nekayah
Rasselas
Johnson

Nekhludov, Prince Dmitri
Resurrection
Tolstoy

Neleta
Anthony Adverse
Allen

Nemo, Captain
Vingt Mille Lieues sous les mers
Verne

Nero
Quo Vadis?
Sienkiewicz

Nessim
Justine; Balthazar; Mountolive; Clea
Durrell

Nesta
One of Our Conquerors
Meredith

Neville, Major
The Antiquary
Scott

Newcome, Brian
Newcome, Clive
Newcome, Ethel
Newcome, Hobson

Newcome, Colonel Thomas
The Newcomes
Thackeray

Newman, Christopher
The American
James

Newsome, Chadwick
Newsome, Mrs
The Ambassadors
James

Newson
The Mayor of Casterbridge
Hardy

Nibbins
The Midnight Folk; The Box of Delights
Masefield

Nickleby, Kate
Nickleby, Mrs
Nickleby, Nicholas
Nickleby, Ralph
Nicholas Nickleby
Dickens

Nimmo, Chester
Prisoner of Grace; Except the Lord; Not Honour More
Cary

Nioche, Noémie
The American
James

Nipper, Susan
Dombey and Son
Dickens

Noddy
Little Noddy Goes to Toyland & others
Blyton

Noggs, Newman
Nicholas Nickleby
Dickens

Noon, Ed
The Tall Dolores; The February Doll Murders; Shoot It Again, Sam
Avallone

Norman, Harry
The Three Clerks
Trollope

Norpois, Marquis de
À la recherche du temps perdu
Proust

Norris, Arthur
Mr Norris Changes Trains
Isherwood

Norris, Mrs
Mansfield Park
Austen

North Wind
At the Back of the North Wind
MacDonald

Nosnibor, Arowhena
Nosnibor, Mr
Erewhon
Butler

Nostromo
Nostromo
Conrad

Nubbles, Kit
The Old Curiosity Shop
Dickens

Nuflo
Green Mansions
Hudson

Nugent, Frank
Billy Bunter of Greyfriars School & others
Richards

Nunn. Jimmy
The Good Companions
Priestley

Nupkins, George
Pickwick Papers
Dickens

O

Oak, Gabriel
Far from the Madding Crowd
Hardy

Oakley, Dorinda
Barren Ground
Glasgow

Oakroyd, Jess
The Good Companions
Priestley

Obadiah
Tristram Shandy
Sterne

Oblómov
Oblómov
Goncharov

Oblowski
Anna Karenina
Tolstoy

Occonestoga
The Yemassee
Simms

Odd, Sergeant-Major
Whisky Galore
MacKenzie

Oddjob
Goldfinger
Fleming

Odette
À la recherche du temps perdu
Proust

O'Ferrall, Trilby
Trilby
Du Maurier

Ogilvie, John
The Four Winds of Love
MacKenzie

O'Hara, Gerald
O'Hara, Scarlett
Gone with the Wind
Mitchell

O'Hara, Kimball 'Kim'
Kim
Kipling

Okonkwo
Things Fall Apart
Achebe

O-Lan
The Good Earth
Buck

Oldbuck, Jonathan
The Antiquary
Scott

'Old Gentleman'
The Railway Children
Nesbit

Olenska, Ellen
The Age of Innocence
Wharton

Olga
Eugene Onegin
Pushkin

Olifaunt, Nigel
The Fortunes of Nigel
Scott

Oliver, Parson
Shamela Andrews
Fielding

Omnium, Duke of
Omnium, Duchess of
see **Palliser**

Onegin, Eugene
Eugene Onegin
Pushkin

Ongar, Lord
The Claverings
Trollope

Opimian, Reverend
Gryll Grange
Peacock

Orestes
Hypatia
Kingsley

Orlando
Orlando
Woolf

Ormont, Earl of
Lord Ormont and His Aminta
Meredith

Oroonoko
Oroonoko
Behn

Orr
Catch-22
Heller

Orville, Lord
Evelina
Burney

Osbaldistone, Francis
Osbaldistone, Sir Hildebrand
Osbaldistone, Rashleigh
Rob Roy
Scott

Osborne, Colonel
He Knew He Was Right
Trollope

Osborne, George
Vanity Fair
Thackeray

Osborne, Lady
Osborne, Lord
The Watsons
Austen

Osmond, Gilbert
Osmond, Pansy
The Portrait of a Lady
James

Ottilia, Princess
The Adventures of Harry Richmond
Meredith

Overmore, Miss
What Maisie Knew
James

Overton, Mr
The Way of All Flesh
Butler

Owen, Frank
The Ragged Trousered Philanthropist
Tressell

Owl
Winnie-the-Pooh; The House at Pooh Corner
Milne

Oxford, Earl of
Anne of Geierstein
Scott

Oxford, Harry
The Egoist
Meredith

P

Pablo
Children of the New Forest
Marryat

Paddock
The Thirty-Nine Steps
Buchan

Paget, Jean
A Town Like Alice
Shute

Palliser, Lady Glencora
Palliser, Plantagenet
Can You Forgive Her?; The Prime Minister; The Duke's Children
Trollope

Palmer, Harry
The Ipcress File; Funeral in Berlin; Billion-Dollar Brain
Deighton

Pancks
Little Dorrit
Dickens

Pangloss, Dr
Candide
Voltaire

Pantagruel
Panurge
Gargantua and Pantagruel
Rabelais

Panza, Sancho
Don Quixote
Cervantes

Paradise, Sal
On the Road
Kerouac

Pardiggle, Mr
Pardiggle, Mrs
Bleak House
Dickens

Pardon, Matthias
The Bostonians
James

Parker, Arthur
Parker, Diana
Parker, Mr
Parker, Mrs
Parker, Susan
Sanditon
Austen

Parker, Stan
The Tree of Man
White

Partridge, Mr
Partridge, Mrs
The History of Tom Jones
Fielding

Pasquier, Raymond
Chronique des Pasquier
Duhamel

Passepartout
Le Tour du monde en quatre-vingt jours
Verne

Paterson, Robert
Old Mortality
Scott

Patterne, Sir Willoughby
The Egoist
Meredith

Pawkie, Mr
The Provost
Galt

Peacocke, Mr
Peacocke, Mrs
Dr Wortle's School
Trollope

Pecksniff, Charity
Pecksniff, Mercy
Pecksniff, Seth
Martin Chuzzlewit
Dickens

Pedlar, Nathan
Barren Ground
Glasgow

Peerybingle, Dot
Peerybingle, John
The Cricket on the Hearth
Dickens

Peggotty, Clara
Peggotty, Daniel
Peggotty, Ham
David Copperfield
Dickens

Pekuah
Rasselas
Johnson

Pelet, M
The Professor
Brontë

Pell, Solomon
Pickwick Papers
Dickens

Pembroke, Agnes
The Longest Journey
Forster

Pendennis, Arthur
Pendennis, Helen
Pendennis, Major
The History of Pendennis
Thackeray

Penniman, Lavinia
Washington Square
James

Pennyfeather, Paul
Decline and Fall
Waugh

Penrose, Robyn
Nice Work
Lodge

Perks
The Railway Children
Nesbit

Perkupp, Mr
The Diary of a Nobody
Grossmith

Perrin, Reginald
The Death of Reginald Perrin; The Return of Reginald Perrin; The Better World of Reginald Perrin
Nobbs

Perrot, Dicky
A Child of the Jago
Morrison

Peter
Heidi
Spyri

Peter
Peter Simple
Marryat

Peter
The Railway Children
Nesbit

Peter
A Tale of a Tub
Swift

Peterson, Carl
Bulldog Drummond & others
Sapper

Petowker, Henrietta
Nicholas Nickleby
Dickens

Petronius
Quo Vadis?
Sienkiewicz

Petulengro, Jasper
Lavengro; The Romany Rye
Borrow

Petworth, Doctor
Rates of Exchange
Bradbury

Peveril, Sir Geoffrey
Peveril, Julian
Peveril of the Peak
Scott

Pew, 'Blind'
Treasure Island
Stevenson

Pfeiffer, Leni
Gruppenbild mit Dame
Böll

Phelps, Mrs
Phelps, Silas
The Adventures of Huckleberry Finn
Twain

Philammon
Hypatia
Kingsley

Philautus
Euphues
Lyly

Phillotson, Richard
Jude the Obscure
Hardy

Phyllis
The Railway Children
Nesbit

Pickle, Gamaliel
Pickle, Peregrine
The Adventures of Peregrine Pickle
Smollett

Pickwick, Samuel
Pickwick Papers
Dickens

Piebald, The
National Velvet
Bagnold

Pierston, Jocelyn
The Well-Beloved
Hardy

Piggy
Lord of the Flies
Golding

Piglet
Winnie-the-Pooh; The House at Pooh Corner
Milne

Pinch, Ruth
Pinch, Tom
Martin Chuzzlewit
Dickens

Pineda
Pineda, Angel
Pineda, Madame
The Comedians
Greene

Pinfold, Gilbert
The Ordeal of Gilbert Pinfold
Waugh

Pinkerton, Miss
Vanity Fair
Thackeray

Pinkie
Brighton Rock
Greene

Pip
Moby-Dick
Melville

Pip
see **Pirrip, Philip**

Pipchin, Mrs
Dombey and Son
Dickens

Pirrip, Philip 'Pip'
Pocket, Herbert
Great Expectations
Dickens

Pocock, Jim
Pocock, Sarah
The Ambassadors
James

Pod
The Borrowers; The Borrowers Afield; The Borrowers Afloat; The Borrowers Aloft; The Borrowers Avenged
Norton

Podsnap, John
Our Mutual Friend
Dickens

Poirot, Hercule
The Mysterious Affair at Styles; The Murder on the Links; Poirot Investigates; The Murder of Roger Ackroyd; The Big Four; The Mystery of the Blue Train; Peril at End House; Lord Edgware Dies; Murder on the Orient Express; The ABC Murders; Murder in Mesopotamia; Death on the Nile; Appointment with Death; Sad Cypress; Evil Under the Sun; The Hollow; The Labours of Hercules; Taken at the Flood; After the Funeral; Hickory Dickory Death; Cat Among the Pigeons; The Clocks; Third Girl; Hallowe'en Party; Elephants Can Remember; Curtain
Christie

Poldark, Ross
Ross Poldark & others
Graham

Pole family
Sandra Belloni; Vittoria
Meredith

Polly, Alfred
Polly, Miriam
The History of Mr Polly
Wells

Polly, Aunt
The Adventures of Tom Sawyer
Twain

Polynesia
The Story of Dr Dolittle & others
Lofting

Ponderevo, Edward
Ponderevo, George
Tono-Bungay
Wells

Pongo
The One Hundred and One Dalmatians
Smith

Pontellier, Edna
Pontellier, Leonce
The Awakening
Chopin

Pontifex, Ernest
Pontifex, George
Pontifex, John
Pontifex, Theo
The Way of All Flesh
Butler

Pooh
see **Winnie-the-Pooh**

Poole, Stanley
Angel Pavement
Priestley

Pooter, Carrie
Pooter, Mr Charles
Pooter, Lupin
The Diary of a Nobody
Grossmith

Poppaea
Quo Vadis?
Sienkiewicz

Pornick, Ann
Kipps
Wells

Porteous, Captain John
The Heart of Midlothian
Scott

Porthos
Les Trois Mousquetaires; Vingt Ans après; Le Vicomte de Bragelonne
Dumas

Portnoy, Alexander
Portnoy's Complaint
Roth

Poste, Flora
Cold Comfort Farm
Gibbons

Pott
Pickwick Papers
Dickens

Potter, Israel
Israel Potter
Melville

Potter, Mr
Potterism
Macaulay

Potter, Muff
The Adventures of Tom Sawyer
Twain

Potts, Caractacus
Chitty-Chitty-Bang-Bang
Fleming

Pottyfar, Mr
Mr Midshipman Easy
Marryat

Poundtext, Reverend
Old Mortality
Scott

Povey, Samuel
The Old Wives' Tale
Bennett

Power, Paula
A Laodicean
Hardy

Poyser, Martin
Poyser, Mrs
Adam Bede
Eliot

Prance, Doctor
The Bostonians
James

Prefect, Ford
The Hitch-Hiker's Guide to the Galaxy
Adams

Prest, Mrs
The Aspern Papers
James

Price, Fanny
Price, Mrs
Mansfield Park
Austen

Primrose, Deborah
Primrose, Dr
The Vicar of Wakefield
Goldsmith

Pringle, Dr Zachariah
The Ayrshire Legatees
Galt

Pringle, Guy
Pringle, Harriet
The Great Fortune; The Spoilt City; Friends and Heroes; The Danger Tree; The Battle Lost and Won; The Sum of Things
Manning

Pross, Miss
Pross, Solomon
A Tale of Two Cities
Dickens

Proudfute, Oliver
The Fair Maid of Perth
Scott

Proudie, Doctor
Proudie, Mrs
Barchester Towers; Framley Parsonage; The Last Chronicle of Barset
Trollope

Prynne
Prynne, Hester
The Scarlet Letter
Hawthorne

Pryor, Mrs
Shirley
Brontë

Psmith
Mike: a Public School Story; Psmith in the City; Psmith, Journalist; Leave It to Psmith
Wodehouse

Puck
Puck of Pook's Hill
Kipling

Pullett, Mrs
The Mill on the Floss
Eliot

Pulling, Henry
Travels with My Aunt
Greene

Pumblechook, Uncle
Great Expectations
Dickens

Pursewarden
Justine; Balthazar; Mountolive; Clea
Durrell

Purun Bhagat
The Jungle Books
Kipling

Pushmi-Pullyu
The Story of Dr Dolittle & others
Lofting

Pyle, Alben
The Quiet American
Greene

Pym, Magnus
A Perfect Spy
Le Carré

Pyncheon family
The House of the Seven Gables
Hawthorne

Q

Quarles, Philip
Point Counter Point
Huxley

Quasimodo
Notre-Dame de Paris
Hugo

Quatermain, Allan
King Solomon's Mines; Allan Quatermain
Haggard

Queeg, Captain
The Caine Mutiny
Wouk

Queen, Ellery
The Roman Hat Mystery & others
Queen

Queequeg
Moby-Dick
Melville

Quelch, Mr
Billy Bunter of Greyfriars School & others
Richards

Quentin, Uncle
Five on a Treasure Island & others
Blyton

Querry, Monsieur
A Burnt-Out Case
Greene

Quest, Martha
Martha Quest; A Proper Marriage; A Ripple from the Storm; Landlocked; The Four-Gated City
Lessing

Quested, Adele
A Passage to India
Forster

Quilp, Daniel
The Old Curiosity Shop
Dickens

Quint, Peter
The Turn of the Screw
James

Quiquern
The Jungle Books
Kipling

Quirk, Jason
Quirk, Thady
Castle Rackrent
Edgeworth

Quiverful, Mr
Barchester Towers
Trollope

Quixote, Don
Don Quixote
Cervantes

R

Rabbit
Winnie-the-Pooh; The House at Pooh Corner
Milne

Rackrent, Sir Condy
Rackrent, Sir Kit
Rackrent, Sir Murtash
Rackrent, Sir Patrick
Castle Rackrent
Edgeworth

Radlett family
The Pursuit of Love; Love in a Cold Climate; The Blessing; Don't Tell Alfred
Mitford

Radnor, Victor
One of Our Conquerors
Meredith

Raffles, AJ
The Amateur Cracksman & others
Hornung

Ralph
Lord of the Flies
Golding

Rama
The Jungle Books
Kipling

Ramorny, Sir John
The Fair Maid of Perth
Scott

Rampion
Point Counter Point
Huxley

Ramsay family
To the Lighthouse
Woolf

Ramsey, Margaret
The Fortunes of Nigel
Scott

Randall, Rebecca
Rebecca of Sunnybrook Farm
Wiggin

Random, Roderick
The Adventures of Roderick Random
Smollett

Ransom, Basil
The Bostonians
James

Raquin, Camille
Raquin, Thérèse
Thérèse Raquin
Zola

Raskolnikov
Crime and Punishment
Dostoevsky

Rasselas, Prince
Rasselas
Johnson

Rassendyll, Rudolf
The Prisoner of Zenda; Rupert of Hentzau
Hope

Rat, Mr
The Wind in the Willows
Grahame

Ratignolle, Adèle
The Awakening
Chopin

Raunce
Loving
Green

Ravenswood, Lord
The Bride of Lammermoor
Scott

Raymond, Mr
At the Back of the North Wind
MacDonald

Razumov, Kirylo Sidorovitch
Under Western Eyes
Conrad

Ready, Masterman
Masterman Ready
Marryat

Reardon, Amy
Reardon, Edwin
New Grub Street
Gissing

Rebecca
Ivanhoe
Scott

Redburn, Wellingborough
Redburn
Melville

Red King
Red Queen
Through the Looking-Glass
Carroll

Redlaw
The Haunted Man
Dickens

Redworth, Thomas
Diana of the Crossways
Meredith

Reed, Mrs
Jane Eyre
Brontë

Reisz, Mademoiselle
The Awakening
Chopin

Remus, Uncle
Uncle Remus; Nights with Uncle Remus; Uncle Remus and His Friends; Uncle Remus and Brer Rabbit; Uncle Remus and the Little Boy
Harris

René
Atala; René
Chateaubriand

Reuter, Zoraide
The Professor
Brontë

Rhayader, Philip
The Snow Goose
Gallico

Riah
Our Mutual Friend
Dickens

Rice, Sammy
The Small Back Room
Balchin

Richard
The Chimes
Dickens

Richard I
Ivanhoe; The Talisman
Scott

Richelieu, Cardinal de
Cinq-Mars
Vigny

Richleau, Duke de
The Devil Rides Out; Three Inquisitive People; Strange Conflict; Gateway to Hell
Wheatley

Richmond, Harry
The Adventures of Harry Richmond
Meredith

Ridd, Annie
Ridd, John
Lorna Doone
Blackmore

Riderhood, Roger 'Rogue'
Our Mutual Friend
Dickens

Riga, Captain
Redburn
Melville

Rigaud
Little Dorrit
Dickens

Rikki-Tikki-Tavi
The Jungle Books
Kipling

Rima
Green Mansions
Hudson

Rintherout, Jenny
The Antiquary
Scott

Ripley, Tom
The Talented Mr Ripley; Ripley Under Ground; Ripley's Game; Ripley Under Water
Highsmith

Rip Van Winkle
The Sketch Book
Irving

Ritchie-Hook, Brigadier
Men at Arms
Waugh

Rivers, Diana
Rivers, Mary
Rivers, St John
Jane Eyre
Brontë

Robarts, Lucy
Robarts, Mark
Framley Parsonage
Trollope

Roberta
An American Tragedy
Dreiser

Roberta
The Railway Children
Nesbit

Robin, Fanny
Far from the Madding Crowd
Hardy

Robinson family
Der Schweizerische Robinson
Wyss

Rob Roy
see **Macgregor, Rob Roy**

Robsart, Amy
Kenilworth
Scott

Robson, Daniel
Robson, Sylvia
Sylvia's Lovers
Gaskell

Rochester, Adèle
Rochester, Bertha
Rochester, Edward Fairfax
Jane Eyre
Brontë

Rodgers, Mildred
Of Human Bondage
Maugham

Roehampton, Lord
Endymion
Disraeli

Rokesmith, John
see **Harmon, John**

Roland, Jean
Roland, Pierre
Pierre et Jean
Maupassant

Rolfe, Helga
An Ace Up My Sleeve; The Joker in the Pack; I Hold Four Aces
Chase

Romford, Facey
Mr Facey Romford's Hounds
Surtees

Romfrey, Everard
Beauchamp's Career
Meredith

Romola
Romola
Eliot

Roo
Winnie-the-Pooh; The House at Pooh Corner
Milne

Rooney, Andy
Handy Andy
Lover

Rosalba, Princess
The Rose and the Ring
Thackeray

Rose
Brighton Rock
Greene

Rose
Eight Cousins; Rose in Bloom
Alcott

Rose, Caroline
The Comforters
Spark

Rosinante
Don Quixote
Cervantes

Rossmann, Karl
Amerika
Kafka

Rottenmeier, Fräulein
Heidi
Spyri

Rougon, Félicité
Rougon, Pierre
Les Rougon-Macquart
Zola

Rover, Ralph
The Coral Island
Ballantyne

Rowena
Ivanhoe
Scott

Roxy
Pudd'nhead Wilson
Twain

Roy, Richmond
The Adventures of Harry Richmond
Meredith

Rubashov, NS
Darkness at Noon
Koestler

Rubehn, Ebenezer
L'Adultera
Fontane

Rudge
Rudge, Barnaby
Rudge, Mrs
Barnaby Rudge
Dickens

Rufford, Lord
The American Senator
Trollope

Rufford, Nancy
The Good Soldier
Ford

Ruggles family
The Family from One End Street; Further Adventures of the Family from One End Street
Garnett

Rumpole, Hilda
Rumpole, Horace
Rumpole of the Bailey & others
Mortimer

Rupert of Hentzau
The Prisoner of Zenda; Rupert of Hentzau
Hope

Rushworth, Mr
Mansfield Park
Austen

Russell, Edwin
Eric, or Little by Little
Farrar

Russell, Lady
Persuasion
Austen

Ryder, Charles
Brideshead Revisited
Waugh

S

Saccard, Aristide
Les Rougon-Macquart
Zola

For **SAINT** also see **ST**

Saint, The
see **Templar, Simon**

Saint-Loup, Marquis de
À la recherche du temps perdu
Proust

Saladin
The Talsiman
Scott

Salar
Salar the Salmon
Williamson

Salavin, Louis
Salavin
Duhamel

Salim
A Bend in the River
Naipaul

Sallust, Gregory
Contraband; Faked Passports; The Black Baroness; V for Vengeance; Come into My Parlour; The Island Where Time Stands Still; Traitors' Gate; They Used Dark Forces
Wheatley

Salteena, Mr
The Young Visiters
Ashford

Salterne, Rose
Westward Ho!
Kingsley

Sampson, Dominie
Guy Mannering
Scott

Samsa, Gregor
Die Verwandlung
Kafka

Sands, Bernard
Hemlock and After
Wilson

Sanger, Albert
Sanger, Tessy
The Constant Nymph
Kennedy

Sanutee
The Yemassee
Simms

Sapsea, Mr
The Mystery of Edwin Drood
Dickens

Sarn, Prudence
Precious Bane
Webb

Sartoris family
Sartoris
Faulkner

Sauron
The Lord of the Rings
Tolkien

Savage, Captain
Peter Simple
Marryat

Sawyer, Bob
Pickwick Papers
Dickens

Sawyer, Sid
The Adventures of Tom Sawyer
Twain

Sawyer, Tom
The Adventures of Tom Sawyer; The Adventures of Huckleberry Finn; Tom Sawyer Abroad; Tom Sawyer, Detective
Twain

Sayer, Rose
The African Queen
Forester

Scales, Gerald
The Old Wives' Tale
Bennett

Scarborough, John
Mr Scarborough's Family
Trollope

Scarecrow
The Wonderful Wizard of Oz
Baum

Scarlet Pimpernel, The
see **Blakeney, Sir Percy**

Scatcherd, Sir Roger
Doctor Thorne
Trollope

Schlegel, Helen
Schlegel, Margaret
Schlegel, Tibby
Howards End
Forster

Schlemihl, Peter
Peter Schlemihl
Chamisso

Schmidt, Anna
The Third Man
Greene

Schroeder, Fräulein
Goodbye to Berlin
Isherwood

Scobie
The Heart of the Matter
Greene

Scott
White Fang
London

Scott, Thomas
Hawbuck Grange
Surtees

Scrooge, Ebenezer
A Christmas Carol
Dickens

Scythrop, Mr
Nightmare Abbey
Peacock

Sea Catch
The Jungle Books
Kipling

Seagrave family
Masterman Ready
Marryat

Seagrim, George
Seagrim, Mollie
The History of Tom Jones
Fielding

Seal, Basil
Put Out More Flags; Basil Seal Rides Again
Waugh

Seaton, Arthur
Saturday Night and Sunday Morning
Sillitoe

Sedley, Amelia
Sedley, Jos
Vanity Fair
Thackeray

Seeonee
The Jungle Books
Kipling

Selden, Lawrence
The House of Mirth
Wharton

Sesemann family
Heidi
Spyri

Seurel, François
Le Grand Meaulnes
Alain-Fournier

Seward, Doctor
Dracula
Stoker

Seyton, Catherine
The Abbot
Scott

Shaddai, King
The Holy War
Bunyan

Shadowfax
The Hobbit; The Lord of the Rings
Tolkien

Shandon, Captain
The History of Pendennis
Thackeray

Shandy, Mrs
Shandy, Tristram
Shandy, Uncle Toby
Shandy, Walter
Tristram Shandy
Sterne

Shardik
Shardik
Adams

Sharp, Becky (Rebecca)
Vanity Fair
Thackeray

Shatov
The Devils
Dostoevsky

Shaw, Sergeant Raymond
The Manchurian Candidate
Condon

Shelby, George
Shelby, Mr
Uncle Tom's Cabin
Stowe

Shepherdson family
The Adventures of Huckleberry Finn
Twain

Sheppard, Jack
Jack Sheppard
Ainsworth

Shere Khan
The Jungle Books
Kipling

Sheringham, Roger
The Poisoned Chocolates Case
Iles

Sherston, George
Memoirs of a Fox-Hunting Man; Memoirs of an Infantry Officer; Sherston's Progress
Sassoon

Shirley, Anne
Anne of Green Gables
Montgomery

Shore, Jemima
Quiet As a Nun & others
Fraser

Short
The Old Curiosity Shop
Dickens

Shrapnel, Doctor
Beauchamp's Career
Meredith

Siddharta
Siddharta
Hesse

Sikes, Bill
Oliver Twist
Dickens

Silver, Long John
Treasure Island
Stevenson

Simcox, Simeon
Paradise Postponed
Mortimer

Simple, David
The Adventures of David Simple; Familiar Letters Between the Principal Characters in David Simple; Volume the Last
Fielding

Sinai, Saleem
Midnight's Children
Rushdie

Sinclair, Emil
Demian
Hesse

Singh, Hurree Jamset Ram
Billy Bunter of Greyfriars School & others
Richards

Singh, Ralph
The Mimic Men
Naipaul

Sisson, Aaron
Aaron's Rod
Lawrence

Sixtus, Eva
Sixtus, Ewald
Alte Nester
Raabe

Skewton, Hon Mrs
Dombey and Son
Dickens

Skimpin
Pickwick Papers
Dickens

Skimpole, Harold
Skimpole, Mrs
Bleak House
Dickens

Skinner, Doctor
The Way of All Flesh
Butler

Skrebensky, Anton
The Rainbow
Lawrence

Slane, Lady
All Passion Spent
Sackville-West

Sleary
Hard Times
Dickens

Slipslop, Mrs
The Adventures of Joseph Andrews
Fielding

Slop, Dr
Tristram Shandy
Sterne

Slope, Obadiah
Barchester Towers; The Warden
Trollope

Sloper, Catherine
Sloper, Doctor
Washington Square
James

Slow-Solid
The Jungle Books
Kipling

Sludge, Dickie 'Flibbertigibbet'
Kenilworth
Scott

Slumkey, Hon Samuel
Pickwick Papers
Dickens

Smallways, Bert
The War in the Air
Wells

Smaug
The Hobbit; The Lord of the Rings
Tolkien

Smeeth, Mr
Smeeth, Mrs
Angel Pavement
Priestley

Smelfungus
A Sentimental Journey
Sterne

Smike
Nicholas Nickleby
Dickens

Smiley, George
Call for the Dead; Tinker, Tailor, Soldier, Spy; The Honourable Schoolboy; Smiley's People
Le Carré

Smith
White Fang
London

Smith, Harriet
Emma
Austen

Smith, Henry
The Fair Maid of Perth
Scott

Smith, Lancelot
Yeast
Kingsley

Smith, Mr
The Comedians
Greene

Smith, Stephen
A Pair of Blue Eyes
Hardy

Smith, Wayland
Kenilworth
Scott

Smith, Winston
Nineteen Eighty-Four
Orwell

Smithson, Charles
The French Lieutenant's Woman
Fowles

Smollett, Captain
Treasure Island
Stevenson

Smorltork, Count
Pickwick Papers
Dickens

Snagsby
Snagsby, Mrs
Bleak House
Dickens

Snailsfoot, Bryce
The Pirate
Scott

Snevellicci family
Nicholas Nickleby
Dickens

Snodgrass, Augustus
Pickwick Papers
Dickens

Snopes family
The Hamlet
Faulkner

Snowball
Animal Farm
Orwell

Snowe, Lucy
Villette
Brontë

Solmes, Mr
Clarissa
Richardson

Somers, Harriet
Somers, Richard Lovat
Kangaroo
Lawrence

Sorrel, Hetty
Adam Bede
Eliot

Souël Père
René
Chateaubriand

South, Marty
The Woodlanders
Hardy

Sowerberry
Oliver Twist
Dickens

Spade, Sam
The Maltese Falcon
Hammett

Spearman, Rosanna
The Moonstone
Collins

Spenlow, Dora
David Copperfield
Dickens

Spitz
The Call of the Wild
London

Sponge, Soapey
Mr Sponge's Sporting Tour
Surtees

Springrove, Edward
Desperate Remedies
Hardy

Square
The History of Tom Jones
Fielding

Squeers, Wackford
Nicholas Nickleby
Dickens

Stackpole, Henrietta
The Portrait of a Lady
James

Stagg
Barnaby Rudge
Dickens

Stalky
Stalky & Co
Kipling

Stanbach, Madame
Linda Tressel
Trollope

Standish, Lady Laura
Phineas Finn
Trollope

Stanhope, Canon
Barchester Towers
Trollope

Stant, Charlotte
The Golden Bowl
James

Starbuck
Moby-Dick
Melville

Stareleigh, Mr
Pickwick Papers
Dickens

Stark, Willie
All the King's Men
Warren

Starkadder family
Cold Comfort Farm
Gibbons

Staunton, Lord
The Heart of Midlothian
Scott

Stavrogin, Nikolai
The Devils
Dostoevsky

St Clair, Augustine
St Clair, Little Eva
Uncle Tom's Cabin
Stowe

St Cleeve, Swithin
Two on a Tower
Hardy

St Columb, Dona
St Columb, Henrietta
St Columb, Sir Henry
St Columb, James
Frenchman's Creek
Du Maurier

Steele, Lucy
Sense and Sensibility
Austen

Steerforth, James
David Copperfield
Dickens

Steinmarc, Peter
Linda tressel
Trollope

Stepanida
The Devil
Tolstoy

St Évrémonde, Charles
St Évrémonde, Marquis
A Tale of Two Cities
Dickens

Steyne, Lord
Vanity Fair
Thackeray

Stiggins, Reverend
Pickwick Papers
Dickens

Stone, Jabez
The Devil and Daniel Webster
Benét

Strangeways, Nigel
A Question of Proof; Thou Shell of Death; There's Trouble Brewing; The Beast Must Die; The Smiler with the Knife; Malice in Wonderland; The Case of the Abominable Snowman; Minute for Murder; The Dreadful Hollow; The Whisper in the Gloom; End of Chapter; The Widow's Cruise; The Worm of Death; The Sad Variety; The Morning After Death
Blake

Strap, Hugh
The Adventures of Roderick Random
Smollett

Street, Della
The Case of the Velvet Claws & others
Gardner

Strether, Lambert
The Ambassadors
James

Strickland, Charles
The Moon and Sixpence
Maugham

Struldbrugs
Gulliver's Travels
Swift

Stryver
A Tale of Two Cities
Dickens

Stubb
Moby-Dick
Melville

Stubbs, Colonel Jonathan
Ayala's Angel
Trollope

Suddlechop, Dame Ursula
The Fortunes of Nigel
Scott

Summerson, Esther
Bleak House
Dickens

Susan, Lady
Lady Susan
Austen

Sutpen, Henry
Sutpen, Judith
Sutpen, Thomas
Absalom, Absalom!
Faulkner

Svengali
Trilby
Du Maurier

Swallow, Philip
Changing Places; Small World
Lodge

Swancourt, Elfride
A Pair of Blue Eyes
Hardy

Swann, Charles
Swann, Gilberte
À la recherche du temps perdu
Proust

Swidger, Milly
Swidger, William
The Haunted Man
Dickens

Swiveller, Dick
The Old Curiosity Shop
Dickens

Sylvie
Sylvie and Bruno
Carroll

Syme, Gabriel
The Man Who Was Thursday
Chesterton

T

Tabaqui
The Jungle Books
Kipling

Tackleton
The Cricket on the Hearth
Dickens

Taji
Mardi
Melville

Talbot, Colonel
Waverley
Scott

Talbot, Edmund
Rites of Passage
Golding

Tallentire family
The Hired Man; A Place in England; Kingdom Come
Bragg

Tantamount, Lucy
Point Counter Point
Huxley

Tapley, Mark
Martin Chuzzlewit
Dickens

Tappertit, Simon
Barnaby Rudge
Dickens

Taran
The Book of Three; The Black Cauldron; The Castle of Llyr; Taran Wanderer; The High King
Alexander

Tarka
Tarka the Otter
Williamson

Tarrant, Selah
Tarrant, Verena
The Bostonians
James

Tartar, Lieutenant
The Mystery of Edwin Drood
Dickens

Tarzan
Tarzan of the Apes & others
Burroughs

Tashtego
Moby-Dick
Melville

Tattycoram
Little Dorrit
Dickens

Tatyana
Eugene Onegin
Pushkin

Taylor, Anne
Emma
Austen

Teach
The Master of Ballantrae
Stevenson

Tellwright, Anna
Anna of the Five Towns
Bennett

Templar, Simon
Meet the Tiger & others
Charteris

Temple, Henrietta
Henrietta Temple
Disraeli

Temple, Miss
Jane Eyre
Brontë

Tench, Mr
The Power and the Glory
Greene

Tetterby, Adolphus
The Haunted Man
Dickens

Tha
The Jungle Books
Kipling

Thaïs
Thaïs
France

Thatcher, Becky
The Adventures of Tom Sawyer
Twain

Thénardier
Les Misérables
Hugo

Theodora
Lothair
Disraeli

Theon
Hypatia
Kingsley

Theopompus, Sir
The Midnight Folk; The Box of Delights
Masefield

Thibault, Antoine
Thibault, Jacques
Les Thibault
Martin du Gard

Thomas, Bigger
Native Son
Wright

Thompson, Rosamund
Thompson, Will
God's Little Acre
Caldwell

Thompson, Sadie
Rain
Maugham

Thornberry, Job
Endymion
Disraeli

Thorne, Doctor
Thorne, Mary
Doctor Thorne
Trollope

Thornton, John
The Call of the Wild
London

Thornton, John
North and South
Gaskell

Thorpe, Isabella
Thorpe, John
Northanger Abbey
Austen

Thrasher, Justice
Amelia
Fielding

Threepwood, Freddie
Something Fresh; Leave It to Psmith; Full Moon; Sunset at Blandings
Wodehouse

Threepwood, Galahad
Summer Lightning; Heavy Weather; Full Moon; Pigs Have Wings; Galahad at Blandings; A Pelican at Blandings; Sunset at Blandings
Wodehouse

Thunder-Ten-Tronckh, Baron
Candide
Voltaire

Thwackum
The History of Tom Jones
Fielding

Tibbs, Virgil
In the Heat of the Night
Ball

Tickletext, Parson
Shamela Andrews
Fielding

Tietjens, Christopher
Some Do Not; No More Parades; A Man Could Stand Up; The Last Post
Ford

Tigg, Montague
Martin Chuzzlewit
Dickens

Tigger
The House at Pooh Corner
Milne

Tilney, Captain
Tilney, Eleanor
Tilney, General
Tilney, Henry
Northanger Abbey
Austen

Timmy
Five on a Treasure Island & others
Blyton

Tin Woodman (Tin Man)
The Wonderful Wizard of Oz
Baum

Tischbein, Emil
Emil und die Detektive
Kästner

Titmarsh, Samuel
The Great Hoggarty Diamond
Thackeray

Toad, Mr
The Wind in the Willows
Grahame

Toby
Typee
Melville

Toby, Uncle
see **Shandy, Uncle Toby**

Todgers, Mrs
Martin Chuzzlewit
Dickens

Toff, The
Introducing the Toff & others
Creasey

Tom
Typee; Omoo
Melville

Tom
The Water-Babies
Kingsley

Tom, Uncle
Uncle Tom's Cabin
Stowe

Toodle
Toodle, Polly
Toodle, Robin
Dombey and Son
Dickens

Toomai
The Jungle Books
Kipling

Toomey, Kenneth
Earthly Powers
Burgess

Too-Too
The Story of Dr Dolittle & others
Lofting

Toots
Dombey and Son
Dickens

Topsy
Uncle Tom's Cabin
Stowe

Torfrida
Hereward the Wake
Kingsley

Toto
The Wonderful Wizard of Oz
Baum

Touchett, Mr
Touchett, Mrs
Touchett, Ralph
The Portrait of a Lady
James

Touchstone, Mr
St Ronan's Well
Scott

Townsend, Morris
Washington Square
James

Tox, Lucretia
Dombey and Son
Dickens

Traddles, Thomas
David Copperfield
Dickens

Transome, Harold
Felix Holt
Eliot

Trant, Elizabeth
The Good Companions
Priestley

Trask family
East of Eden
Steinbeck

Treece, Professor
Eating People Is Wrong
Bradbury

Trefoil, Arabella
The American Senator
Trollope

Trelawney, Squire
Treasure Island
Stevenson

Trendellsohn, Anton
Nina Balatka
Trollope

Trent
Trent, Fred
Trent, Nell 'Little Nell'
The Old Curiosity Shop
Dickens

Trent, Philip
Trent's Last Case
Bentley

Tressel, Linda
Linda Tressel
Trollope

Tressilian, Edmund
Kenilworth
Scott

Trevelyan, Emily
Trevelyan, Louis
He Knew He Was Right
Trollope

Trevelyan, Laura
Voss
White

Triff
Dred
Stowe

Trim, Corporal
Tristram Shandy
Sterne

Trimmer
Officers and Gentlemen
Waugh

Tringle, Emmeline
Tringle, Sir Thomas
Tringle, Tom
Ayala's Angel
Trollope

Tristram, Mrs
The American
James

Troil, Brenda
Troil, Magnus
Troil, Minna
The Pirate
Scott

Trotter, Job
Pickwick Papers
Dickens

Trotter, Tilly
Tilly Trotter; Tilly Trotter Wed; Tilly Trotter Widowed
Cookson

Trotwood, Betsey
David Copperfield
Dickens

Trowbridge, Marquis of
The Vicar of Bullhampton
Trollope

Troy, Sergeant
Far from the Madding Crowd
Hardy

Troy, Virginia
Men at Arms; Officers and Gentlemen; Unconditional Surrender
Waugh

Trulliber, Parson
The Adventures of Joseph Andrews
Fielding

Trumble, Mr
The Vicar of Bullhampton
Trollope

Trunnion, Commodore Hawser
The Adventures of Peregrine Pickle
Smollett

Tuck, Friar
Ivanhoe
Scott

Tuck, Friar
Maid Marian
Peacock

Tudor, Alaric
Tudor, Charley
The Three Clerks
Trollope

Tulkinghorn
Bleak House
Dickens

Tulliver, Maggie
Tulliver, Mr
Tulliver, Mrs
Tulliver, Tom
The Mill on the Floss
Eliot

Tupman, Tracy
Pickwick Papers
Dickens

Turner, Rick L
The Paper Men
Golding

Turpin, Dick
Rookwood
Ainsworth

Turveydrop
Turveydrop, Prince
Bleak House
Dickens

Tweedledee
Tweedledum
Through the Looking-Glass
Carroll

Twentyman, Larry
The American Senator
Trollope

Twinkleton, Miss
The Mystery of Edwin Drood
Dickens

Twist, Oliver
Oliver Twist
Dickens

Tyrold, Camilla
Camilla
Burney

Tyrrel, Francis
St Ronan's Well
Scott

U

Ugly Duchess
Alice's Adventures in Wonderland
Carroll

Ukridge, Stanley Featherstonehaugh
Love Among the Chickens
Wodehouse

Ulrica
Ivanhoe
Scott

Una
Puck of Pook's Hill
Kipling

Uncas
The Last of the Mohicans
Cooper

Underhill, Dr Updike
The Algerine captive
Tyler

Undine
Undine
Fouqué

Ursus
L'Homme qui rit
Hugo

Usher, Madeline
Usher, Roderick
The Fall of the House of Usher
Poe

V

Valjean, Jean
Les Misérables
Hugo

Valsecca, Odo
The Valley of Decision
Wharton

Van Baerle, Cornelius
La Tulipe noire
Dumas

Vance, Philo
The Benson Murder Case & others
Van Dine

Vanderbank
The Awkward Age
James

Van Der Straaten
L'Adultera
Fontane

Van Der Valk, Piet
Love in Amsterdam & others
Freeling

Vane, Ernest
Vane, Mabel
Peg Woffington
Reade

Vane, Lady Isabel
East Lynne
Wood

Vane, Sybil
The Picture of Dorian Gray
Wilde

Van Helsing, Professor
Dracula
Stoker

Vanstone, Magdalen
No Name
Collins

Van Winkle, Rip
see **Rip Van Winkle**

Varden, Dolly
Varden, Gabriel
Varden, Mrs
Barnaby Rudge
Dickens

Varney, Richard
Kenilworth
Scott

Vavasor, Alice
Vavasor, George
Can You Forgive Her?
Trollope

Veck, Meg
Veck, Toby
The Chimes
Dickens

Veneering, Anastasia
Veneering, Hamilton
Our Mutual Friend
Dickens

Venn, Diggory
The Return of the Native
Hardy

Venner, Elsie
Elsie Venner
Holmes

Venus, Mr
Our Mutual Friend
Dickens

Verdurin, Madame
Verdurin, Monsieur
À la recherche du temps perdu
Proust

Vere, Captain
Billy Budd, Foretopman
Melville

Verinder, Lady
Verinder, Rachel
The Moonstone
Collins

Verkhovensky, Pyotr
Verkhovensky, Stepan
The Devils
Dostoevsky

Verloc
The Secret Agent
Conrad

Verney, Lionel
The Last Man
Shelley

Vernon, Diana
Rob Roy
Scott

Vernon, Mr
Vernon, Mrs
Lady Susan
Austen

Verver, Adam
Verver, Maggie
The Golden Bowl
James

Vesey-Neroni, Signora
Barchester Towers
Trollope

Vholes
Bleak House
Dickens

Villars, Mr
Evelina
Burney

Villeparisis, Madame de
À la recherche du temps perdu
Proust

Vincy, Fred
Vincy, Rosamund
Vincy, Walter
Middlemarch
Eliot

Vinrace, Rachel
The Voyage Out
Woolf

Vinteuil
À la recherche du temps perdu
Proust

Vionnet, Jeanne
Vionnet, Madame de
The Ambassadors
James

Vivaldi, Fulvia
Vivaldi, Orazio
The Valley of Decision
Wharton

Von Aschenbach, Gustav
Der Tod in Venedig
Mann

Voss, Johann
Voss
White

Vronski
Anna Karenina
Tolstoy

Vuffin
The Old Curiosity Shop
Dickens

Vye, Eustacia
The Return of the Native
Hardy

Vyse, Cecil
A Room with a View
Forster

W

Wackles, Mrs
The Old Curiosity Shop
Dickens

Waddington, Caroline
The Bertrams
Trollope

Wade, Miss
Little Dorrit
Dickens

Wadman, Mrs
Tristram Shandy
Sterne

Wagg, Mr
Vanity Fair; The History of Pendennis
Trollope

Waggett, Captain
Whisky Galore
MacKenzie

Wait, James
The Nigger of the Narcissus
Conrad

Wakem, Mr
Wakem, Philip
The Mill on the Floss
Eliot

Walker, John
Walker, Roger
Walker, Susan
Walker, Titty
Walker, Vicky
Swallows and Amazons
Ransome

Walkinshaw, Claude
The Entail
Galt

Walsingham, Helen
Kipps
Wells

Walton
Frankenstein
Shelley

Wamba
Ivanhoe
Scott

Warburton, Lord
The Portrait of a Lady
James

Warden, Michael
The Battle of Life
Dickens

Wardle, Mr
Wardle, Rachael
Pickwick Papers
Dickens

Wardour, Sir Arthur
Wardour, Isabella
The Antiquary
Scott

Warren, Nicole
Tender Is the Night
Hemingway

Warrington, George
Warrington, Harry
Warrington, Rachel
The Virginians
Thackeray

Warwick, Diana
Warwick, Mr
Diana of the Crossways
Meredith

Waters, Esther
Esther Waters
Moore

Watson, Elizabeth
Watson, Emma
Watson, Margaret
Watson, Penelope
The Watsons
Austen

Watson, Dr John
A Study in Scarlet; The Sign of Four; The Adventures of Sherlock Holmes; The Final Problem; The Memoirs of Sherlock Holmes; The Hound of the Baskervilles; The Return of Sherlock Holmes; The Case Book of Sherlock Holmes
Doyle

Watson, Miss
The Adventures of Huckleberry Finn
Twain

Waverley, Edward
Waverley, Sir Everard
Waverley
Scott

Waymarsh
The Ambassadors
James

Webster, Daniel
The Devil and Daniel Webster
Benét

Wegg, Silas
Our Mutual Friend
Dickens

Weir, Adam
Weir, Archie
Weir of Hermiston
Stevenson

Weller, Sam
Weller, Tony
Pickwick Papers
Dickens

Wells, Homer
The Cider House Rules
Irving

Wemmick, John
Great Expectations
Dickens

Wentworth, Captain Frederick
Persuasion
Austen

Wentworth family
The Europeans
James

West, Julian
Looking Backward: 2000-1887
Bellamy

Westenra, Lucy
Dracula
Stoker

Western, Sophie
Western, Squire
The History of Tom Jones
Fielding

Weston, Mr
Agnes Grey
Brontë

Weston, Mr
Emma
Austen

Wetheral, Bruce Campbell
Campbell's Kingdom
Innes

Wexford, Inspector Reg
From Doon with Death; A New Lease of Death; Wolf to the Slaughter; Best Man to Die; A Guilty Thing Surprised; No More Dying Then; Murder Being Done Once; Shake Hands For Ever; A Sleeping Life; Put On by Cunning; The Speaker of Mandarin; An Unkindness of Ravens; The Veiled One
Rendell

Wharton family
The Prime Minister
Trollope

`Whisky Priest'
The Power and the Glory
Greene

Whistler, Nicholas
The Night of Wenceslas
Davidson

White Fang
White Fang
London

White Knight
White Queen
Through the Looking-Glass
Carroll

Whiteoak family
Jalna & others
De La Roche

White Rabbit
Alice's Adventures in Wonderland
Carroll

Wickfield
Wickfield, Agnes
David Copperfield
Dickens

Widmerpool, Kenneth
A Dance to the Music of Time
Powell

Wilcox, Charles
Wilcox, Evie
Wilcox, Henry
Wilcox, Paul
Howards End
Forster

Wilcox, Vic
Nice Work
Lodge

Wild, Jonathan
The Life of Jonathan Wild the Great
Fielding

Wildeve, Damon
The Return of the Native
Hardy

Wildrake, Roger
Woodstock
Scott

Wilfer, Bella
Our Mutual Friend
Dickens

Wilkes, Ashley
Gone with the Wind
Mitchell

Wilkins, Mr
Jennings Goes to School & others
Buckeridge

Willett, Joe
Willett, John
Barnaby Rudge
Dickens

William
see **Brown, William**

William of Baskerville
Il nome della rosa
Eco

Williams, Eric
Williams, Vernon
Eric, or Little by Little
Farrar

Williams, Miss
The Adventures of Roderick Random
Smollett

Williams, Mr
Pamela
Richardson

Williams, Parson
Shamela Andrews
Fielding

Willoughby, John
Sense and Sensibility
Austen

Wilson, David 'Pudd'nhead'
Pudd'nhead Wilson
Twain

Wilson, Jem
Mary Barton
Gaskell

Wilson, Mr
The Heart of the Matter
Greene

Wilson, Myrtle
The Great Gatsby
Fitzgerald

Wilt, Henry
Wilt; The Wilt Alternative; Wilt on High
Sharpe

Wimsey, Lord Peter
Whose Body?; Clouds of Witness; Unnatural Death; The Unpleasantness at the Bellona Club; Lord Peter Views the Body; Strong Poison; The Five Red Herrings; Have His Carcase; Murder Must Advertise; Hangman's Holiday; The Nine Tailors; Gaudy Night; Busman's Honeymoon; In the Teeth of the Evidence; Striding Folly
Sayers

Wing, Isadora
Fear of Flying; How to Save Your Own Life
Jong

Winifred
Aylwin
Watts-Dunton

Winkle, Nathaniel
Pickwick Papers
Dickens

Winlow, Marcus
Winlow, Marian
The Go-Between
Hartley

Winnie-the-Pooh
Winnie-the-Pooh; The House at Pooh Corner
Milne

Winterbourne, George
Death of a Hero
Aldington

Winterbourne, Giles
The Woodlanders
Hardy

Winthrop, Dolly
Silas Marner
Eliot

Wiseman, Mr
The Life and Death of Mr Badman
Bunyan

Wititterly, Henry
Wititterly, Julia
Nicholas Nickleby
Dickens

Wix, Mrs
What Maisie Knew
James

Wizard of Oz
The Wonderful Wizard of Oz
Baum

Woffington, Margaret `Peg'
Peg Woffington
Reade

Wolfe, Nero
Fer-de-Lance & others
Stout

Wonka, Willy
Charlie and the Chocolate Factory
Dahl

Won-Tolla
The Jungle Books
Kipling

Woodcock, Adam
The Abbot
Scott

Woodcourt, Allan
Bleak House
Dickens

Woodhouse, Emma
Woodhouse, Isabella
Woodhouse, Mr
Emma
Austen

Woodruff, Sarah
The French Lieutenant's Woman
Fowles

Woodseer, Gower
Woodseer, Minister
The Amazing Marriage
Meredith

Woodward, Mrs
The Three Clerks
Trollope

Wooster, Bertie
My Man Jeeves; The Inimitable Jeeves; Carry On, Jeeves!; Very Good, Jeeves; Thank You, Jeeves; Right Ho, Jeeves; The Code of the Woosters; Joy in the Morning; The Mating Season; Jeeves and the Feudal Spirit; Jeeves in the Offing; Stiff Upper Lip, Jeeves; The World of Jeeves; Much Obliged, Jeeves; Aunts Aren't Gentlemen
Wodehouse

Wopsle, Mr
Great Expectations
Dickens

Worldly Wiseman, Mr
The Pilgrim's Progress
Bunyan

Wortle, Dr
Wortle, Mary
Dr Wortle's School
Trollope

Wotton, Lord Henry
The Picture of Dorian Gray
Wilde

Wrayburn, Eugene
Our Mutual Friend
Dickens

Wulf, Anna
The Golden Notebook
Lessing

Wynne, Sam
Shirley
Brontë

Wyvern, Lady
Wyvern, Lord
Felix Holt
Eliot

X

Xavier, Father
Anthony Adverse
Allen

Y

Yahoos
Gulliver's Travels
Swift

Yakimov, Prince
The Great Fortune
Manning

Yates, Mr
Mansfield Park
Austen

Yavñavalka, Mrs
Valmouth
Firbank

Yeates, Major
Yeates, Philippa
Some Experiences of an Irish RM; Further Experiences of an Irish RM; In Mr Knox's Country
Somerville

Yellan, Mary
Jamaica Inn
Du Maurier

Yeobright, Clym
Yeobright, Thomasin
The Return of the Native
Hardy

Yorick, Parson
Tristram Shandy; A Sentimental Journey
Sterne

Yossarian
Catch-22
Heller

Young, Eugenia
Young, Felix
The Europeans
James

Yram
Erewhon
Butler

Yule, Alfred
Yule, Marian
New Grub Street
Gissing

Z

Zadig
Zadig
Voltaire

Zapp, Morris
Changing Places; Small World
Lodge

Zeitblom, Serenus
Doktor Faustus
Mann

Zhivago, Doctor Yuri
Doctor Zhivago
Pasternak

Zillah
Wuthering Heights
Brontë

Zorba
Zorba the Greek
Kazantzakis

Zuckerman, Nathaniel
My Life As a Man; The Ghost Writer; Zuckerman Unbound; The Anatomy Lesson; The Prague Orgy
Roth